Thomas Edlyne Tomlins

Popular Law Dictionary

Familiarly Explaining the Terms and Forms of English Law

Elibron Classics
www.elibron.com

Elibron Classics series.

ISBN 1-4021-7744-5 (paperback)
ISBN 1-4021-1139-8 (hardcover)

This Elibron Classics Replica Edition is an unabridged facsimile of the edition published in 1838 by Longman, Orme, Brown, Green, & Longmans, London.

POPULAR
LAW-DICTIONARY,

FAMILIARLY EXPLAINING THE TERMS AND FORMS OF

English Law;

ADAPTED TO THE COMPREHENSION OF PERSONS NOT EDUCATED FOR THE LEGAL PROFESSION,

AND

AFFORDING INFORMATION PECULIARLY USEFUL TO MAGISTRATES, MERCHANTS, PAROCHIAL OFFICERS, AND OTHERS.

BY

THOMAS EDLYNE TOMLINS,

ATTORNEY AND SOLICITOR.

LONDON:

PRINTED FOR

LONGMAN, ORME, BROWN, GREEN, & LONGMANS,

PATERNOSTER-ROW.

1838.

LONDON:
Printed by A. SPOTTISWOODE,
New-Street-Square.

PREFACE.

LAW DICTIONARIES have been long familiar to the Public; but, notwithstanding most of them have been carefully compiled and elaborately digested, they have been rendered useful only to the professional student or practitioner.

An attempt has now been made to supply to the Public a familiar exposition of the Law without leading the reader into disquisitions foreign to the purposes of ordinary inquiry.

The subject of English Law and Government is so varied and extended, that the scope of this work has been necessarily confined to those matters and incidents forming the ordinary and daily subjects of discourse, use, and application. But, so far as the limits of such a work would permit, attention has been given to explain many matters which, from their nature, have been hitherto deemed exclusively fit for professional consideration; care has also been taken to familiarise the Public on some few matters involving legal antiquities.

To condense matter of almost indefinite extension, and which is continually accumulating, has been a difficult, and perhaps a hazardous, attempt. The publishers, however, confidently trust that, from the careful and able revision which the whole work has undergone by an eminent Barrister, and considering that all the late alterations and improvements in the Law are noticed, including the Enactments of last Session, it will prove no unsatisfactory offering to the Public.

39. *Paternoster Row,*
January, 1838.

A

POPULAR

LAW DICTIONARY.

A.

ABANDONMENT. In Insurance, is where the assured *abandons* or leaves the cargo or ship insured for the underwriters, resorting to them as for a total loss in the event of a casualty whereby the voyage is lost, the adventure determined or rendered not worth prosecuting, or where unnecessary expense and liability would be incurred by attempts to preserve the cargo or ship; these being, constructively, *total* losses. The damage to the *cargo* must exceed half the value, to entitle the assured to abandon, and thus recover as for a total loss; but if neither the thing insured nor the voyage be lost, and the damage does not amount to a moiety of the value, the assured is not entitled to abandon. The stranding of the ship is a sufficient cause of abandonment, if the ship was on the ground or strand in such a situation as a vessel ought not to be in, while prosecuting the voyage, and sustained actual damage thereby; but the mere striking on a rock and getting off again, which is called "touch and go," is not deemed a stranding. In respect to the abandonment of the *ship*, where a vessel is much injured, that, in order to render her seaworthy, it would cost as much as she was originally worth, or as much as would build a new ship, or it appears upon a survey that the vessel is so shattered by the voyage that the repairs would exceed the value, and she is broken up and sold, the assured may *abandon* and recover for a total loss; the question being, whether the particular injuries could not have been repaired so as to render the ship seaworthy for *the remainder of the voyage*, and not whether the ship was worth repairing generally; and so far the doctrine of abandonment seems settled on tolerably certain principles.

In saving the ship or cargo, the crew are entitled to a compensation payable out of the goods saved, for their labour, if there is sufficient for that purpose.

The assured is bound to act promptly, after he has received intelligence of a casualty, in declaring his intention of abandoning the portion saved: and his notice to the underwriters or their agent, acquainting them of his intention of either abandoning or claiming for a partial loss is irrevocable, and cannot be withdrawn. The not giving a notice within a reasonable time is deemed conclusive of his intention to claim for a partial loss only.

The underwriters, upon abandonment, are therefore entitled to every right the assured had in the things abandoned, or the produce of the sale of the ship made by the captain, who has a general discretion to deal with the ship and cargo in a foreign port as he may think best, but not to sell the ship or cargo, unless in case of absolute necessity. After an abandonment, the captain is of course accountable to the underwriters.

An assured should well consider before he "elects" or chooses to abandon. Unless his case can be brought within the principles of the instances above adduced, it is most advisable for him to make the best of the cargo, and claim for a *partial* loss, the tenor of legal decisions indicating that abandonment and its consequences are not much favoured in the courts.

An abandonment must be total, and not partial, for it is upon the presumption that, although the goods do in fact exist, yet, from some of the perils or casualties mentioned in the policy, they are rendered so unprofitable to the assured as to entitle him to claim as for an absolute loss, leaving the underwriters or assurers to make the most of what is thus *abandoned*, or thrown upon their hands.

In Insurance of goods against fire, the loss may be either partial or total; and many of the offices, if not all, expressly undertake to allow all reasonable charges attending the removal of goods in cases of fire, and to pay the sufferer's loss if the goods are destroyed or damaged by the removal, for no owner is bound under such circumstances to hazard his person, or take extraordinary diligence in saving his goods: the damaged goods are abandoned to the Insurance Office, and they sell them, and carry them to their own account; so that, as far as the nature of these contracts permits, the principles are alike.

ABATE. To overthrow or level. To *abate* a nuisance, means to remove or put an end to a nuisance. This word has another meaning, viz. in respect to the interruption or intrusion by a wrong-doer, called an *abator*, who, on the death of an owner of land, puts out the heir, or interposes a possession adverse to the heir. Also to *abate* a writ or process legally means the showing of some defect therein, and thereby overthrowing it or defeating it. From this last is derived what are termed *pleas in abatement*, which are pleas not much favoured in law, being in many cases answers to the form, not the merits of an action, by showing legal inconsistencies and improprieties in the writ or declaration which sets out the grievance or complaint, such as the omission of necessary parties who should be joined together as plaintiffs or defendants, the original defect of the action, as that a wrong is stated to have been committed by force, when it is clearly a grievance arising upon a breach of contract. Sometimes a circumstance of moral hardship, as that another action is pending for the same cause of action. These, with some others it is not within the scope of the present work, nor would it be practically useful for the reader, to inquire into.

A common plea in abatement, which was styled a plea of misnomer, *i. e.* an objection for erroneously setting forth the Christian or surname of the defendant, and which frequently enabled a defendant to delay his plaintiff, is now abolished. If an error of that nature appears, a Judge will permit the plaintiff to amend his proceedings, not leaving them, as heretofore, to be nullified by the court.

ABATEMENT, is an allowance made for prompt payment, and in this sense it is used in the customs.

ABATEMENT OF LEGACIES. See LEGACIES.

ABDICATE. The renouncing or giving up of an office before the term of service or enjoyment is expired. This word is in common parlance confounded with resignation, but materially differs from it, as *ab-*

dication is done absolutely, whereas *resignation* is in favour of some other person.

ABDUCTION. The taking away of any children from a parent by any sinister means, as violence, deceit, conspiracy, intoxication, or fraud, for the purpose of marrying them, was always indictable as a misdemeanor, and in particular cases was punishable as a capital felony, and an indictment will now lie for a conspiracy to marry an infant in order to obtain the possession of fortune. The case of Edward Gibbon Wakefield called the attention of parliament to this subject; and by the statute 9 *G.* 4. *c.* 31., and in Ireland 10 *G.* 4. *c.* 34. *ss.* 22, 23, 24., the fraudulent or forcible abduction or detaining of *any female* possessed of any interest in real or personal estate, or an heiress presumptive, or next of kin to any person having such interest, *from motives of lucre*, with intent to marry or defile her, is felony, punishable, in the principal, accessories, and abettors, with transportation for life, or not less than seven years, or imprisonment, with or without hard labour, not exceeding four years. Also the taking of *any unmarried girl* under the age of sixteen out of the possession of her father, mother, or person having the lawful care of her, is a misdemeanor punishable with fine or imprisonment, or both, as the court shall award.

A subsequent marriage of a woman or girl to the abductor will not take the case out of the statute, more especially if the marriage was effected by means of fraud, for no person under the influence of fraud can be considered a free agent.

The woman can also, after marriage, be a witness against the offender, and on the other hand can be a witness for him, though she should have cohabited with him from the day of the marriage.

With respect to the taking of an unmarried girl under sixteen, it is an offence within the meaning of the statute to take away a natural daughter from the custody of her putative father. With regard to this offence, it is to be remarked, that as the act is positively prohibited, the absence of a corrupt motive will not be a defence to the charge; and it is no legal excuse that the defendant made use of no other means than the common blandishments of a lover to induce her to elope with him and marry him. Abduction is also used for the offence called child-stealing. By the above statute it is enacted, that the maliciously, by force or fraud, leading or taking away, or decoying or enticing away, or detaining *any child*, male or female, under the age of ten years, with intent to deprive the parents or other person of the lawful possession of such child, or with intent to steal any article, or receiving or harbouring any such child, knowing the same to have been stolen away, is a felony, and punishable, in principals and accessories and abettors, with transportation for seven years, or imprisonment (with or without hard labour) for two years; and if a male, to be once, twice, or thrice publicly or privately whipped, in addition to the imprisonment, if the court think fit; but there is an exception in favour of fathers claiming a right to take their illegitimate children from the mother.

There is a species of abduction which only consists of a civil wrong, such as harbouring an apprentice or servant, wife, child, or relative, in absence of any proof of an original illegal enticing away or detaining, for which action on the case will lie; and as to the restoration of the persons harboured, a writ of habeas corpus can be obtained from the court or a judge, or a warrant from a chief justice authorising search, upon affidavit of the facts; but in the case of an apprentice, impressed or volunteering into the king's service, a *Habeas Corpus* is not grantable unless at his own instance. See Habeas Corpus.

ABETTOR, is an instigator or inciter, a person who promotes or procures the commission of an offence or felony by his counsel, command, or encouragement. In almost all cases of felony, the abettor is now considered as much a principal as the actual felon, especially in the case of murder, and the abettors of offences punishable summarily by justices of the peace are subjected to the same penalties as the principal. See Accessory.

ABEYANCE. When the inheritance to which a party claims to be entitled is not in the possession of any one, it is said to be in abeyance. Titles of honour and dignities are said to be in abeyance when it is uncertain who shall enjoy them; as when a nobleman, holding his dignity descendible to his heirs general, dies, leaving daughters, the king by his prerogative may grant the dignity to which of the daughters he pleases, or on the male issue of one of such daughters. During the time the title to the dignity is thus in suspension, it is said to be in abeyance. A parsonage remaining void, is also said to be in abeyance. In a more loose sense, this term is used to denote that a judgment is pending relative to a matter or right undetermined, and of which no one hath the immediate enjoyment, the right being in a state of suspension. The strict interpretation of this word as to freehold interests has puzzled eminent lawyers; and Mr. Justice Coleridge lately observed, that it was more a matter of curiosity than practical importance.

ABORTION. To administer to any woman being quick with child, any poison or noxious thing, or to use any instrument or *other means whatever*, with the intent to procure miscarriage, is by law declared a capital felony, not only as against the offender, but as against every one counselling, aiding, or abetting therein. And to use the like means to procure miscarriage in a woman *not* quick with child, or not proved so to be, is also declared a felony punishable by transportation for 14 years, or imprisonment, with or without hard labour and whipping. By the words "other means," the administering any herb, or drug, or any act done with the intent to produce abortion, constitutes the offence and it may be remarked, that if death ensue, the party is guilty of murder

ABUTTALS, or BOUNDARIES. The buttings or boundings of lands, East, West, North, or South, with respect to the places by which they are limited and bounded. The sides or the breadth of lands are more properly described as adjacent or bordering, and the ends in length abutting or bounding. Boundaries are of several sorts, such as hedges, ditches, and inclosure of walls, land-marks in common fields, trees and boundary stones in parishes, brooks, rivers, highways, in manors and lordships, &c.

The memory of the boundaries and abuttals of corporation, parochial and church lands, is preserved by annual or periodical processions.

By the Municipal Corporation Act, the boundaries of the boroughs named in the first section of the schedules (A) and (B), are to be those which were settled by the act 2 & 3 *W.* 4. *c.* 64. for settling and describing the divisions of counties, and the limits of cities and boroughs in England and Wales, &c. And the boundaries of those named in the 2d section of the said schedules are to remain until altered by parliament. No place detached from a borough is to be included within it; but, subject to this provision, the boundaries of every borough are to include the whole of the liberties of the same.

By a late Act (2 & 3 *W.* 4. *c.* 80.), passed for the purpose of authorising and enabling ecclesiastical and collegiate corporations to enter into agreements or deeds of reference with their lessees or tenants, or with the owners of lands adjoining to or intermixed with their own, unknown or disputed boundaries or quantities of land can be referred to the adjudication of a person or persons to be nominated by such bodies, and their tenants, or the owners of such adjoining or intermixed lands; and the referees may make maps and plans, and examine parties on both, and call for deeds and writings, and are to make their award on parchment, which is to be approved of by all parties interested, in writing, to be kept in the registry of such ecclesiastical or collegiate corporation, and to be produced to every person interested in the subject-matter thereof, on payment of one shilling, and copies to be furnished.

The granting a commission to ascertain the boundaries of the lands of individuals whose lands lie intermixed, and the fences thereof thrown down, or boundaries ploughed over, is an ancient branch of the jurisdiction of the court of chancery.

It is the duty of a tenant to preserve as he found them, distinct, the boundaries of his landlord, and of landlords of adjoining property; and if he suffer them to become confused, he may be bound to substitute land of his own of equal value, to be ascertained by commissioners.

Where freehold and copyhold land is intermixed, it will be prudent to obtain and mark, from time to time, the boundaries of the different parts of the estate, and that should be done in the presence of the steward or bailiff of the manor, or at least he should have notice to attend. This may save the expense of a commission, which is a chargeable proceeding. In like manner, two owners of freehold, adjoining, may settle the boundaries of each other's land, and prevent future disputes or loss. Plans signed by the owners of adjoining estates, will always evidence a boundary against subsequent possessors of either land, at any distance of time; whereas, if either owner encroach on his neighbour's land, for more than 20 years, and no proceedings are instituted to remove it, in the absence of such written evidence, the encroachment cannot be resisted.

Abuttals, Boundaries of Counties. Felonies and misdemeanors committed on the boundaries of counties, or within 500 yards thereof, or begun in one county and completed in another, may be tried in either. And where the side, centre, bank, &c. of any river, canal, or highway, constitutes the boundaries of two counties, offences committed in any journey or voyage may be tried in any county through which the course of the voyage or journey may have been.

By the Uniformity of Process Act, *writs of summons*, or *capias*, are to be served within the county therein mentioned, or within 200 yards of the border thereof, and not elsewhere. This act does not extend to writs of execution or *attachments* for nonpayment of money; for if the arrest was made out of the proper county, an action of trespass for the imprisonment might be maintained, there being no such exception as to the 200 yards' distance. Places part of a county, but wholly situate within and surrounded by some *other* county, are to be considered as part of the latter county for the purposes of arrest.

The first of the recent acts for building additional churches and chapels enacts, that boundaries of new parishes created by any complete division, and of ecclesiastical districts, shall be ascertained, and the description of such bounds enrolled in chancery, and registered in the registry of the diocese, and notice thereof given, as the commissioners shall direct; and these boundaries may, by special representation made to the king in council, be altered within five years, with the bishop's consent; such alterations to be likewise enrolled. See 58 *G.* 3. *ss.* 21, 22, 23, 24. 30, and 31.

The boundaries of parishes and manors, hamlets or districts, and the boundaries between lands to be enclosed and adjoining lands, are to be settled by commissioners under the Inclosure Act of 41 *G.* 3. *c.* 109. (*s.* 3.), and the General Inclosure Act of 6 *&* 7 *W.* 4. *c.* 115. (*s.* 28.), subject to an appeal at the sessions, in respect of the boundaries of any parish, manor, hamlet, or district.

ACCEDAS AD CURIAM. The title of a writ which removes a plaint from an inferior court, generally the county court, the issuing of which is a preliminary to trying a question of right upon a distress of goods by the proceeding called Replevin, which see.

ACCEPTANCE, signifies the accepting or taking of one thing as a compensation for the payment or performance of another: it is akin to what is termed *accord and satisfaction*, but is distinguished from it by legal subtleties. All that need here be said upon this subject is, that when a party is entitled to a gross sum, he is not bound to accept it piecemeal, and the acceptance of a less sum in satisfaction of a greater may be taken before the day the money becomes due.

ACCEPTANCE, is also an engagement to pay a bill of exchange according to the tenor of the acceptance. It may be either written or verbal. Written, as by the drawee or person to whom the bill is addressed writing on the face of the bill, generally across, "Accepts," "Accepted for £ ." "Accepted, A. B." "Accepted for months," (for the drawee may *accept* for a less sum or for an enlarged period). The words "Presented the (date)," written by a drawee, amounted to an acceptance, and signature is not legally essential. These forms *must* be adhered to in respect of English or Irish bills; though in the case of Scotch and foreign bills, an acceptance need not be in writing on the face of the bill, but it may be given by a letter or any collateral memorandum, or even may be verbal, as where the person drawn upon says "I will accept," "Leave your bill with me and I will accept it," "I will take it up when due." A small matter, it seems, will amount to a verbal acceptface, and any words will suffice which show the party's *unconditional* agreement or assent to pay the bill. A bare promise by a debtor to his creditor that he would pay a bill drawn upon him at a given date, as he would then have the money, does not amount to an acceptance of the bill when drawn; but an agreement to honour or accept a bill will, in many of the latter cases, be equivalent to an acceptance, and it is immaterial whether that agreement be verbal or in writing.

If a bill be drawn payable after sight, the acceptor should in his acceptance state the date, as "Accepted, A. B., 31st August, 1837;" the time is thus fixed.

A book-keeper or other person usually transacting business of this nature for the master, accepting a bill, binds the master.

A mere acceptance, without delivery to the holder, is not sufficient to make this contract binding.

The engagement which constitutes the acceptance is usually made to the holder of the bill, or to some person who intends to receive it, and then the drawee, now the *acceptor*, must answer to him, and any previous or subsequent indorser. If made to the drawer himself, it is binding or not according to the circumstances of the case. Acceptances may be conditional, in contradistinction to the above, which are called absolute; as to pay in the event of a sale of goods; to pay half in money and half in bills, as a contingency shall arise. Similar acceptances may be verbally acknowledged; as if the drawee says the bill will not be accepted until the arrival of a certain ship, or until the sale of certain goods, or that he cannot accept until certain *stores* are paid for, these will amount to acceptances, or, more strictly speaking, an undertaking to accept on the arrival of the ship, on the sale of the goods, on the payment for the stores. However, what is to be considered an absolute or conditional acceptance is a question of law, not of fact, and therefore not within the province of a jury.

The forging the acceptance of any bill of exchange, or the number or sum of any accountable receipt, is a felony, punishable by transportation or imprisonment.

ACCEPTANCE SUPRA PROTEST. Acceptance of a bill is usually made by the party drawn upon (the *drawee*), but it sometimes happens, after the issuing of the bill, that the party drawn upon cannot be found, or that he will not accept at all, or if he do accept, that he does so under terms that impede the negotiation of the bill, or perhaps the drawee's credit may be suspected, or some other circumstance may intervene to prevent his accepting; then, in order to prevent the return of the bill, it is not unusual for some other person to accept the bill for the honour or credit of the person on whose account it was drawn. This transaction is termed an acceptance *supra protest*, and the new acceptor is quite as liable as if he had been the party originally drawn upon, and the holder of the bill is bound to receive this acceptance, if the party thus accepting be a responsible person.

This mode of acceptance is seldom if ever used but for foreign bills, and can only be done *after* the bill has been protested for non-acceptance, or *for better security* (see PROTEST). The method of accepting supra protest is, by Mr. Chitty, stated to be as follows:—The acceptor must in his own person appear before a notary public with witnesses, and declare that he accepts such protested bill *in honour* of the drawer, or for a particular and then named indorser, or generally *for honour*, and that he will pay the same when due, and then with his own hand he must accept thus, "Accepted *supra protest* in honour of *Abraham Wilson*," or which is sufficient, "Accepted, *Timothy Jones*," or "Accepted under protest for honour of *Messrs. Smith and Co.*, and will be paid for their account if regularly protested and refused when due."

The holder as well as the acceptor supra protest should always take care to have the bill *protested* before this acceptance *for honour* is made.

The acceptor *supra protest* has his remedy for the amount against the person for whose honour he accepts, whether the acceptance was made with his knowledge or not.

An act 6 *&* 7 *W.* 4. *c.* 58. declares, that bills protested need not be presented to the acceptors *for honour*, or to the referees *in case of need*, until the day following the day on which such bills of exchange become due; and that if the bills be made payable in one place, and the address of the acceptors *for honour* be in another, they need not be forwarded until the same period; and if that day be a Sunday, Good Friday, Christmas Day, or a Fast or Thanksgiving Day, they need not be presented until the following day.

As to protests for *better security*, see PROTEST.

As to the death of the acceptor, see DISHONOUR, NOTICE OF.

ACCEPTOR. The person who accepts a bill of exchange. He stands in the same relation as the *maker* or drawer, as he sometimes is called, of a promissory note. As he is *primâ facie* a debtor to the drawer of the bill of exchange, or at least by his acceptance admits that he has *effects* of the drawer's in his hands, he is considered as the original debtor, and is *first* liable on the bill, the other parties (who are in law and in fact but so many sureties) being liable in the order they stand upon the bill, they having notice of the *dishonor* or nonpayment of the bill before they can be sued. The liability of the acceptor can therefore but seldom be discharged: it may, indeed, be waived by an express agreement of *all* the parties to the bill that he shall be exonerated, or by an absolute renouncement by the holder, or deliberate acts to that effect. In regard of a foreign bill, if an acceptor be discharged by the law of the place, or custom in respect of the liabilities on these transactions, where the bill was negotiated, he is, as also a drawer or other party, protected *here*. The circumstance of the drawer's name being forged, will not exonerate the acceptor, for, by his acceptance, he induced other parties to take it.

The liability of the acceptor of a bill, or maker of a promissory note, may be temporarily discharged or suspended, by the holders receiving a new bill, or other security, which act will operate as an agreement that, during the currency of the new bill, or till the security become payable, the original bill shall not be put in suit.

The neglect on the part of the holder to present a bill accepted *generally*, that is, payable at a place not exclusively limited, will not release the acceptor, and this even if the bill or note be made payable at a banker's. But by the act 1 *&* 2 *G.* 4. *c.* 78., if the bill be accepted payable at a banker's, or at any other place, and to the acceptance is added these words, "payable at Messrs. Child and Co., 1. Fleet Street, *and there only*," or "*not otherwise, and not elsewhere*," the acceptor will be discharged if no presentment be made at the place so specially appointed on its becoming payable, it being imperative on the holder to present it according to the terms of the *special* acceptance.

On an acceptance payable *generally*, a litigious holder may sue the acceptor without presentment, suit being legally sufficient notice; and the time at which it was payable having elapsed, it becomes, in strictness, incumbent on the acceptor to seek the holder.

If a person, upon whom a bill of exchange is drawn, declines to accept it, but makes a promise to pay the holder on a particular event happening, he may in some cases be sued by the holder for money had and received by the drawer for the holder's use. But it is to be remembered, that it is the *promise to pay*, not, *having the effects*, that constitutes the right of action in this case; for, if funds are remitted to the drawee for the express purpose of answering his acceptance, the holder has no remedy as against him, if he refuse to accept.

Where several persons make a promissory note, or accept, as joint-sureties, the discharge of one of the sureties by a composition will not prejudice the holder's claim upon the others, although the law of principal and surety is generally otherwise.

ACCESSARY, or ACCESSORY, before the fact, is, by Judge Hale, defined to be a person who, being absent at the time of the felony committed, yet procures, counsels, commands, or abets another to commit a felony. After the fact—is a person who, knowing a felony to have been committed by another, receives, relieves, comforts, or assists the felon; but a bare knowledge of the felony will not make him accessory, even if he agree for money not to give evidence against the felon. All who are aiding and abetting when a felony is committed, and as such being accessories, are styled principals in the second degree, in contradistinction to principals in the first degree, who are the persons actually committing the felony. However, it is to be recollected that, in the highest and lowest offences, high treason and misdemeanor, all are principals, and must be indicted as such. In murder also, all aiders, abettors, and accessories before the fact, are treated as principals in the first degree.

It is therefore only in felonies below treason that there can be accessories. The accessory before the fact of any felony is deemed guilty of felony, and punished accordingly. He may be tried before the conviction of the principal, or whether he shall or shall not be amenable to justice; but the best and most usual way is to try the principal and accessory together.

To constitute the offence of being an accessory after the fact, it is necessary that the accessory had notice of a felony being committed by the felon when he assisted or comforted him, and also that the felonious act was complete at the time the assistance was given.

Accessories after the fact cannot be tried before the conviction of their principal, unless they consent to it; but they may be tried with their principal, or separately after the principal has been once convicted.

Accessories having been once duly tried cannot be again indicted or tried in respect of the same felony.

In offences under felony there is no penalty inflicted by the common law for harbouring or maintaining the principal, but in some few cases it is made punishable by statute.

Accessories after the fact to murder may be transported for life, or imprisoned with or without hard labour not exceeding four years: statutory provisions are also made for punishment of accessories where they are not punishable as for the felony committed.

He who counsels or commands any illegal act shall be judged accessory to all the consequences, but not to another distinct thing. As if I command another to beat A, and he beats him so that death ensue, I shall be deemed accessory to his murder; but if I command B to steal a particular horse, and he steals another of a different description, or to burn such a house which he is well acquainted with, and he burns another, I shall not be accessory. See ACCOMPLICE, PRINCIPAL AND ACCESSORY.

ACCIDENTS, or ACCIDENTAL INJURIES. A notion erroneously prevails, that persons are protected from the consequences of injuries or damages they inflict, provided they be unintentional, but several cases in the books demonstrate that the mere absence of an intention to do wrong to another is not sufficient, as far at least as a direct injury is concerned, to protect a party from a *civil* liability for any damage occasioned by his acts. *Criminally*, indeed, he is not liable, because intention is the essence of crime: to this last rule, however, acts done in the prosecution of other acts unlawful or prohibited, form an exception.

The question of liability to civil amends is therefore confined to what are deemed intentional and unintentional injuries in the eye of the law: the solution appears to be, that those acts which are strictly involuntary, *i. e.* being the result of a cause over which the party had no control, exempt the party; all acts being deemed voluntary which proceed from the individual sought to be charged, and are the consequence (directly or indirectly) of any line of conduct pursued by him, such as the bursting of a gun in the party's hand, the running away of a horse under the party's direction, the party's falling against brittle substances, the leakage of a tank or vat, and such like; these *accidents*, notwithstanding the use of ordinary care and circumspection, will subject the party to damages if other persons suffer injury thereby. So coach proprietors are liable to a passenger for injuries sustained by being thrown from their coach if it break down, although the coach is sound as far as human eye can discover. In fact, these cases of *accident* (to use the common phrase) are referrible to *negligence* actual or constructive, or, to speak more strictly and legally, practical or permissive.

Involuntary acts are not only those above alluded to, but may be also considered as those which persons do in the prosecution of some lawful and necessary act, so the firing of a gun in the course of a martial exercise or review will not subject the individual to an action, if a spectator is hit by the wadding or plug; and the running down one boat by another in a tempest, which accident good seamanship could not prevent. Acts arising from the seasons or elements, as the overflowing one man's land by the water from another, by reason of an unusual flood, &c., all exempt the persons sought to be charged either as owners and principals, or servants and agents.

The statute 6 *Ann. c.* 31. has now classed under involuntary *accidents*, "fires," which in principle were referrible to voluntary acts, and the words of which statute now quoted will materially add to the foregoing attempt to explain the law, viz.: —

"No action, suit, or process whatsoever shall be had, maintained, or prosecuted against any person in whose house or chamber any fire shall *accidentally* begin, any law, usage, or custom notwithstanding."

The sum of the foregoing may be concisely stated as follows: — That a mere accidental and involuntary trespass or injury is justifiable at law; and if in the prosecution of any lawful act an "accident" arises, which is purely so, no action can be supported for an injury arising therefrom. However, where *any* degree of blame can be imputed to a party on the score of carelessness, or want of proper caution, he is not exonerated, although there existed no intention to injure.

ACCOMPLICE. Accomplices may be admitted to testify against their companions in guilt, and the principal against the accessory, though such circumstances must necessarily detract from such a witness's credit: indeed, in order to induce the jury to credit his testimony, it is always thought necessary to adduce other evidence directly tending to confirm the leading circumstances of his statement. The evidence of an accomplice for the purpose of furthering the ends of justice, (which ought, however, to flow from pure fountains) is receivable, although his expectation of pardon may depend upon the prisoner's conviction. See APPROVER.

ACCOUNTANT GENERAL. An officer in the court of chancery, being one of the masters in chancery, appointed by act of parliament to receive all money paid into that court; his duty is to convey all money to the Bank, which he does by investing the same in stock, and laying out the dividends in the purchase of fresh stock, generally in 3*l.* per cent. consols. All stock ordered to be paid into court is transferred into his name, and all stock standing in his name in the books of the Bank, is declared by him to be in trust in the particular cause or matter under which it is paid in, or to which it is transferred. He gives certificates of the exact amount of stock or cash so standing in his name to the suitors upon request without fee. He is only to keep account with the Bank, for the Bank is answerable for all money received, and not the accountant general. No fees are to be taken by this officer or his clerks, on pain of being punished for extortion, they being paid certain salaries. The accountant general's salary is paid out of the interest arising from part of the suitors' money, called the suitors' fund. To counterfeit the hand of the accountant general is a felony, punishable by transportation for life.

ACCOUNTANT GENERAL, *Exchequer*, is an officer similarly constituted, and appointed to act for the benefit of the suitors on the equity or chancery side of the exchequer, and to counterfeit his hand is also a felony.

ACCOUNTANT GENERAL, *Bankruptcy*. An officer of the same nature is appointed to act in this court, and his duties are regulated by an order of the Court of Review.

ACCOUNTS, when of a mutual nature, are very fruitful sources of litigation; and if of long standing, unsettled, and of a complicated nature, are more properly made the subject of a bill in chancery. Indeed, accounts between mortgagor and mortgagee, partners, executors, and creditors, tithes, long accounts between principals and agents, scarcely admit of any other mode of investigation, than through the medium of a master in chancery, to whom these matters are always referred. But where one has money of another's in his hands, as bailiff, agent, or receiver, which he ought to pay, an action on promises will lie for such money, as had and received by the defendant for the plaintiff's use. In cases where the items are simple, and the deductions easily ascertainable, such form of action will be the most proper remedy, as the defendant can, in such action brought for the total sum received (in which bail can be obtained), plead and set off his payments; and the jury, upon proof of the money received and paid on both sides, are enabled to give a verdict for the sum actually due. But when the items are numerous, remaining open, and subject to deductions on account of sundry payments, then a bill in chancery must be filed, if arbitration is not referred to. In trials at law for money had and received, where it is apparent that there are cross accounts, the court suggests to the parties the expediency of a reference to arbitration. Indeed, if parties are well advised, this course of settling disputes is adopted in the first instance. As to the mode of proceeding by arbitration, see AWARD.

Accounts between attornies and their clients can, generally speaking, be settled summarily by the order of a Judge, and a reference to the proper officer to tax his bill, and make proper allowances to both. See ATTORNIES.

ACCUSATION. The charging one with an offence. By Magna Charta, no man shall be imprisoned or condemned, on any *accusation*, without trial by his "peers," that is, his equals, or the law of the land.

It is declared by successive parliaments, in the reign of Edward III., that none shall be vexed upon any *accusation*, but according to the law of the land. And no man may be molested by petition to the king, unless it be by indictment or presentment of lawful men, or by process at common law. None shall be compelled to answer an *accusation* to the king, without presentment or some matter of record, viz. by indictment or inquisition.

In treason, there must be two lawful *accusers*. To threaten to accuse another of a crime, for the purpose of extortion, is a felony. See THREATS.

ACKNOWLEDGMENT-MONEY, is a sum paid in some parts of England by the copyhold tenants, on the death of their landlord, as an acknowledgment or recognition of their new lords, much in the same manner as a small sum of money is sometimes paid by a tenant as an acknowledgment of his new landlord on the transfer thereof to a purchaser, or on the entry of the heir, called *attornment*, not so much in use as formerly, and the most common case whereof is this, where a mortgagee enters upon the land for non-payment of his mortgage money, the tenants are required to attorn, viz. to acknowledge the mortgagee as their landlord, by payment of a halfpenny; but the service of a notice upon the tenant is equivalent to this ancient form, in obtaining full possession and receipt of the rents and profits of the land. The effect of the payment of acknowledgment-money (unless obtained by fraud) prevents the tenant from disputing his lord's or landlord's title; and where copyholders or others inclose land, part of the lord's waste, it is usual for them to pay a small sum to the bailiff for the use of the lord of the manor, in order to prevent a twenty years' enjoyment from operating in favour of the party inclosing after that period, unless he is admitted as a copyholder, when the origin of his possession is recorded.

Notices to attorn are often given in order to prevent payment of rent to a party who has parted with his interest in the premises. On the sale of a manor, the freehold tenants who held by payment of a small quit-rent, should in prudence be required to sign a memorandum of acknowledgment, or payment be demanded, and proceedings taken by distress to recover it, or some act done to perpetuate the memory of the payment. It is, however, purely voluntary on the tenant's part, whether he will attorn or not. In rightful cases a written notice to attorn binds him to pay his future rent to the new owner.

ACQUITTAL, is when a person is found not guilty of the offence wherewith he is charged by a jury upon verdict. If a person acquitted be again indicted for the same offence, he may plead *auterfois acquit*, viz. that he has been before tried and acquitted.

If a person is lawfully acquitted on a malicious prosecution, he may bring his action for damages after he has obtained a copy of the indictment; but it is usual for the judges of gaol delivery to deny such copy to him who intends to bring such action thereon, if it appears to them that there was a probable cause for such prosecution.

ACRE. A measure of the surface of land. It used to vary in different parts of the country, especially in Staffordshire, where the acre was nearly one fifth larger than the common English acre, which has generally been estimated as containing in length 40 perches and in breadth 4, and so in proportion, were the length more or less, the general calculation being that there were 4840 square yards in an acre. The acre is now reduced to a certain standard throughout the United Kingdom, by the operation of the late statute for regulating weights and measures, viz. 4 roods, each rood containing 40 poles, rods, or perches of $30\frac{1}{4}$ square yards, or $272\frac{1}{4}$ square feet; and, consequently, each acre contains 43,560 square feet, or 4840 square yards, Imperial measure of surface. The Scotch acre contained 4 roods, each rood 40 falls, and each fall 36 ells; the ell being equal to 37·06 Imperial inches. The Irish acre was equal to 1 acre 2 roods and $19\frac{21}{121}$ poles of the present Imperial surface measure.

The word acre formerly meant an open field or ground of an indefinite size, as *castle-acre*, *west-acre*, *long-acre*.

ACTION, is the remedy to be pursued for a wrong done, or is the right of suing by law for what is due to any one. Actions may be generally classed as criminal and civil.

Criminal actions are proceedings by indictment or inquisition against another, so as to obtain judgment of death, transportation, or imprisonment; or by information in the King's Bench, to have judgment by fine or imprisonment, or both, against another, for misconduct to individuals, breaches of the peace, and acts having that tendency. The first being more a matter of public justice than of private complaint; the latter being instituted or abandoned at the particular instance of the party grieved. See INFORMATION.

Actions which are brought for some penalty or punishment under particular statutes, where the party proceeded against is liable to corporeal or pecuniary punishment, or both, are termed penal actions.

Civil actions are divided into real, personal, and mixed.

A *real* action is the form of suit given for substantiating the title to land or real property, and is generally commenced by ejectment; and in the case of a widow claiming her dower, by a proceeding called a *writ of dower*.

Personal actions are founded upon contract express or implied, as "assumpsit," to recover damages for the nonperformance of a promise or undertaking; upon fraud or wrong, as "action on the case;" "debt," to recover a sum of money owing, for which purpose "assumpsit" is equally available; "detinue," to recover the specific thing claimed; "trover," to recover the thing claimed, or damages; "covenant," for the enforcing of a stipulation by deed or contract under seal; "account," for compelling the statement of an account; "annuity," for recovery of an annuity; which two last actions are now in disuse, the remedies in respect of these claims being obtainable by some of the previous forms of action.

There are also "actions popular," or "qui tam," brought to recover penalties accrued on the breach of a penal statute, and which every one who is willing to prosecute has a right to sue or bring.

In all cases where a loss or damage is sustained, the plaintiff can have a form of action applicable to the nature of the demand or claim, whether it be for injury done to — 1. credit, 2. person, or, 3. property. Actions for injury done to the *credit* are brought *upon the case*, for words spoken or writings published to the detriment of the plaintiff, and affecting him injuriously in the ordinary relations of life: actions on account of the *person* are, assault, battery, imprisonment as affecting his health or liberty: actions on account of *property* are in respect of debts due; claims arising upon contracts, whether under seal or not, made in the ordinary transactions of life; and generally in regard of property, whether real or personal.

Some actions are termed *mixed*, being of a mixed nature, as for trespasses against real property; and where such property is sought to be recovered, together with damages, for the injury done.

By stat. 3 *&* 4 *W.* 4. *c.* 27. all real and mixed actions, except writs of right of dower, writs of right of dower *unde nihil habet*, *quare impedit*, and ejectment, and all plaints in the nature of any such writs or actions except plaints for freebench, or dower, are abolished.

The commencement of a civil action is the issuing a writ or process to compel the party's appearance in court; and the last proceeding is, signing the judgment: the execution which issues to enforce such judgment being, for practical purposes, deemed a new suit.

Many *personal* actions die with the person; that is to say, if the defendānt die, the surviving plaintiff has no remedy against the executors of defendant; but action can be maintained against executors or administrators, as far as their assets will extend, for promises made by their testator or intestate. In actions of trespass, battery, and slander, the death of either party determines the suit. Real actions survive.

In all actions there must be a person able to sue, and a person sueable, and every one must bring his action in the form assigned by law.

The causes for which actions can be sustained are infinite in their varieties, but there is no wrong or injury, or breach of contract, to which a form of action is not applicable.

Actions may be classed under the following heads, to which there are corresponding titles in this Dictionary.

Actions upon promises or mutual contracts not under seal. See Assumpsit, also Agreement, Contract, Carrier, Guarantee.

Actions to recover money in respect of deeds or contracts under seal. See Covenant.

Actions to recover determinate and fixed sums of money. See Debt.

Actions for the recovery of a certain thing detained. See Detinue.

Actions for the recovery of damages on account of forcible wrongs done to the person, wife, children, servants, goods, or property of another. See Trespass.

Actions for the recovery of goods used or converted by another to his own use. See Trover.

Actions on the case for words or writings affecting a person's fame or reputation, or occasioning him *particular* damage. See Libel.

Actions on the case for damages occasioned by fraud or misrepresentation. See Deceit.

Actions for the recovery of land or any interest therein. See Ejectment.

Actions for the recovery of a widow's dower. See Dower.

Actions for the recovery of an advowson or right of presentation to a cure or benefice. See Quare Impedit.

Actions for recovery of damages done to or affecting real property. See Trespass.

Every one, before the commencement of an action, should be assured that the cause of action has actually accrued; that is, that his right of action is perfect, all preliminaries performed, such as notices of dishonour given to drawers and indorsers on bills of exchange, notice of abandonment where requisite, demand made of goods intended to be recovered in an action of trover, and, in cases of *mutual* contract, his part of the agreement fulfilled. It is expedient, in actions to be brought against sheriffs and others for seizing disputed property, to inform them distinctly of the right claimed therein, and it is absolutely necessary that in actions against justices of the peace or magistrates, commissioners of bankruptcy, revenue officers, and many other public functionaries, for acts done by them in the execution of their office, a written notice of action should be duly served at least a month previous to the issuing of the writ, in order to give them an opportunity of tendering amends before action, and which action must be brought within the time limited by the various statutes for that purpose, generally six calendar, and against customs and excise officers within three lunar months.

ADJUDICATION. The act of giving judgment; this term is applied to commissioners of bankrupt, who make a memorandum of adjudicating a party bankrupt, which is called the *adjudication*. Also to the judgment of the Court for Relief of Insolvent Debtors, when they adjudge an insolvent entitled to the benefit of the act. The certificate of that judgment is styled the "adjudication."

ADJUSTMENT, The settlement of a loss claimed of an insurer by the insured. The usual mode of settling a transaction of this nature is for the underwriter or insurer to indorse upon the policy, "Adjusted loss at per cent. payable —— (generally a month)."

The claim of an insured party must necessarily be regulated by the strict terms of the policy, and particularly as to the nature of the policy or insurance; that is, whether the policy was what is termed "open" or "valued:" if the policy was *open*, that is, no price specified, then the insured can claim the prime cost of the goods insured, according to the invoices of the goods. If the insurance was effected on a ship and her outfit, then the total expense of her outfit, including the premiums paid for insurance, is receivable. If the policy be "valued," that is, if the value be agreed upon in case of a total loss, the insurer only pays the sum agreed upon, or in case of a partial loss, an aliquot part corresponding to the loss.

The term "adjustment" applies to the settlement of loss upon a fire policy.

ADMIRAL. A high officer or magistrate that has the government of the king's navy, and the adjudication of all causes of merchants and mariners and things happening on the main sea, and in ships riding in great rivers near the sea, and in his court of admiralty determining the same. The office, since the reign of Queen Anne, has been executed by commissioners, with the exception of His late Majesty, who held the office in the reign of George IV.; the last member of the royal family previously holding this high office being James Duke of York, afterwards James II.: the commissioners are ordinarily styled "The Lords of the Admiralty;" they appoint a judge to perform the judicial functions of the office, which is executed according to what is termed the "civil" or ecclesiastical law, and not according to the common law of England. The jurisdiction of the admiral in his admiralty or vice-admiralty courts will be noticed in the next article.

ADMIRALTY, Court of. This court, or rather the exercise of the ordinary jurisdiction of the admiral, is divisible, and is executed by two courts, who have the same judge, one termed the Instance Court, the other the Prize Court. The one is the ancient tribunal; the other is erected by virtue of a commission from the king, to determine litigations, and to adjudicate upon matters relating to prize ships, captures, seizures, and privateering or reprisals. This latter court only exists during a war, and until the litigations consequent upon it are brought to an end. The other, which is the court generally known by the name of "the Admiralty," is a court for the determination of public or criminal and private wrongs arising at sea, or intimately connected with maritime affairs, where the common law of the land can give no remedy, or at least not so apt and convenient.

As to Offences at Sea.—The admiralty has jurisdiction upon what are termed the high seas, that is, upon all parts of the sea which are not within and do not form a part of any county. And as to offences committed on the coasts, the admiralty have exclusive jurisdiction of offences committed beyond the low-water mark, and between that and the high-water mark. It has jurisdiction of offences done upon the water when the tide is in, and the courts of common law of offences committed upon the strand or shore when the tide is out.

By stat. 27 *H.* 8. *c.* 4. all offences of *piracy*, *robbery*, and *murder* done on the sea, or within the admiral's jurisdiction, shall be tried in such places of the realm as shall be limited in the king's commission directed to the lord admiral, and his lieutenant and deputies, and other persons, to determine such offences after the common course of law, as if the same offences had been done on land. And by another statute in the same year, "all treasons, felonies, robberies, and murders, &c. upon the sea, or within the admiralty jurisdiction, shall also be tried in such shires and places in the realm as shall be limited by the king's commission, as if done on land, and the consequences of the offences are the same.

By the act 7 & 8 *G.* 4. *c.* 28., for the further improvement of the criminal law, and by 9 *G.* 4. *c.* 31. relative to offences against the person, all offences prosecuted in the admiralty are subject to the same punishments of death, or otherwise, as if committed on land. By acts 7 & 8 *G.* 4. *c.* 29. *s.* 30., relating to larceny and other offences connected therewith, and to malicious injuries to property, all felonies and misdemeanors under those acts, committed within the admiralty jurisdiction, shall be tried as any other felony or misdemeanor. See PIRACY.

As to private Wrongs.—The court of admiralty has general power to determine all matters arising upon the seas, which, had they arisen *here*, would have been cognizable by law; therefore seamen's wages, batteries, collision of ships, suits for obtaining possession of a ship, restitution of goods illegally taken on the high seas, questions of possession or right between the part-owners of ships, suits for pilotage, on bottomry and respondentia bonds, for officers' and seamen's wages, and for salvage, and relating to wreck, are properly brought in this court; but on the other hand, generally speaking, the court of admiralty has no jurisdiction over contracts under seal, or deeds (except bonds or instruments which hypothecate or mortgage the ship for money advanced on its credit, and for its use,) or agreements which have no relation to maritime affairs, although executed and signed on shipboard, as a bond, note, or engagement to pay money in London or elsewhere in England.

The judge of the admiralty usually sits at Doctors' Commons, Saint Bennett's Hill, London, and the court is open all the year round: in questions of difficulty or practical seamanship, he calls to his assistance naval and other personages, or two or more Trinity masters. An appeal lies from him to the judicial committee of the privy council, who hold their sittings at Whitehall.

As the ship itself is responsible for the engagements contracted upon it, and also for mariners' wages, which are recoverable in the courts at law and by various summary methods, the court has the power of arresting her and distributing the claims awarded. In cases of salvage the court secures the property saved, and can put claimants with a clear title in possession of a ship; and in cases of part-ownership can interfere upon the application of any one part-owner whose share is fixed and ascertained, to restrain the sending of the ship on a voyage without consent of the applicant, until adequate security to the extent of his interest has been given, to secure him in case the ship should not safely return; but in cases where the shares of part-owners are in dispute, then the admiralty has no power to interfere, but an injunction must be obtained from the chancery to restrain the sailing until the amount of the share for which security is to be given shall have been ascertained, which should in both cases be done *promptly*.

In all other matters the court have power over the persons of individuals, sufficiently necessary for the purposes of their jurisdiction, which is by no means familiar to the public, more especially as the courts of law also have jurisdiction together with the admiralty upon matters of contract and private wrong, although arising on the high seas. It may be remarked that, as the court is open all the year round, a suit in respect of any subject above noticed can be brought and decided while the other courts are closed for their vacations. In many cases, as far as the security against the ship is concerned, it is infinitely preferable to sue in this court, which is moderate in its expenses, and adequately protects its suitors. The practisers are proctors; no attorney at law, or solicitor, as such, being entitled to practise therein, which may in some way account for the apparent predilection suitors have for the courts of common law in cases where equal, and in a multitude of cases more secure right could have been done in this court.

Vice-Admiralty Courts.—A recent statute, the act 2 *Will.* 4. *c.* 51. *s.* 6. declares the matters over which the vice-admiralty courts abroad can exercise jurisdiction; being seamen's wages (which are always, *and under every circumstance*, entitled to a priority), pilotage, bottomry, collision, contempt of the regulations of H. M. service at sea, and *droits* or rights of admiralty, when a ship or its master shall come within the local limits of the vice-admiralty courts abroad, notwithstanding the cause of action arose elsewhere.

Cases of revenue law, it is said, are not within the jurisdiction of the vice-admiralty courts, unless under certain statutes. Questions of that nature are directed by one particular statute to be tried where the offence was committed or seizure made.

The admiralty court has no jurisdiction either criminal or civil (except with contracts for the performance of which the *ship* is liable) within any county, either by land or in rivers; nor, in strictness, of any stranded wreck; for *that* must be cast on land before it becomes a wreck.

Damages are recoverable at law for a wrongful suit in the admiralty, which was not properly triable there.

AD QUOD DAMNUM. A writ directed to the sheriff of a county, to inquire by a jury whether a grant intended to be made by the king will be to the damage of him or others. This writ is also had for the turning and changing ancient highways, which cannot lawfully be done without the king's license obtained by this writ, on the jury finding that such a change will not be detrimental to the public. So of a public river, which is a highway.

ADMINISTRATOR. The person to whom the distribution of the *personal* estate of a deceased is committed by the ecclesiastical court, where there is no executor appointed, or, if named, has renounced. Administratrix, is a female administrator. The instrument by which the ecclesiastical court gives authority to the administrator to act is termed the *Administration*, or *Letters of Administration*. See Executor.

ADULTERATION. The admixture of any preparation or matter of baser substance, or of a different nature, tending to deceive the sight or taste of a purchaser, or in anywise to deteriorate deceitfully things used in the ordinary purposes of life, is a cheat at common law: and in cases where the necessaries of life are made less wholesome by the substitution of any material or ingredient, manufactured or unmanufactured, imitated so as to deceive the purchaser in the quality or quantity; or if beer, wine, or other liquids are diluted, or any infusion be made therein, or are coloured, whereby the public may be deceived in the quality or strength; or if, in any case, the health of the purchaser or the public may by possibility be damnified; various statutes inflict severe penalties, proportioned to the magnitude and circumstances of the offence; and although the persons who commit such pernicious frauds may be indicted for each act, and punished for the misdemeanor by fine and imprisonment, yet it is most expedient to proceed in the manner directed by the several remedial statutes prohibiting by name each offence; more especially as justices of the peace, and in some cases of fraud, equally affecting the revenue and the health of the public, the commissioners of excise, have power to exercise a summary jurisdiction.

ADULTERY. The sin of incontinence between two married persons; or if but one of the parties be married, it is, nevertheless, adultery, but distinguished by the name of *single* adultery. It is only punishable in either by ecclesiastical censure and *penance;* but the husband can have redress by an action on the case for damages, which are assessed by the verdict of a jury. See HUSBAND AND WIFE.

ADVOWSON. The perpetual right of presentation to an ecclesiastical benefice or cure, corresponding to the right of patronage in the canon law. All advowsons formerly belonged to some manor, whose lord, having endowed the church with a house and glebe, obtained the right to present a parson thereto; but in process of time the manor and advowson became separated; and now comparatively few advowsons remain annexed to the manors, which are generally co-extensive with the parish. Thus the distinction of an advowson *appendant* and an advowson *in gross* was created; the former being the advowson as originally annexed to the manor, and the latter in its separated and disunited state. The first disunion of the advowson from the manor was in favour of ecclesiastical corporations, and subsequently of colleges, the annexation to which is styled an *appropriation,* as the acquisition of an advowson by a lay person, *i. e.* not in holy orders, is termed an *impropriation.* The right of presentation may be, and very often is, parted with for one turn only; but such an assignment *must* be made during the life of the present incumbent, and before a vacancy in the church, else the presentation would be void, as an encouragement of simony.

The separation of the advowson from the manor may be effected by the patron, at the present day, by conveying the manor with a reservation of the advowson, by conveying the advowson without the manor, or by presenting to an incumbent as of an advowson in gross, that is, treating it or naming it as already separated.

An advowson can only pass by will or deed, and if appendant to the manor as part of the inheritance, or it may be granted for one or more turns within a limited time.

Advowsons are either vested in ordinary persons, or in a bishop, college, corporation, or in the king, or in any person founding a new chapel by the king's license; and when the patron, not being the king or an ecclesiastical or collegiate corporation, presents his parson to the bishop of the diocese for institution, it is termed a *presentative* advowson. When the advowson is lodged in the bishop, who presents by reason of the patron not presenting in six months, it is termed a *collative* advowson; and when the king or other person does, by a donation in writing, put the parson in possession, by that single act, of a chapel, prebend, or church, for the most part founded by the king, or by a subject with his licence, and exempt from ecclesiastical visitation, it is termed a *donative* advowson.

All persons who have ability to purchase or grant, can likewise present to vacant benefices; but a dean and chapter cannot present the dean, nor may a clergyman who is patron present himself, though, if the bishop admit him on his solicitation, the institution shall be good. A parson about to be admitted makes oath that he has not made *any* corrupt or simoniacal contract. See SIMONY.

If the patron is excommunicate, or outlawed, or attainted, the bishop may refuse to admit his clerk.

If a person present to an endowed chapel, of which he has not obtained a licence of appropriation, the right to present is forfeited to the king, though not the inheritance in the chapel. However, the right to present is restored upon payment of a fine for the contempt.

The king may present by word. or in writing under any seal; a corporation aggregate (*i. e.* of many) must present under seal; and a married woman being entitled, must present with her husband.

Co-heiresses must present by turns, the eldest sister presenting first. Joint-tenants and tenants in common, it seems, must present in like manner; and after partition each shall be separately entitled to their moieties: joint-tenants and tenants in common must *all* concur; but if there are two joint-tenants of a next presentation, one may present the other, and two may present a third, but not a stranger.

An alien born cannot present to a benefice in his own right; he can, indeed, purchase it, but the king upon inquisition shall present.

Roman Catholics cannot grant an advowson, unless made for a valuable consideration to a Protestant purchaser; and devises by them of advowsons are void.

Municipal corporations being possessed of any advowson or right of presentation to any ecclesiastical preferment in their corporate capacity, are directed by the stat. 5 & 6 *W.* 4. *c.* 76. to sell the same under the direction of the commissioners for ecclesiastical revenues, and the proceeds of the sale are to be carried to the account of the borough fund; and any vacancy before such sale shall be effected, is to be supplied by the presentation of the bishop of the diocese. (*s.* 139.)

The mode or course of an ordinary patron's exercising his right of presentation is by his offering in writing, or even by bare words, a clerk (clergyman) in orders to the bishop for institution, which is forthwith done, unless the bishop discover that the presentation was given in performance of a pecuniary or valuable consideration, or that the person presented is illiterate, of evil life, &c.; in which cases he will refuse to admit him, and give prompt notice to the patron, so that he may be enabled to present another "clerk" before six *calendar* months has expired, as the bishop will be entitled to present in default of the patron's presentation of a fit person within that period, which is computed as 182 days from the last incumbent's death or deprivation, or vacancy of the cure. This right of the bishop to present, on default of the patron, is termed "a presentation by lapse;" but if a patron present before the bishop has collated another "clerk," the presentation is good, even though the six months have expired. If the bishop does not collate due time, the presentation "lapses" to the archbishop, and from him in like manner to the king.

Where the incumbency ceases by resignation of the incumbent, or by deprivation, the lapse shall not incur till after 182 days, or six months' notice given by the bishop to the patron; but no such notice is requisite where the church is vacant by the death of the incumbent.

A presentation by lapse does not deprive the patron of any future presentation.

The bishop, it has been observed, is bound to give notice of his refusal to admit; but the patron may contest the cause of the bishop's refusal by a writ of *quare impedit,* which is the process to be used in all cases where the patron is compelled to try his right of presentation against one who injuriously presents a clergyman without title, legally termed an usurper; when, if his turn of presentation be lost, he recovers two years' value of the church.

As no pecuniary profit can lawfully arise to a patron in the exercise of this right (although its estimation is very high, as being a source of provision for relations, or as a means of rewarding learning and virtue), on a mortgage by a patron of the manor to which an advowson may be attached or "appendant," the patron may still present. Also a bankrupt shall present to a benefice vacant at the time of his bankruptcy, though the advowson passes to the assignees. If a parson be turned out of or disturbed in his rectory after induction, his remedy is by trespass and ejectment, his estate being a freehold and corporeal hereditament, although the right of presentation in the patron is incorporeal Where the bishop unduly delays to admit a clergyman, he may have his remedy against the bishop in the ecclesiastical court.

The right to recover an advowson is limited to three incumbencies in sixty years in some cases, and to one hundred years in others.

AFFIDAVIT. An oath in writing; and *to make affidavit* of a thing, is to testify it upon oath in writing. Affidavits are generally *sworn;* that is, the oath is administered by a court openly, or by a judge or some officer or person having competent authority for that purpose, in any other place, and are used to verify various proceedings or acts done in the course of a cause, or to substantiate matter upon motion upon which the courts are applied to for a *summary* decision, *i. e.* an adjudication without the intervention of a jury; for, generally speaking, affidavits are not admissible as evidence in trials. Affidavits are deposited or filed in the courts in which they are instituted or made, and to steal one from its place of deposit is a felony punishable by transportation. Affidavits must set forth the *deponent's* true place of abode, and his *description* or quality and degree or occupation in life. When affidavits contradict each other, the court refers the matters alleged and denied to its chief officers, the master or prothonotaries, whose report will satisfy the conscience of the court; and sometimes issues at law or trials are directed to be had. Persons delegated by the courts of law or equity, or ecclesiastical courts, are termed commissioners. Affidavits are in very many cases made for the purpose of founding a process or preliminary proceeding; as an affidavit *to hold to bail,* an affidavit of nonpayment of money awarded or ordered to be paid, to ground an attachment for contempt, an affidavit to ground an admiralty warrant to arrest a ship, &c. The court of king's bench takes notice of affidavits made in aggravation or extenuation, when a party is brought up to receive judgment; indeed, the conscience of the court can only receive information in that manner.

As affidavits are only made for the purpose of informing the court upon matters upon which it cannot otherwise have judicial knowledge, they should not contain argumentative or inferential matter, as the conclusion or judgment rests with the court; they should also *positively* set forth *all* the circumstances, and not affirm or deny any thing in a loose or insufficient manner. Affidavits thus irregular will be rejected, and the party using them have to pay costs. The fees for taking affidavits vary from 1*s.* to 5*s.*, and depend upon the circumstances and place where taken, and whether papers are annexed, (termed "Exhibits,") or the number of deponents exceed one. Oaths in writing are also termed "depositions," when made before justices of the peace and commissioners of bankrupt. The term "affidavit" seems, in practice, and common parlance, to apply to oaths written, made before the superior courts, or a judge or commissioner thereof. The law allows Quakers and separatists to "affirm" that a statement is true, instead of "making oath;" hence they are said to make a *solemn affirmation*. Affidavits are required by numerous Acts of Parliament; and those affidavits are styled "extra-judicial," as not being in any cause or court, although they were requisite to verify documents, &c.; and notwithstanding a late Act of Parliament, some few are still necessary. However, they are exceedingly limited, for the act of which an abstract is here given, restrains a multiplicity of solemn appeals to the Creator, which it may fairly be presumed had the effect of gradually diminishing the sanctity of an oath, viz.

In any case where, by acts made, or to be made, relating to the revenues of custom or excise, the post-office, the office of stamps and taxes, the office of woods and forests, land revenues, works and buildings, the army pay office, the office of the treasurer of the navy, or of the treasurer of the ordnance, his Majesty's treasury, Chelsea Hospital, Greenwich Hospital, the board of trade, or any of the offices of his Majesty's principal secretaries of state, the office for auditing the public accounts, or any office under the control, direction, or superintendence of the lords commissioners of his Majesty's treasury, any oath, solemn affirmtion, or affidavit, might be required to be taken or made, the lords commissioners of his Majesty's treasury, or any three of them, by writing under their hands and seals, may substitute a declaration to the same effect as the oath, &c.; and the person who might, under the acts imposing the same, be required to take or make such oath, &c., shall, in presence of the commissioners, collector, other officer or person empowered to administer such oaths, &c., make and subscribe such declaration; and every such commissioner, &c. is thereby empowered and required to administer the same accordingly. There is added an exception as to the oath of allegiance, which is to be preserved; and a full exception as to oaths, &c. taken in judicial proceedings or upon proceedings by way of summary conviction before justices of the peace. Declarations are to be substituted for oaths taken by churchwardens and sidesmen respecting acts done under turnpike trusts, on taking out a patent, and respecting lost pawnbrokers' duplicates. The two universities and corporations are at liberty to substitute a declaration instead of the former oaths.

Oaths made voluntarily, that is, made in matters not the subject of legal inquiry, and termed extra-judicial, are abolished.

The fees due upon the oaths are payable for the substituted declarations.

Persons wilfully stating a thing they know to be false upon oath, affidavit, or solemn affirmation, or in the declarations now substituted for oaths, &c., incur the guilt of perjury. See PERJURY.

The making a false declaration in matters relating to the customs, excise, stamps, taxes, or post-office, subjects the party making it to an additional penalty of 100*l.*

The form of this declaration is as follows:—

Surrey, to wit. } I, *James Chilman*, of *Katerham Street, in the parish of Katerham and county of Surrey, labourer*, do solemnly and sincerely declare, that *the paper writing hereunto annexed, and marked* A, *is a true copy of the parish register book, for burials, at Chaldon, in the county of Surrey, as far as relates to the burial of Carew Roffey, therein mentioned, I having examined the same carefully with the said register book; and I further declare, that I knew and was well acquainted with the said Carew Roffey, from the circumstance of my having been a shepherd at Chaldon Court Farm, and a servant of the said Carew Roffey at the time of his decease, which took place, according to the best of my recollection and belief, on or about the — day of —*, 1810, *at Chaldon Court Farm, in the parish of Chaldon aforesaid; and I further declare, that I have this day read the solemn declaration of Michael Rowed, of Katerham Street, aforesaid, carpenter, made by him, and taken and received before John Perkins, Esquire, one of his Majesty's justices of the peace for the said county, at Blechingley, this — day of — instant, touching the death of the said Carew Roffey; and I solemnly declare that I believe the same to be true in substance and matter of fact.* And I make this solemn declaration, conscientiously believing the same to be true, and by virtue of the provisions of an act made and passed in the fifth and sixth year of the reign of his present Majesty, intituled "An Act to repeal an Act of the present Session of Parliament, intituled 'An Act for the more effectual Abolition of Oaths and Affirmations taken and made in various Departments of the State, and to substitute Declarations in lieu thereof, and for the more entire Suppression of voluntary and extra-judicial Oaths and Affidavits; and to make other Provisions for the Abolition of unnecessary oaths.'"

Verification of a register of burial, and death of a party.

Confirmation of the declaration of another as to the same fact.

Taken and received before me, one of his Majesty's justices of the peace for the said county of Surrey, at Blechingley, in the said county, this — day of July, 1836. J. PERKINS. } JAMES CHILMAN.

On the certificate or document verified, should be written,—

"This is the paper writing marked *A*, shown to *James Chilman*, and by him referred to in his solemn declaration taken and received before me, this — day of July, 1836.

"J. PERKINS,
One of his Majesty's Justices of the Peace for the county of Surrey."

AGE. This word has a legal effect in relation to those periods of life which enable persons to do certain acts, which for presumed want of judgment, on account of tenderness of years, they were forbidden to do, and such acts rendered void. For instance, a man at twelve years of age can be called upon to take an oath of allegiance to the king; at fourteen, which is his age of discretion, he may consent to marriage, and choose his guardian for several purposes; and at twenty-one, he may alien his lands, goods, and chattels.

With regard to a woman, at nine years of age, she was, if married, considered entitled to her dower; at twelve, she may consent to marriage; at fourteen, she is at years of discretion, and may choose a guardian; and at twenty-one, she may alien her property. But see the articles, INFANTS, in regard to their acts and liabilities; and CHANCERY, as to the protection afforded them by that court, which assumes the guardianship of their persons and care of their property. Fourteen is the age by law to be a witness; but persons of tenderer years, who understand the nature of an oath, or are sensible of a moral obligation to speak the truth, are now admitted to give evidence.

No one my be a member of parliament under the age of twenty-one years. No man can be ordained priest, till twenty-four, nor be a bishop till thirty years of age. A man cannot be sworn on any jury or inquest, till twenty-one; and it seems a man cannot be admitted, or practise as an attorney, proctor, or notary public, till that age.

Persons under twenty-one, are legally styled "infants under the age of twenty-one years."

A person born on the thirty-first of a particular month attains his full age on the thirtieth of the same month, in the twenty-first year; for majority is completed on the day preceding the anniversary of birth, and the law takes no notice of the fraction of a day.

In criminal law, the discretion of infants varies according to the nature of the offence; though it is laid down as a positive rule, that under the age of seven years, no infant can be guilty of felony, or punishable for a capital offence. But they are presumed capable of doing evil and contracting guilt at fourteen; the law presuming that they are then as capable of discerning good and evil as those of maturer age. Between the ages of seven and fourteen their capacity of doing evil is measured by the strength of the culprit's understanding and judgment; and the law in this case leans to the most merciful construction of the culprit's acts; the chief question being, whether the infant had such a mischievous discretion or judgment, so that it may fairly be presumed the felonious act was the result of deliberation and malice.

It seems that an apprentice may, without any regard to age, be guilty of a felony in taking away his master's goods, if they had not been previously delivered over to his charge.

AGENT. A person who transacts the business of another, either as factor, broker, auctioneer, or servant. Factors and brokers are mercantile agents who have peculiar authorities, and their acts will bind their employers, who are legally termed *principals*, because they are *generally* appointed; servants are more often *specially* appointed, therefore they will not bind their *principal* or employer by acts beyond the limit of their authority. Factors, as a particular class of *agents*, sell and transact the business of their principal in their own name; brokers, in the name of their principal. There are many thousand persons in London who style themselves "agents," or "general agents," who undertake to do the business of others; and attornies and solicitors are styled and deemed "agents" in respect of matters of correspondence, authority, and delegation; but it seems the agency is limited to specific acts, and referable to the general principle of law, which is, that if an agent exceeds his authority, his principal is not bound. These questions are treated of under the article PRINCIPAL AND AGENT.

The continuation of an agent's *authority* may be implied; as if an apprentice, or known representative of another, purchase goods for a principal in his name, and the principal put an end to the agency or employment, the employer or principal should give notice of the revocation or termination of his authority to the agent, else he will continue liable for the agent's subsequent acts; and where the dealings of the agent have been extended to parties not known to the principal, he must give public and general notice, in order that the ordinary presumption of the agent's continued employment should not render him (the principal) liable, or expose others to hazard.

Agents are bound, generally speaking, to account with their principal for the goods sold, &c., and cannot set up the assumed right of a third person, unless a notice has been given, inducing a strong presumption that the goods sold were not those of the employer, or that the proceeds fairly and legally belong to others.

If an agent refuses to account for goods delivered to him for sale, it shall be presumed, after a reasonable time, that he has sold them, and received the proceeds in money.

The authority or employment of an agent cannot be delegated or performed by deputy, unless expressly stated or implied by the terms of the agency.

In all authorities a principal gives to an agent, it shall be intended that the course of dealing with third parties should be according to custom and common usage. If stockbrokers sell stock upon credit, or agents purchase goods to be paid for before delivery, or sell goods to be repaid by other goods; in each case, the broker or agent will not bind the principal, it not being usual to sell stock on credit, or to pay for goods before delivery, or to sell goods on those terms.

Agents who have the possession of goods can pledge them for legitimate purposes; but agents pledging goods for a greater sum than is due to them, and in violation of good faith, are by stat. 7 & 8 *G.* 4. *c.* 29. *s.* 51., punishable by transportation, or fine and imprisonment, at the discretion of the court.

Agents converting to their own use any money, or security for money, having received *written* directions for the application of the same, are by *s.* 49. liable to the same punishment; but no partner of any agent is liable, nor is the agent himself liable, if he has disclosed the fact upon any compulsory process.

The powers and authorities of agents must necessarily depend upon the terms of the employment, and the course of business, which is the subject matter of the agency.

An agent is personally responsible upon a bill or note, unless he states upon the face of it that he subscribes it *for* another, or by procuration of another. An agent selling goods and drawing upon the purchaser for the amount payable to his principals, may be sued by the principals upon the bill.

An agent or contractor for the public, employed by government, cannot be sued upon contracts made by him in that capacity.

The power of agents in a mercantile character is sufficiently defined by the stat. 6 *G.* 4. *c.* 94., which declares—

That persons intrusted, for the purpose of consignment or sale, with goods, and who shall have shipped them in their own names, and persons in whose names goods shall be shipped by others, shall be deemed the true owners thereof, so far as to entitle the consignees to a lien thereon in respect of money or negotiable securities advanced or given by them to or for the use of the persons in whose names the goods are shipped, or in respect of money or negotiable securities received by them to the use of the consignees, just as if such persons were the true owners; provided that the consignees shall not have notice, by the bills of lading or otherwise, at or before the advance or receipt of such money or securities, that such shippers are not the *bonâ fide* owners of the goods.

Persons intrusted with, and in possession of, bills of lading, India warrants, dock warrants, warehouse keepers' certificates, wharfingers' certificates, warrants or orders for delivery of goods, shall be deemed the owners of the goods therein described, so far as to give validity to contracts made by them with others for the sale, deposit, pledge, or disposition of such goods; provided the parties had no notice that they were not the owners.

Provided that no person shall acquire a security upon goods in the hands of an agent for an antecedent debt, beyond the amount of the agent's interest in the goods.

Persons may contract with known agents in the ordinary course of business, or out of that course, if within the agent's authority, notwithstanding notice of their being agents merely; or may take property in pledge from such agents, but they shall only acquire the same right which the agent had.

Agents may pledge to the amount of sums due to them from their principals; provided that the acceptance of bills by agents, drawn by or on account of their principals, shall not constitute any part of such sums, so as to excuse the consequence of improperly pledging, unless the bills shall be paid when due.

AGISTMENT, is where other men's cattle are taken into any ground at so much per week. Agistment is also the profit of such feeding in a ground or field, and extends to the depasturing of barren cattle of the owner, for which tithes are payable to the parson. See TITHES.

AGREEMENT, in a general sense, is taken for any reciprocal contract; but is a term more correctly used to designate a verbal promise or simple contract *reduced into writing*, which is deficient in the formula of sealing and delivery as a deed. The circumstance of the promise being reduced into writing does not confer upon it any priority or greater importance than it originally possessed as a verbal contract; the law only considering the writing as evidence of the promise, not as a new sort or species of contract. An agreement, therefore, being *legally* considered a verbal contract, differs materially from a contract or writing *under seal*, as a deed (termed, par excellence, a specialty contract), which is peculiarly favoured by the law as to priority and other inherent qualities; for instance, a *mutual* and reciprocal consideration or adequate motive (except in the cases mentioned in the statute of frauds, which see below, and under the title CONTRACT) must be always proved, to render an agreement or verbal promise valid; but a deed requires no such consideration to render it valid against the party executing it, even in a court of equity, unless in cases of fraud and bankruptcy.

It is, therefore, a very serious error to believe that an agreement signed, and sometimes stamped, is conclusive evidence of the consideration or motive expressed (except in the cases mentioned below), and to assume that such a writing possesses nearly, if not quite, the efficacy of a deed; for a written agreement, although it may elucidate and render certain the terms of a verbal contract, yet passes or performs no more than such verbal contract could have done without the writing. Where it is desirable to evidence and to confirm matters of importance, a deed or writing under seal, with the requisite formalities, should be prepared; as the time for bringing an action upon the contract will be extended to twenty years instead of being limited to six; the land of the party contracting will be charged, although in the hands of the heir or devisee, in case of his death; and it will also have priority as a special contract over his assets; and in case of putting the same in suit, the required proof is confined to the execution of the deed.

It does not appear necessary to have the express motive or consideration expressed *on the face* of an agreement, though prudence and the desire of avoiding litigation would dictate the practice, as the law will allow it to be supplied by verbal evidence, *except* as to agreements made by executors or administrators in respect of their testators' or intestates' estates; the agreements of third persons for the debt of another; or relating to the sale of an interest in land; or concerning a matter not to be performed within a year (unless earnest given or payment in part be made); contracts for the sale of goods for ten pounds or upwards; acknowledgments or new promises; renewing a debt, which would otherwise be barred by the statute of limitations, or a debt barred by infancy; and contracts or agreements for the sale of goods to be made and delivered at a future time, unless earnest given. Most of these agreements are the contracts which an old statute called the "Statute of Frauds," and a late statute enlarging its operation, require, and should be evidenced by some note or memorandum signed by the party, or in the case of goods, by a part payment or *earnest* given to bind the bargain. These last named memorandums, it is important to observe, *must* contain the motive or consideration, and the substantial parts of the contract, leaving nothing to be supplied by verbal evidence.

It may not be amiss to notice in this place, a decision that an agreement not under seal for a composition is not binding unless the payment be guaranteed by a third person, or the agreement is founded on some *other* sufficient consideration.

Contracts not under seal, though reduced into writing, are styled agreements *by parol.* And agreements of letting for a less term than three years are styled *parol* demises or leases; "parol" signifying verbal. See CONTRACT.

ALE AND BEER. The regulations affecting the *manufacture* of ale and beer are very few: they consist in taking out a licence from the Excise; "entering" the premises, under a penalty of 200*l.* and seizure of the mash-tun and materials; and abstaining from the use of any other article than malt; and ale and beer may be brewed at any degree of strength.

The adulteration of beer is provided against by the act 56 *G.* 3. *c.* 58., which enacts that any brewer, dealer in or retailer of beer, receiving or having in his possession, making, using, or mixing with any worts or beer any liquor, extract, calx, or other material or preparation, for the purpose of darkening the colour of worts or beer, or any liquor, &c., other than brown malt, ground or unground, as commonly used in brewing; or receiving or having in his possession, or using or mixing with any worts or beer any molasses, honey, liquorice, vitriol, quassia, coculus indicus, grains of paradise, guinea-pepper, or opium, or any extract or preparation thereof, or any preparation whatever, as a substitute for malt or hops; forfeits such articles, with the vessels in which they are contained, which may be seized by any excise officer, and 200*l.* for each offence.

Druggists or others selling, sending, or delivering to any licensed brewer, dealer in or retailer of beer, knowingly, any colouring other than unground brown malt, forfeit the same, and are subject to a penalty of 500*l.*

By the act 1 *W.* 4. *c.* 51. for the repeal of the ale and beer duties, brewers are prohibited from having in their brewery, or in any mill connected with the same, any raw or unmalted corn or grain, under forfeiture of the same, and a penalty of 200*l.*

The sale of beer and ale is regulated by the statutes 1 *W.* 4. *c.* 64. and 4 *&* 5 *W.* 4. *c.* 85., by which all householders assessed to the poor-rates, upon a certificate of good character (except sheriffs' officers, or officers executing the legal process of courts of justice), are enabled to sell beer, ale, or porter, or cyder and perry, by retail, to be drunk on the premises, if certificated; and to sell beer off the premises, if uncertificated, on merely obtaining an excise licence; for which a duty of 3*l.* 3*s.* is paid yearly, if the beer, &c. is to be drunk *on the premises*, and if *off the premises*, 1*l.* 1*s.*; and 1*l.* 1*s.* for the cyder and perry. By the former of these acts, the licence from the justices formerly required by 9 *G.* 4. *c.* 61. *s.* 17. is no longer necessary; but the recognizance required by stat. 3 *G.* 4. *c.* 77. *s.* 1., which had been repealed by 9 *G.* 4. *c.* 61., is revived.

By these acts, also, which impose regulations on the sellers of beer and ale, a single justice of the county where any riot shall happen, or two or more justices, where any riot may be expected, are empowered to order any licensed house to be closed at such time as they direct; and justices may permanently regulate the times of opening and closing in Middlesex and Surrey.

The permission by beer or ale sellers, of drunkenness or disorderly conduct in their houses, or the transgression by them of the conditions specified in the licence, subjects them to a penalty of not less than 40*s.*, and not exceeding 5*l.*; for the second offence, not less than 5*l.* nor exceeding 10*l.*; and for the third, not less than 20*l.* nor more than 50*l.*

Licensed houses are not to be opened in Middlesex and Surrey before 5 in the morning, nor after 10 at night; or before 1 o'clock in the afternoon of Sunday, Good Friday, Christmas Day, or any fast or thanksgiving day. In other places, not before 4 in the morning, nor after 10 at night; nor between 10 and 1, and 3 and 5, on Sundays, &c., under a penalty of 40*s.* for every offence; and every sale of beer, &c. is deemed a separate offence.

Nothing in these acts affects the privileges of the two universities, or the vintners in London, or the selling beer in booths at lawful fairs.

ALEHOUSES. See Inns and Alehouses.

ALIENS. Persons *born* out of the king's allegiance, *i. e.* in a foreign state or country not under the dominion of Great Britain. But persons who are the children of fathers, natural born subjects, and their children, even though their mothers were aliens, are considered Englishmen. The issue of an English woman by a foreigner is deemed an alien.

As far as regards the acquisition of property, or its transmission, aliens are able to possess property of what is termed a *personal nature.* Freeholds or estates of inheritance they may indeed purchase, but only for the use of the king, who is entitled to claim the same as a forfeiture. Alien women cannot claim their dower or thirds out of such estates. In matters of trade and commerce they are under no special restraint, and may sue and be sued in the king's courts as British subjects; though it seems the court of chancery will not interfere by injunction to protect the copyright of a foreigner, he being left to prove his *special damage* in an action at law, for the unauthorised sale of his work. This is the condition of *alien friends,* i. e. natives of a country in amity with Great Britain.

Alien enemies, as they are termed in contradistinction to alien friends, natives of a country in actual war with Great Britain, acquire not even a bare right of residence, but by the king's special favour, and are declared incapable of enforcing any contract or suing for any debt due to them.

An alien who is desirous of domiciliating himself in England, must obtain what are termed *letters of denization,* which are letters patent, to make him a British subject, an act which can only be performed by the king's prerogative; or he may apply to parliament to be naturalized, which will be spoken of presently.

Denization, though it relieves the alien of the incapacity to purchase or acquire land, yet does not permit him to *inherit* it, or suffer his heir to take it by descent from him; which is sometimes productive of great inconvenience, and induces legal questions between the foreign born and the English born children of an alien.

Naturalisation, however, puts the alien in the same situation as if he had been *born* in the king's allegiance; a denizen being but in a middle state between a foreigner and an Englishman. The operation of the act of parliament naturalising a foreigner or alien, is consequently more extended in its consequences and operation than denization, and imparts to the alien and his children the birthrights of Englishmen, unfettered by any regulations as to the inheritance of freehold, and only restricting the applicant for denization and naturalisation from ever being of the privy council or either house of parliament, or having any office of trust civil or military, or being capable of any grant of lands, &c. from the crown. The children of a *naturalised* alien labour under not even these restrictions, they apply only to the applicant himself. An alien born cannot accept a benefice without the king's licence. An alien enemy is not entitled to have a writ of habeas corpus, his course is to apply to the secretary of war.

Aliens ought not to be returned on a jury, except an alien is party as a criminal, when the jury are to be half denizens and half natural-born subjects, with the exception of high treason.

In strictness, an alien enemy entering the kingdom during time of war should suffer death by martial law; but this rigour is never exercised unless in extreme cases; for aliens who put themselves under the protection of the king, or, in plainer language, under the surveillance of the secretary of state, may have a general pardon.

Our laws, in their construction, deal mercifully with aliens, who are morally presumed to be ignorant of the interpretation of statutes passed to prevent offences which, but for peculiar or local circumstances, would not be punished with unusual severity. Therefore, in indictments upon such statutes, the judge will direct a conviction upon what is termed the simple or *minor* offence only; but in heinous offences, committed with violence, the law would be allowed to take its course, as ignorance could by no means be presumed. The international restrictions as to the influx or immigration of foreigners are regulated by the political state of the countries. Thus, in 1793, the alien acts, which were continued to 1816 (now repealed), made the regulations following, which are here given, as in case of a war they will doubtless be re-enacted, viz.:—Masters of ships arriving from foreign parts were directed, under penalties, to give an account at every port of the number and names of every foreigner on board to the custom-house officers; and justices and others were to grant passports to such aliens. The king had power to restrain aliens, and to send them out of the kingdom on pain transportation, and on their return of death. Arms of aliens were to be accounted, and if required were to be given up; and aliens were not to go from place to place in this kingdom without passports. The present regulations, regulating aliens in the present time of peace, are, by the alien act now in existence (repealing the 7 *G.* 4. *c.* 5.), as follows:—

The master of every vessel which shall arrive from foreign parts shall immediately declare in writing to the chief officer of the customs at the port of arrival the number of aliens (if any) on board his vessel, or who have, to his knowledge, landed therefrom, and their names, rank, occupation, and description, as far as he shall be informed thereof, under a penalty of twenty pounds, and the further sum of ten pounds for each alien who shall have been on board at the time of the arrival of such vessel, or who shall have, to his knowledge, landed therefrom within this realm, for which the vessel may be detained; with an exception of mariners actually employed in the navigation of the same.

Every alien, after the commencement of this act, arriving from foreign parts, shall immediately show to the chief officer of the customs at the port of debarkation, any passport which may be in his or her possession, and declare in writing to such chief officer, or verbally make to him a declaration, to be by him reduced into writing, of the day and place of his or her landing, and of his or her name, and shall also declare to what country he or she belongs and is subject, and the country and place from whence he or she shall then have come, according to a form approved by one of his Majesty's principal secretaries of state, under a penalty of two pounds.

The officer of the customs to whom such passport shall be shown and declaration made is immediately to register such declaration in a book (wherein certificates shall be printed in blank, and counterparts thereof, according to a form approved by one of his Majesty's principal secretaries of state), and shall insert therein the several particulars by this act required in proper columns, in both parts thereof, and shall deliver one part thereof to the alien who shall have made such declaration, which is to be sent to one of his Majesty's principal secretaries of state; and if such alien shall have arrived from any foreign country in Ireland, a true copy of such declaration and of such certificate is to be sent to the chief secretary for Ireland.

An alien about to depart is to deliver the certificate which he or she shall have received to the chief officer of the customs at the port of departure, who shall insert therein that such alien hath departed this realm. If the certificate should be lost, a fresh certificate may be granted by the secretary of state upon a previous application to a magistrate.

All certificates which are to be given shall be given without fee or reward, under a penalty of twenty pounds; and the wilfully making or transmitting a false declaration, by obtaining a certificate under any other name or description than the true name and description of the alien intended to be named and described, without disclosing to the person granting such certificate the true name and description of such alien, or pretending to be the person intended to be named and described in any certificate, subjects the offender, upon conviction before two justices, to a penalty not exceeding one hundred pounds, or imprisonment not exceeding three calendar months, at the discretion of the justices.

All offences against this act are to be prosecuted within six calendar months after the offence committed, and are to be prosecuted before two or more justices of the peace of the place where the offence shall be committed, who are required, in default of payment of any pecuniary penalty, to commit the offender to the common gaol for any time not exceeding one calendar month, unless the penalty shall be sooner paid, where such penalty shall not exceed the sum of twenty pounds, and forthwith to report to one of his Majesty's principal secretaries of state, or to the chief secretary for Ireland, as the case may require, the conviction of every offender under this act, and the punishment to which he is adjudged; and no writ of certiorari or of advocation or suspension shall be allowed to remove the proceedings of any justice touching the cases aforesaid, or to supersede or suspend execution or other proceeding thereupon.

Foreign ministers or their servants, aliens who have been resident three years, and obtained certificate thereof, and aliens under 14 years of age, are excepted.

Every foreign seaman, who in time of war serves two years on board a British ship of war, by virtue of the king's proclamation, is thereby naturalised under the same restrictions before mentioned as to denizens.

Trading with an enemy is illegal, and of course contracts with them for the purchase or sale of goods cannot be enforced.

Aliens are disqualified by name from being enrolled as burgesses of any corporation. The Bank charter also excludes them from being directors, and nothing short of an act of naturalisation will qualify them for voting in elections for members of parliament.

Aliens, we have seen, cannot present to an advowson.

ALIMONY, is that allowance for maintenance which an ecclesiastical court decrees or orders should be paid to a wife separated from her husband by divorce. See HUSBAND AND WIFE.

ALMANACKS, are legal evidence; and the examination by almanacks (for *one*, it seems, would not satisfy the court) is as conclusive as the verdict of a jury. The Almanack "*to go by*," according to the language of the books, is the calendar prefixed to the Common Prayer, which is part of the law of the land. Since the repeal of the stamp duty upon almanacks, a great variety have been published by irresponsible and ignorant persons, consequently inaccurate. As the Terms are now fixed, and special returns abolished, it seems that judicial reference to almanacks can only be needed to ascertain the days of the month or week, as the courts do not take notice of the courses of the heavenly bodies. The sun's rising and setting, the height of the tide, &c., cannot be proved by almanacks alone.

AMENDMENTS. Corrections of errors in process and pleadings, which the courts generally permit, can be made at almost any stage of the proceedings, at the costs of the party committing the error or slip, or of the attorney, who is in almost every case liable to reimburse or pay to his client what he may have been compelled to expend. In some proceedings, however, errors may be what are termed "fatal," *i. e.* the proceeding is absolutely void, and therefore cannot be amended; but these instances are comparatively rare.

AMENDS, TENDER OF. See TENDER.

ANATOMY. See DISSECTION.

ANCIENT DEMESNE. See MANOR, SOCAGE.

ANCIENT LIGHTS. See LIGHTS.

ANGLING. The taking of fish by a rod and line in the *day* time, in private grounds or waters, is distinguished from a similar act done by night. Although it is deemed a taking of property, yet being done in the day time, without circumstances inducing fear or suspicion, it does not subject the person of the angler to detention, but his rod and tackle may be seized by and forfeited to the owner of the water, who may, by himself or servant, effect the seizure. See FISHING.

ANIMALS, are distinguished by the law into such as are tamed, and such as are untamed or wild (*feræ naturæ*, which see). In such as are tamed and domestic, as horses, cattle, and poultry, these are as much property, and the subjects of ownership, as a table or bed, because they will not stray unless stolen or enticed, *i. e. feloniously led*, away. In wild animals or fish, no one can have a property sufficient for the purpose of an indictment till he has taken possession of them; and some animals are of so base a nature that they will not form the subject of an indictment or action, although the taking them is punishable summarily by statute. See OFFENCES AGAINST PROPERTY, FERÆ NATURÆ, GAME.

ANNUITY. A yearly payment issuing out of land, or charging the person, or both . the first is distinguished by the name of *rent-charge;* the latter are generally annuities, made determinable on life or other contingencies, created for the purpose of securing a greater interest upon a loan than *5l.* per cent. The person receiving the annuity is styled the *grantee;* the paying, the *grantor*. To restrain as much as possible the pernicious practice of borrowing money upon such terms, which not unfrequently absorb the expectancies of heirs and persons in distress, the following regulations have been made by the stat. 53 *G.* 3. *c.* 141. (explained by stats. 3 *G.* 4. *c.* 92. and 7 *G.* 4. *c.* 75.): by which act a *memorial* of every deed, bond, instrument, or other assurance, whereby any annuity or rent-charge shall be granted *for one or more life or lives, or for term of years, or greater estate determinable on lives*, shall, within thirty days, exclusive of the day of execution, be enrolled in chancery, such memorial to contain the date of the deed, the names of all the parties, and of *all* the witnesses; and to set forth the annual sum to be paid, the name of the person for whose life the annuity is granted, the consideration, &c., in the form set forth in a table in the act, otherwise every such deed and assurance shall be void.

In every annuity, deed, &c., where the person to whom the annuity shall be granted or made payable, shall not be entitled thereto *beneficially* (*i. e.* being only a trustee or agent), the name of the party who is *actually* to take the annuity beneficially shall be described in the same manner as is required in the enrolment.

Copies of the deeds or instruments for securing such annuities shall be given to the parties applying for the same; and on refusal may be obtained by an order of a judge of king's bench or common pleas.

If any part of the consideration shall be returned to the party advancing the same, or if notes given as part of the consideration shall not be duly paid, or if the consideration is expressed to be paid in money, if any part shall be paid in goods, or if the consideration or any part of it be *retained*, under pretence of answering future payments, or under any *other* pretence; in any of the said cases the grantor of the annuity may apply to the court in which any action is brought, or judgment entered, by motion, to stay proceedings, and the court may order the assurance to be cancelled, and any judgment obtained to be vacated.

A book of enrolments is to be kept in chancery by a clerk, whose fee for entering each enrolment is *20s.*, and *1s.* for each certificate and search. (The office is next door to the Six Clerks' Office, Chancery Lane.)

All contracts for the purchase of any *annuity* or rent-charge, with any *infant* under 21 years of age, shall be utterly void, notwithstanding any attempt to confirm the same on the infant's coming of age. And all persons soliciting infants to grant annuities, or advancing money to them on condition of their granting annuities when of age, or engaging them by oath or promise not to plead infancy, shall be judged guilty of a misdemeanor. And solicitors or brokers demanding gratuities for procuring money (beyond *ten shillings per cent.*) shall also be judged guilty of *misdemeanor*, and punishable by fine, imprisonment, and corporal punishment, at the discretion of the court.

The preceding act is totally confined to annuities granted for money; therefore other annuities, or arrangements for securing an annuity, need not be memorialised; nor do the foregoing enactments in anywise apply to them, they being placed upon the same footing as ordinary securities. Therefore annuities purchased by the grantees, giving up a business to the grantor, the resignation of an office by the grantee in favour of the grantor, the assignment of freehold premises, book debts, and stock, in trade to a grantor who takes a trading concern from a grantee. The following annuities *expressly* excepted by the act, *viz.*:—Annuities in *Scotland* or *Ireland;* annuities given by *will*, *marriage settlement*, or for the *advancement* of children; annuities secured upon freehold, &c. (as beforementioned); annuities secured by the actual transfer of *stock*, the dividends whereof are of equal or greater annual value than the annuity; *voluntary* annuities, granted without regard to pecuniary consideration or *money's worth;* annuities granted by any body corporate, or under any authority or trust created by Act of Parliament—do not require enrolment.

If an annuity be set aside, the consideration or purchase money may be recovered with 5*l.* per cent. interest, minus the payments made on account of the annuity.

APOTHECARY. See Surgeons and Apothecaries.

APPARITOR. A messenger or officer who serves the processes of the ecclesiastical courts. His duty is to serve citations or summonses, calling upon the parties cited to appear; to arrest them if the court award process of *contumacy*, *i. e.* contempt, against them for not appearing; and to execute the sentences or decrees of the judges of the court.

APPEAL, signifies the removal of a cause from one court to another that is superior, for ultimate decision; and this may, in effect, be done by stating sufficient matters of erroneous judgment in order to have it reversed, which are strictly termed proceedings "in error;" or by appealing to the House of Lords from the decree of the chancellor. *Error* may be applied to courts of law, *appeal* to courts of equity.

A writ of error lies from inferior courts of record in England into the king's bench; and the writ of error on any judgments of the king's bench, common pleas, or exchequer of pleas, is returnable in the exchequer chamber, and from thence to the house of lords, which is the only *final* judgment, and conclusive upon all parties.

In *criminal* cases, judgments may be reversed by writ of error, which lies from all inferior courts of criminal jurisdiction to the king's bench, and from the king's bench to the house of lords.

In *equity*, decrees pronounced by the master of the rolls or the vice-chancellor, may be reversed by the lord chancellor, on a *petition of appeal.* From the lord chancellor a petition of appeal lies to the House of Lords.

In *bankruptcy*, an appeal lies from the decision of the judges of the court of review in bankruptcy to the lord chancellor only; but this appeal is restricted to *matters of law and equity, or on the refusal or admission of evidence only*, on a special case, to be approved and certified by one of the same judges.

APPEAL TO THE SESSIONS, is allowed from the convictions or orders of justices of the peace, or magistrates generally, as a matter of right, where the defendant is dissatisfied with their adjudication; but this right is in many cases barred by various statutes, which render convictions and orders of magistrates final: the statutes taking away the right of appeal must expressly state the prohibition of appeal.

All appeals are subject to various regulations as to security for costs, deposits, bail, &c.

APPEARANCE. It is not necessary in civil causes for defendants to personally appear at the bar of the court, but the appearance is re recorded, viz. by the clerks of chancery and exchequer; by the clerk of the common bails of the queen's bench, at King's Bench Walk, Temple; by one of the filacers in the common pleas, at No. 3. Elm Court, Temple; and by the filacer in the exchequer of pleas, No. 9. Old Square, Lincoln's Inn; who receive a memorandum delivered to them by the attorney, or defendant, at entering the appearance. When a defendant has been personally served with a *writ of summons*, he should, within eight days inclusive after such service, cause an appearance to be entered for him in the court out of which the writ issued; or, in default of his so doing, the plaintiff may, by the terms of the writ, on the morning of the ninth day, cause an appearance to be entered for him (upon an affidavit of the service), and proceed to judgment and execution.

For entering an appearance in the courts of law a fee of 1*s.* is allowed to the clerk or filacer for every defendant, unless an appearance shall be entered for more than one defendant by the *same* attorney, and in that case a fee of 4*d.* for every additional defendant. The memorandum should be written upon a parchment form, which can be bought at a law stationer's, and filled up or written in this form, by a defendant who wishes to save the expense of an attorney at this stage of the proceeding.

"In the Queen's Bench [*or*, Common Pleas; *or*, Exchequer of Pleas.]

James Thompson, Plaintiff, against *John Smith.* [*or*, and another; *or*, and others.]	The defendant, John Smith, appears in person. (J. Smith, 32, Fore-street, Cripplegate.)

Entered the 1st day of November, 1837."

APPORTIONMENT. A division or subdivision into proportional parts of a rent, common of pasture, or a pew, or similar interests; as where a part of the land out of which the rent issues is sold, or the house in right of which the common or pew attaches is sold off, or a partition is made amongst co-heirs, each portion is charged with a proportionate part of the incumbrance, or the benefit is allotted in shares having exact relation to the amount or quantity of the whole. This division or arrangement is termed *apportionment.* Apportionments are also made in point of time in respect of rents reserved by lease; as on the death of a tenant for life of land or houses, of which the rent was reserved payable to him, the executors or administrators are entitled to recover from the undertenant, or reversioner, the whole of the rent, if he died *on* the day it became *payable;* or if *before* that day, a proportion according to the time he lived of the current quarter, or from the last period of payment, making all just allowances. The tenant must live over twelve o'clock at night on the quarter-day, or day appointed for payment, the rent not being payable till the next day.

The same principle attaches on lettings or demises which are verbal, or by *parol, i. e.* by agreement not under seal. See AGREEMENT.

A quit-rent is not apportionable as between tenant for life and the party in remainder.

Interest on a mortgage is apportionable as between the legatee of the mortgage money, or the reversioner, and the executors of the person who had the life interest; so interest and dividends accruing from the public funds are apportionable. The stat. 4 *&* 5 *W.* 4. *c.* 22. extends the law of apportionment of rent (see stat. 11 *G.* 2. *c.* 19.) to *all* rents, charges, annuities, and payments, payable and made at fixed periods.

A tenant for life of property which is liable to the payment of a fine upon renewal, is entitled to have the fine *apportioned* between the reversioner and himself; that is, he can call upon the reversioner to contribute or pay a just proportion of the amount of the fine, to be calculated upon the tenant's life, which is consonant to moral equity, as the reversioner will be entitled, on the death of the tenant for life, to the benefit arising from the renewal. However, such renewals should be *absolutely necessary* in prudence, to preserve the estate from forfeiture, to entitle the tenant for life to the apportionment or contribution; and the reversioner has a right to be informed of the nominees, or other terms of the renewal, if the lease or estate is for lives. This apportionment can be enforced in chancery, by either the tenant for life or his executors.

APPRAISER. A person who values goods. By an ancient statute, appraisers of goods are to be *sworn*, to make true appraisement, and valuing the goods too high, shall be obliged to take them at the price appraised. It seems this statute chiefly applies to distresses for rent, where, by the law at present, an appraiser is sworn by the constable to make a true appraisement; but in other cases where an appraisement is directed by law, an action will lie against the appraiser if a fraudulent valuation be made. A few observations may be here offered as to the vague mode in which appraisements and valuations are made, especially as it appears irregular, and precludes, or at least considerably impedes, inquiry as to the truth of the inventory valued. The values, although taken *singly*, are yet delivered in the aggregate, and different standards of ascertaining the aggregate value prevail, according to the discretion the valuer exercises as to the "circumstances" under which the appraisement is made. As appraisers take specific values, they ought to give or impart them; and therefore it appears any person may refuse to pay for an inventory so appraised. The Insolvent Debtor's Court require appraisements, certified under the hands of their brokers or appraisers, to be made of an insolvent's furniture and wearing apparel, in which the *specific* and *single* values are returned. It would close a great opening for fraud and impropriety, if the public insisted on appraisers returning the single values of articles appraised.

Inventories of a deceased's effects are not, as a *matter of necessity*, to be made and valued by sworn appraisers; any two disinterested and competent persons may make the same upon a paper impressed with the proper stamp, all persons interested concurring: this would save expense, and sometimes a *high* valuation; a double *commission price* on the value being charged, viz., so much for the inventory, which *any* one or two persons may make, and so much for the valuation.

As to the appraiser's valuation on a distress for rent, and his oath, see DISTRESS, also INVENTORY.

APPREHENDING OFFENDERS. Persons so doing are in many cases allowed compensation by the judge on their trial, the order for which is payable by the sheriff of the county; and this compensation may be allowed to the wife, child, father, or mother of a person killed in endeavouring to apprehend, according to circumstances.

APPRENTICE. A young person bound by indenture to a tradesman or mechanic, who undertakes to teach him his trade: there are also agricultural apprentices, factory apprentices, and apprentices to the sea service. This contract is usually effected by a written agreement or indenture stamped as by law is required; but as this contract is almost in every case entered into during the minority of the apprentice, the master has no remedy against him for departing from his service, or commission of any breach of the indenture, or for refusing to serve after 21, so that it is necessary for the intended master to procure the parents or friends of the apprentice to covenant for the performance of the contract. There is an exception in the case of parish apprentices; these, if males, may be bound till 24; females only till 21, or marriage, stat. 43 *Eliz. c.* 2. *s.* 5. See also the custom of the city of London, noticed hereafter. The apprentice is, in the eye of the law, a servant, and may be reasonably chastised by his master or mistress, or, which is more advisable, may be taken before a justice of the peace, who will deal with the refractory apprentice by committing him to the house of correction, for not exceeding one month, to hard labour.

Indentures of apprenticeship made in corporate towns were, till lately, required to be enrolled, as they then evidenced the claim of the apprentice to his freedom; and, in London, indentures of apprenticeship with a freeman are still enrolled at the chamberlain's office within a year from the execution, on the acknowledgment of the apprentice, who is bound by the custom to serve the whole term, notwithstanding the indenture be executed within his minority, and the service exceed that term.* London is now the only city where service to a freeman entitles the apprentice to his freedom; and by the custom of this city, the apprentice may be assigned, or turned over, although strictly speaking, an apprentice is not assignable, the assignment being considered in the light of a contract between the two masters; and it is said upon very old authority, that in case of the master's death, the executor or administrator must put the apprentice to another master of the same trade, by the same custom.

With respect to London apprentices, there are several regulations as regards their indentures and service, which, being of a local and technical

* See Bohun's *Privilegia Londini*, p. 338.; but this has been doubted in a modern case.

nature, are not here mentioned; the chamberlain's clerk, or the clerks of the company of which the master is free, generally affording every necessary information on this subject. Apprentices in London are also under the special control of the chamberlain.

The terms of other apprenticeships are adjusted by the parties themselves; and the regulation of these agreements, as to the conduct of each party, in many cases rests with the justices of the peace, who are empowered by various statutes to make orders between the master and apprentice, either by way of correcting the apprentice, assigning him or her to a new master, discharging him from his indentures, or ordering a return of money to the apprentice; and on death or insolvency, in the case of a parish apprentice, may direct another service.

Whatever an apprentice gains is for the use of his master, whether he was formally bound or not. A master may be indicted for turning away his apprentice, or for not sufficiently maintaining him. If a master gives an apprentice licence to leave him, it cannot afterwards be recalled. If an apprentice marry against a covenant in the indentures, that will not justify the master turning him away, but the master must sue on the covenant. By the custom of London, a freeman may turn away his apprentice for gaming; if a master turn away his apprentice for negligence, the apprentice or his friends can compel a return of a proportionate part of the premium, by bill in chancery. As no apprentice can be made without writing, so none can be lawfully discharged but by writing under the master's hand, and, by statute, with the allowance of a justice of the peace.

Many statutes regulate apprentices put out by public charities, as those put out by the parish; and with regard to a class of young apprentices generally exposed to suffering, the legislature has provided particular protection (see CHIMNEY SWEEPERS); and for preserving the health and morals of apprentices employed in cotton and woollen mills, and other manufactories, by which, amongst other things, the system of night work was abolished as to persons under 21, persons under 18 are not to work more than 12 hours per day, and one hour and a half is to be allowed for meals; and no child under 9 is to be employed; and parents and guardians are liable to penalties for falsely stating their children's ages.

There are, in addition to the numerous statutes regulating apprenticeships, certain acts which authorise justices to compel certain persons under age to be bound as apprentices; churchwardens and overseers may put out poor children apprentices, which, if any one refuse to take, he forfeits 10*l.*; magistrates may also direct apprentices to be put out to the sea service.

Apprentices with whom less than 10*l.* premium is paid, absenting themselves during their apprenticeship, shall serve an equal time beyond their term; 6 *G.* 3. *c.* 25.

APPRENTICES TO FREEMEN OF LONDON. By the custom of London, apprentices that are bound by indenture above the age of 14 years, and under the age of 21, to freemen of London, for the full term of 7 years, are compellable to serve the full term, and an action will lie against the apprentice for breach of any of the covenants; but if the apprentice is under the age of 14 years at the time of his binding, or if he is bound for a less term than 7 years, his indenture is voidable, and he may *sue it out* when he will.*

* See note in the preceding page.

The *binding* of an apprentice is performed at the Hall of the company whereof the master is free: for instance, if the master be a painter-stainer, the apprentice must be taken to the Hall of such company on a court day (generally once a month), when the clerk of the company will make out the indenture, and the master and apprentice will execute it before the court of assistants.

This indenture should be enrolled with the chamberlain of London, which is done by the master and apprentice both attending before the chamberlain at Guildhall, whose fee is 2*s.* 6*d.* If the apprentice refuse to be enrolled within the *first* year of the term (for it must be done then or not at all), the master may, within that time, bring the indenture to the chamberlain or his clerk who will record the same; which record is as good as an enrolment, and shall bar the apprentice from discharging himself. If the master neglect or refuse to enrol the apprentice within the year, such apprentice may be discharged from his service, by what is termed *suing out* his indenture. An apprentice is assigned or *turned over* to another master of the same trade, by the master's consent, or by the special custom, by the executor of his master, who is compellable to place the apprentice with another master.* In either case the *turn-over* must be made before the company where the apprentice was bound, and then before the chamberlain: it is imperative that the apprentice be turned over before the chamberlain as well as the company, else the second master will not be obliged to keep the apprentice, nor is the apprentice compellable to serve such second master; but he may depart when he pleases by *suing out* his indenture against his first master, which can be done without the knowledge of the second master. By the turning over before the chamberlain the first master is discharged from the apprentice, and the second obliged to keep him for the full term of his indentures, however long it may be.

If an apprentice be not enrolled, the master cannot turn him away, for the apprentice shall yet recover damages from time to time upon each refusal to take him back.

The enrolment of an apprentice does not prevent him from *suing out* his indenture for proper and sufficient reasons.

The usual causes for an apprentice *suing out* his indenture are —

1. If the master improperly beat or chastise the apprentice for lawful cause in an unlawful manner.

2. If the master refuse him sufficient necessaries.

3. If the master turn the apprentice away from his service, or leave off his trade, or neglect to instruct his apprentice.

4. If the master do not enrol the apprentice within the first year of the term.

Indentures are *sued out* in the *Mayor's Court* by means of an attorney of the same court; and for any other cause than non-enrolment, the cause of *suing-out* is tried before a jury, who are freemen and masters.

A freeman's widow may take a maid apprentice for seven years, and enrol her just the same as a youth, but the binding must be in all ways conformable to the custom of London as to age, &c.

* The law makes no other provision, in case of the master's death, for the apprentice; so that if the master does not charge his estate by a covenant to return a proportionate portion of the premium in case of his death, the apprentice, whose parents may have paid a considerable sum, are without remedy.

An apprentice, where his master becomes bankrupt, proves for a proportionate part of the premium.

Refractory and disorderly apprentices are punishable summarily before the chamberlain, who has power to send them to Bridewell.

At the expiration of the apprenticeship, the apprentice and the master attend the chamberlain, when the master testifies to the service by the apprentice; if the master refuses, the chamberlain can compel the appearance of the master, or make the apprentice free.

If the master or apprentice commit any fraud, by conniving at a service with a non-freeman, termed a *foreigner*, the master is disfranchised and his shop shut up; the apprentice, as a matter of course, is not admitted to his freedom.

An apprentice's marriage within the term is no cause for disfranchisement or non-admittance to freedom; but he may have a *mandamus*, commanding the mayor to make him free. A writ of *mandamus* is the proper remedy in all cases where freedom is improperly refused.

An apprentice suing out his indenture may compel a return of a proportionate part of the premium, by suing his master in the mayor's court of chancery or equity.

The chamberlain takes upon himself by consent to arbitrate matters between masters and their apprentices, and his decision in such cases is binding.

On an apprentice taking up his freedom, 5*s*. is payable to the orphanage fund, over and above the chamberlain's accustomed fees.

Apprenticeship to a freeman of London confers, after service, the privilege of freedom of that city, and the benefit of carrying on trade therein; as no person, generally, can use any trade, manual occupation, "mystery," or craft therein, except he shall have served an apprenticeship therein for 7 years, upon a penalty of 40*s*. for every month. The words "trade, manual occupation, mystery, or craft," mean such trades or businesses as require skill and experience; and therefore, merchants, husbandmen, and gardeners, or persons following any employment obviously not requiring skill and experience, as a hemp-dresser, are excepted.

In any other place than the city of London, any one may now work in any lawful trade, or in more trades than one, at his pleasure, although he may not have been apprenticed; and discharged soldiers and mariners may carry on and follow trades in London, notwithstanding the charters and bye-laws of the corporation, by virtue of a statute passed enabling persons who have served their country to earn a livelihood without restriction as to place. These persons are in common parlance styled "King's freemen."

Apprenticeship in merchant vessels is regulated by the stat. 5 & 6 *W*. 4. *c*. 19.; and no stamp duty is chargeable.

As to offences by breach of trust committed by apprentices, who are servants in the eye of the law, see EMBEZZLEMENT.

As to securing the rights of the master in case the apprentice should enlist in the king's service, whether army or navy, or in the East India Company's service, reference must be had to the mutiny and to the marine mutiny acts, which require a binding before the age of 14, and direct the indenture to have certain prescribed requisites, and to be indorsed with the certificate of a magistrate within three months from the beginning of the apprenticeship. 3 *W*. 4. *c*. 5. *s*. 42., and 3 *W*. 4. *c*. 6. *s*. 35, 36. 40—42., and the stat. 5 & 6 *W*. 4. *c*. 19. (the Merchant Seamen's Act), the 39th section of which prohibits apprentices to the sea service entering into his Majesty's service without the master's consent; but if the apprentice voluntarily enter on board any of H. M.'s ships of war, and be allowed by the master to continue therein, the master shall receive the balance of the apprentice's wages up to the expiration of the indenture.

As the statutes on apprenticeships would almost fill a volume, the reader is advised in most cases to apply to a magistrate for his direction.

APPROPRIATION. See ADVOWSON.

APPROVER. A party to a criminal offence, who accuses others to be guilty of the same, and is admitted as a witness at the discretion of the court, to give evidence against his companions in guilt: he is vulgarly called "King's evidence." No person who has pleaded "not guilty" to the offence can be such witness; and all persons convicted of felony, and infants under the age of discretion, are equally inadmissible. The testimony given by an approver must necessarily be of an unsatisfactory nature, as the approver's hopes of lenity and pardon must materially depend upon the prisoner's conviction; therefore it is seldom used without offering additional evidence confirmatory of the principal facts of the approver's story. So the accessory may be a witness against the principal, and the receiver against the thief. In misdemeanors a person may be convicted upon the uncorroborated evidence of an accomplice. This mode of obtaining evidence is not now very much in use.

APPURTENANCES. Something belonging to and attached to a freehold, and of a less nature or lower degree, as rights of way, common of pasture, turbary, fishing, &c., outhouses, dovecotes, yards, orchards, and gardens. Land cannot be appurtenant to land, or a house to a house; therefore, by the word *appurtenances* only such things pass of an inferior condition, which usually have been enjoyed together with the house or land.

ARCHDEACON, is an ecclesiastical dignitary immediately under the bishop, and exercising jurisdiction throughout the diocese, or some part. A part of the bishop's power is lodged with him; and in law he is allowed to be an *ordinary* (which see), and consequently has a court where he can inflict penance, excommunicate, suspend inferior clergy, prove wills, grant administrations, and hear ecclesiastical causes. It is admitted that most of this power originally accrued by encroachment. There is a right of appeal to the bishop from his judgments or acts, which practically limits the assumed power of this spiritual functionary.

ARMORIAL BEARINGS, or ARMS. The device depicted on the (now imaginary) shield of one of the British *nobility*, which is divided into the *greater nobility* and the *lesser nobility*. The *greater* containing all titles and degrees of honour from knighthood upwards; the *lesser* all from barons downward, gentry being the lowest degree of nobility. The criterion of nobility is the bearing of arms or armorial bearings received from ancestry and descent.

When the subject of armorial bearings was before parliament in 1798, it was ascertained that there were 9,458 families entitled to bear arms in England, in Scotland 4,000. These families, in the language of the heralds, are *noble*, either by creation as peers, or as gentry who have acquired their armorial bearings from time immemorial.

There is nothing to prevent persons assuming arbitrary insignia and armorial bearings to which they are not entitled; but all persons entitled to *bear arms* can register their genealogies and families at the Herald's College, Saint Bennett's Hill, London, on payment of a moderate fee; the heralds being the examiners of these matters and recorders of genealogies. Persons who cannot show a continual user and bearing of arms by descent from their male ancestors for a century and half, may be generally presumed not entitled. But the heralds grant patents of *nobility*, or grants of arms, as they are commonly termed, upon proper representations and occasions.

A duty is now imposed upon armorial bearings, whether borne on plate, carriages, seals, or in any other way, the regulation of which is under the commissioner of taxes.

ARMS. Any thing that a man wears for his defence, or takes into his hand to strike at another; ordinarily weapons, such as swords, pistols, guns, halberts, lances, javelins, bayonets, &c.

When the wearing of swords was fashionable, and in remoter times, when armour was part of a gentleman's personal equipment even in time of peace, any unusual or dangerous weapons were prohibited; and the *going armed* was punishable by fine and imprisonment; as arms not suitable to the person's quality, or the showing force at unseasonable times, were sure incentives to a breach of the peace, or caused terror. The law, therefore, at this day, allows no man, upon pretence of *protecting his person* or property, to use or exhibit arms but on urgent and publicly acknowledged necessary occasions, upon pain of incurring fine and imprisonment.

The training persons to use arms, or to perform military evolutions, is punishable by a particular statute with transportation or imprisonment.

The frequenting public meetings *armed* is indictable; a justice may hold a party to bail for so doing.

ARRAIGNMENT. The charging a party to plead to an indictment of felony. The party generally is called upon to hold up his hand for the purpose of acknowledgment and identity; if he answers to his name, it is sufficient for the purpose. If a party refuse to plead, the court may order a plea of "not guilty," to be recorded for him.

ARREARS, or ARREARAGES. Money unpaid at the due time, as rent behind-hand; the remainder due on account; or a sum of money remaining in the hands of a party bound to account.

ARREST. The restraint of a person by law, which in civil cases is for securing a debt to an individual, and in criminal or penal cases for compelling the person charged with a crime or offence to appear and submit to justice. Arrest in criminal cases is termed "an apprehension."

All conservators of the peace and magistrates have authority, by their verbal order, or warrant in writing under their seal, to apprehend or cause to be brought before them all persons who are accused of, or suspected to be guilty of, any treason or felony, misdemeanor or breach of the peace, and to commit them to gaol, or deal with them according to law. The sheriff or coroners of a county, also, may apprehend any suspected felon without warrant; a constable or police officer, or policeman, may apprehend any one for a breach of the peace in his presence; and a watchman or beadle may apprehend or detain in custody, for examination, any person he finds in the streets at night, whom there is reasonable ground to suspect of felony, although there be no proof of a felony actually committed.

All persons are enjoined by the law to lay hands on and arrest an offender at the time of his committing a felony, or giving a wound in their presence; and in cases of suspicion, any one having reasonable or probable cause, may apprehend, or charge a constable or policeman or other officer to apprehend the suspected party. In cases of treason or felony, great latitude is allowed to private persons in apprehending parties whom they fairly may have cause to think are guilty thereof; and if any individual does not pursue or assist in taking into custody any person whom he may have seen commit a felony, or do any act of great violence, such as wounding or maiming, or being charged and requested by magistrates, peace-officers, or others, who are actually taking or in pursuit of a suspected felon, to assist in taking or pursuing him, he is liable to fine and imprisonment upon indictment, should the suspected offender escape through his refusal or wilful default. It certainly is the least troublesome and most safe course to charge the offender in custody with a constable or peace-officer, or to give information before a justice, and obtain a warrant for the wrong-doer's apprehension; but where the obvious necessity occurs of securing a transient offender who is actually committing, or has very shortly before committed, a crime, no one can in reason hesitate to arrest him and convey him before a magistrate. It may here be mentioned that the lord chancellor, lord keeper of the great seal, the lord high steward, the lord marshal, and every justice of the queen's bench, have, as incident to their office, authority to keep the peace, and to take recognizances for keeping it. Sheriffs also are, with the above, conservators of the peace; but no duke, earl, or peer, as such, have greater authority than private persons in this respect. The ordinary process of apprehension by warrant is executed by a constable, police-officer, or other person duly authorised, taking the offender and securing him in his own house or common place of confinement for suspected offenders, until he can convey him before a magistrate, which should be done with all convenient speed. Private persons apprehending, may keep the offender in their own houses, or other place of safety, till the party can in like manner be brought before a justice to be dealt with according to law.

In caution, no person should arrest another, unless upon view of the felony or wounding, or on the *hue and cry*, or unless charged so to do by a constable or similar peace-officer, without reasonable and probable cause of suspicion; as every apprehension under other crcumstances is made at the party's *peril*, that is, he will be liable for damages in an action for false imprisonment, if the person apprehended be innocent. What is *probable cause of suspicion* may be generally referred to the party's own intelligence, and common or collected rumour and comparison of facts, the publication of the suspected offender's name in hand-bills, the assertion of credible persons coupled with his knowledge or belief of the suspected offender's character, associations, habits, &c. But as every one is enjoined by law to apprehend a felon upon view of felony or wounding, to join in pursuit upon a *hue and cry*, and to assist a peace-officer in taking or preventing an escape after capture; so the law protects and indemnifies such acts, even if it should turn out that the suspected party was innocent. In other cases, the burden of justification rests upon himself.

In cases of doubt, an application should be made to a justice (when circumstances or time will allow) for a warrant, and the information or suspicions should be stated upon oath. This course will absolutely indemnify informants, provided such statement or information is free from malicious intention. It should always be ascertained that a felony had been actually committed by some one, before a suspicion can be reasonably entertained, or made the foundation of an apprehension.

Constables and peace-officers have, from the nature of their offices, greater latitude and indemnity for their acts; for, upon a bare charge of felony made by a credible person, they may apprehend another, and secure him as an ordinary offender till a justice can determine upon the propriety of committing him or otherwise.

To assist the apprehension, without warrant, of suspicious persons, the propriety of whose arrest might not always be strictly justifiable or readily proved, various statutes have been lately passed, enabling police officers, constables, and private persons to apprehend and seize others *found committing* various petty larcenies or takings of property, committing malicious injuries to property, and committing offences against the game laws and laws for preservation of deer and fish, or conducting themselves in a manner reasonably inducing fear or suspicion of the probable consequences of their deportment. By the Police Act, any policeman, while on duty, is empowered to apprehend certain suspicious persons, as, "all loose, idle, and disorderly persons, whom he shall find disturbing the public peace, or whom he shall have just cause to suspect of evil design, and all persons whom he shall find, between sunset and the hour of eight in the forenoon, lying in any highway, yard, or other place, or loitering therein, and not giving a satisfactory account of themselves," and to deliver any person so apprehended into the custody of the constable appointed under that act, whose duty is to convey the party before the police magistrate, to be dealt with as a vagrant.

The same act contains regulations as to the conduct of individuals at fairs within fifteen miles of Temple Bar, and at coffee-houses in and about the environs of London, and other matters relating to public quiet and convenience, enforcing summary arrest in cases of disobedience, or by warrant afterwards. It also provides that any constable or *other person* may apprehend a *reputed* thief, and convey him before a justice.

The Vagrant Act gives power to *any person whatsoever* to apprehend any person offending against the act, or, as it termed, committing an act of vagrancy. See VAGRANTS.

The Highway Act, and many other acts, give similar power to collectors and subordinate persons.

It seems also that these summary powers may be delegated to others; for persons committing what are termed "malicious" injuries to property, that is, unauthorised damage, may be apprehended by the owner or his servant, or any person authorised by the owner; and the same as to petty takings of property, &c.

Trespassers against game in the day time, *refusing to declare their name and residence*, may be apprehended: with night poachers less ceremony is required.

One thing is imperative upon those private persons who make or command these summary arrests, which is, to take the party arrested before a justice as soon as possible; no time is limited by statute, except as to common trespassers against game, who are not to be detained more than twelve hours: an *unreasonable* preliminary detention would subject the apprehender to an action; but it is unsettled what is reasonable or otherwise; twenty-four hours appears sufficient in general, but circumstances may render a longer detention justifiable.

Many local acts subject persons to summary arrest or payment of a fine; but the persons who arrest must take the person offending before a justice, and the fine must be levied under his warrant, or the offender committed.

Persons making fires or signals to smuggling vessels may be apprehended by any person.

Contempts committed in the face of any court of law or equity, or to any sheriff or coroner in their courts or inquisitions, commissioners of bankrupt, or judges of inferior courts of record, may be punished by a summary arrest and committal.

Persons refusing to enter into recognizances before a magistrate to prosecute, or to give evidence in a case of felony, may be committed, until the sessions or assizes, to the common gaol.

Officers in the army and navy may arrest and imprison in cases of mutiny or gross breaches of duty.

Arrests on civil process are either *provisional*, or a "*holding to bail*," *i. e.* the defendant is liberated on finding bail to answer the action, or *final* or "*in execution*," *i. e.* in conformity to or in execution of a judgment which concludes the suit, in which the defendant cannot be discharged on bail, but must remain in custody till payment or satisfaction of the judgment be made.

The provisional arrest takes place where the plaintiff in any action makes affidavit that the defendant is indebted to him in not less than 20*l.*, exclusive of costs or interest; or where, in cases of special injury, a judge will permit a defendant to be holden to bail for that or a greater amount, upon a writ of *capias*, directed to the sheriff of a particular county or city, who thereupon issues a warrant to his bailiff, authorising the arrest of the defendant, who being captured, is at liberty to demand being taken to any safe and convenient house of any *third** person nominated by himself, being within three miles, and *in the county* where the arrest was made, *not being the defendant's own residence*, there to remain for twenty-four hours. The defendant cannot legally be taken to any gaol or prison, or into any tavern, alehouse, or victualling house, or drinking house, *or to the private house of the officer, until after that time.* If the officer should do otherwise, and within twenty-four hours attempt to take the defendant to prison, he and the principal officer incur the penalty of 50*l.* to the defendant. This important privilege of a defendant, of which it is the bounden duty of the officer (under the same penalty) to inform his prisoner, is usually rendered unavailing by the ignorance of the debtor and the extortion of the officer, who says to his prisoner, "Where will you go?" [naming some place or house of security of his own or of another officer, from the undue and extortionate charges there made called a "sponging house,"] or some similar question leading to an almost involuntary assent on the defendant's part. It is also the officer's duty to deliver a copy of the *capias* and produce his warrant, on request, so that it may be ascertained that the person making the arrest is really an officer, and not a mere assistant, whose arrest would be illegal. There are various extortions practised upon defendants under arrest, which are well known and provided against by an act, which declares that no other fees shall be taken for lodging or accommodation in the officer's or "lock-up" house than those settled by the judges; in the absence of the table of fees, for none have the judges settled, it may be pretty accurately stated that payment for refreshments, after the rate of the charge at a com-

* For instance, the house of a friend, the office of an attorney, &c.

mon inn, is sufficient; and that more than 5*s. per diem*, including a bed, cannot lawfully be demanded, without subjecting the officer to an application to the court for a refund of the excess of lawful charges, or a penalty of 50*l*. Undue charges for "searching the office," "bail-bond," &c., are punishable by an action for treble damages, and a penalty of 40*l*. Any sum charged as a fee for arrest, and paid by a defendant, the court will also, on motion, compel an officer to refund, and make him pay the costs of the application in both instances. Defendants confined in these houses, if taken there *immediately on arrest*, cannot be charged any thing for the first twenty-four hours, save for actual refreshments and bed; and it is imperative on the officer to permit the defendant's provisions to be brought, and his friends and advisers to have access to him. After eight days the defendant must render to gaol, or put in bail.

Upon an arrest in execution the foregoing regulations do not apply, as the sheriff is generally, in strictness, bound to lodge his prisoner within the county gaol immediately after the caption.

As far as regards the remedies against extortion, the defendant taken on final process is much in the same situation with the defendant provisionally arrested, or held to bail. See PRACTICE (Div. 1.).

It is illegal, and a misdemeanor, to arrest a dead body; a vulgar error has obtained to the contrary, founded, perhaps, on the form of the writ, which commands the sheriff to take the "body" of A. B.

Arrests for nonpayment of money, or neglect to perform a thing commanded by or pursuant to a rule of her Majesty's courts, made for the enforcing performance of awards or payments of costs, are in the nature of arrests in execution, being constructive contempts of court.

Arrests for contempt in not answering a bill in chancery or exchequer, are in the nature of holding to bail; which, after render of the party, may be, as it is termed, *purged*, that is, satisfied, by the putting in of the answer; and, in both cases, by payment of the money, or costs, or doing the thing the nonperformance of which constitutes the *contempt*.

Public bodies, or companies incorporated by act of parliament or royal charter, cannot be held to bail. The members of other companies or associations not so incorporated, can be sued as ordinary individuals, and held to bail. Executors and administrators cannot be held to bail in those characters, or for debts due by their testator or intestate, even though they have *assets*, unless they have, by memorandum in writing, charged themselves with a distinct promise, they not being liable by virtue of "the statute of frauds" for more than they receive. See EXECUTORS.

Some persons are privileged from provisional arrest, and some from both provisional and final: such privilege being either temporary or permanent.

Temporary privilege from arrest on civil process (not from criminal) extends to all persons necessarily, or of right, attending, whether as a party interested or summoned as a witness, any court of justice, arbitrator, commissioners of bankrupt, inquisition, or any legal procedure of a public nature, or as barrister, attorney, or juryman. This privilege is not limited to the time of the party's actual attendance on the court, but in going to and returning from the same. Barristers who follow the circuits of the judges are privileged during the whole circuit, although they may not be retained in any cause, it being very possible that they may be so. All ministers, or officers necessarily attending the circuit, are in like manner privileged during the same period, more especially if they are named in the commission of assize. The court upon which the party attends will, upon verbal application and personal examination of the parties, order the immediate discharge of the party arrested; and this is the most usual course; but the court from whence the process issued will do the same.

Attornies, duly certificated, and who have practised within a year, are also permanently privileged from provisional arrest; but they are not privileged in cases of contempt, arrests in execution, or processes of that nature. They are (unless by name excepted in acts of parliament) privileged from all processes issuing from inferior courts; but they should, in the first instance, give due notice of their claim of privilege.

Permanent and absolute privilege from arrests upon both kinds of civil process, is extended to all the queen's servants, her chaplains, or persons liable to attend the queen by reason of their office, as heralds, pursuivants, &c. (unless the Board of Green Cloth otherwise permit). All the royal family; ambassadors and their servants; peers, English, Scotch, or Irish, whether they are entitled to sit in parliament or not; peeresses and widows of peers; members of parliament; judges and the sergeants at law; married women, not having incurred their debts on representations made by *them* of their being unmarried; bankrupts who have obtained their certificate, or whose creditors have proved under their fiats; and insolvents adjudged entitled to their discharge; are privileged from arrest on account of the debts for which they have obtained their certificate or discharge. In cases of the description mentioned in this paragraph, the discharge is obtained by application to the court, or a judge, or by pleading the privilege or special matter. In cases of peerage, and persons having privilege of parliament, judges, and ambassadors, discharge would be given by the houses of parliament. Indeed, in cases of high and notorious privilege, no sheriff or officer dare arrest; the only cases ever known having been those of ignorance and misinformation, and even then the parties were severely censured for the breach of privilege.

A defendant having been served with a writ of summons or serviceable process from any other court, does thereby not acquire a privilege from being held to bail (if the sum will warrant it) on a new suit, the plaintiff being liable to pay the costs of the suit abandoned.

A second arrest cannot regularly take place for the same cause of action; in some cases, however, a judge will permit it. In cases of fraud, a defendant may be twice arrested upon the same affidavit and process.

All writs, and processes of a civil nature, are by law absolutely prohibited to be executed on a Sunday, Christmas-day, and Good Friday. It is a misdemeanor to arrest a clergyman during divine service; he is also privileged in going to and returning from the performance of any religious ceremony he is *personally* obliged to perform. But no such privilege extends to individuals going to or returning from a marriage, funeral, or religious ceremony; although, it seems, to disturb such ceremony by an arrest at the time of its performance would be indictable.

ARREST OF JUDGMENT. To move in *arrest of judgment*, is to show cause why the judgment, whether in a criminal or civil cause, should be stayed on account of insufficiency in the indictment or record. In criminal causes it is done before judgment pronounced; in civil causes, before the successful party can, by the rules of practice, perfect or sign his judgment.

ARSON. The maliciously, and with intent to injure, setting fire to and burning any house, building, ship, stacks of corn, crops, &c. The intention must be to injure or defraud some third person, who is not identified with the defendant. Therefore, a married woman cannot be indicted for setting fire to the house of her husband, with intent to injure him. This offence is felony. See BURNING.

The burning of the house, &c. of another cannot amount to arson, unless it be malicious; it is a trespass, for which the party injured can have his remedy by action: but if a man set fire to his own house, and thereby burn the house of his neighbour, it is arson.

As to negligent burning by servants, see FIRE.

ASSAULT AND BATTERY. A simple assault is an attempt to commit an act of personal violence to another; no words, however provoking will amount to an assault. Battery is the beating or unauthorised touching another, or wilfully putting in motion any substance against him; therefore, any acts done to the person of another in a violent, rude, or revengeful manner, as by spitting upon him, jostling him, or touching him in anger, are batteries: a battery includes the assault. An action of *trespass* is the civil remedy for this injury, which is applicable to the assault only, though this action is generally brought to recover damages for both. Any menace or threat which hinders another in his business by occasion of the fear thereby reasonably entertained, is actionable.

Acts of indecency are assaults, and unauthorised acts done to another who does not resist through fear or misrepresentation, are also assaults; as if a master or medical attendant take indecent liberties with a scholar or patient, even if no resistance is made, it is an assault. Parish officers cutting off the hair of a female pauper are guilty of an assault; and parish officers compelling a youth to submit to a surgical operation against his will, were lately convicted of an assault, although it was shown that the operation was successful. Assaults of these descriptions are more properly subjects of indictment.

In cases where the party assaulted or beaten cannot obtain testimony sufficient to maintain his action, or no special damage can be proved, or where public justice ought to take priority of the private wrong, an indictment is the most apt remedy, as the complainant can give his own testimony in support of the prosecution.

In *common* assaults, or battery of the person, a late statute gives authority to two magistrates, upon complaint made to them by the party aggrieved within three calendar months after the act, to punish the offender by inflicting on him a fine not exceeding 5*l*. payable to the poor, or by committing him to the gaol or house of correction for a term not exceeding two months, unless the fine be sooner paid: but if they find the assault to have been justifiable, or so trifling as not to merit any punishment, they are to dismiss the complaint, unless they find that the assault and battery was in fact an attempt to commit a felony, or shall be of opinion that the case is a fit subject for an indictment; in which case their duty is to bind the party over to appear at the sessions or assizes, there to defend the prosecution.

A decision by the magistrates, or payment of a fine, is a bar to further proceedings. In assaults of a serious nature, and where special damage has been sustained, the aggrieved party can prosecute his indictment, and have his action of trespass; but the punishment in the one case, and the damages in the other, will be materially influenced by the event of the proceeding first tried.

Assaults arising from claims *bonâ fide* made in respect of the right to property, or which involve any similar question, are determinable by magistrates. An action of trespass is the means to try the title to property under such circumstances; and if the assault or violence was serious or unnecessary, the assaulting parties can be prosecuted.

In an action of *trespass*, or indictment for an assault or battery, or both, the party sued must (if he defends) plead, *i. e.* state his matter of defence, either *generally*, that he is "not guilty," that is, that the facts do not amount to an assault, or that he did not commit the assault, which will enable him upon the trial to show matters of extenuation; or *specially*, that he was *justified* in committing the act complained of. This plea involving matters of mere law, and governed by the rules of pleading, it will suffice here to show what is generally deemed matter of *justification*, as it is termed, without entering on the technical incidents of this plea, which is the only available defence to an action or indictment for this cause, extenuation only availing to reduce damages or mitigate punishment; for the denial of the assault by pleading "not guilty," puts the mere fact upon proof, and precludes the defendant from justifying. Matters of justification pleadable to an action or other proceeding for an assault and battery, are, that the defendant was doing some reasonable act in prevention of mischief or damage to himself, or in preservation of his property, wife, family, or others under his protection, or doing some act against the plaintiff which morally or legally he was authorised to do. Therefore, in defence by pleading *justification*, a man may show that the assault complained of arose in preventing a trespass by the plaintiff upon his land or house, or that the plaintiff assaulted his wife, child, or servant, and that the defendant laid hands gently, or with no unnecessary force, on the plaintiff, to prevent his doing so; or that the plaintiff assaulted the defendant, and would have beaten him if he had not defended himself against the plaintiff; or that the plaintiff was his apprentice, child, or scholar, and that the assault complained of was a reasonable correction; or that the defendant had a warrant to arrest the plaintiff, who resisted, and that defendant used no more violence than was necessary to effect such arrest, and such like: the reader always bearing in mind that the burden of this proof is incumbent upon the defendant who pleads it, who must, in using *justification* or *excuse* as a defence, demonstrate that the means used were proportioned to the occasion, or, as it is termed, "reasonable;" it being an established rule that in self-defence, where an injury is to be remedied or prevented by the act of the party aggressed, or apprehending violence, no more should be done than the strict necessity of the case *absolutely* requires.

In actions for assault and battery, if the damages recovered are under 40*s*., the plaintiff can recover no more costs than damages, unless the judge *certify* that a battery was proved, or that the freehold or title to the land came in question. In prosecutions for common assaults, which are punishable by fine and imprisonment only, at the discretion of the court, unless the party accused show that he did not commit the assault, or *justify* the same, upon proof of an attempt to beat, or an actual battery, the party will be convicted; matters of extenuation, such as provocation of the plaintiff, &c., not availing further than to cause a mitigation of the punishment, which is usually moderate.

Some assaults and batteries may, by their consequences, be felony, or the act become felony, as, if a man beat a woman quick with child, and the child be born alive, and die afterwards from the injuries it sustained when the mother was beaten, it will be murder. Many assaults of a very aggravated nature against the person may be felonies. All attempts at robbery and rape, &c., and *all* attempts to commit felonies, are misdemeanors, punishable by imprisonment, with or without hard labour, fine, and compulsory suretiship for the peace, according to particular statutes. See OFFENCES AGAINST THE PERSON.

Every attempt to commit a felony against the person includes an assault; therefore, if the intent cannot be proved, the party may be convicted of the assault.

Assaults, not of so heinous a nature as the last, yet deserving of severe punishment, such as assaults against justices or magistrates, revenue officers, gamekeepers, and public functionaries, &c. in the execution of their duty, are punishable by particular statutes, which generally invest the court with a discretion to inflict severer punishment than for ordinary assaults, and to extend the punishment to transportation.

Common assaults are only punishable by moderate fine and simple imprisonment; the one by Magna Charta, proportioned to the situation in life of the party, the other according to the circumstances of the offence.

We have seen that it is actionable for one to threaten or menace another to the hinderance of his business or detriment of his affairs: but as the law contemplates further prevention as well as remedy, where an injury to the person or dwelling of another, or breach of the peace, has been threatened, and in cases where violence to the person has been offered, and it is apprehended will be repeated, sureties *to keep the peace* or *for good behaviour* can be obtained from the party threatening, by application to a justice or magistrate, or by exhibiting *articles of the peace* at the quarter sessions, or to the court of Queen's Bench, and sometimes to the chancellor, who may direct and cause to be taken a *recognizance to keep the peace*, from the offender, or commit him to prison until such suretiship is found, which in the case of proceeding before a justice is till the next sessions, when articles may be exhibited if further violence is feared; but such suretiship may be extended to two years, or a longer time, by the quarter sessions; the court of Queen's Bench may either require sureties to keep the peace for any term of years (which may afterwards be reduced), or generally, which is for the duration of the party's life.

Articles of the peace must be made upon oath, to which the party complained against may show cause, or make answer. In awarding a *recognizance* and *sureties to keep the peace*, the courts are not exceedingly strict as to the abilities of the sureties. If the party complained against be a peer of the realm, the application must be made to the court of Queen's Bench, or to the chancellor. The articles must state all previous circumstances with particularity and precision, and should also state, that the complaint is made against the party "not from malice or ill-will, but merely for the preservation of the exhibitant's (*i. e.* the complainant's) life, and protection of his or her person from bodily harm."

ASSESSORS. Those that *assess* public taxes, viz. parish dues, highway rates, &c., and also parliamentary taxes.

Assessors are men of law appointed to advise and direct a judge or judges of an inferior court in their decision.

Also see title CORPORATION; this title being given to those barristers who assist the mayor in revising the list of voters in corporate boroughs.

ASSETS, or ASSETZ. Goods or money *enough* (Fr. *assez*) to pay a burthen or obligation cast upon a man in relation to his own transactions, or those of others whose property he has in his hands. A drawee when he accepts is supposed to have assets in his hand, or, commercially speaking, "effects" of the drawer. A drawer of a cheque has assets at his bankers. But the term is more frequently applied to the funds or property in the hands of executors or administrators, applicable for the purposes of paying debts and legacies, or debts only. The law styles property in land come to the heir, assets real; personal property, assets personal; land in the hands of the heir applicable for payment of debts, assets per or by descent.

ASSIGN. To transfer a right to another. It has another signification; as to *assign* a widow her dower, is to allot or portion out a woman the third part forming her dower; to *assign* a perjury, is to state upon what particular false statement of the party the false swearing is intended to be sustained, or, in common parlance, "it is an oath upon which perjury may be *assigned;*" *i. e.* the oath is sufficiently certain and distinct in its allegation, that it can be negatived by evidence of its falsity, and that the party knew it to be false. To *assign* an error; to state an error in legal terms.

ASSIGNEE. The person to whom a thing is transferred or assigned. This word, as well as the word *assigns*, includes the assignee of an assignee, the heir of an assignee, and the assignee of an heir, and so in personal estate, the executors of an assignee, &c. The words "executors, administrators, and *assigns*," so often repeated in deeds relating to personalty, are little better than surplusage; *assigns* certainly is; for what any one takes absolutely by act or deed, he cannot be prevented from alienating. As many erroneously suppose these words to be indispensable, it accounts for their frequent repetition and occurrence; but a power to A. will not extend to his assigns, unless expressly named.

ASSIGNMENT. The transfer by one to another of an interest or power, if specially authorised. The name of a conveyance which, though it may be made of freeholds and interests therein, such as annuities, rent charges, mortgages, &c., yet is generally mentioned with reference to what are termed *personal interests* arising out of land, such as leases, and estates for years; and to simple personalty, *i. e.* goods, chattels, and security for money. This contract is always in law supposed to be founded upon adequate consideration; and therefore, although transfers and assignments may be made verbally, yet in matters of value, and where in caution the transactions should be evidenced and its memory preserved to prevent future claims, they should be made by writing under seal. The statute of frauds provides that no leases, estates, or interests, either of freehold or terms of years, or any uncertain interest, not being copyhold or customary interest, of, in, to, or out of any messuages, manors, lands, tenements, or hereditaments, shall be *assigned, granted,* or *surrendered,* unless it be by deed, *or* note in *writing*, signed by the party so assigning, granting, or surrendering the same, or their agents thereunto lawfully authorised by writing; or by *act and operation of law.*

Some things are not subjects of assignment at law; that is, the law will not permit the person to whom they are assigned to use his own name when he reduces them into possession, as a bond, promissory note, or bill of exchange over-due, beneficial agreements made with the party assigning, arrears of rent, and such like; the person to whom they are assigned, can only sue in the name of the party from whom he took them. In equity, however, an assignee of these *choses* or things *in action* can, provided he prove the adequacy of the price given for them, enforce the payment of the securities against the parties executing them. In transferring or assigning bonds or securities, there is always contained a power of attorney to receive and sue in the assignor's name.

Acts of parliament have, in particular instances, rendered some things assignable which are not in their nature legally so, as bills of exchange, which are transferrible by indorsement, bail bonds, and bankrupt's effects by that name. An assignment of goods or things not it existence at the time of the assignment or transfer, is totally inoperative.

An assignment of a debt may be transferred by order by mere words; as suppose A owes B 100*l*., and B owes C 100*l*., and the three meet, and it is agreed between them that A shall pay C the 100*l*., B's debt is extinguished or satisfied, and C may recover that sum against A, in an action *for money had and received;* but there must be a communication between all parties, and an express agreement by C to accept A *only* as his debtor. Although the law presumes all contracts and transfers to be made upon consideration, yet a *voluntary* assignment by deed, by one, without adequate consideration, is binding, provided he was not in debt at the time; but although *voluntary* assignments do not operate against creditors, yet as against the assignor, the transaction is valid, and he cannot defeat it by a subsequent transfer for value received.

The things that are most ordinarily assigned are, leases and terms of years, legacies, mortgages, goods, and ships, and interests in funded property: transfers of goods and furniture, and ships, are generally styled *bills of sale*. In the transferring of property in general terms, contingencies will not pass unless particularly mentioned.

The person to whom an assignment is made, ought in caution to take possession of the thing transferred, or to notify the change of title, and the right which he has acquired, where future or reversionary property has been purchased, to the trustees or persons in whom the corpus of the fund is vested, or by whom it is payable; and in the case of furniture, stock, or goods, the possession should be open and notorious, for the suffering the assignor to have or continue the possession thereof after sale is generally *primâ facie* evidence of a fraudulent or collusive intent in respect of the claims of creditors, against whom these transfers are often made, and which in many cases are not available for that reason. See Bill of Sale, Fraud.

If a lessee for years assigns his term to another, he cannot reserve a right, or, in fact, any thing to himself; therefore he cannot distrain for rent, if the assignee do not pay to the superior landlord; but he may bring an action either upon the indemnity contained in the assignment, or upon the implied contract. If he underlet, then the case is altered, and he may distrain, although the underlease may practically be an assignment, as being for the remainder of the term wanting one day.

A proviso contained in a lease against underletting or assigning without licence of the lessor is determined by *one* licence being given for either of these purposes; and the lessee or his assigns may underlet, &c.

ad infinitum, unless the licence be limited with a special restriction to that one turn.

The payment of rent, or covenant so to do, is sufficient consideration or value for an assignment of a lease; in other assignments we have seen some money must be paid, or *consideration*, *i. e.* value given. The technical words required in assignments are, *grant, assign, and set over*, which words have also an extended rather than a limited sense. In these deeds, also, the assignor is to covenant to save harmless the assignee from former grants, &c.; that he is owner of the land, and hath power to assign; that the assignee shall quietly enjoy, and to make farther assurance; and the assignee covenants to pay the rent, and perform the covenants, and indemnify the assignor therefrom, &c.

An office of trust is not grantable or assignable to another; and an assignment of all the emoluments of the clerk of the peace for Westminster was held invalid, although the assignment was expressly subject to the deduction of the salary, or allowance to a deputy.

ASSIZES. The court and time where the processes of assize, *i. e. sittings*, are taken and executed.

The judges who are assigned by the king's commission, go their circuits twice a year (England being divided into six circuits, and Wales into two), and hold *assizes* in every county except Middlesex and London, where the Central Criminal Court and the Queen's courts of record are sitting at short periods: and the counties on the home circuit have a criminal assise about Christmas. The commissions of the judges are chiefly of *gaol delivery* and *nisi prius*. The first is to try every prisoner in the gaol for any offence whatever; and the other to try civil causes in which *issues* have been joined in the courts at Westminster, in the county in which the causes have arisen, which stood (formally) appointed for the following term, with this proviso, (*nisi prius;* the operative Latin words of the ancient commission,) *unless before* the day appointed, the judges of assize come into the county in question: this they are sure to do in the preceding vacation—assizes being held between Hilary and Easter terms, and between Trinity and Michaelmas terms; the first known as the Lent assizes, and the other as the Summer assizes.

Assize also signifies a regulation or ordinance, as the "assize of bread."

Assize was also the name of a writ which lay to restore a man to his freehold when he had been forcibly thrust out by what is legally termed a disseisin; now abolished by a late act.

ASSUMPSIT, is the name of the common action "upon promises," which is given for the recovery of damages sustained by the nonperformance of a contract, promise, or agreement, *express* or *implied*. See CONTRACT.

ATTACHMENT, is a process against the person, awarded by the courts at Westminster for contempts, either actual or constructive.

Actual *contempts* are, contumelious or contumacious behaviour in the face of the court, or exhibited towards the king's writs or proceedings of the courts; injustice and deceits by officers and attornies; abuse in the process of the courts; refusals by sheriffs to return writs, or making wilfully a false return: for these and similar matters, attachments will be issued.

Constructive *contempts* are disobedience to the orders or *rules* of the court, which require the payment of money or performance of a particular thing, such as for nonobservance of awards made rules of court, for nonpayment of costs ordered to be paid upon a *motion* or *rule:* for these, attachments issue and are in the nature of civil executions, although the party *attached* is legally considered to be in custody on a criminal procedure.

Attachments out of chancery are issuable for the same causes as the preceding, and also issue on on the nonappearance to a writ of subpœna, the first process in the suit for answering a bill, and for disobedience to the orders or decrees of the court.

The courts deal leniently with *actual* contempts, and make great allowance for the infirmity of human nature. Contempts of this class are generally *purged* or satisfied with a very short imprisonment or fine; and in cases of injustice or deceipt, by reparation being made to the party injured.

Constructive contempts are only *purged* by payment of the money, performance of the thing commanded, appearing or putting in an answer, &c.

Although attachments for nonpayment of costs or a sum of money are in the nature of final process, yet it is said the sheriff *may* take bail. It certainly is not enjoined that he should. On attachments for not putting in answer or not appearing, generally the sheriff takes bail till the return of the writ, which must be returnable on some day in term.

Attachment, Foreign, by the custom of London and some other ancient cities, is the seizure of money, goods, or a debt in the hands of a third party owing to a defendant, to secure a plaintiff his debt. This can only be done within the bounds of the city. This process in London is conducted by the plaintiff entering a *plaint* or suit in the mayor's court (which is more advantageous than in the sheriff's court). The person to whom the money is owing being the plaintiff, the debtor the defendant, and the third party, having goods or money of the defendant, or owing him a debt, is called the *garnishee;* because he is *warned* to show cause why the goods, &c. should not be paid over by him to the plaintiff. The practice is, that when an *attachment* has been served upon the garnishee upon the plaintiff's plaint, and a *return* made by the serjeant, the plaintiff should proceed by his attorney before the next court day, else the defendant may put in bail, and nonsuit the plaintiff for not proceeding. The *garnishee* has a time given him (four court days) to show cause why the plaintiff should not condemn the money, goods, or debt *attached* in his (the garnishee's) hands; and in default of the garnishee's appearance, he is taken, the plaintiff having judgment against him to pay the debt, &c., or the value of the goods as condemned to the plaintiff's use; but the *garnishee* appearing to show cause, may plead that he has no money, &c. of the defendant in his hands, which issue will be tried by a jury, and judgment given accordingly; and after trial the garnishee may *dissolve* the attachment by putting in bail to pay the debt found due. The courts at Westminster have decided that the original defendant should have notice of the attachment, or the judgment will be erroneous, although it has been said that by the custom of the city no notice was ever given him.

A *foreign attachment* cannot be had when a suit is depending in any of the courts at Westminster; and nothing seems attachable but for a certain and due debt, though by the custom of London it may be attached before the day of judgment, but not levied, or recovered.

A bill of exchange is a debt due at its date, though not payable till one, two, or three months afterwards. Goods sold upon credit, the debt is due, but not payable till the expiration of the customary period.

Money due to an executor or an administrator, as such, cannot be attached; it would give a simple contract creditor priority over judgments. Trust money in the hands of a garnishee is not attachable. Money awarded under a rule of court, or due upon a Master's *allocation*, cannot be attached.

It seems the money must be owing to the defendant *alone*, not jointly with others: and goods in the hands of a carrier are privileged.

The debt need not *arise* within the city.

ATTAINDER, is the figurative *taint*, or ideal *corruption of blood*, which attaches on a person capitally convicted of treason or felony. The practical consequence of this doctrine, or rather fiction, which is of feudal origin, formerly was, that it rendered the convict, after judgment, incapable of having heirs, and by this incapacity or civil death obstructed the course of descent, thereby depriving the heir of the land, which the king is entitled to as a thing *escheated* or reverted to him; but now it only operates as a forfeiture for life, and in common parlance is so intended. Attainder for felony also brings with it the forfeiture of goods. As far as the forfeiture of interests in lands of inheritance are concerned, attainder is limited to treason and murder, or the abetting, &c. Bills of attainder are sometimes brought into parliament, and pass into acts, against open rebels, traitors, &c., upon which the party is executed, and his lands and goods forfeited, saving the wife's jointure and dower. The subject of forfeiture for felony is mentioned at the title FORFEITURE.

ATTEMPTS TO COMMIT CRIME, are aggravated assaults: where the object of the offender was to commit an offence which, if completed, would be murder, it is punishable as a capital felony. Attempts to commit felonies generally are misdemeanors, and punishable by statute with imprisonment, with or without hard labour, not exceeding two years, with a fine, at the discretion of the court, and the prisoner may be required to find sureties to be of good behaviour.

The solicitation or incitement to commit a felony, where the felony is not committed, is punishable as a misdemeanor, by fine and imprisonment; if the offence be committed by the person solicited, both parties stand in the relation of principal and accessory, and are punishable accordingly.

Attempts to bribe are mostly considered as the offence of bribery itself. See BRIBERY.

ATTORNIES AT LAW and SOLICITORS, are the immediate agents and representatives of their clients, suitors in the courts of law or equity, retaining or employing them. As their legal knowledge and moral character are made the subjects of examination before admission, and as the necessary qualifications of experience are insured by various enactments, they are considered as persons duly educated, and influenced in their demeanor by honourable principles of conduct. The qualifications chiefly enabling an attorney to practise are, the service of a clerkship for full five years, under a written contract termed articles of clerkship, to some attorney or solicitor duly qualified; but as every encouragement is given by the legislature to procure persons of known liberal education to enter this branch of the legal profession, any person who shall, within four years next preceding the commencement of his intended clerkship, have taken the degree of bachelor of arts or law in the universities of Cambridge, Oxford, or Dublin, may be qualified upon a service of three years; and any articled clerk may serve part of his time, not exceeding one year, as pupil to a practising barrister or certificated special pleader. After such service under articles (upon which there is a stamp duty of 120*l*.), a public examination takes place before certain examiners appointed by the judges, of which the prothonotaries and masters of the courts of law are permanent examiners, with a power of appeal to the judges, of the intended attorney; and after the examination, and the evidencing of the service under the articles, he is admitted in open court, taking certain oaths, — one of which is, "to demean himself properly as an attorney."

The duties of an attorney are those which demand of him probity, activity, and experience; and if he fail in these requisites, he will be visited with the reimbursement to his client of the loss consequent on defaults; and in cases of deceitful and dishonest conduct the courts will summarily interfere, by striking him off the roll, — which punishment, however, is not in all cases to be considered as a perpetual disability to practise, but may be intended to operate as a temporary suspension till he render satisfaction to his client. Yet, though an attorney is bound by law to execute his client's business with care, skill, and dispatch, there must be gross neglect or ignorance to render him liable by action at the suit of his client; indeed, it is established that he is responsible generally for the consequences of ignorance, or nonobservance of the rules of practice of his court, and for the want of such care in the conduct of business as is ordinarily allotted to his department of the profession; whilst, on the other hand, he is not answerable for error in judgment upon points of new occurrence, or of nice or doubtful construction, or of such as are usually intrusted to men in the higher branches of the profession: he is liable, however, if he draw erroneous conclusions from deeds instead of submitting an abstract of them to counsel.

With these remarks the reader is introduced to the following practical information upon the subjects connected with the retainer, or employment of an attorney: —

1. As to his claims for business done; and what charges are taxable, and what are not.
2. As to agreements made with an attorney in respect of business to be done, or extraordinay payment at the conclusion thereof.
3. As to the attorney's liabilities.

I. An attorney, in strictness, should be appointed by a written warrant or retainer; but, in practice, seldom any other than a verbal authority is given by the client to his attorney. His bill of costs and charges for business done in any suit, signed with his name, must be delivered a lunar month before the commencement of any action to recover such charges; and if one sixth part shall be deducted on the taxation, the attorney is liable to pay the costs thereof. The bill may be taxed even after suit commenced, upon the client's undertaking to pay what shall appear due on such taxation, and proceedings will be stayed for that purpose; but if a sixth part should be then struck off, the client will have to pay the costs of taxation, besides the costs of the suit against him. Therefore, in prudence, the bill should be taxed, or at least a proper application made for that purpose, within the lunar month from the delivery, or the amount may be paid within the time, or before action brought, and the attorney then called upon, by motion to the court, to refund such items as are wrongfully charged; but in this last instance, the client's only remedy is to proceed by motion, in which if he succeed so far as to obtain a reduction of more than one sixth part, the attorney, in addition to the refunding, will have to pay the costs of the motion, and the consequent reference to the officer of the court. This reference, which is made to the master, or prothonotary of the court, to tax an attorney's bill, is, in fact, the taking and stating of an account of *all* previous matters; as the attorney is ordered to state upon affidavit all sums, and how and in what manner and on what account they were received by him on account of his client, during his retainer; and upon the balance being found, either party is liable to be attached by the court for nonpayment. The taking of these accounts are conclusive upon both parties, as the *allocatur*, or award of the master or prothonotary to whom these matters are referred, is considered binding, unless error or fraud be subsequently discovered.

The Court of Chancery exercises the like power over its solicitors and clerks in court, and in the same manner.

If the bill should consist of charges not connected with any suit at law or in equity, the same is not subject to taxation or reference, but such demand stands on the same footing as any other cause of action; therefore, immediately after the delivery of any such bill of costs, an adequate tender should be made, should the charges appear, upon advice, exorbitant; or if an action have been commenced, a fit sum should be paid into court.

The payment of an exorbitant demand of this nature, in order to avoid an action, will not preclude the client from disputing it; for the client may bring his action to recover back what has been in ignorance or misinformation paid by him; but a protest of the excess of the demand should be made, where the party prefers immediate payment of a bill not taxable, to avoid inconvenience or annoyance.

II. It seems that an attorney, after the commencement of a suit, may insist on being supplied with the necessary funds for carrying the same to a conclusion, or abandon the same upon reasonable notice; and if taxed costs, termed *costs between party and party*, are paid by the opponent, the sums advanced should be repaid to the client minus any extra costs, which may fairly have accrued to the attorney, termed *costs as between attorney and client;* but it must be remarked, that such demand of money on account is not deemed liberal, unless the client's circumstances are doubtful, or the proceedings are very expensive.

In ordinary cases the remuneration is postponed till the termination of the suit or matter. Stipulations made by the attorney, that the *quantum* of remuneration shall depend on the event of the cause, throw a discredit on the proceedings, and reflect on the credibility of the attorney himself, if his testimony is required in the course of the suit.

It is partly to repress the stirring up of frequent suits, and partly in prevention of the frauds to which it would open a door, were such a practice permitted between persons standing in such a relation, that an attorney is not permitted to take any security or any gift from his client pending an action or suit, although such a security may stand for the amount of costs actually due at the date; and it has been held to extend to future disbursements and advances, but a prospective mortgage for *future* costs will be set aside.

No attorney or solicitor can legally or effectually stipulate to have part of the estate or money to be recovered in lieu of ordinary costs, as that would amount to champerty and maintenance ,and induce the court to suspend his practice; indeed, any stipulation out of the ordinary course of fair remuneration is void and illegal, and all deeds tending to enforce or confirm such bargains may be set aside in equity. The ground on which this principle rests, so far as what is termed maintenance or champerty is concerned, appears to be, that an attorney feeling himself secure as to his costs, might be less attentive to his client's interest, and perhaps be tempted to prolong the litigation. The fact of a security of any nature being given, does not, at least in the absence of any agreement to the contrary, preclude the taxation of the attorney's bill.

In the case of an attorney who takes securities from his client, such securities or instruments cannot be used as *conclusive* evidence of the sum due, or expressed to be due; but additional evidence must be had of the money having been actually advanced, to prove the transaction to have been conducted with good faith.

III. The public are protected from various abuses incident to the office of an attorney, by a penal statute, 2 *G.* 2. *c.* 23., by which persons pretending to be attornies, or practising as such, are punishable by fine. By this act, also, no attorney is to suffer any unqualified person (that is, no person not duly admitted and enrolled) to practise in his name, for the emolument or gain of such unqualified person, upon pain of being struck off the roll, and for the future rendered incapable of re-admission, or again ever practising; and the unqualified person can be committed by the court for not exceeding one year. The courts interfere summarily upon this highly penal statute, and in a very late case the court awarded this punishment against an attorney. No attorney under imprisonment, or confined within the rules of any prison, is to sue out process, or conduct any suit, save those that were commenced by him before his imprisonment, upon pain of being struck off the roll. In Trinity term, 31 *G.* 3. a rule of court was made to prevent the admission of persons under irregular articles of clerkship, &c., chiefly intended to prevent the clerks of attornies from acting as principals.

Persons preparing *conveyances* for gain, not being barristers, solicitors, notaries, proctors, and special pleaders, equity draftsmen, and conveyancers, being members of the four Inns of Court, are punishable by a fine of 50*l.*: there is an exception in favour of persons drawing wills, agreements, or contracts not under seal, and powers (not warrants) of attorney.

An attorney or solicitor trustee cannot act professionally so as directly or indirectly to charge for his personal trouble, or for professional business connected with his trust *in any manner*, for his emolument.

An attorney cannot be called upon to disclose matters communicated to him by his client in that character, in civil as well as in criminal cases; and in *general* business, the attorney is not bound to disclose the secrets of his client. This privilege does not extend to *acts* done in the attorney's presence, as the execution of a deed, the sending of a letter, &c. the giving a direction, &c.; but conversations and communications of every description between the client and the attorney, or his clerks or agents, are privileged, and he may by injunction be restrained from communicating information that came to him confidentially from his client.

As to embezzlement by attornies, see EMBEZZLEMENT.

The attorney should personally conduct his own business, which has been legally decided to be a *profession*, and not a *trade;* he therefore should not delegate matters of importance, and which require skill and experience, to clerks, who are comparatively uninformed, and totally irresponsible.

We have seen that an attorney or solicitor is liable for negligence, but he is not liable for the consequences of a mistake upon points either of law or practice, where doubt may be not unreasonably entertained; yet he is held liable for loss, damage, consequential damage, and prejudicial delay arising from errors in practical proceedings, a competent knowledge of which presupposed his claim to admission; but even in these cases the court will not interfere summarily against the attorney by motion, but will leave the party grieved to his action, in which the question of negligence (subject to the direction of the judge) will be left to the jury. In cases before the court in the progress of a cause, where the negligence of the attorney appears incidentally to have occasioned the application, the court will mulct the attorney in the costs — making him, and not his client, liable.

The client cannot change his attorney in suits *at law* without leave of the court or a judge.

ATTORNEY-GENERAL. A great law officer of the king, made by letters patent. It is his duty to prosecute for the crown, and to exhibit informations of a criminal nature; also to file bills or informations in the exchequer, in respect of matters concerning the revenue or the king's profits. He is the only legal representative of the king in the courts. When he prosecutes in his *official* capacity, he has always the right to reply.

ATTORNMENT, is the acknowledgment of a tenant to a new landlord, either by payment of rent, or a very small nominal sum. There are but few cases in which it confers any legal advantage. See ACKNOWLEDGMENT-MONEY.

AUCTIONEER, and SALES BY AUCTION. An auctioneer is a person licensed to conduct sales by auction, which is most usually done by notifying the conditions of sale, by previous advertisement, or at the time of sale explaining the incidents and qualifications of the property, and receiving the offers or biddings of the persons assembled. The sale is perfected by the auctioneer declaring a certain person entitled to the thing sold at the price nominated by the bidder, and which, from its being originally named, or "put up," at a smaller sum by the auctioneer, and being increased by the succeeding bidders, is called "auction." Auction, however, may be effected by inch of candle, or in fact *in any manner* which allows of successive or increased biddings or offers, for a given time, or till a given sum is accepted. The biddings are closed at the knocking of the hammer in the auctioneer's hand, or by the inch of candle burning out, or by any other termination previously agreed upon, when the contract in the sale of goods is actually complete, and the sale of land, houses, or interests in real property, is perfected from or at the signing of the contract, or more strictly speaking, from the auctioneer writing down the name of the bidder and the sum offered; thus making a memorandum of agreement, which is sufficient to bind the bidder and seller, *i. e.* the purchaser and vendor, if they do not revoke it before its being entered in the auctioneer's book or paper. In the sale of goods, a bidding may be revoked before the knocking of the hammer. As far as regards the biddings, they should be open and unconditional. The procuring persons employed by either auctioneer or seller to increase the price beyond the *real* value of the property, by a collusive competition called "puffing," vitiates the sale.

Verbal declarations by an auctioneer will not control the printed catalogue and conditions of sale, which are generally posted up in the room, or delivered to the persons present, who thus receive sufficient notification of their contents. The auctioneer, however, may, previous to the sale, correct an error or omission lately come to his knowledge; but this should be done in writing, and the correction should be made as publicly as possible, and the copy posted up rendered conformable to that in the auctioneer's hand, and which he should read to the persons assembled.

An auctioneer is a mere agent of both parties; and in his character of agent to the seller, he is responsible to him for any impropriety, indiscretion, or departure from instructions. On the other hand, an auctioneer is not liable as a principal for any other than wilful misrepresentation, or personally warranting the thing sold, or on refusal, after a reasonable request, to disclose the name of his principal. A party absent may employ the auctioneer to bid for him; and the bidding of an authorised agent binds the principal, if his name is disclosed; if not, the liability is charged upon the agent. In the character of agent, if he pay over the produce of a sale to his employer, after receipt of notice that the goods sold were not his property, he will be liable to the real owner.

Auctioneers take out their licence from the excise, renewable on the 5th of July. And if they sell goods for which an excise licence is required, they must take out such licence, unless such goods are sold on the *entered* premises of the seller, and for his benefit. They give security to the excise for the payment of excise duties on sale by auction, for which they are liable, and may deduct the same from the proceeds of the sale; and if no sale, recover the amount as money paid for the seller's use. As far as regards the seller and purchaser, it is generally stipulated that the duty shall be paid by either or both of them, as stated in the conditions to the particulars or catalogue of sale.

An auctioneer who is employed to sell an estate, and who receives a deposit from the purchaser, is a mere stakeholder, liable to be called upon to pay the money at any time; and therefore, although he place it in the funds and make interest of it, he is not liable to pay such interest to the vendor when the purchase is completed, though the vendor (without the concurrence of the vendee) give him notice to invest the money in government securities.

Duties are payable on sales by auction at so much in the pound, varying from 2*d.* to 1*s.* Furniture and fixtures at 1*s.* But no duty is payable on sales by Courts of Chancery, Exchequer, or Great Sessions, in Wales, East India and Hudson's Bay companies, by commissioners of excise, ordnance, or navy victualling offices; on sales by the sheriff, or executions for the benefit of creditors; of goods distrained for rent; nonpayment of tithes; on sale of property of bankrupts *sold by assignees*, of goods imported from a British colony in America, according to 59 *G.* 3. *c.* 54. *s.* 3.; on sales of ships or cargo condemned as prize, and sold for benefit of the captor; on sales of goods abandoned to the insurers, or sold for benefit of the proprietors; on goods saved from a fire and sold for the insurers; on the auction of any copyhold property for lives or years by the lord, or on any similar auction; on letting lands for lives or years; on the sales of wood, coppice, produce of mines or quarries, or materials for working the same, or cattle or dead stock on land, so as the sale be made on the land producing the same, by the owner or his agent.

Owners of property may save the auction duty by buying in the property put up to auction, provided they give a written notice to the auctioneer, previous to the sale, of such their intention. There are some few other exemptions from auction duty upon articles of merchandise, specially named in particular statutes; and auction duty is returned to the parties where the sale is not perfected, for defect of title, or from unavoidable circumstances.

AVERAGE, in its strict sense, is a contribution made by the owners of a ship, and the proprietors of goods, to those whose goods are sacrificed or damaged in the preservation of such ship or cargo, or any part of the merchandize. It is sufficient for the purposes of ordinary information, to state that the averages, which subject the whole of the ship and cargo to this contribution, are either *general* or *particular*. General, when the sacrifice is incurred to prevent a total loss of the ship. Particular, when the loss to ship or goods occurs on the ordinary incidents of a voyage, although they reach their destination; such as accidents to rigging, loss of anchors, &c.; in which case the expenses or loss must be compensated by the parties not immediately concerned in the ship or cargo, viz. the insurers. Particular average, or, as it is commercially termed, average loss, is to be considered only with reference to a particular partial loss, which, when applied to the ship, means a damage sustained from some of the accidents assured against; and when referred to the cargo, has relation to the damage which the goods have suffered from storm, &c., though the whole or the greater part may arrive in port.

The insurance companies and underwriters regulate and limit their liabilities, as to these *particular* averages, by memorandums or conditions attached to their policies (especially as it is only on a partial loss that this question of particular average can occur), to £3. and £5. per cent. upon certain articles specifically named, unless the ship be stranded, which must be an immediate loss.

This restriction as to particular average does not extend to a loss arising from a general average, in which case the insurers are liable, even though the loss is under £3. per cent. The loss arising from general average is always payable by the insurer. The general average appears to be adjusted upon the value of the articles which are to contribute thereto. The ship is valued at the price she is worth on her arrival at the port of delivery. The freight is valued upon a deduction of seamen's wages and petty averages. The goods, saved as well as lost, are valued at the price they would have fetched at the port of delivery. Each person's share of the loss will bear the same proportion to the value of his property, that the whole loss bears to the aggregate value of the ship, freight, and cargo.

When the loss of the ship's rigging or masts is compensated by a general average, two thirds only of the value of the new articles is contributed.

AVERAGE, PETTY, SMALL, or ACCUSTOMED, is a small duty paid to masters of ships, where goods are sent in another man's ship, for their care of the goods, over and above the freight, which comprises the charges of pilotage, towage, &c. It is usual to charge one third of them to the ship and twothirds to the cargo.

AVOWRY. The justifying and *avowing* a distress, *i. e.* a plea by a party making a distress, who is sued in *replevin*, stating why he (the distrainor) took it. See REPLEVIN.

AWARD. When persons refer any matter in dispute to the private decision of another party, such act is termed a *submission*. The party who is to decide upon such submission is the *arbitrator*, and the decision of such arbitrator is termed an *award*. The proper subjects of award are long and unclosed accounts; cases in which it would be difficult to collect several witnesses so as to insure their attendance on a trial; disputes between neighbours as to ancient lights, or drains, or similar circumstances; cases between landlord and tenant upon questions of dilapidations; as to the title of small property, where the claimants are numerous; matters of privacy, arising between family connections; and executors' or trustees' accounts. Cases of slander, or criminal conversation, or where the measure of damages may influence further proceedings, or establish opinion of friends or general acquaintance as to character, do seem fit subjects of arbitration.

Every agreement to submit matters to arbitration should be in writing and unconditional, or, as it is termed, *irrevocable*, and stipulated to be made a rule of some court, else it will be ineffectual.

To carry into effect an intention of referring differences to an arbitrator, an agreement in writing (it is immaterial whether it is under seal or not, but it should bear a 1*l.* 15*s.* stamp if it is) should be prepared, which is less expensive than cross bonds and signed copies exchanged between the parties; the original being given to the arbitrator, according to the following form, which may be varied according to circumstances, viz.—

Form of an Agreement to refer all Matters in Dispute between two or more to a single Arbitrator.

"Memorandum of an Agreement made this ——— day of ———, 1836, between A. B. of —— and C. D. of —— as follows:—

"Whereas differences and disputes have arisen, and are depending between "the said A. B. and C. D. Now this agreement witnesseth, That the said "A. B. and C. D. do, and each of them doth, for himself severally, and not "jointly with others, and for his executors and administrators respectively, "agree to and with each other, his executors and administrators, well and truly "to stand to, obey, abide by, perform, and keep the award, order, and final de-"termination of G. H. of ———, of and concerning the matters aforesaid, "or of any thing in any wise relating thereto; and also of and concerning all "manner of actions, causes of action, suits, contracts, promises, accounts, tres-"passes, damages and demands whatsoever, both at law and in equity, at any "time before or upon the day of the date hereof had, made, or depending by or "between the said parties, or any of them, [and in particular a certain cause "now depending between the said A. B. and C. D. in the Court of ——,] * "and all other matters in difference between them, so as the award of the said "G. H. be made under *his* hand on or before the —— day of ——— next, or "such further time or times as the said G. H. shall from time to time appoint "by indorsement written hereupon, or upon a copy hereof, and signed by him. "And it is also agreed by and between the said parties, that these presents "shall be made a rule of one of his Majesty's courts of law at Westminster, "to the end that the said parties respectively may be finally concluded by the "said arbitration and award thereon, pursuant to the statute in such case made "and provided: Also that the said parties, or either of them, and their wit-"nesses, may be examined upon oath before the said arbitrator: Also *that the* "*costs and charges of the said action shall abide the event, but* † that the costs and "charges attending the present arbitration and award to be thereupon made "shall be in the discretion of the said arbitrator. In witness whereof they have "hereunto set their hands respectively, the day and year above written.

"A. B.
"C. D.

"Signed by the abovenamed A. B. and C. D., in the presence of ——."

---

* The words between brackets need not be used if no action or suit be actually pending.

† If no action pending, the words in Italics may be omitted.

When the matters intended to be settled by an arbitration are the subject of a suit which is pending, and the defendant has not been held to bail, then, upon a short *written memorandum*, signed by both parties, or their attornies or properly constituted agents, a judge will grant an order for referring all matters to the award of an arbitrator named, which order is to be made a rule of court. If the defendant has been held to bail, then the usual course is to carry the cause to trial, and on its being called, to obtain an order of the sitting judge, commonly called "an order of *nisi prius*," for the same purposes: this might be done before that expensive stage of the proceedings has added to the claim, or loss of either party, provided the bail in the action would consent, otherwise their security would be lost, but which is preserved by the plaintiff's obtaining a verdict subject to an award thereafter to be made; a practically useless distinction. The attornies' consent is binding on the client; but well conducted practitioners take care to consult their clients' inclination on this head. The arbitrator cannot, in these cases, award greater damages than those laid in the declaration, and will be much governed by the particulars of demand and sets-off delivered in the action, by the pleadings, &c.

The arbitrator being thus appointed, and being furnished with the papers, accounts, &c., gives notice, or the parties give each other notice, of the meetings he appoints for the consideration of the matters referred to him; and at the appointed time, in the presence of both parties or their accredited agents, he enters upon the subject laid before him, and after hearing both sides, makes his award or determination according to natural equity: but in certain cases, especially when an action is already pending, of which the merits are the subject of reference, the arbitrator, if a lawyer, considers it most suitable to observe the ordinary rules of law and evidence, rendering the proceedings before him similar to the trial of an action; and sometimes, having obtained written statements or briefs from the attornies of each party, forms his conclusion after the examination of the witnesses, or of the parties themselves (if the arbitrator has been so authorised), without hearing the observations of counsel or attornies; and having adopted these or any other methods of inquiry, he *publishes* the award by delivering a copy to each party, or giving notice of his readiness to deliver it, and the award thus published must be decisive and final in its effect.

There are two modes of enforcing obedience to the award: first, by an attachment for nonperformance of the things ordered to be done, after such award shall have been made a rule or order of any court by the usual application, and after formal demand made; secondly, by an action brought to recover damages for what is directed by the award to be done, paid, or performed; or if the submission was by mutual or cross bonds, by a suit upon one of them, and these proceedings cannot be stayed unless it can be shown to the court of which the award is made a rule or order, that the award was not in conformity to, or that it exceeded the objects or the terms of the submission, or that the arbitrator misconducted himself, or some equally strong case, for these agreements receive all possible sanction and assistance from the courts.

It is a very common practice, when parties refer their disputes to the decision of more than one arbitrator, to make provision for the appointment of a person to finally decide in case the arbitrators are unable to come to a decision; which person is called an "umpire." It is very usual for this nomination to rest with the arbitrators; but with more reason, and to prevent all possibility of undue influence, it should remain with the parties, who, together with the arbitrators, it is suggested by an eminent commercial lawyer, should choose the umpire before the subject matter of the reference is gone into. An award made by an umpire is termed an *an award* or *umpirage*.

The law has secured each party against the procrastination or delay of the other, by permitting the arbitrator, on due notice given, to proceed without the attendance of the defaulter: this is termed proceeding *ex parte*.

If partners refer all matters in dispute between them, the arbitrator may dissolve the partnership.

The award cannot affect persons who are not parties to the *submission;* and when limited to particular matters only, it cannot extend to matters beyond.

It is no objection to an award that a certain thing is not formally directed to be performed, if it appear that the same was substantially awarded.

By the operation of the acts relating to servants in husbandry, benefit societies, savings' banks, workmen in certain trades, magistrates are empowered to arbitrate, and decide upon either party demanding the reference; and in case of mariners' or seamen's wages and salvage, similar powers may be exercised by justices of the peace or magistrates. It is imperative on the parties to abide by the determination of the magistrate, where power is given to claim an arbitration; but in the two latter cases the law is not compulsory, more especially as seamen and salvors have security against the ship and the goods saved, for the recompence due to them. The following is a form of award applicable to the foregoing submission, viz.—

Form of an Award upon the previous Agreement or Submission.

"To all to whom this present indenture of award shall come, I, G. H. of "—— send greeting: Whereas there are several accounts depending, and "various differences and disputes have lately arisen, between A. B. of —— "and C. D. of —— [And whereas the said A. B. lately commenced an action "at law in his Majesty's court of *Common Pleas* at Westminster, against the "said C. D. for the recovery of the sum of £ alleged to be due by the said "C. D. to the said A. B. in respect of a certain bill of exchange (*or* pro- "missory note, *or* cheque), drawn by the said A. B. upon and accepted by the "said C. D.; *or*, for goods sold and delivered by the said A. B. to the said C. D.; "*or*, for money lent by the said A. B. to the said C. D.; *or*, for money paid, "laid out, and expended by the said A. B. for the said C. D.; *or*, for money "had and received by the said C. D. for the use of the said A. B.; *or*, as the "cause of action may have been described in the plaintiff's particular of "demand in the action*]: And whereas, for the putting an end to the said dif- "ferences and disputes [and for determining the said action commenced as "aforesaid] they, the said A. B. and C. D., by a certain memorandum of "agreement under their hands, bearing date the —— day of ——, did agree "with each other to stand to and abide the final award, order, and determin- "ation of me G. H., so as the said award was made under my hand, and ready "to be delivered to the parties in difference on or before the —— day of —— "then next ensuing, or at such further times as I, the said G. H., should

* The words between brackets need not be used if no action or suit be actually pending.

"from time to time, under my hand, enlarge the time for making such my "award [And whereas the time limited for making such my award has been "duly enlarged until the —— day of——, as by reference to the memorandum "of such enlargement may appear*]: Now know ye, that I the said arbitrator, "whose name is hereunto subscribed and seal affixed, taking upon me the "burthen of the said award, and having fully examined and duly con- "sidered the proofs and allegations of both the said parties, and also having "examined them upon oath, do, for the purpose of ending all differences "and disputes between the said parties, make and publish that this my "award by and between the said parties, in manner following, that is to "say:— First, I do award and order that all actions [and in particular, the "said action so commenced and prosecuted as aforesaid], writs, and proceed- "ings, and matters in difference shall not be further prosecuted; and I do "award, and adjudge, and determine of and concerning the said matter so "referred to me as aforesaid, that at the time of the making of the said "reference [*or*, at the time of the commencement of the said action], there "was, and still is, justly due from the said C. D. to the said A. B. the sum "of £ , and I do award that the said C. D. shall and do pay the "said sum of £ to the said A. B., and that the said A. B. shall "accept and receive such payment from the said C. D., in full satisfaction and "discharge of all matters in difference between the said parties, to the time "of the said reference: And I do further order, award, and direct, that the "said C. D. do and shall pay all the costs of the said reference, and of this my "award, and that if the said A. B. shall pay the same or any part thereof, "then that the said C. D. shall forthwith repay and reimburse the said A. B. "the same [*or, the arbitrator may direct contrariwise by awarding*, that there is "nothing due from the said C. D. to the said A. B.; *or*, that there is nothing "due from either of the said parties to each other, *or*, that the said A. B. shall "do and perform, *a certain act*, or contrariwise; *or*, that each of the said parties "shall bear and pay his own costs, and also pay equal moieties of the costs "of the reference and this my award, and that if one of the parties should pay "the whole of such costs, then that the other shall reimburse him]: And I "do further direct and award, that after payment by the said C. D. of the said "reference, and of the costs of this my award as aforesaid [*or*, as the case may "be], each party shall, *if required so to do*, at the request, costs, and charges of "the other of them, but not otherwise, execute to him a good and sufficient "release of and concerning all and every of the said matters so referred to "me as aforesaid. In witness whereof I have hereunto set my hand and seal "[*or, subscribed my hand*] this —— day of —— in the year of our Lord 1837.

"G. H. (L. S.)

"Signed and published by the said arbitrator on this —— day of —— A.D. 1837, in the presence of us

"H. J., Accountant, 23. Lucas Street, Commercial Road.
"F. K., Ship and Insurance Broker, 5. Warnford Court, London."

This writing must be impressed with a 1*l.* 15*s.* stamp. If it contain what is termed 30 folios of 72 words, it requires an additional stamp of 1*l.* 5*s.* for every 15 folios.

Forms of Enlargement *of the Time for making an Award, by Indorsement.*

"I, G. H., the arbitrator [*or*, we the undersigned arbitrators] within named, "do, in pursuance of the power given by the terms of submission, enlarge and "extend the time for making my award herein, until the —— day of ——.

"G. H.

"Witness, J. R." [*date*]

---

* If no enlargement was made, the words in brackets are to be omitted.

"We, the within named A. B. and C. D., do hereby agree to enlarge and "extend the time for the arbitrator [*or*, arbitrators and umpire, *as the case may* "*be*,] making their or his award or umpirage in the within, until the —— day "of —— next, and that this may be made a rule of court, if necessary. Dated "the —— day of ——.

"A. B.
"Witness, L. M." "C. D."

The Editor hopes he has suggested sufficient to enable an unprofessional reader to conduct an award where the transactions are simple and not of very great moment. In the settlement of great accounts and transactions, the ubmission and award should *at least* be prepared under professional advice, as the conduct of an award generally requires care and nicety, and oftentimes great legal particularity.

BACHELOR. A man who has never been married; and as such, taxes have been at times levied or increased, as in the case of an increased tax on servants, payable by bachelors.

Bachelor of Arts, is the first degree taken by students at the universities.

BACKING a warrant of a justice or police magistrate, is, where a warrant granted by a justice or magistrate in one jurisdiction or county is required to be executed in another, as where a felony or offence has been committed in one county, and the offender resides or has gone into another; or where goods, for which a search warrant has been obtained from justices or commissioners of bankrupt, are taken from one place to another; in which case, on proof of the handwriting of the justice, magistrate, or commissioner who granted the warrant, the justice in the other county or place indorses or writes his name at the back, thereby giving authority to execute the warrant in his jurisdiction.

Backing, is also used in common parlance (for the practice is legally superfluous), for the indorsement or memorandum which a pawnbroker makes on the back of a duplicate, thereby acknowledging that the party pledging the goods has requested a stay of sale for three months; for this a small sum is asked, but it cannot be enforced—the pawnbroker being obliged to take notice of the request for that purpose, if made by the pawnor in the presence of another, or by a notice in writing. See Pawnbroker.

BAIL. The setting at liberty a party imprisoned in any action, civil or criminal, on surety for his re-appearance.

In civil causes, when a defendant is arrested upon a writ of *capias*, it is incumbent on the sheriff's officer to liberate the defendant on two responsible persons signing a bond (called a *bail-bond*), conditioned for the defendant's "putting in special bail," or, as it is termed, *bail above*, to answer the action within eight days from the arrest; which if the defendant or his bondsmen do not perform, or if the defendant do not return into custody before the end of the eighth day, the bond is forfeited, and the bondsmen are liable to pay the debt and costs. If the defendant procures, at the end of the eight days, the same or two other responsible housekeepers or freeholders to enter into a recognizance before a judge that they will either pay the debt and costs, or render the defendant to prison, the defendant is discharged from custody until the termination of the suit. This second suretiship is called in practice putting in *special bail*, and is the performance of the condition of the first suretiship, the practice of which is attended with considerable expense. A defendant may also, by depositing the sum indorsed on the writ and

10*l*. with the sheriff's officer, who pays it to the sheriff, be relieved of the trouble of finding bail; and at the end of the eight days he may pay 10*l*. more, which is sufficient security for costs, and his person is relieved till the termination of the action. These sums he may also have returned and accounted for, if he desires to pay the claim, or if he chooses to obtain bail; or having given bail, they will be exonerated if the deposit is made by the defendant at any time before issue joined or judgment signed.

The bail have it in their power to render the defendant either to the county gaol or to the prison of the court in which the action is brought (or the defendant may render himself to the county gaol), at any time before judgment in an action or proceedings taken against themselves, upon their bond or recognizance. It is most advisable for bail to render the principal promptly, as, after proceedings taken against themselves, they are liable to costs, not only of suit, but of their application to the court to be permitted to render their principal, *i. e.* the defendant. Bail are of course discharged if they render their principal immediately after judgment signed in the action against him; and also they are discharged if the defendant become bankrupt or insolvent, and obtain his certificate or discharge, or the plaintiff give indulgence to the defendant, which extends in point of time beyond the period by which a verdict could have been obtained; or if the principal die, become a member of parliament, or privileged; or if the plaintiff delay in proceeding. Bail have absolute power over their principal, and can render him to prison without notice, and may even take him on a Sunday, notwithstanding a contrary decision was once given; but bail in inferior courts have no such right, nor persons who have simply executed the preliminary security of a bail-bond. However, persons who are bail should take professional advice, they having need of indemnity or protection; for hard creditors and disreputable practitioners will often endeavour to, what is termed, "fix" the bail, on account of practical errors or inattention on their part.

Bail is also given when a defendant brings a writ of error on account of some defect, real or alleged, in the proceedings of a suit in which judgment has been given against him. It is similar to the giving *special bail*, the recognizance being taken before a particular officer appointed for that purpose; but the bail should remember that nothing *short of absolute payment of debt and costs* will relieve them from this suretiship: the render of the defendant availing them nothing.

In other cases of bail, such as attachments for contempt (not for nonpayment of money), a bail-bond is given to the sheriff, if he chooses to accept of it, for it is by no means imperative on him to take bail in these cases; and at the return of the process the bail of defendant enter into recognizances for the defendant's future appearance. The recognizances are sometimes conditioned for large sums, but are vacated on the defendant's answering the matters of the contempt, &c. Bail is often given to the sheriff on other contempts; and the bond is forfeited if the defendant is not in custody at the return of the attachment, according to the terms of the bond.

In almost all criminal cases, two justices may admit a party to bail, if the evidence be not such as to raise a strong presumption of guilt, but still afford reasonable ground of inquiry. In criminal cases where bail is required, it is taken before a justice or justices, and they have an absolute discretion in admitting parties to bail or committing them, but they are bound to take down the examination in writing. If justices, under pretence of demanding sufficient bail, require very high sureties, the matter can be inquired of by the court of Queen's Bench, who in all doubts should be applied to, as they have power to bail in *all* cases whatever (even capital), where innocence can be fairly presumed, or the charge is not alleged with sufficient certainty. See JUSTICES OF THE PEACE.

Justices generally take two, but on particular occasions they will require more, sureties for the party's reappearance; and the court of Queen's Bench in cases of felony generally require four sureties. See JUSTICES OF THE PEACE.

The courts of Queen's Bench, Common Pleas and Exchequer, in term time, and the chancery in the term or vacation, *may* bail persons by the Habeas Corpus Act.

Persons committed by the Queen's Bench or other warrant for treason or felony, and not indicted the next term, may be bailed.

If a person be dangerously wounded, the offender may be bailed till the party be dead; but it is usual to have assurance from a skilful surgeon that the party is likely to do well.

The recognizance of bail in the Queen's Bench is taken separately, and also that the bail shall be liable *body for body*. It is discretionary with justices whether they will take the recognizance in a particular sum, or *body for body*.

Persons committed improperly by inferior courts can apply to the Queen's Bench to be bailed.

Judges of the Queen's Bench, at chambers, in vacation, admit parties to bail brought up on *habeas corpus*, for misdemeanors, &c.

A person committed by either house of parliament may be bailed by the Queen's Bench after prorogation, but not before. The court of Queen's Bench, as the supreme court of judicature, has bailed persons committed to the Fleet by the lord chancellor, when the cause of commitment was not mentioned, or only in general terms.

By the Police Act, any constable or headborough attending at a watchhouse may take bail from persons charged with petty misdemeanors, without a justice's warrant, and the recognizances are of equal force as those taken before a justice.

The bail can render their principal by taking him to a constable or before a justice.

BAILIFF. This name of office is legally applied to the chief magistrates of some towns, and keepers of royal castles, persons having the conservation of the peace in hundreds, which are subdivisions of counties, and in some particular jurisdictions (as the bailiff of Westminster), and returning officers in the same; but it mostly used to signify officers of the sheriff, who execute all processes directed to him. They are bound in sureties to indemnify the sheriff against misconduct or extortion, for which in most cases he is liable. Their reward consists in some fees payable by the sheriff, and by the attornies who issue the writs, and nominate them to execute the process; but it is to be regretted that their chief profit arises from unauthorised payments, which they obtain from debtors in their custody, and various abuses too well known. See EXTORTION.

BAILIFF OF A MANOR, is one who collects the rents and levies the fines due to the lord, by a precept from the steward, or generally by a bare authority from the lord himself. As an agent, the acts done in derogation of the lord's rights will not bind him, although for manerial purposes he is the known agent. They also summon the courts, and cause notice to be given in the church, or at the church door, and transact all the subordinate business of the manor.

Bailiff of Husbandry. A chief servant to private persons of good estates, in respect of their farms, &c.; a sort of steward in respect of farming business. His contracts in his master's name, in respect of the farm, will bind him.

Bailiff of the Forest, is a keeper of a *walk*, and is immediately subordinate to the verderers. In Epping Forest they are termed keepers.

BAILIWICK, is a county of which the sheriff is legally the keeper, or bailiff. It is also used to signify the precinct of an exclusive jurisdiction distinct from the sheriff, though within his county. In the execution of processes relating to civil matters, this last distinction does not now exist.

BAILMENT, is a delivery by one to another of goods, either by lending, pledging, keeping for safe custody with or without recompence, hiring, or, in fact, any delivery not made on sale, or in contemplation of it. The obligations that arise upon the various deliveries of goods or valuables are contracts either expressed or implied, which will each be noticed sufficiently for the purposes of ordinary information, under the following titles, to which the intelligent reader is referred: — Carrier, Commission, Hiring, Pawn.

The person who delivers goods is termed the *Bailor*, he to whom they are delivered the *Bailee*.

BANK OF ENGLAND. The name of an incorporated body, managed by governors and directors, first established by act of parliament in the reign of King William and Mary, their charter being dated July 27. 1694, and continued by various subsequent acts to the present time, with funds for its support, appropriated to subscribers for stock, which stock forms the debt owing by the nation: upon this the company make dividends half-yearly. The funds, or sums borrowed by government, are redeemable by parliament on payment of the money borrowed; the company continuing a corporation, and receiving the annuities or interest upon the sums lent, till redemption or repayment.

The stock is exempted from taxes, accounted a personal estate, assignable by unstamped transfer, not subject to forfeiture, or liable to be taken in execution.

The great privilege which the Bank of England enjoys, is, that, subject to certain exceptions, no other body can take up, or borrow any sums, on notes, or bills, payable on demand.

The following are abstracts of the most important sections of the 3 *&* 4 *W.* 4. *c.* 98., which regulate its privileges, and determine its existence: —

§ 1. The governor and company are declared to have their exclusive privilege of banking as a body corporate, upon the specific terms mentioned in the act.

§ 2. During the continuance of such privilege, no banking company or partnership exceeding six persons is to issue bills or notes payable on demand in London, or within 65 miles, with an exception in favour of bankers *beyond* 65 miles making their notes payable in London; but if paid in London, they are not reissuable there, or within the 65 miles; and the amount must not be less than 5*l.*

§ 3. Any company or partnership of more than six may carry on banking in

London, or within 65 miles, provided bills or notes on demand are not made for less than six months.

§ 5. The exclusive privileges of the Bank cease upon a year's notice given within six months after the 1st of August, 1845, and repayment of the public debt.

§ 6. Bank of England notes are a legal tender for all sums above 5*l.*, (except with respect to the bank itself), so long as the Bank pay on demand such notes in legal coin.

The management of the corporation is committed to a governor, deputy governor, and 24 directors, elected annually. They must be natural born or naturalised (by act of parliament) subjects of England, and must have in their own name, or for their use, viz. the governor at least 4000*l.*, the deputy-governor 3000*l.*, and each director 2000*l.*, of the capital stock.

Thirteen or more of the directors (of which the governor or deputy-governor must always be one) constitute a court for the management of the company.

Every elector must have in his own name, or for his own use, 500*l.*

There are four courts holden annually—in the months of September, December, April, and July—but a general court can be summoned upon the requisition of nine proprietors qualified as electors.

The forgery of the company's note or *seal* (the "Britannia" on the left hand corner of a bank note,) was shortly afterwards (1697) declared a capital felony; and now to forge or alter, or the offer to dispose of, or put off (with a guilty knowledge), any note, bill of exchange of the Bank of England, commonly called a bank note, bank post bill, or any indorsement on or assignment of any bank note, &c., is a felony, punishable by transportation, &c. 1 *Vict. c.* 84.

The forgery, or assisting to forge, transfers or dividend warrants, or making false entries in the bank books, is a felony.

The making out of false dividend warrants is punishable by transportation for seven years.

Officers or servants of the Bank embezzling bank notes are punishable as for a felony.

The Bank conduct business as private bankers.

The bank note is merely a promissory note payable on demand, signed by one of their cashiers, payable to another person (ordinarily the chief cashier) *or bearer*, upon which the company can be sued as a corporation. They are, however, a sufficient tender, if not refused, and in ordinary transactions considered as cash.

As to bank notes lost or stolen, see Lost and Stolen Bills or Notes.

The Bank of Ireland was established in the year 1782, and the charter continued and the incorporation recognized by acts since the Union.

The Bank of Scotland was incorporated in 1695, and is continued and regulated by acts of parliament subsequently passed.

BANKS FOR SAVINGS. See Savings' Banks.

BANKERS. Persons (for this useful and creditable business is seldom conducted by single individuals) who receive money of others, who draw out the same as their occasions require. They are also incidentally entrusted with *deposits* in the strict sense of the word, when they are affected by the operation of the following act, which applies to all classes of *depositaries*, whom the act 7 *&* 8 *G.* 4. *c.* 29. *s.* 49. describes as follows: —

Any banker (merchant, broker, attorney, or agent), who, being entrusted with money, or security for money, with *written* directions for the application thereof, shall convert the same to his own use; or who, being entrusted with any security, or power of attorney, for safe custody, without authority to sell, &c.; shall sell, negotiate, or apply such security to his own use (in violation of good faith, and contrary to the purpose specified), shall be guilty of a misdemeanor, punishable by transportation for seven or fourteen years, or fine and imprisonment."

But this act does not extend to, or in any way affect,

Trustees, mortgagees, bankers, merchants, brokers, attorneys, or agents, receiving money due on securities, or disposing of securities on which they have a lien."

And such persons are also protected from indictment, if, upon any compulsory process at law, in bankruptcy, or in equity, they should disclose the fact of any such embezzlement having been made. The following observations taken from "M'Culloch's Commercial Dictionary," and "Gilbert's Practical Observations on Banking," supersede the necessity of the editor offering any other practical information on the transactions of individuals with bankers:—

The establishment of banks has contributed, in no ordinary degree, to give security and facility to all sorts of commercial transactions. They afford safe and convenient places of deposit for the money that would otherwise have to be kept, at a considerable risk, in private houses. They also prevent, in a great measure, the necessity of carrying money from place to place to make payments, and enable them to be made in the most convenient and least expensive manner. A merchant or tradesman in London, for example, who employs a banker, keeps but very little money in his own hands, making all his considerable payments by drafts or checks on his bankers; and he also sends the various checks, bills, or drafts, payable to himself in London, to his bankers before they become due. By this means he saves the trouble and inconvenience of counting sums of money, and avoids the losses he would otherwise be liable to, and would no doubt occasionally incur, from receiving coins or notes not genuine. Perhaps, however, the great advantage derived by the merchant or tradesman from the employment of a banker, consists in its relieving him from all trouble with respect to the presentation for payment of due bills and drafts. The moment these are transferred to the banker, they are at his risk; and if he either neglect to present them when due, or to have them properly noted in the event of their not being paid, he has to answer for the consequences."

This circumstance alone must cause an immense saving of expense to a mercantile house in the course of a year. Let us suppose that a merchant has only two bills due each day. These bills may be payable in distant parts of the town, so that it may take a clerk half a day to present them; and in large mercantile establishments it would take up the whole time of one or two clerks to present the due bills and the drafts. The salary of these clerks is, therefore, saved by keeping an account at a banker's; besides the saving of expense, it is also reasonable to suppose that losses upon bills would sometimes occur from mistakes, or oversights, from miscalculation as to the time the bill would become due, from errors in marking it up, from forgetfulness to present it, or from presenting it at the wrong place. In these cases, the indorsers and drawers are exonerated; and if the acceptor do not pay the bill, the amount is lost. In a banking house such mistakes occur sometimes, though very rarely; but when they do occur, the loss falls upon the banker and not upon his customer. It is on other grounds particularly desirable for a merchant or tradesman to have an account with a banking house. He can refer to his bankers as vouchers for his respectability; and in the event of his wishing to acquire any information with respect to the circumstances or credit of any one with whom he is not acquainted, his bankers will render him all the assistance in their power. In this respect they have great facilities; it being the common practice amongst the bankers in London, and most other trading towns, to communicate information to each other as to the credit and solvency of their customers.

The facility which banks afford to the public in the negotiation of bills of exchange, or in the making of payments at distant places, is very great. Many of the banking companies established in different districts have a direct intercourse with each other, and they have all correspondents in London. Hence an individual residing in any part of the country, who may wish to make a payment in any other part, however distant, may effect his object by applying to the bank nearest to him. Thus, suppose A. of Penzance has a payment to make to B. of Inverness, to send the money by post would be hazardous; and if there were fractional parts of a pound in the sum it would hardly be practicable to make use of the post: how then will A. manage? He will pay the sum to a banker in Penzance, and his creditor or correspondent in Inverness will receive it from a banker there. The transaction is extremely simple; the Penzance banker orders his correspondent in London to pay to the correspondent of the Inverness banker the sum in question, on account of B.; and the Inverness banker, being advised in course of post of what has been done, pays B. A small commission charged by the Penzance banker, and the postages, constitute the whole expense."

Banks in the country carry on business much in the same way as those in London, with the exception that they sometimes allow interest on balances or deposits, and also charge interest on over-draughts; and in particular avail themselves of the power of issuing notes payable on demand, now not less than 5*l*., which London bankers cannot. There is no limitation as to the number of partners in a banking business who transact *banking* only; but to exercise the power of issuing promissory notes on demand, and reissuable, there must not be more than six partners in conformity with the act of 1708, which conferred exclusive privileges to the Bank of England, and other statutes since passed regulating notes payable on demand.

Banking establishments having numerous or unlimited partners, are termed *united* or *joint stock banks*, and exist in London and in almost every great town in England. The privileges of the Bank of England do not interfere with the Scotch banks. See Bank of England.

Banks with unlimited partners, *i. e.* more than six, may draw on London on demand, or otherwise, for sums less than 50*l*., which lately they were restricted from doing.

The Act 3 *W*. 4. *c*. 83. directs that quarterly accounts of the issue of promissory notes on demand be sent to the Stamp Office, verified by affidavit, under high penalties; the wilful sending a false return being also punishable as perjury.

Bankers are empowered to pledge bills deposited with them by a customer, and may negotiate them to such an extent as the necessary demands of the customer require, without his express authority. When a banker's acceptances exceed the cash balance in his hands, he may hold collateral securities for the value.

Bankers are bound by law to pay a check drawn by a customer within a *reasonable* time after they have received sufficient funds belonging to the customer. An action will lie for a refusal of such check, even though *special* damage is not proved.

Where money is paid into bankers' hands for the use of third parties, they cannot apply it to the general account of the customer paying it in, who may be indebted to them. If a bill lie due at a banker's, and the acceptor, a customer, pay in the amount for the purpose of taking it up, the money, in law, belongs to the holder of the bill, and he can sue the bankers for money had and received.

Bankers paying money under circumstances which ought to induce inquiry, cannot credit themselves with the amount; and where money is paid in on the joint account of persons not partners in trade, the bankers are not discharged by payment to one of those persons without the authority of the other.

BANKRUPT. A person in actual trade or business (not in a profession), who is unable to perform his engagements with his creditors, the legal presumption of which is inferred from such person having done some one of the following acts, which are termed acts of bankruptcy. (Farmers, graziers, labourers, workmen for hire, buyers and sellers of government stocks, persons buying and selling land, and, as it seems, schoolmasters are not, *as such*, to be deemed bankrupts). The different acts of bankruptcy are,—

Departing from England with intent to delay his creditors.—The departure of a man in embarrassed circumstances is strong, but not conclusive, evidence of such intention.

Being out of England, remaining abroad with the same intent.

Departing voluntarily from his house, or otherwise voluntarily absenting himself, with the same intent.

Beginning to keep house.—A denial to creditors for the purpose of avoiding personal applications for money at his house, or at any other place, is the usual evidence from which this act of bankruptcy can be inferred. The period during which a trader keeps at home is immaterial. It must appear to have been done with the intent to delay his creditors.

Suffering himself to be arrested for any debt not due.

Yielding himself to prison, or suffering himself to be outlawed in England or Wales, or procuring himself to be arrested, or his goods, moneys, or chattels to be attached, sequestered, or taken in execution.—These acts must be done collusively, and have for their object the delaying or defeating creditors in the recovery of their debts.

Making in this kingdom, or elsewhere, any fraudulent gift, grant, or conveyance of his property, or any portion of it, to a creditor or other person.—The word "*fraudulent*" applies to preferences or conveyances made in contemplation of bankruptcy (although to a *bonâ fide* creditor for a moral motive), as well as to those transactions which are obviously done with fraudulent concealment or subtle design. A conveyance in trust for creditors generally comes within this rule, and can be annulled if a fiat issue against such trader within six calendar months from the *execution* thereof by him. If no fiat shall be issued, and such deed be advertised in the Gazette and public newspapers, and the requisites mentioned in the Bankrupt Act of 6 *G*. 4. *c*. 16. *s*. 4. be performed, such deed shall not be deemed an act of bankruptcy.

In the interpretation of these acts, and of the motives with which they are committed, if the intention to delay creditors actually existed at the time of the commission of each act, it is of no moment whether a creditor was delayed or not. However, presumptions of intent to delay creditors are raised by the particular circumstances attending the act, which may nevertheless be rebutted by satisfactory explanations.

An uninterrupted imprisonment for 21 *days, at the suit of a creditor for a legal debt, or an escape from custody under such imprisonment,* is an act of bankruptcy.

The filing by a trader, in the office of the chancellor's secretary of bankrupts, a declaration that he is insolvent, and unable to perform his engage-

ments with his creditors, to be inserted in the Gazette, pursuant to the last-mentioned statute, *s.* 6., is an act of bankruptcy; but no fiat shall be sued out thereon, unless within two calendar months next after the insertion of such advertisement, and unless such advertisement be inserted in the Gazette within eight days after such declaration filed.—This act of bankruptcy may be concerted or agreed upon between the bankrupt or any other person, although all other acts of bankruptcy concerted or colluded between a bankrupt and others, vitiate and cause the proceedings to be annulled.

The filing a petition to the Court for Relief of Insolvent Debtors by a trader, is an act of bankruptcy.

If a trader, after a docket struck against him, pay to the creditor so doing any money, or give any security or satisfaction for such creditor's debt, or any part thereof, so that such creditor receive, or is intended to receive, more than his rateable proportion under the bankruptcy would amount to, it is a new act of bankruptcy, and the chancellor can either order a new fiat to issue, or order the old fiat to be proceeded with; and such payment or security, being illegal, cannot be retained, but shall be delivered up for the general benefit of the creditors. — It is immaterial whether such money or security shall have been given to the petitioning creditor privately or not.

Members of parliament becoming bankrupt are amenable to the law in this respect; but they are not subject to imprisonment or arrest, during the term of their privilege of parliament, except in cases deemed felony. And to facilitate the process of bankruptcy against a class of persons who, by reason of their privilege, could delay and defeat their creditors, it is provided by the above statute, *ss.* 10. and 11., *That if any creditor of a trader having privilege of parliament shall make affidavit that his debt is justly due, and that such debtor is a trader, and shall sue out a summons against him, and serve him therewith, and shall not pay, compound, or secure the same, he shall be deemed a bankrupt. And if any decree or order of any court of equity, or any order in bankruptcy or lunacy, shall have been made, ordering him to pay any sum of money, and he shall disobey such order, after service thereof upon him, and after a peremptory day shall have been fixed for the payment of the same by an order for that purpose; if he shall, after service of the last-named order, eight days before the time finally appointed for payment, neglect to pay the same, he shall be deemed a bankrupt.*

Members of parliament declared bankrupt, are rendered incapable of sitting in the House of Commons for twelve months next after the issuing of any fiat against them, unless their debts are paid in full; which if not done within that time, the election is declared void.

Persons under the age of 21 cannot be made bankrupts, unless they have represented themselves of age. Married women, engaged in separate trade, may become bankrupt.

The process in bankruptcy it termed a *fiat,* and is an authority under the hand of the chancellor, or commissioners, or keeper of the great seal, authorising the petitioning creditor to prosecute his complaint before the court of bankruptcy in London, where the bankruptcy takes place within forty miles from London; or if elsewhere, before certain commissioners nominated by him; in both which cases the following subjects are to be treated of: —

1. The suing out of the fiat of the petitioning creditor's debt, the prosecution of the fiat, and the proof of debts.

2. The property of the bankrupt passing to the assignees; and of their functions and liabilities, and the distribution of the bankrupt's estate.
3. As to the bankrupt's surrender, examination, and certificate; his allowance; and as to the surplus arising from his estate; annulling the fiat, and other incidents.

I. *The suing out of the fiat, &c.*—The creditor suing out the fiat, being assured that the intended bankrupt is a trader, has committed one of the above acts of bankruptcy, and that his debt is sufficient as to amount and legality, petitions accordingly, and makes affidavit thereof, and gives a bond in the penalty of 200*l.*, conditioned for proving the debt and for proceeding in the fiat; which bond can be afterwards used as a means of enforcing reparation to a party against whom a fiat is improperly or fraudulently taken out. This preliminary is called *striking the docket*, an entry whereof is immediately made in a book, to which all persons can have access upon payment of one shilling.

The single debt of the creditor, or of persons being partners, petitioning for such fiat, must amount to 100*l.* at the least; the debt of two creditors must amount to 150*l.* at the least; and the debt of three or more creditors must amount to 200*l.*; and such debt must be one for which, if payable at the time, an action at law could be maintained by the petitioning creditor. But though the petitioning creditor's debt must be due, that is, have an existence at the time of the act of bankruptcy, yet it is not necessary that it should be actually payable at that time. The statute declaring that "every person who has given credit to any trader upon valuable consideration, for any sum payable at a certain time, which time shall not have arrived when such trader committed an act of bankruptcy, may petition, or join in petitioning, whether he shall have any security in writing or otherwise for such sum, or not." So that the holders of notes or negotiable securities not yet arrived at maturity may sue or join in suing out a fiat.

The suing out a fiat prevents the creditor proceeding at law for his debt; and if any proceedings have been taken, they must be discontinued, and the intended bankrupt, if in custody, discharged.

The fiat, being thus issued, must be prosecuted within fourteen days, if the fiat is to be acted upon in London; or within twenty days, if the fiat be directed to country commissioners.

The next step is to get the party adjudged a bankrupt; and this is done by the petitioning creditor attending before the commissioners, deposing to his debt, and the full particulars thereof; and by procuring the trading and act of bankruptcy to be proved by witnesses competent to give testimony according to strict rules of evidence: therefore no creditor of the intended bankrupt is competent for these purposes; the petitioning creditor deposing to his debt being the only exception to this rule.

These proofs being established to the satisfaction of the commissioners, by a personal examination of the witnesses, whose testimony is reduced into writing, they proceed to adjudge the party a bankrupt. (What is sufficent proof upon these matters appears to rest solely in their judgment.) Immediately after the adjudication is made and recorded, one of the commissioners of the court of bankruptcy in London appoints one official assignee, in whom the property of the bankrupt immediately vests, and who acts in concurrence with the assignees subsequently chosen. In country fiats, the commissioners appoint a provisional assignee to carry on the business or trade of the bankrupt, if it be deemed expedient, in whom likewise the bankrupt's property and estate is vested; but he is displaced on the choice of assignees by the creditors. At this time the commissioner in London or the commissioners in the country appoint two or more public meetings (generally two) at which the bankrupt is to surrender and conform; the last of which is appointed on the 42d day after the publication of the bankruptcy in the Gazette; and a notice in writing of his having been declared a bankrupt must be left for the bankrupt at his usual place of abode, or served upon him personally, in case he be in prison; his property his then seized by the messenger of the commissioners, who has very ample powers, enabling him fully to execute the warrant of seizure, which is always under the hand of the commissioner in London or three of the commissioners in the country, as the case may be. These proceedings usually take place at the preliminary, or, as it is usually termed, the "private meeting," at which, if the bankrupt choose, he may attend, and receive written protection from the commissioners from arrest at the suit of his creditors, until the first public meeting.

The acts done at the two public meetings, or adjournment of the last of such meetings, are next to be noticed; and these are, the proof of debts, the choice of assignees, and the examination of the bankrupt.

Proof of Debts.—As the obtaining a knowledge of all claims upon the bankrupt must necessarily precede the distribution of his estate, the commissioners first receive proof by written deposition, upon oath of each creditor, either in person, or by affidavit if he live remote from the place of meeting, in respect of debts due by the bankrupt at the time of the issuing of the fiat; such debts being those for which the creditor has a legal remedy, whether the same be payable then or at a future time. Therefore, bonds conditioned, or covenants by deed, for the payment of money upon a day certain, whether before or after the act of bankruptcy, bills of exchange, or promissory notes not payable, are proveable. So, on the other hand, debts barred by the statute of limitations, or where the consideration cannot be proved, or where the debt is tainted with illegality in its contract, or any legal invalidity, such as want of proper stamp, &c., are not proveable: but a creditor may prove not only a debt due to him before the act of bankruptcy, but also a demand really and with good faith contracted after the act of bankruptcy, and before the fiat was issued, if the creditor had not, at the time the debt was contracted, notice of any act of bankruptcy committed by the bankrupt.

A few observations upon claims by creditors of a particular nature will explain to the reader all that is likely to occur practically on the subject of proof of debts, which may be made while any part of the bankrupt's estate is left undisposed of.

Rent.— The landlord may distrain upon the premises, even although a messenger be in possession, but no more than a year's rent can be levied. The landlord may prove as a creditor for the residue.

Apprentice Fees.—The commissioners may order a proportionate part of a premium paid by the apprentice, or his friends, to be returned, regard being had to the length of time the apprentice shall have resided with the bankrupt, and other equitable circumstances.

Servants' Wages. — The commissioners are also empowered to order any clerk or servant of the bankrupt to be paid his or her wages, or salary, then due, not exceeding six months; the clerk or servant may prove for the overplus due. It has, however, been decided, that workmen employed by the job or piece, under a contract for each particular job, are not entitled to such payment of wages.

Annuities. — Annuity creditors are entitled to prove under the bankrupt's estate for the value of the annuity, to be ascertained by the commissioners, deducting the diminution in value by the lapse of time since its creation or date. If the party entitled to the annuity have security upon land or property, the same may, at his option, be sold; and he will be allowed to prove upon the bankrupt's estate for the balance, if the produce is insufficient.

Contingent Debts. — The commissioners may, upon the application of a creditor who claims a debt payable upon a particular event happening, ascertain its value, and permit the creditor to prove for the amount. This rule is liberally applied to claimants under bottomry and respondentia bonds, and to claimants under insurances effected with the bankrupt. But damages which are in their nature unascertained, and upon which no verdict has been given at the time of the issuing of the fiat, cannot be proved, although the right to recover damages be founded upon a matter of contract. It will be seen hereafter, that the certificate will be no bar to these claims.

Debts and Credits. — Cross accounts are directed by law to be set off, and the commissioners are directed to state the account between the bankrupt and his creditor.

Suretiship Claims. — Any person who has made himself liable for any debt or liability of the bankrupt, *and has paid such debt or liability*, will be permitted to prove to the extent of such payment; and if the principal creditor to whom he paid such debt has already proved under the estate, the surety will be entitled to stand in the place of such creditor, and receive his dividend.

Creditors holding Securities may choose, or, as the law terms it, "elect," to retain such securities; and if such creditor wishes to prove, he must deliver up the security he holds for the general benefit of the creditors. However, the case of mortgagees, or of parties having security upon property, is the same as that of annuity creditors above mentioned. Mortgagees, or parties having property in pledge, being allowed to prove for the balance due after the amount of the debt has been ascertained by the commissioners, and the property sold, such property can be bought in by the mortgagee, or party having it in pledge, upon leave being given (and it is scarcely ever refused) for this purpose.

Bills of Exchange or Notes of Hand. — The holders of negotiable securities may prove against the estate of such of the makers, acceptors, drawers, and indorsers as become bankrupt, and may also bring actions against the solvent parties to the same. The holder may receive a dividend upon his whole claim, from each of the estates upon which he has proved, provided he receives no more than 20*s.* in the pound of the sum actually due. Interest is proveable upon bills, notes, &c. overdue at the time of the fiat, together with costs of protests, commission, exchange, &c.

Costs, recovered by a verdict given, or upon a judgment signed, before the issuing of the fiat, are proveable, if the action were for a debt, although such costs were not taxed at such period. Costs in chancery, equity side of the exchequer, bankruptcy, or lunacy, upon which an order has been obtained for payment, are also proveable in like manner.

Interest is not generally proveable, unless mentioned in the deed, contract, &c., except in the case of bills of exchange, above stated.

A Wife may also prove upon the bankrupt's estate, for money which the bankrupt *bonâ fide*, in consideration of marriage, covenanted to invest; and

A Child may prove for money received by his father for his use. Under particular circumstances, the child has been allowed to prove for the amount of his earnings received by the father, even if the child was living with him.

A Creditor who is not in a situation, from unavoidable circumstances, to prove his debt before a dividend declared, may enter a *claim* for what he may fairly judge to be the probable amount of his debt, and a dividend will be retained for the same; but this claim will be expunged unless substantiated by proof within a reasonable time, of which the commissioners are to judge.

Creditors attending for the purpose of proving a debt, are privileged from arrest, in the same manner as witnesses or parties to a suit attending courts of justice.

The creditor who attends to prove under a bankrupt's estate ought well to consider the expediency of such a course; for by so doing he relinquishes all securities of the bankrupt *alone*, which he has for his debt (except mortgages and property upon which he has a lien, which he may, under direction of the commissioners, cause to be sold, and prove for the balance, as before stated); and he is bound to relinquish the person or the bail of the bankrupt, whether he be then in custody, or afterwards, even if the bankrupt do not obtain his certificate; and such proof cannot be withdrawn, although the securities he has abandoned are of greater value than he was aware of.

On the other hand, the creditor proving his debt is entitled to his fair proportion of the bankrupt's estate, and to interest upon his debt, if there should be a surplus. The bankrupt's effects, not his person, are also liable for so much of the debt as shall not have been satisfied by the dividends, if he do not obtain his certificate. The law recognizes no priority of debts in the distribution of a bankrupt's estate, save those already mentioned, and the case of friendly societies, who are entitled, within forty days after demand made, to receive out of the bankrupt's effects all money or securities which the bankrupt had received for their use, by stat. 33 *G*. 3. *c*. 54. *s*. 10.

A creditor may impeach the validity of a bankruptcy after proof of his debt.

If it is apparent to the assignees, or any two creditors whose separate proofs amount to 20*l*., that the whole or a part of the debt proved is not justly due from the bankrupt, the commissioners, upon an undertaking being given by the assignees or such creditors to pay costs, may inquire into the fact, and according to the result of the inquiry reduce or expunge the proof. But as the determination of the commissioners may be disputed by an appeal to the chancellor, and as a power is given to the assignees or creditors to apply in the first instance, it may be the more prudent and least expensive course for the creditors to raise the intended objections to the obnoxious debt by a petition in the first instance; particularly as the legal right to prove a debt, and the fact of the debt being due, are matters essentially different, and in the former case can only be remedied by the court of review.

II. The choice of assignees must be made at the first public meeting, or at some adjournment thereof, after the proof of debts by the major part in value of the creditors who have proved debts to 10*l*. or upwards, who are personally present at the meeting, or have authorised others to vote for them by power of attorney; and thereupon the commissioners sign an appointment, and a memorandum thereof, at the foot of which the assignees, or the persons deputed by letter of attorney, sign an acceptance of the trust. These persons, whatever their powers may be, are nothing more than mere trustees for the creditors, who, in their discretion, may choose whom they will, subject to the control of the court of review, which will be exercised in the case of an ineligible or unfit appointment. The commissioners also may reject persons apparently unfit; but an appeal lies from their decision. At this stage of the proceedings, in town bankruptcies, an official assignee, who has been previously appointed by the commissioner to preserve the estate, in the character of a sole assignee, now commences to act in concurrence with the assignees chosen by the creditors, save that he is restricted from interfering in the appointment or removal of the solicitor, or in directing the time and manner of selling the bankrupt's effects. Usually two assignees are chosen, though, if requisite, more are appointed. The court will appoint, on application, an agent or inspector, in cases requiring vigilance or attention on behalf of the general body, or a particular class of creditors.

The removal of assignees is a matter of discretion vested in the court of review, who will, upon application, displace an assignee who has been fraudulently elected, has become bankrupt or insolvent, or compounded with his creditors, or is resident out of the jurisdiction of the court; and under terms, an assignee can be removed at his own instance.

The vacancy by death or removal of official assignees in town bankruptcies is provided for by the Bankrupt Act of 1 *&* 2 *W.* 4. *c.* 56. *s.* 24.

Property passing to the Assignees.—The choice of the assignees by the creditors, and their acceptance of the trust, evidenced by the appointment in writing, and the certificate thereof signed by the commissioners, is the act or instrument by which all the bankrupt's personal estate, of which he was possessed *at the time of his committing the act of bankruptcy*, and his real estate from the date of the appointment, whether in possession, reversion, or expectancy, or in action, passes to the assignees; subject, however, in many cases to debts due to the revenue previously accrued, and to any conditions, terms, charges, or incumbrances previously affecting the same before the act of bankruptcy, and to *bonâ fide* payments made since the act of bankruptcy and previous to the adjudication.

It may be remarked, also, that all property of the bankrupt in the possession of others at the time of the bankruptcy, vests in the assignees, subject to any lien or claim the holders may legally possess upon such property. With respect to property in the bankrupt's own possession at such time, but come to the hands of others afterwards, the general rule is, that it vests in the assignees, discharged of any lien or claim. (See Lien.) To facilitate the sale of the real property, freehold or copyhold, various provisions are made by the Bankrupt Act of 6 *G.* 4. *c.* 16., which empower the commissioners to dispose of the same direct to a purchaser, without an intermediate conveyance or surrender from the assignees.

As a term of years, or lease, passes to the assignees, they may, if they consider it valueless, decline the possession; but they are bound to declare their resolution on that head immediately, else they will be considered as having adopted the lease, and consequently chargeable with the covenants, and a very slight holding of the premises will have the effect of making them responsible. It is, however, settled, that if they have improvidently committed themselves, they can relieve themselves of their liability by assigning the lease to another person, however irresponsible he may be, and though this is done for the express purpose of relieving themselves from their responsibility. The landlord, or owner of the premises, has no other remedy than to petition the court of review for the assignees to make their choice either to accept or decline the lease, if he conceives their acts are not sufficiently certain, or declaratory of their intentions.

Property acquired by a bankrupt before the bankruptcy, by means of a criminal false pretence, will not pass to the assignees; but property delivered to the bankrupt in pursuance of a contract of sale, upon a fraudulent representation, will pass to the assignees; for it seems the ownership of the property is changed by the delivery of the goods in pursuance of the previous contract. If there are cross or mutual accounts between the bankrupt and his debtor, the *balance* only is recoverable by the assignees.

Legacies bequeathed to the bankrupt before the allowance of his certificate, will vest in the assignees; and as a bankrupt cannot, under any circumstances whatever, possess any property against his assignees, "all such lands, tenements, and hereditaments, as he shall purchase, or shall descend, be devised, revert to, or come to such bankrupt, *before he shall have obtained his certificate*," and in like manner all personal property in any way acquired by him, will vest in the assignees until he shall obtain his certificate; and this independent of what has passed or is vested in the assignees by having being in his possession at the time of bankruptcy. And although an uncertificated bankrupt may maintain an action for his labour after the issuing of a fiat, yet he cannot sue for after acquired property, if his assignees interfere; otherwise he may. And to prevent the frequency of second bankruptcies, by the statute 6 *G*. 4. *c*. 16. *s*. 127., the assignees under a second fiat, where the bankrupt does not pay 15*s*. in the pound, or has previously compounded with his creditors, or become insolvent, take an absolute interest in all the bankrupt's future property, notwithstanding he obtains his certificate under the second fiat; and this property the assignees may seize or sue for *after any lapse of time*. The bankrupt's person is only protected from arrest, and upon this section it has been held that no action can be maintained against a certificated bankrupt for a debt due before his fiat, although he has compounded with his creditors before his fiat, and his effects have not produced 15*s*. in the pound.

As to reputed Ownership.—To be more particular with respect to the property passing or belonging to the assignees by virtue of the bankruptcy, the reader must bear in mind that the term "at the time of the bankruptcy," or "at the time he becomes bankrupt," has relation to the time of the very act of bankruptcy upon which the fiat is founded. With this introductory remark, it is necessary to premise, that property of other persons in the bankrupt's possession is available for the benefit of the creditors: the words of the act are, "if any bankrupt, at the time he becomes bankrupt, shall, *by the consent of the true owner* thereof, have in his possession, order, or disposition, any *goods or chattels* whereof he was *reputed owner*, or whereof he had taken upon him the sale, alteration, or disposition, as owner, the commissioners shall have power to sell and dispose of the same for the benefit of the creditors under the commission" (*fiat*).

The words of the statute exclude interests in land, which are not so susceptible of reputed ownership as what are legally denominated *chattels*, which are interpreted to be debts, bills of exchange and notes, government stock, and judgments. And to subject the goods of others in the bankrupt's possession to the control of the fiat, it must be clearly shown that the bankrupt had the power of dealing with them as his own, or obtaining credit upon them; or by the simple possession of them at the time of his bankruptcy, with the permission, absolute or constructive, of the true owner; in fact, the bankrupt must have been the reputed owner to all ordinary intent and reasonable presumption. A special proviso excludes this part of the statute from applying to the owners of ships mortgaging a ship to another, and continuing to act as owners, provided the mortgage be registered according to the 4 *G.* 4. *c.* 41. Yet, if the absolute owner of a ship permits the *disposing power* of the ship to be exercised by other persons, who become bankrupts, the ship will pass, even though registered in such owner's name. But the object of this exception in the act is to protect mortgagees of a ship who permit the mortgagor to retain the management and possession, *provided the mortgage be duly registered*, and no further.

To continue the subject. Goods delivered to a bankrupt upon sale or return, and he commits the act of bankruptcy while they remain with him, will pass to the assignees; for he might have had credit upon them, and he stands to the world as reputed owner. It is necessary to notice, that if a person sells goods upon credit to a person whom he hears is in insolvent circumstances, he may, before delivery of those goods, stop them from being delivered to the purchaser; and, consequently, if the purchaser become bankrupt, they will not pass to the assignees. This right of a seller of goods may be exercised any time before delivery; but if the purchaser, or his assignees, once get possession, the seller's right ceases. But as this question is merely incidental, the reader is referred to the title STOPPAGE IN TRANSITU.

Some cases have occurred in respect of household furniture and goods, settled upon a woman in contemplation of a marriage with a person who afterwards becomes bankrupt, the principle affecting which appears to be that the wife's possession should be consistent with the terms of the trust; then if the goods or furniture are in then possession of the bankrupt as apparent owner, at the time of the bankruptcy, they will not vest in the assignees; otherwise, if the furniture is so settled for the purpose of enabling the wife to carry on a *separate* trade or business, and she trade *jointly* with her husband.

The exceptions to the foregoing rules, summarily, are, property in the possession of a bankrupt as trustee, executor, administrator, or assignee; as factor for another; as depositary for a specific purpose; bills lodged for the purpose of collection; money received by a collector of poors' rates, or collector for individuals, if not blended with his general property, but kept apart; and money or property similarly circumstanced, will not pass to the assignees.

In actions by assignees to recover property of others in the bankrupt's possession, evidence of reputation of ownership is receivable; and on the other side, evidence of a contrary reputation can be offered; thus resolving the question into a mere matter of fact for the consideration of the jury, how far the bankrupt had such a disposing power or repute of ownership that he could lawfully, and by the usage of trade or business, have obtained general or specific credit upon the possession of the goods or property so under his power or control.

As to Executions levied on Bankrupts' Property.—If the goods of a trader be seized under an execution before the act of bankruptcy, though on the same day, they may be sold at any time after the bankruptcy to satisfy the judgment; but if seized after the act of bankruptcy, and sold before the fiat (unless the space of two months shall have elapsed before the fiat issued, as will be noticed hereafter), or if such execution was fraudulent or collusive, the goods will pass to the assignees. Upon the same principle, if a creditor of a bankrupt attach money of the bankrupt in the hands of a third party, the assignees may recover it from the creditor.

Voluntary Conveyances.—Goods voluntarily returned by a trader, before an act of bankruptcy, to the creditor from whom he received them, will not pass to the assignees, unless such return was made in contemplation of bankruptcy; and this induces the only remaining question as to what property of the bankrupt not in his possession at the time of his bankruptcy, being previously parted with by him, is subsequently recoverable by his assignees. The 73d section of the Act 6 *G.* 4. *c.* 16. enacts that conveyances to any of his children, or any other person, of hereditaments, offices, fees, annuities, leases, goods, or chattels, or the delivering over in like manner any bonds, bills, notes, or other securities, or transfer of debts to any person, or into any person's name, if made by a bankrupt being insolvent at the time, shall be inoperative as against the creditors. These transactions, generally termed voluntary conveyances, have been declared void, as against creditors, by a statute of 13 *Eliz. c.* 5., and the property conveyed, delivered, or transferred, can be recovered by the assignees. The only exception in the Bankrupt Act of 6 *G.* 4. is in favour of the marriage of any one of his children, or some valuable consideration. It has been settled that the statute does not apply to money given by a parent to his child, to advance him in partnership, or to gifts of money to his children or to others, unless they form specific acts of bankruptcy; but a purchase by a trader for his wife, or a voluntary settlement, or a gift of stock, is plainly within the meaning of the statute. Akin to these voluntary conveyances, are what are termed "preferences;" for it is deemed a fraud upon the bankrupt laws if a trader, in contemplation of bankruptcy, or knowing himself to be insolvent, give money or goods to a creditor, with an intent to prefer him, consequently the assignees can recover such goods or money from the preferred party. The question whether a particular or specific payment has been made "in contemplation of bankruptcy," is a fact purely for the consideration of a jury. The point is, whether the money or goods were delivered under circumstances which might lead the trader to presume his failure probable.

Property of Wife. — A marriage settlement executed by the bankrupt *before* and in consideration of marriage, in favour of his wife, will be valid against the assignees as far as the interest of his wife is concerned. But a settlement made *after* marriage, will be invalid, unless made in consideration of an additional portion, or a sum received in right of his wife, or a sum agreed to be and actually paid; or unless made before the bankrupt entered into trade, and at a time when he was solvent. Generally speaking, the property of the wife coming to the bankrupt on or after marriage, passes to the assignees, subject to a provision in favour of the wife's children out of such funds or property, of which the assignees can only obtain possession by the intervention of a court of equity, or ecclesiastical court, such as legacies, life interests, whether principal, or interest and dividends, to be fixed by the court; but where property is vested in trustees *for the wife's separate use*, no interest whatever will accrue to the assignees therein.

Bonâ fide Payments.—It has been already noticed, that, under certain exceptions, the assignees are entitled to all the bankrupt's property from the time of the commission of the act of bankruptcy upon which the fiat is established, so that, by operation of law, all dealings and contracts by or with him respecting it were wholly nugatory, and could be treated as a nullity by the assignees, however morally just the transactions were. To remedy this inconvenience, which imposed a great hazard upon honest dealings, in cases of secret acts of bankruptcy, the Act 6 *G.* 4. *c.* 16. *s.* 81. enacts, that all conveyances by, and all contracts and other dealings and transactions by and with any bankrupt *bonâ fide* made and entered into more than two calendar months before the date and issuing of the commission (fiat) against him, and all executions, &c. *bonâ fide* executed or levied more than two calendar months before the same period, shall be valid, provided the persons so dealing, or at whose suit or on whose account such execution was so levied, had not notice of any prior act of bankruptcy; and by *s.* 82. a similar provision is made in favour of payments *bonâ fide* made before the date and issuing of the fiat: to understand which fully, as far as notice is concerned, it is to be understood, that, independent of a knowledge or credible information of the intended bankruptcy, the notice of the adjudication published in the London Gazette is, by the sect. made sufficient notice, or intelligence to the party, provided it can be reasonably inferred that he saw the Gazette the same day, or the extract which is inserted in the daily journals; so that the only hazard cast upon a person dealing with a bankrupt, or trader in insolvent circumstances, is in the case of a deed or conveyance, the validity of which cannot be endangered unless the act of bankruptcy is *prior* to *the execution* of such deed, although less than two months may have elapsed before the issuing of the fiat.

Sale of Bankrupt's Estate.—The assignees, having taken possession or prosecuted the recovery of the bankrupt's property, proceed to sell the same by private contract or by auction, as the commissioners may think most advantageous (the official assignee being restricted from interfering); the produce of which must be paid into the hands of the bankers previously appointed by the creditors, and in town fiats, to the official assignee, whose duty it is forthwith to pay the same into the hands of the accountant general.

The bankrupt is compellable to join in executing a conveyance with his assignees (unless he is actually taking proceedings to dispute the validity of the fiat), but not to make a good title.

At the second meeting, being the 42d day from the date of the publication in the Gazette, the bankrupt usually passes his examination after the proof of debts has been concluded.

Audit.—The assignees are compellable to attend at a time appointed by the commissioners at the second meeting, or the adjournment thereof, not sooner than four months from the date of the fiat, nor later than six months from such meeting, for the purpose of producing and auditing their vouchers and accounts upon oath, whereof 21 days notice must be given in the Gazette; and to this notice, if convenient, a notice of declaring a dividend is added; when the commissioners, having examined the accounts with the vouchers, and compared the receipts with the payments, direct what sum shall be retained by the assignees in country fiats, and by the official assignees in town fiats: till this is done, no dividend can be legally declared. After the declaration of the dividend, the sums are paid by the official assignee, and in country fiats by an order of the solicitor upon the assignees, who keep the receipts in a book provided for the purpose. As the assignees have means, further dividends are declared and paid in like manner. And when the amount of the total funds are fully ascertained, and after a final audit, a final dividend is made of the residue of the estate, together with the unclaimed dividends. The creditor's remedy for the detention of a dividend, is declared to be by petition only till the court of review against the assignee.

The creditors are at liberty to prove their debts at every public meeting subsequent to the second; and after a dividend, all who prove before another dividend is actually declared, will be entitled to a sum equal to all the previous dividends paid to their fellow creditors, *if the assignees have enough*, and if there is a surplus it will be paid amongst all the creditors, as well those who proved last as those previously proving.—The claims of creditors not substantiating them by proofs will be struck out at the final dividend, until which time they are generally allowed to remain.

Duties of Assignees.—Independent of getting in and collecting the bankrupt's estate, and prosecuting all claims, rights, and powers vested in the bankrupt at the time of his bankruptcy, it is personally incumbent upon the assignees to be vigilant in protecting the estate against undue or suspicious claims, and not to delegate their trust entirely to their co-assignees; for although they may not generally be personally answerable for any misconduct or misapplication but their own, yet if, by negligence or irregularity, the property be placed in the power of the other assignees, or either of them depute others to fulfil their trust without the express sanction of the court, both and all the assignees are liable for the consequences.

All penalties imposed by the Act 6 *G.* 4. *c.* 16. go to the assignees in aid of the bankrupt's estate.

The assignees may compound with the bankrupt's debtor, or submit disputes arising out of the bankrupt's transactions to arbitration, and may commence suits in equity with the consent of the major part of the creditors present at any meeting notified in the Gazette twenty-one days previous; by this procedure assignees are protected from adverse consequences; for if they take upon themselves to act in these matters without consent of the creditors, they will subject themselves to the costs of suit. A general authority from the creditors will not indemnify the assignees; the consent above alluded to must be obtained for each particular case. All agreements to refer disputes to arbitration are under the immediate control of the court of review.

III. The first duty imposed by law upon the bankrupt is to surrender himself, that is, personally appear before the commissioners, according to the terms of the summons served at his place of abode; if he is not in custody, the act empowering the commissioners, by writing under their hands, to summon him, *whether he shall have obtained his certificate or not;* and in case of his non-attendance, to apprehend and commit him. It is, however, optional with the bankrupt whether he appear or not at the first public meeting, unless he is specially summoned for that day, and in addition to the usual summons left with him upon the adjudication; but it is not very usual to specially summon him for that day. If the bankrupt is in custody he is brought up by warrant of the commissioners; if out of custody he is protected from arrest; and in both cases his books and accounts are to be produced to him by his assignees (if he is not allowed to retain possession of them), in order that he may prepare written particulars of his property prior to his final examination; a copy or sufficient abstract whereof the bankrupt is directed to give them ten days previous. If the bankrupt does not appear and subscribe his surrender before the commissioners by three o'clock on the forty-second day, he will be guilty of a felony. In cases where the bankrupt is desirous but cannot surrender, the time may be enlarged.

When the bankrupt does not surrender a satisfactory account of his estate, or circumstances appear which may fairly warrant the presumption that he has not made a full disclosure, even if no *direct* evidence can be produced, the commissioners may adjourn such examination *sine die*, and in that case his protection from arrest extends no further than the time indorsed upon his summons, not exceeding three months. The commissioners have an absolute discretion in proceeding in this manner.

Commitment of Bankrupt.—The bankrupt may be committed upon his examination, if he refuse to be sworn, or to answer any question put by the commissioners, "relating to his trade, dealings, or estate, or which may tend to disclose any secret grant, conveyance, or concealment of his lands, tenements, goods, money, or debts," or *fully answer* to the satisfaction of the commissioners, and refuse to sign such his examination; and in respect to his nonsurrender, or refusal to sign his surrender, refusal to discover his property, and transactions in regard to the same, books, papers, &c., except his wearing apparel, and that of his wife and children; or if he "shall remove, conceal, or embezzle any part of such estate, to the value of 10*l.* or upwards, or any books of account, papers, or writings, relating thereto, with intent to defraud his creditors; every such bankrupt shall be deemed guilty of felony, and be liable to be transported for life, or for such term, not less than seven years, as the court before which he shall be convicted shall adjudge, or shall be liable to be imprisoned only, or imprisoned and kept to hard labour, in any common gaol, penitentiary house, or house of correction, for any term not exceeding seven years."

Persons who conceal the bankrupt's property, and who do not discover the same before the forty-second day, are subject to a penalty of 100*l.* and double the value of the property concealed. Any persons, after the last examination, making a discovery of concealed property, are allowed 5*l.* per cent. thereon, and any further reward the commissioners or assignees think fit.

The same statute, 6 *G.* 4. *c.* 16., also enjoins that every bankrupt not being in custody shall, at all times after surrender, attend "the assignees in making out the accounts of his estate; and such bankrupt, after he shall have surrendered, may, at all seasonable times before the expiration of the said forty-two days, or such further time as shall be allowed to him to finish his examination, inspect his books, papers, and writings, in the presence of his assignees, or any person appointed by them, and bring with him, each time, any two persons to assist him; and every such bankrupt, after he shall have obtained his certificate, shall, upon demand in writing given to him, or left at his usual place of abode, attend the assignees, to settle any accounts between his estate and any debtor to or creditor thereof, to attend any court of record to give evidence touching the same, or do any act necessary for getting in the said estate, for which attendance he shall be paid *5s.* per day by the assignees out of his estate; and if such bankrupt shall, after such demand as aforesaid, not attend, or on such attendance refuse to do any of the matters aforesaid, without sufficient cause shown to the commissioners for such refusal, and by them allowed,—the assignees making proof thereof, upon oath, before the commissioners,—the said commissioners may, by warrant directed to such person as they shall think proper, cause such bankrupt to be apprehended and committed to such prison as they shall think fit, there to remain until he shall conform to the satisfaction of the said commissioners, or of the lord chancellor."

It may here be observed, that the commissioners possess strictly analogous powers with respect to the calling, and, if in custody, bringing before them all persons who are supposed to be indebted or capable of giving information concerning the bankrupt's estate or transactions, and to compel them to produce papers in their possession, necessary for the disclosure of any matters which they are authorised to inquire into. And the wife of the bankrupt is subject to the same examination, and punishable in like manner for contumacy. But persons so summoned are to be allowed their costs and charges; and where summoned in the character of witnesses, and not as accounting parties, they are to have their expenses previously tendered them, as by law is required, upon service of subpœna.

Protection of Bankrupt.—The bankrupt, if out of custody, has his person protected from arrest from the time of his surrender to his last examination, and is also protected on his return from thence: and we have seen that if the same shall be adjourned *sine die*, the protection is extended, in order that the bankrupt should have every facility in reason for clearing up the suspicion of misconduct, by rendering amended accounts. He is also, after surrender, entitled to an allowance out of his estate, for the maintenance of himself and family until his last examination, at the discretion of the commissioners or assignees; and, after a final dividend made, and obtaining his certificate, he, his executors or nominees, are entitled to the following scale of allowance:—

If the *net* produce of his estate shall not pay *10s.* in the pound, he shall be allowed so much as the commissioners and assignees think fit, not exceeding *300l.*

If the net produce of his estate shall pay *10s.* in the pound, he shall be allowed *5l.* per cent. out of such produce, not exceeding *400l.*

If *12s. 6d.* in the pound, *7l. 10s.* per cent., not exceeding *500l.*

If *15s.* in the pound, *10l.* per cent., not exceeding *600l.*

But the bankrupt is not of right entitled to his allowance of *5l.* per cent., except out of the surplus of the estate, which remains after paying *10s.* in the pound.

The bankrupt is also entitled, upon request, that the assignees declare to him how they have disposed of his estate, and pay the surplus over to him. In the event of a surplus, all specialty creditors, and holders of bills and notes, shall receive legal interest from the date of the fiat; and all other creditors at the rate of *4l.* per cent. The mode of calculation is to charge interest upon the whole till the first dividend, to substract the dividend from the whole, and compute interest upon the reduced principal, to the next dividend.

Certificate.—After the bankrupt has passed his examination, if the creditors are satisfied with his conduct, they usually sign a writing or memorandum termed a certificate, and a consent to the commissioners' signing and sealing it. They, by subscription and sealing, certifying to the lord chancellor and the judges of the court of review that all legal preliminaries have been complied with, and that the same has been duly signed by the requisite number of creditors; viz., four fifths in number and value of the creditors of 20*l.*; or after six months from the examination, by three fifths in number and value, or by nine tenths in number of such creditors, who thereby testify their consent that the bankrupt be discharged from his debts. The certificate cannot be signed by any creditor before proving his debt, and not till *after* the last examination, when it may be signed, either by the individual creditors, by one partner for his copartner, by persons empowered by power of attorney; by the executors or administrators, or one of them, of a deceased creditor; by a surety, where the creditor who has proved, is paid by him; and by a creditor, who, after proof, has assigned the debt: but one trustee cannot sign for his cotrustees; and where a single woman proves a debt, and marries, both husband and wife must sign; also, if a creditor become bankrupt, by such creditor, with his assignee. Upon proof of the signatures by affidavit, coupled with an affidavit that the certificate was obtained without fraud, and after a notice by advertisement in the Gazette that the certificate will be allowed, unless cause shown to the contrary, on or before the 21st day of the appearance of such advertisement, the certificate is allowed by the court of review, unless some creditor in the mean time petition to stay such allowance, and proving on such petition that the bankrupt has lost by gaming in one day 20*l.*, or within one year next preceding his bankruptcy 100*l.*, or by time bargains or similar transactions in the funds, 200*l.* within the same period, or have destroyed or falsified his books, or been privy to the proof of a false debt, or the bankrupt, or any one for him, *even without his knowledge,* have given money or security to a creditor to induce him to sign, or the certificate shall have been obtained by fraud, or signed by a person who had no legal right of proof under the estate. It is to be remarked, that the certificate will not be stayed because other creditors *have proved* their debts under the fiat since its signature; but where creditors of large amount live at a great distance, the certificate, under particular circumstances, may be stayed, to give such creditors an opportunity of proving, and consequently assenting or dissenting to the bankrupt's certificate. And finally, the certificate can be recalled where the fiat is fraudulently issued, and the certificate obtained by the sole preponderance of fictitious debts; but the application must not be a stale one, and nothing but a clear case can induce the court to interfere.

Operation of the Certificate. — The effect of the certificate is to discharge the bankrupt, his person and estate, from all debts due by him at the time of the bankruptcy, and proveable under the fiat, and will not only be a bar to actions for all debts contracted in England, but elsewhere; but it does not prevent an extent against property acquired by the bankrupt since his certificate, the crown not being bound by the bankrupt laws.

We have seen before, that the certificate does not protect the estate, although it does the person, of a bankrupt, who, previously to the fiat, has been an insolvent, or has compounded with his creditors, unless his effects produce clear 15*s.* in the pound on the present fiat; his future estate vesting in his assignees, who may seize the same *without legal process* at any time, the only exception being the bankrupt's tools, necessary household furniture, and clothing of himself and family.

The bankrupt is also liable to unliquidated claims or damages, which can only be ascertained by a jury, and which, consequently, were not proveable under the fiat. Where, therefore, a person who had contracted for a certain quantity of oil, to be delivered to him at a future day at a certain price, became bankrupt before that day arrived, and obtained his certificate, it was held that he was nevertheless liable to a special action of assumpsit, for *not accepting* and paying for the oil. And bankruptcy and certificate are no defence to an action in *tort* against a broker for selling out stock contrary to orders.

The criterion of subsequent liability, is the inadmissibility of proof by the claimant of his demand, either as a debt payable at a future time, as a contingent debt, or as a suretiship debt.

The future estate of a bankrupt assignee obtaining his certificate, remains liable for the amount of the sum owing by him to the estate of which he was assignee.

By the 126th section of the 6 *G.* 4. *c.* 16. any bankrupt who is, after the allowance of his certificate, arrested, or has any action brought against him for any *debt proveable under the commission*, can be discharged upon common bail, and may plead in general that *the cause of action accrued before he became bankrupt.* The bankrupt, also, is not liable upon any promise to pay a debt discharged by his certificate, unless such promise be in writing; and it is settled that the bankrupt cannot be arrested on any subsequent promise, since the 126th section declares, that if arrested for such debt, he shall be discharged on common bail.

Generally speaking, a bankruptcy in another country is not a bar to a claim for a debt contracted in this with an English subject; and with respect to debts contracted in England with a trader residing in Scotland, see SEQUESTRATION IN SCOTLAND.

Annulling or superseding the Fiat.—The fiat can be annulled or superseded, if the proceedings be defective; if improper delay shall have occurred; if a petitioning creditor shall be induced, by payment or security for his debt, to forbear the prosecution of the fiat; if a fiat be sued out to effect a particular purpose, foreign to the ends of this proceeding, as to determine a lease, dissolve a partnership, or force the bankrupt to compromise; or if any undue motive be mixed up with the proceedings: but no bankruptcy can now be annulled by reason of its having been concerted or planned between the petitioning creditor, his solicitor or agent, and the bankrupt.

The payment or satisfaction by a bankrupt of his creditors' demands will entitle him to have the fiat annulled; and particularly if, at any meeting of creditors after the bankrupt shall have passed his last examination, of which twenty-one days notice is to be given in the Gazette, the bankrupt or his friends shall make an offer of composition, which nine tenths in number and value of the creditors at such meeting shall agree to accept, another meeting for the purpose of deciding upon such offer shall be appointed, of which the same notice is to be given; and if at such second meeting nine tenths in number and value of the creditors then present shall also agree to accept such offer, the court of review may order the fiat to be annulled. In deciding upon an offer, a creditor whose debt is below 20*l.* shall not be reckoned in number, but is to be computed in value. Creditors to the amount of 50*l*., out of England must be personally served with a copy of the notice of the meeting to decide upon the offer, in sufficient time to vote thereat in person or by power of attorney. If a creditor agrees to accept a gratuity for his assent he forfeits the whole debt, together with the gratuity or increased sum; and the bankrupt can be called upon to make oath that there has been no such transaction conducted with his privity, and that he has used no undue means to obtain such consent.

In practice, however, these meetings but seldom occur, as it is settled that even the acceptance of the composition does not bind creditors not present at the meeting, and who have proved debts under the fiat, from suing for the remainder of the debt.

The bankrupt has the power to contest or dispute his bankruptcy, by presenting a petition to the court of review for its reversal, within two months from the adjudication, if resident in England, three months if in Europe, or one year if elsewhere; which petition the court can either decide upon by affidavits, or, if the bankrupt prefer it (and find security, if required, for payment of costs), can direct an issue to try the question by a jury before one of themselves: the decision upon the petition, or the verdict on the trial, being conclusive against the bankrupt and all other parties, there being no appeal; but a right is reserved to the chancellor to decide upon any question affecting the legality or materiality of evidence. The death of a bankrupt *before* adjudication annuls the fiat.

As to proceedings in bankruptcy against joint traders, or any member of a firm, see PARTNERS.

BANKRUPTCY, COURT OF, is a court established for the sole administration of the bankrupt law, and takes special cognizance of all transactions relative to a bankrupt's estate, and the debts due from or payable to it. The funds arising from the bankrupt's estate are also committed to the trust and management of this court; the assignees chosen by the creditors still having the sole conduct of the sale, and paying the proceeds over to the official assignee.

The jurisdiction of this court is created and declared by the stat. 1 & 2 *W*. 4. *c*. 56., which transfers the original jurisdiction of the lord chancellor to four judges, who form a *Court of Review*, from which there may be an appeal upon special cases to the chancellor. This *Court of Review* is assimilated to a court of law, as it tries contested facts by a jury. Six commissioners are also appointed, who, though they sit singly, yet may be formed into two *Subdivision Courts* of three each for various purposes, particularly to decide on the propriety of a committal against a bankrupt or witness, and to assist each other: so that the jurisdiction is practically carried into execution by six single commissioners, who each adjudicate on the acts of bankruptcy, and conduct the proceedings under each bankruptcy, each fiat being allotted by ballot; two subdivision courts; and a court of review, controlling all. The officers to this court are a registrar, accountant general, deputy registrars who attend each single commissioner, attornies, official assignees, and messengers, whose duties are incidentally mentioned in the preceding article, or under a corresponding title.

This act also substitutes what is termed a "fiat" for the commission formerly issued; the petitioning creditor being empowered, by the form following, to prosecute his complaint or suit in the court of bankruptcy: —

"Upon reading the petition made to me by A. B. of Oxford Street, in the "county of Middlesex, linendraper, against G. H. of Cheapside, in the city "of London, draper, dealer, chapman, and trader, and, as trader, indebted to "the said petitioner in 100*l.* and upwards, and as having committed an act of "bankruptcy, and the said petitioner having made such affidavit, and given "such bond as by law required; I hereby authorize the said petitioner to "prosecute his complaint in His Majesty's Court of Bankruptcy. Dated "this —— day of —— in the year of our Lord, 1836."

(*Signed by the Chancellor or the Master of the Rolls, or the Vice-Chancellor, or a Master in Chancery appointed by the Chancellor for that purpose.*)

This court is limited to bankruptcies occurring where the bankrupt is resident within 40 miles of London. Fiats in bankruptcy, in cases which occur beyond that distance, are directed to commissioners, who are barristers and attornies (the barristers always forming a quorum). The forms of proceeding are not substantially altered by the present court.

BANS. The publication of matrimonial contracts, which is done in the church before marriage, to the end that if any one can show just cause to the contrary, either in respect of kindred, nonage, bigamy, &c., they may take their exceptions in time. If there is a faculty or licence for the marriage, this ceremony is omitted. See MARRIAGE.

BARGAIN AND SALE. The name of a conveyance by which freeholds were granted. It is required to be enrolled in the courts of law or chancery within six lunar months, exclusive of the day of the date. If made of land or houses in London, it is enrolled in the court of hustings. This mode of conveyance has great advantages, but its publicity has brought it into disuse.

BARON. A degree of the greater nobility of the kingdom next to a viscount. Great proprietors of land were originally termed "barons;" and their title has since been confirmed by patent or prescription, to distinguish them from the lesser barons, being the ordinary gentry, who in former days were the only proprietors of land in common with the greater barons, who were called up to parliament. There are still barons by office, as the barons of the exchequer, and barons of the Cinque Ports. All persons of importance seem to have been known by this name. The burgesses of London in Henry the Third's time were styled barons, and so were persons holding land of the king.

The present barons are — 1. By prescription; for that they and their ancestors have immemorially sat in the upper house. 2. Barons by patent; having obtained a patent of this dignity to them and their heirs male or otherwise. 3. Barons by tenure; holding the title as annexed to land: it is said that it is the possession of their ancient landed territories which imparts the barony to the bishops, thereby giving them a place in the upper house, although they hold by succession, not by inheritance. Another, and, at present, more favoured opinion is, that they sit in the upper house by immemorial usage.

BARONET. A dignity inheritable, created by letters patent to the grantee and his heirs male. It has precedency before all knights, as knights of the Bath, knights-bachelor, &c., except bannerets, who are knights made in the field under the king's standard, and may have supporters to their armorial bearings.

BARON AND FEME. The legal style of husband and wife. See HUSBAND AND WIFE.

BARRATOR. A promoter or instigator of suits and actions in disturbance of the public peace, and for his own gain, without regard to the plaintiff's right. This offence is termed BARRATRY, and is punishable by fine and imprisonment. Instances rarely occur at the present day of a prosecution, though it appears to have given our ancestors great uneasiness, if we may judge from the comments of old writers. The suing another in the name of a plaintiff who has given no authority, or in the name of a fictitious plaintiff, is a contempt of the courts from which the process issued, and summarily punished by them; if in the inferior courts, it is punishable with six months imprisonment, and treble damages.

An attorney knowingly bringing actions where nothing is due, and inciting the plaintiff thus to trouble his neighbours or others, is indictable as a barrator, or the courts will remove him, on summary application, from the roll of attornies.

Public or common informers are not to be considered barrators; though, when frivolous informations or actions are brought by them for the obvious intention to extort money, evidenced by an offer to compound, without leave of the court or a magistrate, or using terrifying language to helpless or ignorant persons, they may be punished as such.

BARRATRY, in insurance, is the commission of any fraudulent or illegal act by a captain or crew, to the damage of the ship, or whereby the ship may be subjected to forfeiture or detention, to the injury of the owners, freighters, or insurers. This is a contingency forming a subject of insurance on ships. The acts done must be fraudulent in intent; for mere indiscretion or ignorance, in the absence of fraudulent motives, will not render the captain chargeable.

Owners, masters, or seamen casting away, burning, or destroying ships, are guilty of felony.

Captains disobeying signals or instructions of the commander of the convoy, or quitting convoy, are subject to prosecution in the admiralty court, which will inflict a penalty not exceeding 500*l.* and imprisonment not exceeding a year.

The loss for which the underwriters are liable in case of barratry must happen during the voyage, and before the expiration of the policy. Smuggling, breach of blockade or embargo, deviation from the course of the voyage, appear to be the barratries of most ordinary occurrence.

BARRISTER. A counsellor learned in the law admitted to plead at the bar of the courts, and to take upon himself the protection and defence of those who retain him. They are either utter or *outer* barristers, that is, plead *without* the bar; king's counsel and serjeants at law, who plead *within* the bar. The judges are chosen from the serjeants at law.

BASTARD. One *born* out of lawful wedlock. The only incapacity of a bastard is, that he cannot be heir or next of kin to any one, save to his own issue. In Scotland, the rule of the civil and canon law is allowed, which legitimates children if their parents afterwards intermarry. The English law does not require that the child shall be begotten in lawful wedlock, but it is indispensable that it should be *born* after matrimony, no matter how short the time, the law supposing it to be the child of the husband; on the other hand, children born so long after the death of the husband, that by the usual course of gestation they could not have been begotten by him, are illegitimate or bastards: the usual course of gestation is 40 weeks, or 280 days; but the law allows some days longer.

If a man dies, and his widow soon after marry again, and a child is born within such a time as that by the course of nature it *might* have been the child of either husband, the child can at the years of discretion adopt or choose which of the fathers he pleases.

Children also born in wedlock may, under circumstances, be illegitimate; as if the husband be away for above 9 months, and no access to his wife can be presumed, the children born during that period are bastards; but the presumption is generally in favour of access, and the contrary must be positively shown. The wife can in no case be admitted to prove the non-access of her husband, though she may be examined as to the fact of criminal conversation.

In a divorce from bed and board, if the wife have children, they are bastards; for there the law will presume the husband and wife conformed to the sentence of separation, unless access be proved. In cases of divorce in the ecclesiastical court, from the bond of matrimony, all the issue born during the marriage are illegitimate, because such divorce is always for a cause or reason which rendered such marriage absolutely void from the beginning.

If a man or woman marry a second wife or husband, the first being living, and have issue by such second wife or husband, the issue are bastards.

If there is an impossibility of procreation on the part of the husband, natural or accidental, there the issue of the wife are bastards.

A bastard may acquire a surname by reputation, though he has none by inheritance.

Though bastards are not looked upon as children for any civil purposes, yet the ties of nature hold as to maintenance, and many other purposes; as, particularly, that a man shall not marry his bastard sister.

A bastard may be made legitimate by act of parliament.

The court of Queen's Bench will grant a *habeas corpus* to bring up a bastard child within the age of nurture, and restore it to the mother. Bastards are within the meaning of the marriage act, which requires the consent of the father, guardian, or mother, to the marriage of persons not married by bans.

As to bastards becoming chargeable to the parish, see POOR.

As to murder of infant bastards by the mother, see MURDER.

BAWDY HOUSES. The keeping a bawdy house or a room, which is the same thing, is punishable by fine or imprisonment, or both, and hard labour. A married woman may be indicted with her husband for this offence. The indictment is determinable at the same sessions or assizes at which it is preferred, unless the court upon special cause shall adjourn the same.

By the 25 *G*. 2. *c*. 36., the expense of prosecuting houses of this kind is payable to the prosecutors by the overseers of the parish in which these houses exist. The sum of 10*l*. is also payable to each inhabitant obtaining a conviction, by the overseers, under a penalty of 20*l*. for refusal. Constables neglecting to prosecute are subject to the like penalty. The indictment is not removable by *certiorari*. Upon oath of any credible person that a house is used as a brothel, a justice may, by warrant, authorise the apprehension of persons found therein, who can be committed for want of sureties.

BEER. See ALE AND BEER.

BEES. A swarm of bees, although they proceed from a particular hive, belong to the first person who takes them, if the owner of the parent hive does not follow them: but he is not justified in entering the land of another for that purpose; for it seems that the occupier of the land may appropriate them if they alight on his trees,—the swarm of bees being in the nature of wild animals, in whom a property will not vest till some one takes possession of them. Trespass will lie for taking from another the swarm he has appropriated, unless the owner of the hive has made pursuit; for after caption they are the subjects of property. It is a larceny to take bees from the hive, or even a swarm after the owner has made pursuit.

BENEFICE. Any ecclesiastical living or promotion, dignity or preferment. They are either elective, as bishoprics, deaneries, prebendaries, &c.; donative, as rectories and vicarages: and these last are more strictly and properly termed "benefices."

BENEFIT SOCIETIES. See FRIENDLY SOCIETIES.

BIGAMY, is the offence of polygamy, *i. e.* the having a plurality of husbands and wives at once. The law provides, that the marrying another during the life of the former husband or wife, no matter *where* the second marriage takes place, is a felony, punishable in principal and accessory with seven years transportation; or imprisonment, with or without hard labour, not exceeding two years. But there are four exceptions. 1. Where the second marriage is contracted out of England by an alien. 2. Where either of the parties have been *continually* absent from each other for seven years, not knowing the other party to be living. (*But this exception only relieves the party from a criminal prosecution; it will not legalize the second marriage, should the first husband turn out to be alive, for he, on his return, may sue in the ecclesiastical court for conjugal rights.*) 3. Where there is a divorce from the bond of matrimony on account of nullity. 4. Where the first marriage has been declared void.

The ecclesiastical courts will also declare the second marriage of any party living, the first husband or wife, void.

BILL. A word applied to many writings which state special or particular matters, such as a bill of complaint, or bill in chancery, a bill of indictment, bill of exceptions, bill of exchange, bill of lading, bill of charges, bill of store, bill of sufferance, &c.

BILL OF EXCEPTIONS. A statement in writing made on the trial of a cause, and before verdict given, of an error in law *not* apparent on the record, but arising upon the evidence before the jury, or the direction of the judge to the jury upon such evidence; which statement being tendered to the presiding judge, he acknowledges it by affixing his seal. It is technically termed a bill of exceptions to evidence, and is in the nature of an appeal to the court superior to that in which the action was brought, upon a writ of error: for error *which is* apparent on the record, a writ of error lies. See APPEAL, ERROR.

BILL OF EXCHANGE, is a transferable order for the payment of money, and obtains its currency by *indorsement*, and in many instances by *delivery* from one to another. A bill of exchange is defined by Blackstone to be "an open letter of request from one to another, desiring him to pay a sum named therein to a third person on his account." The person requesting, is called the *drawer;* the party requested to pay is the *drawee*, who, when he has signified his assent by *acceptance* (see ACCEPTANCE), is styled the *acceptor;* and the person to whom the money is requested to be paid, not unfrequently the drawer himself, is the *payee*.

Bills are either *inland*, viz., those passing from one party to another here; or *foreign*, those passing from one country to another, and either made or payable abroad. The only material difference is, that foreign bills must be protested by a notary before the drawer can be charged, in case of nonpayment; but inland bills need no protest. Foreign bills are often made in *sets* or duplicates, each duplicate, or part, containing a condition that it shall be payable only so long as the others remain unpaid.

The following are various forms of bills of exchange, inland and foreign.

£50. London, January 1. 1837.

Two months after date pay to *Abraham Brown*, or order [*or*, to me or my order], Fifty Pounds, value received.

THOMAS SMITH.

To Mr. James Robinson,
Coppersmith,
31. Houndsditch.

[Indorsed] ABRAHAM BROWN.
or by THOMAS SMITH.
WALTER JONES (the holder, *or* indorsee).

Received March 3. 1837,
for WALTER JONES,
DAVID THOMSON.

£100. London, January 1. 1837.

At sight [*or*, on demand; *or*, at *ten* days after sight,] pay to me or my order One hundred Pounds, for value received in flax.

JACOB ANDERSON.

To Mr. Peter Wells,
Merchant, Bristol.
Payable at London.

London, January 1. 1837. Exchange for £50 sterling.

At sight [*or*, at thirty days after sight, *or*, &c.] of this my sola [*or* only] bill of exchange, pay to *Mr. Hendrick Blumen*, or order, Fifty Pounds sterling, value received of him, and place the same to account, as *per* advice, [*or*, without further advice,] from

J. SALTER.

To Mr. W. Herring, &c.

London, January 1. 1837.

Exchange for 10,000 Livres Tournoises.

At two usances [*or*, —— after sight; *or*, —— after date, at Bourdeaux,] pay this my first bill of exchange (second and third, of the same tenor and date, not paid) to Messieurs ————, or order [*or*, bearer], Ten thousand Livres Tournoises, value received of them, and place the same to account, as per advice from

JAMES STORR.

o Messieurs ————, in Paris,
payable at Bourdeaux.

Au besoin chez Mess. ————. Retour sans protêt [*or*, frais.]

Re-exchange, interest, and expenses, not to exceed £

A French Bill of Exchange.

Paris, le 5 Janvier, 1837. B. P. F. 600.

A trent jours de date, veuillez payer à mon ordre la somme de *six cents francs* que passerez suivant l'avis

de votre devoué,

HERPIN,

`A Monsieur Forneret,
à Marseille (Bouches du Rhône).

Rue St. Honoré, No. 204.

In France, bills of exchange and promissory notes are both styled *billets à ordre.*

A word as to "advice." Every prudent drawer should send a letter of advice for obvious reasons, as well as to let the *drawee* know what provision, &c. has been made for payment. If a bill says, *per advice*, the drawee should not accept till he has received it. These words are not very common in inland bills — but the same reasons apply to both.

As to usance, see title USANCE.

Although it is most prudent to adhere to settled forms, yet particular words are not absolutely necessary in law to constitute a bill of exchange or promissory note; and any writing bearing the proper stamp, which demonstrates the intent to pay to a particular party, will suffice, and even in one case, where a party, either humorously or for the purpose of deception, "promised *not* to pay," &c., the court rejected the word "not."

Promissory notes, being written promises from one to pay a sum of money to another, only bear resemblance to a bill of exchange in the mode of their transfer and negotiation, the form differing from a bill, viz.:—

£50 0 0 London, Jan. 1. 1837.

On demand I promise to pay at *Messrs. Coutts and Co., Strand*, to Abraham Brown, or his order, Fifty Pounds, value received.

THOMAS SMITH.

£50 0 0 London, Jan. 1. 1837.

Two months after date, we and each of us promise to pay Mr. Abraham Brown, or order, Fifty Pounds, valued received.

THOMAS SMITH.
JAMES ATKINSON.

At Messrs. Williams, Deacon, and Co.'s, Birchin Lane, and there only.

A French Promissory Note.

Paris, le 1er Août, 1836. Bon pour F. 321 10.

Au premier Novembre prochain je paierai à Mons. Perier ou à son ordre, le somme de *trois cent vingt et un francs dix centimes*, valeur reçue en marchandises, et pour solde de tous comptes entre nous.

B. MARTIN,
Rue Quincampoir, No. 27.

The party promising being the "maker," the person to whom the sum is payable being the "payee," and the payee indorsing to a third party is called the indorser, who thus directs the maker of the note to pay the money to the indorsee or holder. On these points of resemblance and analogy, the law is precisely the same as with bills of exchange.

Bills and notes may be made payable to bearer, as well as to order; sometimes in the alternative, as to A. B. or bearer. Bills or notes payable to "*bearer only*," need not be indorsed, the transfer being complete without that form.

Bills or notes must not be altered after they have been *drawn* or *made*, unless the alteration is only the correction of a mistake; if made without consent of the party bound, it is void: the stamp laws have made a distinction as to the means of rectifying an alteration; for if *before* negotiation *all parties* consent, the bill or note will be valid; but if made *after* negotiation, no consent will render the instrument valid, as the stamp laws would thereby be contravened.

A bill or note given, accepted, or made, without a date, for the purpose of the holder supplying a date at his convenience, is, for the same reason, void. Where an alteration appears upon a bill or note, it is incumbent on the party claiming, to show that it was made with the consent of the party sued. It seems, an acceptor may consent to an alteration as against himself, he being primarily liable; but the general rule seems to be that *all parties* should consent.

A bill or note must be made for payment of a specific sum of money only, and where a note was worded thus, "I promise to pay J. E. the sum of 65*l*., with lawful interest for the same, three months after date, and all other sums which may be due to him;" Lord Ellenborough was of opinion that the instrument was too indefinite to be considered as a promissory note, and that, since the whole constituted an entire promise, it could not be divided into parts.

A bill or note must not be contingent or conditional, either as to the *time*, or the *fund* out of which it is made payable. The time of the payment being postponed to a particular event which *must* happen, is not such a contingency or condition as will vitiate the instrument:

it is the making the bill or note payable upon a chance or event that may or may not happen, or making its payment depend upon the sufficiency or insufficiency of a fund, that renders it void; for the mention of a particular fund out of which reimbursement is to be made, or the payment to be carried to a particular account, so that the fact of the money being advanced upon the *personal* credit of the drawer is apparent, will operate as an exception.

A bill may be accepted or indorsed by a pencil-writing.

A bill of exchange or promissory note, being essentially negotiable according to the tenor of the instrument, may be transferred or indorsed by one to another, to an unlimited extent, between the periods of date and becoming payable (even before acceptance); and while it is thus running in a negotiable state, every indorsee for value acquires a title to sue the acceptor, and the drawer, and previous indorsers, whatever fraud may have been committed in obtaining the bill by the previous parties: but after the time of its becoming due, the case is otherwise: for though a bill may be indorsed after that time, provided value be given for it, yet the party taking a bill after maturity, takes it subject to all the matters of equity and defence that have attached upon the bill since its making. The circumstance of its being overdue, is in law sufficient to cast upon such a holder the burden of inquiry as to the merits of the bill. Judge Buller lays down this rule in the following words. "There is this distinction between bills indorsed *before* and *after* they become due:—If a note indorsed be not due at the time, it carries no suspicion whatever on the face of it, and the party receives it on its own intrinsic credit; but if it is overdue, though I do not say that by law it is not negotiable, yet certainly it is out of the common course of dealing, and does give rise to suspicion. Still stronger ought that suspicion to be, when it appears on the face of the note to have been noted for nonpayment."

We have seen that bills and notes payable to *order* are transferred by indorsement *and* delivery; bills and notes payable to bearer or payable to order, and indorsed *generally*, *i. e.* payable on demand, are transferable by delivery only. Where a bill or note is transferred by delivery only, the party transferring it cannot be sued thereupon. Simple signature is the usual indorsement; but when indorsed payable to a particular person, it stops the negotiability, restraining the currency to the payee. This indorsement is styled a *full* or *special* indorsement, and generally is thus: "Pay the contents to A. B. (signed) C. D." The ordinary indorsement by simple signature is a *blank* indorsement. The currency of a bill or note may be restricted by other special indorsements, which give notice that the bill is to be carried to a particular account, or the proceeds applicable for the use of a particular person.

The striking out an indorsement *by mistake*, will not exonerate an indorser.

Presentment for Acceptance.—In the case of a bill or note payable at a certain time after sight, acceptance is necessary for the purpose of fixing the time of payment; but in all other cases, though it is usual, it is not necessary, in order to render the bill available against the other parties thereto, to present it for acceptance: it is, however, usual and advisable to present all bills for acceptance, since, in case of acceptance, the additional security of the acceptor is obtained; or in case of refusal, the holder may immediately sue the other parties on the bill.

Where the bill is in the hands of an agent, it is highly advisable that it should be presented for acceptance without delay; since, if not presented till due, and then dishonoured, the holder may lose his chance of recovery against other parties, who may have become insolvent since the time when the bill might have been presented for acceptance; and the agent would, as it seems, in such case, be liable to his principal to the extent of such damage. But this depends considerably upon usage and custom.

If a person hold a bill not addressed to any particular individual, but accompanied with a letter of advice, mentioning the person on whom the bill is drawn, it is said that the bill should be presented to the person mentioned in the letter of advice, who may thereupon accept the bill; and that if he refuses to do so, it may be protested for non-acceptance.

Where a promissory note was made, by which A. B. promised to pay ten days after sight to C. D., or order, the sum of 259*l.*, with interest at the rate of two and a half per centum per annum to the day of *acceptance;* it was held, that the word *acceptance* meant *sight.*

There is no particular time within which a bill payable at sight, or at a certain time after sight, must be presented. The only rule on the subject is, that it must be presented within a *reasonable* time; and what is to be deemed a *reasonable* time, must depend upon the circumstances of each particular case.

The bill, if not payable at a banker's or at a merchant's counting house, may be presented as late as eight o'clock in the evening.

Presentment should be made to the *drawee*, or his authorised or known agent.

Presentment for payment should be made, by the holder or his agent, (or, if the holder be dead, by his executor, within a *reasonable* time,) to the acceptor of a bill, or maker of a promissory note; or to his agent, if accepted by an agent, and the principal be still absent. The presentment should be made at the house or office of the *acceptor* or *maker*, or wherever he can be found; but this, in inland bills, is only necessary to charge the drawer and indorsers with payment. If the bill be made payable at a banker's, or *specially*, it should be presented at the particular place named (see ACCEPTOR), else the other parties will not be charged.—Where a promissory note is made payable in the body of it at a particular place, as, "I promise to pay at Messrs. A. and Co.'s, &c." such special payment is part of the contract, and to charge the *maker* as well as the indorsers, the note must be presented there; and if a note or bill is made payable at two different places, it may be presented at either. All presentments should be made at the usual hours of the party's transacting business of that nature. A presentment after banking hours will not charge the drawer or indorsers, where the bill or note was made payable there.

Where the drawee, acceptor, or maker, is dead, the bill or note must be presented to his executors or administrators; unless where the bill is made payable and is presented at a particular place, in which case it is not necessary to present it also at the house of the executor. In case there be no representative, the holder should demand payment at the house of the deceased.

Where a bill is accepted by an agent, and at the time when it becomes due the principal is still absent, it must be presented for payment to the agent.

Computation of Time.—A month means a calendar month: thus, where a bill is dated the 10th of January, payable two months after date, the two months expire on the 10th of March, to which must be added the three days of grace; so that the bill becomes payable on the 13th of March, and the money is demandable from the acceptor, or maker, on that day. A presentment on one of the days of grace is a nullity, unless on the second, when the third falls on a Sunday, Christmas-day, Good Friday, or a Fast-day. When the time is computed by days, the day on which the event happens is to be excluded; so on a bill or note payable ten days after date, dated the 1st of January, the time does not expire till the 11th. In foreign bills payable at a certain time *after date*, the time is reckoned according to the style of the place where it is *drawn;* but in other cases, according to the style of the place where it is *payable.*

In computing the time upon a bill payable at a certain number of days after sight, the day of presentment must be excluded, and no days of grace are allowed.

As to presentment of checques or notes of bankers, see CHECQUES.

If the last of the three days of grace fall on a Sunday, Christmas-day, Good Friday, or a fast or thanksgiving day, the bill is payable on the Saturday, Thursday, or day before Christmas-day, or the fast or thanksgiving day. If the two latter fall on Monday, the presentment must be made on the Saturday, although the notice of dishonour need not be given till the Tuesday.

If the acceptor does not pay the bill or note upon presentment, notice of the "dishonour" must be given to the drawer and indorsers, by the holder, else he cannot recover the amount from them. (See DISHONOUR, notice of.) The protest of an inland bill is not necessary; but if made at all, it should be made on the day *after* the bill became payable, not on the evening of that day, which is not warranted by the statute. The noting of an inland bill is, in fact, no more than a presentment, when made on the day on which it became due, and therefore may evidence a presentment. There is a necessity, however, in noting and protesting foreign bills, as the notarial protest has credence abroad.

Although a bill of exchange is a contract which imports a consideration or value received, which need not be evidenced in general cases, yet between the persons *immediate* parties to the bill or note, as drawer and acceptor, drawer and indorsee, 1st indorser, and 2nd indorser, &c., and persons immediately contracting with each other, this security cannot be enforced in case of fraud or want of value. Also, if a bill or note be given to another for a special purpose, he cannot sue in his own name. But in cases of third parties holding the bill for value, and who are *innocent* of fraud, no circumstance will avail the acceptor or the previous parties pleading want of consideration, or special matters, in an action brought by such *innocent holders;* and in causes of fraud or want of consideration, it is incumbent on the defendant to substantiate the fact.

Bills or notes given for illegal considerations, or for the furtherance of criminal or immoral acts, or acts against public policy, such as gaming, stock-jobbing in British funds, &c. are not to be enforced between the immediate negotiators of the bill, or parties to the transaction, and as between *them* such bills are void, subject to the same exception as the last mentioned cases, Bills that have not more than twelve months to run, are not subject to the usury laws.

All notes, bills of exchange, drafts, &c., for any sum less than 20*s.* are declared by statute to be void, except bankers' notes, and bank notes, which are also re-issuable, and regulated by other statutes. It is also prohibited to make or draw bills of exchange, or notes, above 20*s.* and less than 5*l.*, unless they specify the names and abode of the payees, and bear date the day they are issued, and are made payable within 21 days, and not negotiable afterwards; and every indorsement (which must be made before the 21 days) is also to be attested according to the form given in the schedule to the statute, viz.:

Paddington, 12th June, 1836.

Twenty-one days after date I promise to pay to *James Thornton*, of *No. 2. Dog Row, Mile End Old Town, Middlesex*, or his order, the sum of *Four pounds nineteen shillings and sixpence*, for value received by

WILLIAM JENKINS.

Witness, *Thomas Willis.*

(THE INDORSEMENT.)

17th June, 1836.

Pay the contents to *John Johnson*, of *No. 4. Pitfield Street, Hoxton*, or his order.

JAMES THORNTON.

Witness, *Peter Selby.*

(This indorsement must be repeated as often as the note is transferred.)

OR,

Islington, June 12. 1836.

Twenty-one days after date pay to *James Thornton*, of *No. 2. Dog Row, Mile End Old Town, Middlesex*, or his order, the sum of *Four pounds nineteen shillings*, value received as advised by

WILLIAM JENKINS.

To *George Gunner*,
of *No. 6. Brown's Lane, Spitalfields.*

Witness, *Thomas Willis.*

(THE INDORSEMENT.)

June 17. 1836.

Pay the contents to *Daniel Ryan*, of No. 7. *Goodge Street, Tottenham Court Road*, or his order.

JAMES THORNTON.

Witness, *James Durant.*

(This indorsement *must* be repeated as often as the note is transferred.)

The regulations affecting bankers' promissory notes or bills under 5*l.*, payable on demand and re-issuable, are beyond the object of this work: it is, however, necessary to notice, that they are, in general, governed by the same rules as other notes and bills; their being *re-issuable* after payment is the most material difference; for after payment, a bill or note loses its negotiable properties, and is extinct or commercial purposes.

Form of Country Banker's Note.

> Norwich, January 1. 1836.
> We promise to pay the bearer on demand, *Five pounds*, here or at Messrs. *Ladbrokes and Co.*, bankers, London.
> For A. B. C. and Company,
> X. Y.

A checque or draft upon a banker is a negotiable instrument, and, though generally governed by the same rules which regulate bills of exchange, is subject to distinctions which will be noticed under the article CHECQUE.

As to bills or notes lost or stolen, see LOST and STOLEN BILLS, or NOTES.

BILL OF HEALTH. See QUARANTINE.

BILL OF LADING. A memorandum signed by the master or captain of a ship, acknowledging the receipt of goods, to be delivered by them at a certain place, subject to certain casualties, for which they are not to be answerable, those being provided for by insurance. The bill of lading is signed in three parts; one part being kept by the consignor, another being sent to the consignee, and the third is kept by the captain.

As the bill of lading confers the right of possession, if lawfully obtained, the captain is justified in delivering the goods to the person who presents it to him, as the bill is transferrible by an indorsement, unless it is presented under unusual or suspicious circumstances.

BILL OF STORE. A kind of licence granted at the Custom House to merchants, to carry such stores and provisions as are necessary for their voyage, custom free. A bill of sufferance is a licence granted to an English merchant to permit him to trade from one English port to another, without paying custom.

BILL OF SALE. A contract under seal, whereby goods and chattels, or any kind of moveables are transferred. This contract is always under seal, *i. e.* a deed; because if any one give or grant goods and valuables, without any consideration, or without delivering the possession, it does not alter the ownership of the property, for a bare promise or undertaking does not found a right of action; but if a party by *deed*, of which a seal is the distinguishing mark, sell or give goods, this changes the property, although no consideration was paid and possession given, a man being always stopped from denying his own deed, at least at law. This deed, therefore, is executed by a party for the purpose of divesting himself of goods and movables, which though it could be done without deed (*i. e.* by mere words, or what is the same at law, mere writing without seal) is more absolutely perfected by this contract and deed; and where the transaction is fair and based on good motives and considerations, nothing can be more secure for the purchaser or person taking them, inasmuch as the party executing the bill of sale is for ever stopped from claiming them, even though possession be not given; but as this deed is often made use of, to colourably and fraudulently transfer to a third person, that property which would otherwise belong to or be taken by creditors, it should be considered that by a stat., 13 *Eliz. c.* 5., all fraudulent conveyances of lands, goods and chattels, to avoid the debt of another, are absolutely void against every one, save the party transferring, unless they are made upon good and valuable, *i. e. adequate* consideration. The interpretation of this statute is easily understood, viz.:—that any conveyance *voluntarily* made for the purpose of frustrating creditors is absolutely void against them and all others, save only the person who assigns, for *he* can never, as we have seen before, claim the property. But on the other hand, if the party be solvent, or have sufficient property remaining on hand to pay his debts, or an adequate consideration, *i. e. full value,* was paid by the buyer, who had no notice of the fraud, the sale is good. As possession is not required to be given under the deed, the contract is perfect without it, though it must be remembered that a party remaining in possession, and thereby appearing ostensibly the owner, after he has actually disposed of his property, is an indication or raises a strong presumption of fraud; yet if by the terms *of the deed itself,* or it can be fairly shewn by other evidence that the party's remaining in possession is not inconsistent with the nature of the transaction, as where the bill is given by way of mortgage, to secure money *bonâ fide* lent, and to be repaid by instalments, the party executing the bill of sale to remain in possession until default made in payment, there such remaining in possession is no badge of fraud.

This act, however, does not extend to conveyances in trust for creditors; and a party not subject to the bankrupt laws, or who does not become an insolvent debtor, may transfer his property to a *bonâ fide* creditor as a security or satisfaction for his debt: but even a *bonâ fide* purchaser or creditor should not in prudence accept the bill of sale, or take the things transferred thereunder, if he know that the vendor has an action pending against him, and that he sells to avoid an expected execution. Indeed, possession should always accompany the sale of goods; at least notice should be given to all parties likely to be claimants upon the vendor.

A bill of sale is the proper and usual conveyance of a ship, which as it cannot always be made the subject of delivery, should be registered as required by the act, and possession taken of all the documents relating to her, and notice of the transfer forwarded to the party in possession. See Fraud, Ship.

BILLINSGATE MARKET is to be kept every day, the toll being regulated by statute. All persons buying fish in this market may sell the same in any other market by retail, but none but fishmongers shall sell them in shops. Persons buying at this market for others, and fishmongers ingrossing the market incur a penalty of 20*l.* See Fish.

BIRD. The stealing of a bird which is ordinarily confined in a cage, or having the same in possession, or the plumage thereof, is punishable before one or two justices, summarily.

BISHOPRICK. See Diocese.

BISHOPS and ARCHBISHOPS. A bishop is the chief of the clergy within a certain district, or sub-division termed a *diocese,* and is the archbishop's *suffragan,* or assistant, in England, Wales, and Ireland.

An archbishop is the chief of the clergy in his division or *province,* in England and Ireland, and has, under the king, supreme power in all ecclesiastical causes.

The ecclesiastical state of England and Wales is divided into two *provinces* or archbishoprics, viz. Canterbury and York, and twenty-four bishopricks (besides the bishoprick of Sodor and Man, the bishop of which does not sit in parliament), and each archbishop has within his province bishops of several dioceses. The archbishop of Canterbury has under him all but four, which belong to the archbishop of York; and are, the bishop of the county palatine of Chester, the county palatine of Durham, Carlisle, and the Isle of Man.

A bishop is elected by the king's *congé d'élire*, or licence, to elect the person named by the king, directed to the dean and chapter: if they fail to make election, the king nominates whom he pleases, by letters patent.

A bishop, when consecrated, must be full thirty years of age.

A bishop (as well as an archbishop) hath his consistory court, to hear ecclesiastical causes; and is to visit the clergy, &c. He consecrates churches, ordains, admits, and institutes priests; confirms, suspends, excommunicates, grants licences for marriage, makes probates of wills, &c. He hath his archdeacon, dean and chapter, chancellor and vicar general, to assist him; and may grant leases for three lives, or twenty-one years, of land usually letten, reserving the accustomed yearly rents. See Lease.

The chancellor to the bishop is appointed to hold his courts for him, and to assist him in matters of ecclesiastical law; who, as well as all other ecclesiastical officers, if lay or married, must be a doctor of the civil law, so created, in some university.

The right of trial by the lords of parliament, as their peers, it is said, does not extend to bishops; who, though they are lords of parliament (except the bishop of Sodor and Man), and sit there by virtue of their *baronies* which they hold in right of the church, or as some think by immemorial usage, yet are not ennobled in blood, and consequently not peers with the nobility.

Archbishopricks and bishopricks may become void by death, deprivation for any very gross and notorious crime, and also by resignation. See Diocese.

BLACK ROD, GENTLEMAN USHER OF, is chief gentleman usher to the king: he has his name from the *black rod*, on the top of which sits a lion in gold, which he carries in his hand. In time of parliament he attends on the peers, and to his custody all peers called in question for any crime are first committed.

BLANKS. Certain void spaces sometimes left by mistake in judicial proceedings or written instruments, and which, if any thing material be wanting, render the same void.

BLASPHEMY, the denying the existence of God or his Providence. Contumelious reproaches of our Saviour are offences punishable at common law; and by a statute of King James the First, the prophanely or jestingly using the name of God, our Saviour, or the Holy Trinity, in any stage play, is punishable by a fine of 10*l*.

BOAT. The stealing of any goods or merchandise from a vessel, barge, or boat of any description whatever, in any port of entry or discharge, or upon any navigable river or canal, or in any creek, is a felony, and punishable with transportation for life, or for not less than seven years, or imprisonment (with or without hard labour, and with or without solitary confinement, for the whole or any part of the imprisonment) for not more than four years; and, if a male, to be once, twice, or thrice publicly or privately whipped, in addition to the imprisonment, if the court shall think fit.

BONA FIDE, "with good faith." An act done *boná fide*, with good faith, without fraud, knowledge or notice of any deceit or impropriety, and in contradistinction to an act done colourably, deceitfully, with bad faith, fraudulently, with knowledge of previous facts rendering the act intended to be set up, invalid.

BONA NOTABILIA, *i. e.* notable or known effects, are such goods as a party dying has in another diocese, besides that wherein he dies, amounting to 5*l.*, which renders it necessary that the will should be proved before the archbishop of the *province*, he having the *prerogative* to grant probate of such wills, unless there is a custom to the contrary. Debts owing to the deceased are *bona notabilia*, as well as goods in possession. See DIOCESE, and EXECUTORS.

BOND, is a writing under seal, styled *obligatory*, because the party signing and sealing binds or obliges himself, his heirs, executors, and administrators, to pay a certain sum of money to another (the *obligee*) at a day appointed. There is generally a condition added, that if the obligor does a particular act, the obligation shall be void or else shall remain in full force, as payment of money, rent, performance of covenants contained in another deed, indemnity, &c. The sum mentioned as payable is generally double the sum actually intended to be secured or recoverable, except as costs, interest, or damages, and is called the penalty of the bond, which is forfeited in law if not paid on the day, though the payment of the sum actually due and costs, with damages (if any have accrued), will always satisfy the same after forfeiture. Generally speaking, nothing at law or in equity can be recovered beyond the total sum mentioned in the obligatory part of the bond; but interest, whether secured by the terms of the bond itself, or not, is recoverable.

A bond is a security of a high nature, and being an instrument under seal is called a specialty, and has priority as such in the administration of an estate.

Infants, married women, idiots, lunatics after inquisition found and not before, can avoid their bonds, but those joined with them in the bond are still liable—but these persons may be *obligees*, for it is to their advantage. An alien also may be an obligee.

As this is a contract under seal the general rule applies that a man may not deny his deed, unless in case of express fraud; so the bond of a drunken man binds him, unless he can show he was made drunk, or made to sign the bond when he was so drunk he knew not what he did; and a bond voluntarily given will be enforced at law, and equity will not relieve the party. A *voluntary* bond will also be paid in administering an estate before legacies, though it has no priority over debts on simple contract.

Persons who execute a bond binding themselves jointly and severally, may be sued either singly, or all together; but the obligors paying can sue their co-obligors for their proportion of the bond, though not of the costs, unless in the case of a principal, who cannot sue his sureties.

Bonds given for illegal considerations are void. Marriage brocage bonds, bonds to secure money lost at play, and all bonds which enforce a contract against public policy, or contra bonos mores, as a bond conditioned not to give evidence against a felon, to indemnify against a legal prosecution, are absolutely void. If a public functionary, such as a sheriff, take a bond as a reward for that which he should have done on request, or for a stated fee, it will be avoided.

Bonds were always presumed discharged and paid, at law and in equity, after twenty years from the time of payment named therein; but the time for suing upon these securities is now by statute limited to ten years, after the Session of Parliament 1833*, or within twenty

* The session ended August 28. 1833.

years after the cause of proceeding accrued, *i. e.* upon bonds forfeited on August 29. 1833, ten years; upon bonds to be forfeited, or upon which the day named for payment should elapse, after August 29. 1833, twenty years is the full term allowed for bringing an action, unless the party bound pay interest, or part of the principal sum, and a *written* acknowledgment is given for the same, to evidence which the obligee should in prudence, *before giving a receipt for the payment*, require the obligor to sign a memorandum indorsed on the bond, stating the amount due thereon at particular times and periods. See LIMITATION.

The stealing a bond is a felony, being a larceny.

Bonds are often given by parties *conditioned* for the good behaviour or faithful service of another, and accounting for money received as clerk or servant; in such cases it is extremely difficult for the obligors of such bond to discharge themselves, other than by the termination of the service of the party serving. A notice to the employers that they will not pay or be liable after a certain period, it seems, would be of no avail unless caution or notice was given of misconduct, which the employers could by strict inquiry upon such notice have prevented; indeed, unless a very strong case could be made out, almost amounting to an actual permission, by the employer, of the clerk's embezzlement, the sureties or obligees will be liable. All that they can do by way of precaution beforehand is, to expressly stipulate with the master or employer not only for a power to determine the liability at reasonable notice, but that the master himself shall inspect the clerk or servant's accounts at stated periods, and give notice of any deficiency in the same when discovered; and the sureties should obtain a counter-bond from the clerk or his relations or friends, otherwise bonds or guarantees for these purposes may be ruinous in their consequences. The prosecution by a master for embezzlement will not discharge the sureties.

Payment, after the day, of a less sum, is not good, as the bond is deemed forfeited, unless it can be shown that such payment was accepted by the obligee.

If a single woman obligee marry the obligor, this amounts to a release.

If an obligor make the obligee his executor, and leave assets, the bond is deemed satisfied, for he may retain the money. But if two obligors are bound jointly and severally to another, and the executor of one of them makes the obligee his executor, yet the obligee may sue the other obligor.

If two are jointly and severally bound, and the obligee give a release to one of them, both are discharged. But a covenant not to sue one of several obligors has not this effect. If three are jointly and severally bound, and the seal of one is torn off with a view to his discharge, this act will release the other two, the bond or obligation being deemed cancelled.

BOOK DEBTS. There is a notion afloat among tradesmen that debts entered in their books are entitled to a priority, or rather, that they prove themselves, the books being evidence of the contents; but this is a very erroneous opinion, and against the rules of evidence, which prohibit statements in writing, by absent persons, from being testimony of the facts therein mentioned. It certainly is true, that entries made *at the time* by a shopman or clerk (not by the tradesman himself) have been admitted as evidence after the death of the writer, and a shopman or clerk may be allowed to refresh his memory in giving evidence of the delivery of the goods, or payments made, or other matter stated in such books, upon the principle that the writer thereby furnished proofs of a charge against himself, and a tradesman's books may be evidence against him for the same reason. It would lead to great frauds, if the tradesman by his own entry, created evidence for himself; or, if the entries of a shopman or clerk, who could be produced, if living, should prevail in his absence. Entries in books of account certainly deserve credit before commissioners of bankruptcy, and courts, where testimony by the party's own deposition, or affidavit is allowed; but at law, they are considered as mere memoranda, to refresh the memory of the writer, who must *himself* be produced, to prove all the circumstances connected with the entry, and the transaction to which it alludes; if dead, his handwriting *must* be proved.

BOROUGH. See BURGAGE.

BOROUGH COURTS OF RECORD. The jurisdiction of ancient courts for the trial of actions, formerly held in boroughs now governed by the operation of the Municipal Corporation Act, are preserved by the same act, but the jurisdiction is extended to twenty pounds, under certain provisions which ensure the good regulation of such courts, and place their rules under the *surveillance* of the courts of Westminster. The judges are either a barrister of five years' standing or the recorder of the borough. The clerk of the peace summons the jury.

BOROUGH-ENGLISH. A mode of descent, or inheritance, which prevails in some ancient boroughs and copyhold manors, which is that estates shall descend to the youngest son; or if the owner has no issue, to his younger brother. If no son or brother, then the daughters or sisters jointly and severally inherit. By this custom the widow has for her dower the whole of her husband's lands holden by this tenure, instead of a third, for her life, as dower. This extended dower is called freebench.

This custom goes or runs with the land, and cannot be avoided by the owner making a will.

BOTTOMRY BOND, a contract in the nature of a mortgage, or, as it is termed, *hypothecation* of the ship, as a security for money lent or expended upon her without reserving any claim against the owners in person, and usually made by the master abroad, stipulating that the money advanced, together with the agreed premium, shall be paid within a stipulated number of days after the safe arrival of the vessel at a named port of discharge in England, or at any port within the Admiralty jurisdiction. To entitle the lender abroad to proceed against the ship itself, there must be a *written* instrument or mortgage. The principle upon which bottomry bonds are sustained, although they reserve a great interest for the use of the money, is that the loan is made on the credit of the vessel when in distress, in a foreign country, and where the master has neither funds or credit for that purpose. If the ship is lost, the money is not recoverable. In adjudging on priorities of claim in the admiralty, in case the ship is ordered to be sold to pay the claims upon her, the last mortgage is paid in preference to the first, upon the principle that if the loan had not been made, the former lenders would have utterly lost their security, but it must be shown that the *last* loan was essential for the preservation of the vessel.

It is a matter of discretion with the captain, as agent of the owners, whether he takes up money on bottomry, or not; to justify his doing it the ship *must be in a foreign port*, and in a state of necessity.

Bottomry is not to be confounded with a simple loan, upon the success of an adventure, although it may be coupled with an assignment of the party's interest in the ship, which is in some cases forbidden.

Bottomry is allowed upon the extraordinary risk that is run: therefore, if there is no risk incurred, the law allows no premium; and contracts made colourably by bottomry, in order to cover an extraordinary rate of interest, are within the usury laws. Bottomry is insurable. The lender receives all or nothing. The loan of money on the cargo of goods is called respondentia; in this contract the only security is the credit of the borrower. See RESPONDENTIA.

BOUGHT AND SOLD NOTES. The practice of licensed brokers is to keep books, wherein they *enter* or register the terms of any contract they effect, and the names of the parties, which is legally binding; as when the broker for a seller treats with a buyer, he is deemed the agent of both, and he, in strictness, should sign the book, and deliver a transcript or memorandum thereof to each party, which is called a "bought and sold note," and contains all particulars. As these notes contain the essential parts of the bargain, they will suffice in the absence of a corresponding entry in the broker's book, but if these notes describe the particulars differently or incorrectly, as one species of goods for another, or erroneously state the terms, no contract arises, and a variation of this nature cannot be corrected by a reference to the broker's book.

BOUNDARIES. See ABUTTALS.

BRAWLING, or QUARRELLING, IN THE CHURCH. Indecent conduct in a church is punishable upon indictment, at the discretion of the court. Striking with a weapon in a church, or church-yard, was severely punished by an old repealed statute, with cutting off the ears, and branding and excommunication. *Smiting* and *chiding*, or brawling and assault, &c. in a church or church-yard, are punishable by the ecclesiastical court with suspension, or prohibition from entering the church, admonition, and (what is most remembered) payment of costs, and a sum, sometimes as high as 35*l.* and also imprisonment if the *smiting* was actually within the church, or within a room in a church-yard. A clergyman chiding, or brawling, is suspended from his office. Recrimination, or extenuation, or justification, is not allowed in these proceedings, (as the sanctity of the place is the only thing considered) which are seldom resorted to but in vestry disputes, and matters giving rise to malignant passions.

BREAD, BEER, and ALE, THE ASSIZE OF, was formerly granted to the lord mayor of London, and some other corporations, but it is at present repealed. Under various statutes bakers cannot carry on their trade on Sundays, within certain hours.

BREWERS. See ALE and BEER.

BRIBERY. An offence signifying the receiving or offering any undue reward to a person concerned in the administration of public justice, whether judge or officer, &c., to influence his behaviour in his office, and it sometimes signifies the appointment of another person to a public office, upon undue consideration or reward. The giving or offering a bribe is as much *bribery* as the offence of taking the reward or receiving the consideration. This offence is punishable at common law; but several statutes have superadded penalties and punishments, upon which prosecutions most usually take place.

The sale of offices concerning the administration of justice, with the exception of a very few patent or freehold offices, is specially prohibited, by penalty and perpetual disability to enjoy the office sought thus to be obtained. The offer to privy councillors, or officers of state to procure offiees, or the reversion of offices, &c. in the gift of the crown, is punishable as a misdemeanour upon information.

Undue practices at elections are provided against by statute, although the common law crime in all cases remains; the bribing, or the attempt, which is the same thing, a custom-house officer, is punishable by a penalty of 200*l.*; and bribery at corporation elections subjects the party to a penalty of 50*l.*, and perpetually incapacitates him from voting in any election whatever.

BRIDGES. Public bridges, which are of general convenience, are of common right to be repaired by the whole inhabitants of that county in which they lie; but this does not relieve corporations or others, who by reason of tenure, are bound to repair them. If a bridge is not repaired, the remedy is by indicting the vill, or the county, or any particular inhabitant of a county, or tenant of land, charged to the repairs of the bridge; and the person or persons indicted will be liable to pay the fine assessed by the court for the default of the repairs, who in their turn, can by action call for a contribution or apportioned share from those who are bound to pay their share, and who might have been indicted also. Wherever the county or the inhabitants of the county are liable to the repair of a public bridge, they must repair 300 feet of the highway at each end of the bridge; but, by a late statute, this will not extend to future built bridges. The bridges which the inhabitants of a county are at law bound to repair, are all bridges used by the public for twenty years, or which are a part of a turnpike road, even though the trustees built the bridge, unless the bridge was built since 1803 by the trustee of the roads; though if the county surveyor directed the building, it will render the county liable. And it has been held, that a company empowered by act of parliament to render a river navigable, and to alter such highways as hindered the navigation, were bound to repair a bridge which they had substituted for a public ford. The control of these buildings is under the justices of the peace in general sessions.

No persons are compellable to make a new bridge but by act of parliament; and the inhabitants of the whole county cannot, of their own authority, change a bridge from one place to another.

The rendering impassable, pulling down and destroying a bridge, is a felony punishable by transportation, or imprisonment and whipping.

BROKERS. Agents, and mediators of bargains and sales of goods, between merchants and others, on commission. They are licensed by the lord mayor and aldermen in London and Bristol, and acting without such license subjects them to heavy penalties; and in Bristol, the party employing them is liable to a penalty of 50*l.* They give bond in a high penalty, and receive a medal as the evidence of their qualification. Twelve persons of the Jewish persuasion are also licensed and appointed by the lord mayor, who chiefly act for those of the same belief. As agents, they are bound to reveal the name of their principal or employer, and are prohibited from dealing on their own account, in goods, or taking any other profit than their brokerage or commission.

They are also bound to register their contracts in a book, and to deliver transcripts thereof to the seller and the buyer. Their acts will bind their principal: indeed they are, in strictness, the agents of both parties, but if a bill of exchange is to be given as payment, the seller may, if he chooses, dissent from the contract. The statute regulating their official duties in London, is the 6 *Anne*, *c.* 16.; in Bristol, 3 *G.* 2. *c.* 31.

As agents, they are specially punishable for embezzlement.

Persons who distrain goods, sell or appraise them, and deal in furniture, are also called brokers. See Distress for Rent.

There are also bill-brokers, who buy, sell, and deal with merchants, in respect of bills of exchange, selling to those who draw on, and buying bills of those who remit to foreign parts; from their knowledge of the rate of exchange, they fix the average rate of exchange in these securities, by which merchants consider themselves bound.

Brokers, Ship and Insurance. Ship-brokers are persons who negotiate the buying and selling of ships, procure cargoes on freight, adjust the terms of charter parties, settle with the master or captain. Insurance brokers negotiate between the merchant or freighter, and the underwriter or insurer, and act generally therein as agents, in which capacity they are liable to their principals. They do not seem to be brokers within the meaning of the statute, but are rather agents.

Brokers of Stock, commonly called Stock-Brokers. Their business is to transact business in the funds for stock-holders, and conclude contracts or bargains in government or other stock. They are brokers within the meaning of the statute regulating-brokers, and must be admitted by the lord mayor and aldermen. Stock-brokers are paid by a brokerage or commission, which they are entitled to deduct from the produce of the sale; generally, an $\frac{1}{8}$ per cent. (2*s.* 6*d.*). But agreements for the sale of stock are generally made at the Stock Exchange, a building at the east end of the Bank, in Lothbury, which is frequented by a set of middlemen, called jobbers, who make it their business to accommodate the buyers and sellers of stock with the exact sum they want. A jobber is generally possessed of considerable property in the funds, and declares a price, at which he will either sell or buy, being the market price. Thus, he declares he is ready to buy 3 per cent consols, at $85\frac{1}{2}$, or to sell at $85\frac{5}{8}$; so that in this way, a person wanting to buy or sell any sum, however small, has never any difficulty in finding a purchaser or seller.—*Macculloch's Comm. Dict.*

BROTHEL, or BAWDY HOUSE. A house, room, or other place, kept for the resort of lewd persons of both sexes. The keeping of one is punishable by fine, imprisonment, and any other infamous punishment, at the discretion of the court. Any person going to these places is subject to be imprisoned, till he give security for good behaviour, by recognisance, according to circumstances. A woman is punishable with her husband for this offence, notwithstanding the general rule, that where a wife commits an offence in concert with her husband she acts under his control and coercion, and therefore to be acquitted on that ground or presumption. See Bawdy Houses.

BUBBLES, the familiar name for chimerical projects carried on by joint stock companies for the purpose of enriching the projectors at the expense of the subscribers for shares. Statements deceitfully published, and made for the purpose of fraud, subject the contrivers to indictments for a misdemeanor, or cheat, on the prosecution or information of a party grieved.

Where a society or company is formed upon principles, which, with reference to the number of subscribers, and the nature of the subscriptions, makes the whole a *bubble*, it seems that a member or shareholder may apply to chancery for dissolving the same, and for giving to each member a proportion of the sums subscribed for purposes, which, from the nature and object of the society, cannot possibly be answered.

BUILDINGS. If a house newly built exceeds the ancient foundation, so that the air and light of another house is obstructed, action on the case will lie against the party building.

The laws relative to building and party walls in London and Westminster, and places within the bills of mortality, Pancras, Marylebone, Paddington, and St. Luke at Chelsea, are reduced into one act, called the Building Act, 14 *G.* 3. *c.* 78., the provisions of which, being very minute and technical, the reader is referred thereto. See PARTY WALLS.

BUOY-ROPE and BUOY. The cutting away, wilfully injuring or destroying, is a felony punishable by transportation for seven years, or imprisonment at the discretion of the court. The running down, or making fast to a buoy, subjects the offender to a penalty of 50*l.*, which may be mitigated to not less than 10*l.*, besides making recompence for damage.

BURGAGE, the name of a tenure by which all tenements in *burgs*, or walled towns, were formerly held, and which is not entirely lost. This tenure was a rent certain, payable to the king or the lord to whom he had granted it, and differed nothing in effect from socage tenure. The citizens of London held in burgage of the kings of England, till they had a grant to hold in *free* burgage, which is the same as free socage, the almost universal tenure of land in England. Burgs are the ancient corporate towns who sent members to parliament, the electors being the occupiers of the tenements in such burg, since called a *borough*, to distinguish it from a *town* which had no such privilege. *Borough* is more usually applied to those towns and places now admitted to send members to parliament under the terms of the *Reform Act*, such as Lambeth, Birmingham, &c.; which last may be distinguished by the term of modern boroughs, to distinguish them from the ancient boroughs. Also see CORPORATION, SOCAGE, TENURE.

BURGH-ENGLISH, or *Borough*-English, is a tenure and custom that has obtained in ancient boroughs, and in some manors of great antiquity, viz.:—That the youngest son shall inherit, or, if the owner has no issue, then the younger brother; in default of males, the daughters, taking as at common law. As in the manor of Lambeth, Surrey; in the manors of Hackney, St. John of Jerusalem in Islington, Heston and Edmonton, in Middlesex, and in other counties. See BOROUGH-ENGLISH.

BURGLARY, is the offence of breaking and entering a dwelling-house between nine o'clock at night and six o'clock in the morning, with intent to commit a felony therein. And whether or not this is proved on the trial, the prosecutor may prove a larceny of his goods, and the defendant will be convicted of the simple stealing.

The both breaking and entering between the hours of nine at night and six in the morning, constitute the essence of this offence, and the breaking may be on one night and the entering on another.

Every permanent dwelling-house, in which the owner or occupier, or his family, dwell and lie, is deemed a dwelling-house; the *temporary* absence of the owner and his family will not deprive the house of the protection the law gives it. The building must be of a permanent nature, not a booth or tent.

A man cannot be indicted for burglary in his own house. Therefore, if he break and enter the room of his lodger and steal his goods, he can only be convicted of the larceny.

By a late act it is declared that a church may be the subject of a burglary.

There may be a constructive breaking, the law not suffering itself to be trifled with by cunning evasions in a matter which so highly concerns the protection of the public. Therefore, if any one obtain admission to a dwelling-house by any artifice or sleight, he is adjudged a burglar; or if a servant conspire with a robber to let him in by night, both shall be adjudged guilty of burglary. Obtaining admission through the chimney is a burglarious entry, for the chimney is closed as far as its nature will permit, and the breaking need not be of an outer door or wall, the breaking of an inner door or wall completing the offence. The breaking must be of some part of the house, else it will not be burglary.

The entering a dwelling-house with intent to steal, or stealing in the house, and in either case *breaking out*, is declared a burglary by statute.

The stat. 1 *Vict. c.* 86., which took effect on the 1st of October, 1837, enacts that whosoever shall burglariously break and enter into any dwelling-house, and shall assault, with intent to murder, any person being therein, or shall stab, cut, wound, beat, or strike any such person, shall be guilty of a capital felony.

The crime of simple burglary is by this act punishable at the discretion of the court, by transportation for any term not less than ten years, or imprisonment for any term not exceeding three years. *s.* 2. *c.* 8.

BURIAL in *some* part of the churchyard is the strict legal right of every parishioner, without even paying for breaking the ground; and that right will be enforced by the queen's bench, who will grant a writ of mandamus to the rector, vicar, or perpetual curate, for that purpose, upon refusal; but no parishioner can bury in stone or iron but upon the permission of the parson, and the ecclesiastical court will regulate the fees concerning such burials, if the parson will permit such coffins to be deposited in the churchyard. The place of burial is also entirely at the discretion of the parson, who cannot be compelled to bury the body of a parishioner in a family vault or grave, although he may have given permission to erect it, for nothing but a *faculty*, or license, from the bishop or ordinary will secure to any one the unreserved right of burial in a particular spot in a church-yard or church; and even that faculty fails where the family cease to be parishioners.

Black cloth and ornaments placed round the pulpit on the occasion of a funeral, or mourning, do not belong to the parson, but to the persons at whose cost they were placed there; and if the parson take them, an action of *trover* will lie against him.

No creditor can arrest the body of a deceased debtor, and the doing such an act is indictable as a misdemeanor, as well as a conspiracy to prevent a burial, or wilfully obstructing it.

It has been supposed, that permitting a funeral procession to pass over private grounds creates a public right of way, but this is a vulgar error.

A funeral is exempt from toll.

By the 68th canon, "*No minister shall refuse, or delay, to bury any corpse that is brought to the church or church-yard (convenient warning being given him before) in such manner and form as is prescribed in the Book of Common Prayer.*"

Persons who are dissenters, and persons baptised by persons *not clergymen*, are entitled to Christian burial, equally with those who are baptised in the Established Church. So suicides, acquitted by the coroner's jury of felo de se, are likewise entitled to burial : but excommunicated persons, or persons found by a coroner's jury felo de se, are not entitled to have the office for the burial of the dead performed.

Burial *within* the church is at the discretion of the parson, who generally has a fee for his permission, and by custom a fee is sometimes payable to the churchwardens for such a burial, as the parish is at the charge of repairing the floor.

But with respect to the additional churches and chapels, built and building in populous parishes, various regulations are made by seven acts of parliament, which, with regard to burials, enact that none are to be permitted in any church or chapel erected under these acts, or in the adjacent cemetery, at a less distance than twenty feet from the external walls, except in vaults wholly arched with brick or stone, under the church or chapel, and to which the only access shall be by steps on the outside of the external walls, under the penalty of 50*l*. And by these acts the burial-places under the church and cemetery may be sold, and fees are payable, which appear to be regulated by a comparison of what the parson *would be entitled to of vaults or burying places of the like description in the church*, which gives no information at all, for the fee is not specially regulated, and it is entirely optional with the parson to permit or prohibit a burial in his church; so that a reference to the abuses of the mother church, in which the new or district church is situated, only appears indirectly to sanction an abuse in such mother church; for if burial in a church ought to be prohibited on the grounds of public health, the parson should refuse every one; and if he is allowed to permit such burials, the fees should be stated or approved by legal if not canonical authority.

The building and repairing, &c., the walls of church yards and cemeteries to the new churches, are particularly under the provision and regulation of the commissioners appointed by the acts.

BURNING. The offence of arson, at common law, extended not only to the burning of dwelling-houses, but of all outhouses part thereof, although not contiguous thereto, such as barns, stables, &c. The dwelling-house was also required to be proved that of *another* person. Later statutes have extended the offence to other descriptions of buildings, and the stat. 1 *Vict. c.* 89., which amends the laws relating to burning or destroying buildings and ships, has made the offence of setting fire to any dwelling-house, any person being therein, a capital felony; and with respect to the setting fire to a church, chapel, house, stable, coach-house, outhouse, warehouse, office, shop, mill, malthouse, hop-oast, barn, or granary, or any building or erection used in carrying on any trade or manufacture, or any branch thereof, whether the same be in the possession of the offender, or of any other person, with intent to defraud or injure any person, is declared a felony punishable at the discretion of the court, by transportation for life, or for not less than fifteen years, or imprisonment, with or without hard labour, in a gaol or house of correction, for not exceeding three years, and with or without one month at a time, and not more than three months in a year, of solitary confinement. Also the unlawfully setting fire to, or otherwise destroying a ship or vessel with intent to murder any person, or whereby the life of any person shall be endangered, is declared a capital felony; and the setting fire to ships or vessels, either complete or unfinished, with intent to injure or defraud others, is a felony, and subjects the offender to the secondary punishments above-mentioned. The setting fire to coal mines, and vegetable or agricultural produce, is also a felony, and subjects the offender to the last-named punishments.

The words of the act are "set fire to" merely, so that it is not necessary to complete the offence that the house or property be consumed.

Principals in the second degree, and accessories before the fact, are, by this act, punishable as principals in the first degree; and accessories after the fact are subject to imprisonment as before named, for not exceeding two years.

The above acts, to constitute them offences, must be committed wilfully or maliciously, and that intent must be proved.

BUTTER and CHEESE. The shipping of butter and cheese for the London market is regulated by the stat. *4 & 5 Will. & Mary, c. 7.* The sale of butter at York and New Malton are regulated by particular acts; and the butter trade of Ireland is also under numerous statutory regulations, it being a staple commodity.

Butter is directed by a stat., 36 *G.3.*, to be packed as follows:— In a *tub* 84lbs., in a *firkin* 56lbs., in a *half-firkin* 28lbs., and each sort of butter to be packed separately, and salted with small fine salt, and of that no more than is necessary for the preservation of the butter. Cheesemongers and dealers in butter are to deliver the quantities required in a tub, firkin, or half-firkin, or else are liable to damages for the deficiency, with costs. The makers of the casks, and the dealers in the butter, are to have their names branded on the casks, under penalties; and all penalties not above 3*l.* may be recovered before one justice, above 5*l.* by action at law, for the benefit of the complainant or informer. But the acts do not extend to butter packed in quantities not exceeding 14lbs.

BY-LAWS. The orders and regulations of corporations for the government of their members, being private laws, which may also be made by courts-leet and courts-baron, persons having right of common, &c. which are binding upon themselves, unless contrary to law or public policy, and then they are void. But there should be a custom authorising the making, especially if a penalty is incurred for non-observance. By-laws, by whomever made, should be reasonable and for the common benefit, not for the advantage of any particular individuals. The by-laws of some of the companies of London have lately been noticed by the courts of law, and a nice distinction has been drawn between by-laws made in *restraint* of a trade, and by-laws to *regulate* a trade. These questions occurred in the cases of the Pewterers' Company, who assumed a power to prevent a person, not being free of the company, being a pewterer within the city, which was holden void, unless a special custom could be proved, and the Painter-stainers' Company, who claimed similar privileges, but with more reason, as they have the power to *regulate* the art of painting, which is beneficial to the public.

Where a by-law of a corporation is made in restraint of trade, it seems the custom and usage must correspond with it.

Generally speaking, by-laws imposing fines on their members for disobedience to, or neglect of, any particular duty necessary for their government, can be supported, and an action can be maintained for the penalty; but, unless warranted by a special custom, it cannot be levied by distress or sale of the party's goods.

By an ancient statute, by-laws of corporations should be approved of by the lord chancellor.

The power of making by-laws is included in the very act of incorporation; and with respect to private corporations, it would be expedient that they were now sanctioned by the authority of the lord chancellor, as formerly. But with regard to corporations of towns now regulated by the Municipal Corporation Act, the council have express power by that statute to make such by-laws as to them shall seem meet for prevention and suppression of any nuisances not already made punishable in a summary manner, and to inflict a fine, not exceeding 5*l.*, which by-laws cannot be made unless two thirds of the whole council are present; and cannot come into operation till forty days after the same have been sent to the secretary of state, for approval by his majesty in council, who may disallow the same; and after public notification thereof has been made in the borough, by affixing the same in some public place, usually the town-hall. But the by-laws must be consistent with reason and law, else no approval of his majesty will give them validity.

CANON LAW. The ecclesiastical law, partly founded upon the imperial or Roman law, also called the *civil* law, which has place in the courts of admiralty and in the courts of the two universities.

CANONS. Rules framed by the clergy for their own governance, but which do not bind the laity, unless sanctioned by parliament; but the clergy are bound by canons made in convocation and confirmed by the queen.

CAPIAS. The name of a writ, taking its name from the operative Latin word, *that you take*, directed to the sheriff, commanding him to arrest the defendant and to keep him until he gives bail, or is liberated by due course of law; therefore, under this writ the sheriff detains the defendant till he gives bail, &c. This *capias* is called mesne process, as also all writs before one of the final processes in a suit, called a *capias ad satisfaciendum* (called, from its abbreviation, a *ca. sa.*), under which writ the sheriff takes the defendant, and keeps him till he pays the debt.

There is also a writ of capias, which issues to apprehend a party against whom an indictment is found, in order to outlaw the party; but in ordinary cases, persons indicted, not in custody at the finding of the bill, are apprehended by warrant from the chief justice, called a *bench warrant*, or by other warrant if for a felony or misdemeanor.

CAPITAL FELONIES. Crimes for which the party indicted is liable to suffer death. By a late statute the court before whom any offender may be capitally convicted may in all cases abstain from pronouncing sentence of death; and may, instead thereof, order sentence of death to be *recorded* against such offender.

The following is a list of offences punishable with death by the recent acts for the amendment of the criminal law:—

1. High treason. 2. Murder. 3. Attempting to murder, by administering to, or causing to be taken by, any person, poison or other

destructive thing. 4. Attempting to murder, by stabbing, cutting, or wounding, or by any means whatsoever causing to any person any bodily injury dangerous to life. 5. Rape. 6. Unnatural offences. 7. Piracy, whenever accompanied with an attempt to murder any person. 8. Robbery of any person, accompanied with an attempt to murder the person robbed, by stabbing, cutting, or wounding. 9. Burglary (*i. e.* housebreaking between nine o'clock at night and six o'clock in the morning), accompanied with any attempt to murder any person in the house; or if any person in the house shall be stabbed, cut, wounded, beaten, or struck by the *burglar*. 10. Unlawfully and maliciously setting fire to any dwelling-house, any person being therein at the time. 11. Unlawfully and maliciously setting fire to, casting away, or in any wise destroying any ship or vessel, either with intent to murder any person, or whereby the life of any person, *lawfully* being therein, shall be endangered. 12. Exhibiting any false light or signal with intent to bring any ship or vessel into danger, or unlawfully and maliciously doing any thing tending to the immediate loss or destruction of any ship or vessel in distress. 13. Every accessary *before the fact* to any of the above offences is punishable as a principal.

The felonies punishable capitally under the unrepealed statutes are very few. Among those, however, is the offence of an assembly of persons remaining together after they have been commanded by proclamation, under the *riot act*, to disperse, which is still capital.

The substitution for capital punishment is transportation for life, or for any term not less than fifteen, and in some cases seven years, or imprisonment, with or without hard labour, in a gaol or house of correction, for not less than five years. Some part of the imprisonment may be directed to be in solitary confinement, but it is limited to one month at a time, and to the extent of not more than three months in the year.

CAPTURE. This word has peculiar relation to *prizes* taken by privateers in time of war, but it is equally applicable to prizes taken by the army or navy.

CARRIER. A person carrying goods for others, whether in ships, boats, barges, carts, waggons, coaches, or *otherwise*, for hire. A man may be a *common* carrier, or a carrier for the particular occasion. The taking a reward or hire founds the contract. The liability and duties of carriers *generally*, at common law, *i. e.* by the custom of the realm; and their liability, particularly or specially, under an act lately passed, limiting their charge where certain notice is given, may be concisely stated.

The liability of a carrier commences with the delivery of the goods to him or his servant, or to some one intrusted by him to receive them; for after receipt of the goods, he cannot, if they are lost, plead that they were improperly secured. The liability itself extends to all loss and injury of the things carried, unless occasioned by accidents, not happening through the intervention of human means, usually termed the act of God, or the king's enemies. He is therefore liable, if robbed, if the goods are destroyed by fire, or wrongfully seized by third persons; and this under every circumstance.

Goods conveyed by a carrier, whether *common* or hired for the particular purpose, are privileged from distress or attachment, on account of the debts of the persons sending them, or of the carrier.

The responsibility of the carrier does not charge him, in case any fraud, wilful mis-statement, or concealment is made by the sender o.

owner of the goods, or where it can be shown distinctly, that the damage or loss complained of arose by his own neglect or interference with the conduct of the carriage. And the responsibility of the carrier ceases when the goods have reached their place of destination, and the control of the carrier has thereby terminated, or when he has done all that in him lies to effect a delivery, either actual or constructive, *i. e.* giving the party notice of their arrival, where he has not either expressly or impliedly contracted to deliver them at the premises. In the case of a wharfinger who undertakes to *ship* goods *left* with him to be sent *coastwise*, his responsibility does not cease till he has delivered them to the mate or captain of the ship.

The remedy against the carrier is to be enforced by the person to whom the goods were sent or consigned, unless, by the terms of agreement between the sender and the purchaser, they were to be at the risk of the sender till actually delivered, or the consignee obtained the sending of the goods by fraud, which at law vests no property in the hands of the fraudulent party; in these two latter cases, the sender must sue; the general principle of law being, that the consignee acquires the property from the time the sender delivers it to the carrier, the intermediate risk being borne by the carrier, who for this purpose may be considered an insurer for the person to whom they are sent, unless specially agreed to the contrary.

In cases of goods consigned by shipping, the bill of lading (subject, of course, to the same exceptions) will decide the question, who is to sue the carrier. If it be to deliver "to A," then he should be the plaintiff; if "to A, for the use of B," B must sue; if "for A (the consignor) and in his name to B," A. is to sue the carrier, although B. may have insured.

Where goods have been lost which have been put on board a ship, the owners or captain are liable severally, and the action may be brought against either. It is often safer to bring the action against the captain, if he is substantial, and all the owners are not known, for if *all* the owners are not sued, they may plead it in abatement.

Agents for persons abroad, and who freight the goods, may, it seems, bring an action in their own name, for the non-delivery thereof, according to the bill of lading; the action arising from a contract expressed by the bill of lading, more than from the liability at law.

To make the carrier liable, the goods must be lost while under his care: he is only liable as far as he undertakes to be accountable. The two latter propositions bring under the reader's notice the act before alluded to, being the stat. 1 *W.* 4. *c.* 68., passed "for protection of mail-coach contractors, stage-coach proprietors, and other common carriers, against loss of parcels, *the value of which shall not be declared by the owners*, which in effect puts at rest many questions on this branch of law, as far as regards carriers by *land*, to which it solely extends. This act protects carriers from liability in case of the loss of the articles hereafter specified, *exceeding* 10*l.* in value (except loss by the felony of the carrier's servants, or his personal default, which remains as it did at common law), unless the party delivering the goods declare the value and offer to pay, if required, an extra charge for carriage; but requires that the notice of the increased charges that may be required shall be notified by some notice affixed in legible characters in some conspicuous place in the office, of which all persons sending goods, &c. are bound to take notice. The act specially states, that *other* notices shall not protect a carrier from liability; but the act does not exclude special contracts, or particular agreements, which can be enforced as ordinary rights of action. And as to any *other* goods, and even those goods and articles hereafter specified, when *under* the value of 10*l.*, carriers cannot, unless by special contract or notice, protect themselves from their common law liability (from which they indemnify themselves as they did before the act, by their *booking* fee, and their rate of carriage). Actions for loss may be brought against any *one* proprietor, though the contract is legally made with several; and the act provides that the *declared* value, and the insurance money, is recoverable in case of loss; but the carrier may still require proof of the value of the lost package, and may pay money into court. The articles specified in the act are as follows; —

Bills of Exchange.
China.
Clocks.
Coin (gold or silver) of this or any other state.
Engravings.
Furs.
Glass.
Gold coin, or gold manufactured or otherwise.
Jewellery.
Lace.
Maps.
Notes, of any Bank, or for payment of money.
Orders for payment of money.
Paintings, Pictures.
Plate (gold or silver).
Plated articles.
Precious stones.
Promissory notes.
Securities for payment of money.
Silks, manufactured or unmanufactured, or wrought up, or not with other articles.
Silver.
Stamps, English or foreign.
Time-pieces of every description.
Title-deeds.
Trinkets.
Watches.
Writings.

The office or place appointed by the carrier for the receipt of goods is deemed his warehouse or receiving-house; and the "booking" office keeper is bound to give a receipt on request, which is free from stamp duty.

The postmaster-general is not a carrier, and is not liable, in his official capacity, for loss of bills, notes, &c., stolen or lost.

Carriers by water, being owners of ships, are by certain statutes exempted from liability in respect of loss by robbery, embezzlement, or making away with gold, silver, jewels, &c., unless the shipper insert the true nature and quality of such valuables, in the bills of lading. And neither owners nor masters are answerable for a loss happening by fire.

A carrier by water impliedly undertakes or promises that the vessel shall be tight, and fit for the purpose; therefore cannot exempt himself from the consequence of having an unfit vessel, that being a *personal* default, even if he limit his responsibility by special notice to a particular damage or loss.

Carriers have a *lien* upon the goods they carry, but it is limited to the carriage of each individual parcel or package, and not *general, i. e.* for the general balance due to the carrier from the sender, for successive packages, or for a debt due to him by the consignee, unless full notice have been given by the carrier of receiving goods only on the terms of their being subject to this general lien, which notice should be made as public as possible, otherwise it will not operate; indeed, any notice which intends to restrain the legal responsibility of a carrier, which is very extensive, and is not materially altered by the act of 1830, should be made as public as possible, by cards, advertisements, bills, &c.; as an *implied* agreement that the sender consented to waive the carrier's responsibility in certain respects, can only be inferred from the fact of the sender's receiving *actual* notice.

Carriers are subject to a penalty of 20*s*. for travelling on Sunday, or for not tying up any dog attending them, to the cart or waggon. They are also, with all other owners of carts and carriages, liable to the penalty of 5*l*. if they do not paint their christian and surname, and place of abode, on the cart or carriage.

CART. The driver riding upon a cart without having reins, or a person on foot to guide it, forfeits 10*s*.; and if the owner is the offender, he forfeits 20*s*. On changing property, new owners' names are to be affixed, and various regulations are made as to the painting of their names by the stat. 1 & 2 *W*. 4. *c*. 22. *s*. 59, 60.

CASTS. See SCULPTURE.

CATTLE, BUYING AND SELLING. No salesman, broker, or factor, employed in buying cattle for others, shall buy and sell for himself in London, or within the bills of mortality, on penalty of double the value of the cattle bought or sold.

Cruelty to cattle is repressed by various statutes. See CRUELTY, DROVERS. The killing and maiming, with intent to steal, cattle, is a capital felony. The killing and maiming, or wounding cattle without such intent, is a felony for which the offender may be transported for life, or for a less term, imprisoned, or whipped.

Horses or cattle brought to slaughter-houses, are to be killed within three days, and in the mean time provided with sufficient food. They are to be entered in a book. See SLAUGHTER-HOUSES.

CAVEAT, in the ecclesiastical court, is a process to stop the institution of a parson, and more frequently the probate of a will or grant of letters of administration; it holds good for three months. Also see PATENTS.

CEMETERY. A place of burial. It appears to be distinguished from a churchyard by its locality and its incidents: by its locality, as it is separate and apart from any sacred building used for the performance of divine service; as to its incidents,—that inasmuch as no vault or burying-place in an ordinary churchyard can be purchased for a perpetuity, in a cemetery a *permanent* burial-place can be acquired. There is a public cemetery at Kensal Green, near London, which is under the direction of a company incorporated by act of parliament.

By the acts for building *new* churches, &c., it seems that something like a permanent right may be acquired in a burial-place, for thereby the life trustees or churchwardens of such new churches or chapels may sell the burial-places underneath such church or chapel, and in the *cemetery*, upon payment to the incumbent of *such dues* as he would be entitled to of vaults or burying-places of the like description in the church; a very uncertain mode of ascertaining the price payable. See BURIAL.

CENTRAL CRIMINAL COURT. A court of criminal jurisdiction for the exclusive trial of offenders in London, Middlesex, and in certain parts of Essex, Kent, and Surrey, being within ten miles of St. Paul's cathedral.

Offences committed on the high seas, within the jurisdiction of the admiralty, are also to be tried in this court.

The court holds its sessions, according to the act by which it is constituted, at least twelve times in the year, at the Sessions House, Old Bailey, London; but the sessions *may* be holden in the suburbs of London.

CERTIFICATE. The certifying or giving notice of a thing done. This term is applied to many legal acts. A judge *certifies* a particular fact on the back of a nisi prius record, in order to entitle to or deprive a plaintiff of costs. A clerk of assize gives a certificate of a former conviction of felony, in order that a party, if found guilty upon a present indictment, should undergo a cumulative punishment. Magistrates *certify* or give certificate of witnesses' expenses in attending before them, or give a certificate to a party convicted of a petty assault, of his having paid the fine, or suffered the imprisonment, to bar an action at law. Questions of law, referred to the judges from chancery, are answered by *certificate.* Officers inferior *certify* or report to officers superior, or to a court, facts officially known to them. Certificates are always in writing, with the exception in the case of the recorder of London, who certifies or verifies the certificate or report of the mayor and aldermen concerning the customs of London, by word only, upon a question sent by the courts to them in respect of such customs. This is called Trial by Certificate.

CERTIFICATE (Customs). No goods can be exported by *certificate*, except foreign goods, formerly imported, on which the whole or a part of any customs paid by importation is to be drawn back. This proceeding is regulated by the act which relates generally to the customs.

CERTIORARI. The name of a writ issuing out of the chancery or queen's bench, directed in the queen's name to the judges or officers of the inferior courts, commanding them to *certify*, or return the records of a cause depending before them into the chancery, king's bench, or common pleas, to the end the party may have the more sufficient justice. It lies to justices of the peace, and removes convictions and orders made by them; also indictments at the sessions. When directed to inferior courts, it removes the cause and all the proceedings to the superior court, and judgment must be given there. This writ is only grantable on matters of law, and cannot be had to remove causes after issue is joined; consequently is only allowed by a judge, or the court, upon a proper representation. Indeed, this writ, in both civil and criminal cases, is very often brought for delay; yet, as it lies in all judicial proceedings where a writ of error cannot be had, erroneous convictions of justices, and false judgments in inferior courts, would otherwise be without remedy. The regulations affecting these writs, some restraining it, some absolutely prohibiting its being issued in particular instances, are numerous, and purely technical.

CHALLENGE. An exception taken to jurors in civil or criminal cases. In civil, where a juryman is of kin to either party, or has an interest in the matter in question; in criminal, where the prosecutor or culprit, without assigning any reason, causes jurymen to be set aside, or, after a limited number have been set aside, makes some special exception, as that the intended juryman is prejudiced or biassed for or against the prisoner, and has so declared his mind, or alleges with certainty any other facts, such as relationship, affinity, favour, infamy, disqualification, &c. See Jury.

CHALLENGES TO JURORS, are those exceptions or objections which a prisoner makes to the jury which are to pass upon him, which are either individually or collectively: the first is termed a challenge to the *polls*, the second to the *array;* and he may challenge individually a certain number for his own dislike, without alleging any reason; but after he has challenged his full number, he must allege special matter of objection before he can be allowed to object to any more. But see tit. JURY.

CHAMPERTY. See MAINTENANCE.

CHANCELLOR, the highest judicial officer in the kingdom, and, when there is no lord high steward, the first officer of the kingdom. He is created by the king's will, and not by patent or writ; therefore holds his office during pleasure. He is keeper of the great seal of the United Kingdom, which office of keeper has the same power as the lord chancellor, but they are usually vested in one and the same; though instances have occurred of a lord keeper being a judge of one of the courts: but there cannot now be a lord keeper and a lord chancellor. This high office is sometimes put in commission, and the commissioners are by statute empowered to exercise all the authority, jurisdiction, and execution of laws, which the lord chancellor or lord keeper, of right, ought to use and execute. There is a lord high chancellor of Ireland; but this officer appears appointed solely for judicial purposes.

The chancellor or lord keeper takes precedence of every temporal lord; is a privy councillor by virtue of his office; and prolocutor or speaker of the house of lords by prescription; he appoints all the justices of peace; he is visitor, in right of the king, of all hospitals and colleges of the king's foundation, and patron of all the king's livings under the value of 20*l.* a year in the king's books. He is the general guardian of all infants, idiots, and lunatics, and has the superintendance of all charitable uses in the kingdom. To this he exercises that jurisdiction which is known as the chancery.

In his judicial capacity, he has various assistants and officers, viz.:—The vice-chancellor, the master of the rolls, the masters in chancery in England and in Ireland. (See these titles.) The subordinate officers are,—The *six clerks*, who transact and file all proceedings by bill and answer, and also issue out some patents that pass the great seal; which business is done by their under clerks, each of whom has a seat there, and whereof every six clerk has a certain number in his office, usually about ten; the whole body being called the *sixty clerks*. *Twenty-four cursitors*, who make out various writs, which are termed original, and which are sent to or *made returnable* in the courts of king's bench or common pleas; the business of the several counties is distributed among them. The *registrar*, who is hereditary, he has sufficient deputies, who enter and draw up all orders and decrees. *The master of the subpœna office* issues out all writs of *subpœna*. The *clerk of the affidavits* files all affidavits, and delivers out office copies thereof, without which the affidavits themselves will be of no avail. The *three clerks of the petty bag office*, who make out writs of summons to parliament; writs of *congé d'élire* for the election of bishops; patents, and various technical businesses upon recognizances acknowledged in the court of chancery. The *accountant-general*, who is also a master in chancery, receives the money paid into court, and conveys it to the Bank to be invested in stock for the suitors of the court. A serjeant-at-arms, who executes processes of contempt by his substitute, and brings up the parties before the court, who are committed to the *warden of the Fleet*, who receives and detains them; and various other secretaries and clerks, who are appointed for particular purposes, such as bankruptcy, appeals, &c., all nominated by the chancellor. See tit. CHANCERY.

CHANCELLOR OF A DIOCESE; or, of a Bishop. A person appointed to hold the bishop's courts, and to assist him in all matters of ecclesiastical law. He is generally a doctor of the civil law, created in some university.

CHANCELLOR OF THE DUTCHY OF LANCASTER, an officer before whom the *Dutchy Court*, or *Chamber of Lancaster*, is held. The court concerns only the lands holden of the king in right of his dukedom or dutchy of Lancaster, and is quite distinct from the jurisdiction of the County Palatine. This jurisdiction comprises much property lying out of the *County* of Lancaster—in Yorkshire, Nottinghamshire, Leicestershire, Staffordshire, Essex, Herts, Northamptonshire, Monmouthshire, Derbyshire, and particularly a tract of land surrounded by Westminster (the Savoy, &c.). The proceedings of this court are assimilated to those of the chancery, and equity or chancery side of the exchequer; indeed, it seems those courts may take cognizance of the same matters, or that the court is not so much in use as it was formerly. It is holden in Westminster Hall, at the end of a corridor, by the left-hand entrance, as you go into the hall.

CHANCELLOR OF THE EXCHEQUER. A great officer, who sometimes sits with the barons of the exchequer in the exchequer chamber; but his office, in fact, is rather with the practical management of the revenue, he being, generally, first commissioner of the treasury. His name is still preserved in all bills of complaint, which are preferred to him and the barons of the exchequer on the equity side, where a jurisdiction is exercised similar to the chancery, in practice and effect; but beyond his formal appearance on stated occasions, his judicial functions are scarcely ever called for. The chief baron, or other barons, make orders, decrees, &c., although it was originally intended that the treasurer (whose office is in commission), chancellor, and barons should sit together. When there is a lord treasurer, the chancellor of the exchequer is under treasurer. There are other chancellors; such as chancellors of universities, chancellors of orders of knighthood, &c. They may be termed, rather, recorders.

CHANCERY, is the court wherein the lord chancellor, or lord keeper, exercises his jurisdiction, which is divided into what is termed the common law and the equitable jurisdiction. The *first* being that in which he is bound to observe the method of the common law, by issuing various writs returnable in other courts, writs of *habeas corpus* and prohibition to inferior courts, and taking cognizance of a variety of formular matters in respect of bankruptcy, letters patent, sureties of the peace against peers, &c. The *second* being the equitable jurisdiction, which is the most extensive, in which he proceeds by the rules of equity and good conscience, and moderates the rigour of the common law, considering rather the *intention* than the words of the law, equity being the correction of that wherein the law, by reason of its universality, is deficient. On this ground, therefore, to maintain a suit in chancery, it is always alleged that the plaintiff is incapable of obtaining *relief* at common law, in cases of accidents, mistakes, &c., without fault of his own, *equity* never acting *against*, but in conformity to the common law, supplying its deficiencies, not contradicting its rules—a judgment at law not being reversable in chancery. It may here be noticed, that there are in England two supreme courts of *equity*, the high court of *chancery* and the *exchequer*, the latter affording equal relief with the former, though, for various reasons, it is not so much used. The objects of equitable jurisdiction will first be noticed; secondly, the constitution of the court.

1. Private rights and remedies (for no criminal jurisdiction, not even for the prevention of crime, is exercisable in this court) are here decided on principles of universal justice, where the interference of a court of judicature is necessary to prevent a wrong and the law is silent. These subjects occur in cases of accident and mistakes or omissions; in respect of accounts of various descriptions, as between mortgagor and mortgagee, principal and agent, partner and partner, tithes and other matters of account which are complicated *and unsettled*, consequently not readily ascertainable before a jury; in fraud of every description, such as corrupt, unjust, deceitful, oppressive, or catching bargains, which includes of itself an infinity of jurisdiction and interference; for every misrepresentation and act against good faith, or contrary to the obvious rules of justice, is within the reach of equity; where forfeitures in strictness have accrued from the nonpayment of rent, mortgage money, fine on admission to copyholds, &c. &c.; where a division or apportionment of property or liabilities cannot in ordinary means be effected; in respect of the property of infants, and their personal care and maintenance, and persons of unsound mind; when an agreement, for the breach of which damages could only be given at common law, is desired to be specifically performed; in all cases of trust and confidence, executorships, payment of creditors and marshalling of assets (see tit. EXECUTOR); and, lastly, in cases where by particular statute the court is required to interfere, as in bankruptcy appeals from the court of review, charitable trusts, friendly societies, and references under particular local acts to ascertain titles of land, or preserve the fund where the owner is not known or indemnity is required: these, and many more, forming the instances where the interference of this high and enlarged judicature is called for and sustainable. The *prevention* of wrong being the main object in view, as will be observed under the title INJUNCTION, also a proceeding of a very frequent and important nature. But the great peculiarity in the jurisdiction of this court is the exclusive jurisdiction it entertains over cases of uses and trusts unexecuted, as courts of law do not in general recognise any other party than the person in whom the property is *legally* vested; who, although he takes no beneficial interest, yet is the *legal* owner, the person who is the object of the trust having no power to sue his own trustee at law, or by any other process than by a bill in equity; hence the distinction of a *legal* title and an *equitable* title or right. The first being in the trustee, devisee, or executor, the latter being in the party who is really intended to be benefited by the will, instrument, or trust deed. See tit. TRUST.

The course of proceedings in courts of equity is either formal or summary. Formal, by the usual course or mode of suit, which shall be hereafter noticed. Summary, being applications made by motion or petition, supported by affidavit, upon which orders are made binding upon both parties, who appear by counsel, much in the same way that applications are made to the courts of common law upon motion. Various statutes, which affect the disposition of property, endue this court with power to make orders as to the security of any part belonging to infants, persons of unsound mind, or other individuals over whom the court assume jurisdiction. The granting an injunction for the prevention of particular wrongs, which the complaining party reasonably anticipates. In cases of disputed annuities, this court exercises a jurisdiction when the deed is absolutely void. However, the courts of common law appear by the annuity act to have greater powers of *summary* remedy; but where suits at law are apprehended, it may be expedient to institute a suit in this court in cases where the deed is *voidable*, *i. e.* fraudulently obtained, though perfect in its technical requisites.

2. This court is composed of three tribunals, respectively presided over by the lord chancellor, the master of the rolls, and the vice-chancellor. Before either of these judges may be brought any causes or motions, except such as relate to lunatics, which are always heard by the chancellor. The vice-chancellor is compelled to hear all matters which the chancellor may direct, in addition to those originally set down for hearing in his own court. The master of the rolls is independent of the vice-chancellor, and decrees or orders in causes decided before him cannot be varied by the vice-chancellor, though they are subject to be reversed or altered by the lord chancellor, upon petition, in the nature of an appeal. The master of the rolls takes precedence of the vice-chancellor; indeed he is so far a separate judge, that plaintiffs may choose whether they will have their cause decided by the master of the rolls, who is not bound to hear any other causes than those set down before him, as we have seen the vice-chancellor is.

A suit in chancery is commenced by a bill of complaint, which is a sort of petition methodically drawn, praying relief on account of the matters included or set forth in such bill, and a writ to compel the defendant under a certain pain (*sub pœnâ*), whence the name of the writ, to appear and answer the matters of the plaintiff's complaint. The bill having been filed, a writ of *subpœna* issues, commanding the defendant that "within four or eight days after the service of that writ on him, he should cause an appearance to be entered for him, and to answer concerning such matters as shall be alleged against him, &c., upon pain of an attachment issuing against his person," &c. To this the defendant answers, or pleads to the bill (unless the bill is insufficient in law, when he may *demur*—see tit. Demurrer), upon which issue is joined (*i. e.* the point in dispute can fairly be collected from the pleadings). Witnesses are then examined upon interrogatories (viz. questions in writing) prepared by counsel, the answers to which are delivered verbally by the witness, who is, in London, examined by an officer, called the examiner; if in the country, by commissioners specially delegated, and immediately reduced into writing. The depositions are afterwards published, as it is termed, *i. e.* copies are given out to the plaintiff or defendant; the statements of the bill, answer, and depositions of the witnesses are then abbreviated, and, with proper observations, delivered to counsellors who attend for each party upon the hearing of the cause, which, having been heard by the chancellor, vice-chancellor, or master of the rolls, as the case may be, judgment is pronounced; and the judgment, or *decree*, as it is usually called, is drawn up by the registrar from written notes or minutes which he makes in court, and from the senior counsel's brief, which is handed to him for that purpose.

It should be remembered that equity will not retain a suit for any thing under 10*l*. value, except in cases of charity, nor concerning lands under 40*s*. per annum.

☞ The courts of equity (for the court of exchequer, in its equitable jurisdiction, has precisely the same practice) have a peculiarity which does not exist in the courts of law (except upon motions made upon affidavit, which the party is obliged to answer by another affidavit), which is, that they enable a plaintiff to compel a defendant to *answer,* that is, deny or discover matters which could not be attainable in evidence by any other proceeding—in fact, state matters, and facts which may tend to his own detriment, but not so as to subject himself to penalty or punishment. But as questions of fact are not, when disputed, ascertainable in these courts, because their constitution, which follows the civil law, does not admit of the common law proceeding of a trial by jury, they have power to send an issue, *i. e.* a disputed fact, to the courts of law for decision by a jury, reserving to themselves their *equity,* that is, the right of framing a judgment upon that verdict, which, according to the language of these courts, shall be "according to equity and good conscience." Courts of equity also have the power of sending a case to be stated to the judges of one of the courts at law, for the better guidance of their judgment and decision, it being a maxim or established principle, that "equity follows the law." See INJUNCTION, SUBPŒNA, PRACTICE.

In administering relief, the court of chancery has frequently to unravel a long chain of fraud, and, by a comprehensive decree, to counteract the unjust consequences which have arisen or may arise from it; to investigate accounts, frequently complicated, between persons who employ all their art to perplex and resist; to enforce agreements for the conveyance or transfer of property in which many persons are interested, and long examinations of title are necessary; to compel the correction of mistakes by which rights have been acquired, according to the strict letter of the common law, but contrary to justice; to administer a large property encumbered with debts, and involved in various difficulties, and to draw out a surplus to be distributed according to the complicated rights of creditors, and various other claimants. (*Chanc. Commission Rep.* p. 13.)

CHARITIES. There is no restriction whatever upon persons giving in their lifetime, or bequeathing by their will, money or property *strictly personal, i. e.* not connected with land or houses, provided it is to be continued or appropriated as such, for charitable purposes; but as the locking up of land and real property from being parted with is against public policy, and as much private misery might arise from persons in their dying moments giving away their real estates from their families, the stat. 9 *G.* 2. *c.* 36. provides, that no lands or tenements, or money to be laid out thereon, shall be given for or charged with any *charitable* uses whatsoever, unless *by deed indented,* executed in the presence of two witnesses, *twelve calendar months* before the death of the donor, and enrolled in chancery within six months after its execution (except stock in the public funds, and which must be transferred at least *six calendar months* previous to the donor's death), *and* unless such gift be made to take effect immediately, and be without power of revocation; and that all other gifts shall be void. The two universities, their colleges, and the scholars on the foundation of the colleges of Eton, Winchester, and Westminster, are exempted from the operation of this act, which has for its object the appropriation of *any interest* in land or hereditaments, *i. e.* property partaking of the qualities of real estate, by will to a charitable institution. And this intent has been to the utmost extent executed by the courts, as a numerous train of decisions will show; but the act does not extend to Scotland. Therefore the following property cannot be devised for charitable purposes.

1. Land, whether freehold, copyhold, or leasehold.

2. Money charged upon or arising from such property.

3. Money to be laid out in the purchase of such property, or in paying off any incumbrance thereon, or to be invested by way of mortgage upon such property.

4. Dock, canal, or railway shares, tolls or dues, and turnpike tolls or bonds.

5. Money due upon mortgage of the preceding, or upon poor-rates, church-rates, county-rates, or any assessment.

6. Rents, or other profits arising upon all the foregoing species of property.

The following is the form of a bequest to a charitable institution :—

"I give and bequeath unto the treasurer for the time being of an institution known by the name of '——' the sum of £——, to be raised and paid out of my *personal* estate and effects, and not out of any part of my freehold or copyhold lands, tenements, or hereditaments, to be applied towards carrying on the charitable designs of the said institution."

Whether the charity is intended for England or some other country.

Corporations may, notwithstanding this act, take real property, if they have a licence by the terms of their incorporation to take land in mortmain.

A citizen of London may, by the custom, devise land *in the city*, but not elsewhere, to charitable uses, notwithstanding the act.

Also, any one is at liberty to devise land, &c. for the augmentation of Queen Anne's bounty; and, to a limited extent, five acres of land or 500*l*. money, for the building or repairing of a church or parsonage-house; but a glebe of fifty acres can be augmented by one acre only.

A grant of lands in trust, to rebuild or repair a tomb or vault, is not within the *meaning of the statute*.

Notwithstanding these special prohibitions, a statute of 2 *Eliz.* permits land to be given for the maintenance of houses of correction, or of the poor.

The lord chancellor has special jurisdiction over all charities, and he, upon the *relation* of the attorney-general, who is instructed by some informant (technically termed the *relator*), to file an *ex-officio* information, will establish the charity, and inquire into misappropriation or nonapplication of the funds, and administer the same. From his decision there is an appeal to the lords: but the court will not interfere in respect of a foreign charity.

Charitable funds in Ireland are administered by the commissioners appointed by an act passed for tha tpurpose shortly after the union.

Whenever a charitable purpose fails, the Crown has a right to interfere, and direct to what similar fund or purpose it shall be applied; but where a particular charitable purpose is not named, or being named is too indefinite to admit of explanation from the words of the will, or is illegal in itself, or against public policy, there the court of chancery will decree a distribution of the property according to law amongst the next of kin, or otherwise, according to the bequest of the residue.

In all cases of breach of a charitable trust, or whenever the interference of a court of equity is necessary, any two persons may present a petition to the lord chancellor, master of the rolls, or court of exchequer, praying relief in a summary way, upon affidavits, the order upon which is conclusive, unless an appeal be allowed by the attorney or solicitor-general, and made to the house of lords within two years.

All charitable donations whatever ought to be registered with the clerk of the peace, together with full particulars of the objects, names of benefactors, persons having custody of deeds, &c.

By a statute passed in 1831, commissioners were re-appointed to examine and investigate all charities for the education of the poor, or for beneficent purposes in England and Wales, and to investigate frauds and abuses, for the execution of which commission ample powers are given. The commissioners are to report half-yearly, and to report specially upon charities whereof the funds cannot be applied according to the original intentions of the donor.

CHARTER. Written evidences or deeds, a term formerly applied to all writings under seal, and now applied to letters patent royal, under the great seal. The form of action for detaining deeds is "detinue of *charters*."

CHARTERPARTY, is a contract under hand, or sometimes under hand and seal, made between the freighter, *i. e.* he who charters or hires the ship, or a part, for the carriage of his goods, and the owners, or master on their account (he generally having authority, written or implied, from the terms of his employment), containing the terms upon which the ship is hired to freight; and in this contract the owners or master bind themselves, the ship, tackle and furniture, that the goods freighted shall be delivered (dangers of the sea excepted) at the place of consignment; and they also covenant to provide seamen, rigging, &c., and to equip the ship completely, which they also warrant seaworthy. The freighter, on his part, stipulates to pay the freight. It is not *at law* considered a deed, unless under seal, but its efficacy is not materially lessened for want of this formality. It is distinguished from a bill of lading, inasmuch as the charterparty states the terms and conditions of the freight or carriage, whereas the bill of lading only ascertains the contents of the cargo.

The freighters may underlet, if not prohibited by the terms of the charterparty, or may put in other persons' goods. The owners are, not liable for any other than gross neglect in their captain or master, who is, for all legal purposes, their agent; and their responsibility as carriers commences on the master's receipt of the goods.

The freighters generally insure.

CHASE. A place for keeping beasts of the chase, deer, &c. It is of a middle nature, something between a forest and a park.

A chase, park, or warren cannot in strictness be made without the king's licence.

CHATTELS. All property, moveable or immoveable, which is not freehold, copyhold, or inheritable. They are in law distinguished as *real* and personal; chattels real, or chattel interests, are interests or minor estates, carved out of greater; as terms of years, leases, &c., which are but chattels, or personalty, in the eye of the law.

Chattels personal are all other property not connected with what is termed freehold. All chattels, both real and personal, go to the executor or administrator on the death of the owner; whereas *realty*, *i. e.* freehold, copyhold, or other inheritance, descends to the heir. A man is technically said to be *possessed* of chattels, *seised* of freehold or inheritance.

Leases, as have been said before, are chattels, even though they are for a thousand years; it is a vulgar error to suppose that a lease beyond ninety-nine years constitutes a freehold.

CHATTELS PERSONAL, are things moveable, such as animals, household furniture, money, jewels, corn, clothes, and every thing else that can properly be put in motion, and transferred from place to place.

CHATTELS REAL, are things which immediately concern, and in some degree partake of the nature of real property, as by being immoveable and of a lasting nature; as terms for years, viz. leases, the next presentation to a church.

There is another sort of chattel, which, though personal, yet is often called by another name, viz. chose in action, *i. e. a thing in action*, being mere rights arising from contracts not yet brought into possession, therefore outstanding; such as a reversionary interest concerning money or personalty, money due on simple contract, note, bill, bond, or other security.

CHEATS, are dishonest practices, in defrauding or attempting to defraud another of his property; such as using false weights or scales, fraudulently gaming, &c.; and are either punishable at common law, or, as in the case of obtaining money or goods by false pretences, punishable by statute: in either case they are deemed misdemeanors, and termed cheats.

Where the cheat is committed by means of a false pretence, the conduct and acts of the party will be sufficient, without any verbal representation; but to constitute the offence of cheating generally, the deceit practised should be proved to be such, against which no ordinary prudence could avail; and therefore a mere act of bad faith upon a previous confidence in the party will not constitute the offence, as the person injured has his civil remedy. That part of the statute law which provides for the punishment of cheats, declares, that if any person shall by any false pretence obtain from any other person any chattel, money, or valuable security, with intent to defraud any person of the same, he shall be deemed guilty of a misdemeanor, and at the discretion of the court may be transported for seven years, or suffer such other punishment by fine or imprisonment, or by both, as the court shall award.

CHECK, or CHEQUE. A check or draft is a written order, addressed to the bankers of the drawer, payable to a person therein named, or bearer, for payment of a sum of money. It is drawn in the following form, and is exempt from stamp duty if drawn upon a banker or person acting as such, within fifteen miles of the place where drawn, (which *place* must be specified therein), and bearing date on or before the day of its being issued, and if it does not direct the payment to be made by bills or notes. The deviation from these regulations invalidates the check, and subjects the party issuing it to a high penalty.

London, January 1. 1837.

Messrs. ———

Pay *Thomas Wilson*, or bearer, Thirty-five Pounds, Two Shillings, and Two Pence.

JOHN NOKES.

£35. 2. 2.

Checks resemble bills of exchange and promissory notes; and the rules respecting them affect checks, they being transferrable as bills or notes, though in strictness not due before demand is made at the banker's by presentment. They are taken as cash by mercantile men, but, legally, they cannot be described as such.

In the usual course of business, a check cannot be negotiated, so as to affect the drawer, after banking hours of the day after it was issued, and cannot charge the person delivering the check to another till after the next day from the delivery; and where it has been received at a place distant from the place of presentment, then it should be forwarded for presentment on the day after it was received.

Bankers on whom a check is drawn, having funds sufficient of the drawer in their hands, are bound to honour it, else they will be liable in an action for damages, whether *actual* loss has been sustained or not by the drawer; but, on the other hand, the bankers should be reasonably satisfied that the party presenting the check came honestly by it, at least they are justified in refusing to pay it under suspicious circumstances; and of course they are bound to ascertain that the sum in figures corresponds with the sum named in the body of the check, and that it has not been altered, for they may have to bear the loss of the difference, unless the drawer created the opportunity for fraud by the manner in which he drew the check.

A banker should not pay a check after the death of the drawer; but if he pay before notice of that circumstance, he is indemnified, and may credit himself with it, and the holder is not liable to refund.

A check should be presented at the banker's within the usual hours of business, that is, before five o'clock on the day it is given; and in case of distance from the place of presentment, before five o'clock on the day *after* the receipt of it.

A check is not protestable on non-payment, though the holder is bound to give the same notice as upon the dishonour of a bill of exchange or promissory note.

Where an acceptor pays his acceptance by a check, the bill should not be given up till the draft or check is paid, as all parties but the acceptor would be thereby discharged.

The notice which the holder of a check should give the drawer, or those who delivered it to him (the holder) since the issuing, may be the same as the form given under the title "DISHONOUR," with the following variation:—"Sir, the check for £———, drawn by you [*or* by Mr. B., and by you delivered to me] the day before yesterday, was yesterday presented at Messrs. ———, the bankers, for payment, which they have declined to honour. I request your immediate payment thereof. Yours, &c." If a holder pay a check into his banker's, and the same be not paid when by them presented for payment, the holder's banker has a day allowed him to give notice to his customer, which customer, being the holder, has a day allowed him to give notice, so that the holder's banker is considered as a distinct party; as is the case in bills or notes, and therefore, practically, the notice of dishonour is postponed a day. Therefore, when a bill, note, or check, in the hands of a banker, on behalf of his customer (the holder), falls due on a Saturday, he need not give notice of the dishonour to his customer till the Monday following, nor the latter till the Tuesday. Indeed, the rules which are applicable to the dishonour of bills or notes, and the notice which must be given by the holders of their dishonour, refer equally to checks, for it is quite as incumbent on the holder of an unpaid check to give notice to the drawer and indorsers, or parties transferring or delivering it, in due time, as in any other case; the law making the same allowances in cases where ignorance of address has caused a delay, although due diligence has been used to discover the residence.

CHILD-STEALING. See ABDUCTION.

CHIMNEYS and FLUES. By the 18th section of 4 & 5 *W.* 4. c. 35., called the *Chimney-sweepers' Act*, it is enacted, that all withs and partitions between any chimney or flue which shall be built or rebuilt, shall be of brick or stone, and at least equal to half a brick in thickness; and every breast, back, and with, or partition of any chimney or flue, shall be built of sound materials, and the joints of the work well filled in with good mortar or cement, and rendered or stuccoed within; and also every chimney or flue hereafter built or rebuilt in any wall, or of greater length than four feet out of any wall, not being a circular chimney or flue of twelve inches in diameter, shall be in every section of the same not less than fourteen inches by nine inches; and no chimney or flue shall be constructed with any angle therein which shall be less obtuse than an angle of 120 degrees; and every salient or projecting angle in any chimney or flue shall be rounded off four inches at the least, upon pain of forfeiture, by every builder, master, or master-workman, who shall make or cause to be made such chimney or flue, of 100*l.*, to be recovered, with full costs of suit, by any person who shall sue for the same in the courts at Westminster, with an exception in favour of chimneys or flues being built at angles with each other of ninety degrees and more, such chimneys or flues having therein proper doors or openings, not less than six inches square.

CHIMNEY-SWEEPERS. The last act regulating this neglected class of apprentices, enacts, that no child under ten years of age is to be apprenticed to a chimney-sweeper, and chimney-sweepers taking apprentices are to be householders. Apprentices *under* fourteen years of age are to be so designated by a brass plate on a leathern cap. A penalty is imposed, of not exceeding 10*l.*, or less than 40*s.*, on a chimney-sweeper for employing children under fourteen years of age, not apprentices. It is a misdemeanor to require any person to ascend a flue to extinguish a fire. The binding or assignment of apprentices shall take place by consent of two justices; the boy is to have a trial of the business previous to his apprenticeship, and justices are to refuse their sanction if, by an examination previous to the binding, they are unwilling to be bound. Chimney-sweepers are not to have more than two boys on trial, or more than four apprentices at the same time, and they are not to let them out for hire. Complaints by apprentices against their masters are to be heard by two justices; fine upon masters for ill-usage, 10*l.*, and not less than 40*s*.

Streets are not to be hawked or called by chimney-sweepers, under a penalty of 40*s*.

CHURCH-RATES. Rates assessed for the repairs of a parochial church by the parishioners in vestry assembled. The churchwardens are the persons who collect and levy this rate, and they are the persons whose duty it is, as ecclesiastical officers, to call the meeting, or vestry, to consider of the amount necessary. At this vestry, or meeting, the churchwardens are mere parishioners, the churchwardens not being empowered to make the rate themselves; but if they give notice of a vestry for that purpose, and if no other parishioners attend, they may alone, or with those who do attend (however few in number), make and assess the rate.

The courts of law have no power to enforce the assessment of a church-rate. Ecclesiastical censure and punishment (*i. e.* imprisonment for three months) is the penalty for disobedience in a parish, or rather the churchwardens, for not calling a vestry. The statutes for building fifty new churches in and about London and Westminster (9 *Anne*, *c.* 22., 10 *Anne*, *c.* 11., 1 *G.* 1. *st.* 2. *c.* 23., 5 *G.* 1. *c.* 9.), make provisions for the apportionment and assessment of church-rates, upon which the court of queen's bench may exercise jurisdiction in the shape of a mandamus, to enforce an assessment. And the seven late statutes for building additional churches in populous parishes in England, provide, that "The repairs of district churches or chapels shall be made by the districts to which they belong, by rates to be raised within the districts in like manner as repairs of churches by parishes; and such district is to be deemed a separate parish, for that purpose; and the repairs of chapels, not made district churches, shall be made by the parish in or for which the chapels shall be built. (58 *G.* 3. *s.* 70.)

Districts are to remain subject to the repair of the original parish church for twenty years after the district church shall be consecrated; after which, the parish church shall be repaired by the remainder of the parish; and each district shall afterwards make separate rates for such repairs, as if separate parishes. (*Ib. s.* 71.)

So that the court of queen's bench may exercise jurisdiction in respect of the repairs of the churches comprised in the last-mentioned statutes. But with respect to the original parishes, and so much of those not divided into districts, the law is as above stated.

The subject of the liability of parishioners to repair the church has lately been the subject of much disquisition, the result of which has been briefly summed up by a learned gentleman (Mr. Arnold, of Lincoln's Inn), whose investigation has not a little tended to disencumber the subject of many doubts and apparent inconsistencies, viz.: —

1st. The reparation of the body of the church belongs, by the peculiar law of England, to the parishioners; and the power of taxing themselves for that purpose is vested solely in them: it follows hence,

2dly. That the churchwardens of a parish cannot, in their capacity as churchwardens, impose a church-rate on the parishioners.

3dly. There are no means (except in the cases of the new churches, as before mentioned) of compelling the parishioners so to tax themselves; though, if a church-rate has been duly levied, any parties who refuse to pay it may be punished by the ecclesiastical courts.

4thly and lastly. The church-rate is not a charge upon the land.

CHURCHWARDENS, are persons appointed for the purpose of performing all acts requisite for the repairs, management, good order, and decency of behaviour in a church. They are called in some parishes *sidesmen*, a corruption of synods-men, because they formerly presented immoral offences to the episcopal synod; they are still in the nature of ecclesiastical officers, though they are laymen, being sworn in by the archdeacon or bishop of the diocese.

Since the appointment of overseers of the poor, their functions have been enlarged, and by various acts of parliament various duties are imposed upon them. They are a corporation by custom, and may sue and be sued for the goods of the church; but in their corporate capacity they may not take land, except in London, by special custom, for the use of the church. They may receive and pay for the benefit of the church, and may even dispose of the goods of the church *if the parishioners consent*. They are therefore liable to their successors in office, who may call them to account for improper expenditures or waste.

Although the churchwardens have the property of the church in their possession, they have no interest in the church, the freehold of that being in the parson, except in London, where it is vested in the churchwardens, who consequently have to repair the chancel, a duty which the parson, in other places, has to perform, the churchwardens repairing the remainder of the church. But by the act for building new churches, they are created a body corporate, for the purpose of holding all lands and buildings on behalf of the parish.

Their appointment is by election; for it is usual to appoint two churchwardens for every parish, who should be chosen by the parson and the parishioners, and if they disagree, then one should be chosen by the parson or his curate, and the other by the parishioners; but by *custom*, on which the right of choosing these officers entirely depends, the parson may choose one and the parishioners another; or (as in London) the parishioners may elect both. By the late act for building new churches, one churchwarden is annually chosen by the incumbent, and one by the parishioners. Under the word "parson" a curate is included. The parishioners choose churchwardens in or at the vestry, where the majority bind the rest of the parish. Sometimes a *select vestry* has the power of appointment. See VESTRIES. They are chosen annually in Easter week.

Churchwardens are overseers of the poor by virtue of their appointment, though, on the other hand, overseers are not churchwardens.

The following description of persons are exempt from serving the office of churchwarden or overseer of the poor, viz.:—Aldermen, apothecaries, or members of the apothecaries' company by charter, attornies and solicitors, barristers, clergymen, clerks in court, dissenting teachers, militiamen, members of parliament, peers, physicians, prosecutors of felons, surgeons, magistrates, revenue officers, officers of the courts of law, captains of the guards, persons attendant on the king, officers in the army, navy, or marines, whether on full or half-pay; and no person living out of the parish, although he has or occupies property within it, can lawfully be chosen churchwarden or overseer.

For their powers and duties in respect of the poor, the reader is referred to tit. OVERSEERS.

Their authority with respect to the church and parish is multifarious, but reducible to a few heads.

1st. They are to place the parishioners in pews or seats in the body of the church, as conveniently as they can, appointing pew-openers and gallery-keepers, subject to the power of the archdeacon or bishop, or as he is technically termed, ordinary, because having *ordinary* jurisdiction.

2d. In case of a vacancy of the benefice, they are to apply to the chancellor of the diocese for a sequestration, which entitles them to the management of all the profits and expenses of the benefice, subject to an account to be rendered to the ordinary; and they have also the appointment of a curate.

3d. They may make a rate to repair the church, giving the parishioners due notice to attend a vestry for that purpose; the majority of parishioners controlling the propriety of granting the rate. The pound-rate, as it is termed, is the most usual mode of taxation.

4th. With respect to the church and church-yard, in strictness, their consent should be had for burying a person in a different parish from that in which he dies. They having the care of the church, can refuse to open it to any other than the parson, or his servant or authorised agent. And it is their duty to keep the church clean, and prevent improper or irreverent conduct in the church or church-yard. They provide register books and chests for the registers and parish muniments.

Churchwardens are compellable to do specific acts enjoined by acts of parliament, by a writ of *mandamus;* and in respect of matters which they perform by virtue of their office, they can be punished or sued in the ecclesiastical court of the diocese where the parish is situate. Action can also be brought in the courts at Westminster for monies mispent. To secure them against vexatious actions, they have double costs allowed them on a judgment in their favour.

All other matters concerning these officers may be referred to tit. OVERSEERS.

CINQUE PORTS. Five ports or havens that lie on the south-east coast of England, towards France; namely, Dover, Hastings, Hythe, Romney, and Sandwich, to which were afterwards added Winchelsea, Seaford, and Rye. They were distinguished from other ports, on account of their superior importance, in consequence of which they are governed by a *lord warden of the cinque ports*, and have divers privileges granted to them as a particular jurisdiction, their warden having the authority of admiral among them, and sending out writs in his own name.

By the Municipal Corporation Act, their jurisdiction is preserved, although all chartered admiralty jurisdictions are abolished.

CLERK. The law-term for a clergyman, and by which all of them who have not taken a degree are designated. In another and more ordinary sense, it signifies a person who is employed by his pen in any court, or by private individuals.

CLERKS and SERVANTS, stealing any chattel, money, or valuable security belonging to or in the possession of their master, may be transported for fourteen years, and not less than seven years, or imprisoned not exceeding three years (and, if male, whipped). Also clerks and servants, or any person employed for or in such capacity, taking into their possession any chattel, money, or valuable security, on account of their master, and embezzling the same, or any part, are liable to the same punishment.

CLERK OF ASSIZE. The chief clerk or clerk of the crown for the counties included in a particular circuit. He is included in the commission of assize, or, as it is termed, "associated" with the justices of assize and gaol delivery. He is a barrister, and is prohibited from being counsel to any on the circuit. He keeps the indictments, and all records of the criminal proceedings on the circuit, and appoints the clerk of indictments, clerk of arraigns, and other officers of the circuit. The clerk of indictments is generally included in the commission. The duties of this office also comprehend the granting of certificates, and various businesses connected with the circuit. His, or rather the clerk of indictment's, fee for drawing an indictment, is settled by act of parliament at 2*s*.

CLERK OF THE PEACE. An officer belonging to the quarter sessions. His duty is to read the indictments, enrol the proceedings, and issue processes, and transact a variety of business incident to the sessions, he being in fact the clerk of assize for the quarter sessions; at least, his office corresponds therewith as far as the jurisdiction of the quarter sessions of the county or riding is concerned. His fees are settled by the justices of the peace. His place cannot be sold, and he holds his office till deemed incompetent, or discharged for misconduct by the justices, who thereupon appoint another.

By the Municipal Corporation Act, the council of any borough who have a separate court of quarter sessions, are empowered to appoint a clerk of the peace, whose duties are similar to other clerks of the peace: he may be considered as chief clerk to the recorder of the borough, as far as the criminal jurisdiction of the recorder or borough is concerned. The jury of the borough courts of record are summoned by him.

CLUBS, or CLUB HOUSES, are associations to which individuals subscribe for purposes of mutual entertainment and convenience; the affairs of which are generally conducted by a steward or secretary, who acts under the immediate superintendence of a committee.

It has hitherto been supposed that these societies, in a legal sense, partake of the character of a commercial partnership, and that, consequently, members paying their subscriptions, or partaking of the advantages held out by such associations, are liable for engagements entered into by the manager or committee.

This question has been recently set at rest, it being unanimously held in the court of exchequer, that the members of a club, *merely as such*, were not liable for debts incurred by the committee for work done, or goods supplied to the club. The following is a condensed report of the action, and of the judgment of Lord Abinger, which decided the fate of two other suits, pending for similar causes of action.

Flemyng v. *Hector, Esq. M.P.* The Westminster Reform Club was established in London in the year 1834, for the ordinary purposes of the clubs existing at the west end of the town, and on a similar footing, except that the members were to be chosen from among those professing political opinions in accordance with the principles of the Reform Act. The plaintiff, Flemyng, was a wine merchant who had supplied wine to the club. Mr. Hector was elected a member in April 1835, and paid his entrance and subscription, and continued to frequent and dine at the club until its dissolution; *it was proved, also, that he was in the habit of asking for Flemyng's wine.* An action having been brought for the wine supplied to the club against the defendant, the jury, under the direction of Lord Abinger, found for the plaintiff, leave being reserved to the defendant to move to enter a nonsuit; and a similar verdict was found in another case; and the general question came on for argument in Michaelmas Term, 1836, in the Court of Exchequer, when the full court were unanimously of opinion that the members of a club, merely as such, were not liable for debts incurred by the committee for work done, or goods supplied for the use of the club—for that the committee had no authority to pledge the personal credit of the members.

Lord Abinger, in delivering judgment, said, "I had thought, but without much consideration, at the assizes, that these sort of institutions were of such a nature as to come under the same view as a partnership, and that the same incidents might be extended to them; that where there were a body of gentlemen forming a club, and meeting together for one common object, what one did in respect of the society, bound the others, if he had been requested and had consented to act for them. Trading associations stand on a very different footing. Where persons engage in a community of profit and loss, as partners, one partner has the right of property for the whole; so, any of the partners has a right, in any ordinary transactions, unless the contrary be clearly shown, to bind the partnership by a credit; he might accept a bill of exchange in the name of the firm, and as between the firm and strangers, the partnership would be bound, although there might be an understanding in the firm that he was not to accept. It appears to me that this case must stand upon the ground on which the defendant put it, as a case between principal and agent. I apprehend that one of the members of this club could not bind another member by accepting a bill of exchange, acting as a committee-man, even where there might be an apparent necessity to accept, as in the case to a purchase of a pipe of wine: the party might draw a bill, but I do not think he could accept the bill to bind the members of the club. It is, therefore, a question here how far the committee who are to conduct the affairs of this club as agents, are authorised to enter into such contracts as that upon which the plaintiffs now seek to bind the members of the club at large; and that depends on the constitution of the club, which is to be found in its own rules; and upon two of the cases, those that were tried before me at Guildford, looking at these general rules, it certainly does strike me that it is impossible to interpret them so as to give the committee the power of dealing on credit, even for the purposes of the club. It appears by the rules, that every member is to pay his subscription of 10 guineas as entrance money, before he can become a member, and a yearly subscription of five guineas; so that by the provisions of the club, there is to be a fund in hand in order to bear the expenses. But then, again, every member who makes use of the club, who either eats or drinks there, or takes any sort of refreshment, is to pay ready money. That shows again, that the club was not disposed and not intended to have any transactions on credit, even with its own members; and it also shows that care was taken to provide ready money to meet every expense, so that if a party, or a gentleman of the club, were to order any particular thing that the club did not contain, he is to pay for it *instanter*; so that no occasion was expected to be necessary for the committee's pledging the credit of the club, or even their own. Under these circumstances, as the rules of the club, which are in writing, must be taken to form the constitution of the club, and are to be construed as matters of law, I do not not see what there was to go to the jury. I do not see any thing in these rules of which the jury are to be the judges. The words are, "to manage the affairs of the club;" the question then is, what the affairs of the club are. They are to have in their hands a subscription, and they are to take care that every member pays it before he comes into the club, and pays for every thing he has in the club. It therefore appears, that the members in general intended to provide a fund for the committee to call upon. I cannot infer that they intended the committee to deal upon credit; and unless you infer that that was the intention, how are the defendants bound? It is very true that an order was made to pay Mr. Flemyng so much on account; but the moment you state the case as one of principal and agent, you see that something more was necessary in order to fix the defendant, than the mere fact that the committee did not pay the money the moment they ordered the wine. It has been decided in several cases, that where a party gives his agent money to obtain goods, which the agent obtains on credit, the principal is not liable; so that even if the defendant knew — supposing that he was presumed to know from the books of the commitee — that there was a payment made to Flemyng, yet there is no account by which it has been proved that the committee had no money to pay it; there has nothing been proved which is required to be proved in order to fix the principal. Suppose a man gives money to his coachman to enable him to purchase hay and corn, — if the coachman takes the money and obtains the things either on his own or his master's credit, having the money in his pocket, his master is not bound; but if no money has been given, we must suppose it matter of necessity, and that he did buy on his master's credit. It appears, then, there is no evidence to show that at the time this wine was ordered, or the sum of 100*l.* paid, the committee had not funds in hand, or at least, Mr. Hector had no reason to suppose they had not funds in hand. If they had, it was immaterial to him whether they chose to pay immediately, or whether they rather chose to pay at stated periods. I therefore think upon these grounds, that in both these cases there ought to be a nonsuit entered.

COAL MINE. The wilfully setting fire to a coal mine is a capital felony, but sentence of death may be recorded. It is not a capital offence for a party to set fire to his own coal mine, but it would be punished as a high misdemeanor.

CLOCKMAKERS are bound to engrave upon the dial-plate their name and residence, and are liable, under stat. 3 *&* 4 *W*. 4. *c*. 52., to various penalties for frauds on the importation or exportation of clocks. Workmen in their employ embezzling any metal or diamond, forfeit 20*l*. upon conviction before a magistrate; and for every subsequent offence 40*l*., or suffer imprisonment in the House of Correction.

COIN. Offences against the current coin of the realm, or any other coin not current here, are punishable by a new law, which had for its object the determination of various technical doubts, which had arisen upon a multiplicity of acts passed for repressing false money, and punishing the makers or coiners thereof.

With respect to the gold and silver coin, the counterfeiting, or unfinished attempt to counterfeit, the current gold and silver coin of the kingdom, is declared a felony, and is punishable by transportation for life, or for a shorter term, not less than seven years, or imprisonment for not less than four years.

The act also subjects to the like punishment those who, by gilding, silvering, or colouring any coin, piece of inferior silver, gold, or metal, with the intent to counterfeit the gold or silver coin, or to make it pass for silver or gold coin, or by filing or altering copper coin with the like intent, produce, or attempt to produce, the resemblance of the gold and silver coin.

The impairing the gold or silver coin is also an offence punishable as a felony by transportation for fourteen years, or imprisonment for three years.

The buying and selling false coin, or importing the same, is also a felony punishable with transportation for life, or imprisonment for four years.

The uttering false coin is a misdemeanor, punishable by a year's imprisonment; and if the party has other counterfeit money in his possession, or has uttered, within ten days, more counterfeit coin, two years; second offences, after a former conviction, are felonies, punishable by transportation for life, or imprisonment for four years.

The having in possession three or more pieces of false coin with the intent to utter, is a misdemeanor, punishable with imprisonment for three years; and the second offence, felony, punishable with transportation for life, or imprisonment not exceeding four years.

Similar offences against the copper coin are punishable by transportation for seven years, or imprisonment. The uttering counterfeit copper coin is a misdemeanor, punishable by a year's imprisonment.

With regard to foreign silver coin, not current here, the counterfeiting or importing is a felony, punishable by seven years' transportation. The counterfeiting foreign copper money is also a misdemeanor, punishable with imprisonment for one year, and for the second offence, transportation for seven years. The knowingly making or mending coining tools, is a felony, punishable by transportation for life or for a less term, or imprisonment for not less than four years.

The act of which the above is but a very imperfect summary, is so comprehensive that no offence against the coin can be out of the scope of its provisions.

COLLEGE. A corporation or society of men having certain privileges by the king's licence.

COLLISION OF SHIPS. Ships running foul of each other. For damage occasioned by this circumstance, it is more usual to bring an action at law, but the admiralty has jurisdiction, and, for technical reasons, hereafter mentioned, it may be expedient to bring the suit in that court. The late Sir William Scott, in a suit for collision, states the possibilities under which an accident of this sort may occur.

"In the *first* place, it may happen without blame being imputable to either party; as where the loss is occasioned by any other greater body, in that case the misfortune must be borne by the party on whom it happens to light; the other not being responsible to him in *any* degree. *Secondly*, a misfortune of this kind may arise where *both parties are to blame*, where there has been a want of due diligence or of skill *on both sides;* in such a case the rule of law is that the loss must be *apportioned between them*, as having been occasioned by the fault of both of them. *Thirdly*, it may happen by the misconduct of the *suffering party only*, and then the rule is that the *sufferer* must bear his own burden. *Lastly*, it may have been the fault of the ship which ran the other down, and in that case the *injured party* would be entitled to an entire compensation from the other." It is further a general rule that "the law imposes upon the vessel having *the wind free* the obligation of taking proper measures *to get out of the way* of a vessel that is *close hauled*, and of showing that it has done so, and if not, the owners of it are responsible for the loss which ensues."

It frequently happens in cases of that kind that there is a great discordance of evidence as to the facts upon which the court has to form its decision. The testimony of the witnesses is apt to be discoloured by their feelings, and by the interest which they take in the success of the cause; and the court too frequently has to decide upon great diversities of statement as to the courses the vessels were steering, or the quarter from which the wind was blowing, at the time when the accident occurred. In these cases the course of proceeding in the admiralty court is for the witnesses on each side to give their testimony, which is considered, by two at least Trinity Masters, who assist the court and state their opinion upon the testimony which vessel was to blame, and then the admiralty judge gives judgment. In a cause of collision against a *steam vessel*, the court, assisted by Trinity Masters, pronounced for damages and costs, holding that a steam vessel, not receiving her impetus from sails, but from steam, is, or ought to be, more under command, and manifestly, having seen the other vessel, was to blame. It should seem that usually *steam boats* should go to the starboard; whilst the general rule of navigation is, that when other ships are crossing each other in opposite directions, and there is the least doubt of their going clear, the ship on the *starboard tack* is to persevere in her course, while that on the *larboard* is to bear up or keep more away from the wind. When it is doubtful which vessel was to blame, or whether such a degree of blame may not be imputable to each as to render it difficult to decide, who, if either, ought to make compensation, then it seems to be preferable to proceed in the Court of Admiralty; because, if it should then appear that the navigators of both the ships were equally to blame, but that only one was materially damaged, this court has a peculiar and singular jurisdiction, to decree that the owners of each vessel shall make good a moiety of the entire damage, although in a court of *law*, when the mischief done was the result of the combined neglect of both parties, both are *in statu quo*, and neither could recover any compensation from the other. (*Chitty's Practice of the Law.*)

In cases of *collision*, the ship and tackle may be arrested by admiralty process, provided the collision took place at sea, not in a river or place which is within a county: in the latter case the remedy is by action at law.

COLLUSION, is a deceitful agreement or contract between two or more persons, for the one to bring an action against the other, &c. to some evil purpose, as to defraud a third person of his right, &c. This collusion is either apparent, when it shows itself on the face of the act or, which is more common, it is secret, when done in the dark, or covered over with a show of honesty. And it is a thing the law abhors;

therefore, when found, it makes void all things dependent upon the same, though otherwise in themselves good.*

Collusion also is a varied deceit wrought by means of an action or legal proceeding, in which parties, having *apparently* adverse interests, exclude or defraud some person by means of the judgment given in such suit.

COLONIES. The trade of Great Britain with her colonies is regulated by the statute 3 & 4 *W.* 4. *c.* 59. The British colonies in North America are, the provinces of Lower and Upper Canada, Nova Scotia, and New Brunswick; in the West Indies, Jamaica, Barbadoes, St. Lucia, Antigua, Grenada, Trinidad, and some other islands; in South America, Demerara and Berbice. Great Britain has also colonies and settlements elsewhere, as Columbo, Port Lewis, Cape of Good Hope, the island of Mauritius, Sydney, the island of Van Dieman's Land, and some others.

COMBINATION, is the organising any number of persons, from two to an unlimited extent, to do an unlawful act, or, more distinctly speaking, to do an act to the wrong of another. The term is usually applied to workmen who combine to raise their wages by a sudden refusal to work except on certain stipulated conditions, which is only unlawful where means of intimidation and threat are used, or where contracts of a definite and precise nature are sought to be avoided. The present statute affecting workmen only extends to the offence of any one or more persons forcing or *endeavouring* to force workmen by violence, intimidation, &c., to leave their service, or to quit their work, or return it unfinished, or to prevent their hiring themselves; of compelling others to belong to clubs, pay fines, or of forcing any master to alter his mode of work, or limiting his apprentices (the settling rates of wages or hours of work are expressly excepted), and punishes offenders with three months imprisonment, with or without hard labour, on a conviction before two justices within four months. Offenders also are compellable to give evidence for the Crown, and are indemnified. On the construction of this statute it has been held illegal for workmen to combine for the purpose of dictating to the master whom he shall employ.

COMMISSION, is the term used for a *bailment*, or delivery, of something to another, who undertakes *without recompence* to do some act concerning the thing delivered, or, as it is technically termed, "bailed;" such as to carry it. Therefore in all such gratuitous acts, as the party delivering the thing, called the "bailor," derives an advantage, the bailee is not responsible but for gross negligence; for example, a stage coachman who gratuitously engages to carry a parcel, is not liable for the loss of it, unless he is guilty of great or extraordinary carelessness in regard to the thing entrusted to him.

All voluntary promises concerning the doing of any act do not impose any liability upon the party promising if he omit to do it; but if he commence the act promised to be done, and injure the promisee by his wilful neglect, he is liable in an action for the consequences.

COMMISSION. Brokerage, factorage, or agency. An allowance or remuneration given by principals, or employers, to their brokers, factors, or other agents, which allowance is generally established by the usage of some particular trades or businesses; it varies, accordingly, with the nature of the employment, and is sometimes chargeable upon the thing,

* By stat. 1 & 2 *W.* 4. *c.* 56. *s.* 42., a fiat of bankruptcy may issue by concert between the bankrupt and petitioning creditor or their agents.

or price of the thing, sold or dealt with; and where the transaction does not admit of that mode of payment, it is a direct claim upon the employer or purchaser, as the case may be. It is not unfrequently fixed by a special agreement, especially where the duty to be performed by the agent is ascertained, and no liability incurred; but where an agent, on the sale of his employer's goods, guarantees the responsibility of the purchaser, he is entitled to a higher rate, settled by usage of trade, called *del credere*. Where there is no express agreement, the law presumes that the parties contracted for the usual remuneration due by custom; and if there is no custom or usage, or no express agreement evidenced, then it is a matter of consideration for a jury to ascertain what was the value of the services rendered. Of course, no remuneration can be recovered if, from the negligence or misconduct of the broker, the employer derived no benefit.

It is usual with auctioneers and others to charge extravagant prices, by way of "commission," on the letting of houses, &c., according to the rental; but this cannot be supported unless a particular agreement be proved, there being no usage of trade or business in these contracts, which does not equally apply to or concern the sale of goods or merchandise; therefore, the auctioneer can only claim a sum proportioned to the value of his services, or rather the business actually performed; and so it was held by the late Lord Tenterden, in an action brought by an auctioneer for commission. On the sale of goods, however, a commission may reasonably be charged by the auctioneer.

An agent cannot recover a commission for effecting the sale of shares in an illegal association or undertaking; and it seems that a person who acts in London as a sworn broker, within the city regulations and laws, as to brokers, but who is not legally qualified to act as such, cannot recover his commission; nor can commission be recovered upon private treaties, where the object is to conceal any fact from the purchaser, whereby he is induced to give a higher price, even though that excess does not extend beyond the commission, such being a fraud on the purchaser.

The annuity act regulates the commission to be taken for procuring the sale of an annuity, being 10*s.* per centum, whether by solicitors, brokers, or other agents; the breach of which is a misdemeanor, and subjects the party to fine, corporal punishment, and imprisonment.

Where the usage of trade is not known to an employer, he should, in prudence, make an agreement with his broker, unless he consents to abide by the custom. Indeed, all persons not in business should be on their guard against unauthorised demands, not from the city brokers, for they are reputable and responsible, but from a variety of persons who style themselves commission agents, and who suppose they can charge or retain what sum they think proper, under pretence of "commission."

COMMISSION. The warrant or letters patent which all persons exercising jurisdiction, either ordinary or extraordinary, have to determine any cause or action, as the commission to the judges, special commissions of oyer and terminer, gaol delivery, &c. From this word is derived Commissioner, who is any one that has a commission, letters patent, or other lawful warrant, to examine any matters, or to execute any public office, of which there are an infinite number.

COMMITTEE, are those to whom the consideration or ordering of any matter is referred.

COMMITTEE of a lunatic, idiot, or one of unsound mind, is the person to whom the care and custody of such lunatic, &c. is *committed* by the chancellor, upon the report of a master in chancery, or other evidence of his fitness, and of his having entered into security, to account for the rents, &c. of the lunatic's estate. Generally some near relation is approved of.

COMMISSIONERS OF BANKRUPT. SEE BANKRUPT.

COMMISSIONERS OF SEWERS. SEE SEWERS.

COMMITMENT. The sending to prison. In civil cases, where a debtor, or person in *contempt*, has been taken by the sheriff of the county, to whom the process is directed, he may be taken by writ of habeas corpus before a judge, who commits him to the prison of the court from whence the process issues, which is a custody distinct from the sheriff. Persons rendered in discharge of their bail may be *committed* by a judge, to either the prison of the court, the King's Bench prison, or the Fleet; or they may be rendered, at the option of the parties, to the custody of that sheriff who originally took them.

In cases of criminality, persons charged with non-bailable offences, or who are unable to give bail, are *committed* by justices of the peace to the county gaol. See JUSTICES. But in towns having a recorder and a fit prison magistrate, must commit to the town prison. (*4 & 5 W. 4. c. 27. s.* 3.)

In cases of high crimes against the state, the privy council or the secretary of state may *commit;* but the papers of the persons committed must not be seized.

Coroners *commit* persons found by the jury guilty of murder and manslaughter.

The speaker of the house of commons *commits* members or others behaving disrespectfully to the house, or impeached by the house, to any gaol or place at the discretion of the house, or to the custody of a particular person, the serjeant-at-arms, which is a preliminary custody.

COMMON. There are several kinds of *common*, which word signifies a right which persons have or use in the land, woods, or waters of another. It is one of those properties legally termed *incorporeal hereditaments*, which presumedly commenced by some deed between lords and tenants, now lost, but being by age formed into a prescription, continues good. See PRESCRIPTION.

Common is of five sorts: — 1. Common of pasture, which is a right that one or more have to feed or fodder their cattle in another's land. 2. Common of turbary, or the liberty of cutting turves in another's soil to be burnt in a house. 3. Common of piscary, or a right of taking fish in another man's pond, pool, or river. 4. Common of estovers, or *botes*, which is a right of taking trees, loppings, or underwood, in another's woods, for fire or reparation, or mending of husbandry implements, viz. *house-bote* or *fire-bote*, sufficient allowance of wood to repair the house, or for fuel; *plough-bote* and *cart-bote*, allowance of wood for mending carts, ploughs, &c.; *hay-bote* and *hedge-bote*, wood for repairing hays or hedges. 5. A liberty to dig for gravel and sand, stone, &c. in another's soil, which is still the custom in many manors; and, in addition, the right that some have in turning their cattle out to pasture, for a limited time in the year, upon the land of another, and to his exclusion, known in some parts of the country by the names beastgates or Lammas land. Common of pasture is the most usual, and is distinguished in law by being either *appendant*, belonging to the *occupiers* of arable land, for putting beasts commonable, *i. e.* horses, sheep, cows, and oxen; *appurtenant*, belonging to an estate for all beasts commonable or not commonable, *i. e.* swine, goats, geese; *in gross*, belonging to a person who is neither occupier nor freeholder; *by cause of vicinage*, the intercommoning by reason of neighbourhood. These commons of pasture, generally, are subservient to the title of the lord of the manor, who may dig pits and grant inclosures, if he has immemorially exercised that right, provided he leave sufficient herbage; but, after all, the commoner has but a very limited interest in the soil, for, though he may bring an action on the case, if the lord or any one else surcharge the common, *i. e.* put in an unreasonable number of cattle, and he may throw down hedges wrongfully erected, and drive away the beasts of a stranger mixed with those of a commoner, yet the lord may what is termed *approve*, *i. e.* improve, or inclose for himself, leaving a sufficiency of herbage; and its lying on him to show that there *is* sufficient, will not always help the case: this leads to the subject of approvement and inclosure generally, whether by lord or tenant. An unqualified custom for the lord of a manor to inclose, is bad; and it is said there can be no approvement by the lord in derogation of a right of common of turbary; but this depends much upon local circumstances. Also, any one who has a freehold in part of the waste (although he is not lord) may enclose part, leaving a sufficiency for the commoners. With respect to the commoners, they are driven by law to an action against the lord in almost every case, except for his hedging in the common, which they may lay open; but they cannot cut away bushes, furze, or fern, or do any similar act, even to the amelioration of the land; nor can they dig a trench to drain off stagnant water, as they have no freehold in the waste. If the lord make a warren, the conies must not be killed, an action must be brought; and the commoners cannot justify the cutting down of trees, though sufficiency of waste is not left, for their remedy is by action. An adverse possession of twenty years, of an inclosed waste by the lord, is a complete bar to a person claiming right of common.

A right of common is absolutely acquired by sixty years' enjoyment; and presumptively, by a thirty years' user.

Where there are *common-field-lands*, all the arable lands in such fields are directed by the stat. 13 *G.* 3. *c.* 81. to be cultivated by the occupiers under such rules as three-fourths in number and value (with the consent of the land and tithe owners, the latter not to receive any fines, only rents) shall appoint by writing, the expense to be borne proportionably under the management of a *field-master* or *field-reeve*, to be appointed annually in May.

Persons having right of common, but not having lands in such fields, and persons having sheepwalks, may compound for such right by written agreement, or may, with their consent, have parts allotted them to common upon, and the balks, slades, and meres may be ploughed up.

Lords of manors, with consent of three fourths of commoners, may let, for not more than four years, any part of wastes not exceeding one twelfth part, the clear rents being applicable for the improvement of the remainder.

In every manor where there are stinted commons, in lieu of letting part, assessments may be made on the lords of manors, and the owners or occupiers of the commons, and the money employed in the improvement of the commons, under the direction of the majority, which (or in some instances two thirds) may regulate the depasturing, opening, shutting up, breaking, and unstacking the commons, and the kind of cattle to be allowed the commoners.

All previous rights are saved by this act, except as to the class of persons who are expressly subjected to the provisions of this act.

Inclosures of wastes and commons have been heretofore made by local statutes, which are subject to, and regulated by, the provisions of the General Inclosure Act, the stat. 41 *G.* 3. *c.* 109., amended by 1 *&* 2 *G.* 4. *c.* 23.; but these being found insufficient, the act 6 *&* 7 *W.* 4. *c.* 115. has been passed, which, with the two former acts, now form a code of laws relative to inclosure of commons and open fields. See INCLOSURES.

Allotments under an inclosure act are freehold, unless otherwise directed by the act of inclosure; though many of these acts declare that the allotment shall be of the same tenure as the land in respect of which they are set out, and are by the last declared to be subject to the same incumbrances. Strips of land outside of old inclosures, and between them and a highway, are to be presumed to belong to the copyholder or proprietor; but now the commissioners appoint and determine as to whom the herbage upon the private roads to be set out shall belong.

A person inclosing waste acquires a right of possession, or presumptive title, after twenty years, as against the lord of the manor, and absolutely against the commoners.

By the inclosure act last mentioned, enclosures from common or open lands which have been made for more than 20 years will not be liable to be allotted, or laid open for the purpose of distribution; but such as have been made within that period must be deemed part of the lands forming the subject of allotment or award of the commissioners: but this will not authorise the allotment to any other than the proprietor of any land built on, or cultivated as an orchard or garden, or which has been previously enclosed by an agreement between the proprietor and other persons, then having right of common; and enclosures made for schools, or charitable purposes, are not to be disturbed.

COMMON LAW, is the term used for the law of this kingdom, simply without other laws, as it was generally administered before any known act of parliament made to alter or qualify it. According to Judge Hale, the common law of England is the common rule for administering justice within this kingdom, and asserts the king's royal perogatives, and likewise the rights and liberties of the subject. It is generally that law by which the determinations in the king's ordinary courts are guided; and this directs the course of descents of lands; the nature, extent, and qualification of estates, and therein the manner and ceremonies of conveying them from one to another; with the forms, solemnities, and obligation of contracts; the rules and directions for the exposition of deeds and acts of parliament; the process, proceedings, judgments, and executions of our courts of justice; also, the limits and bounds of courts and jurisdictions, the several kinds of temporal offences and punishments, and their application.

COMMON PLEAS. One of the queen's courts at Westminster, now constantly held in Westminster Hall. It is, as its name imports, a court for determining "common pleas," *i. e.* pleas between subject and subject. It takes no cognizance of crimes, or matters of a public nature, but it can restrain inferior courts who proceed beyond their jurisdiction;

and causes from those courts can be removed into this. It has in all civil actions the same power and authority that the queen's bench has.

COMPANY. This word in common parlance applies to a partnership of more than two persons; but it is more particularly used to designate a body, or number of persons associated for the purpose of carrying on some particular undertaking, commercial or otherwise. Some great companies are incorporated by royal charter, and their privileges thereby are confirmed by act of parliament, as in the case of the Bank of England, Royal Assurance, East India Company, and many others; and these are deemed *corporations*, and partake of the advantages and privileges incident to that condition. Other companies are created or associated by mutual agreement, declared by a deed of trust and arrangement. In these associations, each subscriber is a partner, and consequently liable for all the contracts of the company. These are distinguished by the name of *Joint Stock Companies*, and have very often letters patent granted them for the purpose of investing them with necessary powers for the conduct of their affairs, *but no further*, and sometimes (but seldom) the liability of shareholders is limited to the amount of their shares. A late act, however, declares that companies which it would be inexpedient to incorporate by royal charter, may yet, at the pleasure of the Crown, have certain privileges granted them, such as the power of suing and being sued by particular officers of their own; but it nevertheless declares that every member of the company is liable to the decrees and judgments awarded against it, limiting the power of issuing execution against any person at the discretion of the court, and to three years after the defendant shall have ceased to be a member. (4 & 5 *W.* 4. *c.* 94.)

The test of a corporation is the having a common seal. Unincorporated companies generally have not a common seal granted them.

Although partnership liabilities will be explained under the appropriate title, yet the marrow of a few decisions in respect of the liabilities of subscribers to unincorporated *companies*, or, in plainer language, unincorporated *partnerships*, may be given. The mere subscribing, or offering to subscribe, to an intended company, will not constitute a partnership, either as between themselves, or as regards the public, even though the first deposit be paid, unless the subscriber had *personally* interfered with the concern, or had signed the deed which regulated the conduct of the company, or otherwise held himself out as a partner, the entry by a secretary of the party's name in a book not being deemed a sufficient publication of a partnership; but, although the concern prove abortive, and is never carried into effect, the parties and directors interfering or signing the deed are liable; but after the formation of the company, or the carrying on the works contemplated, there the party by holding a share has an interest in the profit and loss, and is, to all intents and purposes, a partner: he may, indeed, transfer his share to another, but that will not protect him from the liabilities incurred in the interval of his purchase and transfer.

A cotemporary writer correctly observes, that the great distinction in law between joint stock companies or partnerships and corporations is, that in the first the law looks to the individuals of whom the partnership is composed, and knows the partnership no otherwise than as being such a number of individuals; while in the second it sees only the creature of the charter, the body corporate, and knows not the individuals. Hence, on a judgment against a corporation, execution can only be levied on the corporate effects; or supposing a trading corporation to become wholly insolvent, the individual members or proprietors will only lose their stock or share in the capital of the body corporate, and do not become answerable for the debts in their individual capacities. But it is far otherwise with the members of unincorporated partnerships, who may be made liable for the debts of the firm, to use an expression of Lord Eldon's, "even to their last shilling, and their last acre."

Civic *companies* are *corporations* when they possess letters patent, but not else, although they have possessed a common seal, and have received, centuries ago, a charter from the city, they being only *fraternities*, although partaking of the nature of a corporation, no one but the king having power to create a body corporate. Most of the companies of London obtained charters from royalty, which enabled them to do various acts out of the city, and be recognised elsewhere, as well as to enforce performance of their by-laws; which, after all, do not give them a right of action in the superior courts in respect of forfeiture incurred, though the city courts take cognisance of them. See CORPORATIONS.

The stat. 4 *& 5 W.* 4. *c.* 94. has not been found effectual for the purposes intended (many companies being still obliged to resort to parliament for private acts), and it is now altogether repealed by the stat. 1 *Vict. c.* 73., which enables the queen to confer certain powers and immunities on trading and other companies; to effectuate which the sect. 2. authorises the crown to grant, by letters patent, to "any company or body of persons associated for a trading or other purpose," such privileges as might be granted by a charter of incorporation. Sect. 3. provides for the carrying on of suits by and against the patentees in the name of a registered officer: this clause contains an express provision that the body may sue one of their own members. By sect. 4. the individual liability of the members may be defined by the letters patent. There are numerous other clauses in the act, detailing the provisions which the company will be bound to observe. Upon the whole, it now appears that letters patent, granted in pursuance of this statute, will be quite as efficient to found a trading or other company as a private act, except where compulsory powers to take land, &c. are required, or some protection not conceded by the ordinary rules of law.

Unincorporated companies having transferrable shares, thereby pretending to act as corporations, are, and always have been illegal, independent of the bubble act, 6 *G.* 1. *c.* 18. (now repealed); for that act only subjected the concoctors and persons connected with them to penalties, in addition to those to which they were before that time liable at law: consequently, they are still indictable as nuisances; for, being bodies perpetually shifting and changing, they cannot conveniently sue or be sued in courts of justice; however, all shareholders in such companies are not only liable to the creditors of the company, but are liable to contribute equally with their co-partners to the losses and debts of the company, and these liabilities cannot be evaded by shareholders assigning their shares; but the liability does not extend beyond the charges existing at the period of their assigning or transferring the shares.

COMPOSITION. An agreement for money in lieu of tithes, and it can be made with the parson when it is only of a temporary nature, such as for three years, or a lesser period, and is then termed a *personal* composition; *real* compositions are, when the land is perpetually exempted from the payment of tithes, by payment of some small sum, which is called a *modus*. Compositions for a longer term than three years, and not exceeding twenty-one years, or three lives, must be made with the concurrence and consent of the parson, the patron, and the ordinary, else the contract will not be binding upon the successor to the benefice. See TITHES.

COMPOSITIONS BETWEEN DEBTOR AND CREDITOR, are agreements or contracts tending to ensure an equal distribution of a debtor's estate to his creditors; who, in consequence, are bound to release him from his engagements.

As equality of distribution is the basis of this contract, any partial or underhand agreement to secure individual creditors a greater dividend than others, no matter how attempted to be secured, is in law deemed fraudulent, and consequently of no effect. Even any misrepresentation by a creditor as to the amount of his debt, in order to induce the others to accede, will bind him so as to limit the amount in accordance with his statement. Sureties, also, to any such fraudulent contract are exonerated.

It may, however, be arranged that one class of creditors may be paid in full, or receive more than another class; but this arrangement must be at least communicated to the other less favoured creditors, and then they cannot afterwards set aside the composition.

The points that arise upon these transactions are, generally, those arising from collusive or fraudulent agreements, by those creditors who "stand out;" for these arrangements of composition, by their terms, include all the debts *due* by the debtor at the date of the contract, although not then *payable*, as bills of exchange; consequently, "compositions" are so far prospective in their effect, the creditor signing the agreement or deed being bound to accept the composition upon all his debts.

Agreements for this purpose not under seal are not binding, unless a consideration be therein expressed, or the consideration is paid or performed, or, in technical language, "executed." So, verbal promises or simple agreements to accept less than a debt, will not bind a creditor. The holder of a bill or note compounding with the acceptor, without the concurrence of the drawer and indorsers, loses his remedy against them.

The creditors are not bound to accept the composition if the terms of the composition are not strictly complied with, and equity will not relieve the debtor. So, if one payment or instalment be made of a sum payable by instalments, and the remainder are not paid, the creditors may resort to their securities, and enforce the full sum due from the debtor, giving credit only for the sum actually received; or if the debtor be bankrupt, or insolvent, prove as for the total sum in like manner.

The debtor is not entitled to a previous demand to perform his engagements.

A deed of trust, or assignment of a debtor's property, for the benefit of *all* his creditors, is different in its operation from the simple agreement for a composition agreement; for such assignment only extends to such debts as are actually owing at the time of making the deed. This arrangement is one which is not deemed fraudulent, as against judgment creditors; but it is otherwise with respect to the operation of the bankrupt laws, unless the deed be advertised as directed by the Bankrupt Act (6 *G.* 4. *c.* 16. *s.* 4.), and six months elapse before a *fiat* is issued. See Bankrupt.

An assignment in trust of all the debtor's property is generally associated or blended with a composition agreement, or a release of all debts, on the produce of his estate being divided. The arrangement then is of the nature of a "composition," as to the exoneration of the debtor from all the debts due but not yet payable to those creditors who sign, not simply from the debts actually due and payable at the date of the deed, as before mentioned.

It is not unfrequently declared, in deeds of assignment for benefit of creditors, that those creditors who do not sign by a day specified shall be excluded; but this is not to be understood literally, the meaning and legal effect of this declaration is, that those creditors who do not sign can, at the specified time, be called upon formally to renounce all benefit by the deed; for till that is actually done, any creditor may come in and execute, and entitle himself to a dividend.

COMPOUNDING A FELONY, is where the party robbed not only knows the felon, but takes back his goods, or agrees not to prosecute for some compensation or amends made him. This is a misdemeanor, and punishable by fine and imprisonment, the private wrong being absorbed by, or as the lawyers term it, *merged in* the public injury. It is a felony by statute to take any reward for helping a person to stolen goods without bringing the offender to justice; and the advertising a reward for the return of things stolen, or *no questions asked*, or printing or publishing such advertisement, incurs a penalty of 50*l.* It seems that compounding prosecutions for misdemeanors does not come within the above statutes, provided they are not of a *public* nature, in which case any compromise or compounding must be had with the sanction of the court of queen's bench, and not otherwise. All informations for penalties can only be compromised by leave of the court, under a penalty of 10*l.* and imprisonment; but in most cases of summary conviction before magistrates, there is no legal impropriety in compounding an information; indeed, in cases concerning petty larcenies and small injuries to property, magistrates have power to discharge the offender upon his making a pecuniary compensation. It is not uncommon for the court of quarter sessions, or justices elsewhere, to permit a defendant on a prosecution or complaint for assault or battery to *speak* with the prosecutor, and upon his being satisfied, to inflict a nominal fine as an amends to public justice.

COMPROMISE, OFFER OF. An offer of compromise, if made for the sake of peace, and for the purpose of determining litigation, will not be taken as an *admission* of a sum due, or that any thing is due; but it would be prudent for parties willing to make a payment in a peaceable spirit to stop litigation or annoyance without reference to the sum claimed to be due, so to qualify their offers, that no misapprehension may arise as to the inducement of the offer; else a litigious and ungenerous adversary, or his attorney, which is just the same, will rather proceed in his claim, considering that the offer may operate as a strong presumption in the minds of the jury that something is due. See Evidence, where this point is particularly alluded to.

The compromising a criminal act, or anything that savours of it, is termed "compounding." See COMPOUNDING A FELONY.

CONCEALMENT OF BIRTH. The concealment, or the bare endeavour by a woman to conceal the birth of her child, by secret burying or otherwise disposing of the dead body, is a misdemeanor which subjects her to be imprisoned, with or without hard labour, for not exceeding two years.

This crime is perfected by any suspicious concealment, whether the child be born alive, and afterwards die without any fault of the mother, or even if the child be still-born and she does any act to conceal the birth.

Although the concealment is a matter of suspicion, yet the coroner's jury should never return a verdict of wilful murder against the mother unless there is decisive proof offered them of the child having been born alive. The mother, if arraigned upon an inquisition or indictment for the murder of her child, although acquitted of the murder, may be convicted of the concealment.

CONDITION, is a stipulation, or precise technical words in a deed, sometimes operating as a restraint, and sometimes referrible to a contingency or thing to happen at a future time, and limiting the advantage or benefit to the performance of a particular act. In this case, a condition is either *precedent*, *i. e.*, the condition or stipulation must be performed before the advantage can arise; or *subsequent*, where the advantage immediately arises, but the stipulation remains *to be performed*. Much legal learning is wrapt up in these distinctions.

CONDITION OF A BOND, is that part of a bond following the formal part of that instrument, and commencing thus: "The *condition* of this obligation is such, that 'if' the party bound do such and such a thing, then the *obligation*, and consequently the penalty annexed (and which in law becomes due on the non-performance), is to be void and of none effect; otherwise, to remain of full effect and virtue."

CONFEDERACY, is the same as Combination and Conspiracy, only that the two former words denote particular offences, of which a confederating or unlawful union is the essence. In all acts of this nature the offence is complete on proof of the confederacy, though nothing be concluded, the intent and not the effect being the criterion of the offence. All confederacies for the purpose of wronging another are unlawful; indeed the word is used in the law in an adverse sense, as well as in common parlance. See CONSPIRACY, COMBINATION.

CONSANGUINITY, is kindred by birth or blood; affinity being kindred by marriage, the relations of the husband standing in the same degree of affinity to the wife in which they are related to the husband by consanguinity, but there is no affinity between the kinsmen themselves.

Consanguinity is either *lineal* or *collateral*. Lineal consanguinity is where one is descended in a direct line from the other, as father, son, grandson, great-grandson, &c., descending; and father, grandfather, great-grandfather, ascending; every generation in this *direct* line constituting a different degree or step, reckoning either upwards or downwards. Thus, in the annexed table, the father and the son of the Propositus (deceased intestate, or last possessed) are both related to him in the first degree; his great-grandfather and great-grandson, in the third degree. This mode of reckoning degrees in the lineal or *direct* line, is used by the common law in cases of descent of real property, and by the ecclesiastical or canon law in cases of distribution of the property of intestates, or dividing residues undisposed of amongst the next of kin.

Collateral consanguinity is where the kinsfolk all spring from the same lineal ancestor as the deceased, but are not in the direct line with him; and, therefore, instead of being father, grandfather, son, grandson, &c., they are brothers, sisters, uncles, aunts, nephews, nieces, cousins, &c.; thus the father of a deceased, is also *lineally* related to the deceased's brother; but the deceased and his brother are *collateral* kinsmen only. So a person and his first cousin are *collaterally* related, because they descend from the same great-grandfather or grandfather; indeed, the rule is simply this, all a man's kindred springing from his ancestors (*excepting only the ancestors themselves, who of course are lineal,*) are collateral relations; but all a man's descendants are lineally related to him. Thus far as regards the consanguinity or relationship, as reckoned at common law, which will be elucidated further under the title DESCENT, and by the table thereto.

When the next of kin, or degrees of relationship in the collateral line, are to be found for the purpose of granting administration, the reckoning of degrees is that adopted by the ecclesiastical law, which does not count them as the common law does in regard to descent; for the canonists, in accounting degrees between two persons, count upwards from one of them to the common ancestor from whence both relations spring, and then downward to the other, reckoning a degree for each person both ascending and descending; as, in the following table, if the reader wishes to ascertain in what degree was the deceased related to his brother, he will find that from the deceased to his father (who, being father to both, is the common ancestor) he is to count upwards *one degree;* and from the father to the brother, downwards, *another degree;* thus he is related to his brother in the second degree. In the same manner he will find in what degree of relationship the deceased was to his first cousin or cousin-german; from the deceased to his father *one*, to his grandfather *two* (who being the grandfather to both is common ancestor); then downwards from grandfather to uncle *three*, from uncle to cousin *four*, degrees. In like manner as to the second cousin; from the deceased to his father *one*, to his grandfather *two*, to his great-grandfather (the common ancestor) *three;* then descending from great-grandfather to great-uncle *four*, to the great-uncle's son (the cousin-german of deceased's father) *five*, from the great uncle's son to the second cousin *six*, degrees.

It may be remarked that the husband and wife are not next of kin, but are related only by affinity.

A TABLE

OF LINEAL AND COLLATERAL CONSANGUINITY OR RELATIONSHIP.

The Roman figures represent lineal relationship, the Arabic figures collateral. In both the degree of relationship to the deceased is demonstrated.

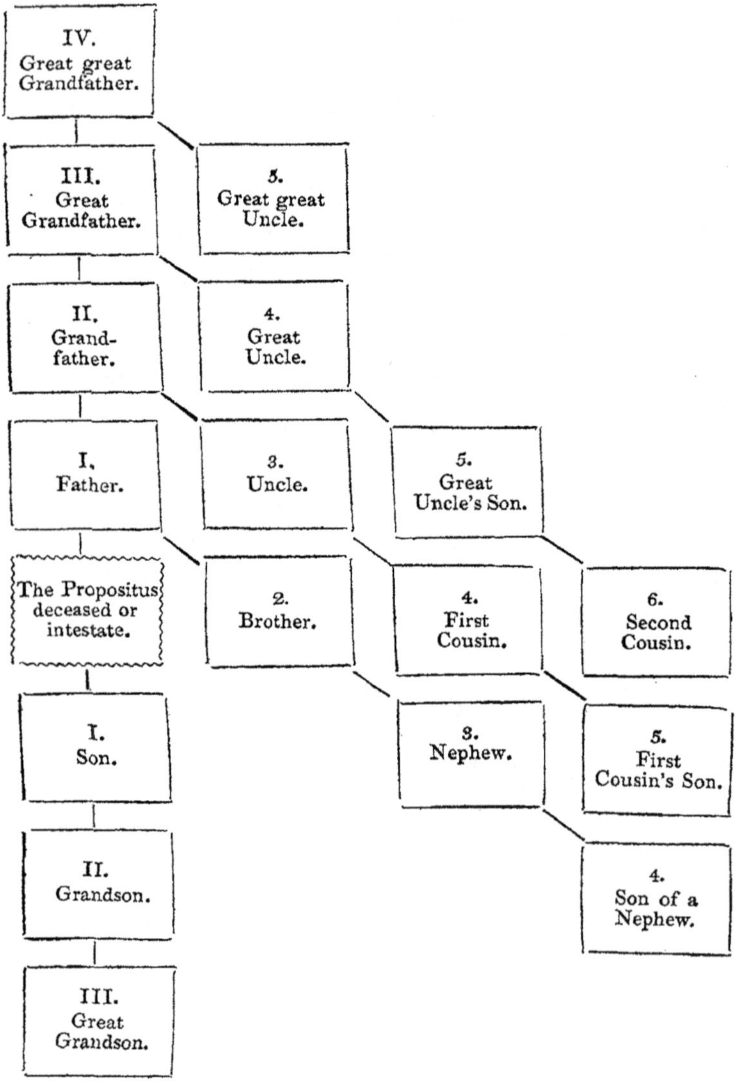

CONSIDERATION. The quid pro quo; the matter of inducement to a contract or transaction; the object in view which is introductory to the dealing. *Considerations* are by law required to be lawful, and not have for their object the carrying into effect any fraudulent or injurious act.

CONSISTORY COURT, or DIOCESAN COURT, is the court of every diocesan bishop, held in his cathedral, or other convenient place within the diocese, concerning all ecclesiastical causes arising within his diocese; and in this court probate of wills and letters of administration are granted, where the deceased's *personal* property is only in that diocese, and he hath not goods to the value of 5*l.* (10*l.* if in London) elsewhere. The bishop's chancellor is the judge in this court, and in places remote from the court he appoints a commissary with a register to enter his decrees. From the sentence of either an appeal lies to the archbishop of the province, or metropolitan of the diocese, (either Canterbury or York,) and from them the case can be removed to the judicial committee of the Privy Council.

CONSPIRACY. The term used for an unlawful confederacy to prejudice a third person. Formerly, and in its strict legal sense, it was used for an agreement of two or more falsely to prosecute another for felony, which is a crime not very frequent now. There must be two at least to form a conspiracy. For acts which are in the nature of false accusations, the party grieved can have his remedy by action *on the case.* Combinations or confederacies, which are entered into for the purpose of wronging third persons, are of various natures, and, consequently, these offences bear different shades of guilt; but, ordinarily speaking, all conspiracies, combinations, and confederacies are misdemeanors, punishable by fine and imprisonment. See COMBINATION.

CONSTABLE, or petty constable as he is termed, to distinguish him from the high constable or bailiff of a hundred or other district, is a very ancient officer, appointed in every village or township throughout the kingdom for the purpose of keeping the peace, or, more practically speaking, for the purpose of taking into custody those who commit breaches of the peace, or more serious offences. The office of a constable is chiefly to obey the warrants and precepts of the justices of the county, or those who *back* any warrant to be executed by him in the limit of his power, within the village, township, or parish, or other place for which he is chosen or appointed. The constable is chosen at the court leet, or, where there is no leet, then at the tourn which is not much in use: if there is no tourn, or the custom is that the inhabitants or parishioners should choose their constable, such choice is made accordingly; and he is then sworn before a justice of the peace to well and sufficiently execute his office. On other occasions he is sworn in the court leet or tourn.

In London there is a constable to each precinct in every ward, nominated by the inhabitants of the precinct; and each constable may execute warrants throughout the whole city.

The person appointed to this office should be an inhabitant housekeeper of the place for which he is chosen; and any person appointed may be indicted for not taking the office upon him. On just cause the court of quarter sessions may remove a constable, and by warrant compel him to appear and be sworn.

By 1 & 2 *W.* 4. *c.* 41. two or more justices, on information on oath that tumult, riot, or felony has taken place, or may be apprehended, in any parish,

&c., may nominate householders (not exempt) to be special constables, who shall take the oath required by the act; and notice of the nomination shall be forwarded to the secretary of state and lieutenant of the county. Secretary of state may, on representation of the justices, order persons exempt to be sworn in. The justices may make orders for rendering such special constables more efficient, and may remove them for misconduct. Such special constables to have all the powers and immunities of ordinary constables. On representation from two justices of adjoining county that extraordinary circumstances render it expedient, the justices of the county wherein constables are acting may order them to act in the adjoining county.

Aged persons, or persons weak of body, should not be elected; and persons who are exempted from being chosen as churchwardens or overseers are also relieved from the office. But it seems settled that masters of arts, justices of peace in another county, officers of the guards, officers or watchmen at the custom-house, tenants in ancient demesne, (who are by custom exempt from almost every other public duty,) and younger brothers of the Trinity House, are liable to serve; but if a gentleman of quality, or such persons last-mentioned, are chosen where there are other sufficient persons, it has been said they may be relieved on application to the court of queen's bench.

No person is liable to serve unless *resident* in the parish, *i. e.* sleeping there.

A constable may make a deputy when sick or unable, but the constable is answerable for his misdeeds if his deputy be not sworn.

The power and authority of the constable is very great; and it is said, upon high legal authority, "That he hath as good authority in his place as the chief justice of England hath in his;" indeed, it should be remembered, that as the office is for the purposes of *prevention*, he must necessarily have a reasonable discretion.

His duty is to apprehend all persons committing assaults, or suspected of felony or other offences, and carry them before a justice of the peace, which course is always the most advisable, as well as the most usual; but he may (especially if he apprehend a rescue) carry a party arrested for felony to the common gaol, and the gaoler is bound to receive him; or he may, if no justice is near the place of caption, secure the arrested party in some safe place. He may compel any one whom he sees committing an assault or breach of the peace to give surety to him in his own name (not otherwise) for keeping the peace; he may break open doors of houses wherein there is an affray or riot, *if entrance on demand be refused;* also he may imprison to *prevent* a felony; in fine, he is empowered to repress all public disorders and trespasses.

When the constable has a warrant he is tied up thereby to act only as it directs. If he arrest on a general warrant (before some justice) he may carry his prisoner to what justice he will. He is not obliged to return his warrant, but may keep it for his own justification, upon certifying what he shall have done by virtue of the warrant. A constable may imprison or put in the stocks any one insulting, assaulting, or opposing him, though only verbally, in execution of his office.

The constable is the proper officer to a justice of the peace, and bound to execute his lawful warrants; and, therefore, where a statute authorises a justice to convict a person of any offence, and to levy the penalty, &c., without saying to whom such warrant shall be directed, the constable is the officer to execute the warrant, and must obey it. The constable must, at his peril, take notice that his warrant is signed by a person in the commission of the peace, and, if guilty of misdemeanor in executing a lawful warrant, he becomes a trespasser. But a warrant properly penned, (even though the magistrate who issues it should exceed his jurisdiction,) will, at all events, indemnify the officer who executes it.

The constables and churchwardens levy the poor-rate; it seems they and the churchwardens may assess it where the churchwardens and parishioners disagree.

A variety of other duties are imposed upon constables.

If a constable does not perform his duty he may be fined by two justices in session; on the other hand, he is to be allowed his lawful expenses by the county; and special constables have an allowance by two justices when appointed to execute warrants in cases of felony.

It is a misdemeanor to discharge an offender brought to the watch-house by a watchman in the night; and if he wilfully let a felon escape it is felony. And it seems generally agreed that all voluntary escapes in the constable or peace-officer amount to the same crime as the offender was guilty of, whether treason or felony.

All persons are bound to assist a constable in apprehending and securing a person suspected of, or charged with, a felony.

In actions brought against a constable on account of an act done by virtue of his office he shall have double costs on verdict; and it is specially provided by another act of parliament that no action shall be brought against any constable or other officer, or any person acting by his order and in his aid, for any thing done in obedience to any warrant of a justice of peace, until *demand* of the perusal and copy of such warrant, and the same hath been refused or neglected by the space of six days; and in case after such demand and compliance therewith any action shall be brought against such constable, &c., without making the justice a defendant, then, on producing and proving such warrant, the jury shall give a verdict for the defendant, notwithstanding any defect of jurisdiction in such justice; and if such action be brought jointly against such justice, and also against such constable, &c., then, on proof of such warrant, the jury shall find for such constable, &c.; and if the verdict shall be given against the justice the plaintiff shall recover his costs against him, to be taxed so as to include costs plaintiff shall be liable to pay to such constable, &c. No action shall be brought against any constable, &c., unless commenced within six calendar months after the act committed.

A constable cannot break open and enter a house to distrain for poor's-rate or church-rate, or for other penalties, unless authorised by the act of parliament authorising the levy; even then he must first demand entrance. In cases of trespass for excess of authority he is not entitled to a notice or demand of his warrant. A constable is every three months, and within fourteen days after he goes out of office, to deliver to the overseers of the poor an account, entered in a book kept for the purpose, and signed by him, of all sums by him expended and received on account of the parish, &c.; which overseers are, within fourteen days, to lay the same before the inhabitants, and, if approved, are to pay the money due out of the poor's-rates, but, if disallowed, are to deliver the book back to the constable, who may produce it before a justice of peace, giving reasonable notice to the overseers; which justice is to examine the account, determine objections, settle the sum due, and enter it in and sign the account, and the overseers are to pay such sums out of the poor's-rate, but may appeal (giving notice) to the quarter sessions.

Constables also have a duty to perform with regard to distresses for rent. See DISTRESS.

CONSUL. An officer appointed by government to reside in foreign countries for the purpose of extending and facilitating commerce and communication between the two countries. Also, merchants or other persons appointed by foreign princes to reside here for the same purpose. The duties of British consuls abroad, and their fees, are regulated by the stat. 6 *G.* 4. *c.* 87. A foreign consul resident here is not protected from arrest as an ambassador's servant.

CONTEMPT. An act of insult or contumely offered to a court of justice, for which the party can be *attached*, or, if the insult be offered in the face of the court, instantly committed. Contempts may be *constructive*, that is, as an act of disobedience to an order of a court is deemed to be a contempt of its jurisdiction. A person who refuses to pay or do what the court orders should be paid or done is said to be *in contempt;* and though the contempt may be, and mostly is, a mere matter of default of payment, yet it is treated as an affront offered to the court; but as the courts can only enforce their orders or *rules*, as they are termed, in this manner, it is not so unreasonable a fiction as many at first sight would suppose. The process that issues to take a person guilty of contempt is called an *attachment*.

CONTINGENT REMAINDER. See REMAINDER.

CONTRABAND GOODS are those articles or commodities which are prohibited by act of parliament or the queen's proclamation to be exported or imported, bought or sold.

CONTRACT. An agreement made, or engagement entered into, upon adequate inducement.

Contracts are *in law* classed as contracts under seal and contracts not under seal. The former being termed *specialties*, the latter *parol* or *simple contracts*.

Contracts under seal comprehend all deeds, conveyances, mortgages, bonds of all kinds, annuities, leases, apprenticeship indentures, charterparties, and insurances, and all instruments which are delivered or executed with the formality of sealing, which only gives them the properties and privilege of specialties. See DEED.

There are also contracts or obligations which are termed *of record*, because recorded and enrolled in some court of judicature, being a court of record; such are judgments, recognizances of bail or other recognizances, which bind the land of the party, and for which there need no consideration be shown to render them binding, except that fraudulent records may be treated as nullities by third parties.

Contracts not under seal comprehend all verbal promises, bills, notes, and policies, charterparties (if not sealed), and every species of written contract not sealed as a deed; indeed, all unsealed writings rank in the eye of the law as mere *parol* or verbal contracts, the writing only being evidence of the promise or contract, or controlling its terms, not as the contract itself, which (under certain exceptions, in particular sorts of promises,) is as valid without writing as with it. This secondary sort of contract is divisible into

1. Contracts or promises purely and *actually* verbal.
2. Contracts evidenced by or reduced into writing, and those contracts which are under the operation of the statute of frauds.

1. All sealed writings, generally termed deeds, assume or import adequate consideration or value from the solemnity of the contract, but it is precisely the reverse with every other sort or kind of contract; therefore, to constitute a sufficient contract or agreement there must be a reciprocal or mutual assent of two or more persons competent to contract, a good and valid consideration, and a thing to be done which is to be the subject of the contract, which must be strictly lawful, or, more distinctly speaking, not unlawful, either in doing a forbidden thing, or omitting the performance of an act enjoined by the law to be done; and it is a general rule that a simple contract need not be reduced into writing, unless in the cases where a written promise is in express terms required by the law, as by the statute of frauds.

Simple contracts are either expressed or implied. *Express* contracts being in the language of Judge Blackstone, "where the terms of an agreement are openly uttered and avowed at the time of the making, as to deliver an ox, or ten loads of timber, or to pay a stated price for certain goods. *Implied*, are such as reason and justice dictate, and which, therefore, the law presumes that every man undertakes to perform; as if I employ a person to do any business for me, or perform any work, the law implies that I undertook or contracted to pay as much as his labour deserves. If I take up wares from a tradesman, without any agreement as to price, the law concludes that I contracted to pay their real value." Practically, there is no difference in these distinctions, farther than as to the mode of substantiating a contract. *Express* contracts are more often reduced into writing, whereas *implied* arise from the course of dealing between the parties, or the particular circumstances attending each transaction.

It would be nearly impossible to enumerate every case in which, to use legal phraseology, "an implication can be raised," *i. e.* a promise peremptorily supposed or presumed; but to demonstrate that the law acts in accordance with natural equity and moral sense a few cases may be noticed, which will sufficiently explain to the reader the doctrine of *implied contracts*. If I have and receive money belonging to another without any valuable consideration given on my part, and I do not pay it over to the owner, he can have an action against me "*on the case*" upon this *implied* undertaking; for the law construes this to be money had and received for the use of the owner only, and *implies*, *i. e.* presumes, that I undertook to account for it to the true proprietor; and in such action I shall have to recompense the owner in *damages* equivalent to his loss in violation of my (*implied*) promise; and this action is to be brought in almost all cases where money has been received by one for the use of another, or which the receiver ought, in justice, to refund or pay over. If another man pays money for my use, at my request, the law implies a promise, *i. e.* that I will repay him; as if in my absence A. incurs an expense in burying my deceased wife in a manner suitable to my situation in life, though without my knowledge, the law will imply a promise by me to reimburse A.; and promises to a particular extent or effect may be implied in many cases from the circumstance of the parties having invariably, on similar occasions, adopted any particular terms or course of dealing. The law will also raise special implications from the acts of a party, or from a legal duty imposed upon him, which (specially implied) promises the law infers the party will consequently perform, the actual fact being that the party never promised or intended to perform what the law enjoins he should do. Thus if a party seduce away and harbour an apprentice, the master may sue such party for the work and labour of the apprentice. So an action lies to recover the value of goods, as sold to the defendant, if he by fraud induces the plaintiff to sell them to an insolvent person, and afterwards obtains them for his own benefit, upon the principle that no one shall take advantage of his own wrong. Upon the same principle seems the doctrine to be founded that if a husband wrongfully expel his wife or desert her, leaving her unprovided with necessaries, he is liable upon an implied promise to any person who supplies her with them, although the husband give public notice not to credit the wife. In short, many promises are implied by law, where there is a moral or equitable obligation incumbent on a party to fulfil. So far with respect to contracts purely verbal.

2. With respect to contracts reduced into writing, in regard of their being reciprocal, and of being founded upon adequate recompense and considerations, they stand in precisely the same situation as mere word of mouth promises or contracts; and as the promise is only evidenced by the writing, which is in common parlance called an "agreement," such writing does not, like a deed, of itself import a value received, nor is the party executing it stopped from disputing the validity of the contents; far otherwise: the adequacy of the consideration must be proved just as if it was verbal. If no consideration be expressed, (and it is not in all cases absolutely necessary that such consideration should be apparent on the face of the contract when in writing,) it may be supplied by verbal evidence, though, when the consideration is expressed fully, there the courts do not allow of opposite evidence, that being, in effect, to substantiate a contract different in essentials from that before them.

But the legislature has long since interfered with regard to verbal contracts which tended to charge, by parol evidence solely, parties (especially those who were not primarily liable) upon fictitious or misrepresented transactions, upheld by frauds and perjuries (whence the statute took its name), by enforcing certain requisites to charge particular parties; for the statute of frauds, 29 *Car.* 2. *c.* 3., provides that no action shall be brought—1. To charge any executor or administrator upon any special promise to answer damages out of *his own* estate. 2. To charge one with the debt or default of another. 3. To charge any one upon an agreement made in consideration of marriage. 4. Upon any contract or sale of lands, tenements, or hereditaments, or *any interest* therein; or, 5. Upon any agreement not to be performed within the space of one year from the making—*unless* the agreement upon which such action shall be brought, or some memorandum or note thereof, shall be in *writing*, and *signed* by the party to be charged therewith, or some other person thereunto by him lawfully authorised. And with respect to the sale of goods, that no contract for sale of any goods for 10*l.* or upwards shall be good, except the buyer shall — 1. Accept part and *actually receive* the same; or, 2. Shall give earnest to bind the bargain or in part payment; or, 3. Unless some memorandum or note of the same bargain be made and signed by the parties to be charged, or their agents (such as auctioneer, broker, &c.,) thereunto authorised.* Also,

* For instance, if A. *orders* goods of B. to the value of 10*l.* This contract cannot be enforced against B. if he refuse to accept and pay for the goods, unless one of these legal requisites shall have been complied with, and *vice versâ.*

there are certain contracts which by late statutes require signature; such as the promise of a bankrupt to pay a debt barred by his certificate, of a debtor to pay a debt barred by the statute of limitations, and of an adult to pay a debt due, contracted during his nonage, and which he was not bound to discharge. See Bankruptcy Act, 6 *G*. 4. *c*. 16. *s*. 131.; Lord Tenterden's Act, 9 *G*. 4. *c*. 14.

The writing a letter containing a proposal to which a party assents, is a conclusive memorandum; but a verbal promise of marriage is not within the meaning of the statute, the conduct of the parties, and a general though definite and reciprocal understanding between them, their friends and relations, evidencing the conduct which implies this promise. In the case of guarantee, where a *verbal* promise is given by one to pay the debt of another, or rather to send goods to another, the person sending the goods can yet recover from the party giving the order, provided he trusted him *originally*, and it can be shown that the credit was given to the party ordering the goods, not to the party to whom they were sent. The question being *to whom was the credit given?* For if A. verbally promise to pay B. the debt owing him by C., the credit having been given to C, there the promise is void.

In all agreements and memorandums upon contracts entered into of the nature referred to in the statute of frauds, it is necessary that the consideration should be fully and explicitly stated; for though we have seen that an agreement concerning a contract of another nature may be explained or evidenced by verbal testimony, as it might have been had it not been reduced into writing, yet, the statute requiring the formality of a signature by the party chargeable, the agreement or undertaking in these cases must expressly state the value, recompense, or consideration; and then the signature of the party chargeable is sufficient in these agreements, although in all other cases the contract is reciprocal, and must be *accepted* by both, or acts tantamount or leading to the presumption of the assent of both assumed.

Illegality of Contracts. Agreements generally, when in accordance with legal forms and requisites, have the force of laws over the makers of them; but this rule does not apply where the interests of the public or of morality are affected by the contract, and may be injured by the observance of its provisions; but, as the presumption of law is in favour of a contract, if it is reasonably susceptible of two meanings, one legal and the other illegal, that interpretation shall be put upon an agreement which will effectuate its operation, for illegality of consideration shall not be inferred or implied. It is for the party who takes that objection to prove it clearly, the burden of the proof resting on him. The contracts that the courts have repudiated, as being against the interests of morality or public policy, or on account of their generally injurious tendency, are contracts in consideration of *future* illicit cohabitation, or for the purposes of prostitution; for printing libellous or immoral publications; in restraint of trade; in contravention of the bankrupt or insolvent laws, as affecting the equal distribution of the estate; restraint of marriage; to procure a marriage for reward; for future separation of, or tending to prevent a reconciliation between, married persons; sale of offices, having for their intent the obstructing the course of justice; in trade made with an enemy; and wagers against public policy, or on the subject of illegal games, or tending to the injury of third parties, are invalid.

Fraud.—Misrepresentation or concealment to the manifest deceit of another avoids a contract written or unwritten; but the misrepresentation will not generally be deemed fraudulent unless made with the knowledge of the party, or the contract is based upon it. As the law enforces the observance of honesty and good faith in all transactions, so, where a defect is of the nature called *latent, i. e.* such a defect that the buyer cannot with the greatest attention discover it, the contract may be set aside, even though the thing was purchased *with all faults;* whereas a different rule applies where the defect is *patent, i. e.* observable and apparent by the exercise of ordinary caution and inquiry, so that nothing short of a concealment amounting to actual fraud will vacate a contract, trifling defects not being sufficient foundation for the rescinding of a contract where the seller is not cognizant of them. The noncommunication of intelligence which would materially influence a party in making a contract is certainly a fraud in the eye of the law, whether the party actually knows of its importance or not; for he is bound to communicate every fact of which he is cognizant, or upon which he can reasonably be supposed to possess full information. These questions generally resolve themselves into mere matters of fact, upon which the jury, not the law, have to decide. For the point is, was the thing suppressed material or not?

Misrepresentation by a party of the *legal* effect of an agreement does not constitute fraud, upon the principle that ignorance of the law is not to be presumed in individuals; for if it were, every one would plead it, and there would be no means of confuting him.

Some contracts are rendered voidable at law by reason of the inequality, or particular condition or relation of the contracting parties; so a guardian shall not purchase of his ward; an attorney shall not purchase of his client, or shall not purchase the subject of dispute; and assignees cannot, without leave of the court, purchase the bankrupt's estate.

In general, inadequacy of price does not of itself absolutely vitiate a contract; but, coupled with other circumstances, it may establish a case of fraud. Gross inadequacy of price of itself amounts to evidence of fraud, and will form a ground for cancelling a contract.

The alteration of a written contract in a *material* part by a party, even if all other parties consent, invalidates it.

However, in the case of written agreements, misrepresentations cannot be urged, unless the subject of the misrepresentation formed part of the agreement, *i. e.* such misrepresentation was the basis of the contract; for if that were allowed, it would be tantamount to permitting verbal testimony to contradict or add to what is written; therefore, in all cases where a contract, or the heads of it, are reduced into writing, it behoves both parties to state in such writing all the matters of inducement to such contract, so that if a *substantial* misrepresentation has been made it can be referred to a particular fact upon which the delusion exists, or which lulled the suspicions of a careful person, who, but for that special representation, would have satisfied himself by an inquiry.

Indeed, matters not embodied in a *written* contract, cannot ever be questioned so as to contravene the express terms of an agreement in writing. In verbal contracts, that which is not particularly specified cannot afterwards be noticed, unless, as before observed, particular statements are made which lull inquiry and quiet suspicion. Finally, it may be necessary to observe, that a misrepresentation is unimportant if the party to whom the false statement was made knew the real state of the facts, for in such case he was not deceived.

As to misrepresentation, concealment, and other matters of deceit, especially in written contracts and deeds, see FRAUD.

CONVEYANCE. A deed which passes or conveys land from one to another. The conveyances now in use are the "lease and release," "bargain and sale enrolled," and "settlements." A deed that conveys what is termed an *incorporeal* hereditament, that is, some advantage or right issuing out of or chargeable upon land, is legally styled *a grant*, as a grant of annuity, grant of advowson, &c.

CONVEYANCERS, are those who employ themselves solely in the preparation of deeds and conveyances of land, &c. No person is deemed qualified by law to act as a conveyancer unless he is a barrister or attorney, or a student, or member of some *Inn of Court* duly certificated, *i. e.* paying 12*l.* stamp duty for his licence. The drawing wills or powers of attorney does not subject the party to any penalty for practising as a conveyancer without payment of the 12*l.* duty imposed by the stamp acts.

CONVOCATION. The assembly of the representatives of the clergy of the two provinces of Canterbury and York, formerly convened, and now *pro formâ* held, but adjourned *sine die*, to consult of ecclesiastical matters in time of parliament. It was prorogued in 1717, and has never sat again for any business.

CONVOY. Ships of war appointed by government in time of war to escort merchants' ships to various ports. It is against law for ships to sail without convoy in war time. It is also made one of the stipulations in shipping policies that the insured sail with convoy; and, to perform this warrantry or stipulation sufficiently, the insured must obtain, if possible, the *sailing instructions*, which afford full information as to signals, place of rendezvous, &c.

COPARCENERS. Heirs female and their issue, who are all entitled to have an equal portion in freehold or copyhold estates in default of heirs male. The issue taking no more than what would have originally come to their parent. The female issue in the same degree are usually called co-heiresses. See PARCENERS.

COPPER-PLATE ENGRAVINGS, COPYRIGHT IN. See LITERARY PROPERTY.

COPY. The transcript of an original writing, as the *copy* of a patent, charter, deed, &c. See EVIDENCE.

COPYHOLD. A tenure of lands in *England* (for it is rare in Ireland), for which the tenant or owner has nothing to show but the *copy* of the *rolls* made by the steward who holds the lord's court, which rolls contain special entries and memoranda of the *admission* of a tenant, his surrender to the use of another, or *alienation*, his *death*, and the claim and admission of the heir or devisee. There are two sorts of copyhold. The first, which is styled ancient demesne, or a customary freehold, which are only subject to a very small quit-rent, and an occasional nominal heriot. The second, a base tenure or mere copyhold, holden, as the *copy* says, "at the will of the lord," and subject to a two years' value as a fine on death, or alienation, or *heriot*, and a yearly quit-rent superadded, which shows the baseness of the tenure, it being a relic of the servile tenure of *villeins*, or bondsmen, who held their lands at their lord's will, that is, while they performed base or servile offices, and paid an acknowledgment for the profits of the land. The "will of the lord" is now practically a nullity, it being qualified by "the custom of the manor;" and the liberal construction courts have put upon the formular words, which are still useful as they designate the tenure, and, consequently, the nature, of the services attendant upon this inferior inheritance.

A copyhold cannot now be created; for the essence of the tenure is that it has been holden, let, or demised, as the case may be, *time out of mind*, by copy of *court roll*, and that the tenements are parcel of or within the manor.

The customary freeholders, formerly called *barons*, whence the name "court baron," are a superior sort of copyhold, and anciently held of the lord by some *honourable* service, such as accompanying the lord to the wars against the Scots for forty days or more, which was called *escuage*, and similar services. When they are termed tenants in ancient demesne, these freeholders hold of a manor which had existence at the time of king Edward the Confessor, and holden of the crown at the time of the conquest: these manors are all mentioned in doomsday book: they had also peculiar local privileges. It is not usual in many manors to formally admit the freehold tenants; but they are enrolled by name and the amount of quit-rent. In ancient demesne manors greater particularity was observed, as, till the abolition of fines and recoveries, these proceedings were had in the lord's court, and brought pence to the steward. The mere copyholders have their only evidence of tenure by copy. "A court baron and customary court" generally signifies the tenure of the manor, the first being for the freeholders, the second for the mere copyholders. "A view of frank-pledge," or "court-leet or law-day," signifies that the lord has power to exercise, or formerly exercised, peculiar jurisdiction within his manor for petty wrongs, &c.

Copyholds are often let for lives, renewable for ever upon certain fines, but more frequently they are *of inheritance, i. e.* they descend according to the course of the common law in respect of descent, unless in some particular manors where there are contrary customs of great antiquity, such as Borough-English and Gavelkind.

If a lord of a manor refuse to *admit*, he can be compelled by the court of chancery; also, if he seizes the land for nonpayment of a fine, the tenant can be relieved in equity against the rigour of the forfeiture; and if the lord refuse to admit a person to whom a surrender has been made, on account of a disagreement about the amount of the fine, the queen's bench will grant a *mandamus* to the lord, commanding him to admit, without examining the right to the fine; for which the lord can seize the land, bring an action of debt, or distrain for it, and so put the question at issue; for the tenant may defend himself against the lord's proceedings.

One who has a *primâ facie* title to a copyhold is entitled to inspect the court rolls, and take copies of them so far as relates to the copyhold claimed, though no cause be depending for it at the time.

Copyholds *escheat* and are *forfeited* in many cases. Escheat of a copyhold estate is where the lands fall into the hands of the lord for want of an heir. *Forfeitures* arise by alienation by *deed*, or if the heir does not come in, perform his service, or pay his fine, upon three proclamations made for that purpose; denial of lord's right, refusal to pay quit-rent, leasing without licence, and similar acts, which must be noticed or presented by the *homage*, or jury, at the lord's court.

Courts baron, or copyhold courts, must be notified publicly in the parish church or other public place before they can be lawfully held or proclamations made; but special courts for particular purposes may be held, which will bind the parties at whose particular instance they are convened. The lord may do many single acts out of court, and surrenders may be made out of court by custom into the hands of the steward, or two copyholders in his place, and many matters may be transacted for individual purposes by the steward or the lord, but matters concerning the tenants at large must be transacted at courts publicly held and properly notified.

Copyholds cannot be taken in execution; but if a party is outlawed the rents may be seized for his life. See MANOR.

COPYRIGHT. The exclusive right of printing and publishing *copies* of any literary performance; extended also to music, engravings, calico-prints, designs, and most works of art. See LITERARY PROPERTY.

CORN. The trade of Great Britain in corn is at present regulated by the provisions of the statute 9 *G.* 4. *c.* 60., which act contains a series of regulations for ascertaining the average price of British corn, by means of weekly returns from the corn-dealers in London, and 150 other cities and places in England and Wales. These returns are made in each place to local inspectors, and by them transmitted to a comptroller of the returns in London, appointed by the crown. The inspectors in towns being appointed by the corporations, and in other places by the justices of the peace.

All duties and bounties on the exportation of corn are repealed.

Corn may be imported upon payment of certain duties, regulated by the average.

CORN-RENTS. By statute 18 *Eliz. c.* 6. on college leases, one third of the old rent then paid should for the future be paid in wheat or malt, reserving a quarter of wheat for each 6*s.* 8*d.*, or a quarter of malt for every 5*s.*; or that the lessees should pay according to the price on the market-day next before the rent becomes due: this was devised for the upholding the revenues of the colleges. The value of money having been observed to sink much, and the price of provisions to rise greatly, on our communication with the Indies, so that presuming the quarter of wheat to be 50*s.*, and the colleges receiving a quarter of wheat or its value for every 13*s.* 4*d.*, which they are paid in money, it follows that the corn-rent will be in proportion to the money-rent nearly as four to one; but both these rents united are very far from the present value. Colleges, therefore, in order to obtain the full value of the term, take a fine upon the renewal of their leases, though the corn-rent has had the effect of making the old rent approach nearer its present value. (2 *Blackst. Comm., by Christian.*)

CORONER. An ancient officer, whose duty is chiefly to make inquiry or *inquisition* upon violent or unnatural deaths, and to perform certain acts relating to the execution of process where the sheriff is a party. His duty is limited to a county or a division of a county. Coroners are chosen by the freeholders of a county in a full county court, summoned by the sheriff, who is the judge, upon receipt of the queen's writ for that purpose. The election takes place upon view, or by a poll, if demanded, which shall be determined in ten days. The coroner, when elected, is chosen for life, or during good behaviour, or till incapacity: he is generally a man of substance and repute, and very often a lawyer by profession, the office requiring adequate legal information.

There are also special coroners. Municipal and other corporations have power by acts of parliament and prescription to choose and appoint their own coroners: some are appointed by the admiralty, and some are appointed by charter, and some persons are coroners by virtue of their offices. The chief justice of the queen's bench, the lord mayor of London, some lords of manors and officers, are either coroners in their manors or liberties, or have the appointment of them; for instance, the marshal of the Queen's Bench has the appointment of a coroner.

Coroners are judges when they take an inquisition, and are *ministers* or officers when they act in lieu of the sheriff.

The judicial functions of a coroner are regulated by an ancient statute, which directs him to go to a place where any person is slain or *suddenly dead*, and, by his warrant to the bailiffs or constables of a place, summon a jury out of the neighbouring places or towns to make inquiry *upon view of the body*; and he and the jury are to inquire into the manner of killing, and all circumstances that occasioned the party's death; who were present, whether the dead person was known, where he lay the night before, &c., and to examine the body for signs of violence. The coroner may send his warrant for witnesses, and is to take their examination in writing; and if any appear guilty of murder he is to inquire what goods and lands he has, and commit him to prison, or cause him to be apprehended. When the jury have brought in their verdict, the coroner is to return the inquisition to the next assizes or commission of gaol delivery in the county, or (but it is rarely done) certify it (*i. e.* file it in the crown office) to the court of queen's bench, where the murderers may be proceeded against.

By a late statute, every coroner, upon inquisition taken before him for manslaughter, murder, or for being accessory to murder before the fact, shall put the evidence in writing, and bind the witnesses by recognizance to appear at the next court of oyer and terminer, or gaol delivery, or superior criminal court of a county palatine, and certify and subscribe the evidence, recognizances, and inquisition, and deliver the same to the proper officer of the court before its opening; and for neglect he is liable to be fined.

A coroner is not bound, *ex officio*, to take an inquisition, but he must be sent for. He has a discretion as to admitting or excluding persons from his court. If he act corruptly or maliciously he is liable to a criminal information; but, as he is a judge of record, an action does not lie against him for turning a person out of a room when he was about to make an inquisition. A coroner's inquisition being *final* (*i. e.* as far as its being a deliberate accusation upon record), he ought to hear counsel and evidence on both sides; for he is bound to admit evidence against the queen's interest as for it; but it has been decided, that if one be killed by another, and it is certainly known that he did it, the jury are only to hear the evidence for the queen, and inquire whether the killing were by malice or otherwise; and, where a coroner would not admit of evidence against the queen to prove a *felo de se* to be *non compos mentis*, his inquisition was set aside. The words *suddenly dead* are not to be understood of a fever, apoplexy, &c., and ought not in such cases to warrant an intrusion into private families. Death by the kick of a horse is not a case for an inquest: violent and unnatural deaths are what the law intends.

The coroner may, in convenient time, take up a dead body in order to view it; but if it is in such a state that it cannot be seen, the inquest should be taken by the justices of peace upon testimony, for the coroner can only inquire *upon view* of the body. It is a misdemeanor, and consequently indictable, to bury a dead body, liable to the coroner's inquest, without sending for the coroner.

Coroners are also to make inquisition upon *all* persons who die in prison.

A coroner is entitled to certain fees, generally 20*s.* 9*d.* a mile for every mile he *goes* (his *returning* cannot be computed) from his house, and 13*s.* 4*d.* out of the murderer's goods, or out of any fine levied upon the township, if the murderer escape by day. If he takes more he is guilty of extortion.

Coroners can be attached summarily by the court of queen's bench for false or illegal inquisitions, but except in cases of *felo de se*, their inquisitions, if legal in form, cannot be questioned; for corruption or extortion, the court before whom he shall be convicted may deprive him of his office. Also the court of queen's bench or the justices of assize may fine coroners for irregularities committed by them in their office.

Coroners make inquisition as to found or hidden treasure. By custom in some places they may make inquisition of other felonies than homicide. The *ministerial* functions of a coroner are to execute writs where the sheriff is either plaintiff or defendant, and to return juries where the sheriff is in any manner interested, or is of kin to either party.

It seems a newspaper statement of a coroner's inquisition, *accompanied with comments*, is libellous, although the report be strictly true, and no malicious motive is apparent.

THE CORONER OF THE QUEEN'S HOUSEHOLD is to take all inquisitions upon the bodies of all persons slain in the queen's palace, or in any house where she may happen to be: he has exclusive jurisdiction of the county coroner, whose inquisition, if taken there, would be void.

CORONER OF LONDON AND SOUTHWARK. The lord mayor is coroner of London; but the corporation of London may grant exclusive jurisdiction to a coroner of their own appointment, and may choose two persons to be coroners in Southwark. The inquisition of any other coroner would be void. In London, the practice is for the *ward beadles* to summon the jury upon the coroner's warrant.

The writs which lie for election or discharge of a coroner are termed a writ *de coronatore eligendo*, and a writ *de coronatore exonerando*.

CORPORAL OATH. An oath administered to one upon his *personal*, not written, testimony.

CORPORATIONS. A body politic or incorporated, consisting of a number of persons, empowered by law to act under one name and as one person. They are established by royal charter or act of parliament, not unfrequently both, and they may claim to be a corporation by *prescription* (which see): London is a corporation by prescription. It is one of the royal prerogatives to constitute a corporation, but the parliament may exercise this power singly or collectively; singly, with respect to a particular body, and collectively, by incorporating all establishments endowed for particular purposes, as was done in the reign of Queen Elizabeth, and since, in the cases of charitable foundations, to avoid the charges incident upon the grant of incorporation; but this power is rarely used, as trenching upon the queen's prerogative.

Corporations are either *aggregate*, that is, composed of many, who are in the eye of the law but one natural body, or *sole*, which consist of one person only, incorporated by law, and having a certain perpetuity and endurance which in their natural persons they could not have; in this sense a king is a corporation sole, so are bishops, deans, and prebendaries distinct from their several chapters, and so are parsons and vicars.

Corporations aggregate are most commonly the mayor and burgesses of a city or town, the head and fellows of a college, the master and brethren of an hospital, the dean and chapter of a cathedral church. They are termed *ecclesiastical* corporations when the members are all spiritual or clerical persons, or, rather, act in that capacity. When the corporation has for its object the relief of the sick or poor, as an hospital, or the advancement of learning, as a college, it is termed an *eleemosynary* corporation: the latter are not *spiritual*, though all the persons may be clerical, but, like other corporations, *lay*, *i. e.* the members are devoted to worldly affairs.

Corporations, when created, must have a name given to them, by which they must sue or be sued, or acquire or part with property; and by virtue of their incorporation they have the power of making reasonable and consistent by-laws for their governance. They are not liable, personally or individually, for their engagements, but their property is alone answerable. However, they may be compelled by writ of *mandamus* to perform specific acts. They can hold property in mortmain, and have perpetual endurance and continuance for the purpose of transmitting the property of the corporation to their successors. All acts done by corporations of many are evidenced by their common seal.

Corporations cannot commit felony or treason, and cannot be excommunicated. They cannot appear but by attorney. An action for trespass will not lie against a corporation, but it does against those individuals who act in the names of the corporation. Corporations, or incorporated bodies, cannot be outlawed, but their corporate property can be taken in execution, which is the utmost remedy that can be had against them, the persons of the members being exempt.

With respect to acts done amongst themselves, they may sue each other for acts done in their individual or natural capacities. Members cannot be witnesses for a corporation, except where the interest is very remote. They can enfranchise and disfranchise for acts done to the prejudice of the body, or contrary to the member's oath; but they cannot enforce a forfeiture by their by-laws, unless empowered so to do by act of parliament. A writ of *mandamus* lies against them at the suit of a member wrongfully disfranchised. In acts done by them the major part binds the minority.

As a corporation is, in fact, an investing persons with a local jurisdiction, its laws are binding upon strangers; but "companies" or fraternities, such as the civic companies of London or other towns, cannot bind strangers, unless empowered by act of parliament, for they have no local power.

Corporations are controlled by what is termed the right of *visitation*, which is vested, in the case of *lay* corporations, in the queen, and in the case of spiritual corporations, as well as those of charitable foundation, in the bishop of the diocese. But where a founder of a charitable corporation has named a *visitor* or *visitors*, there the crown or the church have no right to interfere, while the corporation is properly conducted.

The queen exercises her right of control or *visitation* by means of the court of queen's bench; and in cases of impropriety in foundations, where a *visitor* is appointed, the attorney-general, on the queen's behalf, acts on the *relation* of some person, who is technically termed the "relator," and reforms the abuse complained of. Our colleges are, however, deemed *lay* corporations, notwithstanding they consist of ecclesiastical persons.

Corporations may be dissolved by forfeiture of their charter in cases of abuse, by surrender, or by act of parliament, or by the natural death of all the members of the corporation.

Corporations are not bound, generally, but by their common seal: they cannot bind themselves by their bill or note, except in the case of trading companies, or by having express powers for that purpose given them by act of parliament. The *head* of a corporation, such as a dean or a mayor, in many cases binds the chapter or the corporation in the execution of ordinary contracts; but no title can be obtained upon purchase of their property, except the conveyance be under their common seal. And companies who have no *head* are extremely restrained by operation of law in their simple contracts.

The proper remedy for a burgess, or officer, who claims admission to a corporation, in either capacity, is an application to the court of queen's bench for a writ of *quo warranto*, calling upon the person "usurping," to show *by what warrant* he exercises or enjoys the franchise or office. See MANDAMUS, QUO WARRANTO.

All corporations are to be understood here as *aggregate*, except described as *sole*.

The corporations of towns, termed municipal corporations, from the Latin word *municipium*, a *walled town*, are regulated by a late act of parliament, which forms a new constituency, subject to the claims of those who are or were freemen at the passing of the act (Sept. 9. 1834); "freemen," corresponding to the title "burgess," now adopted in all town corporations; *London*, to which the act does not extend, being the simple exception.

This act repeals so much of all laws, usages, grants, and charters, relating to the boroughs hereafter mentioned, as are not in conformity with the provisions of the present act; but reserves to inhabitants, apprentices, and freemen, and burgesses, and to the sons, sons-in-law, daughters, wives and widows of freemen and burgesses, certain rights and interests in the charitable funds, and the right of the latter to vote for members of parliament pursuant to sect. 4. of the Reform Act; prohibits *future* admissions, *by gift or purchase;* and provides for the perpetual succession of freemen and burgesses by admission and enrolment under one general style of "the mayor, aldermen, and burgesses of ———."

The government of a borough, or municipal corporation, is thus constituted: —

1. There are the *freemen*, or burgesses, in existence on the 9th of September, 1834, whose rights are reserved, and the burgesses now, or hereafter, to be enrolled under the present act. From these proceed 2. The councillors. 3. The aldermen. 4. The mayor.	On this corporate body are attendant a town clerk, two assessors, and two auditors, besides other officers appointed by "the council," *i. e.* the mayor, aldermen, and councillors.

1. *As to the Burgesses.*—The overseers of every parish, on the 5th of September, yearly, are to make out an alphabetical list of every male person of full age, who has been rated to all poor-rates in respect

of a *house*, *warehouse*, *counting-house*, or *shop* within the borough, for two years and eight months immediately preceding the 31st of August, *and* who has been during the same time an inhabitant householder within the borough, or seven miles thereof, and has been rated in respect of such premises within the borough ; and, lastly, has paid on the 31st of August all rates and borough taxes payable on or before the preceding 1st of March. And the overseers having made such list, and kept a copy for perusal by any one, between the 5th and 15th of September, are to deliver the *original* list to the town clerk, who is to print and deliver copies at a reasonable price, and fix a copy on the outer door of the town-hall, or in some public and conspicuous station within the borough, on every day between the 5th and 15th of September. If there should be no town clerk, then this duty devolves upon the person filling an analogous situation in the corporation ; and if the borough is situate in a precinct, or extra-parochial place, the list is to be made out by the overseers of the adjoining parish or parishes.

The list, as published by the town clerk, is as follows :—

"THE LIST OF BURGESSES of the Borough of in the Parish [or Township] of

Christian Name and Surname of each Person at full Length.	Nature of the Property rated.	Street, Lane, or other Place in this Parish (or Township) where the Property is situated for which he is now rated.
Ashton, John - -	*Shop* - -	*No. 23. Church Street.*
Bates, Thomas - -	*House* -	*Brook's Farm.*

"(*Signed*) *A. B.* } Overseers of the said parish
C. D. } [or township.]"

Persons who are omitted must, before the 15th of September, give the following notice in writing to the town clerk :—

"To the Town Clerk of the Borough of

"I hereby give you notice, that I claim to have my name inserted in the burgess list of the borough of . That I occupy [*here describe the house, warehouse, counting-house, or shop then occupied by the claimant*] in the borough, and that I have been rated in the parish of —— [*here state the parish or parishes, and the time during which the claimant has been rated in each of them within the borough.*] Dated the —— day of —— in the year 1837.

"A. B. of [*place of abode, and number of house*]."

And persons objecting to any name, must, on the same day, give notice to the town clerk, and also to the party objected to, or leave on the premises rated, the following written notice :—

"To the Town Clerk of the Borough of —— [*or* to the person objected to, *as the case may be.*]

"I hereby give you notice, that I object to the name of C. D., of ——, in the parish of —— [*describe the person objected to, as described in the burgess list*], being retained on the burgess list of the borough of ——. Dated the —— day of ——, in the year 1837.

"E. F., of [*here state the place of abode, and property for which he is said to be rated in the burgess list*]."

N. B. This notice, if not left on the premises, should be *personally* served.

The town clerk makes out a list of the claims and objections, according to the following forms :—

"LIST OF CLAIMANTS.

"The following Persons claim to have their Names inserted on the Burgess List of the Borough of ——.

Christian Name and Surname of each Claimant.	Nature of the Property for which he is now rated.	Situation of the Property for which he is now rated.	Parish (or Parishes) in which he has been rated, as stated in the Claim.
Allen, John .	*House* -	*No.* 17. *High Street.*	*Rated in the last year in Saint Mary's parish, in the borough, and in the two preceding years in Saint James's parish, in the borough.*

"(*Signed*) *G. H.* Town Clerk."

"LIST OF PERSONS OBJECTED TO.

"The following Persons have been objected to as not being entitled to have their Names retained on the Burgess List of the Borough of ——.

Christian Name and Surname of each Person objected to.	Nature of the Property for which he is now rated.	Situation of the Property for which he is said to be now rated in the Overseer's List.	Parish in which is the Property for which he is now said to be rated in the Overseer's List.
Bates, Thomas -	*House* -	*Brook's Farm* -	*Saint James's.*

"(*Signed*) *G. H.* Town Clerk."

And causes copies of such lists to be fixed as the original lists, during the eight days next preceding the 1st of October; he also is to make out a list of the claimants and persons objected to, to be perused *gratis*, and deliver copies at 1*s*. each.

The revision of these lists then takes place on some day between the 1st and 15th of October (on three clear days' notice), by the mayor and two assessors, holding an open court for that purpose; the town clerk attending, and producing the lists and copy of the lists of claims and objections; and the overseers, vestry clerks, collectors of poor-rates, also being present, for the purpose of answering all necessary questions.

The court finally determines all claims and objections, and names are inserted, expunged, or retained, accordingly. This being completed, the burgess lists, thus revised and signed, are delivered by the mayor to the town clerk, who keeps them, and copies them into an alphabetical book, with every name numbered in a regular series. This book is to be completed on the 22d of October, and is called "The Burgess Roll."

It has been observed, that freemen and burgesses are still permitted to exist as a separate body *for certain purposes*, but the *future* admission to this separate body is limited to those who shall become entitled in respect of birth, servitude, or apprenticeship, or marriage; therefore, to preserve the evidence of their claims, a list is to be made by the town clerk of every borough on the 1st of December, yearly, of all those who have already been admitted burgesses or *freemen;* which list will in future comprise those who claim by birth or patrimony, apprenticeship or servitude, and marriage, as last observed. This list is called "The *Freemen's* Roll," and the examination of the claims is referred to the mayor, against whom the ancient remedy, by a writ of *mandamus*, will still lie, in case of a refusal to admit the applicant as a freeman. The roll may be perused at all reasonable times, without fee, and the town clerk is bound to deliver a copy on a reasonable price being tendered.

This "freemen's roll" does not distinguish those freemen who are entitled to vote for members of parliament. The town clerk, or other person executing his functions, is required, by the 46th section of the Reform Act, to prepare and publish the lists of freemen entitled to vote, and he must still do it by a separate list.

2. *The Election of Councillors next takes place.*—The qualification of a councillor is the being entitled to be on the burgess roll, and, in boroughs of four or more wards, being possessed of an estate to the value of 1000*l.*, or being rated to the poor upon an annual value of 30*l.*; and in boroughs not divided into wards, or being divided into less than four, the being possessed of an estate to the amount of 500*l.*, or rated to the poor upon an annual value of not less than 15*l.*

The number of councillors is a number divisible by 3, for, on the 1st of November, in every year, one third part of the whole number of councillors go out of office; those going out who have been longest in office without re-election, for any councillor going out of office may be forthwith re-elected if then qualified.

The election of councillors takes place on the 1st of November, yearly, when so many are chosen as will supply the places of those going out of office; and is held before the mayor and two assessors, or, in case of the death or incapacity of the mayor, before an alderman appointed by the council; and in case an equality of votes for two or more persons, the mayor and assessors are to name from such persons so many as shall be necessary to complete the requisite number;—for instance, if ten councillors are to be chosen, and there are eleven voted for, of which eight have a clear majority of votes over the other three, between whom there is an equality of votes, the mayor and assessors are to name two out of the three.

A list of the persons elected as councillors is published by the mayor, not later than two o'clock on the day next but one after the election, and allowing for an intervening Sunday; and the voting papers may be inspected at the town clerk's office, by any burgess, for six months at least, upon payment of 1*s.*

3. The aldermen, who are in number one fourth part of the councillors, are elected on the 9th of November in every third year, computed from the 9th of November, 1838, on which day one half of the aldermen go out of office, and the number filled up by a new election, the half going out of office being always those who have been in office longest without re-election. The *council, i. e.* the mayor, the half of the aldermen remaining in office, and the councillors, electing sufficient to supply the places of those going out.

Extraordinary vacancies in the office of councillor and alderman are filled up by a new election; the person elected to supply the vacancy only staying in office until the time when his predecessor would have gone out of office.

4. The mayor is to be elected by the *council, i. e.* by the mayor, aldermen, and councillors, out of the aldermen or councillors. His election takes place on the 9th of November, and he continues in office one year. He is, by virtue of his office, a justice of the peace during the year of his office and the next year, and returning officer in cities and boroughs returning members to parliament, not being counties of themselves; and he is entitled to a salary. In case of a vacancy by death, or refusal, the aldermen and councillors are, within ten days, to elect another person for the remainder of the current year.

The *auditors* and *assessors* are elected on the 1st of March, yearly, by the burgesses, from the persons qualified to be councillors (being burgesses), who continue in office one year. The form and manner of their election, and the filling up a vacancy, are the same as the election and filling up the vacancies with respect to councillors, only a burgess is limited to one vote for an auditor and one for an assessor. The duties of the auditors are very important. They audit the accounts of the corporation, and guard against any misappropriation of the borough fund. The assessors are to act with the mayor in the revision of the burgess lists, and in the election of councillors, auditors, and assessors.

It is compulsory on every person elected to accept office, if duly qualified, or to pay a fine.

The town clerk (who is not to be a member of the council) is to be appointed by the council, and holds his office during pleasure. His duty is to advise the corporation in the absence of the recorder, and he acts as clerk at the meetings of the corporations; and they are to appoint, once in every year, a treasurer, who is likewise not to be a member of the council, who is to pay no money but under special directions.

Other necessary officers are appointed by the council, and removed by them.

On the 1st of November, yearly, the councils of the following cities and towns are empowered to appoint sheriffs, viz. — Oxford, Berwick-upon-Tweed, Bristol, Canterbury, Chester, Coventry, Exeter, Gloucester, Lichfield, Lincoln, Norwich, Worcester, York, Caermarthen, Haverfordwest, Kingston-upon-Hull, Newcastle-upon-Tyne, Nottingham, Poole, and Southampton, — who are to execute the office in the accustomed manner.

No person can be lawfully registered as a burgess, who, within a year preceding the 31st of August, shall have received parochial relief, or alms, or any charitable allowance from the borough funds; but medical assistance, or instruction in an endowed school, does not disqualify.

No person in holy orders, or any dissenting minister, can be elected councillor, alderman, or mayor, or any person holding any other office than that of mayor in the disposal of the council, nor while sharing directly or indirectly in any contract or employment from the council; but being a shareholder in any company lighting or supplying with water or insuring from fire in the borough, will not operate as a disqualification.

Any mayor, alderman, or councillor, being declared bankrupt, insolvent, or compounding with his creditors, or being absent during his mayoralty for more than two months, or an alderman six months (illness excepted), becomes disqualified and liable to a fine, as for non-acceptance of office, and the council are thereupon to declare the office to be void by a written notice; but any such person, on obtaining his certificate, or on payment of his debts in full, or on his return, may be re-elected.

Every person elected a mayor, alderman, councillor, auditor, or assessor, must subscribe a declaration of his acceptance of office, and a promise to fulfil its duties; if qualified by estate only, that he is possessed accordingly to the requisite amount; and on or before admission, make and subscribe the declaration required by the Test Act, and take the oaths of supremacy and allegiance, or, if a Catholic, the oath appointed in lieu thereof. Aldermen may, once in three years, be required to re-subscribe their declaration of qualification. The breach of these forms disqualifies the party, and subjects him to a penalty of 50*l*.

The penalty upon persons acting as mayor, alderman, councillor, auditor, or assessor, after disqualification, is 50*l*. Persons convicted of bribery at any election in the borough are subject to the same penalty, and are perpetually disqualified from voting in any parliamentary or *other* election, and forfeits his franchise as a burgess; but no person is liable to the penalty or incapacity of voting unless a prosecution be commenced in two years from the time of incurring the penalty; and offenders discovering others offending in the same manner are discharged from all penalties or disabilities in respect of the offence. There is, however, a very important direction in this act, applicable to the larger boroughs, which are all in schedule A. of the act; and that is, their division into wards, and the assigning a number of councillors to each, which number, for the reason before mentioned, must be a number divisible by 3.

In such boroughs, divided into wards, the burgesses in each ward are, on the 1st of November, separately to elect the whole number of councillors assigned to each ward, one third of whom go out of office by annual rotation; and these ward councillors will, when elected, form part of the general body of the councillors of the borough. Assessors are likewise, on the 1st of March, yearly, to be chosen by the burgesses for each ward. The persons presiding at the ward elections are to be one alderman and the two assessors of the ward: the assessors who revise the burgess lists, with the mayor, being the assessors of the mayor's ward; all other proceedings being assimilated to the elections for councillors or assessors of the whole borough.

Burgesses are only to vote in the ward in which they are registered, the burgess roll being made out in lists of each ward, called "Ward Lists." If a person is elected a councillor or assessor in two wards at once, the mayor is to declare in what ward he is to serve.

Vacancies in the office of councillor or assessor, occurring in the wards, are supplied in a similar manner to undivided boroughs, the aldermen and assessors taking the place of a mayor.

After the borough has had its full complement of councillors, there can be no election to supply a vacancy, as long as the remaining number exceed two thirds of the whole number of the council.

The general meetings of the council are directed to be held quarterly, one on the 9th of November, and the other three on such days as shall, on the 9th of November, be appointed; and of those meetings no *public* notice need be given, as the proceedings are entered in a book, to which access can be had. But extraordinary meetings may be called by the mayor upon his own direction, or, on his refusal, upon a requisition signed by five councillors, who give the same public notice which the mayor would have been obliged to give, *i. e.* a notice signed by him, fixed on or near the town-hall door three clear days before the meeting; and in addition, they must give,—what, it seems, is not imperative upon the mayor,—a notice of the business to be transacted, and also give a summons specifying the business to be transacted (signed by the town clerk), to be left, three clear days before the meeting, at the usual place of abode of every member of the council, or at the premises in respect of which he derives his qualification.

At all meetings, the mayor, or, in his absence, an alderman, or, in the absence of all the aldermen, a councillor specially chosen, presides, and has a second or casting vote. The minutes are entered in a book signed by the president, and open to every burgess upon payment of 1*s.*

The council, being the mayor, aldermen, and councillors, exercise those powers which were previously inherent to the privileges of every corporate town. They have power, subject to revision by her majesty in council, to make bye laws for the government of the borough, and suppression of nuisances; and to appoint in certain cases a coroner, not a member of the council. They have the regulation of the borough courts of record, police, and gaols; the management of the revenues of the corporation; and have the powers of certain trustees, under paving and lighting; and other acts transferred to them. They may make rates, and, upon petition to her majesty in council, may have quarter sessions, with a recorder (who is the sole judge), and other appendages necessary for the execution of justice. On the other hand, they are liable to the county rate, and to pay the overseers for their lists, and discharge their share of prosecutions at the assizes, for felonies and misdemeanors committed within the borough; to the salaries of their recorder, mayor, officers, and payment of all corporate expenses; and bound to account for the surplus funds, which are to be expended in the improvement of the borough. As trustees for charitable purposes, they only act provisionally, and till the administration of those funds is provided for by parliament.

The county justices have jurisdiction in boroughs to which a separate quarter sessions is not assigned. The mayor, we have observed, is a justice during his office, and for one year afterwards; and her majesty's commission may issue appointing justices in boroughs, which, upon the petition of the council, are entitled to a separate commission of the peace, who are to have salaries; but, though barristers, not to sit at *general* quarter sessions, or at any court of general gaol delivery. The queen can still grant charters of incorporation upon petition of the householders of any town; which charters will be, if granted, subject to the provisions of this act, as far as the circumstances of this new borough are applicable.

All capital jurisdictions, and criminal jurisdictions, and exemptions from the admiralty jurisdiction, other than those specified in the act, are abolished, saving the privileges of the Cinque Ports, and excepting also the adjudication upon salvage rights. See CINQUE PORTS, SALVAGE; also see BOROUGH COURTS OF RECORD, BY-LAWS, CLERK OF THE PEACE, CORONER, POLICE, POLLING BOOTHS.

The boroughs and towns upon which this act has operation, are in the two following schedules (A.) and (B.): the style of each now now being "the mayor, alderman, and burgesses of———" [the following cities and towns].

SCHEDULE (A.)—England and Wales.

Boroughs which are to have a Commission of the Peace.

Section I. Parliamentary Boundaries to be taken until altered by Parliament.

Borough.	Wards.	Aldermen.	Councillors.	Borough.	Wards.	Aldermen.	Councillors.
Aberystwith - -	-	4	12	Macclesfield - -	6	12	36
Abingdon - -	-	4	12	Monmouth - -	-	4	12
Barnstaple - -	2	6	18	Neath - -	-	4	12
Bath - -	7	14	42	Newark - -	3	6	18
Bedford - -	2	6	18	Newcastle-under-Line	2	6	18
Berwick-upon-Tweed	3	6	18	Newcastle-upon-Tyne	7	14	42
Bridgewater - -	2	6	18	Newport (Monmouth)	2	6	18
Bridport - -	2	6	18	Newport (Isle of Wight) - -	2	6	18
Bristol - -	10	16	48	Northampton - -	3	6	18
Bury St. Edmond's -	3	6	18	Norwich - -	8	16	48
Cambridge - -	5	10	30	Nottingham : -	7	14	42
Canterbury - -	3	6	18	Oxford - -	5	10	30
Cardiff - -	2	6	18	Pembroke - -	2	6	18
Carlisle - -	5	10	30	Poole - -	2	6	18
Caermarthen - -	3	6	18	Portsmouth - -	7	14	42
Carnarvon - -	2	6	18	Preston - -	6	12	36
Chester - -	5	10	30	Reading - -	3	6	18
Chichester - -	2	6	18	Ripon - -	-	4	12
Colchester - -	3	6	18	Rochester - -	3	6	18
Dartmouth - -	-	4	12	St. Alban's - -	-	4	12
Denbigh - -	-	4	12	Sarum, New [Salisbury] - -	3	6	18
Derby - -	6	12	36	Scarborough - -	2	6	18
Devizes - -	2	6	18	Shrewsbury - -	5	10	30
Dorchester - -	-	4	12	Southampton - -	5	10	30
Dover - -	3	6	18	Stafford - -	2	6	18
Durham - -	3	6	18	Stamford - -	2	6	18
Evesham - -	-	4	12	Stockport - -	7	14	42
Gateshead - -	3	6	18	Sudbury - -	-	4	12
Gloucester - -	3	6	18	Sunderland - -	7	14	42
Guildford - -	-	4	12	Swansea - -	3	6	18
Harwich - -	-	4	12	Tiverton - -	3	6	18
Haverfordwest -	-	4	12	Truro - -	2	6	18
Hereford - -	3	6	18	Warwick - -	2	6	18
Hertford - -	-	4	12	Wells - -	-	4	12
Ipswich - -	5	10	30	Weymouth and Melcombe Regis -	2	6	18
Kendal - -	3	6	18	Wigan - -	5	10	30
Kidderminster -	3	6	18	Winchester - -	3	6	18
Kingston-upon-Hull	7	14	42	Windsor - -	2	6	18
King's Lynn - -	3	6	18	Worcester - -	6	12	36
Leeds - -	12	16	48	Yarmouth, Great -	6	12	36
Leicester - -	7	14	42				
Leominster - -	-	4	12				
Lichfield - -	2	6	18				
Liverpool - -	16	16	48				

SCHEDULE (A.) — (*continued*).

SECTION II. — Municipal Boundaries to be taken until altered by Parliament.

Borough.	Wards.	Aldermen.	Councillors.	Borough.	Wards.	Aldermen.	Councillors.
Andover - -	-	4	12	Lincoln - -	3	6	18
Banbury - -	-	4	12	Liskeard - -	-	4	12
Beverley - -	2	6	18	Louth - -	2	6	18
Bewdley - -	-	4	12	Ludlow - -	-	4	12
Bideford - -	-	4	12	Maidstone - -	3	6	18
Boston - -	3	6	18	Maldon - -	-	4	12
Brecon - -	-	4	12	Newbury - -	-	4	12
Bridgnorth - -	-	4	12	Oswestry - -	2	6	18
Clitheroe - -	-	4	12	Penzance - -	2	6	18
Chesterfield - -	-	4	12	Plymouth - -	6	12	36
Congleton - -	3	6	18	Pontefract - -	-	4	12
Coventry - -	6	12	36	Richmond - -	-	4	12
Deal - -	2	6	18	Romsey - -	-	4	12
Doncaster - -	3	6	18	St. Ives - -	-	4	12
Exeter - -	6	12	36	Saffron Walden -	-	4	12
Falmouth - -	-	4	12	Stockton - -	2	6	18
Grantham - -	-	4	12	Tewkesbury - -	-	4	12
Gravesend - -	2	6	18	Walsall - -	3	6	18
Grimsby - -	-	4	12	Welchpool - -	-	4	12
Hastings - -	3	6	18	Wenlock - -	3	6	18
Kingston-upon-Thames - -	3	6	18	Wisbeach - -	2	6	18
				York - -	6	12	36
Lancaster - -	3	6	18				

SCHEDULE (B.)—ENGLAND AND WALES.

Boroughs which are not to have a Commission of the Peace unless on Petition and Grant.

SECTION I. Parliamentary Boundaries to be taken until altered by Parliament.

Borough.	Wards.	Aldermen.	Councillors.	Borough.	Wards.	Aldermen.	Councillors.
Arundel - -	-	4	12	Ruthin - -	-	4	12
Beaumaris - -	-	4	12	Tenby - -	-	4	12
Cardigan - -	-	4	12	Thetford - -	-	4	12
Llanidloes - -	-	4	12	Totnes - -	-	4	12
Pwllheli - -	-	4	12				

SECTION II. Municipal Boundaries to be taken until altered by Parliament.

Borough.	Wards.	Aldermen.	Councillors.	Borough.	Wards.	Aldermen.	Councillors.
Basingstoke - -	-	4	12	Calne - -	-	4	12
Beccles -	-	4	12	Chard - -	-	4	12
Blandford Forum -	-	4	12	Chippenham - -	-	4	12
Bodmin - -	-	4	12	Chipping Norton -	-	4	12
Buckingham - -	-	4	12	Daventry - -	-	4	12

SECTION 2. Municipal Boundaries, &c. (*continued*).

Borough.	Wards.	Aldermen.	Councillors.	Borough.	Wards.	Aldermen.	Councillors.
Droitwich - -	-	4	12	Marlborough - -	-	4	12
Eye - - -	-	4	12	Morpeth - -	-	4	12
Faversham - -	-	4	12	Penryn - -	-	4	12
Folkstone - -	-	4	12	Retford, East -	-	4	12
Flint - -	-	4	12	Rye - - -	-	4	12
Glastonbury - -	-	4	12	Sandwich - -	-	4	12
Godalming - -	-	4	12	Shaftesbury - -	-	4	12
Godmanchester -	-	4	12	South Wold - -	-	4	12
Helstone - -	-	4	12	South Molton - -	-	4	12
Huntingdon - -	-	4	12	Stratford-on-Avon -	-	4	12
Hythe - -	-	4	12	Tamworth - -	-	4	12
Launceston - -	-	4	12	Tenterden - -	-	4	12
Llandovery - -	-	4	12	Torrington - -	-	4	12
Lyme Regis - -	-	4	12	Wallingford - -	-	4	12
Lymington - -	-	4	12	Wycombe, Chepping	-	4	12
Maidenhead - -	-	4	12				

CORRUPTION OF BLOOD. An ideal infection which, in contemplation of law, attached upon all persons committing felony, rendering their heirs incapable of inheriting or claiming through them: by this fiction, the heir was rendered incapable of taking his parent's land, which, together with his goods, were forfeited to the superior lord, not then unfrequently, and now almost always, the queen. However, this corruption is taken away by a late act, the felon only forfeiting his life estate and his goods, except in cases of high treason or murder, in which the law remains unaltered. See FORFEITURE OF GOODS.

COSTS. In almost all cases where a man recovers debt or damages, he is entitled to recover his expenses or *costs*, which consist of fees payable to the officers of the courts, counsel, and attornies. And where a defendant has a verdict, or the plaintiff discontinues his suit, he is, on the other hand, entitled to his costs, and *execution* may be levied for them.

Costs may be considered either as between *attorney and client*, being what are payable in every case to the attorney by his client, whether he succeed or not; or as between *party and party*, being those costs only which are allowed in some particular cases to the party succeeding against his adversary. In either case they are assessed, or, as it is termed, *taxed*, by one of the masters of the court, before they are leviable upon either party by execution in the suit in which they have accrued.

But the plaintiff's general right to costs is, for the purposes of moral justice, limited by various statutes, which have for their object the prevention of trifling and malicious actions for *words*, for *assault and battery*, and for *trespass*, so that where the jury who try any of these actions shall give less damages than 40*s*. the plaintiff shall be allowed no more costs than damages, *unless* the judge before whom the cause is tried shall *certify* under his hand, on the back of the record, that an *actual battery* (and not an assault only) was proved, or that in trespass the *freehold* or *title* of the land came chiefly in question: but there is also another exception; as a verdict for wilful and malicious trespasses, or trespasses in hunting by inferior tradesmen, always carry costs, although less than 40*s*. be given.

If actions for *debt* be brought against defendants living within the jurisdiction of courts of request, for sums less than 40*s*., the plaintiff cannot recover costs; but to this there are some exceptions, which will be noticed under the tit. COURTS OF CONSCIENCE.

Where the defendant is arrested, and the plaintiff does not recover the amount of the sum for which the defendant is arrested, the defendant is entitled to costs, provided it appears on affidavit that the plaintiff had not reasonable or probable cause for arresting the defendant for that amount.

Costs are not given to informers in actions brought by them upon penalties, unless the act in question expressly gives them.

Costs in equity are given according to discretion: they do not attach as a mere matter of right; they follow the conscience of the court according to the special circumstances of the case, and very often are payable out of a fund in the cause, over which the court may have a control.

COVENANT. The agreement of two or more by deed under seal, whereby either or one of the parties promises to the other that something is done already, or shall be done afterwards. He that makes the covenant, is called the *covenantor;* and he to whom it is made, the *covenantee*. A *covenant* is generally either *in fact* or *in law*. In *fact*, is that which is expressly agreed between the parties, and inserted in the deed. In *law*, is that covenant which the law intends and implies, though it be not expressed in words; as if a lessor demise and grant to his lessee a house or lands for a certain term, the law will intend a covenant on the lessor's part, that the lessee shall, during the term, quietly enjoy the same against all incumbrances.

Covenant is also the name of an action adapted for the recovery of damages for the breach of any deed or covenant.

COTTONS, PRINTED. See PRINTED LINEN, &c.

COUNTY, or SHIRE. A district containing a circuit or portion of the kingdom, into which the whole land is divided for the better government of it, and the more easy administration of justice; so that there is no part of the kingdom which lies not within some county, and every county is governed by a yearly officer, — the sheriff. Of these counties the numbers have been different at different times: there are now in England 40, besides 12 in Wales (6 in North Wales, and 6 in South Wales), making in all 52. It is said that this division of the kingdom was made by King Alfred.

Many of these counties are subdivided, for the purposes of representation in parliament by election, by a statute called the Boundary Act. (See tit. PARLIAMENT.) And for the purposes of government, by quarter sessions and petty sessions of the justices, by two other acts.

There are three counties termed *palatine* — Chester, Durham, and Lancaster — because the bishop of Durham, the earl of Chester, and the duke of Lancaster had those counties as feudal dominions, they holding immediately of the crown; and two of these still have a species of separate jurisdiction, viz. Durham and Lancaster; the jurisdiction of the county palatine of Chester being lately abolished. The courts of Durham and Lancaster are reckoned among the superior courts:

they decide questions on debts and property, and the judges of assize sit therein by virtue of a special commission.

Some counties are also *corporate*, being certain cities and towns (12 cities and 5 towns) which by charter are counties of themselves, and are not comprised in any other county, being governed by their own sheriffs and magistrates.

By the *Reform* Act, thirteen cities and towns, which are counties of themselves, are, for the purposes of representation, included in the adjoining counties. See schedule G. of the act.

COUNTY COURT. There are two courts of this name; one being the ordinary court for pleas of debt under 40*s*., and to any amount above 40*s*. by *plaint* or writ of *justicies* (but in this case there is no process against the *person* of the defendant, only against his goods). Under 40*s*., the county court has power in Middlesex, and *sometimes* elsewhere, to arrest the person of the defendant by virtue of particular acts of parliament, which put it on a level with courts of request generally. (See COURTS OF CONSCIENCE.) The other court is called the tourn, or turn, and is a public assembly held twice in every year, viz., within a month after Easter and Michaelmas, where constables are chosen, high constables, or bailiffs of hundreds, &c.

COUNTY RATES. Rates which are levied upon the county, and collected by the high constables of hundreds, and by them paid to treasurers appointed by the justices, for the purpose of repairing bridges, gaols, or houses of correction, prosecutors' and witnesses' expenses, and purposes of public convenience. By a recent statute, all business relating to the assessment and application of county rates shall be transacted at the quarter sessions, in open court, and two weeks' notice shall be given by advertisement in two county papers of the time of holding such sessions, and of the day and hour when such business will be transacted.

COURTS, are places where justice is administered. There are a great number of courts, the jurisdiction of some of which, especially the greater ones, are in some respects co-extensive and concurrent with each other; others have a more limited jurisdiction, and are either subordinate to or controlled by the superior courts. Some administer the law as between party and party; others as between the king and his subjects, in respect of criminal offences. However, the chief legal distinction exists between such courts as are *of record* and such as are *not of record*: the first being those which are held by course of common law in pleas of or above 40*s*., with power to fine or imprison; the second are chiefly those which are subject to the control of other courts when they exceed their jurisdiction. These are subdivided into courts superior and courts inferior. The courts superior are the lords' house of parliament, the chancery, queen's bench, common pleas, and exchequer; then, those courts holden by commission, such as gaol delivery, assizes, &c., central criminal court for London and its environs, and nisi prius; then courts established by custom or charter, such as the courts of Lancaster, Durham, or marshalsea, or by acts of parliament, as the courts of bankruptcy or insolvency; lastly, such courts as act by virtue of the queen's commission and acts of parliament, as the quarter sessions, court of sewers, courts of conscience, &c.

The courts not of record, are the courts of equity, courts baron, county courts, hundred courts, &c.

The inferior courts of record, are corporation courts, courts leet, and what is termed the sheriff's tourn.

From these divisions and distinctions questions sometimes arise, but they are mostly referrible to the question above stated, viz., how far are they subject to the control of the king's superior courts?

For the purposes of ordinary information, courts of judicature are either—1. Civil, or 2. Criminal.

The superior courts, or, as they are frequently termed, "The Courts of Westminster," are those of law and equity. Of the former, are the queen's bench, the common pleas, and the exchequer. As far as regards the recovery of debts, or damages, the jurisdiction and process of these courts are similar, and governed by much the same principles.

The courts of equity *, principally for enforcing mere *equitable* claims, or claims in some respects imperfect at law, and for giving effect to *mere equitable* defences, are the court of chancery, held before the chancellor, the court of the master of the rolls, the vice-chancellor's court, and the equity side of the court of exchequer, holden before the chief baron, or before one other of the barons.

The *ecclesiastical* courts have jurisdiction principally over rights and injuries, private or public, of a *spiritual* or *ecclesiastical* nature; as questions upon the legality of a marriage and the propriety of divorce, and the right of a wife to alimony; questions relative to wills of personal property, probates, letters of administration, legacies, and distribution of assets; defamation, imputing a *spiritual* offence, *i. e.* fornication, lewdness, &c. and not actionable or punishable at law; and certain spiritual offences themselves, as adultery, incest, fornication, brawling in churches, and many other offences against religion or morality. The courts are principally the archdeacon's, consistory, peculiars, arches, and prerogative courts. The practice of these courts is noticed under the tit. PRACTICE.

The court of *exchequer chamber* is a court of *error*, for revising the judgments of the three superior courts of *law* in matters of *law*, and is holden before the judges of the two other courts not concerned in the judgment impeached. The judges of the court of common pleas, together with the barons of the exchequer, constitute the court of error, upon a writ of error from the judgment of the court of queen's bench; and the judges of the queen's bench, together with the barons of the exchequer, constitute the court of error upon a writ of error in the judgment of common pleas; and the judges of queen's bench and of common pleas constitute the court of error from a judgment of the court of exchequer.

The high court of parliament is a court of error, not only from judgments in error of the court of exchequer chamber, but also the court of appeal from decrees and proceedings in chancery.

The court of error, or appeal, from the decrees and proceedings of the superior ecclesiastical courts and the court of admiralty, courts of judicature in the East Indies, colonies in America, and other British dominions abroad, is the judicial committee of the privy council, which is composed of—1. The president of the council; 2. The chancellor, or first lord commissioner of the great seal; 3. The chief justice of the king's bench; 4. The master of the rolls; 5. The vice-chancellor; 6. The chief justice of the common pleas; 7. The lord chief baron; 8. The judge of the prerogative court; 9. The judge of the high court of admiralty; 10. The chief judge in bankruptcy; 11. The members

* *Chitty's Practice of the Law.*

of the privy council, who shall have held any of the offices before-mentioned; 12. *Two* other privy councillors, appointed by her majesty, who shall have held the office of judge in the East Indies, or any of the queen's dominions beyond seas; 13. *Any other* members whom her majesty may summon. Four members constitute a quorum.

The courts of bankruptcy and review. See BANKRUPTCY, COURT OF.

2. The court of queen's bench is the most extensive of all the courts, for it not only has cognizance of all civil injuries, but has the supreme criminal jurisdiction, and also the control of public proceedings; therefore this ranks first as a court of criminal justice.

The courts of assize, gaol delivery, oyer and terminer, &c., holden by commission for each circuit, twice in the year, and once in the winter for the home circuit.

The central criminal court, constituted for the purpose of administering justice in criminal matters in London, Middlesex, and certain parishes near London.

The court of quarter sessions, holden for each county.

Courts of corporate cities, who by charter are empowered to try all offenders within their precincts, borough courts of quarter sessions, courts of petty sessions of justices, courts leet, police courts or offices in towns and cities, where magistrates exercise, by virtue of many acts of parliament, summary jurisdiction over offences of a light character, in addition to their provisional functions.

See titles KING'S BENCH, COMMON PLEAS, EXCHEQUER, CHANCERY, SPIRITUAL COURTS, ADMIRALTY, PRIVY COUNCIL, QUARTER SESSIONS, ASSIZES, JUSTICES, MARSHALSEA, COURTS OF CONSCIENCE.

COURTS MARTIAL, are courts who sit in pursuance of martial and naval articles of war.

They are amenable for damages (individually) to any person injured, for the consequence of any unjust sentence. Lieutenant Frye, of the marines, in 1746, brought his action against the president of a court martial, and recovered damages, and sued the other members, who, reflecting in intemperate language on the chief justice of the common pleas, were committed. See *Gazette* of Nov. 15. 1746.

COURTS OF CONSCIENCE. Courts for the recovery of debts, mostly under 40s., and consequently beneath the notice of the superior courts; but some extend to *5l.* and upwards, to *10l.*, and in Bristol to *20l.* They appear to have been modelled upon the plan of the county courts and hundred courts, but have an extended jurisdiction; for they can award execution against the person, which those courts cannot. The county court is by no means superseded by those courts which have local jurisdictions; in Middlesex, the county court for recovery of debts under 40*s.* is assimilated to these courts. The number of courts of request now instituted, not including other courts, such as the county courts and chartered courts, are about 60, and are instituted by various acts of parliament in populous and commercial districts. These courts are directed by commissioners, except in Middlesex, where the sheriff appoints a barrister as his deputy in the various courts for the hundreds in his county. If persons sue in other courts, where the defendant is within the jurisdiction of one of these courts, he is deprived of costs; and in some cases the plaintiff is liable to pay costs to the defendant; and, generally speaking, both parties must be living within the limits of the court; but these rules vary, there being an act of parliament for each particular court.

CREDIT, LETTER OF. Sometimes termed a bill of credit, because it is by merchant-law a contract as binding as a bill of exchange, and indeed resembles it in many particulars, save its negotiability. The following form of a *special* letter of credit is taken from Marius's "Advice concerning Bills of Exchange:" the date and style is given to show its long usage. With a slight variation in the address, it is perfectly applicable to the purposes of the present time.

"Mr. William M.

"Sir, Laus Deo, in London, this 29th of February, 1654.

"*My last unto you was of the* 12 *January, wherein I wrote you what needful in answer to yours of the* 7*th of the same month.* This serves chiefly to desire you to furnish and pay unto Mr. John G., English gentleman, to the value of two thousand crowns, at one or more times as he shall have occasion, and desire the same of you, taking his receipt or *bills of exchange* for the monies which you shall so furnish him with, and put it to my account. And this my letter of credit shall be your sufficient warrant for so doing. Vale.

"To Mr. William M. "Yours, Thomas P.

"Merchant, at Paris."

The words in italics serve to identify the writer, and therefore, supersede the necessity of a letter of advice, which otherwise would be sent. A *general* letter of credit is an open writing or letter to the same purport, but is directed to all merchants or more than one in a particular place, and makes the writer responsible for the bills of exchange that are drawn upon him by the merchants who furnish the bearer of the letter with money or goods, although the writer does not accept, or refuses to accept, such bills.

CRUELTY to animals is punishable by a recent act, which declares that any person wantonly and cruelly beating, ill-treating, abusing, or torturing any horse, mare, gelding, bull, ox, cow, heifer, steer, calf, mule, ass, sheep, lamb, dog, or any *other* cattle or domestic animal, or improperly driving the same, whereby any mischief shall be done, shall upon conviction be fined or imprisoned. That any person keeping or using any house, room, pit, ground, or other place for running, baiting, or fighting any bull, bear, badger, dog, or other animal (whether of a domestic or wild nature or kind), or for cock-fighting, shall be liable to a penalty of *5l.* for every day he shall so keep and use the same. That persons impounding cattle or animals shall provide them with sufficient food, and may recover the amount from the owner, with penalty for neglect, and remedies for recovery thereof.

That if any cattle or animal shall remain impounded for more than twenty-four hours without sufficient daily food, any person may enter the pound and supply such food, &c.

That all horses or cattle brought to slaughter-houses shall be killed within three days, and in the mean time be provided with good and sufficient daily food.

It also provides that one half of the penalties for offences against the provisions of the act shall go to the informers, and renders greater facility in the apprehension and punishment of offenders. See DROVERS.

CUMULATIVE, or ACCUMULATIVE, signifies *additional*, and is applied to judgments or sentences, which add or impose an additional punishment to commence after the expiration of the first, which formerly could only be done with persons convicted of misdemeanor, but now in all cases of felony; for instance, if a man is convicted, or is under sentence of seven years' transportation, on a second conviction he is now liable to be sentenced to an additional term of seven or fourteen years, or for life, as the case may be. This term is also applied to the additional legal remedy a person is sometimes entitled to, upon a wrong done him, as an indictment for the breach of social order, and an action at law for damages, which, in some instances, will attach upon offences not felonies. A legacy is said to be cumulative, where an intention is apparent that the legatee should receive two sums, or that the thing given should accumulate.

CURATE. He who represents the incumbent of a church, parson or vicar, and takes *care* of divine service in his stead; in case of pluralities of livings, or where a clergyman is old and infirm, it is requisite there should be a curate to perform the cure of the church. He is to be licensed and admitted by the bishop of the diocese, or by an ordinary having episcopal jurisdiction; and when a curate hath the approbation of the bishop, he usually appoints the salary too; and in such case, if he be not paid, the curate hath a proper remedy in the ecclesiastical court, by a sequestration of the profits of the benefice, but if he hath no licence from the bishop, he is put to his remedy at common law, where he must prove the agreement, &c. But, by a particular act, the bishops are empowered to license curates, and to assign them salaries in no case less than 80*l.* a year, and increasing up to 150*l.* according to the population of the parish, &c. The occupation of the parsonage house may, in certain cases, be assigned to the curate, who is not to quit his curacy without three months' notice to the incumbent and the bishop. These regulations are to operate on persons having become incumbents after July 20th, 1813, and in case only of the non-residence of the incumbent on his living for more than three months in the year.

There are *perpetual curates*, as well as temporary, who are appointed where tithes are impropriate, and no vicarage endowed; these are not removeable, and the impropriators are obliged to find them, some whereof have certain portions of the tithes settled on them.

No curate (or minister) ought to perform the duties of any church before he has obtained a licence from the bishop.

CUSTOM, is a law or right not written, which, being established by long use and the consent of our ancestors, hath been and is daily practised. If it is to be proved by record, the continuance of a hundred years will serve. *Custom* is either *general* or *particular*. General, when allowed through all England.

Particular, is that which belongs to this or that county or manor; as *gavelkind* to *Kent*, *borough-English* to *Lambeth*.

General customs, which are used throughout *England*, and are the common law, are to be determined by the judges; but *particular customs*, such as are used in some certain towns, boroughs, cities, &c., shall be determined by a jury. But the judges of the courts of queen's bench and common pleas can overrule a custom, though it be one of the customs of *London*, if it be against natural reason or the general good.

The requisites of a custom are, antiquity, continuance, acquiescence, reasonableness, certainty, and consistency. To which may be added, that they must be *compulsory*, although established by consent, for an optional custom is no custom at all. Concerning the customs of London, see LONDON; also see PRESCRIPTION.

CUSTOM-HOUSE. The house or office where exports and imports are entered, and where the duties, drawbacks, and bounties payable or receivable, are settled; and where ships are, as it is termed, *cleared out*. The principal office is in Thames-street, near the Tower, London. There are minor or subordinate custom-houses in seaport towns.

CUSTOM-HOUSE BROKERS, are persons authorised by the commissioners of customs to act for parties in the entry or clearance of ships, and the transaction of general business. They give bond to the commissioners in a sum of 1000*l.*, conditioned for their good conduct, and for the purpose of enabling restitution to be made of any loss accruing by their negligence or misconduct. However, the appointment of these persons, who are of good credit, does not prevent a party, or his clerk, from transacting his own business or affairs at the custom-house.

CUSTOMS, are duties charged on commodities on export or import. The customs are regulated by various acts, in which specific directions are given for the entry, discharging, and shipping of all goods, inwards and outwards, with certain prohibitions and restrictions as to the import and export of certain goods; also for regulating the *coasting trade*, which term designates *all trade by sea* from any one part of the United Kingdom to any other part thereof. Also see SMUGGLING, and NAVIGATION, and PLANTATION.

The management of the customs is regulated by various acts, and is under the direction of eleven commissioners. One for Scotland and Ireland, with two assistant commissioners; the latter acting under the control of the English commissioners, who are, in their turn, under the control of the lords of the treasury.

CUTTING and STABBING. See WOUNDING.

DATE OF A DEED, is the description of the time, viz. the day, month, year of our Lord, and year of the reign (but this last is not so usual as formerly) in which the deed was made. If there is no date to a deed, it can take effect from the signature or delivery.

A deed can be dated back, but not on a day that is to come, for that would render it void.* A deed also may be dated at one time, and signed, sealed, and delivered, or, as it is more concisely termed, *executed*, at another.

DAY. The legal or common day (as distinguished from the astronomical day) is a space of 24 hours, commencing from midnight. In law proceedings, if a fact be done in the night it is stated as being done in the night of such a day. In legal proceedings, generally, the law does not notice the particular time of a day when any act is done, unless it be an act which is criminal or penal from the circumstance of its being done by night. The law does not, except in cases of necessity, or in considering special and consecutive acts on *one* day, admit of any division or fraction of a day; therefore, when a thing is to be done on a particular day, the party has all that day, that is till 12 at night, to do it in. Upon this principle, a man cannot distrain for rent till the day after, that is, after sunrise on the day after that on which the rent was reserved or made payable.

The Burglary Act, 1 *Vict. c.* 86., declares, that so far as the same is

* Where a deed to which several persons were parties, purported to bear date on the 20th of November, and was executed by one of two defendants on the 16th of that month, and by the other on a previous day; it was held to be immaterial, it not appearing that a blank was left for the date at the time of the execution. *Cockell* v. *Gray*, 6 *Moore*, 482.

essential to the offence of burglary, the night shall be considered to commence at 9 o'clock in the evening of each day, and to conclude at 6 o'clock in the morning of the succeeding day.

DAYS OF GRACE. When a bill or note is payable at one or more usances, or at a certain time after date, or after sight, or after demand, it is not payable at the precise time, but three days of grace are allowed. This indulgence the acceptor can claim as a right; and it now seems to be settled that, in England, bills payable at sight or on demand have this indulgence. (*Roscoe on Bills.*)

A check, bill, or banker's note, having no day named, is payable on presentment.

DEATH. The death of a plaintiff or defendant in an action at law, causes it to *abate*, that is, to fall to the ground or cease. In a suit in chancery, if a party die, the suit is *revived* or renewed by or against the survivors.

The death of the holder of a bill of exchange does not supersede the necessity of protesting a bill of exchange or promissory note, or doing any act which charges the drawer or indorser with the payment, in default of the payment by the acceptor or maker of the bill or note. See Bill of Exchange, *Presentment.*

DEBATING SOCIETIES. See Lectures.

DEBT, is the title of an action which lies where one owes another a sum certain upon a specialty contract, or for any determinate sum whether upon specialty or simple contract, where the contract arose immediately between the plaintiff and defendant: so this action will not lie for an indorsee of a bill against the acceptor, as there is no immediate contract between them; but the indorsee shall have his action on the case upon the implied promise, more concisely termed an action on promises.

This action has some advantages in practice of a purely technical character, which need not be here noticed.

DECEIPT. See Fraud.

DECLARATION. See Practice.

It is also the designation of a species of deed where property is vested in a trustee, and the trustee, by the same or a separate deed, *declares*, *i. e.* acknowledges, the trusts or purposes of the deed, or the mode in which the property shall be applied.

DEFEAZANCE, is the condition or terms annexed to a warrant of attorney, or recognizance, differing in effect nothing from what is termed the condition of a bond.

DEED, is the general term applied to a contract under seal, and has its essence by sealing, signing, and delivery; which last is the manual or constructive giving it to the party, with or to whom the deed is made, and is generally presumed to be done where other essentials concur. Deeds are of various natures; deeds of lease, assignment, covenant, settlement, &c. See Contract.

A deed must be written on parchment or paper duly stamped, and must not be interlined or altered *after* the delivery.

Some deeds are required to be enrolled at length, as deeds of bargain and sale; some only should have a *memorial*, *i. e.* a memorandum, containing the date, parties, and land or property conveyed, enrolled, as lands and long leaseholds in York and Middlesex. A deed is a more general term than *conveyance*, which signifies only a deed conveying or assigning lands and houses.

DEER. Summary punishment may be imposed by fine, not exceeding 20*l.*, upon any person who shall have possession, or upon his premises, with his knowledge, any deer, or the head, skin, or other part thereof, or any snare or engine for the taking of deer, without satisfactorily accounting for such possession; or who shall set or use any snare or engine whatsoever, for the purpose of taking or killing deer, in any part of any forest, chase, or purlieu, whether inclosed or not, or in any fence or bank dividing the same from any land adjoining, or in any inclosed land where deer are usually kept, or shall destroy any part of the fence of any land where deer are then kept.

The hunting for deer in *inclosed* places, is a felony punishable as larceny. The hunting for deer in *uninclosed* places subjects the offender to a penalty not exceeding 50*l.*; the second offence to be deemed a felony, punishable as a simple larceny, *i. e.* by transportation for seven years, or imprisonment for a less term, and (if a male) whipping, at the discretion of the court.

Persons entering forests or places, whether inclosed or not, for the purpose of hunting deer, must give up their guns on demand, which can be seized in case of refusal. The beating of keepers is declared a felony, punishable as before. (7 *&* 8 *G.* 4. *c.* 29. *s.* 26—29.)

DEFAMATION. See Libel.

DEL CREDERE, Commission of. *Del credere* is an Italian mercantile phrase, signifying the same as the English term guarantee, or *warranty*, or the Scotch term warrandice; and, when applied to the situation of a factor, is understood in the following sense:—A factor who has general orders to dispose of goods for his principal to the best advantage, is, like all factors, liable only to that degree of diligence which a prudent man uses in his own affairs; and, consequently, a factor is authorised to dispose of the goods according to the best terms which can he obtained; and if it shall appear that he has done so, and that he has sold his goods to persons in *reputed* good circumstances at the time, and to whom he would reasonably have given credit in his own affairs, he will not be liable to his principal, although some of these persons should fail; and for such trouble, the factor is generally paid by a per centage upon the goods sold, and in this case the principal runs the risk of the credit of the person to whom the goods are so sold. Many merchants do not choose to run this risk, and to trust to the prudence and discretion of the factor; and therefore the agreement called *del credere* was invented, by which the factor, for an *additional premium*, when he sells goods on credit, becomes bound to warrant the solvency of the purchasers, and renders himself liable in all events for the payment of the price of the goods sold.

It should, however, be remembered, that a factor or broker, receiving *del credere* commission, is not primarily liable, that is, he is not to be had recourse to but after proceedings have been taken in vain against the purchaser of the goods, or his bankruptcy or insolvency; the law considering the *del credere* factor or broker but as a surety for the purchaser's payment to the owner of the goods. Therefore, where a purchaser has been sued by the owner, and nothing, or only a part recovered upon verdict, the factor is to be called upon to make up the deficiency; and in bankruptcy or insolvency the owner must prove his debt before he can call upon the factor for the balance, after payment of the dividend, or, what is more usual, the factor pays the whole demand, and proves as a surety upon the bankrupt's estate.

DEODAND. Any *personal* chattel, that is, any thing not forming part of the freehold by its annexation to house or land, which is forfeited by "moving to the death" of a person, no matter whether the owner were concerned in the killing or not, which killing is generally by an accident occasioned by negligence. In strictness, if the thing which kills is *in motion*, not only that part which gives the wound (as the wheel which runs over a man's body and kills him), but all things which move with it, and help to make the load more dangerous (as the cart and loading, which increase the pressure of the wheel), are forfeited. Where a thing *not in motion* is the occasion of a man's death, as if a man fall from a cart wheel, the thing alone, *i. e.* wheel, is forfeited. Where there does not appear to have been negligence in the owner, the jury will (though not strictly warrantable) mitigate the deodand. The deodand, viz. the produce of the sale, generally belongs or is forfeited to the queen, but, by prescription or custom, it may belong to the lord of a manor or franchise; in either case it should, by ancient law, be laid out in *pious*, *i. e.* charitable, uses, not for superstitious or even religious purposes.

DEPOSIT, is a *bailment* or delivery of goods to another to keep without reward. The *bailee*, *i. e.* the person to whom the goods are delivered, is only liable for *gross* neglect; but his duty is of a more serious nature, and he is responsible for ordinary neglect, if he *spontaneously* and *officiously* propose to keep the goods, or when he changes the description of his character, by taking the charge of the goods in consequence of any reward or lucrative contract. In such cases, however, the bailee is only bound to take the same care of the goods as he would of his own; and therefore, if, notwithstanding such care, they be stolen by his servants, he is not liable.

Where the bailee alone receives benefit from the deposit, he is liable for slight negligence.

DEPOSITARY. The person with whom any thing is deposited.

DESCENT. The transmission of real estates of inheritance, freehold or copyhold, by heirship or hereditary succession, which, in both cases, is governed by particular rules of law, and in many instances, in the latter, by special custom. The rules of descent having been lately altered in three important particulars by an act which took effect, in respect of descents after the 31st of December, 1833, renders it necessary that this subject should be noticed more fully than the object of this work would otherwise demand, as there are now two laws of inheritance, viz. one respecting descents before the 1st of January, 1834, and another regulating descents taking place on or after that day.

By the rules of common law, which is the ancient custom of the land, a real estate descends, on the death of the last proprietor, to the eldest or only son, or his descendants, if he should be dead leaving issue, and next to the second and other sons, according to priority of birth, and their descendants: in default of sons and their descendants, it descends to daughters in equal shares, if more than one, and to the descendants of any deceased daughter collectively; such descendants, therefore, taking the share which would have gone to the parent if living.

When there is no lineal descendant, the estate goes to the eldest or only brother of the *whole* blood, that is, to him who was born of the same father and mother as the deceased proprietor, and to his descendants, if he should be dead leaving issue, and to the other brothers in succession and their descendants. If there be no brother or descendants of a brother, the sisters of the *whole* blood succeed in equal shares, and the descendants of deceased sisters; such descendants taking their parents share as before.

In the case of the failure of brothers and sisters and their descendants, it becomes necessary to inquire whether the deceased proprietor took the estate himself by inheritance, termed *descent*, or whether he acquired it immediately by a deed or will, — in technical language, was a *purchaser*. In the former case (*i. e.* by *descent*) the heir is to be sought in the family from which the estate descended to the deceased proprietor, that is, on the father's side or on the mother's side, as it happened: in the latter case (*i. e.* by *purchase*) the law gives the preference to the relations on the paternal side; but if there be none such, then it directs the inheritance to go to the relations on the maternal side.

At this point a rule occurs, which is deduced from feodal principles, which is, that every lineal ancestor of a deceased proprietor, whether near (as father) or remote (as grandfather), is excluded from *immediately* inheriting. But the father may take his son's estate by an *intermediate* descent *; but sooner than the estate should go at once, or *immediately* as it is termed, to the father or mother of the deceased, the law directs it to escheat, *i. e.* go to the king if freehold, or to the lord of the manor if copyhold or ancient demesne, or in any way holden under him.

In default, however, of lineal and immediate collateral heirs and their descendants, the inheritance is to be traced *through* the nearest ancestor, that is, the father, unless it be a maternal inheritance, and if it be a maternal inheritance, *through* the mother; and therefore it will pass (by the old rule) to his or her eldest brother of the whole blood, or his descendants, and the other brothers in succession, and their descendants; and if none such, to sisters of the whole blood, and their descendants, in equal shares as before: on failure of this line, the next more remote ancestor on the same side is made the stock or root in the same manner, and then the next more remote, and so on; the rule being still observed that the paternal line has the preference in ascending from the first purchaser, and that up to the first purchaser the inheritance must be traced back through the line of ancestors by which it descended.

If heirs in the pure male line, ascending from the first purchaser, should fail, then, in compliance with the rule above stated, a female ancestor, or some ancestor of a female ancestor, is to be made the *stock*, *i. e.* the person through whom the descent is to be traced: and first, it is a rule that such female ancestor is to be taken on the paternal side, if any such can be found; and therefore the brother of the paternal grandmother (the father's mother) is preferred to the brother of the mother of the deceased proprietor, he having been the first purchaser; and the pedigree is still to be traced up as far as possible on the paternal side through males, and the female ancestor of the remotest male ancestor is to be preferred as a stock to the female ancestor of a less remote male ancestor; for instance, the paternal great-grandmother to the paternal grandmother.

On failure of relations on the paternal side of the first purchaser, the maternal line is let in, that is, the mother of the first purchaser is con-

* For instance, if the son has neither issue, nor brothers or sisters, the estate will descend to an uncle or some collateral relation to whom the father may, on his decease, be the next heir.

sidered as the stock, and her ancestors, first on the paternal and then on the maternal side, as before.

It is to be observed, that on failure of heirs of the last proprietor on the side of the first purchaser, the estate does not pass to the heirs of the last proprietor on the other side, but *escheats* as before ; so that an estate descended (the reader will mark the distinction between *descent* and *purchase*) to the deceased proprietor from his mother, can never pass to his collateral relations on the father's side.

It has been laid down in the above statement, that collateral relations, in order to be let in to inherit, must be of the *whole* blood of the person from or through whom they are to derive their claim. Thus, a brother of the deceased proprietor, by the same father but a different mother, cannot inherit to the deceased proprietor, whether he took by purchase or descent; the estate will rather escheat; and the same is the case with an uncle, half brother of the father, and so on. This rule, like that which excludes the lineal ancestor, has its origin in feodal principles, and, like the rule which excludes the father, is diametrically opposite to the course of distribution in personal property, where we shall see, under title "EXECUTORS," that the father takes the whole property of a deceased son, leaving no wife or issue, or the half if he leaves a widow; and that the half blood (*i. e.* issue by different wives) take the same proportion as those of the whole blood, *i. e.* those who have the same father and mother. This rule of not admitting the half blood to inherit as heirs to the whole blood, did not, however, extend to females ; for though they could not inherit to each other, yet they could take in common with the sisters of the whole blood, where the last proprietor was their father or other ancestor, whether lineal or collateral, as uncle, &c.

The reader will by this time have drawn the conclusion that the law of descent, as it stood at common law, and as it affects claims by descent where the last proprietor died on or before the 31st of December, 1833, depended, or does now depend, upon various circumstances.

1. Whether or not the last proprietor took his estate by *descent* or *purchase*.

2. That land could not lineally ascend, that is, the father or grandfather could not take "*immediately*" as heir to his child dying without issue; but that the brothers singly, or sisters collectively, or, if they failed, the uncles or aunts, or other collateral relations of his child, excluded him.

3. That the distinction of whole and half blood, and the prohibiting a lineal ancestor to inherit, created exceptions to the uniformity of descent, founded upon principles not generally understood, indeed, diametrically opposite to the feelings of the people.

With regard to the *first* question, which, being a strictly legal and technical distinction, raised matters of law which it is not expedient here to discuss, the present act provided that, from the 1st of January, 1834, a *descent* shall always be traced from the purchaser, but the last owner shall be considered to be the purchaser, unless the contrary be proved, that is, that such last owner inherited the title; in which case the descent must be traced from the last preceding proprietor or person entitled, from whom it can be proved the last owner inherited the same according to the laws of descent, who in his turn will be presumed in law to have taken by purchase and not by descent, until the contrary be proved ; and so on, without reference to any one particular ancestor, thereby confining the inquiry to a very narrow circle, and consequently demonstrating how far back the pedigree shall be deduced, and the course of descent to be adopted.

The *second* circumstance which breaks in upon the otherwise uniform course of descent at law, viz. that the lineal ancestor, *i. e.* the father or grandfather of a deceased proprietor, may not inherit, is, from the 1st of January, 1834, abolished; for by the statute it is provided that the lineal ancestor of a deceased proprietor without issue may be heir-at-law to him, in preference to the brothers or sisters of the deceased, or other collateral relations.

The *third* circumstance, viz. the distinction of whole blood and half blood is done away with from the 1st of January, 1834; so that in descents after that time, when the *whole blood* of the same degree, as brothers and sisters, is exhausted, the brothers and sisters of the half blood may succeed to the inheritance or title in the course of succession displayed in the annexed table of descents.

There is one more thing to be impressed on the reader's mind, which is, that by one of the rules of descent already alluded to, the lineal descendants, *in infinitum*, of a person deceased shall *represent* their ancestor; that is, shall stand in the same place as the person himself would have done, had he been living. Thus the child, grandchild, or great grandchild, either male or female, succeeds before a younger son, and so *in infinitum;* and these representatives shall take neither more nor less, but just so much as their principals would have done: as if there be two sisters, and one dies leaving six daughters, and then the father of the two sisters dies, without other issue, these six daughters shall take amongst them exactly as much as their mother would have done had she been living; that is, a moiety of the lands as coparceners, *i. e.* co-heiresses; so that, upon a division made, if the land be divided into twelve parts, the surviving sister shall have six parts, and her six nieces one part each, or one half to the surviving sister, and the other half to the nieces. This taking by representation is called succession *in stirpes*, according to the roots, since all the branches inherit the same share that the root whom they *represent* would have done. So, if the next heirs of a man be six nieces,—three by one sister, two by another, and one by a third, his inheritance by the law of England, is divisible only into three parts, and distributed *per stirpes* thus, one third to the three children who represent one sister, another third to the two who represent the second, and the remaining third to the one child, who is the sole representative of her mother.

However, in dividing the inheritance to which females are entitled in the same degree, as daughters, grand-daughters, nieces, aunts, &c., the rule of descent is kept uniform and steady as far as regards the subdivided parts,—the same preference to males, and equal division amongst females, as would have obtained amongst the roots themselves. 1. As if a man has two sons, A and B, and A dies leaving two sons, and then the grandfather dies, now the eldest son of A shall succeed to the whole of his grandfather's estate; and if A had left only two daughters, they should have succeeded also to equal portions of the whole, in exclusion of their uncle B and his issue. 2. But if a man has only three daughters, C, D, and E, and C dies leaving two sons, D leaving two daughters, and E leaving a daughter and a son, who is younger than his sister, here, when the grandfather dies, the eldest son of C shall succeed to one third, in exclusion of the younger, in conformity with the laws of descent, the two daughters of D to another third in partnership, and the son of E to the remaining third, in exclusion of his elder sister; and this same *right of representation*, guided by the same rules of descent, prevails downwards *in infinitum*. The following diagrams illustrate practically the above position.

I.

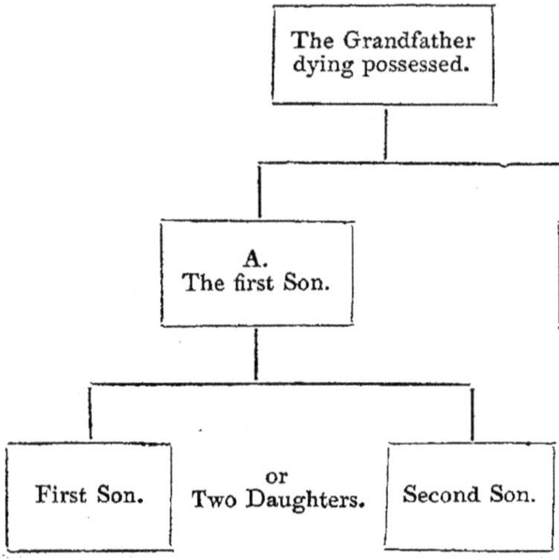

II.

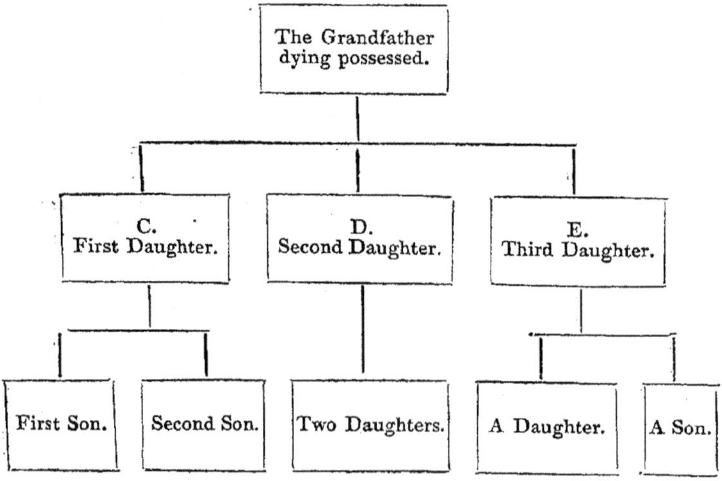

The last proprietor, or person last entitled, and whether in possession or not, is considered in the table, according to the legal presumption, to have come to the property as a purchaser, whereby the estate is

To face page 185.]

TABLE OF DESCENTS,

According to the COMMON LAW, and as altered by the Stat. 3 & 4 Will. IV. c. 106.*

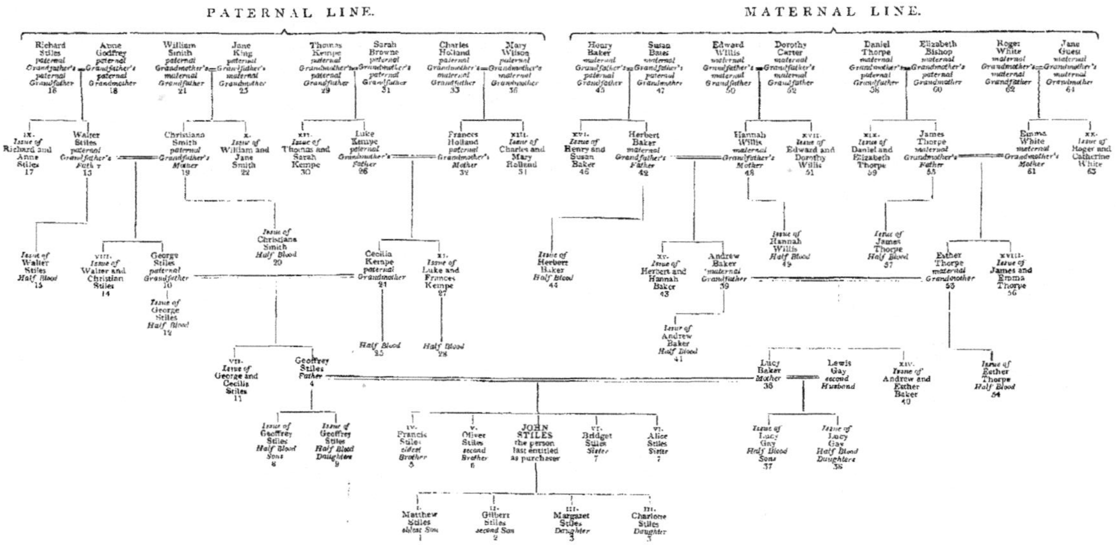

The persons in the highest line have been numbered as persons capable of inheriting in the new course of parental or lineal *ascent*; but this has been done more as a means of continued illustration, than as supposing the probability of their actual succession; for, in the exemplifying all genealogies, the name of every person, who, if alive, would inherit, is stated, in order that the title may be deduced *through* him.

The issue by the half blood of Nos. 32. and 61. have not been designated in the table, because the principle of descent has been illustrated by the preceding examples of Nos. 21. and 54.; more especially as the former numbers are in the remoter degree.

* By § 11. this act does not extend to any descent on the death of any person *before* the 1st of January, 1834. The Roman numerals show the late, and the Arabic figures the present mode of succession.

descendible to the kin or blood of such last owner in *general*, *i. e.* not to the kin or blood of any *particular* ancestor, which would be necessary if the last owner took the estate by descent; but even supposing that the last owner is shown to have taken by *descent*, the party from whom he took is presumed to have been a *purchaser*, until the contrary be shown.

The table prefixed to this page, which was originally framed by Sir William Blackstone, according to the late law of descent, and is still in operation as to descents up to the 31st of December, 1833, goes back but a very short way; indeed, it has been observed by one of his annotators, that a few generations more would necessarily make it diverge over an immense space. Sir William Blackstone, in this table, also takes it for granted that all the names in the top of the table have no collateral relations, for, if they had, all the figures above IX. 17. must have been placed differently. The figures in Roman numerals show the priority of descent in each individual according to the late law; the figures in Arabic demonstrate the order of descent as at present regulated by the late statute 3 & 4 *W*. 4. *c*. 106. Those compartments which have no Roman numerals were formerly excluded from the inheritance, being either lineal ancestors or half blood. The figures, it must also be observed, denote the order in which the several classes would succeed to *John Styles*, and not to each other; and, before an heir is searched for in the higher figures, we must first be assured that all the lower classes, from No. I. 1. to No. VII. 11., were extinct at *John Styles's* decease. Subject to these observations, this table will be exemplified, in the language of the learned commentator, with some variations now rendered necessary, and premising that the *general* heirs of *John Styles* are sought for, he having taken by *purchase*.

In the first place succeeds the eldest son, *Matthew* Styles, and his issue (No. I. 1.) : if his line be extinct, then *Gilbert* Styles, and the other sons respectively, in order of birth, or their issue (No. II. 2.) : in default of these, all the daughters together, *Margaret* and *Charlotte* Styles, or their issue (No. III. 3.) : on failure of the descendants of John Styles, his father, *Geoffry* Styles (No. 4.), takes the inheritance ; and afterwards his issue by his wife *Lucy*, the mother of *John* Styles, is called in, viz., first, *Francis* Styles, the eldest brother of the whole blood, or his issue (No. IV. 5.); then *Oliver* Styles, and the other whole brothers respectively, in order of birth, or their issue (No. V. 6.); then the sisters of the whole blood all together, *Bridget* and *Alice* Styles, or their issue (No. VI. 7.) ; then the brother of the half blood, *William* Styles, and his issue (No. 8.) ; and next all the daughters of the half blood together, being half sisters to the issue of Geoffry and Lucy Styles, come in; then, in defect of these, the inheritance ascends to his father, *George* Styles (No. 10.), and then descends to his issue by his wife *Cecilia*, the grandmother of John Styles, being No. VII. 11., respect being had to their age and sex : in default of such issue of *George* Styles, the males of the half blood singly, and their issue, according to priority, and then the females collectively, inherit (No. 12.) : in default of issue of the half blood, the inheritance ascends to *Walter* Styles, the paternal great-grandfather (No. 13.), and then descends to Walter's issue by his wife Christiana Styles, the great-grandmother of John Styles (No. VIII. 14.) : in default of the issue of Walter and Christiana Styles, the issue of Walter Styles of the half blood (No. 15.) succeed, according to legal priority: for want of such issue, the inheritance mounts up to

Richard Styles, the paternal great-great-grandfather (No. 16.), whose issue by his wife Anne Styles succeeds (No. IX. 17.); and so on in the paternal grandfather's paternal line, or blood of *Walter* Styles (No. 13.) *in infinitum:* on failure of these, the mother of the paternal grandfather, Christiana Smith, is let in, and her issue by another husband, being the half blood (No. 20.): in default of these, the inheritance ascends to *William Smith* (No. 21.), father of Christiana Smith; and from him the inheritance descends to his issue by Jane Smith (No. x. 22.), William and Jane Smith being the parents of John Styles's paternal grandfather's mother, and so on, in the paternal grandfather's maternal line, or blood of Christiana Smith, wife of Walter Styles, *ad infinitum*, till both the immediate bloods of George Styles, the paternal grandfather, are spent. Then we must resort to Cecilia Kempe (No. 24.), wife of George Styles, the paternal grandmother, and her issue by another husband, being the half blood (No. 25.); then to Luke Kempe, father of the grandmother (No. 26.), and then to his issue (No. XI. 27.); and, in default of issue by his wife Sarah, then to his children of the half blood (No. 28.): then there is an ascent to Thomas Kempe, the paternal grandfather of John Styles's grandmother (No. 29.), and his issue by his wife Sarah (No. XII. 30.): the inheritance then ascends to Sarah Browne (No. 31.), and any other issue of the half blood she may have, and in default we reckon on in the paternal grandmother's paternal line, or blood of Luke Kempe, *in infinitum:* in default of which we must call in Frances Holland (No. 32.), and her issue of the half blood (if any); then ascending to her father, Charles Holland (No. 33.), and descending to the issue of Charles and Mary Holland, the parents of John Styles's paternal grandmother's mother (No. XIII. 34.), and so on, in the paternal grandmother's maternal line, or blood of Frances Holland, *in infinitum*, till the immediate bloods of Cecilia Kempe, the paternal grandmother, are both spent; whereby the paternal blood of *John* Styles entirely failing, recourse must then be had to his maternal relations, or the blood of the *Bakers*, *Willises*, *Thorpes*, and *Whites*, in the same regular and successive order as in the paternal line.

DESERTED PREMISES. The possession of premises deserted (there being a half year's rent due, and the rent reserved being three fourths of the yearly value) can be restored to the landlord by two magistrates.

This remedy is only applicable in these cases, viz. 1. Where the rent is three fourths or more of the yearly value. 2. Where there is no sufficient distress, and the land is uncultivated and unoccupied. 3. Where there is a half year's rent due.

A tenant ceasing to reside on the premises, and leaving nothing to satisfy a distress, is said to desert the premises, although a man is in possession.

DETAINER, is the name of a writ, directed to either the marshal of the Queen's Bench or the warden of the Fleet, commanding him to *detain* a particular person named therein. This process may be the commencement of a suit, when the party in custody is indebted 20*l*. or upwards to a plaintiff, but he may be liberated on bail, just as if he was in the custody of the sheriff.

If a person is already in the custody of the sheriff, ordinary bailable process, *i. e.* the writ of *capias*, will detain him. The distinction being, that the custody of the sheriff, who has one prison, and the custody of the court, who has another, are practically different; the one having no control over the other. Persons in custody may also be sued by a writ of summons, which is serviceable process. See PRACTICE.

DETINUE. The name of an action which lies against him who *detains* a specific article or chattel from another. But the thing sought to be recovered must be identified; therefore money or coin, unless in a bag or box, cannot be recovered; *trover* being the remedy applicable for this injury. In detinue, the plaintiff can only recover the thing sought for. In *trover*, the plaintiff can either recover the thing claimed or damages.

This action is mostly brought to recover deeds and papers, and such things, the loss of which could not be recompensed in damages.

DEVISE, is the bequest or gift by will of realty, or things of that nature, being immoveable. The term *bequest*, applies in strictness to personalty.

DILAPIDATIONS. See WASTE.

DIOCESE, or BISHOPRICK. The extent of every bishop's jurisdiction. This kingdom has two sorts of divisions, one into counties or shires, for temporal purposes; another into dioceses, for ecclesiastical purposes, of which there are twenty-three in England and three in Wales. The kingdom is also, in respect of ecclesiastical government, divided into two provinces, viz. Canterbury, which has twenty bishopricks; and York, which possesses the remaining six. Every diocese or bishoprick is divided into archdeaconries, these again into deaneries, and the deaneries are subdivided into parishes. The bounds of dioceses have been settled by the report of the commissioners appointed by K. Will. 4., to consider the state of the established church.

A bishop may perform divine offices, and use his episcopal habit in the diocese of another without leave, but may not perform therein any act of jurisdiction without permission of the other bishop.

For many purposes of a temporal nature, regard must be had to the extent or limit of a diocese, as the office of proving a will or granting administration belongs to the bishop of the diocese in which the deceased died, if all his goods and chattels happened to be there; otherwise, if he had what are termed *bona notabilia, i. e.* known goods, in another diocese, to the value of 5*l.* (or 10*l.* if in London), the metropolitan, or archbishop of the province in which he died, has the prerogative of granting the probate or administration, which will be mentioned under the title EXECUTOR.

In various dioceses, however, there are particular ecclesiastical jurisdictions for proof of wills, unless the deceased possessed *bona notabilia* out of the diocese; and a very few lords of manors have the privilege of proof of their tenants' wills. These ecclesiastical jurisdictions are called *peculiars;* they are mostly archdeaconry courts; the archdeacon often having a jurisdiction independent of the bishop. The *courts of peculiars,* as they are styled, are exceedingly numerous, and of too local a character for mention here; but a table of the dioceses is subjoined, in order that the reader may be guided in some degree upon the extent or locality of jurisdiction.

	Diocese.	Jurisdiction.
The Province of Canterbury.	Canterbury - -	All Kent, except the city of Rochester and deanery of the same, the parishes of Addington and Croydon, together with the district of Lambeth Palace, in the county of Surrey.
	Bath and Wells -	The whole county of Somerset.
	Chichester - -	The county of Sussex.
	Ely - - -	Cambridgeshire, Huntingdonshire, Bedfordshire, and part of Norfolk and Suffolk, adjacent to Cambridgeshire.
	Exeter - - -	Cornwall and Devonshire.
	Gloucester and Bristol	Gloucestershire and city of Bristol, a part of Wiltshire adjacent to Gloucestershire, and the parish of Bedminster.
	Hereford, Lichfield, and Coventry - -	Herefordshire and part of Salop, including Peculiar of Bridgnorth, Staffordshire, and Derbyshire.
	Lincoln - - -	Lincoln and Nottingham shires.
	London - -	London, Middlesex, and parishes in counties of Surrey, Essex, and Kent, about ten miles round London.
	Norwich - -	All Norfolk and Suffolk, with the exception of the Archdeaconries of Norwich and Sudbury.
	Oxford - - -	Oxfordshire, Buckinghamshire, and Berkshire.
	Peterborough - -	Northampton, Rutland, and Leicester shires.
	Rochester - -	The deanery and city of Rochester in Kent; Hertfordshire and Essex, except the parishes in the latter within eight or ten miles of London.
	Salisbury - -	Wiltshire (the deanery of Malmesbury excepted) and Dorsetshire.
	Winchester - -	Surrey (except parishes near and in diocese of London, and parishes of Addington and Croydon, and district of Lambeth Palace), Hants, Guernsey, and Jersey.
	Worcester - -	Worcester and Warwick shires.
Wales.	Asaph and Bangor	Anglesea, Caernarvon, Merioneth, Denbigh, Montgomeryshire, and part of Flintshire.
	Llandaff - -	Glamorgan, Monmouth, and part of Brecknock shire.
	Saint David's -	Pembroke, Cardigan, Caermarthen, and Radnor shires, and part of Brecknock.
Province of York.	York - - -	All the county of York not in the diocese o. Ripon.
	Durham - -	The counties of Durham, Northumberland, and the district called Hexhamshire.
	Carlisle and Man -	The Isle of Man, counties of Cumberland and Westmoreland, and that part of Lancashire adjacent to the latter.
	Chester - -	Cheshire, and parts of the counties of Flint and Salop.
	Manchester - -	The whole of Lancashire, except the Deaneries of Furnes and Cartmel.
	Ripon - - -	The greatest part of the West Riding of Yorkshire.

DISHONOUR. The nonpayment of a bill of exchange or promissory note, check, or any negotiable instrument, on the day when it becomes due, and after presentment duly made. It also means the nonacceptance of a person drawn upon by his correspondent or other person in favour of the drawer, or some particular payee. The consequences of which are, that, on dishonour for nonpayment, if the holder use due diligence, all parties are liable to pay the amount; and, on nonacceptance, the holder has an immediate right of action against the drawer and indorsers. Under the article BILLS OF EXCHANGE, it has been observed that it is necessary in all *foreign* bills that they should be protested; but there does not exist the same necessity in inland bills, though, as a *noting*, which is a preliminary or imperfect protest, often evidences the presentment, it is usual to send all dishonoured bills to a notary who merely *notes* the inland, but *protests* the outland or foreign bill.

In order to fully charge the drawer and indorsers, on nonpayment by the acceptor, *due* notice *must* be given by the holder; and this may be done by word of mouth, or, what is the more usual and circumspect practice, by writing in the form of a letter. An eminent mercantile lawyer has so tritely embodied the law and practice on this subject, that I shall use almost his own words. The notice of nonpayment must be given or forwarded to the drawer and indorsers of the bill, and the indorsers of the note, and even to the mere transferer of a check. The time is fixed by law: the notice *may* be given upon the day of refusal, but it *must* be given or forwarded *on the day after the dishonour*, to all parties, or to such of them to whom it is intended to resort for payment, or, at least, to the last indorser; and each indorser must, in his turn, *on the day after he receives* notice, give or forward to his next or immediate indorser, notice of such dishonour. Each indorser, without regard to the number of them, or the nearness of their residence, is, for the sake of certainty, allowed a day, or in other words, *his* day, that is, until the day after that on which he received notice, to communicate the intelligence to the others; but if a holder of a dishonoured bill or note, or any other party, receive notice of the dishonour on one day, he must, if the drawer or next indorser reside in the *same* town, or in London, within the limits of the threepenny post, give the notice, or put the letter containing it into the post, so soon on the day after dishonour, or notice thereof, that it may be actually received and read *on that day*. Where the drawer, or next indorser, does not reside in the same town, then the notice is to be sent by the general post, or, if none, by a special messenger, or next best conveyance; and it suffices to put the letter giving the notice into the post-office on the day after the party so doing has himself had knowledge of the dishonour of the bill or note; and in this last case it is not necessary to forward notice on the *same* day as that on which he received notice, though there may be abundant time to do so; and if there be no post on the day after, then it suffices to put the letter into the post-office on the second day. With respect, however, to the holder's giving notice to a drawer, and to all other parties, it is advisable to give the earliest notice the circumstances will allow; indeed, next to the acceptor, the drawer is deemed liable, and, in practice, looked to on the default of the acceptor. If these rules are not strictly observed, the remedy against the drawer and indorser will be lost, unless it can be shown that the bill was drawn for the accommodation of the drawer, or particular circumstances can be proved excusing neglect in the holder or his agents, or, rather, showing that the delay arose from unavoidable occurrences, or matters which the holder could not have guarded against; but these latter instances are rare, and not to be relied on.

Verbal notice may also be given of the dishonour for nonpayment or nonacceptance, and the giving such verbal notice to a servant at the party's house, there being no clerk in the counting-house, will suffice; and where a person drawn upon has a counting-house where he transacts business, and at which the bill is addressed, it is sufficient to apply there for the purpose of giving notice, without attempting to give or leave notice at the private residence. Also, it is sufficient, in the case of an inland or foreign bill, to send twice *during the hours of business*, and to knock there, and wait a short time and then go away without leaving any written notice; but prudent holders will generally leave or send *written* notice, according to the rules already noticed; for even if the letter miscarry, the notice will be good, if accurately directed.

Where parties entitled to notice are abroad, notice may be given of the dishonour at their residence in England, or demand of acceptance or payment may be made upon wives or servants.

A few cautions may be added as to the mode of evidencing the delivery or sending of a written notice; for things not capable of legal proof may, in effect, be said not to be done at all; and as to what the letter or notice should contain.

A duplicate or copy of the letter containing the notice (if sent in the form of a letter), and of the address or direction, should be made, and examined with the original by the person who puts the original into the post, and a memorandum or minute should be made on the duplicate letter or notice of the time the original was delivered or put into the post, for any doubt as to the time would nullify the whole and prove fatal. It would also be prudent to let the same person who saw the holder sign his name to the original, and to the duplicate letter or notice, deliver the same, or put the same into the post-office; and not to employ any other person who could not give legal evidence as to the contents, thereby rendering the proof of notice insufficient.

The letter or notice (whether verbal or otherwise) should state three things:—1. The particular bill or note to which it alludes, and how the person addressed is a party thereto, whether as drawer or indorser. 2. It *must* state *distinctly* the fact that a presentment for payment has been made. 3. That payment has been refused. The following is a form of written notice adapted for ordinary occasions, viz.—

"No. 2. Skinner Street, Snow Hill,
"Sir, July 2d, 1836.

"The bill on Mr. T. D. for £58. 2*s*. 6*d*. *drawn by* [or *indorsed*] by you, and which fell due *yesterday*, and whereof I am the holder, was *yesterday* duly presented for payment, and was dishonoured by him, and lies in my hands unpaid. I request your immediate payment of the amount, and am, Sir,

Your obedient servant,
"To Mr. A. S. G. H.
No. — Upper Thames Street, London."

If a promissory note, say "The promissory note for Mr. T. D. for £58. 2*s*. 6*d*." &c.

When a bill or note is presented, it is usual, though not legally necessary, to leave a short memorandum containing particulars, thus: "January 3. 1837. Bill [*or* note] by H. on D. for £58. 6*s*. 2*d*. lies due for payment at ———." See Bill of Exchange.

As to dishonour of checks, see Check.

Where a bill, note, or check comes into the hands of the crown, no notice of dishonour is necessary to an indorsee or transferrer, as no neglect can, in law, be imputed to the crown.

There is one legal consequence attached to a dishonour, which is, that if the dishonoured bill or note has been given in satisfaction of another bill or debt, the original consideration or value is *revived*, that is, called again into operation as if the new bill had not been given, or no bill had been given for the debt; and yet, where a renewed bill is given, if notice of dishonour is not given to the drawer on the second bill, the holder cannot recover in an action brought upon the first, the plaintiff abandoning the renewed bill, which, under other circumstances, he would be at liberty to do.

DISSECTION. As the preventing the burial of a body is an indictable nuisance, great difficulty was till lately experienced in procuring subjects for the use of those who studied or delivered lectures on practical anatomy; and the schools themselves, where this science was taught, rather existed by sufferance than otherwise. A great odium and prejudice also attached on public dissection, because it constituted part of the punishment of murder. To obviate this prejudice, and to provide for the regulation of anatomical schools, the act 2 & 3 *W*. 4. *c*. 75. was passed, which, after reciting that "a knowledge of the causes and nature of sundry diseases which affect the body, and of the best methods of treating such diseases, cannot be acquired without the aid of anatomical examination," and alluding to the crimes that had been practised for the purpose of procuring "subjects," empowers the secretary of state for the home department in England, and the chief secretary in Ireland, to grant licences to practise anatomy, to *any fellow or member of any college of physicians or surgeons, or to any graduate or licentiate in medicine, or to any person lawfully qualified to practise medicine, or to any medical professor, or to any student attending any school of anatomy*, on application by the party, countersigned by two magistrates of the county or borough where the party resides. And inspectors of schools of anatomy are to be appointed by the secretary of state, for certain districts, who are to make a full return of all subjects removed for anatomical examination to any place in their districts, and visit such schools. (*Sects*. 1—12.)

The obtaining a proper supply of bodies is attained by the act providing that "any executor or other party *having lawful possession* of the body of a deceased person, and not being an undertaker or other party intrusted with the body for the purpose only of interment," may permit such body to undergo anatomical examination, unless the deceased shall have expressed his wish not to be so examined, either in writing, or verbally in the presence of two or more witnesses, during the illness whereof he died. So that persons not having expressed their will in writing, persons dying suddenly, and persons dying in workhouses or elsewhere without known relatives, may be handed over by those who have the lawful custody of the body, for anatomical examination.

Provisions are made for the case of an express direction by a person, that, after his decease, his body is to be anatomised; but, under the terms of the act, it is impossible for a person to leave his body for dissection, if the wife, husband, or nearest known relatives object thereto. (*Sects*. 8. & 9.)

So much of the act 9 *G*. 4. *c*. 31. as directs that the bodies of murderers may be dissected, is repealed, and their bodies are directed henceforth to be hung in chains [this direction is since repealed], or buried within the precincts of the prison in which they were confined before conviction, as the judge may direct. (*Sect*. 16.)

The act requires that bodies to be dissected shall, before removal, be placed in a decent coffin; and the party removing the same is to make provision that, after examination, it is to be interred in consecrated ground, or a public burial-ground, a certificate whereof is to be transmitted to the inspector within six weeks after the receipt of the body. (*Sect.* 13.)

Offences against the act are declared misdemeanors, and punishable by imprisonment for three months, or by a fine of 50*l.*, at the discretion of the court.

The act came into operation on the 1st of August, 1832.

DISTRESS, is the taking of a personal chattel out of the possession of the wrong-doer into the custody of the injured party, to procure a satisfaction for the wrong committed. It is of two kinds: the taking or distraining for cattle trespassing and doing damage (termed *damage feasant*), or for nonpayment of rent, quit rent, or other dues or services. The most usual injury (which after all is only constructive) for which a distress can be taken, is that of nonpayment of rent. Distress also signifies the thing taken. This is a remedy which all persons may have who possess an ulterior interest in the house or premises let, or, as the law terms it, a reversion; but it may be well to remark, that no landlord, who has not reserved to himself the superior estate (as where he has assigned *all* his interest, not underlet), or where the rent is not fixed, can avail himself of this means of recovering the rent; therefore, where a tenant is let into possession under an agreement for a lease, and no lease has been executed, *and no rent paid*, the landlord cannot distrain, though, if the tenant has paid rent, it would be otherwise. Remedy by distress and sale is given for poor's rates, taxes, and various penalties and dues imposed by act of parliament. The distress must be of something valuable on the premises or land, and which can be restored in as good a plight as it was at the time of making the distress (corn and crops only excepted): fixtures, utensils of trade in actual use, the books of a scholar, corn in a mill, goods exposed to sale in a market, materials in a weaver's shop for making of cloth, the cloth of another being made up at a tailor's, horses with riders on their backs, or drawing a cart, the cart itself if in use, if one be riding in the cart, but not the corn in it, cattle being driven to market (not put up in a field or place by the way), or at an inn, which is always privileged, are exempt; but implements of trade, and the books of a scholar, it seems, are only exempt where they are in actual use, and where a sufficient distress can otherwise be had. Beasts of the plough and sheep should not be taken, if other sufficient distress can be found; if not, they may be distrained. Clothes on the person, goods in the custody of the law, things pledged with a third party, goods in a carrier's waggon or in his warehouse, goods sent to an auctioneer's for sale, and, generally speaking, property of third persons *bonâ fide* delivered to another in the exercise of his trade, are also exempt; but this privilege does not, it seems, extend to distresses made for queen's taxes, and the collector, in distraining, may prefer distraining on whichever he thinks most saleable. In other cases, the property of third parties is exempted till it is ascertained that the tenant's goods prove deficient, unless in the cases before noticed, where the exemption is absolute. Trees of a nurseryman are not distrainable, though he removes them from time to time. By a particular statute with respect to corn or crops ripe or unripe, it is lawful for any person having an arrear of rent due to him, to seize and secure sheaves or cocks of corn, or corn loose, or in the straw or hay, lying in any barn or granary, or otherwise, and to detain the same in the place where found till sale or replevy; and by another statute, the landlord is empowered to seize as a distress all sorts of corn, and grass, hops, roots, fruits, pulse, or other product, growing upon any part of the estate demised, and the same to cut, gather, make, cure, carry, and lay up, *when ripe*, in the barns, or other proper place on the premises; and if no such barn or proper place, then in any other barn or proper place, as near as may be to the premises, and in convenient time (*i. e.* when cut, gathered, and made,) to appraise, sell, or otherwise dispose of the same towards satisfaction of the rent and charges of distress and sale; but notice of the place where such distress may be lodged, shall, in one week after the lodging thereof, be given to the tenant, or left at his last place of abode; and upon tender of payment of the arrears of rent and costs of the distress before the corn, &c. be cut, the distress shall cease, and the corn, &c. be delivered up.

Landlords are also empowered to take as a distress, cattle or stock of their tenants feeding upon any common belonging to any part of the premises demised.

Distresses (except for damage feasant) must be made by day, that is, after sunrise and before sunset, and a distress cannot lawfully be made after tender of payment; and it is the duty of every landlord or agent, broker, &c. to make a formal demand before making the distress; at all events, if the tenant then tender the rent *and no more*, the distress will be unlawful. The landlord must not break open a house to make a distress, but when he is inside he may break open an inner door; and where goods have been fraudulently removed, he may, in presence of a peace-officer, break open *in the day-time* any place whither the goods have been fraudulently removed, and locked up to prevent a distress, oath being first made, in case it be a dwelling-house, of a reasonable ground of suspicion.

Persons distraining for rent, may impound the distress on any convenient part of the land chargeable with the distress. Goods or cattle cannot be used by the party distraining, for they are but as a pledge: this leads to the consideration of the mode of making a distress for rent.

The landlord himself, or any other person, as his bailiff, generally a broker or person accustomed to this business, by an authority in writing, may make the distress for rent. The form of an authority may be thus:—

" To Mr. C. D., my bailiff.

" I do hereby hereby authorize you to distrain the goods and chattels of " Mr. E. F. [the tenant] in the house wherein he now dwells [*or*, on the pre- " mises in his possession], situate in ———, in the county of ———, for " —— pounds, ——, being [one] year's rent due to me for the same at [Christ- " mas-day] last, and for your so doing this shall be your sufficient warrant and " authority. Dated the —— day of ———, 1837.

" Witness, S. L. [Landlord's signature] J. S."

Being legally authorised to distrain, you make a demand upon the premises of *£. s. d.*, the exact rent due, which, if not paid, you may enter, and make a seizure of the distress. If it be made in a house, seize a chair or other piece of furniture, and say, " I seize this chair in " the name of all the goods in this house, for the sum of ——— pounds, " being one year's rent due to me [*or*, to J. S. the landlord] at Christmas- " day last, by virtue of an authority from the said J. S. for that purpose " [*provided you distrain as bailiff*]."

Then take an inventory of so many goods as you judge will be sufficient to cover the rent distrained for, and also the charges of the distress. Make a copy thereof, as follows:—

"An inventory of the several goods and chattels distrained by me A. B. "this —— day of ——, in the year of our Lord ——, in the houses, out-houses, "and lands [*as the case is*] of E. F., situate in ——, in the county of ——, "by the authority and on the behalf of J. S. [*provided you distrain as bailiff.*] "for the sum of —— pounds, being one year's rent due to me, or the said J. S. "[*as the case is*] at Christmas-day last.

"In the dwelling-house, two tables, two chairs, &c.

"In the barn, six hurdles [*and so on*].

"In the upper field, two cows, &c.

"In the stable, two horses, &c.",

At the bottom of the inventory subscribe the following notice to the tenant:—

Notice to Tenant.

"Mr. E. F.

"Take notice, that I have this day distrained [*or*, that as bailiff to J. S. your "landlord, I have this day distrained] on the premises above-mentioned, the "several goods and chattels specified in the above inventory, for the sum of "—— pounds, being one year's rent due to me [*or*, the said J. S.] at Christ-"mas-day last, for the said premises; and that unless you pay the said rent, "with the charges of distraining for the same, within five days from the date "hereof, the said goods and chattels will be appraised and sold according to law. "[*If the goods are removed, state the place to which they are removed.*] Given "under my hand the —— day of ——, in the year of our Lord ——.

"C. D."

If the sum distrained for be for arrears of rent-charge, you may give this notice: —

"Mr. E. F.

"Take notice, that by the order and on behalf of Mr. J. S. I have this "day taken and distrained, in and upon the farm and lands called ——, in "your possession, in the parish of ——, in the county of ——, all the severed "corn, grain, and effects, in the inventory hereunder written mentioned, for "the sum of £——, being [one] year's annuity or rent charge of £—— per "annum, due to the said C. D. at [Michaelmas] last, and charged on, and "issuing and payable out of, certain manors, farms, lands, and premises "called ——, in the said parish of —— in the county of —— aforesaid, of which "the farms and lands first above mentioned are part and parcel; and that "unless the said arrears of the said annuity or rent-charge, together with the "expenses of this distress, are paid and satisfied, the said corn, grain, and "effects will be disposed of according to law. Dated this —— day of ——, "1837.

"To Mr. E. F. and all whom it may concern. C. D."

Growing crops, or cattle on a common, cannot lawfully be distrained for a rent-charge, unless an express power to that effect be reserved in the deed creating the rent.

If growing crops are seized, this form will be applicable: —

"Mr. E. F.

"Take notice, that I have this day taken and distrained, [*or*, that I, "bailiff to Mr. J. S. your landlord, have taken and distrained,] on the "lands and premises above mentioned, the several growing crops specified in "the inventory for the sum of £——, being [two] quarters' rent due to me, "[*or* to the said J. S.] at [Michaelmas] last, for the said lands and pre-"mises; and unless you previously pay the said rent, with the charges of "distraining for the same, I shall proceed to cut, gather, make, cure, carry, "and lay up the crops, when ripe, in the barn, or other proper place on the "said premises, and in convenient time sell and dispose of the same, towards "satisfaction of the said rent, and of the charges of such distress, appraise-"ment, and sale, according to the form of the statute in such case made and "provided. Given under my hand, this —— day of —— 1837."

A true copy of the inventory and notice must either be given to the tenant himself, or left at his house; or, if there be no house, on the most notorious place on the premises, in the presence of a witness. It is expedient to have a person with you when you make the distress, and also when you serve the inventory and notice, to examine the same, and to attest the regularity of the proceedings.

The goods may be removed immediately, and in the notice the tenant may be acquainted where they are removed; but it is now most usual to put a man into possession, and let them remain on the premises till you are entitled by law to sell them, which is on the sixth day inclusive after the distress made, *i. e.* goods distrained on the Saturday, may be removed and sold on the Thursday afternoon following.

If the tenant require further time for the payment of the rent, and the landlord chooses to allow it, it is best to take the following memorandum in writing from the tenant:—

"I, E. T. do hereby consent that J. S. my landlord, who on the —— day of "———— distrained my goods and chattels for rent due to him, shall continue "possession thereof on the premises for the space of seven days from the date "hereof, the said J. S. undertaking to delay the sale of the said goods and "chattels for that time, in order to enable me to discharge the said rent.

"Witness my hand this —— day of ——, 1837.

"E. T."

This memorandum prevents the landlord from being deemed a trespasser, which, after the expiration of five days, he otherwise would be, and subject himself to an action of trespass for staying longer upon the premises.

If there is no allowance of, or agreement for further time, search at the expiration of the five days at the sheriff's office, to see if the goods have been replevied; if not, and the rent and charges still remain unpaid send for a constable and two sworn appraisers, who having viewed the goods, the former must administer to the latter the following oath.

"You, and each of you, shall well and truly appraise the goods and chattels "mentioned in this inventory [*holding it in his hand*] according to the best of "your judgment. So help you God."

Then indorse on the inventory the following:—

"Memorandum, that on the —— day of ——, in the year of our Lord ——, "A. B. of, &c., and M. N. of, &c., two sworn appraisers, were sworn upon "[the Holy Evangelists,] by me J. K. of, &c., constable, well and truly to "appraise the goods and chattels mentioned in this inventory, according to the "best of their judgment. As witness my hand,

"J. K., Constable.

"Present at the time of
"swearing the said A. B.
"and M. N. as above, and
"witness thereto. } P. Q.
R. S."

After the appraisers (neither of whom must be the person making the distress) have valued the goods, continue the indorsement on the inventory as follows:—

"We, the above named A. B. and M. N., being sworn upon [the Holy "Evangelists,] by J. K. the constable above named, well and truly to appraise "the goods and chattels mentioned in this inventory, according to the best "of our judgment; and having viewed the said goods and chattels, do appraise "the same at the sum of —— pounds. As witness our hands the —— day of "——, in the year of our Lord ————.

"A. B.
"M. N. } Sworn Appraisers."

When the goods are thus valued, it is usual for the appraisers to buy them at their own valuation; and a receipt at the bottom of the inventory, witnessed by the constable, is usually held a discharge. But if the distress be of considerable value, it is much more advisable to have a proper bargain and sale between the landlord, the constable, the appraiser, and the purchaser.

The goods being disposed of, deduct the rent in arrear, and all reasonable charges attending the distress, and return the overplus (if any) to the tenant.

If the produce is not sufficient to cover the demand, you may distrain again.

Note. — The man in possession of the goods, &c. is to be paid 2*s.* 6*d.* *per diem* if the tenant keep him, and 3*s.* 6*d.* if he keep himself.

The law being thus, that persons who distrain for rent of any kind, may sell the things distrained for payment of the rent in arrear, if the tenant or owner fails to replevy, (see tit. REPLEVIN) within five days after taking of the distress, and giving the tenant notice of the cause, the constable is bound to assist, by swearing two sworn appraisers (not being concerned in making the distress) to fairly appraise the goods, and the overplus, if any, is paid to the constable for the use of the owner; all which may be done upon the premises, the oath *must* be administered there.

The impounding of the goods, if cattle, *may* be on the premises, and most usually is so; but otherwise, the distrainors must place the cattle in either a pound overt, that is open, being some notorious or common pound within the county, or in some special or covert pound, a stable, or private building. If cattle are impounded, the distrainor must feed them, and charge the owner with the expense.* Goods must be impounded in some *pound covert*, to use the legal phrase, which is either on the premises, or in some place within the county, which, as well as in the case of cattle or beasts, must not be more than three miles distant from the place where the distress was made. In all cases, too, notice must be given of the distress and of the things taken.

The landlord must remove the goods from the premises at the end of five days, and will be deemed a trespasser for any time beyond it that he keeps them. The five days allowed before a distress can be sold, are inclusive of the day of sale; wherefore, it seems, the distress may be removed on the sixth day. A reasonable time is also allowed the landlord for appraising and selling after the five days have elapsed.

Goods fraudulently removed by the tenant from off the premises, may be followed or pursued by the landlord, who is empowered to seize the same within thirty days, unless the goods are first sold for an adequate consideration to a *bonâ fide* purchaser. He may, with a magistrate's warrant, and with a peace-officer, break open places in the day-time, as before observed, upon reasonable suspicion. It should be remembered, that only the goods of a *tenant* can be thus pursued; any one else may lawfully remove his property from the premises, if he is apprehensive of a distress, at any time.

A devisee is empowered to distrain for a rent devised or bequeathed to him out of the lands or premises, if the same are chargeable; and he is just the same as a landlord, save that he cannot distrain upon growing crops, and cattle upon the common appurtenant, or attached to the premises.

* By the Cruelty Act, *5 & 6 W. 4. c. 59. s. 45.*, penalties are recoverable for neglect in furnishing sufficient food, and any person may enter the ground and supply such food.

A distress for damage feasant has been incidentally mentioned: it is a distraining of cattle whilst actually upon the distrainor's land, and *in the very act of* doing damage, for else they may not be seized; or if they are, the owner may retake or rescue them, the distrainor being always entitled to his action for trespass if he does not distrain; but a horse with its rider, or cattle in the actual use of the party, cannot be taken, because such a distress might lead to a breach of the peace; nor can they be distrained after a tender of adequate amends. Cattle distrained in this manner are generally put into some pound overt, or public pound; but they may be privately kept as other distresses, and upon the following notice being given the owner, he must pay reasonable amends to the distrainor, or replevy them :—

" *Form of Notice of having distrained and impounded Cattle damage feasant.*

" Mr. A. B.

" Take notice, that I have this day distrained three horses [*or*, cows, oxen, " pigs, &c., *according to the fact*], which, I am informed, are your property, " whilst the same were trespassing and doing damage to and upon my crop of " wheat [*or*, oats, &c. *according to the fact*], and other crops and herbage, grow- " ing and being in a close in my occupation, called *Goswells*, in the parish of " *Chaldon*, in the county of Surrey; and I have impounded the said horses, " [*or*, cows, &c.] for such trespass and damage, *in the common pound, situate at* " *Katerham Street in the said county* [*or*, in my stable adjoining my house, called " Chaldon Court, in the parish and county aforesaid], where you must feed " and provide for the same, otherwise I shall do so for you, and charge you with " the amount, in addition to my claim for the damage done. And I further " inform you, that the damage done by the said horses to and upon my said " close, amounts to £——, the payment of which I hereby require; but I am " ready to concur with you in having the same valued in your presence, if you " require; but this notice is given you without reference to a further claim I have " upon you for damage previously committed. Yours, &c.

" To Mr. A. B., Tolsworth Farm. T. W."

In addition to the distresses for rent, rent-charge, and damage feasant, various acts of parliament authorise distresses upon the order of a justice or justices, for sewers rate, poor's rate, highway rate, and also for various penalties recoverable or payable under certain other statutes. Lords of manors can also distrain for their fines, heriots, quit-rents, and other dues or amerciaments assessed by the court jury or homage; also deodands may be distrained for, in all which the previous forms are applicable. The right to distrain does not injure the party's right to an action, except in the cases of parliamentary or parochial assessments leviable or distrainable under warrant of a justice, which limit a time for the sale of the goods.

Executors and administrators may distrain for rent due to their testator or intestate, as such testator or intestate, if living, might have done. (*3 & 4 W. 4. c. 42. s. 37.*) And within six months after the end of any term or lease at will, provided it be during the continuance of the tenant in arrear. (*s. 38.*)

If a distrainor take an excessive distress, *i. e.* a great deal more than necessary to satisfy the rent and charges, or omits the formalities above mentioned, turns the tenant out of possession, sells fruit or corn before it is ripe, continues more than five days in possession, or if the distress is made after a tender of the rent only (for the broker is entitled to nothing for his simple demand which he is bound to make), an action can be sustained by the tenant, not only against the party actually making the distress, but against the landlord, or whoever else warranted or authorised it, the landlord being liable for any excess of authority by his agent or bailiff.

The charges for a distress can always be added to the amount distrained for, and the property is liable to pay them; but they should be reasonable, for any exorbitance will subject landlord and broker to an action. The law regulates the sum to be taken for charges of a distress not exceeding 20*l*., and persons aggrieved by charges beyond can be relieved on application to a single justice, who will adjudge the transgressor to pay treble the amount received contrary to the act. The charges allowed are, for levying the distress, 3*s*.; for a man in possession, 2*s*. 6*d*. a day; for advertisements (if any such), 10*s*.; for appraisement, 6*d*. in the pound on the value of the goods; the amount of the stamp; and for catalogues, sales, commission, and delivery of the goods, 1*s*. in the pound on the nett produce of the sale. And these regulations are specially extended to all distresses for rates or taxes not exceeding 20*l*.

Rent cannot be lawfully distrained for till the day *after* that on which it is made payable.

Distress is also a term signifying the things taken under a writ of *distringas*, being a writ which issues to compel a party's *appearance*, by distraining upon him for his contempt in not previously *appearing*; it is in common cases 40*s*. See DISTRINGAS.

DISTRINGAS. In practice, the operative Latin word for a writ of distraint, commanding the sheriff *that you distrain*. It is used for the purpose of compelling the appearance of a defendant who has had notice of, but cannot personally be served with, process. The object of this writ is to enable a plaintiff to proceed with the action, just as if the defendant had appeared, *or* to outlaw him, but *both* cannot be done. The most usual case is of a defendant, who having a residence or tangible personal property, *and* being in England, has evaded the personal service of a *writ of summons*, which evasion, if shown to the court or a judge, is the occasion of issuing a *distringas*, which authorises the sheriff to distrain upon defendant's goods for 40*s*., which, if the sheriff cannot personally serve, or execute by distraining, or if the sheriff do distrain, and the defendant still refuses to appear, the plaintiff may, by leave of the court or a judge, enter an appearance for him, *i. e.* just as if the defendant had authorised his attorney to have appeared for him, and therefore the action proceeds to judgment: or if the plaintiff prefer it, and it certainly has its advantages, he can proceed to outlawry. If a defendant is out of England, and has an establishment here, this writ can still be obtained, so as to enable the plaintiff to proceed in his action against the goods; though, where a defendant has no personal but real property, in England, and is himself out of the country, it is most usual to outlaw him. See OUTLAWRY.

Distringas is also the name of a process which issues out of the chancery or equity side of the exchequer, to compel the appearance of corporations to bills or injunctions filed against them.

DISTRINGAS CORPORA JURATORUM, or HABEAS CORPORA JURATORUM, *i. e.* that you (the sheriff) *distrain* or *have* the bodies of the jurors. The title of the writ which compels the sheriff to have, by means of the compulsion supposed to exist by means of the fictitious distress of all the jurors' lands and chattels, the jurymen in court appointed to try a cause, if special jurors, or set of causes, if common jurors, in court on a particular day, being those named in an oblong square piece of parchment called a *panel*.

Other compulsory processes against the sheriff are termed *distringas*.

DIVORCE. Divorces are of two kinds, namely, *à mensâ et thoro* (from bed and board), and *à vinculo matrimonii* (from the bond of marriage).

A divorce from bed and board does not dissolve the marriage; for the cause of it is subsequent to the marriage, and supposes the marriage to be lawful: this divorce may be by reason of adultery in either of the parties, for cruelty of the husband, &c. And as it does not dissolve the marriage, so it does not debar the woman of her dower, or bastardise the issue, or make void any estate for the life of husband and wife.

The woman under separation by this divorce, if she sue in any court, must sue by *her next friend;* but she may sue her husband in *her own name* for alimony, which is the allowance made to a woman for her support out of the husband's estate, and settled at the discretion of the ecclesiastical judge, on consideration of all the circumstances of the case. If the husband refuse payment of the wife's alimony, the amount may be recovered at common law, and he is besides subject to excommunication. It is generally proportioned to the rank and quality of the parties. But in case of the wife's elopement and living in adultery, the law allows her no alimony, except during a suit for divorce.

Divorces for causes *precedent*, are confined to the ecclesiastical court. But divorces from the bond of matrimony for causes *subsequent*, are very common by act of parliament, *e. g.* for adultery.

A divorce from the bond of marriage, absolutely dissolves the marriage, and makes it void from the beginning, the causes of it being *precedent* to the marriage, as precontract with some other person, consanguinity or affinity within the Levitical degrees, impotency, &c. This divorce enables the parties to marry again; but this is not the case with respect to a divorce from bed and board only.

DOCUMENTS. To steal, obliterate, take away, or destroy any documents belonging to *any* court of record or equity, is a misdemeanor, and punishable by transportation or fine and imprisonment.

DOG. Every person has a right to keep a dog for the protection of his house and yard, and for that purpose may let it loose *at night*, and if a person incautiously go into the yard after it has been shut up, and he be hurt, he has no remedy: but if the owner *knew* the dog to be ferocious, and leave his yard-gate open, he must not let the dog loose in the day-time, or let it have a chain so long as to be able to reach and hurt a person entering the yard, and he should give a verbal, or written or printed caution against coming too near, or he will be liable for any damage. In one case it was held, that where a fierce and vicious dog is kept chained for the defence of premises, and any one incautiously, or not knowing of it, should go so near as to be injured by it, no action can be maintained by the person injured, though he was seeking the owner, with whom he had business. In a still later case it was held, that a person is not entitled to recover compensation for an injury received from the bite of a dog placed in the yard for the protection of outhouses, unless he had such reasonable and justifiable cause for being in the place where the dog was, as might be pleaded in answer to an action of trespass. But that, if he had such cause, the circumstance of there being a notice on a board, in large letters, warning persons to "beware of the dog," will not be an answer to an action by him for the injury, if it appear that he was not able to read. And that if no suspicion be thrown upon the plaintiff by the defendant, in such a case, it may be taken that he had such cause, and he is entitled to recover, provided the dog be put in a place forming part of one entrance to the house of the defendant, although there may be other entrances of a more public description by which the plaintiff might have proceeded; and the plaintiff, in the particular case, having been injured by the dog whilst proceeding to the defendant's house for a lawful purpose, recovered a verdict for 70*l.* damages.

A person may justify killing a dog in a *warren*, whilst pursuing the rabbits there, or whilst pursuing deer in a park, if he cannot otherwise prevent the destruction of the rabbit or deer; but if he could, then he must not kill the dog. But neither the occupier of other lands, nor the lord of a manor, or his gamekeeper, has any right directly to shoot or seize a dog illegally pursuing a hare when *self-hunting*; and it is very questionable whether an occupier of land can legally place *dog-spears* on his land to protect game, and *kill* dogs in pursuit thereof, even with public notice. (*Chitty's Practice of the Law.*)

By the game act, gamekeepers are empowered to seize all dogs that shall be used for killing game, by any person not authorised by want of certificate.

The stealing of a dog subjects the offender to pay the value, and a sum not exceeding 20*l.* on conviction before two justices; and on a second conviction, to be committed to a common goal, or house of correction, to hard labour, not exceeding twelve calendar months, and whipping, if a male; and persons found in possession of a stolen dog, (knowing the same to have been stolen) or the skin thereof, are liable to the same punishment.

Action will lie to recover the value of a dog wantonly destroyed; and to recover the animal itself, action of trover will lie.

It is indictable as a misdemeanor to suffer a mastiff dog to go in the street or highway unmuzzled, especially if it has been accustomed to bite.

There is a tax imposed upon the possessor of a dog, unless excused on account of poverty.

DOMESDAY, or DOOMSDAY BOOK. An ancient register compiled by order of King William I., containing a survey of all the lands in England, except some small portion now remaining in the Chapter-house, Westminster Abbey, amongst the exchequer records. It is often referred to for the purpose of ascertaining what lands are *ancient demesne* which is found by their being described as land holden of King Edward the Confessor, therein noted T. R. E. See MANOR, SOCAGE.

DONATIO MORTIS CAUSA. *A gift by reason of death.* A gift made of personal property in the last illness of the donor. A note not payable to bearer cannot be given, or receipts for South Sea annuities will not pass the stock, though a bond or mortgage will operate as a legacy of the money secured by those instruments. Duty is payable to government upon this species of gift, as a legacy; in fact, it is to all intents and purposes a legacy, as the delivery does not operate till after the giver's death. A gift without reference to death, is not a *donatio mortis causa*, and may be made at one time as well as another; and these are the only distinctions that can ordinarily arise as far as the gift itself is concerned. The gift may be made to a third person in trust for an absent party.

DOWER, is a third part, or other customary share of such lands of inheritance whereof the husband was owner during the marriage, which the wife is to enjoy during her life, unless she acknowledges a deed parting with this right, which attaches on all land not conveyed to the husband in a special manner, for the purpose of barring this right, or where the wife has not released it before marriage in consideration of a jointure or other provision, whether he sold it during the marriage or not. But women married after the 1st of January, 1834, cannot claim dower out of land disposed of by their husbands in their life-time, or by their will. Again, any partial incumbrance effected by their husbands, are good against dower. Husbands also may defeat their wives dower by any prospective instrument during them arriage, or by will; so that in the marriages taking place on or after the 1st. of January, 1834, this estate will not so frequently attach. See HUSBAND and WIFE.

DRAMATIC LITERARY PROPERTY. By 3 *W.* 4. *c.* 15.,

"The author of any tragedy, comedy, play, opera, farce, or any other dramatic piece or entertainment, composed, and *not printed and published* by the author thereof, or his assignee, or which hereafter shall be composed, and not printed or published by the author, or the assignee of such author, shall have as his own property the sole liberty of representing, at any place of dramatic entertainment in any part of the British dominions, and shall be deemed and taken to be the proprietor thereof: and the author of any such production, printed and published within ten years before the passing of this act, by the author or his assignee, or which shall hereafter be printed and published, or the assignee of such author, shall, from the time of passing this act, or from the time of such publication respectively, until the end of twenty-eight years from the day of such first publication of the same, and also, if the author or authors, or the survivor of the authors, shall be living at the end of that period, during the residue of his natural life, have as his own property the sole liberty of representing, or causing to be represented, the same, at any such dramatic entertainment as aforesaid, and shall be deemed and taken to be the proprietor thereof. (*s.* 1, 2.)

The act saves the right of those whom the author has authorised previous to the passing of the act, to represent his production.

The remedy which is given by the act is an action, in which the least damages are 40*s.* (and double costs), up to the full amount received from the representation; but the time for bringing the action is limited to twelve months.

DRAWER. The person who makes or draws a bill of exchange. When the bill drawn is made payable to the party's own order, he of necessity must indorse: he is then technically termed the drawer-indorser. On the dishonour of a bill, he is entitled to notice thereof, within the time limited by law: if such notice be not given, he is discharged. See BILL OF EXCHANGE, DISHONOUR.

By the 2 & 3 *W.* 4. *c.* 98., bills of exchange expressed to be payable in any place, other than the residence of the drawer, if not accepted on presentment at such specified place, may, without further presentment to such drawer, be protested there, unless the amount be paid to the holder on the day when they should have become payable, had they been duly accepted.

DREDGE. The using a dredge net or engine within the limits of the oyster fisheries, for the purpose of taking oysters or oyster brood is a misdemeanor, and punishable by fine and imprisonment.

DREDGER-MEN. Fishers for oysters. See OYSTERS.

DRIFT OF THE FOREST. An examination of what cattle are in the forest, that it may be known whether it be surcharged or not, and whose the beasts are, and whether they are commonable, &c. There is also a drift of common and half-year or Lammas land for the same purposes. This examination is made by *driving* (whence the term) all the beasts into an enclosure or pound.

DROVERS. Those who buy cattle in one place to sell in another. They are traders, subject to the bankrupt laws. The term is more commonly applied to persons who drive the cattle from or to the markets previous and subsequent to their sale. See CATTLE.

DROVERS OF CATTLE. The following rules and orders respecting drovers were made by the mayor and court of aldermen, London, 29th of November, 1831, pursuant to an act enabling them so to do:—

All drovers must be licensed, and wear a ticket, or badge, visible on the upper part of the left arm, with a *letter* and *number*, and the city arms, painted white on a black ground.

No person (not being the owner) to be employed or assist in driving cattle, unless licensed, and wearing such ticket (consequently no boys are allowed, on any pretence, to assist in driving).

No licensed drover is to pawn, or permit any other person to use, his ticket.

No licensed drover, or any other person, to beat or strike any cattle, sheep, calves, or lambs, *on or below the hock*, or *otherwise* beat, bruise, or illtreat such cattle.

No goad, or other pointed instrument, to be used, or *had in possession* by the driver, the point of which shall be longer than a quarter of an inch.

Only one dog allowed with each drove of sheep; and *no* dog allowed in driving other cattle.

A licensed driver, ticketed as above; must precede every drove of cattle exceeding ten in number.

A penalty of from 5*s*. to 20*s*. for a breach of each of the above rules, or one month's imprisonment; and if the driver cannot be found, the master shall be liable for the offence committed by him. These regulations extend five miles round London by virtue of the act 21 *G*. 3. *c*. 67.

Drovers are not to travel with cattle on Sundays, under a penalty of 20s.

DRUNKENNESS. A drunken person can be fined by a single magistrate on the oath of one witness, or on his own view, 5*s*. for the first offence, to be levied by distress and sale of his goods, and for want of a distress shall sit in the stocks six hours; for the second offence, he can be bound in two sureties of 10*l*. each for his future good behaviour, and imprisoned till the next sessions, unless he sooner provide the required sureties.

A person may be indicted at the sessions for drunkenness, and also punished for it in the ecclesiastical court, it being a *spiritual* offence.

Drunkenness is no legal excuse for a crime or misdemeanor committed.

At law, or in equity, a man cannot avoid his act or deed executed by him when drunk, unless he was made drunk by the contrivance of the person to whom the deed was given, or with whom the transaction took place.

DURESS. When a deed or contract is entered into, or signed under any unlawful detention or imprisonment, or under fear from any threat or menace, such deed or contract is said to have been executed or entered into under *duress*, and is void, for all legal acts should be performed by the free assent of the party.

DUEL. See MURDER.

EJECTMENT, or "*trespass* and ejectment" as it is legally termed, is the name of an action that lies to recover all real property, or houses, lands, &c., and minor interests therein. It depends or is framed upon several fictions to facilitate the process and bring the question of right before the jury: thus, if John Allen claims land or house of Thomas Roberts, it is feigned that one John Doe had demised or let to Allen the premises claimed, for a term of years at present unexpired, from which one Roe ejected Allen ; Allen therefore serves a *declaration* (the first process in ejectment) upon the tenant in possession, stating these fictitious matters, and the tenant or the real defendant's name is, by leave of the court, inserted in the place of Roe, so that the plaintiff claims, by reason of his fictitious lease, the premises from Roberts, the real defendant or party interested, who is *let in* to defend, the cause being intituled as "*Doe on the demise of* Allen against Roberts," instead of Allen against Roberts, as in other cases.

Within what time this action may be brought, see title LIMITATION.

ELECTION. A choice.

ELECTION OF MEMBERS FOR PARLIAMENT. See PARLIAMENT.

ELEGIT. The name of a writ of execution whereby the sheriff is empowered to seize and (not to sell but) deliver to the plaintiff, at an appraisement, all the goods of a debtor *except his oxen and beasts of the plough*, and if that is insufficient to liquidate the debt or damages, then to deliver one moiety, or half of the land, or interests in land, to the plaintiff to receive the rents and profits until his debt be discharged. This writ is executed by means of a jury, whom the sheriff summons for that purpose.

EMBEZZLEMENT. The pilfering or purloining money or property entrusted to any one as a servant or agent, or for a particular purpose. Clerks and servants receiving and embezzling the money or property of their employers, shall be deemed to have stolen the same, and may be transported for fourteen years or imprisoned. With respect to clerks and servants, it must be noted that to bring a servant or clerk within the law, it must be shown that he was authorised to receive it ; and if a person, not being a clerk or servant, in a single instance is requested to receive money, receives and embezzles it, he cannot be convicted of embezzlement. The embezzlement by a servant or clerk must be of the particular sum to be received ; for if he embezzles a sum he was not authorised to receive, the crime is not complete.

As to embezzlement by agents, see AGENTS.

EMBLEMENTS. When a tenant from year to year, tenant for life, parson having glebe land, or any person whose tenancy is not determined by the tenor of the lease or agreement under which he holds the land, sows the land, the tenant or executors shall reap the crops which have been so sown; but it is otherwise in respect of leaseholders, or those whose tenancies expire at a particular day, as at the end of the lease or other specific time agreed on at the commencement of the tenancy, except by custom as to *way-going, crops, &c.* These crops are termed *emblements.*

ENGRAVINGS. See LITERARY PROPERTY.

EQUITY, is the relief afforded to parties by our courts of equity (see COURTS), where the common law, from its constitution and practice is unable to afford the suitor substantial justice. It is particularly exercised in cases of trust and matters arising from the mutual faith and confidence which man is obliged to repose in man. It is almost impossible to define its boundaries, or to state with precision in a work of this nature the extent of its jurisdiction. The mode of procedure and proof is adapted to cases of the above nature, and addresses itself to the conscience of a party complained of, as he is obliged to answer upon his oath all matters relating to the transaction.

ESCAPE, in a civil case, is where the sheriff or his officer, which is the same thing, lets, voluntarily or negligently, his prisoner go at large after the return of the process, and which renders the sheriff liable for the debt in an action on the case to be brought against him by the creditor. Also if a prisoner for debt escapes out of the Queen's Bench prison, or Marshalsea, or the Fleet, the marshal, keeper, or warden, is to be answerable; if the escape be from a *sheriff's* prison, the sheriff is liable; and it matters not whether the debtor is retaken. Debtors escaping may be retaken upon warrant and committed to the county gaol: it is indictable for a person to attempt an escape from prison. If a debtor is rescued, the sheriff is not liable, but he must *return* it; *i. e.* he must report the same to the court, who will commit the rescuers.

In criminal cases, if the gaoler or officer having custody of a party charged with a felony, permit him to escape *voluntarily*, he is punishable in the same degree as for the offence of which the party was guilty; but the person permitting the escape, cannot be so punished until the conviction or outlawry of the offender himself.

The mere *negligent* escape of a prisoner subjects the gaoler to fine and imprisonment proportioned to the circumstances of the offences.

ESTATE, signifies an inheritance, freehold, for term of life or years, or any interest that a man has in tenements, or things holden, as a mortgage estate, an estate at will, from year to year, or at sufferance, &c. As to what is real and what is personal estate, see REAL ESTATE.

EVIDENCE, is the demonstration to a jury of facts necessary to be proved on the trial of matters forming the subjects of legal decision; and this demonstration is either afforded by testimony of witnesses upon oath, or by writings: the facts thus authenticated and brought before the jury are called *evidence*, as being *evident* and made plain to them from these sources of information. Evidence is produced to a jury on the trial of any alleged facts, criminal or civil, which are affirmed by one party and denied by another, legally termed an "issue," or "issues in fact;" and these *issues*, as they are styled, are peculiarly subjects on which the jury are to form a direct judgment or opinion; the propriety or *admissibility* of such *evidence* being a matter of pure law, which, if disputed, is an *issue in law*, triable by the judges, and with which the jury can have nothing to do.

The evidence, therefore, presentable to a jury is based upon a system of judicial or legal learning now established in our courts, upon principles which are very full, comprehensive, and refined; evidence not being what a jury may consider to be evidence, but such as is directed by the presiding judge to be received as such, or rejected; the matters offered to the consideration of the jury being submitted to the test of evidence affording the only ground upon which they can according to their oath, which is "to give a verdict according to the evidence," come to a lawful decision.

The limits of this work can only enable the editor to give a partial, yet he hopes practical, outline of this diffuse, although necessary, branch of legal learning; he therefore proposes to consider evidence apart from refined distinctions, and as, 1. Written and unwritten. 2. As regards the rules by which evidence is governed, and to evidence in its absolute and presumptive character.

1. Written evidence or proofs are public records and ancient deeds (*i. e.* deeds thirty years old), the simple production of which substantiate the facts therein mentioned; and modern deeds and other writings, which must be verified as to their essentials and forms; and if not under seal, as to the facts, by the verbal testimony of witnesses.

Records and public writings are *proved* by the production of the originals, or certified and examined copies if inrolled; but common deeds cannot be proved ordinarily by copies or counterparts, where the originals can be procured, for it is a rule that the best evidence the nature of the case will admit shall be produced; for, if it appear that better evidence might have been brought forward, the very circumstance of its being withheld, induces a suspicion that it would have prejudiced the party in whose power it is, had he produced it. Thus, if a written contract be in the custody of the party, no verbal testimony can be received of its contents. Private writings, being deeds not thirty years old, are put in evidence, by thetestimony of execution of the deed by the subscribing witnesses, and in other cases by proof of the handwriting of the party, or of those whom they purport to be: thus, contracts or agreements, or bills of exchange, when authenticated by the testimony of the attesting witnesses, or proof of the handwriting of the parties, are strong evidence of the facts they mention, though not so conclusive as a deed, because not so solemnly executed.

The *letters* of individuals are evidence *against* the writers, as admissions of the facts and circumstances stated in them, but not *for* them, as that would in effect permit a party to make evidence for himself; but they may always be explained, or contradicted, by evidence of the circumstances under which they are written. They are evidence only against the immediate parties, unless they appear to be written by an agent duly authorised, or by a clerk, shopman, &c. in the ordinary course of his employer's business, which must, in that case, be previously shown by evidence.

Private memoranda, made when, or recently after, the events occurred, by competent persons interested in them, are evidence on their coming into question at a future period, provided the person who made them be dead, or cannot be produced as a witness; but if he can, he must be called.

Tradesmen's books are good evidence of the facts mentioned in them against the tradesman, because it cannot be ordinarily presumed that he will make any entry therein injurious to himself; and, on the other hand, entries made therein by the tradesman himself, his shopman, &c., will be evidence against his customers as of the delivery of goods, sale, price, &c., if they appear to have been regularly made according to the course of business, and nothing is apparent to induce suspicion of incorrectness: but they can only be used as what is termed secondary evidence; and if made by the tradesman *himself*, without evidence of the delivery of the goods named, they are inadmissible. See Book-debts.

The books of a steward or collector are evidence against himself, and his estate after his death.

Where it is necessary that written or documentary evidence of a private nature should be produced, such as deeds, agreements, writings, letters, memoranda, &c., before a party shall be permitted to give copies, or other evidence of their contents, it must be shown that the originals are burnt, lost, or destroyed, or in the possession of the other party, having an interest to suppress them, and that such party has had notice to produce them; which if he does not do, then the next best (*i. e. secondary*) evidence will be allowed to be given, which may be done by attested or examined copies, or verbal evidence of the contents. An ancient deed proves itself; but it should be shown that the party seeking the benefit of it has the custody of it, or that it was procured from the proper custody.

The *depositions*, or memorandums of what witnesses have sworn before magistrates, coroners, examiners in chancery or the exchequer, officers of the ecclesiastical courts, are good evidence, if the persons mentioned in them as deponents be dead; but there is some exception as to proceedings or depositions, which cannot be produced against any person not a party to the suit in which they were taken. In criminal cases, the confession of a prisoner before a justice (unless obtained by threat or promise) is evidence against himself, as well as the depositions, which last are only receivable as evidence if the witnesses be dead, or unable to travel; such last facts to be duly evidenced.

There appears to be no difference, as to the production of papers in evidence, between civil and criminal cases; in neither case is the party bound to produce evidence against himself; but, in a criminal prosecution, as well as in civil cases, notice may be given the party to produce papers in his possession, and in case of his refusal or neglect, and on proof of their being in his possession, other or secondary evidence may be given of their contents.

A *receipt* is not conclusive evidence against the party signing it; but he may show he did not receive the sum or thing therein named. *Receipts in full* are conclusive, when given by any one with a knowledge of all circumstances; but if such receipt was obtained by fraud, it is otherwise.

Entries in family Bibles, Prayer, or other books, when made by the parent, head of a family, or other competent person, of births, marriages, deaths, and other facts, happening within his own knowledge, are good evidence of such facts.

In conclusion, with regard to written proofs or evidence, the principle appears to be, with none other than a few necessary exceptions, that every instrument, to the signing of which there is a witness, must be proved by that witness, if living and to be found, or by proving the handwriting of the witness, in case he is dead, or domiciled in a foreign country, or absconded from his creditors and not to be found after a diligent search, or cannot be found in such a manner as to raise a presumption of his death, or is blind, insane, or felon-convict, or was interested at the time of the signing or execution of the writing, which rendered his attestation a nullity, or has become interested since, or has set out to leave the kingdom.

To facilitate the carrying various statutes into execution, certain acts are declared to be sufficient evidence of particular transactions, and the courts of law have made rules, with a view to saving of expense, in respect of the production of evidence, which, if unnecessarily produced or insisted upon by either party, after certain notice, will expose the party receiving such notice to all the costs attendant upon the party requiring particular evidence, whatever the event of the cause may be.

Unwritten evidence is required in cases where the subject of the action or prosecution does not arise from any matter in writing, and consequently, the only evidence which can be given of it is verbal testimony, by the examination of living witnesses, who are credible or competent..

In judging of credibility or competency, all persons, of whatever religion or country that have the use of their reason, and believe in God and a future state, are to be examined, except persons deemed *infamous* (*i. e.* convicted of perjury or felony, and some other offences of an odious nature, and not pardoned, or undergone the punishment), and those who have a direct interest in the event of the cause; all others are legally competent, though it lies with the jury to judge of their credibility.

In civil cases, one witness is sufficient evidence to a jury of any one single fact; but in criminal prosecutions for high treason and perjury, two witnesses at least are necessary.

Counsellors, attornies, or solicitors, are not to be examined against their clients, because they are obliged to keep their secrets; but they may be examined as to any thing known previously to them, not in that capacity; for it has been held, that only what is communicated to an attorney for the purpose of bringing a suit, or relating to a suit, is privileged from disclosure. The counsellor or attorney cannot waive this privilege, but the client can.

A witness shall not be examined, where his evidence tends to clear, or accuse himself of a crime; nor is he bound to give any answer which would expose him to punishment, penalty, or forfeiture, or to a criminal charge, as to convict him of usury; neither is he compellable to answer questions which are degrading to his character, although such questions may be legally asked; but a witness cannot refuse to answer on the ground only that his answer may establish a debt due from him to the king or any other.

A witness cannot be examined as to any fact that does not relate to the point in issue.

The wife cannot be examined in any cause in which her husband is a party; though it is otherwise where third persons have an interest, even though her testimony may make her husband liable to a legal demand, and, contrariwise, the husband cannot be examined where the wife is a party, save in actions or prosecutions for offences concerning the separate interests of the wife, but not to involve her in any personal consequences, as for crime; although in criminal cases, especially in high treason, there are some necessary exceptions to this rule.

If a witness has been promised a reward, or other advantage, by the party in support of whose case he is called, on the condition of his success, the witness shall not be examined; but the mere fact of the witness having received pecuniary or other assistance from one of the parties before the trial, is no ground of objection to his competence, nor will a general promise of money or advantage on any event, destroy his competence, though the jury may consider the testimony of such a witness strictly in point of credibility.

Trustees, guardians, executors, and administrators, who have no personal advantage from the property confided to their care, are competent witnesses in all questions connected with their trusts.

Informers are not deemed good witnesses, because they are manifestly interested in the result of the trial, or inquiry, though persons entitled to rewards on conviction of criminals are competent.

2. With regard to the rules by which evidence is governed, some have already been noticed; and one especially, which is, that the best evidence of which the nature of the case admits must be adduced, and that a party must not attempt to rely on what is termed *secondary* evidence, at least, without proving that *primary* evidence cannot be given, and the reason why it cannot be adduced.

Presumptions, or inferences, are not allowed; but positive proof is always required, where, from the nature of the case, it appears it might possibly have been had; but, next to positive proof, *circumstantial* evidence, or the doctrine of *presumptions,* must take place; for positive or absolute evidence is *direct*, and is in affirmance or denial of any particular fact; but presumptive evidence is *collateral*, and arises from the conclusion to be drawn by the conscience of a jury conversant with the affairs and business of life, from the conduct of the parties affording an inference that such a particular fact did or did not occur.

Violent presumption is many times equal to full proof; for there those circumstances appear, which *necessarily* attend a fact which cannot be absolutely demonstrated.

Probable presumption arises from circumstances which *usually* attend a fact; and this has its weight; as where a bill of exchange, negociated after acceptance, is produced from the hands of the acceptor after it is due, the presumption is that the acceptor has paid for it.

Light presumptions have no weight at all.

All presumptive evidence of felony should be admitted cautiously, for the law holds it better that ten guilty persons escape, than one innocent suffer; and Sir Matthew Hale, in particular, lays down two rules most prudent and necessary to be observed: 1. Never to convict a man for stealing the goods of a person unknown, merely because he will give no account how he came by them, unless an actual stealing be proved of such goods: and, 2. Never to convict any person of murder or manslaughter, till, at least, the body be found dead; on account of two instances he mentions, where persons were executed for the murder of others, who were then alive, but missing. Indeed, to conclude the doctrine of presumptions, no fact should be inferred, without premises that will warrant the inference: some more certain grounds than mere *thinking*.

The party making any affirmative allegation, which is denied by his adversary, is in general required to prove it, unless, indeed, a man be charged with not doing an act which by law he is required to do, for there a different rule must necessarily prevail.

As the evidence must in all cases be applied to the fact in dispute, no evidence unconnected with it can be received, nor can the character of the parties be called in question, unless brought before the court by the proceedings themselves, as in action for slander, libel, &c.

Hearsay, or the repetition by one person of what he has heard another say, is not generally deemed admissible evidence; but there are circumstances when it will be allowed, as where a person at the point of death, conscious of his being so (which is question of law, not of fact), makes a statement, or declaration, relating either to former transactions of his life, or to the cause of his death, when he dies by violent means; but declarations of a criminal at the time of execution, cannot in any case be admitted. Also declarations made by the parents, or other relations of a person whose legitimacy is in question, or respecting the state of the family in questions of pedigree, are admissible in evidence after their death, provided they were made before the doubts arose; for if made after the subject has become a matter of dispute, they are inadmissible; and hearsay evidence, by hearsay, may also be allowed concerning public rights and local custom, as if such evidence were not allowable, it is hardly likely that any local custom could be established. In like manner, the general reputation of the country is admissible evidence on questions respecting the nature and existence of public rights and customs, and of the boundaries of manors, parishes, &c.; but it is no evidence of *private* rights, or of particular facts or instances of individual enjoyment of public rights; and, lastly, with regard to this species of evidence, the general reputation in a family as to the birth, legitimacy, marriage, death, and descendants of any particular member of it, is admissible evidence, on those facts coming into dispute at a subsequent period, because after a lapse of years such facts seldom admit of direct proof.

There is a more certain and admissible *hearsay* evidence, which perhaps cannot be strictly so termed, as the declarations or statements made by a person or party interested *at the time* (not prior or subsequently), respecting the motives or objects he had in view in doing a particular act, and the statements or declarations of the parties to a suit, which are termed "admissions," and where a criminal act has been committed, "confessions," which, if not explained, or in the case of a *confession*, if it was voluntary and no improper influence or inducement was used or held out, are evidence against the parties admitting or confessing; but if there be no proof of a dealing or transaction prior to the admission, and no proof of a crime actually committed before the confession, it is not a conclusive evidence; in fact, may fairly be considered as no evidence at all.

A few words may be added as to the effect of offers or statements made by a person who is sued for a demand which he is defending, which, though made for the sake of *peace* and in good faith, are often cunningly wrung into an admission of the justice of a claim or set-off by an unjust or dishonourable adversary, in order that a distinction should be drawn between *offers of compromise* and an *admission of a demand*, after a dispute has arisen; for an offer to pay a sum of money in order to get rid of an action is not of itself evidence of the justness of the demand, as many suppose, though it may be, and often is, a question for the jury to determine, whether an offer was or was not made to stop litigation, without regard to the question whether any thing was or was not really due, especially after some indistinct evidence has been offered in favour of the claim. Therefore, persons who have disputes upon their hands would do well to introduce into any letter or statement which may be written or made with an amicable intent, a declaration that "the offer is made and to be received without prejudice," or "that the present offer or statement is made without regard to the real fact whether any thing is or is not legally due," or that the offer is made "to purchase peace:" in these cases the communication in any subsequent letter referring to the first, so guarded, cannot be used against the writer, or even influence the jury against him, if he is driven into court. Generally speaking, verbal evidence shall not be adduced to add to, vary, or contradict the terms of a written contract, upon the principle that the court and jury cannot make a new agreement for the parties, unless the terms were written fraudulently. The law of England always presumes against fraud, and that, till the contrary be shown, things have been duly and properly transacted; so the legal presumption is, that a person's character is good until the contrary is shown, or that he is innocent of an imputed offence till his guilt be proved. Also, where a person is bound to do an act, the omission of which would be criminal, his performance of that act will be presumed until the contrary appear; but if a criminal act has once been proved, the law infers malice, and requires exculpatory evidence from the party. Thus, in a case of homicide, on proof of the prisoner having killed the deceased, the law presumes malice unless the prisoner can justify or extenuate the deed.

Persons are presumed to be dead at the expiration of seven years if not heard of, or if after diligent inquiry they cannot be found, the seven years being calculated from the time they were last heard of.

As to the summoning of witnesses, and their examination, see WITNESS.

EXCISE. The revenue arising from duties and taxes laid on articles, the produce of, or consumed in, this country. This part of the public revenue is regulated by the stat. 7 & 8 *G.4. c.* 53.; amended by 4 & 5 *W.* 4. *c.* 51.

EXCOMMUNICATION. A sentence of the ecclesiastical courts prohibiting offenders from mixing with the congregation, or participating in the offices of the church: this sentence in early times was only directed against felons and irreclaimable persons, but afterwards (for obvious purposes) was directed against those who did not perform the decrees of an ecclesiastical court. The word *excommunication*, indeed, has been taken away by a late statute, and the term *contumacious* is now applied to a party who does not or cannot pay what is enjoined by an ecclesiastical court *for his soul's health*, in lieu of penance: under the process for this constructive contumacy, a man may be *perpetually* imprisoned, whatever the amount may be, and though under 20*l.*, as the insolvent debtors' act does not extend to these contempts or contumacies, which the ecclesiastical court insists are *actual* contempts. The decrees or orders of these *Courts Christian*, or *Spiritual Courts*, are always prefaced, amongst other recitals, with "and having set God before our eyes."

EXECUTION is the final process or writ by which the judgment of a court is executed. It issues from the court where the judgment was obtained, and is either, 1. Against the body of the defendant alone (see CAPIAS AD SATISFACIENDUM). 2. Against his goods and chattels (see FIERI FACIAS). 3. Against the goods of the defendant, and the profits of all his lands (see LEVARI FACIAS). 4. Against the defendant's goods, and the half of his lands (see ELEGIT). In the cases where the lands are seized, the profits only are taken, or rather the land is in pledge for the debt, in case of a deficiency in the goods which are primarily liable. Execution is styled *final process:* all previous process is called *mesne process*. As to what the sheriff may seize, see SHERIFF.

The execution of judgment in criminal cases is performed by, or under the direction of the sheriff, who is bound to provide an expert executioner.

EXECUTORS AND ADMINISTRATORS. An executor is a person appointed by a party's last will and testament, to perform and *execute* it after his decease. An administrator is one who administers either the effects of a deceased person who has made a will, but has not appointed executors, or has survived them if appointed, or *where* those appointed refused to act, or of a deceased person *intestate, i. e.* who has made no will whatever. The administrator in the former instance is styled *administrator with the will annexed;* in the latter case *general administrator:* an executor is in some points an administrator, for he administers or distributes the effects of the party making the will, who is styled the " testator.'

There is also the executor *de son tort*, i. e. *in his own wrong*, which is, if a stranger takes upon him to act as executor without any lawful authority, as by intermeddling with the goods or personal property of the deceased, and by many other transactions which will be noticed hereafter.

The duties of executors and administrators closely resemble each other, and in many points are the same: they will therefore be noticed together; the only distinctions that the reader need carry in his mind being that the executor and administrator *with the will annexed*, distribute the effects of the testator as appointed by him, and the undisposed of *residue*, according to law; and the *general* administrator of an intestate distributing the whole of the estate or effects according to law, as in the case of a residue just now noticed, that is, according to the various acts regarding the distribution of intestate's effects, commonly called the "Statute of Distributions." It is also to be remembered, that unless for the purposes of sale and distribution of the proceeds as personalty, executors and administrators have nothing to do with real estate, *i. e.* freehold or copyhold, offices hereditary, interests charged on freehold, &c., their dealings being only with chattels, or chattel interests, so termed in contradistinction to *real* interests. These terms are fully explained under the titles PROPERTY, CHATTELS.

The acts necessary to be done by executors will be noticed in the order in which they have to be performed; the distribution of the residue, and the law of intestacy, being lastly considered.

On the death of a person, any one, in the absence of the nearest relation or the executor, may take care of and secure the property, and provide daily necessaries for the household, and even bury the deceased without incurring any liabilities whatever to the creditors or legatees of the deceased: indeed, such person must be reimbursed by the executors or administrators what he may reasonably expend in the performance of such friendly office, *if they possess assets;* the law implying a contract upon which an action will lie against them upon refusal, or he may retain sufficient for these necessary purposes if any thing has fairly come to his hands.

The executor is, generally speaking, at hand, or can be sent for, and it is his office to order the deceased to be buried in a manner suitable, not so much regarding his quality, as to the estate he leaves behind him, for any excess will have to be borne by the executors in case there is a deficiency for payment of debts and legacies; if the testator is insolvent, 20*l.* would be the utmost amount, except he was a person of condition, when more might be allowed, but honesty suggests the strictest economy in such cases.

An executor should well consider as to his accepting this friendly but yet troublesome office, and therefore ought in prudence to peruse the will carefully, in which, if there are many trusts, he should look to his indemnity by the clauses of such will, against liabilities by acts of third parties, and for which he would otherwise be liable; if there are children, or persons comparatively helpless, he should not hastily refuse, but carefully ascertain the means left by the testator for their provision, and who may be joined with him in the trust. If there appears a slight deficiency for which a sale is to be made of real estate, which is not as such generally within the scope of an executor's dealings unless devised in trust for such sale; it behoves him to consider the title to such estate, and how the money may be raised without much delay, and without interfering with other charges upon it, unless provided for in the will. If there appears a deficiency unprovided for, *i. e.* if the estate is insolvent, then prudence would suggest the throwing up the trust altogether, especially if any substantial creditors step forth who are willing to administer, or the family are willing to take the property and distribute it themselves. The refusal to act is termed a *renunciation* or *renouncing* of administration; and the declining to receive freehold or real property upon trust, is termed *disclaiming*, which is done by deed, both which the executor should do as soon as circumstances will permit, for he ought not to delay; indeed, his acting without proof of the will, will bind him, and after proof of the will by him, the duty is absolutely cast upon him.

If an executor take possession of, and administer any part of the *personal* estate, and omit to prove the will within six calendar months after the death of the testator, he is liable to forfeit 100*l.* and 10*l.* per cent. upon the stamp duty, payable on the probate.

Where there is more than one executor, on the refusal of one, administration may be granted to the other or others, and those who neglect may come in at any period of time and act, unless specially foreclosed. Executors may, if they choose, *disclaim* by deed the real property devised, and administer the personal property.

If the executor has made up his mind to act in the executorship either solely or jointly with others, and is satisfied with the indemnities afforded him by the will against the acts of his co-executors, and other liabilities incident to the performance of trusts, especially for minors, he will take peaceable possession of the testator's effects, and may enter the house of the heir for that purpose, and may, even before probate or proof of the will, pay and receive debts, and do various other acts incident to his executorship, he may *commence* actions, and file bills in equity, but cannot proceed further without first obtaining the probate under seal of the ecclesiastical court. On the other hand, if he has chosen to act, he may before *probate*, be sued by the creditors of the deceased, and may in equity be compelled to answer and discover respecting the *personal* estate of the testator, and concerning the proceeds of any real estate devised to him upon trust.

He should make an inventory for the purpose of exhibiting it to the ecclesiastical court, pursuant to the bond given for that purpose, which in practice is not often called for, but which, for other considerations, should be made upon an appraisement stamp according to the value. If the executor do not cause the effects or personal estate to be carefully appraised and reduced into an inventory, the law will suppose him to have enough to pay *all* debts and legacies until he does away with that presumption; but if he files his inventory, it lies upon his adversaries to show that he hath received more than the inventory contains.

The inventory need not be made by "*sworn* appraisers;" any two "honest," *i. e.* credible and disinterested persons, is sufficient. See Appraisement, Inventory.

At this period it may be necessary to advert to the executor or administrator *de son tort*, before alluded to, who is not unfrequently some pragmatical, certainly some legally unauthorised person, who, upon pretence or colour of acting for the widow and children, or in some such manner, interferes in the conduct of the deceased's affairs, and supposes himself sheltered from account or liability by qualifying his acts as done for others; but it should be known, that any one who intermeddles in a deceased's affairs, beyond doing the immediate acts of charity and kindness before mentioned, renders himself liable to the creditors at large and other claimants, without reserving to himself any legal rights, for his acts, as they are done presumedly at his own instance, are to his own liability and wrong, and, therefore, he is liable to debts, whether there are assets or not, and to the costs of proceedings instituted by the claimants.

The criterion of an executor *de son tort* is his doing those things that executors usually perform in the course of their functions, and which, in fact, lead to the common and public inference that the party so acting has the authority of an executor. If an administration be afterwards granted to an executor in his own wrong, that will render valid all the *lawful* acts he has done in his former administration, but will not sanction any illegal or improper disposition that may have been made by him of the deceased's property. All persons, however nearly related to the deceased, or even the widow of a deceased, who intermeddle with the effects, are executors of this class.

The will must be proved, we have seen, within six months after decease of the testator, or within two calendar months after the termination of any suit or dispute respecting the will or the right to administer, if there be any such, which shall not be ended within four calendar months after the death of the deceased, under a penalty of 100*l*., and 10*l*. per cent. on the amount of the probate duty.

The will must be proved in the proper ecclesiastical court, that is, in the diocese, or in one of the districts of a diocese, called *peculiars* (which has jurisdiction and power to grant probate exclusive of the bishop), where the deceased's effects are situate; but if the deceased left *known goods*, termed *bonâ notabilia*, out of the diocese or peculiar, the will must be proved in the court of the archbishop of the province in which he died, the archbishop, or *metropolitan* as he is styled, having the *prerogative* to grant probate in such cases. For instance, if a person dies in Wilts or Berkshire, probate ought to be obtained out of the bishop's court at Salisbury, those counties being within the diocese of the bishop of Salisbury, unless the testator should happen to die at Great Farringdon, where there is a peculiar, in which last case the will will have to be proved there; but if the testator had known goods, *i. e. bonâ notabilia*, out of those places, *in divers dioceses* as it is termed, to the value of 5*l*., or 10*l*. in London, the metropolitan, viz. the archbishop of Canterbury, grants, by his prerogative, probate to executors. So, if a man die in a diocese in the province of York, and have *bonâ notabilia* in different or divers dioceses in that province, the archbishop of York grants a prerogative probate. See DIOCESE.

Sometimes it is necessary to have two probates from separate provincial courts, as, if a man die having property within the province of York and the province of Canterbury, and sometimes there must be a probate in the court of peculiars and in the court of the archbishop of the diocese in which the court of peculiar jurisdiction is situated, in respect of property situate out of the peculiar.

A bishop's will is always proved before his archbishop, wherever his personal property may happen to be.

The common form of proving a will is usually conducted by a proctor, registrar, or agent, in the ecclesiastical courts, and is as follows: — The executor takes the will of the deceased, and in strictness should also take the inventory, and presents them before the judge of the ecclesiastical court, or more usually his surrogate, and produces witnesses, who make oath that the will produced is the *true, whole, and last will and testament of* the deceased. The executor or administrator with the will annexed, is required to make oath that he or she will dispose of the goods of the deceased according to law. When wills are proved with no subscribing witness, there must be the affidavit of *two* persons, that the signature is the testator's handwriting; if *one* subscribing witness, the affidavit of one person only is required; if there be two subscribing witnesses, the oath of the executor alone is sufficient.

Where a subscribing witness takes a legacy, or any interest under the will, he is considered by the ecclesiastical courts as no witness at all, and the want of such witness must be supplied by affidavit as above.*

There is what is termed the solemn form of proving a will when it appears imperfect upon the face of it, or when any person having an interest under the deceased's estate, or next of kin, wishes to invalidate it, the process is as follows:—The persons who would have been entitled to administer the effects, if the testator had died without a will, must be cited to be present when the will is presented in court for probate; and the party presenting it, being generally the executor or some one claiming under it, prays the court that witnesses may be examined upon it, and that the will may be published and confirmed: whereupon the witnesses are secretly, and apart from each other, examined; and their testimony, reduced into writing, termed *depositions*, is afterwards published or notified in court, and then the judge pronounces for or against the validity of the will, according to the evidence. If the executor himself, to ease himself of all responsibility in the case of adverse claimants, or parties claiming interest, as in case of intestacy, choose this method, he cites or summons the next of kin, and all others claiming general interest, and the proceedings thereupon are conclusive upon all parties.

It is usual when there is a contest about a will, or when the right of administration comes in question, to enter a *caveat* in the ecclesiastical court, which prevents administration for three months.

There is a duty payable to government upon probates of wills, letters of administration with the will annexed, and administrations generally, which is chargeable upon all the executor or administrator expects or has a right to receive, without making any deduction for debts owing by the deceased. This duty can be returned if too much has been paid.

After the proof of the will and the making an inventory, though the latter is not absolutely necessary, nor can it always be performed till after collection, the executor is to collect the effects inventoried, and has ample power given him by the law for that purpose, he being the representative of the deceased, and may therefore take without force or violence all the goods of the deceased, and the writings relating to the *personal* estate; for this purpose he may open any open door, or lock, or the key being in, although the house, box, or chest be in the possession of the heir-at-law, and whatever is recovered, being of a saleable nature, may be sold or mortgaged. Funds at the bank may be transferred to an executor or administrator on production of the probate; in fine, every thing that the deceased could have lawfully done with the property, the executor or administrator may do, so that it be in conformity with the testator's will. The chattels, *real* and *personal*, of an intestate or testator, coming to the hands of an executor or administrator, are leases for years rent due which may be distrained for, corn growing and cut, grass cut,

* The common law adopted a contrary course; it rendered the gift void, and admitted the testimony of the witness. The late statute of wills, 1 *Vict.* c. 26. *s.* 15, 16, 17., nullifies the bequest to a witness, and renders him, as well as other parties, competent to prove the execution of the will. See WILLS.

&c., cattle, money, securities for money, plate, household goods; and even a plantation, although of an inheritance and a freehold, yet being in a foreign country is considered a chattel in the hands of executors or administrators applicable for the payment of debts. These things are termed "assets," as are all sums directed by the will of a testator to be raised out of real estate by either mortgage or sale.

The executors or administrators having obtained assets, are next to distribute or administer the same, according to the will of the testator, or the statute of distributions after payment of funeral expenses, debts, and legacies.

In payment of debts, executors or administrators must observe the rules of priority in this respect, else on a deficiency of assets or means, if they pay those of a lower degree first, they must answer those of a higher degree unpaid, out of their own estate; and for that reason, if an action be brought against them for debt of inferior degree, and a debt of higher degree be still unpaid, they must defend themselves by pleading that fact, or they will have to pay both. Therefore they must,

1st. Pay or retain all funeral and testamentary expenses, and the costs of administering the estate by a suit in chancery.

2. Debts due to the king on record or specialty; being fines, duties unpaid on the probate or administration, and debts arising upon deed under seal. Debts due to the king, not specialties, stand upon the same footing as other debts due to individuals.

3. Debts which various statutes have declared, shall have particular preference, viz. debts due to the post-office, debts due by overseers for money received by them, debts due by a trustee or treasurer to any benefit or friendly society duly enrolled, and debts due by collectors of metropolis paving acts, as receivers thereunder.

4. Debts of *record* due to ordinary individuals, viz. judgments docquetted (for if not docquetted they rank as simple contracts), decrees in equity, *i. e.* in chancery or equity side of the exchequer, and recognisance of bail or such like.

5. Debts due by deed or by a contract under seal, being bonds, mortgages, &c.; but rent, though not reserved by deed, ranks as a specialty debt, and ranks in this degree of priority, though the landlord has a better remedy by distress.

6. Simple contract debts—that is, debts upon notes and verbal promises, or contracts simply ranking as such, though in writing (the *seal* constituting the specialty): of these, debts due to the king are first to be paid, the wages of servants or labourers, and the remainder may be paid as the executor or administrator may choose; but if the executor have no knowledge of a specialty debt, or debt of higher degree, he is at liberty to pay a simple contract creditor upon suit, which suit the creditor may commence immediately after the deceased's death; but, generally speaking, it is unsafe for executors or administrators to pay simple contract creditors before they have ascertained that there are no debts of higher degree. A simple contract creditor who obtains a judgment is, however, entitled to his priority; and if the executor cannot plead liability to higher debts, he acts wisely in paying upon a *bonâ fide* action.

Executors or administrators may retain debts due to them, if they are not administering in their own wrong, or take out administration as creditors, but the retaining can only be in respect of a debt of *equal* degree; and a retaining cannot be supported which operates against debts of a *higher* degree or priority. Also amongst creditors coming under any particular class, and being of equal degree in respect of legal priority, the executor or administrator may pay whom he chooses in full, to the detriment of his brother creditors, who stand upon the same footing with the favoured creditor. Executors or administrators are also bound to reserve a sufficient fund to meet the performance of any contract which the deceased may have made in his lifetime, which of course is payable before legacies.

The administering of a testator's or intestate's estate may be, indeed in some cases *must* be, effected by the court of chancery, or the equity side of the exchequer, which will by a decree order all parties to come in and prove their debts and claim their legacies, and then, as it is termed, " marshall the assets," which shall be noticed hereafter. The executors or administrators, with the will annexed, as the case may be, having disposed of the claims of their testator, by payment of the debts and by reservation or retention of a sufficient sum to meet ordinary expenses to pay legacy duties, and to fulfil any continuing or outstanding contract made by the deceased, or for carrying on the trade of the deceased for a convenient period, have next to turn their attention to the legacies payable under the will, a branch of their duty which presents many legal difficulties, most of which may be obviated or remedied by a due and careful attention to all the circumstances attendant on the bequest, and the legal interpretation of the words in which it is framed. This subject will be treated of under the title LEGACIES; and all that is here necessary to observe is, that the executor should not, on payment of legacies above 20*l.*, take a receipt stamped as in the ordinary course of business, but should make application to the legacy duty office for printed forms, which will be given him *gratis*, and must be filled up according to circumstances, and then forwarded to the same office; and when the legacy duty has been paid, the receipt will be stamped and returned. Particular attention should be paid to this, otherwise high penalties will be incurred. See LEGACIES.

The reader has been informed, that the executors or administrators have nothing to do with *real* estate, but only with estate of an inferior degree, viz. chattels, real or personal, and, generally speaking, where a testator devises land for payment of debts, or to raise a specific fund for a particular purpose. Questions upon the *marshalling of assets*, as it is termed, do not arise but where a testator or intestate dies insolvent; that is, if the personal estate (which is the only fund chargeable at *law*) will not pay the debts due by specialty and legacies, or either of them, then the simple contract creditors and legatees, together with the remainder of the specialty creditors (*who are to be paid in full before the simple contract creditors receive any thing*), may obtain satisfaction in a court of *equity* out of the real estates of the deceased, to the extent of the debts that remain, whether special or otherwise: these assets are therefore termed *equitable* assets, in contradistinction to *legal* assets, which is the personal estate, come to the hands of the executor or administrator; and the court of equity, in administering these assets, adheres to the rules to be observed as to the priorities and privileges of the kinds of debt before mentioned. This proceeding may commence by either a creditor or legatee filing a bill in chancery or in the exchequer against the executor or administrator for an equal division of the deceased's legal as well as equitable (*i. e.* the proceeds of his real estates) assets, for we have seen the executor or administrator may favour whom he chooses in a particular class of creditors; or such a proceeding may emanate from the executor or administrator himself, who, when pressed by numerous creditors bringing actions at law to obtain judgments against him for the legal assets (*i. e.* the personal estate), before he has, or whether he has or has not, assets to pay all, procures a friendly creditor to institute such a suit, to prevent the accumulation of costs and litigation; or, if he is himself desirous of applying the assets as far as they will go in satisfying the debts equally, may file a bill against all the creditors, so that they may contest each other's debts, and that their rights of priority may be settled. This proceeding also may, without impropriety, take place where an estate is perfectly solvent, and consists of personalty only, or personalty and realty; and the persons chiefly entitled are minors, or persons of unsound mind, or where from particular circumstances the opinion or direction of the court of chancery (where most of these suits are pending) or exchequer is desired as to particular matters, or the executor is desirous of being indemnified in the discharge of an onerous trust, or relieved from it altogether. In either case his reasonable costs are allowed him out of the balance in his hands, and his accounts are audited before one of the masters of the court, who invests the fund for the benefit of the parties entitled, or pays it them if immediately entitled, or distributes it amongst the creditors, having regard to the priority of their claims, specialty creditors being always paid in full before those by simple contract.

The land is not to be resorted to for payment of simple contract debts until the personal estate is exhausted by payment of debts of higher degree; and in the case of a solvent estate, the land is not to be charged with the payment of legacies unless it can be fairly collected that the testator intended that his land should be sold or charged with the payment of such legacies; and even then the personal estate, which is the legal and primary fund, must be first drained, unless it can be shown that he meant to exempt his personal estate; but where legacies are payable out of particular funds, on failure of those funds the legatee is disappointed: the questions arising upon these matters often render an appeal to a court of equity more necessary than the public seem to allow.

When the debts and legacies are discharged, the residue or surplus must be paid to the residuary legatee, *i. e.* the person appointed by the will to receive the remaining surplus; and if there is no person entitled under the will, then the executor is bound to distribute it amongst the next of kin, under the statute of distributions, and precisely as a distribution is made by the general administrator of the whole amongst the next of kin in cases of intestacy. The executor cannot be compelled to pay over the residue till the end of one year, after which time it seems he will be liable to pay interest. In cases of intestacy, the statute of distributions declares that no distribution shall be made till after one year, and that even then the persons receiving their distributive shares shall give bond to refund in case debts should appear. In practice, it is usual before dividing a residue amongst the next of kin, to advertise for creditors or for legatees, or next of kin undiscovered, so that the appearance of a legatee or unpaid creditor should not cause a refund by the residuary legatees or next of kin.

A TABLE

SHOWING HOW THE UNDISPOSED OF RESIDUE OF A TESTATOR OR THE PERSONAL ESTATE OF AN INTESTATE IS TO BE DISTRIBUTED.

If the testator or intestate dies, leaving,	*His personal representatives or next of kin shall take the residue or the whole, in the proportions following: viz.—*
Wife and child, or children.	One third to wife, rest to child or children; and if children are dead, then to their representatives (*i. e.* their lineal descendants), except such child or children, not heirs-at-law, who have been advanced by intestate, in his lifetime, to an amount equal to the separate shares of the other children.
Wife only.	Half to wife, rest to next of kin, in equal degree to intestate, or their legal representatives.
No wife or child.	All to next of kin and their legal representatives.
Child, children, or representatives of them.	All to him, her, or them.
Children by two wives.	Equally to all.
If no child, children, or representatives of them.	All to next of kin, in equal degree to intestate.
Child, and grandchild, or grandchildren.	Half to child, half to grandchild, or grandchildren, who take, by right of representation, their father's share.
Husband.	The whole to him.
Father, and brother, or sister.	Whole to father, and he need not administer.
Mother and brother, or sister.	Whole to them equally.
Wife, mother, brothers, sisters, and nieces.	Half to wife, residue to mother, brothers, sisters, and nieces.
Wife, mother, nephews, and nieces.	Two fourths to wife, one fourth to mother, and the other fourth to nephews and nieces.
Wife, brothers or sisters, and mother.	Half to wife, half to brothers or sisters and mother.
Mother only.	The whole.
Wife and mother.	Half to wife, half to mother.
Brother or sister of the whole blood, and brother or sister of half blood, *i. e.*, half brother and half sister. See *Table of Descent.* DESCENT.	Equally to both.
Posthumous brother or sister, and mother.	Equally to both.
Posthumous brother or sister, and brother or sister, born in lifetime of father.	Equally to both.
Father's father, and mother's mother.	Equally to both.
Uncle or aunt's children and brother, or sister's grandchildren.	Equally to all.
Grandmother, uncle, or aunt.	All to grandmother.
Two aunts, nephew, and niece.	Equally to all.
Uncle, and deceased uncle's child.	All to uncle.
Uncle by mother's side, and deceased uncle or aunt's child.	All to uncle.
Nephew by brother, and nephew by half sister.	Equally *per capita*, *i. e.* in their own right and singly.

Brother or sister's nephews or nieces.	The whole to nephews and nieces taking *per stirpes*, *i. e.* as representing their parents, and collectively, (see PER CAPITA), and not in their own right and individually.
Nephew by deceased brother, and nephews and nieces by deceased sister.	Each an equal share in their own right (*per capita*).
Brother and grandfather.	Whole to brother.
Brother's grandson, and brother or sister's daughter.	To daughter.
Brother and two aunts.	To brother.
Father and wife.	Half to father, half to wife.
Mother and brother.	Equally.
Wife, mother, and children of a decaased brother or sister.	Half to wife, a fourth to mother, and a fourth collectively, (*per stirpes*) to deceased brother's or sister's children.
Wife, brother, or sister, and children of a deceased brother or sister.	Half to wife, ane fourth to brother or sister, in their own right singly (*per capita*) one fourth to deceased's brother or sister's children, by right of representation, collectively (*per stirpes*).
Brother or sister and children of a deceased brother or sister.	Half to brother or sister *per capita*. Half to children of deceased brother or sister, *per stirpes*.
Grandfather and brother.	All to brother.

The *next of kin* referred to are to be traced by the table of consanguinity.

No persons shall take collectively as representatives, or standing in the place of a deceased parent, beyond brothers' and sisters' children among collateral relations. This will be sufficiently exemplified by the foregoing table.

Administrations are granted either for *special* purposes, where there is a will and executors named, but from particular circumstances they are unable to act, or *generally*, where there is no will at all, as noticed at the commencement of this article.

Special or limited administrations, with the will annexed, are grantable for particular purposes, or until a disability or impediment is removed or purpose satisfied; as where one or more under age are appointed executors, or there is a suit pending to try the validity of the will, or the executor named is an uncertificated bankrupt, or out of the country, administration is granted to some one, which determines or is concluded on one of the minors coming of age, the end of the suit, the executor's obtaining his certificate or superseding his fiat, or return into this country, on the happening of which events the executor named enters upon the trust and completes the distribution of the testator's property. The residuary legatees, or one of them, are entitled to administration with the will annexed, in preference to the next of kin, although it may be uncertain whether there is a residue or not, when no person is appointed executor, or he is dead before the testator, where the executor or executors refuse to act, or themselves die before obtaining probate, or where an executor who has obtained probate dies without leaving an executor, or is lunatic, or convicted of felony before the completion of the executorship. In the other cases the administration may be granted to the residuary legatee or next of kin; and where it is plain that the next of kin can derive no benefit, they may be cited to accept or refuse it, and, on their refusal, a creditor may be appointed; and where an executor resides out of the kingdom, administration may be granted to a creditor, next of kin, or legatee: but where the court grant administration to one of several creditors, he can be compelled to pay debts of equal degree without preferring his own, which an executor or administrator can otherwise always do.

Administrations are also granted, limited to a particular thing, such as a term of years, of which the deceased was possessed as trustee, or for the purpose of selling goods, and the like; but two administrations cannot be granted of the same thing or chattel.

Administrators with the will annexed, who have administration granted them for the purpose of carrying the will into execution, are in effect as much executors as those originally appointed by the testator, or, if he appointed none, as fully as if he had. So far of *limited* or *special* administrations, which are every whit executorships, and governed by the same rule.

General administrations are grantable when a person dies intestate, *i. e.* without a will, in which case the husband has a right to administration of his wife's effects, or of the residue, if she by settlement or otherwise have a special power of disposing of her property; if the husband die before administration actually granted, his executors or administrators are to be preferred before the wife's next of kin.

If the husband dies, the administration is grantable to his widow or next of kin, or to both, at the discretion of the court from which probate issues, or of the judicial officer granting it, termed the *ordinary;* or administration of part may be granted to the wife and of the residue to the next of kin. If the wife *renounce, i. e.* decline administration, the children, or other next of kin are entitled to administer in preference to creditors, who can only administer where every person entitled renounces or declines, or refuses to appear when cited or summoned before the ecclesiastical court for that purpose.

The next of kin are the relations of the deceased intestate by blood, not by affinity, which is only relationship on the side of the wife. The kindred are preferred in taking administration, by their nearness in degree of relationship or consanguinity to the deceased; but among persons of equal degree the ordinary may use his discretion, but usually puts the administration into the hands of the person to whom the greater part of the parties interested wish to intrust the estate. It may here be remarked, that the husband and wife are not next of kin, but only related by *affinity*. A statute of Henry VIII. expressly provides for administration being granted to them in the first instance.

A *caveat* may be entered by an interested party in the same manner as before mentioned with respect to executors.

The table of consanguinity at that title can be referred to for the computation of the nearness of degrees; also the tables at the titles Descent, Kindred.

Of the next of kin, first, children; on failure of them, the father of the deceased; if he is dead, the mother is entitled to administration; and though parents and children are both in the first degree, children are preferred; then brothers (primogeniture making no difference); then grandfathers, paternal or maternal, but though they are both in the second degree, the paternal grandfather is preferred: next come uncles or nephews, and lastly cousins, and the females of each class respectively. Relations by fathers' and mothers' side in equal degree are equally entitled: there is no difference or preference in respect of half or whole blood; but the ordinary may use his discretion to which of the two he will grant administration, as well as in all cases where the degrees are equal.

A married woman entitled to administration cannot administer without her husband's permission, because he must join in the administration bond; but if he is abroad, lunatic, or bankrupt, a stranger may join in his stead. The wife is administratrix solely; and if a married woman, is the only next of kin and a minor, her husband may be appointed her guardian during her minority, and administer as such till she comes of age; but on her attaining full age, a new grant of administration should be made to her.

An administrator cannot, as we have observed an executor can do before probate, perform various acts incidental to his trust before administration granted; indeed, *letters of administration* do not issue till after fourteen days from the intestate's decease, unless perishable goods are required to be particularly protected. The same officer who grants probate of wills also grants administration; and before administration with the will annexed is granted, the executors should formally renounce before him, or evidence of their death or incompetency be produced.

Administrators on intestacy enter into a bond with two sureties, in a penal sum, double the amount of the effects sworn to, of the whole amount of which an affidavit must be made, without deducting any thing for debts due by the intestate. The stamp payable is mentioned under the title STAMPS.

In getting in and collecting the estate of an intestate, the administrator stands in precisely the same situation as an executor, only, instead of distributing, as an executor would do, the estate according to the terms of the will, and the residue to the residuary legatee or next of kin, the *general administrator* has to pay the debts and distribute the balance or residue amongst the next of kin and wife (if any) of the deceased, according to the table above set forth, which will give the reader every requisite information. No distribution should be made till a year after the intestate's death, for the purpose of protecting creditors; and any one receiving a distributive part and shares can be called upon by the ecclesiastical court to refund and pay back to the administrator a rateable or proportionate part of any debt of the deceased which may afterwards appear, with costs of suit and administrator's charges.

There is also, by the customs of London and province of York, a mode of distribution which is recognised by law in cases of intestacy, where the intestates are freemen of those cities; viz.—If a freeman of London die intestate, leaving a widow and children, his personal property (after deducting the widow's apparel and the furniture of her bed-room, called the *widow's chamber*, or 50*l.* in money if the estate be above 2000*l.*, unless the estate be in debt,) is divided into three equal parts, one to the widow; one to the children, called the *orphanage part;* and the third to the administrator, called *the dead man's part.* If there be neither wife nor children, the administrator takes the whole. This *dead man's part* is now divisible, according to the statute of distribution, amongst the next of kin, so that if a man dies worth 1800*l.* personal estate, leaving a widow and two children, his estate (subject to the widow's chamber) is divisible into eighteen parts, of which the widow shall have eight, viz. six by the custom and two by the statute; and each of the children five : three by the custom and two by the statute. If a freeman intestate dies leaving a widow and one child, the widow is still entitled to eight parts as before, and the child is entitled to ten, viz. six by the custom and four by the statute. If the freeman leaves a widow and no child, the widow shall have three fourths of the whole : two fourths by the custom and one fourth by the statute; the remaining one fourth being divisible amongst the next of kin. It is also to be observed, that the widow may, by settlement before marriage, be barred of her share, either customary or distributive; and if she be divorced for adultery from bed and board, she loses her customary share. Also as to the children of a freeman, if any of them are advanced by the *father* in their lifetime with any sums not amounting to the shares they would be entitled to on their father's death, they must give credit for the sum advanced before they are entitled to any share of their customary or *orphanage* part, for it is to this part only that the doctrine of *advancement* extends, the share in the third part called the dead man's part, being distributable and claimable by the children as other personal estate, and the advancement must have been made in money or personalty, not in land or money to be laid out for that purpose. If any child is so advanced to the extent of his share in the *orphanage* part, he is not entitled to any part of that fund; and where a child has been advanced, the presumption is that the advancement is what is termed *complete*, *i. e.* to the extent of his orphanage share, unless he produce a writing under his father's hand, showing the contrary. The children are, however, not entitled to their *orphanage* share till 21, so that the share of a child dying under that age survives, *i. e.* increases the shares of the survivors who attain that age, nor can the minor dispose of it by will till that age; though with respect to the *dead man's part*, which is distributable by law, a daughter might dispose of it at 12 and a son at 14 years of age, as he or she could of other personal estate before January 1. 1838; but if a female orphan marry and die before she attains 21, the husband will be entitled in her right to her customary or orphanage share.

A freeman of London has the power to prevent the custom from attaching, by making his will, which, unless he is satisfied with the custom, he should in prudence prepare, as his residence out of the city will not prevent the distribution, according to the custom. However, an intestate must reside within the province of York (viz. within the dioceses of York, Durham, Carlisle, Chester, Sodor and Man), to render his personal estate liable to that custom; but it matters not where a freeman of London resides at the time of his death.

The custom of the province of York does not disagree with the custom of London but in one or two particulars, respecting the bequest of the *orphanage* part and as to the *advancement*. In the first place, a minor might, before the 1st of January, 1838, bequeath or dispose of his or her orphanage part at 14 or 12; and, in the second, an advancement by a gift of *land* shall be credited in account by the minor as an advancement in *money;* the heir also, who inherits any land in fee or fee tail, is excluded from any filial portion.

A few words may be said concerning charging the child with his "advancement," which is legally termed "bringing into hotchpot," and applies only to cases of *intestacy;* though in *wills* carefully penned, where the testator intends that substantial gifts and benefits conferred in his lifetime should or should not *be* considered as *advancements*, provision is made for excluding from or bringing into *hotchpot* advances by way of settlement, as the testator happens to be either desirous of further preferring or bringing down to a rateable share those of his family he has peculiarly noticed in his lifetime. The hotchpot in money is more regularly defined to be the bringing of a previously advanced share into the general mass of *personal* property at the death of an intestate. The first article in the table will explain this, and remind the reader that any advancement, or provision, or settlement made for the heir-at-law *in land* is always excepted, though if his advancement is made *in money*, he must bring it into hotchpot.

It has been determined, that small sums occasionally given to a child by a father, or presents, such as a gold watch or wedding clothes, are no advancement; neither are maintenance money or allowance at school or an university, or putting him out apprentice, this being only for the minor's education. The principle being, that only marriage portions, sums or substantial gifts, considerable as regards the intestate's estate, and which manifestly had for their object the settling or providing for in life of a child, shall be considered as advancements. And this consideration should not be forgotten by the administrator of an intestate, when he is about to make distribution. In cases of wills it must be specially noticed by the testator; the doctrine only applying to intestates.

Executors and administrators are liable, *as far as their means or assets extend, but no further*, for all contracts and debts upon or for which their testator or intestate might have been sued in his lifetime: these must, of course, be all paid before legacies. The law protects an executor or administrator from being liable for the debt of the deceased out of his own property, as the promise, according to the Statute of Frauds, must be in writing; and even this promise must be supported by an adequate consideration or motive expressed in the writing itself, as a promise to pay, if the creditor will not sue, or when sufficient money comes to his hands, or the like: but where an executor or administrator carry on the deceased's trade, he makes himself liable for all losses, though the profits must be accounted for. If an executor, &c. does any wasteful or improvident act, or is negligent in his trust, he is liable out of his own estate, though *moral* fraud may not be imputed to him. Executors are not unfrequently liable for the acts of each other; for if an executor be *completely passive*, he can discharge himself: and it has been settled, that if several executors agree together that one shall intermeddle with and receive one part of the estate and another with another part, each becomes liable for *the whole*. So, if all join in selling the goods and one receive the money, all are liable. If an executor be present when money is paid to his co-executor, it seems he is liable; however, his mere joining in a receipt will not render him liable, though it was considered so. Where executors are trustees, they must *all* join in giving receipts, but executors may *each*, as executors or administrators, give a receipt, which will bind the other. The best course for an executor to take, is not to act in the sale of goods or in the dealings of the estate, unless he is indemnified by the terms of the will against all liabilities on these accounts, or unless he retains a control over the money; for if he can show that he was not present when the money was paid, and that he never had any control over it, he will not be liable for any loss arising from the misapplication or improper conduct of his fellow-executors.

As executors and administrators are considered as *trustees*, courts of equity take particular cognisance of all matters concerning their trust, whether expressed or implied; *expressed*, as being named in the will, or implied, as imposing a moral duty upon them, such as paying equitable demands which existed against the deceased, or any part of his property at his decease; and, consequently, they can be compelled, by bill in chancery or equity side of the exchequer, to set forth and fully to account for all property and assets actually come to their hands, or for so much, which but for negligence or breach of trust would have been realised and applicable for the purposes of the will, or for payment of debts, at the suit of legatees, next of kin, or creditors.

The ecclesiastical court has power to compel executors and administrators to exhibit their inventories and pass their accounts; and this court has the power of distributing the personal estate of an intestate: but, unless in a few cases, this court has no power of assisting legatees, and in no case whatever has it the power to enforce the payment of debts. So that the legatee must, in almost every case, resort to equity for his legacy, and the creditor *in all cases* to either law or equity for his debt.

Although executors and administrators may claim money out of pocket, and may receive or retain interest when they pay a demand out of their own pocket, to prevent a suit and to save the estate, yet they are allowed nothing for trouble or loss of time. And where executors retain more money than is reasonably sufficient to answer demands on the estate, they are chargeable with interest, particularly after a year has expired; in strong cases, where the retention of a very large sum has been unreasonably detained, *compound* interest will be allowed against them in favour of the estate. In conclusion, as executorship is a trust and confidence, any departure from it, however slight, subjects the executor to loss, for the nature of the burden is not to be recompensed by any gain or profit from the estate, which in legal and natural justice is to be considered as the principal fund: indeed, the keeping a balance at a banker's in the executor's own name, and thereby increasing his credit, is an indirect gain, which will charge him with interest.

The probate of wills and administrations of seamen and marines are regulated by the stat. 11 *G*. 4. and 1 *W*. 4. *c*. 20.

EXECUTORS' AND ADMINISTRATORS' ACCOUNTS. *Directions as to payment of the duties upon legacies and residues, and accounting for the latter.*

There is a certain sum payable to government upon *every* legacy bequeathed by a testator's will and in cases of intestacy, in respect of the sum to be actually distributed, or, where there is a will, of the undisposed of residue divisible amongst the next of kin or relations of the deceased, where the legacy or the sum to be divided is of the amount of 20*l*., according to the table No. 1.; and this duty is to be paid by the executor or administrator *upon retaining* or paying over the legacy or residue: for, if the duty is not retained, the executor is personally responsible, together with the party who receives it. Should the bequest be by way of annuity, then the value and the duty is to be calculated according to a table subjoined to the act, and the same is payable by four equal payments, at the ends of the first, second, third, and fourth years of payment of the annuity, without regarding other contingencies or chances; but in case of death or the failure of the annuity, the duty ceases or is returnable, as the case may be; but where a legacy is given to purchase an annuity, the duty is payable out of the gross sum: and where legacies are given in such a manner or upon such terms that the value can only be ascertained as the sums actually accrue or are paid, the duties are then payable from time to time out of the principal fund chargeable with the legacy. Where different persons, all standing in the same degree, and consequently liable to pay the same rate of duty, take a legacy or residue or part of *in succession*, the duty is payable in one sum; but when the persons are in different degrees and pay different rates of duty, the duty is only payable as they become entitled, and in the same manner as an annuity;—the rule being, that the duty on successions and partial interests, when chargeable upon persons taking at *one rate*, shall be paid out of the capital by the executor or administrator, or person retaining it, who are, together with the persons entitled to a legacy and receiving it, liable for the duties, which can be recovered in a very summary manner, as hereafter noticed.

Furniture, plate, &c., which does not yield an income, is not chargeable with duty till sold, or come to the hands of any person having a right to sell the same, when the duty is chargeable upon such legatee only, and not upon the executor; and this appears the only case where an executor is not liable for the duties.

Persons taking any legacy or residue *jointly*, pay, or rather the legacy is chargeable, in proportion to their separate interests; and legacies payable upon contingency are chargeable with a duty payable out of the capital, unless payable as an annuity.

Money bequeathed for the purpose of paying certain legacies which are desired to be paid duty free, is not liable.

The act contains various provisions for settling disputes as to legacies on property not reduced into money (legally termed specific), and to prevent evasions by particular contrivances.

The communications necessary for the assistance of executors and administrators are to be made to the distributor of stamps in the country, or to the head office, or Legacy Duty Office, Somerset House, Strand, London.

We have observed in the commencement of this article, that *every* legacy is liable to duty, so that there is no species of legacy that is exempt (bearing in mind that land devised is always exempt) from duty; even a debt forgiven, though not the interest, or a bond or note given up, either in contemplation of death or otherwise, are chargeable. Although land itself is exempt, yet where it is directed to be sold the duty attaches; and where land was directed to be sold to pay a legacy, and the legatee took the land, it was held that the duty was payable, though, had the land been devised, it would not have been chargeable.

Those interests in land which are called chattels real, such as terms for years, mortgages, &c., are considered as personalty, and as such become chargeable.

Where a party dies in England, being domiciled here, all his personal property elsewhere is chargeable with legacy duty, as if it was situate in England; otherwise, if he died abroad and the property administered there; but if the will is proved in England, the charge to duty attaches.

An executor or administrator, when he proves his testator's will or takes out administration, makes oath that the personal property (not taking debts into account) is under a particular sum; and as a copy of such affidavit and the will or administration is transmitted from the ecclesiastical court to the commissioners of stamps in London, they have very ample information as to the residence of the executors and other necessary particulars, and they, very shortly after probate or administration, send the executor or administrator a printed form of letter, generally as follows:—

R. ——No. 1.

*Reg. A. B. No. 2. 1835. Folio 528.	No letter in answer to this can be noticed unless this reference be copied therein.

Stamp Office, Somerset Place,
Legacy Duty Department,
——1835.

Sir,

The copy of the will of *Peter Simpson* deceased, to which you, Mr. *James Skinner*, and Mr. *Wm. Atkinson*, are executors, having been received at this office, and the legacy duties payable under the said will charged to your account, the commissioners of this revenue think it proper to apprise you thereof, in order that you may not, for want of information, or through inadvertence, incur the penalties imposed by the act on defaulters, by neglecting to pay the duty on the legacies and residue, when, and as you shall pay, deliver, or otherwise discharge the same, or when the same shall be retained by you, either to your own use, or for the use and bendfit of others.

And to the same intent, the commissioners direct me further to inform you, that before executors can legally retain the residue, or any specific proportion thereof, either to their own use, as residuary legatees, or as trustees for the use and benefit of others, or pay over, or otherwise satisfy the residue, or any specific proportion thereof to the residuary legatees, they, or their agents, must personally deliver (not transmit) into this office, or to the stamp distributer for the county or neighbourhood in which they reside, an account of the particulars of such residue, with the amount or value thereof, and the duty offered to be paid thereon; and they are to pay the duty, either at the head office, or to the said distributer, within fourteen days after the same shall have been assessed, under a penalty of treble the amount of duty. And that if, contrary to these directions, receipts and accounts shall be transmitted by post, or sent to agents to deliver under cover (which is in effect the same thing), the receipts and accounts so transmitted or delivered, will invariably be laid aside, or returned to the agents unnoticed, and will be considered in all proceedings instituted against the executors, as not having been received by, or presented to this office; it being quite obvious that receipts and accounts cannot possibly be examined, unless persons attend with them competent to give such information as may be required, and to answer whatever queries may arise in investigating the accounts, and to take the direction of the office on such points as need alteration.

For your guidance and information in rendering an account of the residue, printed office forms and instructions are provided, with which you may be supplied, on applying at this office, or to the distributer of stamps for the county or neighbourhood in which you reside.

In cases where two probates of the same will shall be taken out, the executors should give notice thereof to this office, stating, at the same time, when and in what court the first probate was granted, in order to prevent application being made to them for duties which may have been accounted for, and settled under the first entry of the will in the books of this department.

* You are requested particularly to notice, that the register and the folio thereof, in which your account is entered, is given at the head of this letter, and must be inserted at the head of the residuary account, and every legacy receipt for property passing under this will, and also at the head of every letter which you address to this office; for which purpose it is very material

that this letter should be preserved; as no answer can be given to any letter in which such reference shall not be inserted.

I am,

Your obedient servant,

———

Comptroller of the legacy duties.

Mr. *Abel Jenkins*,

Milbank Street, Westminster.

N. B. Letters from persons residing in the metropos or i ts vicinity, will not be answered, it being expected that such persons will personally apply to this office for whatever information they may require.

Your attention is particularly requested to the following Information.

1. The duties on legacies are to be paid at the time of paying, delivering, or otherwise discharging the legacies; but if by reason of infancy, or the absence of the legatees, or any other cause, the legacies cannot be paid, but are retained by executors for the use of the legatees, the payment of the duties is not to be deferred till such legacies are actually paid, but the duties are to be accounted for when the legacies are so retained.

2. A legacy payable to a legatee on his attaining the age of 21 years, or at some other future period, the interest of which is directed by the will to be applied for the benefit of such legatee until the legacy becomes payable, being a vested legacy, the duty is payable on the amount or value of such legacy, immediately, and the office form for the payment of the duty is to be filled up and signed by the executors, as retaining the legacy in trust for the use of the legatee.

3. The value of any legacy given by way of annuity for any life or lives, or for years determinable on any life or lives, or for years or other period of time, must be valued by the tables annexed to the 36 *G.* 3. *c.* 52., and the duty is to be paid on such value by equal instalments out of the first four annual payments of the annuity.

4. Any legacy or residue given to different persons in succession, liable to the same rate of duty, is to be charged with duty on the amount thereof, as in the case of a legacy to one person. And any legacy or residue given to different persons in succession, liable to different rates of duty, they who take for life only, or other temporary interest, are to pay as annuitants; and when any person or persons shall become entitled to the principal, or when upon the death of a tenant for life, all the remaining persons in the succession shall be liable to the same rate of duty, then the duty must be paid upon the principal, as if the same had come to them immediately on the death of the testator.

5. A legacy given subject to any contingency which may defeat the gift, is nevertheless to be charged with duty as an absolute bequest, and the duty is to be paid out of the capital of such legacy; and should the contingency afterwards happen, and the legacy go to one liable to a higher rate of duty, such legatee is to pay the difference. Note. — Of this description is a legacy to an infant on his attaining the age of 21 years, with the interest in the mean time for his benefit, and in the event of his dying under the age of 21 years, the legacy is given over to another; — therefore upon such a legacy, the duty is payable immediately, according to the infant's rate of duty; and the office form for the payment of the duty is to be filled up and signed by the executors as retaining the legacy in trust for the legatee; and should the infant die under the age of 21 years and the legacy go to one liable to a higher rate of duty, such legatee is to pay the difference between the duty before paid, and the rate of duty to which he shall be liable.

6. Leasehold estates for lives applicable by law, in the same manner as personal estate, are chargeable with duty: *i. e.* when the estates are granted to the lessee only, without naming heirs, executors, or administrators after him; or where, by the grant being made to the executors or administrators of the lessee, the estates go to the executors or administrators, and are assets in their hands. In the estimate of such estates, the ages of the respective lives must be stated.

7. For the payment of the duty on the residue, a statement of the deceased's personal estate, and the monies arising from the sale or mortgage of real estate, or the value of the real estate if not sold, when the same is directed by

the will or codicil to be absolutely sold or mortgaged, and of all payments made thereout, is to be rendered on the office printed residuary form, which together with a duplicate thereof, is to be delivered (not transmitted) by the executors, or their agent, into this office, or to the stamp distributer, in whose district the executors reside, and the duty paid on the amount or value of the clear residue within fourteen days after the assessment, under a penalty of treble the value of the duty.

8. It having been determined by the court of exchequer, in Trinity Term, 1810, in the case of the Attorney General *v.* Lord George Cavendish, that the duty is chargeable upon the amount or value of the property as it stands with its accumulations at the time of the residuary account being delivered, and not as it stood at the time of the death of the deceased, it follows, that in rendering an account of the residue, all investments which shall have been made of any part of the deceased's personal estate, together with the rents of leasehold estates, and all dividends, interests, and profits arising from the personal estate of the deceased, subsequent to the time of the deceased's death, and all accumulations thereof down to the time of the executor's delivering the account, and offering to pay the duty thereon, must be considered as part of the deceased's personal estate, and accounted for accordingly.

9. Effects not consisting of money, or securities for money, are to be valued at the time the account is rendered; when inventories, and proper valuations thereof will be required to be produced; the stocks are to be valued at the medium price of that day. In the estimate of leaseholds, the following particulars must be stated: viz. —

Whether held for years certain, or for years determinable on any life or lives.

If for years certain, the unexpired term for which they are held.

If for years determinable on any life or lives. — The number of years, and the age or ages of the life or lives.

The ground rent per annum.

The rent per annum at which they are let, or if not let, the estimated annual value.

The conditions of renewal.

If let, whether let on lease, or from year to year.

The unexpired term of the under tenant's leases.

10. Where the residue of personal estate is given to one for life, and afterwards to others, a distinct account must be given of the rents, dividends, and interest accrued subsequent to the death of the testator, and of the payments thereout for interest of legacies, and for interest of the testator's debts, accrued after his decease, so that the balance due to the residuary legatee for life may be clearly ascertained, and the proper duty charged thereon.

11. If any legacy specifically bequeathed shall be included in the account of residue by reason of the same being given to the residuary legatee; or of the person entitled to the legacy, and the residuary legatee being liable to the same rate of duty, it will be indispensably necessary, in order that such legacy may be discharged in the books of this office, and to prevent the executors from being afterwards called upon to account for the duty on such legacy, to attach a note to the residuary statement, describing the legacy and stating the same to be included in the account.

12. In cases of insolvency, or when the shares of the residuary legatees shall not be of the value of 20*l.* each, an account must nevertheless be rendered by the executors in the manner before directed, in order that the commissioners may satisfactorily ascertain that the estate is not chargeable with duty.

13. Executors or their agents personally applying at this office, or to the stamp distributer in whose district they reside, will be supplied with the necessary forms, and receive whatever further information they may require.

14. Executors and administrators resident in the country, who may be desirous of delivering their legacy receipts and residuary accounts, and of paying the duty thereon to the stamp distributer of the county or neighbourhood in which they reside, are desired particularly to notice that each distributer transmits the receipts and residuary accounts left with him, to the head office every month, and that such receipts and residuary accounts are returned to him on that day month following, duly stamped and registered, to be delivered back to the persons to whom they respectively belong.

15. Persons paying or receiving any legacy, residue, or share of residue

liable to duty, without taking or signing a proper receipt for the same, in which the duty thereon shall be expressed to have been deducted, will be subject to a penalty of 10*l.* per cent. on the amount or value of such legacy, residue, or share of residue. Every legacy receipt must be dated on the day of signing, and the duty thereon paid within twenty-one days from the date thereof, under a penalty of 10*l.* per cent. on the amount of the duty; and if the duty shall not be paid within three months from the date of the receipt, a penalty will then be incurred of 10*l.* per cent. on the amount or value of the legacy.

As penalties are frequently incurred through inadvertence, you are particularly requested to attend to the information given under this head.

Appraisements or valuations of any property made for the purpose of ascertaining the legacy duty, payable in respect thereof, are, by the last Stamp Act, exempt from duty.

Note. — It is absolutely necessary that the time when the intestate died, and when, and in what court the will was proved, should be inserted in each receipt and residuary account.

In cases where an executor or administrator shall have paid debts due and owing from the deceased to such an amount as, being deducted from the gross value of the estate and effects, would reduce the amount thereof to a less scale of probate or administration duty than that on which duty has been paid, it is lawful for the commissioners to return the difference, provided application be made for the same within three years after the date of the probate or letters of administration. *Vide 55 G.* 4. *c.* 184. *s.* 51.

The regulations and form of affidavit necessary to be observed, in order to obtain such return, may be had at the office.

It is absolutely necessary that this reference at the head of the letter should be used at the head of every letter or communication which may have to be addressed to the Legacy Duty Office, as no notice can be taken of it for want of such reference, it being a difficult task to search amongst many thousand wills for the person named; the same consequences, therefore, will attach on sending a letter without this reference, as if none had been sent at all.

At the end of a year another letter is forwarded to the executor or administrator; and, unless the residue is bequeathed to a husband or wife of the deceased (which is exempt from duty), peremptorily calling for an account of the deceased's estate within a month. In default of this demand not being complied with, and perhaps after one more notice, the solicitor of stamps proceeds against the executor or administrator, and the legatee himself, if he has received the legacy, or the next of kin, if they have received their share, and not paid the duty; by obtaining a rule or order of the court of exchequer, calling upon the executors and parties interested, why, on the day named in such rule, they should not deliver an account upon oath of legacies and personal property paid or to be paid or administered by them, and why the legacy duties thereon should not be paid; and if the parties served with this rule do not show sufficient cause or reason, a process called an attachment issues against them, and the parties are committed to prison as debtors without bail.

The distributor of stamps in the country, who may be found in every great town, and the porter at the Legacy Duty Office, in Somerset House, will deliver, gratis, forms of legacy receipts, forms of legacy receipts where an annuity is given, and forms of the account of the residue of a testator's or intestate's estate. Sufficient of each of these forms should be obtained, which will be filled up according to the circumstances of the case, and with particular attention to the written directions, which will be shown by the parts in *Italics* in the subjoined forms.

Every possible information will be given at the head office in Somerset House, and by the distributors in the country; and it may be observed, that executors will always do well to promptly apply to the head office in cases of doubt, where their questions will be answered with the utmost courtesy.

Whenever it is requisite that the estate of a deceased should be administered in chancery, the executor or administrator is relieved from future liability in respect of legacy duties after he has passed his accounts in that court.

Executors can also pay the duties *in parts* as the legacies are paid.

Where too much or too little duty has been paid in respect of probate or legacies, application should be made to the head office, who will give a form of affidavit and instruct the applicant as to the proper course to be pursued.

The following are the forms used as receipts for legacy or residue, or on retaining the same, receipts to be given by annuitants, or executors on retaining the same in trust (a separate form being required to be filled up and signed for each legacy, and for the first four payments of the annuity or retainings thereof), and a form in which the residuary account should be demonstrated and balanced, so as to show the exact sum divisible, either amongst the residuary legatees or next of kin, as the case may be, or the gross amount of an intestate's estate, and the degrees of kindred among whom the same is divisible, and who pay duty according to their degree of relationship with the deceased:—

Form No. 1.

STAMP OFFICE.

Legacy Receipt.

Register *A. B.*	No. 2.	1835.	Folio 528.

On Account of the personal (*if the Legacies are payable out of real estate, say* real) estate of *Peter Simpson*, late of *Upper Baker-street, Marylebone, in the county of Middlesex, grocer*, who died on the *seventh* day of *July, One thousand eight hundred and thirty-five.*

Names of the executors, or administrators, devizees, in trust, or heir at law, with their residence and profession.	Abel Jenkins, of Milbank-street, Westminster, grocer, James Skinner, of No. 53. Whitechapel, in the county of Middlesex, upholsterer, and William Atkinson, of Staple Inn, in the said county, gentleman, executors [*or* administrators].

Acting under probate of will, [or *letters of administration*,] granted by the *Prerogative* Court of *the Archbishop of Canterbury*, on the *tenth* day of *August, one thousand eight hundred and thirty-five.*

Name of the Legatee or next of Kin.	Degree of Relationship to be here stated as on the other side.	Describe the nature of the Bequest, and if Residue, state what Part or Share.	Price of Stocks.	Value.			Rate of Duty per Cent.	Amount of Duty.		
				£	s.	d.	£	£	s.	d.
Obs.--The name of the legatee should be stated as in the will, and with sufficient precision, as "A. B.;" or, if the legatees are described as a particular class, "A. B. one of the children of C. D." (as in the will); or, if the legatee be married, "Elizabeth, the wife of E.F., late Elizabeth Jones, spinster, one of the children of G. I.;" where the legatee is named, without any description, of course none beyond his name is necessary, though if *misdescribed*, it should be noticed.	The description should be in the words of the act, as child of the deceased, descendant of a child of the deceased, father or mother of the deceased, brother or sister of the deceased.	One-fourth part of 333*l*. 6*s*. 8*d*. 3*l*. per Cent. Consolidated Bank Annuities, [or, a specific legacy of 3000*l*. New 3½ per cent. Bank Annuities.	91¾	57	0	0	6	3	9	5
		A pecuniary legacy of 1000*l*., subject to the payment of an annuity of 10*l*. for the life of Thomas Smith, aged 60, the value of which being deducted —*l*. leaves—*l*. The third part of the residue of the intestate's estate. A pecuniary legacy of 1000*l*. A specific legacy of all the household furniture in testator's house, at Upper Baker-street. A specific legacy of testator's interest in the moiety of leasehold premises at Camberwell, Nos. 17. 19, 20, and 21. in ——— Street. A release of a debt due to the testator upon the note of hand of the legatee for 75*l*. The fourth-part of the proceeds of a freehold estate at Ryegate directed to be sold, being the residue of the testator's estate. A pecuniary legacy directed to be laid out in land to be conveyed to the legatee and his heirs. A specific legacy of testator's horse.]	90½ (The price on the day of transfer.)							

In this space insert any special matter necessary to explain the mode in which the legacy is given.

Where the legacy is bequeathed to trustees or to the executors, upon trust for the benefit of infants or minors, or for persons in succession chargeable with the *same* duty, or who do not take but in the event of particular contingencies, or where the trusts are special or for the benefit of more than one person, it is necessary to state concisely the terms of the bequest from the words of the Will; but if given simply in trust for infants, state "in trust for the legatee, a minor."

Received (or *retained* in trust) ——— the ——— day of ——— 1836, the *said* 3000*l*. *New* 3½ *per Cent. Bank Annuities*, being the Legacy [or *third part or* share of residue] above mentioned, having first allowed or paid ——— for the duty thereon.

A. B. (*Legatee, next of Kin*), or
C. D. }
E. F. } (*Executors.*)

PENALTIES.

The receipt must be dated on the day of signing, and the duty paid *within* 21 *days after*, under a penalty of 10*l*. per cent. on the amount of the *duty;* and if the duty be not paid *within three months* from the date of the receipt, a penalty will be incurred of 10*l*. per cent. on the *amount or value of the legacy:* —and the commissioners of stamps cannot, *under any circumstances*, stamp a receipt on which the duty shall not be paid within the time limited, unless the penalty be also paid.

STAMP OFFICE.

Received the ——— day of ——— 1836, the sum of ——— for duty on account of the within-mentioned legacy.

£———

Registered | Comptrolled

Rates of Duty payable on Legacies, Annuities, and Residues, &c. of the Amount of 20*l*. and upwards, by Stat. 55 Geo. 3. cap. 184.

The Description of the Legatee, Annuitant, Residuary Legatee, or next of Kin, *must be in the following Words of the Act.*	Out of or on Personal Estate only, if the Deceased died any Time *before* or upon the 5th April, 1805.	Out of or on Real or Personal Estate, if the Deceased died *after* the 5th April, 1805.
To children of the deceased, and their descendants, or to the father or mother, or any lineal ancestor of the deceased	(no legacy duty)	1*l*. per cent.
To brothers and sisters of the deceased, and their descendants	2*l*. 10*s*. per Cent.	3*l*. do.
To brothers and sisters of the father or mother of the deceased, and their descendants	4*l*. — do.	5*l*. do.
To brothers and sisters of a grandfather or grandmother of the deceased, and their descendants	5*l*. — do.	6*l*. do.
To any person in any other degree of collateral consanguinity, or to strangers in blood to the deceased	8*l*. — do.	10*l*. do.

Where any legatee *shall take two* or more distinct legacies or benefits under any will or testamentary instrument, which shall altogether be of the amount or value of 20*l*. each shall be charged with duty although each or either may be separately under that amount or value.

The husband or wife of the deceased is not chargeable with duty.

Form No. 2.

STAMP OFFICE.

Annuity Receipt.

Obs. — *On legacies given to be enjoyed by persons in succession, chargeable with a different rate of duty, the persons entitled for life only, are to pay duty as annuitants, and must therefore give their receipts in this form.*

REGISTER *A. B.* No. 2. 1835. Folio 528.

On Account of the personal [*or* real] estate of *Peter Simpson*, late of *Upper Baker-street, Marylebone, in the county of Middlesex, grocer*, who died on the *seventh* day of *July, One thousand eight hundred and thirty-five.*

Names of the executors, or administrators, devizees, in trust, or heir at law, with their residence and profession.	*Abel Jenkins, of Milbank-street, Westminster, grocer, James Skinner, of No. 53. Whitechapel, in the county of Middlesex, upholsterer, and William Atkinson, of Staple Inn, in the said county, gentleman, Executors,* [OR, *Administrators;* OR, *Administrators with the Will annexed.*]

Acting under probate of will [or administration with will annexed], granted by the *Prerogative* Court of *the Archbishop of Canterbury*, on the *tenth* day of *August, One thousand eight hundred and thirty-five.*

Name of the Annuitant, with the Name and Age of the Life or Lives or the Number of Years for which the Annuity is to endure.	Degree of Relationship if any, must be stated in the Words of the Act, as on the other Side.	Amount of the Annuity.			Age or Ages, or No. of Yrs.	Value of the Annuity.			Rate of Duty per Cent.	Amount of Duty.		
		£	s.	d.		£	s.	d.	£	£	s.	d.
John Allen, aged 40, *for his life,* [*or John Allen, for the life of Maria Allen, his wife, aged* 32.	*Stranger in blood.*	150	0	0	40	1979	11	0	10	197	19	0
Winifred Jenkins, for 10 *years certain.*	[*Sister of the mother of the deceased.*											
Mary Jones, aged 60, *for her life;* [*or as the case may be, according to the words of the will.*]	*Descendant of a sister of the deceased.*]											

			£	s.	d.
In this space insert any special matter necessary to explain the mode in which the annuity is given.	[See note in preceding form.]	Amount of the 1st, [2d, 3d, 4th,] year's annuity	150	0	0
		Allowed the 1st, [2d, 3d, 4th,] payment of duty	49	9	9
		Balance received £	100	10	3

Received [*or* retained in trust] the *seventh* day of *July*, 1836 [7-8-9], the *sum of one hundred pounds ten shillings and three pence,* being the 1st [2d, 3d, or 4th] year's payment of [my] annuity above mentioned, having first allowed or paid *forty-nine pounds nine shillings and nine pence* for the duty thereon.

J. A. (*the Annuitant*), or
A. J.
J. S. } (*Executors.*)
W. A.

Obs. — *If the annuitant die before these payments are due, of course they are not made.*

The following is the " Residuary Account," *to which (though it sufficiently explains itself) a few additions have been made, and a few articles filled up, so that the reader should have no doubt in applying it for the requisite purpose.*

No. 3.

STAMP OFFICE.

Form of account to be delivered (in duplicate) by executors and administrators retaining the residue, or any part or share of the residue, of personal estate; and by executors and trustees retaining the residue, or part of the residue, of monies arising from real estate, devised to be sold, &c. for the purpose of having the duties charged and assessed, pursuant to the acts of 36 Geo. 3. c. 52. and 45 Geo. 3. c. 28. and 55 Geo. 3. c. 184.

DIRECTIONS.

1. Executors and administrators, before the retainer of any part of the property to their own use, are to deliver the particulars thereof to the commissioners of stamps, or to the stamp distributor in whose district they reside, and pay the duty thereon within 14 days after, under the penalty of treble the value of the duty.
2. All rents, dividends, interest, and profits arising from the personal estate of the deceased, or his real estate, directed to be sold, subsequent to the time of his or her death, and all accumulations thereof, down to the time of delivering the account, and offering to pay the duty on the residue, must be considered as part of the deceased's estate, and must be accounted for accordingly.
3. Any account transmitted by post, or left under cover at the office, will either be returned to the parties, or thrown aside unnoticed.

REGISTER *A. B.* No. 2. 1835. Folio 528.

An Account of the Personal Estate [and of Monies arising out of the Real Estate], of *Peter Simpson, late of Upper Baker-street, Marylebone, in the County of Middlesex, grocer,* who died on the *Seventh* Day of *July, One thousand eight hundred and thirty-five,* exhibited by Abel Jenkins, James Skinner, and William Atkinson, the Executors [or Administrators] of the Deceased [or Trustee of the Real Estate, directed by the Will to be sold, &c.], acting under the Will, or Letters of Administration of the Effects of the Deceased, proved in, or granted by the *Prerogative Court of the Archbishop of Canterbury,* on the *Tenth* Day of *August,* 1835.

			No. 1.			No. 2.		
	Description of Property.	Dates of Sales, if Sold.	Money received, and Property converted into Money.			Value of Property not converted into Money.		
			£	s.	d	£	s.	
Money and property converted into money are to be inserted in column No. 1., and the date when converted affixed. Property not converted into money is to be valued at the time the account is rendered, and inserted in column No. 2., and inventories and proper valuations must be produced.	Cash in the house		78	10	4			
	Cash at the bankers		3840	2	6			
	Furniture, plate, linen, china, books, pictures, wearing apparel, jewels, and ornaments	Sold at ——— on ———, 1835,	1080	8	4			
	Wine and other liquors	Do. do.	276	0	0			
	Horses and carriages, farming stock, and implements of husbandry, as by valuation of Messrs. B. and T., 38. Fenchurch-street..............	....	..	..	..	246	0	0
	Stock in trade	Purchased on — by Mr. —— of Aldgate.	7470	14	6			
The unexpired term of years, the number and age of the lives, the terms of renewal, and the clear net residue reserved must be stated.	Fixtures in shop at ————, and do. in house, as by valuation of Messrs. B. and T., 38. Fenchurch-street	Sold at this valuation to Mr. —— of ——, on —— Nov. 1835.	400	0	0			
	Leasehold estates at Camberwell	....	....	..	..	700	10	0
	Do. — at Mile-end	....	....	..	..	458	9	0
	Carried forward........							

Note	Particulars	Dates of Sales, if Sold.	No. 1. Money received, and Property converted into Money. £	s.	d.	No. 2. Value of Property not converted into Money. £	s.	d.
Note. If there should not be room in this form for the particulars of any description of the property, the total only of the amount or value of such property is to be inserted here, and the particulars are to be stated on a separate paper (*which may be referred to as* A. B., C. D., *&c.*)	Brought forward....							
	Rents due at the death of the deceased		272	3	5			
	Mortgages and interest due at the death		108	10	0			
	Bonds, bills, notes, and interest due at the death............		2749	0	0			
	Book and other debts		3840	0	0			
	Canal and other shares............							
	Ships or shares of Ships					468	0	0

Note	Stocks	£	s.	d.	Price of Stocks.
The stocks unconverted (i. e. *unsold*) are to be valued at the medium price of the day on which the account is dated.	Exchequer Bills				
	Bank Stock				
	East India Stock				
	East India Bonds (*specifically bequeathed.*)*				
	Reduced 3 per Cents..				
	Consols, 3 per Cent...	6475	17	2	91½
	New 3½ per Cent.	2840	0	10	97¾
	Reduced 3½ per Cent.				
	New 4 per Cent. Annuities				
	Bank Long Annuities	69	0	0	

* *Obs.—If the stocks are sold, the amounts are carried to the first column, if unsold, to the second; if a sum in stock is specifically bequeathed, and consequently transferred to the legatee, it need not be brought out, but simply noticed as a specific bequest.*—Ed.

Note	Particulars	Dates of Sales, if Sold.	No. 1. £	s.	d.	No. 2. £	s.	d.
	Dividends on the above stocks due at the death							
	Policy of assurance, per directors of Atlas Assurance Office							
Here specify any other stocks, funds, or property converted or not converted.	*Proportionate part of annuity of £— secured to testator (or intestate) by deed of annuity, dated 6th of February, 1811, from L. M. Esq., for the life of the testator, accrued since 6th February last up to the 7th July last, the same being payable half-yearly*							
	Stock invested in the trading fund of the ——'s company, London							
	Dividend due thereon, on the 6th July last							
When directed by the will to be sold or mortgaged.	Real estate directed to be sold							
	(Insert the total of column No. 1. in column No. 2.)	.. ..	..	..	..	£		
	Total of property		..	..	..	£		

Note	PAYMENTS.	£	s.	d.			
	Probate of administration						
	Funeral expenses						
A schedule of these deductions *signed by the executor or administrator* to be annexed.	Expenses attending executorship or administration						
	Debts on simple contract, rent and taxes, wages, &c. due at the death of the deceased, per schedule annexed						
	Debts on mortgage, with interest (if any) due at the death						
	Debts on bonds, and other securities with ditto						
	Pecuniary legacies per account annexed						
Here state the particulars of any other lawful payments, and of the funds, or other securities purchased, and when.	3333*l.* 6*s.* 8*d.* *3 per cent. Consols*, purchased on the *28th of October*, at 90¼						
	333*l.* 6*s.* 8*d.* *like stock, purchased on the same day, appropriated for payment of Mrs. W.'s annuity during her life*						
	(*Deduct the Total of the Payment from the Total of the Property*)..						
	Net amount of property carried forward......£						

TO SHEW THE BALANCE OF CASH, IF ANY.

Total of column No. 1...... £
Total of payments .... £
Cash balance .. £

No. 3.

Note. — Upon reversions falling in, state the date of the death of the tenant for life.

Separate papers are to be annexed to the account to show how these totals are made up.

	£	s.	d.
Net amount of property brought forward......			
ACCUMULATIONS OF INTEREST, DIVIDENDS, RENTS, &C.			
Rents of leasehold estates sold, to the time of sale, and of those remaining unsold (after deducting ground rents, &c.), to the date of this account			
Rents of real estate directed to be sold to the time of sale if sold, if not, to the date of this account			
Dividends on the stocks and funds sold to the time of sale, and of those remaining unsold, including the last dividend			
Interest on exchequer bills sold or paid off to the time of sale or payment, and of those remaining unsold to the date of this account			
Interest on bonds, mortgages, and other securities paid off, to the day of payment, and of those outstanding, to the date of this account			
Interest at 4 per cent. on £ being the balance of cash in hand, as on the other side, to the date of this account			
Interest on canal and other shares to the time of sale, and of those remaining unsold, and on other property yielding an income not included in any of the above items, to the date of this account			
The value of the benefit accruing to the executor or other person entitled to the residue from the interest of money or dividends of stock retained to answer vested or contingent legacies payable at a future day without the intermediate interest or dividends.			
Total			

PAYMENTS OUT OF INTEREST, &C.	£	s.	d.
Interest on mortgages, bonds, and other securities due from the estate			
Interest on pecuniary legacies..........			
Payments on account of annuities..........			

	£	s.	d.
(*Deduct the total amount of these payments from the preceding total*)			
Balance............... £			

The value of Annuities must be calculated by the tables in the act of 36th Geo. 3. at the age of the annuitants at the time of passing the account.

DEDUCTIONS FROM RESIDUE.	£	s.	d.
The value of annuities given by the will, and now remaining a charge on the residue, viz.			
10*l.* to *Mrs. W.*, age 60, value	90	7	6
150*l.* to *Mr. John Allen*, age 40, value	1979	11	0
Debts still due from the estate } A schedule or particulars of these deductions to be annexed			
Retained to pay outstanding legacies .... }	676	9	2

	£	s.	d.
Total deductions .... £			
Net residue .... £			
Deduct any portion of the residue not liable to duty, or for which duty is paid on separate receipts, viz.			
Residue on which duty is chargeable			

DECLARATION.

State whether this sum is the whole or what part of the residue. Describe the relationship of the residuary legatee, or next of kin, in the words of the act, as set forth on the other side.

We do declare that the foregoing is a just and true account; and *we* offer to pay to the commissioners of stamps the sum of £—— for the duty, after the rate of £—— per cent. upon the sum of £——, being of the said residue and monies to which entitled and intend to retain to own use, [or for the use of], being a to the deceased.

Dated the day of 1836.

STAMP OFFICE ASSESSMENT.

The duty on the within-mentioned sum of £—— is assessed after the rate of per centum, at the sum of £——.

By the Commissioners,

RECEIPT.

Received on the day of , 1836, the sum of for the duty assessed as above.

Registered. Comptrolled.

EXPOSURE OF PERSON, is an indictable offence, and by a particular act of parliament every person wilfully exposing his person in a public street, &c., with intent to insult any female, shall be deemed a rogue and a vagabond, and may be committed to the house of correction to hard labour for any time not exceeding three months.

EXTENT is a writ at the suit of the queen, or it may be at the suit of a person indebted to the queen. In the first instance it is styled an extent *in chief*, in the second case an extent *in aid*.

It is in the nature of a writ of execution, and binds all the defendant's lands and property. Copyholds, however, cannot be taken. The body of the defendant may be also taken unless otherwise directed, which is generally the case.

EXTORTION is the demanding a fee or present by colour of office. It is punishable by fine and imprisonment at the discretion of the court.

In actions against attorneys for extortion, treble damages and costs may be recovered.

Officers may be indicted jointly for extortion, as they may be jointly guilty of the offence; and he who assists is equally guilty, for there are no accessaries in extortion.

There are various statutes punishing extortion by under-sheriffs, bailiffs, gaolers, clerks of assize, &c.

FACTORS. Those who are concerned in the *sale* and *purchase* of commodities, are either *brokers*, specifically so termed, or factors. The former have not the possession of goods, but simply conclude the bargain in the name and on the account of some other person. When the agreement for sale or purchase has been made, the broker gives to the seller a memorandum of the sale, to the buyer a memorandum of the purchase, and the delivery of these notes (which are called *bought* and *sold* notes) at once binds the bargain, and confers on the principal the same rights and liabilities as if the transaction had been carried on by himself in person. Factors are contradistinguished from these, principally by having possession of the goods, and dealing with them as their own, and in their own names. They are persons specially appointed to receive and make consignments of goods on account of merchants residing either in another country, or in some distant part of the same country. In the former case, they are called *foreign*, in the latter, *home factors*.

The direct profit of brokers and factors consists, generally, in a commission of so much per cent. on the amount of their sales or purchases. Occasionally, however, they render themselves answerable to their principal for the credit of the person to whom the sales are made, and are then said to act under a commission of *del credere* or guarantee, in which case an additional premium is stipulated for, in consideration of the self-imposed liability. The duties and liabilities of a factor, as distinguished from a broker, will be fully disclosed by the following cases and extracts from the *Lex Mercatoria.*

Goods remitted to a factor ought to be carefully preserved; and he is accountable for all lawful goods which shall come to his hands; yet if the factor buy goods for his principal, and they receive damage after they come to his possession, without negligence of his, the principal shall bear the loss; and if a factor be robbed, he shall be discharged in account brought against him by his principal.

A factor is not answerable against all events for the safety of goods which he has in charge; but it is sufficient if he do all that by his industry he may, for their preservation.

He is not liable in cases of robbery, fire, or any other accidental damage happening without his default.

If the principal gives the factor a general commission to act for the best, he may do for him as he thinks fit; but otherwise he may not. Though in commissions at this time, it is common to give the factor power in express words to dispose of the merchandise and deal therein as if it were his own, by which the factor's actions will be excused, though they occasion loss to his principal.

If the factor has orders from his principal not to sell any goods but in such a manner, and breaks those orders, he is liable to the loss or damage that shall be received thereby; and where any goods are bought or exchanged without orders, it is at the merchant's courtesy whether he will accept of them, or turn them on his factor's hands. When a factor has bought or sold goods pursuant to orders, he is immediately to give advice of it to his principal, lest the former orders should be contradicted before the time of his giving notice, whereby his reputation might possibly suffer; and where a factor has made a considerable profit for his principal, he must take due care in the disposition of the same, for without commission or particular orders he is answerable. A factor shall suffer for not observing orders; and no factor acting for another man's account in merchandise, can justify receding from the orders of his principal, though there may be probability of advantage by it; if he make any composition with creditors without orders, he shall answer it to his principal.

Factors ought to observe the contents of all letters from their principals, or written to them by their order. A merchant is answerable in action upon the case for the deceits of his factor, in selling goods abroad; and as somebody must be a loser by such deceit, it is more reasonable that he who employs and puts confidence in the deceiver should lose, than a stranger.

A bare commission to a factor to sell and dispose of merchandise is not sufficient power for the factor to intrust any person, or to give a further day of payment than the day of the sale of the goods; for in this case, on the delivery of the one he ought to receive the other; and by the general power of doing as if it were his own, he may not trust an unreasonable time, viz. beyond one or three months, &c., the usual time allowed for the commodities disposed of; if he doth, he shall be answerable to his principal out of his own estate.

By the Factors Act, 6 *G.* 4. *c.* 94., a person intrusted with and in possession of a bill of lading, or any of the warrants, certificates, or orders mentioned in the act, is to be deemed the true owner of the goods described therein, *so far* as to give validity to any contract or agreement made by him for the sale or disposition of the goods, or the deposit or pledge thereof *as a security for any money or negotiable instrument*, if the buyer, disponee, or pawnee, has not notice by the document or otherwise, that such person is not the actual and *bonâ fide* owner of the goods.

The words in *Italics* are important, for it has been held that a person with whom goods had been pledged *as a security for India warrants*, which he had intrusted to the factor who pledged them with him, was held *not* to be protected by them.

FACTORAGE. See COMMISSION.

FACTORS DEL CREDERE. See DEL CREDERE.

FACTORIES. The employment of young persons in mills and factories, is regulated by two late statutes, the most material provisions of which are as follows:—

The employment of children under nine years of age, after the 1st of January, 1834, is prohibited, except in silk mills. No child is to be employed more than 48 hours in one week, or more than 9 hours in one day, who, six calendar months after the passing of the act, has not attained 11; 18 months after 12, or 30 months after 13 years of age, except in silk mills, where children under 13 may work 10 hours every working day. No person under 18 is to work in the night between half-past 8 in the evening and half-past 5 in the morning; or more than 12 hours a day, or more than 69 hours a week, except in certain cases mentioned in the act; and every such person is to have one hour and a half for meals.

No child under 13 is to be employed without a certificate from a surgeon as to its strength and appearance, countersigned by an inspector or justice; and no person above that age, and under 18, is to work more than 9 hours a day, or between 9 in the evening and 5 in the morning, without a certificate of age.

Children in factories are to attend schools for two hours at least for six days in the week, to be witnessed by the schoolmaster's voucher.

Four inspectors are to be appointed of places where children are employed in factories to enforce the provisions of the act, who are to have access at all times to the factories, and to possess the same powers over constables as justices, and to make reports twice a year to a secretary of state.

Certain penalties are imposed for an infringement of the provisions of the act as to working; and the forging of any certificate is made a misdemeanor, punishable with two months' imprisonment. All proceedings and convictions may take place before one inspector or magistrate, from whose decision there is no appeal, except in cases of forgery of certificates.

The act extends to all factories in the United Kingdom, where machinery is used for dressing or weaving cotton, wool, worsted, hemp, flax, tow, or silk, with the exception of mills used solely for the manufacture of lace.

FAIR. A greater sort of market granted to towns, places, or persons by royal grant, or used by prescription which implies such a grant or charter; and without these qualifications, every *fair* now so termed, is a nuisance, and the parties frequenting indictable. See MARKET.

FALSE PRETENCES. See FRAUD (Div. 3.).

FEES. Certain perquisites or pecuniary sums or rewards allowed to officers in the administration of justice, for their labour and care, and are either ascertained by acts of parliament or ancient usage. All fees allowed by acts of parliament become established fees, and the several officers entitled to them may have an action of debt for them; and those fees which courts of justice allow their officers are *established* fees, and cannot be taken away but by act of parliament.

FELONY. All crimes (not mere misdemeanors, however high) above simple larceny to treason. Larceny is a felony by statute, which it never was at common law, or as the law, till lately, stood; but it is not punishable as a felony, nor hath it a superadded to its punishment forfeiture of goods and chattels, which is the distinguishing criterion of felony in the eye of the law.

FENCES. See HEDGES and DITCHES.

FEOFFMENT. The name of a conveyance of freehold lands, now not much in use, because it must be accompanied by an open and known delivery of possession at the time of executing the deed, termed "livery of seisin." It is mostly used for gifts, or where no pecuniary consideration is given or money paid, as where corporate property is vested in a certain number of persons of whom very few survive, the survivors by this deed enfeoff some new nominees.

FIERI FACIAS. A writ of execution, by which the sheriff is directed *to cause to be made of the all goods and chattels* of the party named in the writ, a certain sum, being the sum awarded by the judgment. Under this writ the sheriff takes and sells all the goods and chattels (strictly so termed) of the party; but he cannot take what are termed *choses in action*, which are banknotes or securities for money, or money itself lying loose.

FINES AND RECOVERIES. See RECOVERIES.

FIRE. To prevent fire, workmen in London, Marylebone, Paddington, Pancras, and Chelsea, and within the bills of mortality, must erect party-walls between buildings of brick and stone of a certain thickness, under penalties inflicted by the Building Act (14 *G.* 3. *c.* 78.).

The same statute gives rewards for assistance in cases of fire, viz. to the first turncock 10*s.*; to the first engine *not exceeding* 30*s.*; the second not exceeding 20*s.*; the third 10*s.*; payable by the churchwardens or overseers, but not without the approbation of a justice of the peace. The churchwardens are to be repaid by the inhabitant if the fire begins in a chimney.

Servants burning houses by negligence forfeit 100*l.*, or suffer eighteen months' imprisonment. (§ 84.)

No action shall be had against any person in whose house a fire shall accidentally begin. (6 *Ann. c.* 31.) See ACCIDENT.

FISH, FISHERY, &c. All persons who peaceably demean themselves have a right to take fish in great rivers, being arms of the sea, and where the tide ebbs and flows; indeed, there are few navigable rivers where the public have not a right of free fishery. Where the right to the *soil of the river, i. e.* the ground over which the river flows, is in the queen, it is pretty certain that the subject may fish there, but where the soil is the property of another, as it generally is in a private river, there no one can lawfully fish unless he is interested in a right of *common* of "*piscary*" (the legal term for fishery), or can by *prescription* claim a particular right to fish in exclusion of others, or without leave first obtained of the owners of the adjoining lands, the ownership of the ground evidencing a presumptive right, the disturbance whereof is a trespass for which an action will lie. By custom or prescription, many persons, such as the owners or occupiers of neighbouring land, or the inhabitants of a township or city, may have an exclusive right of fishery in a river, although the ground or soil belongs to the owners of the land on both sides, and sometimes an individual may claim an exclusive right by prescription to have a *several* fishery, *i. e.* a right of exclusive fishing in creeks or arms of the sea, where otherwise all would be entitled in common. Unless the privileges of lords of manors, or claims by prescription interfere, every one has a right to take fish left on the shore between high and low water mark. However, no trespass must be committed on the lands of another, in the assertion of this right.

With respect to fish as private property, by being enclosed in ponds or private waters, the law provides by statute 7 & 8 *G.* 4. *c.* 27. 1. That the taking or destroying fish in water running through, or in land adjoining, or *belonging* to the dwelling-house of any person who is the owner of such water or has a right of fishing therein, is a misdemeanour; 2. The taking, or attempting to take, or destroy fish in any *other* water, but which shall be *private* property, or in which there shall be any *private* right of fishery, is an offence punishable summarily before one magistrate with a penalty of 5*l.* An officer fishing without written leave is punishable under the mutiny act with the same penalty.

But if any person by *angling in the day time* take, or attempt to take, or destroy fish in the first mentioned water, he is liable, on summary conviction before a magistrate to a penalty of 5*l.*; if in the second and last mentioned water 2*l.*: and power is given to seize the rods, lines, and fishing tackle for the use of the owner, but this seizure exempts the angler from the payment of any penalty or damages for such *angling*.

Acts tending to the destruction of fish, ponds and dams, or the fish therein, are classed as malicious injuries, and punishable accordingly by another statute.

An infinity of statutes have been passed for the preservation of salmon and river fish, commencing at the reign of Edward I., many of them local, but all empowering justices and lords of court leets to inflict penalties for injuries done to the fry of fish, and taking fish out of season or unsizeable.

The Fishmongers' Company, in London, have power by statute to regulate abuses in fishery, and to register the Thames fishermen, mark their boats, &c. The court of assistants sits once a month or oftener.

The Lord Mayor of London, as conservator of the Thames, hath a water bailiff, whose duty it is to protect the fry and fishery from unlawful and detrimental practices of the fishermen, who are punishable by fine and seizure of nets, &c.

The supply and sale of fish as an article of provision in London, is regulated by various statutes, which have for their object the prevention of salesmen buying at first hand to sell again at exorbitant prices in the same market, or elsewhere, and the punishment of persons taking or selling unsizeable fish, or fish out of season. The stat. 2 *G.* 3. *c.* 15. declares that any person, whether a fishmonger or not, may buy fish in season and sizeable, but that no fish bought shall be re-sold by the first purchaser before conveyance to London or Westminster, or any other place whereto it is consigned under a penalty of 20*l.* Fish carriages or machines to be registered and marked "fish machine," which may travel on Sundays and Fast days, are exempt from toll when empty, but no game or anything else to be put in under a penalty of 5*l.*; and if the owner sell the fish before arrival within the *bills of mortality*, he is liable to a penalty of 10*l.*

Fish, by the same statute, brought to London are directed to be sorted and sold in some open market, and till exposure for sale no part to be sold by retail under a penalty of 10*l*. Buying up fish (except salmon and lobsters) subjects the party to 50*l*. penalty.

The purchase of fish to be shared in lots among fishmongers, and then to be retailed, or fishmongers buying more than necessary for their own sale or use, penalty 20*l*.

The combination by salesmen, fish proprietors or others, not to sell to any particular person, any fish publicly exposed for sale, subjects the parties to a penalty of 10*l*.

Persons selling at first hand in the London markets, must put up a board describing the sorts and number received (except as to the *number* of flounders, plaice, dabs, mackerel, maids, herrings and pilchards); if further supplies received the same day, they must also be likewise published under penalties of 10*l*.

By 36 *G*. 3. *c*. 181. *s*. 1. the sale of fish in Billingsgate market by wholesale, can only take place *once*, if in that market again the sale must be by retail. Purchasers of fish in that market may sell them again by *retail* in that market or *elsewhere*, except that none but fishmongers may sell in public, or in fixed shops or houses.

By the act 42 *G*. 3. *c*. 19. every master of a vessel is to give account of the sorts of fish brought alive to the Nore in his vessel, and if after such arrival he wilfully destroy or throw the fish away, (not being unwholesome or unmarketable), he is liable to be committed to the house of correction, and kept to hard labour for not less than one, and not exceeding two months.

By an act of the 11 *G*. 4. *c*. 70. provision is made for the sale of fish in Hungerford market.

The national fisheries are regulated by various statutes too numerous even to quote, but they are specified as the Newfoundland fisheries, Greenland fishery, Southern whale fishery, British white herring fishery, Scotch fisheries, Scotch salmon fisheries, lobster fishery on the coast of Scotland, fisheries on the coast of Ireland. pilchard fishery in Cornwall, &c.

All fish of foreign taking or curing, or in foreign vessels (except turbot and lobsters, stock fish, live eels, anchovies, sturgeon, botargo, and caviare) are prohibited. Also, See OYSTERS.

FISH-POND. The breaking down the dam of a fish-pond or private water, or of any water in which there shall be a private right of fishery, and the putting lime or *any* noxious material into a fish-pond, or such water, is a malicious mischief, and misdemeanour punishable by 7 years' transportation, or imprisonment with or without hard labour, and with or without solitary confinement, not exceeding two years, and (if a male) whipping.

FIXTURES are those things which are fixed to house or land by a tenant or occupier, either for purposes of domestic comfort or ornament, or for the convenience of trade, more commonly known as house-fixtures and trade-fixtures.

With respect to every thing annexed to the land, the rule of law formerly was, that the thing annexed to the land formed portion of the land itself upon the same principle which is still acknowledged, that if one build upon the land of another, the improvement or addition belongs to the proprietor of the land, because the land could not be enjoyed without the building or annexation, but it has been held convenient for the purposes of trade and convenience that this rule should be relaxed; therefore fixtures put up for the purposes of ornament or convenience, and the disannexing of which will not cause material damage in the removal, belong to a tenant. So a building erected for carrying on a trade for whatever purposes, and however substantial in itself, so that it is not in a situation to be considered as affixed to the freehold, in the eye of the law (for unless a thing is absolutely attached to the freehold or premises by being let into the ground, or united by means of nails, screws, bolts, or the like, the law considers it as a mere loose and movable chattel) is consequently removable by the tenant. Indeed, for convenience of trade, a very liberal construction prevails as to what shall be deemed an annexation to the freehold or premises sufficient to deprive the tenant of the power of removal: thus, if a tenant erects a barn, granary, stable, or any *other* building upon blocks, rollers, stilts or pillars, it is removable; so a varnish house laid upon a wooden plate resting on brickwork, the quarters being morticed into the plate; a post-windmill, if laid on cross traces *not attached to the ground;* vessels, or utensils supported on brickwork; frames or horses standing on the ground; and the like of machinery let into caps or steps of timber, and even, as it seems, although fastened by pins. By adopting these or similar modes of construction, a tenant may not only make valuable additions to his premises with perfect safety, but avoid the effect of a covenant in his lease to repair buildings erected after the commencement of his tenantry. Mr. J. Chitty Jun., in his "Law of Contracts" has presented his readers with the following useful alphabetical list of those fixtures, which, as between landlord and tenant, have been decided to be removable or not.

The first list comprises things *not* removable by the tenant; the second, things removable, but *not being mere trade fixtures;* and the third comprehends *mere trade fixtures,* held to be removable.

1. *List of things held* not *to be removable.*

Agricultural erections.
Alehouse bar.
Barns fixed in the ground.
Beast house.
Benches.
Carpenter's shop.
Cart house.
Chimney pieces (in general.)
Conservatories.
Doors.
Dressers.
Foldyard walls.
Fruit trees.
Fuel house.
Glass windows.
Hearth.
Improvements, permanent.
Jibs.
Keys.
Locks.
Millstones.
Partitions.
Pigeon house.
Pineries substantially affixed or erected on brickwork.
Pump house.
Racks in stables.
Strawberry beds.
Waggon house.
Windows.

2. *List of things held to be removable (not being trade fixtures.)*

Arras hangings.
Barn on blocks.
Beds fastened to ceiling.
Bells.
Bins.
Blinds.
Book-cases.
Buildings on blocks, rollers, pillars, &c.
Cabinets.
Chimney backs.
Chimney glasses.
Chimney pieces (ornamental.)
Cider mills.
Cisterns.
Clock cases.
Coffee mills.
Cooling coppers.

Coppers.
Cupboards.
Dutch barns.
Furnaces.
Furniture (fixtures, put up as.)
Granary on pillars.
Grates.
Hangings.
Iron backs to chimneys.
Iron chests.
Iron malt mills.
Iron ovens.
Jacks.
Lamps.
Looking-glasses.
Malt mills.
Marble chimney-pieces.
Marble slabs.
Mash tubs.
Mills on posts.
Mills *laid* on brick foundations.
Ornamental fixtures.
Ovens.
Pattens, erections on.
Pier glasses.
Posts.
Presses.
Pumps slightly attached.
Rails.
Ranges.
Sheds.
Shelves.
Sinks.
Slabs of marble.
Stable on rollers.
Stoves.
Tapestry.
Tubs.
Turret clocks.
Vessels, &c., on brickwork.
Wainscot, fixed by screws.
Water tubs.
Windmill on posts.

3. *List of Trade Fixtures decided or said to be removable.*

Accessory buildings, that is, accessory to a removable utensil.
Brewing vessels and pipes.
Cider mills.
Cisterns.
Closets.
Colliery machines.
Coppers.
Counters.
Cranes.
Desks.
Drawers.
Dutch barns.
Engines.
Fire engines.
Furnaces.
Gas pipes.
Glass fronts.
Iron safes.
Machinery let into caps or steps of timber.
Partitions.
Plants and pipes of brewers, distillers, &c.
Presses.
Pumps.
Reservoirs.
Salt pans.
Shelves.
Shrubs planted for sale.
Soap works, fixtures in.
Steam engines.
Stills.
Trees planted for sale.
Varnish house.
Vats.

There are also certain fixtures as to which the right of removal is unsettled. They may be classed as *doubtful.*

Brick-kilns.
Frames in nursery grounds.
Furnaces in smelting-houses, and glass-houses.
Glasses in nursery grounds.
Green-houses.
Hot-houses.
Lime-kilns.
Malting floors, stoves, &c.
Pavements.
Sheds.
Storehouses.
Tables, fixed or dormant.
Verandas.
Wind or water mills.
Workshops.

The right of removal of fixtures has only been considered hitherto without reference to leases or agreements, which govern the right of removal of fixtures more than those who hastily sign such contracts are generally aware of. For a tenant by lease, under covenant to repair *erections* thereafter to be built, *and to surrender* them at the end of the term, cannot remove additions to the premises, though made for the purposes of trade, or any other additions or fixtures, though not of a permanent and substantial nature. If a tenant covenant or agree to leave at the end of his term "all fixtures, fastenings, and *improvements* set up, &c., during the term," this restriction will operate against the tenant's right of removal; so that every intended lessee should be careful in considering how far he may be affected by the lease or agreement in regard of his fixtures; he should not attend to what brokers and illiterate persons may tell him: every thing affecting the right to remove fixtures should be carefully excluded from the contract; and those fixtures of the landlord which may be let, should be set forth in a list or schedule, so that his demand may be limited at the expiration of the tenancy. Agricultural improvements always belong to the landlord, unless it is otherwise arranged.

A tenant must remove his fixtures *before the expiration of the tenancy*, or at least, before he quits the premises, in case he holds over; for he has no remedy for them against the landlord, if he is prevented taking them away afterwards.

The fixtures of a dwelling-house are often sold to an incoming tenant on the commencement of his tenancy. In this case the sheriff or assignee may seize and take them, if the tenant be bankrupt, insolvent, or there is an execution issued against his goods; but no mischief must be done to the premises by their removal. If a tenant replace his landlord's fixtures, such as stoves, &c., it seems he cannot, on his departure, retake the improved additions, and put in the old fixtures.

Where an agreement respecting fixture is about to take place between an outgoing and an incoming tenant, it is advisable that the landlord be made a party to the transaction; for otherwise the latter may, perhaps, insist, that as the fixtures were not removed during the outgoing tenant's term, they fell in with the lease; and that the incomer took them as part of the demised premises, and, consequently, is not entitled to remove them. If there be no immediately incoming tenant at the end of a term, and the outgoer wishes to leave his fixtures to be valued to the next tenant, he must obtain the consent of his landlord to allow them to remain on the premises; for, if the fixtures remain on the premises after the expiration of the term without such consent, the tenant loses his property in them. *J. Chitty, jun. on Contracts.*

Fixtures being considered as part of the house or premises, no compensation can be demanded by a landlord for their use. It would spare much litigation to landlords and loss to tenants, if the public discountenanced the custom of paying for *fixtures* on entering a house; for the tenant very often purchases what he cannot readily sell at the same price, or conveniently take away, and the landlord sells what he may often have to replace (in case of a sale by, or execution against, the tenant, or his bankruptcy or insolvency) at a considerable loss; indeed, landlords seem to be intuitively aware that as *house fixtures* are a great incumbrance on the tenant, he is generally glad to part with them at almost any rate, and where there is no incoming tenant to take them off his hands, the landlord obtains them as a compensation for some alleged dilapidation, small allowance of rent, &c., and finds his account in selling them to a future occupier at the old price.

With regard to fixtures, as between the executors or administrators, and the heir or remainder man entitled to the premises, it seems that the old rule of law, viz., that all additions or improvements are part of the premises, is not so much relaxed as in the case of landlord and tenant, which are governed by principles of public convenience and trade: therefore, as between executors and the heir or remainder man, it seems that stoves, grates, and cupboards, or any thing fixed for the better enjoyment of the premises, although they might be removed by a tenant during his tenancy, yet, form part of the freehold or premises descendible to the heir, to the exclusion of the executor who claims the chattels or personal property. The claim of an executor appears very unsettled, although it seems pretty well decided, that erections for the purpoess of *trade* belong to the executor, though additions for convenience or comfort generally do not. Coppers, tubs, and brewing utensils and blinds go to the executor, because the premises may be enjoyed without them; whereas, stove grates and shelves are indispensably necessary, and go to the heir. The intelligent reader will therefore note the principles upon which the old rule of law is relaxed or enforced in these cases.

It often happens that upon the purchase of premises it is agreed that "the fixtures shall be taken at a valuation" or "*fair* valuation," *i. e.* that the valuer should exercise his discretion as to the *price* to be paid, which must not exceed a reasonable sum; but valuers or appraisers often exceed their authority, and place in their specifications what things *they adjudge fixtures;* a very unwarrantable discretion, for, in the absence of any previous agreement what are to be deemed "fixtures," only those things can be valued which are "trade fixtures," and the purchaser will only have to pay for those, almost every other annexation or fixture attached to the premises, for the purposes of convenience or enjoyment belonging to the purchaser; so that the purchaser is entitled to as much as could be claimed by an heir against the executor, which is a very favourable rule in respect of a purchaser.

The stealing of any chattel, or fixture, let with any house or lodging, is a felony, and punishable as a larceny, by transportation for seven years, or imprisonment not exceeding two years (with or without hard labour or solitary confinement), and whipping, if a male, at the discretion of the court.

FLEET. The name of a prison so called from its standing by the river Fleet, now bricked up and paved over. It is the prison to which persons are committed by the ecclesiastical courts, courts of equity, exchequer, and common pleas. It is governed by an officer called the warden, who is answerable for the custody of his prisoners, and is summarily amenable to the courts, whose prisoners are sent there for any abuse, extortion, or misconduct.

FOOTPATHS. Persons riding on, or driving cattle on, forfeit 40*s.* and damages under the highway act; and this penalty is incurred for damaging any footpath near the road, although not maintained by the trustees of turnpike roads.

FORFEITURE OF GOODS was formerly the punishment of all felonies; to which was superadded some other punishment of a corporal nature, generally death; and it still attaches on all felonies above larceny, and upon cases of *felo de se;* the law contemplating the act of suicide, as a felony committed by a man upon himself. Lands are forfeited now, as far as regards the profits, during the life of the offender; and are absolutely forfeited by the owner's committing murder or treason: but suicides, strictly so termed, do not forfeit lands, or any interest therein.

A person outlawed for murder or treason forfeits lands and goods; and a person outlawed for debt also forfeits the profits of his land

and all his goods, which are distributed by the treasury among the creditors prosecuting the outlawry.

In manslaughter the offender forfeits goods and chattels.

After a conviction by judgment, or outlawry for high treason, or murder, a commission issues to nominees of the attorney, to inquire what lands or tenements the offender had, at the time of the treason, or murder committed, and to seize them for the use of the king. The goods of a felon cannot be seized before forfeiture; but they may be inventoried.

There are two instances in which a person forfeits goods and chattels, and the profits of his lands during life; namely, the drawing a weapon on a judge in court, and striking any one in the presence of the queen's courts of justice.

In præmunire a party forfeits lands absolutely, and goods and chattels. See PRÆMUNIRE.

Forfeiture also is the term used, where, upon the breach of a condition, or for some illegal act, the owner loses all interest in real or personal property. As if tenant for life commit waste, or make leases for more than three lives, or twenty-one years; or if a copyholder refuse to do suit and service, or pay his quit-rents and fines to the lord; or, if tenant for life grant a greater estate than he himself possesses, his estate is forfeited: in the case of the copyholder, to the lord; in the case of the tenant for life, to the person next in remainder or reversion.

FORGERY is the making, or alteration of, any instrument, with a fraudulent intent; and the uttering a forged instrument, with perfect knowledge of its being forged, is also forgery; and, with very few exceptions, rendered equally penal with the act of forgery itself. Therefore, the intelligent reader will bear in remembrance, that not only the fabrication of the *whole* of a written instrument, but a fraudulent insertion, alteration, or erasure, even of a letter, in any material part of a true instrument, is a forgery; and it matters not, whether the signature be true, and the matter contained in the instrument false, or *vice versa.*

The making of a false instrument in the name of a fictitious person, is as much forgery, as if it were made in the name of a person known to be in existence.

The offence of forgery is a felony punishable in the cases hereafter named.

Accessories *before the fact* are mostly treated as principals; *after the* fact, are punishable with imprisonment, not exceeding two years; but persons executing distinct parts of a forgery, whether in immediate connexion or concert, or not, are all principals.

Persons punishable for forgery are classed according to the nature of the documents altered or forged; viz:

1. *As to the seals, &c.* Forging the great seal of the United Kingdom, her majesty's privy seal, any privy signet of her majesty, her majesty's sign manual, the seals of Scotland, the great seal, and privy seal of Ireland; treason: transportation for life, with or without previous imprisonment.

2. *As to Records, &c.* Avoiding records; felony. Forging a court roll, or copy of a court roll; felony: transportation or imprisonment. Forging a memorial or certificate of registry of lands, in Yorkshire or Middlesex; imprisonment for life, forfeiture of lands, &c. Forging an entry in a register relating to baptism, marriage, or burial; felony: transportation or imprisonment. Uttering a false certificate of a previous conviction; felony: transportation, or imprisonment, and whipping. Forging a will; felony: transportation for life or years, or imprisonment for not exceeding 4 nor less than 2 years.

3. *As to the revenue, &c.* Forging the stamps on paper, &c., playing cards,

almanacks, plate, &c., newspapers, &c.; felony: transportation for life. Forging debentures or certificates for payment or return of money, required by statutes, relating to the customs or excise; felony: transportation for life.

Forging the stamps denoting the duty to have been paid on paper, pasteboard, &c., fine. Forging the stamp on linens, calicoes, stuffs; felony. Forging the stamp on cambrics, &c.; felony: transportation for life. Forging the mark of postage on letters; fine and imprisonment. Forging franks; felony: transportation for seven years. Forging a hawker's license, 300*l.* fine. Forging declarations of return of insurance; felony: transportation for seven years.

4. *As to public securities, &c.* Forging an entry, &c., in the books of the Bank of England or South Sea Company, forging a transfer of stock of the Bank of England, South Sea Company, or of any other body corporate, company, or society, now or hereafter to be established, or a power of attorney to transfer it, or transferring it by personating the proprietor; felony: transportation for life or years, or imprisonment for not exceeding four nor less than two years. Forging the names of witnesses to such power of attorney; felony: transportation or imprisonment. Clerks, &c., employed in the Bank of England or South Sea Company, wilfully making or delivering any dividend warrant for a greater or less sum than the party is entitled to; felony: transportation or imprisonment. Forging exchequer bills on debentures; felony: transportation for life, with or without previous imprisonment.

5. *As to public offices,* forging the name of the registrar of the high court of admiralty, on the bank receipts for suitors' money; felony. Forging the hand of the accountant, general registrar, &c., of the high court of chancery, or of the cashier of the bank, to any instrument relating to suitors' money; felony. Forging the hand of the accountant-general of the exchequer; felony. Forging the handwriting of the receiver-general of the excise, or excise controller of cash, or other person duly authorised, to any draft, &c., upon the Bank of England; felony. Forging the handwriting of the receiver-general or comptroller-general of the customs, or any person acting for them, to any draft, &c., upon the bank; felony. Forging the handwriting of the receiver general of the stamp duties, or of his clerk, or of the commissioners of stamps, to any draft, &c., on the bank; felony. Forging the handwriting of the treasurer, or other signing or vouching officer of the navy, to any paper whereby his majesty's naval treasure or stores may be paid or disposed of. Forging the handwriting of the treasurer of the ordnance, &c., to any draft, &c., on the bank; felony. Forging the handwriting of the receiver-general of the post office, &c. to any draft, &c., on the bank; felony. Forging the handwriting of the adjutant-general of the volunteers and local militia, &c., to any draft, &c., on the bank; felony. Forging the handwriting of the surveyor-general of the woods and forests, &c., to any drafts, &c., on the bank; felony. Forging any contracts, certificates, receipts, &c., relating to the redemption of the land tax; felony, and all punishable by transportation for life, or for a less time.

6. *As to officers in the navy and army.* Forging any letter of attorney, order, assignment, last will, &c., in order to receive pay or prize-money due to any officer or seaman, or any marine officer or marine; felony. Forging any letter of attorney, order, last will, &c., in order to receive money due on account of any out-pension granted by Greenwich hospital; felony. Forging bills, &c., drawn by officers of the navy for their half pay; felony. Forging the signature of the parish minister to the certificate to obtain probate of a seaman's will, or administration to him; felony. Forging the name of any officer of the navy, entitled to allowances on the compassionate list, or any marine officer entitled to half pay, to any remittance bill, certificate, voucher, or receipt, in relation to the same; felony, and the same as to marines. Forging the name of any officer's widow to any remittance bill, certificate, voucher, or receipt, respecting her pension; felony: transportation. Forging seamen's remittance bills; felony: transportation. Forging receipts or certificates of annuity for military and naval pensions; felony: transportation.

7. *As to public companies, &c.* Forging a bond of the East India Company; felony: transportation for life, with or without previous imprisonment. Forging a receipt or warrant of the South Sea Company for subscriptions; felony. As to forging the stock of these and other corporate bodies; felony: transportation or imprisonment.

8. *As to public trade.* Foreign Mediterranean passes; felony: transporta-

tion for life or years or imprisonment. As to forgeries on the London and Royal Exchange Insurance Company, the Globe Insurance, the English linen Company, the British Society for extending the fisheries; and the British Plate Glass Manufactory, &c. There are other statutes with respect to forgeries upon particular companies, but these are now immaterial; for the acts 11 *G.* 4. *&* 1 *W.* 4. *c.* 66. extend to bodies corporate, or companies or societies of persons not incorporated, and to any person or numberof persons whatsoever who may be intended to be defrauded, whether they reside and carry on business in England or elsewhere. Forging a shipping license; penalty 500*l.* Forging quarantine certificates; felony. Forging certificates, &c., mentioned in the act for the abolition of the slave trade; felony: transportation. Forging the assay marks on gold and silver plate; transportation for 14 years. Forging alehouse certificates; misdemeanor.

9. *As to the instruments of forging.* To make or have any frame, &c., for the making of paper with the words "Bank of England" visible on the substance, or to make paper with curved or waving bar or wiry lines, &c., or to make, &c., or sell, &c., such paper, &c.; felony: transportation for 14 years. To engrave on any plate, &c., any bank-note, &c., or blank bank-note, bill, &c., or use and have possession of such plates, &c., or utter, or have paper upon which a blank bank-note, &c., shall be printed; felony: transportation for 14 years. To engrave on any plate any word, number, figure, character, or ornament resembling any part of a bank note, &c., or use or have such plate, &c., or utter or have any paper on which there shall be an impression of any word, &c.; felony: transportation for 14 years. To make use of or have possession of any frame, &c., for the making paper, with the name or firm of any person or persons, body corporate or company, carrying on business as bankers appearing on the substance, or to make, sell, &c., or have possession of such paper; felony: transportation for 14 or 7 years, or imprisonment for 3 years or 1 year. To engrave on any plate, &c., any bill of exchange or promissory note of any bankers, &c., any words resembling the subscription thereto, or use such plate, &c., or sell or have any paper on which any part of such bill, &c. shall be printed; felony: transportation for 14 or 7 years, or imprisonment for 3 years or 1 year. To engrave plates, &c., for foreign bills or notes, or use or have such plates, or utter any paper on which any part of such bills, &c., may be printed; felony: transportation for 14 or 7 years, or imprisonment for 3 years or 1 year.

The stat. 1 *Vict. c.* 48. abolishes the punishment of death in all cases of forgery; and the mitigated punishment for these offences is the one provided by the 11 *G.* 4. *&* 1 *W.* 4. *c.* 66., which is above particularly mentioned with respect to the forging of wills and powers of attorney for the transfer of stock, those being the two exceptions in the alteration of the law effected by the latter statute, and now placed on the same footing with the offences named therein.

FRAUD and DECEIT. As the law impliedly prohibits all dishonest practices, it will never permit an individual to acquire, through the medium of fraud, any right or interest, and it matters not whether a fraud be committed by a principal or agent.

The committing a fraud in the dealings which must necessarily take place between man and man are infinitely varied, and it is difficult to accurately class them, though, for the purpose of a summary, they may be noticed. 1. Frauds arising from misrepresentation. 2. In respect of deeds in fraud of creditors. 3. Criminal frauds, commonly termed false pretences.

1. *Misrepresentations.* A misrepresentation may be effected in regard to a contract or dealing, by either stating what is known to be false or delusive, or by the suppression of material facts, which, if known, would enable the party to form a clearer judgment or dispel a delusion which exists by reason of the concealment; and any device naturally calculated to induce a careful person to forego inquiry into a matter

upon which the other party has information is a fraud. However, a misrepresentation is unimportant, if the party to whom the false statement is made knew the real state of the facts; for in such case he was not deceived.

It, however, may be generally asserted, that a particular representation, although *false in effect*, is not consequently *fraudulent*, unless the misrepresentation formed part of the contract itself and the object was to deceive; for that would be, in the case of a written agreement, to permit unwritten testimony to vary or alter a written contract; and in unwritten contracts, if the misrepresentation does not bear immediately upon the substance or material inducement of the contract, it cannot be said that a party is defrauded, unless fraud appears to have been intended.

It is a question of fact entirely for the jury, whether or not a fact is material, and should have been communicated. Where both parties are upon equal terms in respect of judgment and information, no fraud can be said to be committed.

A misrepresentation of the *legal effect* of an agreement does not constitute fraud.

A great inadequacy of price in a thing sold is not of itself sufficient to vacate a sale or agreement for that purpose, unless other circumstances of fraud are apparent, as weakness of intellect in the party selling, an evident intention to make a catching bargain, &c.

Frauds of this nature are mostly relievable in a court of equity.

The courts of law can in many cases assist those who have been the dupes of designing and knavish men, where the fraud has been committed by means of written contracts or specialties; and in unwritten contracts, where damages have been sustained from a fraudulent misrepresentation or suppression of material facts, a court of law is the proper place for a remedy.

The object of a fraud may be to injure third persons, which is more properly termed a collusion, as where the creditors of a debtor agree to accept a composition for their claims, and one of the creditors joins in the arrangement that the debtor, or another for him, shall pay a greater sum of money as a price for his concurrence; this is a fraud upon third parties, viz. the creditors who all execute upon the faith that they each have the same share; so where two parties *collude*, *i. e.* contrive to injure a third party by their mutual acts, they being apparently hostile agreements or contracts entered into for these or similar purposes, are voidable, and cannot be enforced either at law or equity between either of the contracting parties.

2. *Deeds in fraud of creditors.* In the last division it was noticed that acts between two, to prejudice a third person, were collusive and fraudulent; and the law acting upon this principle, has at very early periods declared by statute, that all acts, judgments, and deeds, with the intent to defraud and delay creditors, or their actions or suits, are void, as against the creditors of the party so executing any deed, or suffering any judgment to be executed against his goods or lands, *i. e.* the act or deed stood valid with regard to the party himself and barred *him*, but left it open for the creditors to dispute a transaction which had but one intent, viz. to defraud them. All parties concerned are also subject to a penalty of a year's value of the land, and the whole of the money in the deed or judgment, together with half a year's imprisonment: the forfeiture being divided between the crown and the informer.

The object of the legislature was evidently to protect creditors from those frauds which are frequently practised by debtors under the pretence of discharging a moral obligation; for as to those gifts or conveyances which want even a good or meritorious consideration for their support, their being voluntary seems to have been always a sufficient ground to conclude that they were fraudulent; but though the statute protects the legal right of creditors against the fraud of their debtors, it anxiously excepts from such imputation the *bonâ fide* discharge of a moral duty. It, therefore, does not declare all voluntary conveyances, but all fraudulent conveyances to be void; and whether the conveyance be fraudulent, or not, is declared to depend on the consideration being good, and also *bonâ fide*.

Certain deeds, although moral in their consideration, are deemed fraudulent by the bankrupt and insolvent laws; as if a bankrupt convey property for a valid consideration, after an act of bankruptcy upon which a *fiat* is founded, and within two months of the issuing of the same fiat, this deed or transaction is set aside, as well as all executions levied under the same circumstances. Indeed, all deeds by a man in insolvent circumstances tending to prefer another who has a moral claim for such preference, and although the party preferred be not aware of his debtor's insolvency, are void as against creditors under these laws, which operate for the benefit of creditors, by a rateable division of the debtor's property.

3. *False pretences.* The obtaining of any thing, money, or valuable security, with the intent to cheat and defraud another, is a misdemeanor, punishable by transportation for seven years, or by fine and imprisonment. The offence of defrauding by a *false pretence* is very common, and as each case depends upon particular circumstances, it is necessary to state the principles of law and evidence affecting this offence.

To constitute a false pretence, there must be a pretending by the offender of some particular fact which has no existence, made in order to induce the party injured to part with his property, which pretence, as in the case of a cheat, need not be made in words: thus, if a person obtain goods from another upon giving him in payment his cheque upon a banker with whom he has no account, this is a false pretence; but, on the other hand, a declaration by the party that he would do an act he did not mean to do, as a pretence to pay for goods on delivery, is not a false pretence within the meaning of the act, but is merely a bare promise of future conduct referrible to the performance of a contract. In one case, where a party, to induce his bankers to honour his cheques, drew a bill on a person on whom he had no right to draw, and which had no chance of being paid, in consequence of which the bankers paid his cheques, it was adjudged not to be a false pretence, because he only obtained *credit*, it would have been held otherwise had he obtained *money* upon the bill.

In many cases, where there is an intent to defraud, coupled with a deliberate intent of stealing, and the party receive the goods, he may be convicted of *larceny*, *i. e.* the stealing, even though legally entitled to his acquittal for the false pretence, a statute specially providing that where the offence turns out to be a larceny or simple stealing, and not a false pretence, that the defendant should be convicted of the *larceny;* it being difficult in many cases to distinguish between a larceny and a false pretence, and the law not allowing both offences, which are of a different degree, to be joined in one indictment.

FRAUDS, STATUTE OF. See CONTRACT.

FREIGHT. The money paid for a carriage of goods by sea; or, in a larger sense, it is taken for the price paid for the use of a ship to transport goods, and for the cargo, or burthen of the ship. Ships are freighted either by the *ton* or by the *great;* and, in respect of time, the freight is agreed for, at so much per month, or at a certain sum for the whole voyage. If a ship, freighted by the *great*, happens to be cast away, the freight is lost; but if a merchant agrees by the *ton*, or at so much for every piece of commodities, and by any accident the ship is cast away, if part of the goods is saved, it is said she ought to be satisfied her freight *pro rata;* and when a ship is *insured*, and such a misfortune happens, the insured commonly abandons, that is, transfers those goods over to the assurers, which they carry to their own account. See ABANDONMENT, CHARTER-PARTY.

FRIENDLY SOCIETIES, or BENEFIT CLUBS, are associations chiefly among the lower classes of tradesmen, "for the purpose of mutual relief, and maintenance of the members, their wives, or children, relations, or nominees, in sickness, infancy, advanced age, widowhood, or any other natural state or contingency, whereof the occurrence is susceptible of average, or for any other purpose which is not illegal;" regulated by two statutes, viz: 10 *G.* 4. *c.* 56., and 4 & 5 *W.* 4. *c.* 40., and which, in encouraging associations of the above nature, extend the subjects of relief to losses by fire, shipwreck, substitutes, if drawn for the militia; a weekly allowance, if reduced to a workhouse, or imprisoned for debt; and for any contribution towards an annual feast, or any reasonable or lawful purpose; but these last-named subjects are to be separately and distinctly contributed to, as an extra subscription, and not to be identified with the primary purposes for which these societies are erected. Also, the money payable on the death of a member, may be disposed of by will at his pleasure.

The only restriction in their formation is the enrolment and approval of their rules by the barrister appointed to certify their correctness and freedom from irregularity or erroneous principles; which costs no more than a guinea, the transmission of the packet enclosing them being free of postage.

The rules, which must be proper and wholesome, and not illegal or repugnant to the acts, may be made by the major part of the members, and may inflict reasonable fines, and can be amended upon a notice given to the barrister (at present, J. T. Pratt, Esq., 3. Elm Court, Temple); they should also distinctly declare the purposes for which the society is established, and direct the employment of the subscriptions, and impose a penalty upon their misappropriation.

They should also in distinct terms declare the place of meeting, the number and the duties of the officers, and the liabilities of the members at large, and how long the officers shall continue in office, the number of members who form a committee, and the powers and duration of such committee.

The rules *must* direct how the treasurer is to lay out the funds, and in what manner the consent of the society to such laying out, is to be signified. The rules should provide for references or awards, in cases of disputes; whether to, or by justices of peace, or arbitrators; if the latter, the number of them, and how chosen.

Provision must be made that the steward, or principal officer, shall *at least* once in the year, lay a particular statement of the funds of the society, with an account of receipt and expenditure since the preceding statement, for the use of the members generally, who may have a copy on payment of 6*d*. And a copy of the form of return, prescribed by the former act, must be annexed to the rules of the society; another copy of which return should be sent to the barrister, who lays the same before parliament.

Rules should also be made for the payment of sums under £20, in cases of members dying without a will.

These acts also give remedies to the members, or those claiming in their right against the society; or any fraudulent dissolution, or division of the funds. The votes of 5-6ths in value of the members being requisite to effect this purpose; and no division can take place, but for the purposes of the society, clearly stated, and approved by justices of the peace.

The funds of the society are vested in the trustee or treasurer, who may, with respect to the property of the society, sue and be sued in his own name.

Any frauds committed with respect to claims upon, or payments by, the society, are specially cognizable by magistrates.

If the trustee or treasurer refuse to transfer stock, standing in his name for the use of the society, or abscond, the court of exchequer will, on summary petition, transfer the funds to the new treasurer, free from council's or official fees.

Provision is made for settling disputes, by referring the same to arbitrators or to justices, which is to be final and conclusive.

Power is also given to these societies, to invest their funds in savings' banks, or with the commissioners for the reduction of the national debt (the office is in the Old Jewry, London,) at the interest of £3 16*s*. 0½*d*. per cent.

If the steward, trustee, treasurer, &c., of the society is insolvent, bankrupt, or his property is taken in execution, or he dies, a priority is given to the society for the payment of any demand the society may have against him, in respect of the funds in his hands, on the happening of either of these circumstances.

Sums not exceeding £20 may be paid on the death of members to wife, children, nominee, or, if none, amongst next of kin, without the expense of letters of administration; or, otherwise, in conformity with the rules which must be made for that purpose. And no stamp duty is payable in respect of the transactions, payments, receipts, or deeds of this society.

Minors, who are admitted into these societies with consent of their guardians or parents, may act therein and enjoy all the privileges, and, on the other hand, are liable to all the responsibilities, attaching on members of full age.

The responsibility of a treasurer or trustee is limited to the money actually received by him, and, therefore, he is not liable for any deficiency in the funds, unless he shall have, *under his hand, and by a writing registered in like manner with the rules of the society*, declared his willingness so to be answerable; and by such writing the treasurer may express that his liability or responsibility shall not exceed a given sum beyond what he shall *actually* receive by virtue of his office. If required, treasurers or officers receiving money are to give a bond to the clerk of the peace, with sufficient sureties, which may be put in suit by the society in the name of the clerks of the peace, on the society's indemnifying him from costs of suit.

As all rules are to be entered and registered in a book, accessible to every member, and as every act of a committee appointed by the society is to be entered in like manner, publicity of all circumstances connected with the regulation and disposal of the funds of the society is adequately secured to every member, who may always, in addition to these advantages, have the benefit of a magistrate's decision in cases of fraud or refusals to arbitrate, which decision being by the statute declared final cannot give rise to a litigation in the superior courts.

Persons who are desirous of obtaining information respecting the means of establishing or creating these societies on true and advantageous principles, should carefully peruse the two acts, the latter of which repeals a few directions which imposed a needless expense on the society; or become the purchasers of an excellent book on this subject by the certifying barrister, the price of which does not exceed by many pence the costs of the two acts of parliament at the queen's printers.

FURNISHED LODGINGS. The stealing from furnished lodgings is a larceny, punishable by transportation for seven years, or imprisonment for two years, and (if a male) whipping.

The illegally pawning of property so circumstanced, which is a species of theft, is punishable under a clause in the pawnbrokers' act in a summary manner. See PAWNBROKER.

FURZE. The wilfully setting fire to corn, grain, or pulse (whether standing or cut down), or any part of a wood, coppice, or plantation of trees, or any heath, gorse, or furze, is a felony, punishable by transportation for seven years, or imprisonment with or without solitary confinement, and (if a male) whipping.

GAME are hares, pheasants, partridges, grouse, heath or moor-game, black game, and bustards. The taking of which is regulated, and the selling legalized, by act 1 & 2 *W.* 4. *c.* 32.; and the unlawful taking by night punishable under another recent statute, called the night-poaching act, 9 *G.* 4. *c.* 69. The provisions of the former act may be noticed under two heads. 1. As to the right and qualifications to kill game. 2. As to the buying and selling of game. 3. As to Trespasses. Poaching will be considered under the title POACHERS.

1. Any person is at liberty to kill game on his own land, or on that of another person, with the leave of the person entitled to the *game*, upon obtaining a game certificate: for which 3*l.* 13*s.* 6*d.*, or for a menial gamekeeper, 1*l.* 5*s.*, is payable to the collector of the king's taxes of the place where the applicant resides.

The restrictions as to *time* or *season* are, sunday or christmas-day, under a penalty of 5*l.*, with costs for each offence, recoverable before two magistrates; and with regard to *season*, the taking or killing *partridges* between the 1st of February and the 1st of September; *pheasants*, between the 1st of February and the 1st of October; *black-game*, (except in Somerset, or Devon, or in the New-Forest, Hants,) between the 10th of December and the 20th of August, and in Somerset, Devon, and the New-Forest, between the 10th of December and the 1st of September; *grouse, or red-game*, between the 10th of December and the 12th of August; or bustards, between the 1st of March and the 1st of September, subjects the party to a penalty of 1*l.*, for every head of game, with costs of conviction; recoverable before two magistrates. Hares may be killed all the year round.

Poisoning game subjects the party to a penalty not exceeding 10*l.* with costs, recoverable in like manner.

Any person not having the right of killing game upon the land, or permission from the person having such right, taking, or destroying the eggs of any bird of game, swan, wild duck, teal, or widgeon, or having the same in his possession, is liable on conviction, before two magistrates, for every egg taken, destroyed, or found in his house or possession, 5*s.*, and costs.

The enabling all *certificated* persons to kill game, only gives them power to sport on their own land, or that of another, with leave of the person entitled to the *game* (for the possession of the land and the right of sporting are distinct matters), and renders them liable to the restrictions, as to the place of sporting, considered under the third head, as to trespasses; for there are only three cases, where the occupier of land under a lease or agreement, can kill game himself, (if certificated) or give permission to other certificated persons, to sport thereon. 1st. Where such right has been by express words granted in his lease or agreement. 2d. Where a fine was paid on the granting, or renewal of such lease; and 3dly, where the lease or agreement, is for a term exceeding twenty-one years: and in the two latter cases, the right is taken away, by the landlord or tenant for life, or party entitled, reserving to himself the right of sporting. But, subject to these exceptions, the superior landlord, or the party who may have the reserved right, has the power of not only sporting himself, but permitting others to sport: and the right, of all parties claiming by any grant, or in right of any lord or owner of a forest, chase, or warren, or the steward of any manor, forest, &c., where the property is in the crown, are particularly saved by the act.

The act, also, does not abolish the provisions of former game acts with reference to game-keepers, or keepers of manors, which extend to game-keepers appointed under the present act.

Persons killing or taking game without a certificate are subjected to a penalty of 5*l.*, in addition to the penalties imposed for not taking out a certificate.

If an occupier kill or take game, or permit others to do so, he is liable for the penalty of 2*l.* for the pursuit, in addition to a penalty of 1*l.* for every head of game; and the persons to whom he gave permission, are also liable for any proceeding the landlord may institute for the trespass.

The appointment of game-keepers.— The lord of a manor is now empowered to appoint as many game-keepers as he may think fit; which game-keepers have power to seize for the lord of the manor's use, dogs, nets, guns, and *any* instruments used for killing game, within the limits of the manor, by persons not having taken out a certificate; indeed, none but a game-keeper can do this, for a private person is not justified in seizing a dog, which is coursing a hare on his own premises, nor can he legally shoot a dog trespassing on his lands in pursuit of game. A game-keeper cannot legally seize a gun, unless the uncertificated person be using it in the destruction of game, nor can he kill the dog of a person following game within the manor, unless indeed the hare or game is put in danger of being killed; in which latter case, it may be justified. When a game-keeper makes a seizure of a dog or gun, he should in prudence demand to see the certificate of the person using the same; which, if he fails to produce, he becomes liable to the penalty of 20*l.*

The power of a game-keeper is limited to his own manor, and if he kill or take game, or sport out of the manor, he may then be proceeded with as against any other individual who has no certificate; but one game-keeper cannot seize the dogs, &c., or gun of another game-keeper for trespassing out of his manor, upon the principle that the dogs and gun are in fact the lord of the manor's, not the game-keeper's.

A game-keeper having a certificate, upon which less than 3*l.* 13*s.* 6*d.* has been paid, (viz. 1*l.* 5*s.*,) is not authorized to kill game for any other person than he who appoints him; whereas, a game-keeper receiving a *deputation*, may kill game for any person, but the person who appoints him; for this game-keeper, a certificate of 3*l.* 13*s.* 6*d.* must be paid, and the lord or steward appointing him, will not be chargeable for the duty payable on male servants on his account; whereas in the first instance he is chargeable.

A person entitled to kill game upon land in Wales, of the annual value (clear) of 500*l.*, to which he is entitled, can *appoint* a game-keeper with the same powers of seizure as other game-keepers appointed in manors.

These appointments and deputations must be registered with the clerk of the peace.

Although persons having an annual game-certificate, have power to sell game to any one licensed to sell it, as hereafter mentioned, yet only the game-keeper whose certificate costs 3*l.* 13*s.* 6*d.*, can sell game *without* the written authority of his master; but the game-keeper whose *appointment* is chargeable with only 1*l.* 5*s.*, if he sell game, must have the written authority, *and* sell the same on the account of his master, else he may be proceeded against, as if he had none. The former game-keeper, having a deputation and a 3*l.* 13*s.* 6*d.* certificate, being considered as a game-keeper only; the latter is considered a mere menial, evidenced by his master's paying only 1*l.* 5*s.*, and being chargeable to the duty on male servants in respect of his service.

The act regulating certificates is the 52 *G.* 3. *c.* 93., which places the duties under the regulation of the commissioners for assessed taxes, and is not disturbed by the present game act. The operation of the duties as affecting the appointment and deputation, has been already noticed; but the most penal effect, is that according to the 11th rule annexed to the act, viz., any person refusing to produce and show his certificate, or in default thereof, to give his christian and surname, residence, parish, and place, where assessed to these duties, or producing fictitious certificate, or giving a false name, is liable to forfeit 20*l.*, which cannot be mitigated to lower than 10*l.*

2. *As to the sale of game.* Persons who have obtained an annual certificate, or appointed as game-keepers, or having deputations, may sell game under the restraints previously noticed with respect to game-keepers having *appointments* only. But the magistrates at a special session for that purpose in the month of July, may grant to any householder, shop, or stall-keeper, (not being an innkeeper or seller of beer or the owner or driver of any mail-coach or public conveyance, or carrier, or higler, nor in the employment of such persons,) a license to buy and sell game, but a board with the words "licensed to deal in game,"

must be affixed, with the party's christian and surname. The license is only in force for a year; and, in addition thereto, the party licensed must pay 2*l.* for a certificate, which is in force for the same period as the, license. The penalty imposed for dealing in game, before the certificate is paid for, is 20*l.*

Persons in partnership need only take out one license and certificate.

The sale of game by persons not certificated (not being dealers) subjects the party to a penalty not exceeding 2*l.* for every head sold or offered to sale; but this does not prevent innkeepers selling game for consumption in their own house, they having previously purchased the same from a licensed dealer.

The purchase of game from any one not licensed, or not having the board affixed to the front of his house, shop, or stall, subjects the buyer to a penalty not exceeding 5*l.* and costs: and the purchase by licensed dealers from persons not authorized to sell game, or the selling without the board being affixed, or in any way pretending to be a dealer in game, is subject to a penalty not exceeding 10*l.* and costs. These penalties being recoverable before two magistrates.

3. Trespasses. The committing any trespass, by entering or being in the daytime on any land in pursuit of game, or woodcocks, snipes, quails, landrails, or conies, subjects the party to a penalty of 2*l.* and costs; and where the trespassers amount to five they may each be fined 5*l.*

The trespassing on any land, or upon any of her majesty's forests, parks, &c., and not quitting the same forthwith at the command of the occupier, and refusal to tell name and residence, subjects the party to apprehension, and being taken before a magistrate; who will, on conviction, inflict a penalty of 5*l.* and costs of conviction.

If such trespasser be apprehended, and not taken before a justice of the peace within twelve hours of the arrest, he must be discharged; otherwise the party keeping him in custody will be liable to an action for false imprisonment; but whether arrested or not, or after discharge, if the party cannot convey the trespasser before a magistrate in time, he may be proceeded against for the trespass, by summons or warrant before a magistrate.

No trespasser who gives his real name and address can be lawfully arrested, or subjected to a higher penalty than 2*l.*, unless the trespass was committed by four or more.

It is incumbent on the trespasser, in all cases, to show that he was authorised to sport on the land trespassed upon; for otherwise the oath of the occupier, or person having the right to kill game on such land, will warrant a conviction.

It is also incumbent, in prudence, on every person who has obtained permission of an occupier or tenant of land, to ascertain that he can lawfully grant such permission; for if it turn out that the landlord, lessor, or other person having right to the game, have not granted the occupier permission, the sportsman will be liable to the penalty of trespass, at the complaint of such landlord, &c.

The occupier of land is himself liable to a penalty of 2*l.*, if he pursues or kills game without permission or grant from the landlord or other person to whom the right is reserved; and a further penalty of 1*l.* for every head killed.

The cases in which an occupier can lawfully sport have been previously noticed. Where he is not authorised to sport he is in law a trespasser, or, rather, punishable by the fines of 2*l.* and 1*l.*, independent of the penalties incurred for not having an annual certificate.

But no persons can in any case be considered trespassers *under this act* (for the remedy by action is not taken away) hunting or coursing, and being in fresh pursuit of any deer, hare, or fox, already started, upon other land; persons claiming and exercising a right of free-warren (which see) or free-chase, lords of manors, stewards of royalties, (such as forests, &c.,) and gamekeepers, within the limits of the manors or places mentioned in their appointments or deputations.

The penalties for trespasses and offences in respect of game may be enforced by any two commissioners of assessed taxes, or any one magistrate, who can issue a summons at any time not exceeding three months after the commission of the offence, and also enforce the attendance of witnesses; and upon his appearance, or in his absence after summons, can give judgment for the whole penalty, or mitigate it to one-half, and cause the adjudged penalty to be levied, together with the costs, on his goods; and in default of goods, can commit him to the house of correction, for any time not exceeding six calendar months. To these convictions an appeal is allowed to the sessions, on the party's giving security to double the amount of the penalty: but at the sessions the decision is final, and cannot be removed.

The penalties for sporting without a game certificate are 20*l.*, and 3*l.* 13*s.* 6*d.*; which any two commissioners, or a single justice, as the case may be, have power to mitigate to 10*l.*

GAMING is the term used for excessive, and, consequently, unlawful playing at games, or with cards and dice. The inference of their being excessive exists when the stake is above a moderate sum of money, and the game is protracted for a longer period than is ordinarily supposed necessary for the purposes of amusement or purely pleasurable excitement.

From the destructive and pernicious consequences which must necessarily attend excessive gaming, both the courts of law and equity have shown their abhorrence of it; but the playing at cards and dice, &c., when practised innocently and as a recreation, the better to fit a person for business, is not at all unlawful, nor punishable as an offence.

And as the gaming in the manner as has been mentioned may be lawful, yet if a person be guilty of cheating, as by playing with false cards, dice, &c., he may be indicted for it at common law as a cheat, and fined and imprisoned according to the circumstances of the case, and heinousness of the offence.

Also, all common gaming-houses are nuisances in the eye of the law, not only because they are great temptations to idleness, but also because they are apt to draw together great numbers of disorderly persons, which cannot but be very inconvenient to the neighbourhood: it was, therefore, by 16 *Car.* 2. *c.* 7. enacted, that

If any person, of what degree soever, shall by fraud, deceit, or unlawful device, in playing at cards, dice, tables, bowls, cock-fighting, horse-races, foot-races, or other games or pastimes, or bearing a share in the stakes, betting, &c., win any money or valuable thing, he shall forfeit treble the value, one moiety to the crown, and the other to the party grieved, if he shall sue within six months; in default whereof, the last mentioned moiety is to go such other person as will prosecute within one year, &c. If any person shall play at cards, &c., other than for ready money, or bet, and shall lose above 100*l.* at one time or meeting, upon tick (*i. e.* tickets), he shall not be bound to make it good, but the contract or tick and security shall be void, and the winner shall forfeit treble the value.

By the 9 *Anne*, c. 14. all *notes, bills, bonds, judgments, mortgages, or other securities* given for money won by playing at cards, dice, tables, tennis, bowls, or other games; or by betting on the sides of such as play at any of those games, or for repayment of any money knowingly lent for such gaming or betting, shall be void: and where lands are granted by such mortgages or securities they shall go to the next person who ought to have the same as if the grantor were actually dead, and the grants had been made to the person so entitled after the death of the person so incumbering the same.

If any person playing at cards, dice, or other game, or betting, shall *lose the value of* 10*l. at one time to one or more persons*, and *shall pay the money*, he may *recover the money lost by action for debt* within three months afterwards; and if the loser do not sue *any other person may* do it and recover the same, and *treble the value, with costs*, one moiety to the prosecutor and the other to the poor, and the person prosecuted shall answer upon oath on preferring a bill to discover what sums he had won.

Persons by *fraud* or *ill-practice* in *playing* at cards, dice, or by bearing a share in the stakes, &c. or by *betting, winning* any sum or valuable thing whatever, or winning at one sitting above 10*l.*, shall, being convicted thereof on indictment or information, forfeit five times the value of the sum or thing won; and in case of such ill practice shall be deemed infamous, and suffer such corporal punishment as in case of wilful perjury, the penalty to be recovered by action by such persons as will sue for the same.

Any two or more justices of peace may cause such persons to be brought before them as they suspect to have no visible estate, &c., to maintain them; and if they do not make it appear that the principal part of their expenses is got by other means than gaming, the justices shall require securities for their good behaviour for a twelvemonth, and, in default of such security, commit them to prison until they find it; and playing or betting during the time to the value of 20*s.* shall be deemed a breach of good behaviour, and a forfeiture of their recognisances.

Although under the statute of *Anne* a bill of exchange or note given for a gambling debt is void, yet now the same is valid in the hands of a *bonâ fide* holder, who did not before it came into his hands have notice of the circumstances; but this is under the operation of a late act of parliament; for, as the consideration was unlawful, the security was void by the statute against all parties, innocent or not.

Betting and wagers on horse-races are illegal within the meaning of the above statute, and can be recovered back; but wagers on a horse-race run for 50*l.* or upwards are legal, and can be recovered, where the sums betted by both parties amounts to no more than 10*l.*

Although the statute of *Anne* enacts that the loser cannot recover his goods or money after three months, yet if money be paid on a security for money lost at play or any game, it may be recovered back; the limitation of three months not extending to payments made on account of void securities, the principle being that a payment under a security absolutely void cannot be supported.

With respect to what is deemed a *one sitting*, where two persons played at cards from Monday evening to Tuesday evening without interruption, except for an hour or two at dinner, and one of them won a balance of 17 guineas, it was held to be *one sitting* within the meaning of the above statute.

There are other statutes denouncing certain games now unfashionable, and inflicting penalties upon parties setting them up, and persons playing thereat.

Persons keeping common gaming-houses can be indicted at common law, and punishable as for a misdemeanor, at the discretion of the court; and, by a particular statute, persons convicted of keeping a common gaming-house may be sentenced to imprisonment with hard labour, in addition or in lieu of any punishment which might previously have been inflicted.

By another act, two inhabitants of any parish may require the constable, in a particular manner, to prosecute any person for keeping a common gaming-house, and a copy of the notice requiring such prosecution is to be served upon the overseer.

Persons playing or betting in any street, road, &c., or open place, at or with any table or instrument of gaming, at any game or pretended game of chance, are punishable summarily as rogues and vagabonds.

GAOL. A place for the keeping of debtors, and persons "attached," belonging to each county; in which, also, (but in a different part or side of the prison,) prisoners are confined to answer offences committed.

All gaols, whether in the keeping of the sheriff of a county or city, corporation, lords of liberties or persons claiming by prescription, as the dean and chapter of Westminster, to whom belonged the prison of the gate-house, belong to the queen.

There must be one common gaol in every county, and at least one house of correction: where a county is divided into ridings having distinct commissions of the peace, or distinct rates in the nature of county rates, there must be a house of correction for each riding.

The houses of correction are for the custody of persons being rogues and vagabonds, and for custody of such who are convicted upon summary convictions before magistrates, or convicted of minor offences at the quarter-sessions, and the justices have specially the keeping of such gaols. But all murderers and felons are to be imprisoned in the common gaol, of which the sheriff has the keeping. Debtors are also confined in the county gaol, if not removed by writs of *habeas corpus* to the prison of the court from whence the process issued.

The court of queen's bench, being the supreme court of criminal jurisdiction, can commit a person to any prison which they shall think proper, who cannot be bailed or removed by any other court or person.

Persons in a county gaol for debt are relieved by a county rate, but in other gaols they must apply for parochial relief through a justice.

The justices of the peace, or such of them as are termed visiting justices, regulate the economy of gaols and prisons within the county, unless the gaol belong to a corporation or town.

No untried prisoner shall on any pretence be put upon the tread-wheel or compelled to labour, but he may labour in any employment if he choose, and untried prisoners, unable to work, are allowed sufficient food.

There are a great many statutory regulations which are extremely humane, and enable a discharged prisoner to be passed to his settlement, and with respect to those whose imprisonment has been shortened by recommendation of court of quarter-sessions, they are supplied with clothing and a small sum of money on their discharge.

The offence of breaking out of prison is mentioned under tit. PRISON-BREAKING.

A gaoler is bound not only by the law, but by principles of charity and humanity, to treat his prisoners with due care, and attention to those personal comforts that are requisite to secure health, especially with regard to the untried prisoners; for if a prisoner die through abuse or ill usage of the gaoler he will be guilty of murder. Gaolers are also punishable summarily by the courts for ill usage or misbehaviour to the prisoners.

The prisons of the Marshalsea, of the Queen's Bench, commonly called the Queen's Bench prison, the prison of the Marshalsea of the queen's household, called the Marshalsea, and the prison of the Fleet, are immediately under the cognisance of the courts to which they belong; and upon complaint made to the judges the marshal, keeper, or warden will be attached and fined, if the complaint is well founded.

Any one assaulting a gaoler for keeping a prisoner in safe custody may be fined and imprisoned.

No one can purchase the office of gaoler, or any other office under the high sheriff, under a penalty of *500l.*

The duties of gaolers, and the government of county and other prisons, are regulated by the stat. 4 *G.* 4. *c.* 64.; and by *s.* 10. the following rules are established: —

1. The keeper of every prison must reside therein: he must not be an under-sheriff or bailiff, or concerned in any occupation or trade whatever; nor is he, or any other officer of the prison, allowed to sell any article to any prisoner, nor have any interest, directly or indirectly, in any contract or agreement for the supply of the prison.

2. A matron must be appointed to superintend the female prisoners.

3. The keeper must, as far as may be practicable, visit every ward, and see every prisoner, and inspect every cell, once, at least, in every 24 hours; and, in visiting the female prisoners, he shall be accompanied by the matron, or by some female officer of the prison.

4. The keeper must keep a regular journal of all occurrences of importance within the prison, which must be laid before the justices at every quarter-sessions.

5. Due provision must be made in every prison for the enforcement of hard labour, in cases where prisoners shall be sentenced to it. *

6. The male and female prisoners must be confined in separate buildings or parts of the prison, so as to prevent them from seeing, conversing, or holding any intercourse with each other; and the prisoners of each sex must be divided into the following classes: —

First. Debtors, and persons confined for contempt of court in civil process.

Second. Prisoners convicted of felony.

Third. Prisoners convicted of misdemeanors.

Four h. Prisoners committed on charge or suspicion of felony.

Fifth. Prisoners committed on charge or suspicion of misdemeanors, or for want of sureties.

Sixth. Vagrants.

Prisoners intended to be examined as witnesses for the crown must also be kept separate.

But the justices may authorise the employment of any prisoner in any menial office within the prison, or for the purpose of instructing others. And the keeper may confine a prisoner with another class, if he shall deem it improper for him to associate with others of the class to which he belongs.

7. Female prisoners must in all cases be attended with female officers.

8. Every prisoner sentenced to hard labour, must, unless prevented by sickness, be employed not exceeding 10 hours in every day, except on Sundays, Christmas Day, and Good Friday.

9. Prayers selected from the Liturgy of the Church of England must be read every morning by the chaplain, the keeper, or some other person.

10. Provision shall be made for the instruction of prisoners of both sexes in reading and writing.

11. Prisoners shall attend divine service on Sundays, and on other days when performed.

12. No prisoner shall be put in irons by the keeper, except in cases of

---

* This regulation is not carried into effect in Newgate; in fact these regulations are only partially observed in that prison, which, however, is in a state of extreme improvement, by the great exertions of the late sheriffs.

urgent necessity, and then not longer than four days, without an order in writing from a visiting justice specifying the cause.

13. Every prisoner shall be allowed a sufficient quantity of plain and wholesome food, to be regulated by the justices in session; and prisoners under the care of the surgeon shall be allowed such diet as he shall direct.

14. Prisoners before trial, who shall not receive any allowance from the county, may procure for themselves, and receive at proper hours, any food or other necessaries, subject to a strict examination.

15. But no prisoner who is confined under the sentence of any court, or in pursuance of any conviction before a justice, shall receive any food or necessaries other than the gaol allowance, except under special circumstances.

16. Due provision shall be made for the admission, at proper times, of persons with whom prisoners committed for trial may desire to communicate; and rules and regulations shall be made by the justices at sessions for the admission of the friends of the convicted prisoners.

17. The surgeon must examine every prisoner before he is passed into the proper ward; and no prisoner shall be discharged if labouring under any acute or dangerous distemper, unless he himself requires it. No prisoner before trial shall be compelled to wear a *prison dress*, unless his clothes be deemed insufficient, or necessary to be preserved for the purposes of justice. But no prisoner not convicted of felony, shall be clothed in a party-coloured dress.

18. Every male prisoner shall be provided with a separate bed, hammock, or cot, either in a separate cell, or in a cell with not more than two other male prisoners.*

19. The walls and ceilings of the wards, cells, rooms, and passages, used by the prisoners, must be scraped and lime-washed at least once in the year, and the rooms, passages, and sleeping cells shall be cleansed once a week, or oftener if requisite.

20. All prisoners shall be allowed as much air and exercise as shall be deemed proper for the preservation of their health.

21. Forbids the admission of spirituous liquors for the use of prisoners; and by *s.* 40. a penalty of 20*l.* is inflicted on persons carrying, or attempting to carry, spirituous or fermented liquors into any prison. And any gaoler selling, lending, or giving away any such liquor, is liable to forfeit 20*l.*

22. No gaming shall be permitted; and the keeper may seize and destroy all cards, dice, or other instruments of gaming.

23. No money, under the name of *garnish*, shall be taken from any prisoner on his entrance into the prison, under any pretence whatever.

24. Upon the death of a prisoner, notice shall be given by the keeper forthwith to one of the visiting justices, as well as to the coroner of the district, and to the nearest relative of the deceased where practicable.

By *s.* 11. none of the prisoners can serve upon the coroner's inquest.

By *s.* 12. the court of lord mayor and aldermen may make further regulations, with the sanction of the two chief justices, for the management of the prisons in London; and five justices may do the like in regard to those of any county. Copies of these rules must be put up in a conspicuous part of the prison; and such rules shall be binding upon the sheriff, so as not to interfere, however, with his right or duty to appoint or remove any keeper of a county gaol.

By *s.* 15. the chairman of the Michaelmas quarter-sessions shall transmit to the secretary of state copies of the rules and regulations then in force, for the government of every prison in the county, together with plans of any additions to the building of the prison.

By *s.* 24. a general report is required to be prepared at such sessions by the clerk of the peace, and signed by the chairman, and by him transmitted to the secretary of state to be laid before parliament. By 5 *G.* 4. *c.* 85. *s.* 8. the chairman must also at the same time transmit a correct statement of any increase or diminution in every such establishment of officers and servants, or in their respective salaries or emoluments.

---

* This regulation is only adhered to as far as the accommodation of the prisons will allow, as in Newgate, Giltspur-street prison, and other houses of correction.

By *s.* 16. visiting justices shall be appointed by the sessions, and their duties are prescribed by this and the following sections.

By *s.* 14. the gaoler must attend every quarter-sessions, and make a report in writing of the actual state and condition of the prison, and of the number of the prisoners.

By *s.* 19. he must also make a return at every assizes of the persons sentenced to hard labour.

By *s.* 20. he must, under the penalty of 20*l.*, on the second day next after the termination of every sessions or assizes, transmit to the secretary of state a calendar containing the names, crimes, and sentences of every prisoner tried, distinguishing with respect to all prisoners capitally convicted such of them as may have been reprieved by the court, and stating the day on which execution is to be done upon those who have not been reprieved.

By *s.* 21. he must deliver to every court of quarter-sessions a certificate how far the rules for the government of the prison have been observed, under the penalty of 10*l.*

And by *s.* 22. he must, one week before every Michaelmas sessions, make a return of the state of the prison to the clerk of the peace.

By *s.* 41. the keeper of every prison has power to hear all complaints touching any of the following offences: 1. Disobedience of the rules of the prison. 2. Assaults when no dangerous wound or bruise is given. 3. Profane cursing and swearing. 4. Any indecent behaviour, and irreverent behaviour at chapel. 5. Absence from chapel without leave. 6. Idleness or negligence in work, or wilful mismanagement of it. For any of these offences the keeper may punish the offender by ordering him to close confinement in the refractory or solitary cells, and by keeping him upon bread and water only, for any term not exceeding three days.

By *s.* 42. any criminal prisoner being guilty of any repeated offence against the rules of the prison, or of any greater offence than the gaoler is empowered to punish, any one of the visiting, or any other justice of the county or district, may inquire upon oath and determine the offence, and may order the offender to be punished by close confinement not exceeding one month; or by personal correction, in case of prisoners convicted of felony or sentenced to hard labour.

By *ss.* 28. and 33. the justices at quarter-sessions are to appoint a chaplain and a surgeon to each prison within their jurisdiction, the latter of whom is to keep a regular journal.

By the 4 *G.* 4. *c.* 64., and the 5th *G.* 4. *c.* 88., those acts are declared not to extend to the prisons of the Queen's Bench, or the Fleet, Bridewell, the Marshalsea, the Penitentiary at Millbank, or that at Gloucester.

As to gaolers permitting prisoners to escape, see tit. ESCAPE.

GARNISHEE. The person warned not to pay money which he owes to another person, which person is indebted to a creditor, and attaches the money in the hands of the person warned or summoned, called the *Garnishee*. See ATTACHMENT.

GAVELKIND. A custom which holds in Kent, concerning the descent of lands in most parts of that county, whereby the lands of the father are equally divided at his death amongst all his sons, or the land of the brother among all the brothers, if the brother has no issue. Females inherit jointly and severally as at common law. Many parts of Kent are *disgavelled* by various statutes, and the mode of descent rendered conformable to the course of inheritance at common law, but it still prevails to a considerable extent. The widow of a *gavelkind man*, as he is termed, takes a life interest in the half of her husband's gavelkind lands, and the husband is tenant by courtesy of his wife's land, (which see,) whether he has issue by her or not. This custom cannot be avoided by making a will, for the custom cannot be separated from the land: as the term is, the custom runs with the land.

As this tenure causes land to be divided into minute divisions, it is said practically to produce inconvenience, though this distribution of the land is more in accordance with natural notions of inheritance than the common course of descent, which excludes the younger children.

GIFT. A conveyance or deed which passes or transfers either land or goods: it signifies a gratuitous transaction, purely voluntary. Although the words "give and grant" are often used together in deeds, yet *grant* means the transfer of a thing for an adequate consideration. Gifts, when a person is in insolvent circumstances, are generally void, as against creditors.

GRANT is the name of a conveyance or deed which passes things of an *incorporeal* nature, or things which are not of a permanent or substantial nature. See HEREDITAMENT.

GUARDIAN. See INFANT WARD.

HABEAS CORPUS (*i. e. that you*—meaning the person to whom this writ is directed—*have the body of*).—The name of a writ which is used for various purposes, but the chief of which is the release or bailing of a person who considers himself illegally imprisoned, or entitled to be discharged upon bail. It is also applicable to all cases where the party confined in private, or *any custody whatever*, is desirous of being released; but the application must, generally speaking, be made by the person himself by a request attested by two witnesses. In cases of infant children, the father or guardian may apply. With regard to the preservation of public liberty, which is guarded by this writ, it need scarcely be observed, that if any person, no matter who, had the power to imprison *arbitrarily*, there would soon be an end of that civil liberty which is an Englishman's birthright; and, therefore, the following statute, called the *Habeas Corpus Act*, 31 *Car.* 2. *c.* 2., was passed, not for the purpose of making a *new concession* to the public, but rather of enforcing and declaring what had immemorially been the common law of this land, particularly since the great charter, the language of which is, that no "freeman" (all persons are *now* free) shall be taken or imprisoned, but by the lawful judgment of his *peers*, *i. e.* his equals,) or by the law of the land. The immediate cause of the passing of this statute was the various encroachments which had been made upon the liberty of the subject, in that and the preceding reign, as well as in the interregnum. This writ was by no means a new writ. It had been a long time before the process by which a person brought himself before the superior courts to be discharged from unlawful or continued imprisonment; but gaolers and others delayed executing or returning the writ by bringing up the party imprisoned; and the courts of law, the judges of which were not so independent as now of regal influence or popular clamour, interposed sundry devices, ill-accordant with the spirit of the English constitution, to refuse this writ, which every one *then* had of *right*, and every one now has of right and law, as declared by the nation in parliament assembled, the highest recognition of this liberative process.

The statute 31 *C.* 2. *c.* 2. enacts,

1. That on complaint and request in writing, by or on behalf of any person committed and charged with any crime (unless committed for treason, or felony, expressed in the warrant; or as accessory, or on suspicion of being accessory before the fact, to any *petit* treason or felony, plainly expressed in the warrant; or unless he is convicted, or charged in execution by legal process), the lord chancellor, or any of the twelve judges in vacation, upon viewing the copy of the warrant, or affidavit that a copy is denied, shall (unless the party has neglected for two terms to apply to any court for his enlargement,) award a *habeas corpus* for such prisoner, returnable immediately before himself or

any of the judges; and, upon the returns made, shall within two days discharge the party, if bailable, upon his giving security to appear and answer to the accusation in the proper court of judicature.

2. That such writs shall be indorsed, as granted in pursuance of this act, and signed by the person awarding them.

3. That the writ shall be returned, and the prisoner brought up, within a limited time, according to the distance, not exceeding in any case twenty days, upon tender of the charges, not exceeding 1*s*. per mile, and security by his own bond to pay the charges of his return, if remanded, and not to escape.

4. That any officer or keeper neglecting to make due returns, or not delivering to the prisoner or his agent, within six hours after demand, a copy of the warrant of commitment, or shifting the custody of a prisoner from one to another, without sufficient reason or authority (specified in the act), shall for the first offence forfeit 100*l*., and for the second offence 200*l*., to the party grieved, and be disabled to hold his office.

5. That no person once delivered by *habeas corpus* shall be recommitted for the same offence, on penalty of 500*l*.

6. That every person committed for treason or felony, expressed in the warrant, shall, if he requires it, the first week of the next term, or the first day of the next session of *Oyer* and *Terminer*, be indicted in that term or session, or else admitted to bail, (unless the queen's witnesses cannot be produced at that time,) and if acquitted, or if not indicted and tried in the second term or session, he shall be discharged from his imprisonment for such imputed offence; but that no person, after the assizes shall be opened for the county in which he is detained, shall be removed by *habeas corpus* till after the assizes are ended, but shall be left to the justice of the judges of assize.

7. That any prisoner may move for and obtain his *habeas corpus*, as well out of the chancery or exchequer as out of the queen's bench or common pleas; and the lord chancellor or judges denying the same, on sight of the warrant, or oath that the same is refused, shall forfeit severally to the party grieved the sum of 500*l*.

8. That this writ of *habeas corpus* shall run into the counties palatine, cinque ports, and other privileged places, and the islands of Jersey and Guernsey.

9. That no inhabitant of England (except persons contracting, or convicts praying to be transported, or persons having committed some capital offence in the place to which they are sent to be tried) shall be sent prisoner to Scotland, Ireland, Jersey, Guernsey, or any other place beyond the seas within or without the queen's dominions, on pain that the party committing, his advisers, aiders, and assistants, shall forfeit to the party grieved a sum not less than 500*l*. to be recovered with treble costs, shall be disabled to bear any office of trust or profit, shall incur the penalties of *præmunire*, and shall be incapable of the queen's pardon. This is the substance of that great and important statute, which extends only to the case of commitments for such criminal charge as can produce no inconvenience to the public justice by a temporary enlargement of the prisoner, and leaves all other cases of unjust imprisonment to the *habeas corpus* at common law. By 56 *G*. 3. *c*. 100. "for more effectually securing the liberty of the subject," reciting that the extending the remedy of the writ of *habeas corpus*, and enforcing obedience thereto, will be advantageous to the public, and that the provisions of the existing acts extend only to cases of detainer on criminal charges, it is enacted, that when any person shall be confined, or restrained of his liberty (except for crime or debt), any baron of the exchequer, as well as any judge of either bench in England or Ireland, shall, on complaint or behalf of the party confined or restrained, if reasonable cause appear to them, award in vacation time a writ of *habeas corpus ad subjiciendum*, returnable immediately before the judge awarding the same, or any other judge of the same court.

The party to whom the writ is directed refusing to make a return or pay obedience thereto is declared guilty of a contempt of the court, and may be apprehended on the judge's warrant, and held to bail or committed, to answer such contempt. Such writs issued in vacation may be made returnable in the ensuing term; and writs issued by the court of queen's bench, common pleas, or exchequer, in term time, may be made returnable in the vacation, before one judge or baron. The judge before whom the writ is returnable may examine the truth of the fact in the return, and do therein as to justice shall appertain;

or, if he has any doubt, may bail the party detained to appear before the court, who shall finally determine on the discharging, bailing, or remanding such party, and the like proceedings may be had by the court on such writs awarded by the court. These writs shall run in counties palatine, the cinque ports, and all privileged places, and into ports, harbours, creeks, and bays, though not within the body of any county; and, lastly, the provisions of this act are extended to writs of *habeas corpus* awarded in pursuance of the former existing acts.

In matters not of criminal or political offences, the ancient writ of *habeas corpus* is still used, which is, as all writs of this nature are, directed to the person detaining another, and commanding him to produce the body of the person detained, with the day and cause of his detention; and it is by this process that a prisoner for debt removes himself from the custody of the sheriffs to the custody of the court, *i. e.* is removed from the sheriff's prison to the prison of the court; for upon the sheriff bringing his prisoner before the judge, he commits the prisoner to the Queen's Bench prison or the Fleet, whichever court it may be.

Applications are made to a judge or the chancellor upon affidavit, and may be made in vacation: in term time they should be made to the court sitting at Westminster. It should be remembered, that all writs of *habeas corpus* should be issued, or, rather applied for, at the request of the party detained. In cases where a person is detained for a criminal matter, or by a warrant of a justice, he must sign a written request to the judge, requesting him to peruse a copy of the warrant or commitment, and this request must be signed in the presence of two witnesses.

Writs of *habeas corpus* are used at law for various purposes, such as to bring persons confined for debt before the court as witnesses, or to commit them absolutely to custody after judgment obtained against them, which is in the nature of a writ of execution; also causes are removed from inferior courts to the superior courts by this writ, which, as it removes the body of a defendant, removes the *cause* also. The object of removal of a cause from an inferior court to a superior is, that more efficacious justice be done; but this writ is not unfrequently sued out for delay, to prevent which, the party removing the cause, whether in custody or not, must enter into recognizances, and no cause under 5*l.* can be removed from an inferior court.

HEDGES, FENCES, and DITCHES. Where a hedge and ditch join together, in whose ground or side the hedge is, to the owner of that land belongs the keeping of the same hedge or fence, and the ditch adjoining to it on the other side, in repair and scoured. An action on the case or trespass lies for not repairing of fences, whereby cattle come into the ground of another and do damage. No man making a a ditch can cut into his neighbour's soil, but usually he cuts it to the very extremity of his own land; he is of course bound to throw the soil which he digs out upon his own land, and often, if he likes it, he plants a hedge on the top of it; therefore, if he afterwards cut beyond the edge of the ditch which is the extremity of his land, he cuts into his neighbour's land, and is a trespasser.

Persons stealing, or throwing down with intent to steal, any live or dead fence, post, rail, pale, stile, or gate, are punishable summarily before, one magistrate by a fine not exceeding 5*l.*, besides the value of the thing stolen or the injury done. To break, or throw down, or cut any fence, wall, stile, or gate, is punishable in the like manner.

The stealing, ripping, or cutting with intent to steal, any lead, iron, or other metal fixed for a fence to any dwelling-house, garden, river, or in any public street, is a felony, punishable as a larceny

HEIRESS, stealing, see Abduction.

HEREDITAMENT is a very comprehensive term, including whatever may be inherited, be it *corporeal* or *incorporeal*, *real* or *personal*. *Corporeal* hereditaments consist wholly of substantial and permanent objects, all of which may be comprehended under the general denomination of land. An *incorporeal* hereditament is a right issuing out of a thing corporeal, whether real or personal, or concerning or annexed to the same — such as rights of way, advowsons, rights of common, annuities, &c.

As to prescriptive rights on "incorporeal" hereditaments, see Prescription.

HERIOT is a due to the lord of a manor, rendered at the death of a copyhold tenant, or on a surrender or alienation of his estate, being the best beast or goods found in the possession of the tenant deceased, or otherwise according to custom. The copyholder who holds by a *free* tenure, not a *base* tenure, as the mere copy holder, seldom pays a heriot, but only something *certain* in the name of a heriot, such as a penny, &c. See Copyhold. For heriots, the lord may either seize, distrain, or bring action of debt: the seizure may be out of the manor, but the distress (which may be of any third party, goods, or beasts upon the land) *must* be made within the manor, viz. on the land itself.

HIGH CONSTABLE or CONSTABLE OF THE HUNDRED. The chief officer of a division of a county called a hundred: his office formerly was and still seems to be to assist the sheriff in the conservation of the peace. He is chosen at the sheriff's town, and for many purposes represents the district for which he is appointed, being the hundred. He returns jurors for the county court and for the quarter-sessions. He is the person who is to be sued, or, if the claims be not more than 30*l*., is to have notice of claim for compensation, in consequence of damage sustained by public riots or tumultuous assemblies.

HIRING. A *bailment* or delivery of goods to another for recompense or *hire*, to be paid by the *bailee* or person to whom they are delivered, who is liable for any damage, however occurring, he being bound at law to take the utmost care of them.

As to the hiring of servants, see Master and Servant.

HOMICIDE. See Murder.

HORSES. Every horse for sale in Smithfield must be openly exposed for one whole hour together, between ten in the morning and sunset, and afterwards brought by both buyer and seller to the booker of the place of sale, that the toll may be paid if due, and, if not, one penny to the book-keeper, who shall write down the price, colour, and marks of the horse, with the names, additions, and abodes of the buyer and seller. Nor shall such sale take away the property of the owner, if within six months after the horse is stolen he puts in his claim before some magistrate where the horse shall be found, and within forty days more proves it to be his property by the oath of two witnesses, and tenders to the person in possession such price as he *bona fide* paid for him in the open market. But in case any of these points are not observed such sale is utterly void, and the owner shall not lose his property; but at any distance of time he may seize or bring an action for his horse wherever he happens to find him. Stat. 2 *P. & M. c.* 7., 31 *Eliz. c.* 12.

If my horse is taken away, and I find him in a fair, a common, or a public inn, I may lawfully seize him to my own use; but I cannot justify breaking open a public stable, nor entering the grounds of a third person to take him, except he be stolen.

Contracts as to the sale of horses. The rule at law is, that every one who purchases goods takes them at his own judgment; and unless induced to purchase by representations which are false within the knowledge of the seller, or by arts used to disguise them, has no remedy against the seller, if the goods turn out, upon a future trial or more considerate inspection after the purchase, to be worth less than the sum given, for relief can only be afforded in cases of fraud, *i. e.*, where defects are artfully suppressed, and false statements knowingly made. The same rule of course applies to the sale of a horse; for if a man sell me a horse with a secret malady, without warranting it to be sound, he is not liable, *i. e.* if there be no fraud, which fraud consists in the seller's not disclosing the defect, if it was within his knowledge; but as the fact of the patent defect being within the seller's knowledge is a matter which the purchaser must prove, and as the organic structure of this animal is very delicate, it is a matter of difficulty to fasten a fraud of this nature upon an experienced dealer in horses, more especially as the adequacy of the price does not at law raise the presumption of an express warranty or assurance that the animal is worth the price paid. Therefore it is usual to insert in the receipt for the purchase money an assurance or undertaking, which may be general, as that the horse is *sound;* and, where that general warranty is given, it extends to all faults known and unknown to the seller, and whether of secret infirmity or patent defect (merely temporary defects or accidents of a slight nature excepted). As the assurance or warranty is a contract in writing, it cannot be varied or contradicted, and, practically, is the only indemnity a purchaser has in case of a deceit having been practised, it being remembered that the purchaser must positively prove that the horse was unsound at the time of the sale; the producing doubtful evidence of the soundness, even of experienced judges, will not do.

Warranties are general, as just now mentioned, and special or particular, which only undertake that the description as to age, colour, and the work to which the horse is to be put, accord with the real qualities of the animal.

However, a general warranty will not extend to guard against defects that are plain and obvious to the senses of the purchaser, and require no skill to detect them, as if a horse be warranted perfect, and yet want an ear or tail, &c. But if on the sale of a horse the seller agree to deliver it sound and free from blemish at the expiration of a specified period, the warranty is broken by a fault in the horse when delivered, although such defect was obvious at the time of the sale; and, as some *splints* cause lameness and others do not, a *splint* is not one of those plain defects against which a warranty will not indemnify; and where a seller warrants a horse sound *at the time of the sale*, and the horse afterwards become lame from the effects of a *splint*, visible when the horse was bought, it is certain that the warranty is broken.

All warranties on the sale of a horse can only undertake for his qualifications *at the time of sale*, and cannot extend to a future period, at least such is the general opinion.

What is soundness or unsoundness is a matter of fact, not of law; and the term "unsoundness" ought undoubtedly to apply to the real nature of the defect, and its construction as to general opinion, and the rules of honesty and good faith based upon the *actual* terms of the bargain; which, being difficult to be ascertained, must, after all, be referred to the written warranty, if there was one, or to the conflicting testimony which is usually offered in trials arising from this transaction; but the principles to be deduced from the numerous cases appear to be, that *unsoundness* includes every defect by which the horse is rendered less fit for present use and enjoyment; any defect of a temporary nature, and not interfering with such enjoyment, and any matter of exception introduced into the warranty, a form of which is hereafter given, always excepted. So disagreeable tricks or habits, not inducing disease, or accidents in shoeing, a complaint proceeding from change of diet, slight cold, &c., are not unsoundnesses; but if at the time the animal was purchased, which is the time when all defects must be shown to have had existence, he had any complaint which induced organic disease, although not visible at the time of purchase, the warranty is broken. If the *cause* existed at the time of sale it is sufficient, although its existence does not appear till two months afterwards.

In warranties from vice or blemish, if the animal has any disposition or habit incompatible with the safety of an ordinary rider the warranty is broken.

A *cough*, though not an organic disease, yet is an unsoundness, if it had existence at the time of the purchase. *Roaring* and *crib-biting* are unsoundnesses, but the latter appears not strictly so if the habit is only incipient. *Splints* having existence at the time of sale are unsoundnesses if they terminate in lameness; and as to *thrushes* and *quidding* there appear to be conflicting opinions among the veterinary surgeons; but the question is simply this, do they induce organic or permanent disease? If dealers in horses or sellers are candid, they will point out these defects; if purchasers are cautious, they will insist upon having any dubious or incipient unsoundness inserted in the warranty.

The following is a form of receipt and warranty, which, of course, must be varied according to circumstances, and requires no other stamp than the duty required for the purchase money.

"Received this 2d of February, 1837, of Mr. L. M., *seventy pounds*, the price of a *bay mare*, warranted free from vice and blemish, [*or* thorough broke for gig or saddle, *or* sound, quiet, free from vice and blemish, four years old last ———, *or* has been constantly driven in harness, warranted, *or* warranted sound in every respect] except, [*here the matters of defect and blemish may be set forth, which the seller should do as precisely as he can.*]

As a buyer can recover damages for the expense he has been put to in the keep of a horse which turns out to be unsound, he must, as soon as the unsoundness is discovered, immediately tender back the horse to the seller; and the refusal of the seller to receive it will not affect the purchaser's right of action for breach of the warranty; and it is clear law, that if a person purchase a horse which is warranted, and it afterwards turn out the horse was unsound *at the time of the warranty*, the buyer may, if he please, keep the horse, and bring an action on the warranty, in which he will have a right to recover the difference between the value of a sound horse and one with such defects as existed at the time of the warranty, or he may return the horse in the same state he was when sold, and bring an action to recover the money paid.

A person hiring a horse is bound to ride it as carefully as a discreet person would treat his own horse, and, if by negligence or imprudence it is lost, he must answer for it. Also, if the hirer administer medicines to the horse, without calling in a farrier, by which the horse is damaged or dies, he is legally answerable for the full value, and if he over ride it, or even continue his journey after the animal has refused his feed. In all actions by horsekeepers for negligence of the hirers, they must show some actual negligence by the hirer; for where, in an action of this nature, the horse having been returned with the knees broken, the hirer only proved that the horse had often been let to hire, but had never fallen down, it was held insufficient, for that some evidence of negligence should have been given.

If a man borrow a horse of another, he is liable for *slight* neglect; indeed, in almost every case the borrower of a horse is answerable to the owner.

The sale of horses in markets and fairs is regulated by two ancient statutes, passed for the prevention of stealing horses, and selling them again in private, which direct that the names of the buyer, seller, and voucher of the seller's identity, shall be entered in the toll-taker's book, and a note delivered to the buyer; and if these requisites are not complied with, or the keeper of the toll-taker's book permit a person not known to him to make a sale, the sale is void, and a forfeiture incurred of 5*l.*; and the owner may, by force of the statutes, seize and retake the horse, or have an action of detinue for the same; but these statutes are not strictly enforced.

By various acts, duties are imposed upon horses kept for drawing carriages, or for riding, or letting on hire, race-horses, &c.

By a statute 26 *G.* 3. *c.* 71., which was passed to put a stop to the practice of stealing horses for the sake of their hides, persons keeping places for slaughtering horses or cattle must take out a license at the quarter-sessions, upon the certificate of the minister or church wardens that the applicant is a proper person, which license, if granted, is to be entered with the clerk of the peace; and all persons so licensed are to have painted over their gates their name, and "licensed for slaughtering horses, pursuant to an act passed in the 26th *G.* 3."

By this act inspectors are appointed, who are chosen by the parishioners in vestry, annually or oftener, and books are directed to be kept, and powers given to constables, and other provisions made for the preventing the above practice. But the act does not extend to curriers, &c., or farriers or persons killing horses to feed their own dogs.

The stealing, or killing with intent to steal, the carcase or skin of any horse, is a felony, punishable by transportation for life.

The maliciously killing, maiming, or wounding *any* cattle is a felony, punishable by transportation for life or imprisonment.

HORSE-RACING. By statutes 13 *G.* 2. *c.* 19., and 18 *G.* 2. *c.* 34., which regulate horse-races, it is enacted,

That no person should enter any horse which was not *bonâ fide* his own property, and no more than one for the same plate, upon forfeiture of the horse or its value: no plate to be run for under the *intrinsic* value of 50*l.*, under a penalty of 200*l.*, and those who advertise such plate to forfeit 100*l.* That every race should be begun and ended on the same day; and that no race should be run except at Newmarket and Black Hambleton, and for not less than 50*l.* under a penalty of 200*l.*; and that the sums paid for entering should be paid to the second best horse:

Horse-racing not in conformity with these provisions is, in legal language, "an unlawful game," and as such within the statutes made against *gaming*, which see, under that title; therefore, no sum above 10*l.* can be betted upon any race whatever, even though the odds above 10*l.* have been betted against sums *under* 10*l.*; and although a horse may be run for 50*l.*, betting on him is unlawful if above 10*l.*, and even bets under 10*l.* must be upon a legally constituted race, *i. e.*, for 50*l.* and upwards. All trotting matches are unlawful, and wagers upon them, if paid, recoverable back. See also WAGERS.

Money lent to pay a bet or wager is recoverable.

HOTCHPOT. The bringing in all monies and estates into one sum or account, in order to effect a more equal distribution. A sum advanced to a child is to be brought into hotchpot, with an intestate's effects, so that the party advanced is debited therewith on the division of his father's property. See EXECUTORS.

HUNDRED. A part or division of a shire or county, which is governed by a high constable or bailiff, and formerly there was regularly held in it the hundred court, which was held before the bailiff or deputy of the sheriff in the same manner as the county court is now held. The constitution of this hundred court is still preserved in Middlesex, for the county courts of that county are, by the act which extends the jurisdiction of the Middlesex county court to execution against the person, distributed according to hundreds, the deputies sitting in courts appointed for such hundred. The hundred is liable for damage occasioned to property by riotous or tumultuous assemblies of the people by action, the process in which is served upon the high constable: if the plaintiff recovers damages, the sheriff, on the receipt of the writ of execution, makes out a warrant to the treasurer of the county, directing him to pay the amount; and he also reimburses the high constable for his expenses.

In damages under 30*l.*, the party damnified gives a notice, stating his claim for compensation (pursuant to the form mentioned in the act 7 & 8 *G.* 4. *c.* 31., which every party damnified ought to procure from the queen's printers immediately after the riot), to the high constable, and the claim is settled by the justices at a special sessions.

HUSBAND and WIFE. The law of England considers marriage in no other light than as a civil contract, although it is accompanied with a religious ceremony and formalities. The sanctity of this contract is only considered in ecclesiastical courts; the courts of law and equity, or temporal courts, viewing unlawful or incestuous marriages not as a crime, but merely an inconvenience, excepting the case of bigamy, which, though it be a matter of ecclesiastical jurisdiction as respects the annulling of the marriage, is by the statute law classed as a crime, of which the law takes special notice. Marriage, with its various incidents, is noticed under that title. The law of husband and wife, as relates to their mutual property, liabilities, and contracts, being summarily defined under the present article.

1. By marriage, the husband and wife are one person in law; that is, the very being or legal existence of the woman is deemed suspended during marriage, or at least is incorporated and consolidated into that of the husband, under whose protection she performs every thing: by reason of this fictitious unity, it is a rule of *law* *, that a married woman

* *Equity*, it will be noticed hereafter, admits under certain restrictions the possession by the wife of a separate personal estate. See DIVISION 2.

cannot possess *personal* property; so every thing of that nature to which she is entitled at the time of her marriage, and which accrues in her right, whether by gift, bequest, or otherwise, during the marriage, vests solely in the husband; so that it does not require the aid of any court of law or equity to declare his claim, or give him by its decision the possession of it: he takes it free from any right of survivorship in the wife; he may dispose of it during his life, or bequeath it at his death; and, if he does not dispose of it, his executors and administrators, and not his wife exclusively, although she may survive him, will be entitled thereto.

All sums of money which the wife earns by her own skill and labour belong to the husband, and after his death they form part of his estate, though the wife survive: this right of the husband is so strongly recognised, that, where the wife had been actually paid for her services, it was held that the husband had a right to recover the amount, if it had been paid after notice given by him to the parties employing not to pay her. All money lent by the wife, or which another may receive on her account during the marriage, belongs likewise to the husband, and he alone is the proper person able to sue for it.

But with respect to a certain kind of *personal* property (real estate will be mentioned presently) called *choses in action*, the husband's interest is of a more limited nature than it is in other personalty.

Choses in action are mere rights arising from contracts expressed or implied, which must be asserted at law for the purpose of being reduced into possession, or, more plainly speaking, those things of which the possession can, in case of refusal, be recovered by legal process, being outstanding dues, such as money due on *simple contract*, specialty, damages for breach of contract, reversionary interests in personal property, &c. When these rights belong to a woman at the time of her marriage, or come to her since, they are only the husband's *conditionally*, *i. e.*, provided he get them into absolute possession in *her* lifetime, which if he does not do, and she die first, his right would only accrue as her administrator; but, if *he* should die first, she would be entitled, by what is termed her right of survivorship absolutely, even if she had concurred in the sale or mortgage of them by her husband; though, after they are reduced into possession, the sale by the husband seems good enough at law; yet in this last case the wife's concurrence is necessary to bar her of her right of settlement or *equitable* relief or allowance.

With respect to leases, and what are termed chattels real, the husband has power to dispose of them during her life, and, if he survive, they are his absolutely; they are, while he and the wife are *both alive*, liable for his debts, and subject to an outlawry obtained against him. If the wife survive, of course they belong to her.

The husband is entitled to all rents due in his wife's right, in the same way as to her leases, and by his surviving he will be entitled to the arrears accrued due before and since the marriage; if she survive, she is entitled by her right of survivorship.

After the death of the wife, the husband is entitled to administration of her personal property. After the death of the husband, the wife can, with the next of kin or reserving their right, take out administration. See Executors.

With respect to the real or inheritable estate of the wife, if a wife be possessed of such estate at the time of or during her marriage, the husband thereupon becomes entitled to the rents; and after his death the estate remains entire to her or her heirs, should she die before him, unless by the birth of a child, *born alive* and capable of inheriting the property, the husband become entitled to a previous estate for life, which is termed tenancy by the courtesy of England. This tenancy, however, only entitles the husband to a bare estate for life, in which he is restricted from impoverishing or wasting the estate, and cannot anticipate the profits by granting leases upon fines, though of course there is nothing to prevent his taking a fine upon a lease for his own life, reserving a nominal rent.

Four things must concur to render this estate for life perfect:—1. The marriage, which must be lawful. 2. The title or possession of the wife. 3. The birth of such issue, which by course of law would inherit the land. 4. The death of the wife.

This tenancy does not attach as a *legal* or *necessary* consequence upon lands of copyhold tenure; it generally holds by custom.

The custom of gavelkind in Kent allows of this life-tenancy, but it is only of *half* the land, and is forfeited by the husband's marrying again.

The wife may, with the concurrence of her husband, convey her inheritable estate to a purchaser, by acknowledging the same before a judge, master in chancery, or commissioner, and being examined privately as to her consent.

The husband and wife are restricted from granting unreasonable leases, tending to deteriorate an entailed estate, viz. leases for not more than 21 years, or longer than three lives.

On the other hand, the husband, in recompense of the benefit he derives from courtesy, &c., is bound to discharge all obligations entered into by the wife before marriage; for otherwise her creditors might lose their just debts; but this responsibility is confined to the wife's engagements while unmarried; for, if made during a former marriage, her after-taken husband is not liable for them, upon the principle that during marriage she is incapable of making any contract. And again, this liability on the part of the husband lasts only as long as the marriage; for, should she die before her husband has paid the debts, he is released from further responsibility; and should he die before the recovery of them, *i. e.* before judgment obtained, she alone will be liable, and the husband's estate exonerated. Yet for debts contracted by her during the time she was unmarried, in consideration of the personal fortune he has received with her, he may be liable as her administrator; for if there is any outstanding property not realised (choses in action) they are *assets* in the husband's hands as such administrator; and to those debts he will be liable in that character, not as husband, as far as those assets or property will extend, but no further. And, lastly, the husband is liable to debts contracted by his wife as executrix before marriage, either by waste or mismanagement; consequently the husband is chargeable therewith, and, upon a judgment in an action sued against them for such a cause, he may be taken in execution after her decease.

Though the husband is liable during marriage for the debts of his wife contracted when unmarried, yet the form is, that the action should be brought against them both. If, however, an action should have been commenced against the woman while unmarried, and she should marry *after judgment* had against her, the execution must issue against her alone. If she marry *before* judgment, the first action can be abandoned and the husband joined with the wife in a second.

The sum is, the husband is liable for all debts contracted by his wife while she was unmarried, though he had no fortune with her; and if she die *before a judgment* is obtained in action brought for recovery of such debts, he is not answerable for them, although he may have had a fortune with her, unless in this last case he is administrator to her: he is also, in like manner, responsible during their joint lives in respect of property wasted by her at any previous period to the present marriage, whether then unmarried or not.

By law, every man is obliged to supply his wife with necessaries, such as meat, drink, medicines, necessaries suitable to *his* degree and circumstances; and if he fail so to do, having sufficient means, the ecclesiastical court will grant a divorce from bed and board, and give her *alimony* for her support.

Although the contract of a married woman is absolutely void, yet with respect to certain contracts, namely, such as relate to suitable necessaries for her husband's family, she will be regarded as his agent, generally constituted for that purpose; a presumption perfectly accordant with his own liability, and the duty of both, and which consequently implies his assent; for, with respect to other contracts, she is not his agent, unless his authority be expressly proved; yet an *implied* assent will be disproved by evidence that a positive order or notice was given by the husband, that his wife should not be trusted by the party seeking to charge him, except where the husband has improperly turned her out of doors, or abandoned her, in which case a promise will be *implied*, notwithstanding the husband's notice; for otherwise the wife might suffer intolerable hardships. The chief point to be considered by tradesmen is, are the things purchased *necessaries?* If they are such, it matters not whether the husband and wife cohabit: the husband is liable, unless the goods be furnished under his express notice to the contrary, or credit be given to the wife alone, or the tradesman is fairly presumed cognisant of particular circumstances, such as a separate allowance to the wife, previous and abundant supply to the wife by the husband, &c. However, the case of desertion, and notice not to trust given by the husband, is no reason why the husband should not be liable for her maintenance and necessaries duly furnished: if the things purchased are *not necessaries*, or not suitable to the apparent situation in life of the wife, which of course follows that of the husband, then it is incumbent on the tradesman supplying them to make inquiry as to the power of the wife to bind the husband, and to prove the husband's *express* direction to her to make the purchase, or, at least, that he saw her use the articles bought without expressing any disapprobation.

If a wife have illegally absented herself from her husband's house, or conducted herself extravagantly when there, and is likely to endeavour to obtain necessaries or goods on the credit of her husband, he may, and should, in order to protect himself from liability, give a *public* notice in the Gazette, or newspapers circulated in the neighbourhood, prohibiting third persons from trusting her on his credit; and it is advisable, also, in such a case to give, and be prepared to prove, a *particular* and private notice or prohibition to every tradesman and person who had been accustomed to deliver goods to the wife on credit; for otherwise, unless in cases where the wife has been guilty of adultery, the husband may be liable until the tradesman has received actual notice; and though no notice is absolutely necessary when the wife has been guilty of adultery, yet it is always expedient to give the same. If such a notice have been given, and the husband receive back his wife, he thereby revives her authority to contract on his credit for necessaries, and impliedly revokes his previous notice. When the husband has causelessly turned away his wife, or improperly refused her necessaries, a general notice, or even a special prohibition, is of no avail; and necessaries may be delivered to the wife in defiance of such notice, so as to fix the husband.

Upon the principle of agency in the wife, a man is responsible for necessaries or goods furnished to any woman whom he represents to be his wife, and whom he permits to use his name. Lord Kenyon, in a case of this nature, said, "It is certain that if a man has permitted a woman to whom he was not married to use his name, and to pass for his wife, and in that character to contract debts, he is liable for her debts; and I am of opinion that he is liable, whether the tradesman who furnished the goods knew the circumstance to be so or not. He gives her a credit from her name and cohabitation." Yet it should be remembered, that, if action be brought against a man for goods furnished to a woman *after* she has ceased to cohabit with the defendant, the plaintiff cannot recover, if there be proof that they never were married, though they may have lived together as man and wife for several years, and she may have been always introduced into society by him as his wife. And if a man, being already married, marries a second woman, he will be liable for necessaries furnished to the second wife during their cohabitation; and he cannot discharge himself by proof of the previous marriage. But, if it could be proved that a person bringing an action in such a case knew of the celebration of the first marriage, such knowledge would be a bar to the action.

Not only clothes, meat, medicine, and lodging, but proper legal advice, and proctor's charges, in a suit necessarily instituted against the husband, are *necessaries* with which the law says, upon the doctrine of implied contracts, a husband is bound to provide his wife; and for which, if another should supply her, he is liable to pay.

The law in estimating what are necessaries, with a view of charging the husband, does not take account of the fortune brought by the wife, but only considers what the husband's circumstances were at the time when the articles were supplied. It is also decided, that a woman of her own authority may borrow money for necessaries, so as to charge her husband.

The liabilities to which a husband is subject in respect of his wife, whether for debts contracted by her during the existence of the marriage, or for necessaries, or by reason of such previous responsibilities in respect of executorship, &c., as have been previously noticed, cease altogether when the ecclesiastical court pronounces the marriage void from the beginning; for from the date of the sentence the woman becomes as much a *feme sole, i. e.* single woman, as if she had never been married.

Although a married woman is by the common law generally incapable of suing or being sued, yet there are a few necessary exceptions to this rule. Therefore, the wife of a person transported for any period, however short, or imprisoned by a commutation of punishment, voluntarily exiled, an alien, enemy, or a foreigner, who has left England, is in each of these cases equally capable of suing and being sued as a *feme sole, i. e.* single woman; and a woman whose husband is banished for life, by act of parliament, is empowered to make a will. But a wife, whose husband, a natural-born subject, departs of his own accord from the kingdom, is not rendered *sole* and separate by such departure; indeed, if the wife were liable, every person who left the kingdom for a short time, and went to live in Scotland, or Ireland, France, or elsewhere, would be exonerated from all debts which his wife might contract in the meantime. And it has been held, with respect to the wife of an alien friend, that she could be sued as a single woman, in cases only where her husband had never been in England, or, having been there, had left it under a legal disability to return to it.

By the custom of London, a married woman is capable in some instances of binding herself by contracts; that is, by being what is termed a *feme sole trader*, or trader on her own account, in the city of London. She, as such, is liable to the bankrupt laws. But the custom operates only on her buying and selling, or, more technically speaking, on debts by simple contracts not under seal.

A married woman will be discharged from an arrest, or holding to bail, unless it should appear that she has represented herself as a single woman: but where she has given a warrant of attorney to confess a judgment as a *feme sole*, she will not be discharged from an execution issued upon that judgment, for by that very act she represented herself as a single woman. If a married woman, sued as such jointly with her husband, be held to bail *alone* on process issued against both, she will be entitled to her discharge, or, if she is arrested on similar process with her husband, she will still be entitled to her discharge, but the husband must remain in custody until he puts in bail for both. And lastly, if a married woman be arrested on execution, or final process, issued against herself and husband, either alone, or with him, she will not be discharged, unless there should be some collusion between the plaintiff in the suit and the husband to detain her in confinement.

Although a married woman has no personal property during her marriage, unless her husband be transported, or any circumstance occur by which she is presumed single, yet, on her husband's death, previous interests, which had lain dormant, revive, and come into operation, and she takes all her bonds, bills, debts, and mortgages to herself absolutely, and, also, all her leases which have not been disposed of by the husband in his lifetime. In addition to her own property, she is entitled to what is termed her paraphernalia, her jointure, and dower, or thirds. Paraphernalia are the furniture of her chamber, in London called "the widow's chamber," her wearing-apparel, and ornaments of her person, being jewels or pearls, the quantity of which last seems to depend upon her husband's circumstances; the general rule being, that, if he dies solvent, she may retain all, otherwise she relinquishes the most valuable, or much the greatest part. Wearing-apparel is always exempt from claims of creditors; and, as personal estate is the fund for payment of debts in exoneration of the real estate, the widow may recover from the heir the amount which she has to pay in consequence of her husband's specialty creditors out of her paraphernalia, which otherwise would have been payable out of the real estate.

For the interest which a widow has in her deceased husband's personal estate, see EXECUTORS.

2. As to the separate estate of the wife, pin-money, jointure, dower, and what is termed *equitable* provision for the wife out of property bequeathed to her, — a married woman may, notwithstanding her marriage, have property secured to her by means of trustees, under a deed executed before her marriage, and not in such a manner as to be

a fraud upon him. Indeed, property of any kind may be bequeathed or settled to her use in the same manner; and, where no trustees are appointed for that purpose, a court of equity will give effect to the will, bequest, or instrument which declares the intention that the wife shall have a separate interest. Where the intention is so evident, and trustees are not appointed, the husband is considered as a trustee for his wife, and is accountble in equity, which takes cognisance of the interests of married women, and requires their consent to any disposal of them by the husband, if placed at all within its jurisdiction. But, although the law is so far qualified by the jurisdiction of equity, as to permit a married woman to take and enjoy property to her separate use, *when given with that intent*, yet such a trust must be very explicitly expressed before the rights of the husband will be so materially interfered with. "For her sole and separate use," "to be at her disposal for her livelihood," "independent of her husband, and not to be liable for his debts or engagements," are the words oftenest used, and which clearly demonstrate such an intention, which the courts of equity will see perfected if no trustees be appointed. As an incident to this separate property, the creation of which is often, in this commercial country, of beneficial consequences, the savings belong to the wife, if kept apart from other money allowed by the husband for expenditures on her own or domestic account.

Pin-money is an annual income settled by the husband before marriage on his intended wife, or gratuitously allowed by the husband for the wife's private expenditure: this is usually secured by a covenant on the part of the husband, with nominees of the wife, being trustees, who can, if withheld, sue the husband for arrears; but the arrears cannot, unless frequently from time to time demanded, be carried back beyond a year; nor can arrears, under any circumstances, be recovered, where the husband has been compelled to supply her with the articles which it was the object of that allowance to furnish her with, viz., clothes and ornaments.

Pin-money is forfeited by elopement, leaving home without good cause, and adultery; and the trustees will be prevented from using legal measures to enforce payment by an *injunction.*

Jointure is a provision for the wife, made by the husband out of his land or houses, in case she survives her husband: it is generally executed by a settlement by deed, and in ancient practice gave the husband and wife a *joint* interest (hence the term) during their lives in the land or houses settled.

The effect of a jointure is to bar the wife's dower or thirds in her husband's lands.

Dower is an estate for life which the widow acquires in a certain portion (generally a third, but by the custom of various manors it is half, and then called free-bench, sometimes the whole,) of her husband's freehold or copyhold land of inheritance, to the intent she may properly maintain and bring up the children. This legal provision for the wife may be lost by the act of the wife; as if she elopes, and is not afterwards reconciled to her husband; by her obtaining a divorce from the bond of marriage; by withholding the title-deeds of the property from the heir or devisee; by acknowledging a conveyance of the land with her husband; and by accepting any other provision, either by gift or bequest in which it may be expressly stated that it is given in lieu of dower. Dower is taken from the wife, also, by the act of the husband, by his disposing of the land in his lifetime; by his declaring by deed or will that his wife shall not be entitled to dower; by his bequeathing the land, or any part of it, to his widow; and, lastly, by his obtaining a divorce from the bond of marriage.

Dower is also now void against creditors of the husband.

Jointure is more advantageous for the wife, not only for its certainty, but because it cannot be forfeited if the marriage be valid. Dower is subject to a variety of contingencies, but few of them attach in respect of women married after December 31. 1833. With respect to the dower of those women married *before* January 1. 1834, dower attaches on *all* real property acquired by their husbands, unless they took it by a particular form of conveyance which excludes the wife; and is only forfeitable by elopement, or lost by their joining in and acknowledging a conveyance with their husbands, or accepting a certain provision.

If a married woman should by any accident lose her jointure, she is entitled to her dower, subject to the restrictions imposed by the late law, if she was married on or after January 1. 1834. See MARRIED WOMEN.

As to *equitable* provision, the court of chancery will, in all cases where the husband requires its assistance in obtaining his wife's property, compel him to settle some part of it upon his wife, and children by her; or, where the wife parts with her estate for the purpose of relieving her husband, a commensurate provision will be secured by the interference of the court out of the husband's property: but these *equitable* claims of the wife can be waived by her upon a competent provision, or by her specially releasing and giving up her right thereto, unless she is a ward of the court, or a clandestine marriage has taken place. But it must be noticed that it is only in cases of legacies and trusts, and where the husband has not obtained the property, that the court will interfere; and if the husband does not apply for the principal, but is content with the interest, to which he is undoubtedly entitled, the court will not compel him to make a settlement.

The court will interfere as against assignees, if the husband be bankrupt or insolvent; for, as the assignees could not obtain the fund without the interference of the court, the court will dictate the terms upon which the fund shall be paid them.

As against a purchaser of the fund the same *relief* will be given; so that every one who purchases a wife's legacy or bequest, exceeding 200*l.*, should be satisfied that her *equity* is satisfied by an adequate provision, or that some provision is set apart for her out of the fund about to be sold.

When a married woman has her property in the hands of the court, the court will also secure her a separate allowance in case her husband illtreat or desert her.

Married women, who have been wards in chancery, and over whose property the court of chancery exercises special jurisdiction, have their property secured to them by settlement made under the direction of the court. See WARD.

If a husband, on his marriage, make an adequate settlement on his wife, she has no claim for any further allowance, for by that act he becomes in equity the purchaser of her fortune; but with respect to future property, of any *very great* amount, the court will still exercise its jurisdiction, if the fund comes under the distribution of the court, though perhaps not so strictly as where no settlement was ever made.

A wife is excused in law from criminal misconduct, when she commits any offence in concert with her husband, because she is charitably presumed to act under his influence and coercion, whether the real fact be so or not; but to this the crimes of manslaughter, murder, and treason are exceptions; for the husband's authority or command can in nowise extenuate her guilt in these cases. Also in misdemeanors another exception is made, which is, that a wife may be indicted for keeping a brothel, and punished with her husband, unless evidence of coercion be substantiated; for this is an offence which concerns the domestic management of a house; and offences of this nature are presumed to be generally conducted by the intrigues of the female sex.

Adultery or criminal conversation with another's wife is left by our law to the punishment of the ecclesiastical or spiritual courts; but, as adultery is a wrong to the husband, the law gives a remedy for it by action, in which, upon the trial, all circumstances of aggravation or extenuation are brought forward; for the jury are to collect, from a review of those circumstances, the extent of the *real* injury sustained by the husband in his peace of mind and happiness, and give damages accordingly.

A husband can obtain a divorce in the ecclesiastical courts for the adultery of his wife; but, if she can show a case of recrimination, he will not be permitted to have the relief he seeks for. Upon the same principle, a bill for a divorce can be obtained in parliament, if the husband has made out a case of heartless infidelity on the part of his wife, otherwise not.

Divorces in the ecclesiastical courts are from bed and board only; and, by private acts for divorce, maintenance is given to the wife, provided she does not continue to live in adultery.

IDIOT, is a natural fool, a person who has never had any understanding or reason, and has not enjoyed lucid intervals. The queen has the protection of an idiot, or rather of his estate, which, by prerogative, is vested in her during the idiot's life, though it is usual for the crown to grant the surplus profits to his family or next of kin. In the case of a *lunatic*, the queen acts as a mere trustee, through the medium of the lord keeper of the great seal; in that of an *idiot*, she is entitled to that surplus which she grants to his relatives. As an idiot can be only declared so by inquisition, and view of his person by the jury, it seldom happens that the jury return that the party is an idiot, but simply that he is of unsound mind; and it seems that such inquisition cannot be traversed, for the material object is obtained, and the general term includes the more particular inquisition.

These distinctions will be noticed under the title Lunatics, to which the reader is referred.

IGNORAMUS. A Latin word, signifying "we are ignorant," formerly indorsed on a bill of indictment by the grand jury, when they rejected the evidence as too weak or defective, so as to put the person accused on his trial: the words now used, since the abolition of Latin proceedings, are "not a true bill," or "not found;" upon this, the person against whom the bill or presentment is made is delivered from gaol, by proclamation or otherwise.

IGNORANCE of the law is no excuse, for, if it were, every man would plead it as an excuse; and, as the learned Selden asks, who could confute him? Ignorance of a *fact*, however, is a different thing; but no breach of law must be committed upon such ignorance, for that would nullify the rule.

If parties pay money under erroneous impressions respecting the *law*, they cannot recover it back; otherwise, if under a mistake of *facts*. Deeds executed under a misapprehension of *facts* may be relieved against in equity; but, in these cases of mistake, it should be shown that the party seeking relief has acted with ordinary caution or promptitude. A mistake, where occasioned by the person who receives the money, or derives benefit from the transaction, making a false representation, or suppressing facts, in his knowledge only, is remediable as a fraud. See Payment of Money.

IMPEACHMENT. The accusation and prosecution of a person for treason or other crimes and misdemeanors. Any member of the house of commons may not only impeach one of their own body but also any lord of parliament. The mode of proceeding and practice is settled, and the same evidence is required, as if the proceedings were before other courts; this proceeding being in the high court of parliament, *i. e.* in the lords' house, the commons exhibiting articles, and appointing managers to conduct the prosecution.

A peer may be impeached for any crime, for he is liable by his peers only; but a member of the house of commons cannot be impeached before the lords (who, in fact, are the judicature) but for high misdemeanors.

Till the house of commons demand judgment on an impeachment exhibited by them, the lords cannot pass sentence.

Impeachment of Waste, is a restraint of committing waste. See Waste.

IMPLICATION. A necessary inference of something not expressly declared between parties in deeds, agreements, contracts, &c., arising from what is therein already expressed. Implications or inferences will not, in general, in deeds (which, being under seal, are of great concernment in law) create or alter estates; but in wills, wherein greater amplitude of construction is allowed, they frequently may; but the inference must be necessary and inevitable. Conditions and covenants may be implied in law, and in legal proceedings defects may be supplied.

IMPOSSIBILITY. A deed or bond requiring the performance of an impossible thing is void; but if a thing originally possible become, by death or inevitable accident (absurdly styled the "act of God") impossible, the party bound must perform the condition, and do the requisite act, as near as possible to the intent of the deed or bond.

IMPOTENCY. Marriages can be dissolved absolutely by the ecclesiastical courts for this disability: the marriage is only void from the sentence pronounced, and the complaining party is at liberty to marry again.

IMPRISONMENT. A restraint or detention of the person; an arrest. None shall be imprisoned but by the lawful judgment of his peers, or by the law of the land—*Magna Charta;* and no person is to be imprisoned but as the law directs.

False Imprisonment, is arresting or imprisoning without just cause, contrary to law; or where a person is unlawfully detained, without legal process. If a person be any way unlawfully detained, it is false imprisonment; and considerable damages are recoverable in these actions. The law favours liberty, and the freedom of a man from imprisonment; so that false imprisonment is a great offence; and lawful imprisonment is so pitied, that by several statutes, as well as by the common law, defaults are saved on that account.

If a person be imprisoned on any by-law of a corporation, &c., it is false imprisonment; because a by-law to imprison is against

Magna Charta. If a justice of peace commit a person without just cause, it is false imprisonment; and a constable cannot imprison a man at his pleasure, to compel him to do any thing required by law, but is to carry him before a justice. When any justice sends for a man, and commits him to gaol without any examination, the party may have action of false imprisonment against him; and if a justice of peace sends a general warrant to arrest a person, and say not for what, action lies against him, but not against the officer.

In false imprisonment, brought against an officer of an inferior court, if he *justify* an arrest by virtue of their warrant, he must show that the court has jurisdiction, or the action lies against him. If erroneous process issue out of a court that hath jurisdiction of the matter, and the bailiff or officer execute it, whereby the party is imprisoned, the officer shall be excused in action of false imprisonment; but, if the court out of which the process issues hath no cognisance of the cause, it is otherwise; for, in such case, the whole proceedings are *coram non judice, i.e.* not before a judge, and the officer will not be excused.

If an arrest is made by one who is no legal officer, or not named in the warrant, it is false imprisonment, for which action lies. An action of false imprisonment lies against a bailiff for arresting a person without warrant, though he afterwards receives a warrant; and so it is if he arrest one after the return of the writ is passed, or without showing the warrant.

If a sheriff, or any of his bailiffs, arrest a man out of his county, or after the sheriff is discharged from office, or a person arrest one on a justice's warrant, after his commission is determined, &c., it will be false imprisonment. And if the sheriff, after he has arrested a man lawfully, when a legal discharge comes to him, as *supersedeas* or the like, do not discharge the party, he may be sued by this action.

In case the plaintiff in a suit brings an unlawful warrant to a sheriff, and shows him the defendant, requiring him to make the arrest; or if he bring a good warrant, and direct the sheriff to a wrong man, &c., for this the action for false imprisonment will lie against both. If a warrant be granted to arrest or apprehend a person, where there are several of the name, and the bailiff or other officer arrests a wrong person, he is liable to action of false imprisonment; and he is to take notice of the right party at his peril.

A man arrested on a Sunday, or after the sheriff's officer has broken into his house, may bring his action for false imprisonment against the sheriff's bailiff; but the party arrested will not be released, except the court will notice the arrest on the Sunday, &c., as an irregularity, and then, it seems, the party must waive his action.

Mere irregularities in lawful process against the person may be considered as wrongful imprisonments, and the judges will discharge the party, if he agree to waive his right of action. If a bailiff demand more than his just fees, when offered him, and keep a person in custody thereupon, it is false imprisonment, and punishable; and if a sheriff or gaoler keep a prisoner in gaol after his acquittal, for any thing except for lawful fees, it is unlawful imprisonment.

Unlawful or false imprisonment is sometimes called duress of imprisonment, where one is wrongfully imprisoned till he seals a bond, &c.

All persons concerned in a wrong imprisonment can be sued in action of false imprisonment, and the party grieved may sue any one of them for it.

The action for false imprisonment is, in some cases, an action "on the case," where there is colour of authority; in other cases, the action is "trespass."

In all cases where a man is falsely imprisoned, he may bring a *habeas corpus;* and upon return of the writ, setting forth the cause of the commitment, if it appear to be against law he shall be discharged; or, in criminal cases, he may be bailed, if it be doubtful, &c. See ARREST.

INCENDIARIES. Persons who burn houses, barns, ricks, &c. See ARSON.

INCEST. The marriage of persons within the Levitical degrees; in fact, those degrees of collateral consanguinity, or affinity, prohibited by our law; being the third degree in consanguinity, and the fourth degree in affinity. (See KINDRED.) These marriages are void from the act itself, and the issue are deemed bastards. A divorce can be sued for in the ecclesiastical court at the instance of any one.

INCH OF CANDLE, is a species of auction, notice being given upon the exchange, or other public place, of the time of sale. The goods to be thus sold are divided into lots, printed papers of which, and the conditions of sale, are also published; and when the goods are exposed to sale, a small piece of wax candle, about an inch long, is burning, and the last bidder, when the candle goes out, is entitled to the lot or parcel so exposed. See AUCTION.

INCIDENT. A thing necessarily depending upon, appertaining to, or passing with, another that is more worthy or principal.

A court-baron is inseparably incident to a manor, and a court of piepowder to a fair: these are so inherent to their principals, that by the grant of one the other is granted.

Rent is *incident* to a reversion; timber trees are *incident* to the freehold, as also deeds and charters, and a way to lands; distress to rent, and amercements, &c. And there are certain *incidents* to estates-tail, as to be dispunishable of waste, to bar the tenant's issue by deed acknowledged, &c.

INCLOSURES of common fields, or improvements of open commons, wastes, and common fields, are generally effected by the authority of private acts of parliament, where all the parties interested have concurred in the arrangement; but the expense attending the application, and other circumstances, induced the legislature to pass the General Inclosure Act, 41 *G.* 3. *c.* 109., which was amended by 1 *&* 2 *G.* 4. *c.* 23.; the object of which acts was not only to methodise and regulate inclosures, but to afford other facilities; and, in addition to two acts for limited purposes and partial amendment, the act 6 *&* 7 *W.* 4. *c.* 115. has been passed, "for facilitating the inclosure of *open* and *arable fields* in England and Wales," so that a complete general law of inclosure has been formed.

Therefore, the only modes by which an inclosure can now be effected of open and common arable and meadow fields are established by the last statute, which provides,

1. That open and common fields may be inclosed, with the consent of two third parts in number and value of the parties interested therein as freeholders or tenants, for any term of years, whereof one hundred years are unexpired; or as holders of copyhold or customary-hold tenure of an estate equal in quantity to such estates; or as guardians, trustees, husbands, or committees of any person under legal disability, entitled in *possession* to any rights of common, or other rights in open

and common arable fields, or open meadow and pasture or fields known by metes and bounds, or occupied according to known legal rights in *England* or *Wales*, and the right of intercommoning extinguished. Commissioners are to be nominated by the parties consenting (or, rather, who shall have previously expressed their consent in writing), which commissioners are to appoint an umpire, and give public notice of a meeting to be holden in one of the parishes or townships wherein the lands to be inclosed are situate, or within seven miles of the boundaries of one of them. At such meeting, the major part of the proprietors may agree for the payment of a gross sum to the commissioners or surveyor for the performance of their future duties; and four fifths of the proprietors may also agree upon the adoption of any plan or valuation, as well as of rules for the guidance of the commissioners or umpire; both which are to be binding upon the commissioners and umpire, subject to be appealed against at the quarter-sessions; and the commissioners are enabled to decide upon disputes between interested parties, from which decision an appeal also lies to the quarter-sessions.

2. Seven eighths in number and value of the persons similarly interested, as before-mentioned, are empowered to effect an inclosure, without the intervention of commissioners, if they by themselves, or by their known agents, or (if under legal disabilities) by their husbands, guardians, or committees, at a public meeting, or adjournment thereof, of which public notice is to be given, enter into an agreement for such inclosure, and for the granting compensation to persons possessed of rights, whether they be consenting parties or not; and shall sign or seal a schedule containing a description of land intended to be inclosed, to be deposited with the clerk of the parish, and with the clerk of the peace; and a notice of such deposit is to be affixed on the church door on three successive Sundays, and published in some newspaper, circulating in the county, thrice in three subsequent successive months after such schedule shall have been so deposited; the act declaring that such inclosure shall be as valid and effectual as if the same had been effected by means of commissioners, subject, however, to an objecting party's right to appeal to the quarter sessions.

The subsidiary provisions and enactments relate to the manner of the commissioners' proceedings, where the inclosure takes place by their intervention, and their power in relation to boundaries, surveys, rules for adopting a course of husbandry, encroachments, compensations for standing crops, public and private paths and roads, turnpike roads, ditches, &c., fences, expenses, accounts, penalties, witnesses, costs, the publication of their award. The methods also of determining objections to the inclosure, where the same is effected without commissioners, are very numerous, therefore cannot be here further noticed.

The act itself does not extend to the inclosure of any open or common arable fields, or of any open or common meadow, or pasture, or fields, of London, or

Within one mile of any city or town of -	5,000	inhabitants.
Within one mile and a half - -	15,000	—
Within two miles - - - - -	30,000	—
Within two miles and a half - -	70,000	—
Within three miles - - - - -	100,000	—

Therefore such lands are not liable to be inclosed at all. See Approvement, Common.

Inclosure also means any place inclosed within a wall, hedge, fence, ditch, or the walls, hedge, fence, or ditch itself, &c.: any person injuring these, by taking, with intent to steal, or without such intent, is punishable, summarily, before one justice of the peace, as for a malicious injury to property. *Stat.* 7 *&* 8 *G.* 4. *c.* 29. *ss.* 40, 41.

INCORPOREAL HEREDITAMENTS or RIGHTS. See HEREDITAMENTS, PRESCRIPTION.

INCUMBENT, from Lat. *incumbo*, minding diligently. A clerk resident on his benefice with cure; and is so called, because he does, or ought, to bend all his study to the discharge of the cure of the church to which he belongs.

INCUMBRANCE. A mortgage, annuity, rent-charge, a condition or covenant affecting an estate, or, in legal language, "following the land," the concealment of which from a purchaser is fraud.

INDECIMABLE. Not tithable, or by law ought not to pay tithe.

INDEFEASIBLE. That which cannot be defeated or made void; as a good and *indefeasible* estate, &c.

INDICTMENT is a formal *inquisition* or accusation made by twelve men at the least, called a grand jury, whereby they find and *present*, namely, notify, that such a person, of such a place, in such a county, and of such a quality or situation in life, has committed such a treason, misdemeanor, felony, trespass, or other offence, against the peace of the queen (namely, the general peace, of which the queen, as chief magistrate, is the conservatrix), her *crown* and *dignity* (mere words of form and respect). Before the jury have inquired into the facts, it is termed a "bill," but after they have come to the conclusion that the matters should be answered and disproved it is termed an indictment, and thereupon is a matter of record, and the party is arraigned upon it. So a coroner's inquisition is a matter of record, because found by the oath of twelve men at the least; and the party may be arraigned upon it, as upon an indictment, an indictment being but an inquiry, legally termed an "inquisition;" and, by the law, no man can be put upon his trial for a felony but by an indictment, or something equivalent thereto; for lesser offences he may *be tried by* information. See tit. INFORMATION.

The sheriff of every county is bound to return to every session of the peace, and every commission of *oyer* and *terminer*, and of general gaol delivery, twenty-four good and lawful men of the county, some out of every hundred, "to inquire, present, do, and execute all those things, which, on the part of our lady the queen, shall then and there be commanded them." As many as appear upon this panel are sworn of the grand jury, to the amount of twelve at least, and not more than twenty-three, that twelve may be a majority. This *grand* jury are previously instructed in the articles of their inquiry by a charge from the judge on the bench. They then withdraw from court to sit and receive indictments, which are preferred to them in the name of the queen, but at the suit of any private prosecutor: and the grand jury are only to inquire upon their oaths, whether there be sufficient cause to call upon the party to answer it.

When the grand jury have heard the evidence, if they think it a groundless accusation, they used formerly to indorse on the back of the bill *ignoramus*, namely, "we know nothing of it;" intimating that, though the facts might possibly be true, the truth did not appear to them; but now they assert in English, more absolutely, not a true bill, or (which is the better way) "not found;" and then the party is discharged by proclamation without further answer; but a fresh bill may afterwards be preferred to a subsequent grand jury. If they are satisfied of the truth of the accusation, they then indorse upon it "a true bill." The indictment is then said to be "found," and the party stands indicted. But to find a bill there must be at least twelve of the jury agree; for so tender is the law of England of the lives of the subject, that no man can be convicted at the suit of the queen for any capital offence unless by the unanimous voice of twenty-four of his equals and neighbours; that is, by twelve, at least, of the grand jury, in the first place, assenting to the accusation, and afterwards by the whole petit jury of twelve more finding him guilty upon his trial. But, if twelve of the grand jury assent, it is a good presentment, though some of the rest disagree. (2 *Hawk. P. C.* 161.) And the indictment, when so found, is publicly delivered into court.

Although a bill of indictment may be preferred to a grand jury upon oath, they are not bound to find the bill if they find cause to the contrary.

A grand jury, where there are different counts or paragraphs in an indictment, alleging distinct offences to have been committed, may find a *true bill* for one count and *not found* upon another. But it is only in cases under felony, where the judgment upon each count is the same, that different counts for different offences are allowed.

A party under prosecution may except to, or challenge, any of the grand jury summoned by the sheriff, as being outlawed, returned at the instance of the prosecutor, or being akin to him.

Persons indicted may employ counsel for them as in civil cases.

Persons indicted not appearing, or not putting in bail where the offence is bailable, are outlawed, and forfeit all their goods and chattels. See OUTLAWRY.

Several defendants cannot be joined in one indictment for perjury; for perjury is a separate act in each.

A person indicted of felony, &c., may plead, generally, a former acquittal or conviction, a pardon, or other special plea, or the general issue, *not guilty*, or may plead, in abatement of the indictment, that the court has no jurisdiction, which is now the only plea in *abatement* allowed.

Indictments must not only be precise in form as to name, place, date, and fact, but the offence itself must also be set forth with clearness and certainty; and, in some crimes, particular words of art must be used, which are so appropriated by the law to express the precise idea which it entertains of the offence, that no other words, however synonymous they may seem, are capable of doing it. Thus, in treason, the facts must be laid to be done "treasonably, and against his allegiance;" else the indictment is void.

In indictments for murder, it is necessary to say, that the party indicted "murdered," not "killed" or "slew," the other. In all indictments for felonies, the adverb "feloniously" must be used; and for burglaries, also, "burglariously;" and all these to ascertain the intent. In rapes the word "ravished" is necessary, and must not be expressed by any periphrasis, in order to render the crime certain. So, in larcenies, the words "feloniously took and carried away" are necessary to every indictment; for these only can express the very offence. All capital crimes whatsoever, after any lapse of time, and also all inferior crimes of a public nature, as misprisions, and all other contempts, all disturbances of the peace, all oppressions, and all other misdemeanors whatsoever, of a public evil example against the common law, may be indicted; but no injuries of a private nature, unless they some way concern the public as nuisances, oppressions, disturbances, assaults, &c.; for an indictment is the queen's suit, which is the reason why the party who prosecutes is a good witness to prove it. And no damages can be given to the party grieved upon an indictment, or other criminal prosecution, unless particularly grounded on some statute; but the court of queen's bench, by the queen's privy seal, may give to the prosecutor a third part of the fine assessed for any offence; and the fine to the queen may be mitigated, in regard to the defendant's making satisfaction to a prosecutor for costs of prosecution, and damages sustained by the injury received.

INDORSER, INDORSEE. When a transfer is made of a bill of exchange or note, if made by indorsement, *i.e.* a writing on the back, the person making it is called the indorser, and the person in whose favour or to whom it is made is called the indorsee, who, when in possession of the bill, is called *the holder*. There is no limit to the number of indorsees, for, if there be not room on the bill, others may be added on an annexed paper.

An infant may be an indorsee.

Indorsements of bills are usually made after acceptance and before payment; but a man may indorse a blank bill, and it will render him liable to the amount thereafter expressed, not exceeding the limit of the stamp. Indorsements can be made after the bill falls due, but it carries suspicion; and, if the payment of value be disputed in any action brought to recover the amount, such indorsee must be prepared to prove that the defendant had value, and must in that respect stand in the shoes of the party from whom he took it. But this rule does not extend to notes payable on demand, unless the indorsee knew that a demand of payment had been made and refused.

When a bill is payable to a particular person, or to *bearer*, it is transferable by mere delivery, without indorsement.

When a bill or note becomes the property of the queen by an extent, she may transfer it by sign manual; and a pencil writing is a sufficient indorsement.

The indorsement is generally the signature of the party transferring, which is termed an indorsement in blank. When the indorsement mentions the person in whose favour it is made, it is termed a *full* indorsement, in which none but the indorsee himself can transfer it; though if he indorse by his simple signature, without specifying any particular person to whom the contents are to be paid, it is transferable as other bills are. Indeed, a bill can be transferred by one to another after the first indorsement has been made, which is by the *drawer* or *payer;* but no liability attaches, save by actual indorsement.

A bill may be indorsed by one of several partners in the partnership name, and also by an agent, who should state his capacity, else he may render himself liable; as "A. B. as agent for C. D.," or C. D. *per proc.* A. B.; or he may write the name of C. D., which will be sufficient; but the two former are the most safe and usual; and it might be difficult, in case of a misunderstanding, for A. B. to prove that he had authority to sign C. D.'s name.

An indorsement may be *restrictive* or *qualified, i. e.* by limiting the payment to a particular person; as "pay E. F. for my use;" "pay to H. I. only;" which restricts the currency of the instrument; or the liability of the party indorsing may be nullified by adding words to that effect, such as "without recourse to me;" meaning that the party indorsing will not be personally responsible: this indorsement is chiefly available to agents, or persons who are obliged to indorse and yet have no interest in the amount. See BILL OF EXCHANGE.

INDORSEMENT. Any thing written on the back of a deed; as receipts for consideration-money, the attestation of the sealing and delivery, &c. On sealing of a bond, any thing may be *indorsed* or subscribed upon the back thereof as part of the condition, and the *indorsement* and that shall stand together.

INDORSEMENT OF BILLS OR NOTES. The writing of a *payee* on the back (*in dorso*) of the bill or note, for the purpose of transfer to a third party. An indorsement which mentions the name of the person in whose favour it is made is called an *indorsement in full*, and an indorsement which does not is called an *indorsement in blank*. After an indorsement in *full*, the indorsee or person in whose favour the indorsement is made can only transfer the bill by *his own* indorsement in writing; but after an indorsement in blank, which is only the *mere signature* of the payee or subsequent holder, the bill may be transferable by mere delivery only; in effect, making it payable to any holder or bearer into whose hands it may be lawfully delivered or honestly come. The name of the drawer, or person to whom it is made payable, must appear in the first indorsement, which, if it be made, as is with us ordinarily the case, in *blank*, by mere signature, may be handed from one to the other without any further indorsement, and give a good title to the holder of the bill; otherwise if the indorsement be in full, or special.

Indorsements, it is noticed under the title BILL OF EXCHANGE, can be made in different forms, and can be framed so as to avoid personal liability, or to suit particular purposes.

The following are forms of indorsements applicable to every possible case of mercantile expediency:—

1. *Ordinary form in blank by drawer or payee, partner and agent.*

"Jacob Anderson."

"Whitmore & Co."

or,

"For self, (*or* "self and partners,")
William Whitmore."

"℘ procuration Jacob Anderson,
Abel Watkins."

or,

"As agent for Jacob Anderson,
Abel Watkins."

2. *Indorsement to avoid personal liability.*

"Jacob Anderson,"
sans recours.

or,

"Jacob Anderson, with intent only to transfer my interest, and not to be subject to any liability in case of non-acceptance, or non-payment, *as the case may be.*"

3. *Indorsement* in full.

"Pay Charles Haswell, or order,
Jacob Anderson."

or,

"Pay to Messrs. Jones, Lloyd, & Co., or order, value in account.
Jacob Anderson."

4. *Restrictive Indorsements, in favour of the Indorser, and also in favour of another person.*

"Pay Charles Haswell for my use, (*or* for my account,)
Jacob Anderson."

or,

"Pay to Charles Haswell only."

or,

"The contents must be credited to Henry Jones."

The residence of the indorser might very well be mentioned in all the foregoing forms (except No. 2.), as the holder might without difficulty be enabled to give the proper notice in case of dishonour. The words "in case of need at *Messrs. Childs', Temple Bar,*" form the usual reference to an indorser's banker, if he is not known in the commercial world, or is not resident in London. In French "au besoin chez Mons. Daly, Place Vendôme, (No. 8.) à Paris."

Bills indorsed in France state the place and precise date, else they will not be current. The following are forms of such indorsements: The words "au besoin," &c. are already explained; the words "retour sans protêt," or "sans frais," mean, that in case of a dishonour the bill shall be returned without protest or without expense. We will suppose a bill drawn in France by an English merchant or traveller in the following customary form: —

"£50. 0*s.* 0*d.* (1250 francs.) "Abbeville, 2d Nov. 1836."

"Ten days after sight of this my sola bill of exchange, pay to the order of *Jules Hypolite Singetigre* fifty pounds sterling, value received.
Thomas Ryall."

"To Messrs. ——
"London."

Indorsement 1. "Payez *Leroy Mabille*, ou ordre, valeur reçu en argent." [*or,* "en marchandises," *or* "en compte."] "*Jules Hypolite Singetigre,* à *Abbeville,* 2 Décembre, 1836, retour sans protêt," *or* "sans frais."

2. "Pay to the order of Messrs. *Al. Adam & Co.*, value received, Boulogne, 4 Décembre, 1836. *Leroy Mabille.*"

3. "Pay to Messrs. Jones, Lloyd, & Company, *or* order, value in account. Boulogne-sur-mer, 5 Décembre, 1836. *Al. Adam and Co.*"

4. "Jones, Lloyd, & Company."

INDUCTION, *inductio, i. e.* a leading into. The giving a parson possession of his church. After the bishop has granted institution, he issues out his mandate to the archdeacon to *induct* the clerk, who thereupon either does it personally, or usually commissions some neighbouring clergyman for that purpose. It is induction which makes the parson a complete incumbent. See Institution.

INFANT. A person under the age of twenty-one years; whose acts the law in many cases pronounces *void,* or *null,* or *voidable, i. e.* good until dissent had, and which may be ratified, after the infant's attaining full age, or set aside, at the infant's option. However, many acts of considerable importance may be done by minors in relation to their persons or affairs. A male at fourteen is at years of discretion, may consent to marriage, and may choose his guardian; and also could, before Jan. 1. 1838, bequeath his personal estate, if his discretion was sufficiently proved. He may also take up goods, being necessaries, and suitable to his circumstances in life, and bind him by what is termed a *single* bond, *i. e.* bond without penalty, for their payment. A female at twelve is by the law considered at maturity, may consent to marriage, and could, before Jan. 1. 1838, bequeath her personal estate, if discretion be fully proved; at fourteen may choose a guardian, and is considered at years of legal discretion. At twenty-one years of age (which age is completed on the day preceding the birthday) infants arrive at "full age," and may dispose of their lands by will or otherwise, and do all other acts.

As far as regards marriage, persons under age must conform to the present laws respecting marriage, and obtain consent of parents or guardians, or publish bans, or procure a licence, else the marriage will be deemed invalid; but infant widowers or widows need no consent, whatever their age may be. See MARRIAGE.

With respect to the guardianship of minors, the law, considering the imbecility of judgment in children of the age or fourteen, provides by a stat. of *C.* 2., that any *father*, under age, or of full age, may, by deed or will, attested by two witnesses, dispose of the custody of his child, either born or unborn, to any person except a popish recusant, either in possession or reversion, till such child attain twenty-one. These guardians are commonly termed *testamentary guardians*, or guardians by statute.

The consequence of this statute is to vest in the guardian all the infant's estate, both real and personal.

If a *mother* happens to be a surviving parent, the children must seek their guardian at common law, that is, some near relation may take care of the infant's *person* till twenty-one, unless at fourteen years old or afterwards they appoint a guardian. The near relations who undertake this charge, to which they may be appointed, can only undertake the custody of the *person* of the infant; and the guardianship of the parents in their lifetime extended no farther. These guardians are termed "guardians by nurture."

If no person will undertake the guardianship, although the infants are under fourteen, yet they must appoint their guardian under hand; but, if the children have property, the jurisdiction of the chancellor on the part of the crown arises, and he protects, by the process of the court of chancery the infant's person and property, by delegating the care of the same to some proper person. Indeed, not even the power of the father to appoint guardians to his children supersedes the chancellor's right of interference for the infant's protection; and this is extremely necessary, as in cases of incapacity or misconduct, or reasonable apprehension by reason of the guardian's bankruptcy, &c., loss and injury are prevented; but the court cannot *remove* the testamentary guardian: all that can be done is to appoint a proper person to superintend the education, and to receive and duly account for the proceeds (under sureties) of the infant's estate; and this protection and interference will be continued after the infants have attained full age, if circumstances require it.

The court of chancery exercises this jurisdiction by delegation from the crown, who is the universal guardian of infants, idiots, lunatics, and persons of unsound mind; and the court of chancery is the only proper court which can appoint and remove guardians, and prevent them and others from abusing their persons or estates. Indeed, this wholesome jurisdiction, which is cheaply administered, is extended to deprive parents morally unfit for the guardianship of the custody of their children.

Guardians are, in fact, trustees where they receive the profits of the infant's property, and, consequently, are accountable as such, and have the same allowances; and this trust is not assignable, being a personal trust.

An infant is incapable of acting as executor till twenty-one.

By the custom of gavelkind, which holds in some parts of Kent, and in some manors near London, an infant at fifteen may sell his lands; and similar customs are said to exist elsewhere.

By the custom of London, an infant unmarried, and above the age of fourteen, may bind himself apprentice to a freeman of London with proper covenants; which covenants, by the custom, shall be as binding as if he were of full age.

With respect to crimes, see Age.

Infants under twenty-one are privileged in some cases as to misdemeanors so as to escape fine or imprisonment, particularly in cases of omission, as for not repairing a highway, bridge, or the like; but for misdemeanors evidencing moral turpitude there is no favour shown them.

The incapacity of infancy does not attach upon the queen, mayors of corporations, or heads of public bodies, lords of manors, and peers, in respect of their appointing chaplains, (even if not ten years of age,) or patrons of churches.

An infant cannot be an attorney, steward of a manor, bailiff, factor, receiver, or hold any official situation of discretion or trust, though it seems as to some situations or offices which may be executed by deputy, or which only require skill or diligence, there is an exception; such as the offices of park-keeper, gaoler, forester, &c. The rule is positive as to excluding infants from places of public and pecuniary trust.

An infant cannot be a common informer; for an informer must sue in person, not by attorney, which an infant cannot do.

Infants cannot be jurors or members of parliament.

The incapacities of infants are but after all so many privileges; for, though he may not alien or charge his property, he may inherit, acquire, purchase, and obtain any property whatever, and may avoid his contracts when he comes of age, if he find them disadvantageous, save those for necessaries, and in the case where he has paid money with his own hand.

Those acts which are void, and those which are voidable, need not be considered in a work of this nature: the distinction is purely legal; and as both can be rendered unavailing to bind the infant, so he may contract anew in case of a void contract, or confirm the voidable on his attaining age.

The law, however, in its favour towards infants, has rendered a memorandum in *writing* necessary to charge the infant upon a promise after he has attained his age, in respect of contracts entered into by him during his nonage.

As to Necessaries. — An infant may bind himself to pay for his necessary meat, drink, apparel, physic, and such other necessaries, and likewise for schooling; but, in respect of this liability, the infant is not chargeable if the credit was given to his parents, or he was under their protection at the time he was instructed, or living in their house.

It must appear that the things were actually necessary, and of reasonable prices, and suitable to the infant's degree and expectations.

Although an infant shall be liable for his necessaries, yet, if he enters into an obligation with a penalty for payment thereof, this shall not bind him ; otherwise, upon a bond or single bill for the *exact amount* of necessaries furnished.

Necessaries for an infant's wife are necessaries for him ; but, if provided only in order for the marriage, he is not chargeable, though she use them after. An infant is liable for the nursing of his child. Debts contracted during infancy form, however, a good consideration to support a promise made to pay them when a person is of full age, provided that promise is in writing.

Though a promise *by* an infant will not bind him unless for necessaries, yet he shall take advantage of any promise made *to* him, though the consideration was his promise when an infant.

And an infant plaintiff has been allowed to recover on mutual promises of marriage.

If one lends money to an infant who actually lays it out in necessaries, yet this will not bind the infant, for it is upon the *lending* the contract must arise.

INFANTS WITNESSES. See WITNESS.

INFERIOR COURTS. The courts of judicature are generally classed as superior and inferior. The former being the courts at Westminster, the latter, the marshalsea, lord mayor's court, sheriff's court, courts of conscience, &c., having limited jurisdiction, whose proceedings are controllable by the queen's bench specially, and also by the common pleas. Where final judgment is obtained in any inferior court of record, and the defendant cannot be found in their jurisdiction, the superior courts at Westminster may remove the record, and issue execution as in judgments in such superior court.

INFORMATION, CRIMINAL, is a formal written suggestion or relation of an offence alleged to be committed, filed by the queen's attorney-general (or, in the vacancy of that office, by the solicitor-general,) in the court of queen's bench, without the intervention of a grand jury, and it lies for misdemeanors alone. These informations are termed *ex officio*, because it lies peculiarly within the official duty of the attorney-general to proceed against those who commit enormous misdemeanors, such as disturbing the government and peace of the kingdom by gross and scandalous libels upon the queen's ministers, blasphemies, seditious and outrageous acts or riots, briberies, and oppressions, and such other matters of public concern.

Informations may be filed, with leave of the court of queen's bench, with the master of the crown office ; and these are similar to those *ex officio*, and for misdemeanors ; only that these are at the instance of private persons, and cannot be obtained without a particular representation of the facts made by the party applying ; it resting entirely with the court whether they grant leave or not. The subjects of this *private* sort of information are misdemeanors, batteries, libels, and improprieties of a gross kind, but such as tend particularly to the injury of the individual, while by their example they have a pernicious tendency to corrupt morals, or incite breaches of the peace.

The application is made upon affidavit; and the court, where the crime suggested and sworn to by the affidavit is *primâ facie* apparent, grants a rule calling upon the party complained of to show cause why a criminal information should not be filed ; and, if the party does not show sufficient cause or reason, the rule is made absolute, *i. e.* the application is granted, and the complainant files his information.

It will be seen that this proceeding is without the intervention of a grand jury; and, in the case of an *ex officio* information, without any oath at all.

When the information in either case is filed, the party, having obtained a copy of it, (which, in *ex officio* cases, is granted him free of expense upon application to the court) appears and pleads thereto; and, upon issue joined, it is tried at nisi prius with the civil cases; and if the defendant is found guilty upon the prayer of the complainant or attorney-general, as the case may be, he has sentence passed upon him, either immediately, if at the assizes, or in the next term, if the information was tried in London or Middlesex.

The party complaining may be, and almost always is, a witness for the prosecution; indeed, as the information is never granted upon libels or scandalous matters without a denial by the prosecutor of the truth of the libel or scandal, it is fit that he should be cross-examined by the defendant.

As no damages are recovered, and as the party himself is exposed to the ordeal of a strict examination, it is most advisable for persons grossly injured in their fair reputation to proceed against the libeller by this proceeding. In indictment for libel or slander the defendant must be convicted on proof of the words spoken without more; and in an action for damages the defendant is much restricted by the form of pleading and evidence; for if he do not make out a plea of justification, or show he did not speak the words, a verdict must pass against him.

A criminal information, therefore, is more satisfactory.

The discretion of the court in granting informations is guided by the merits of the person applying, by the time of the application, by the nature of the case, and by the consequences which may possibly result from the granting it.

As to informations before justices of the peace, see JUSTICES OF THE PEACE.

INFORMER, is the designation of a person who takes upon himself the public duty of enforcing penal statutes. *Common* informers are so styled from their obtaining a livelihood by their taking upon themselves this task. The evidence of an informer is not receivable where he would, in the event of a conviction, be entitled to any part of the penalty; and upon this principle it is that complainants, who complain of assaults and other injuries summarily cognisable before justices of the peace, cannot receive any part of the fine or penalty if they appear as witnesses, but the compensation is payable in aid of the poor's-rate.

INITIALS. Persons who draw, accept, or indorse bills or promissory notes, or in other writings are designated by the initial letters, or any contraction of their christian name, may be held to bail, sued, and described by such initial or contracted name.

INJUNCTION, is a writ issuing out of a court of equity, and is said to be — 1st, Remedial or preventive; 2d, Judicial or decretal.

1st. Courts of equity have assumed the right to interfere (in cases where the courts of common law cannot assist), by restraining the commission of a wrongful act, to which an action at law might afford but a very unsatisfactory remedy, or where damages are not capable of complete proof, or the wrongdoer is insolvent, or where the consequences of the wrong committed or apprehended would be incalculable, or not easily repaired. The cases in which applications are mostly made are those of irreparable waste, plain nuisance, infringement of a clear copyright, forcible entry, wasteful trespass, executors wasting property, the danger of a bill being unjustly negotiated by partners or others, and to stay proceedings at law manifestly unjust; and in similar cases where prevention, absolute or conditional, is necessary.

These proceedings are sometimes heard *ex parte*, *i. e.* on the affidavits of the complaining party alone, or on a day appointed, on which both parties attend, when the injunction is either granted or refused conclusively: in the former case the injunction is provisional, or can be dissolved on the party complained of giving the plaintiff notice of his intent, and filing affidavits in full answer to those of the plaintiff. *Ex parte* injunctions are granted upon urgent matters sworn to, and the necessity of immediate interposition suggested or apparent.

To detail the cases in which courts of equity will grant relief by a preventive interposition would far exceed the bounds of a work of this nature; but the jurisdiction of the courts of equity, especially the court of chancery, is so ample, that almost every case of fraud or wrong, the commission of which would cause injury of an irremediable nature, is within the scope of its authority.

The process is generally by a bill of complaint, which being the usual commencement of a suit, by calling upon the defendant to answer, gives the plaintiff a right to apply to the court on motion and affidavit; but, as is said before, on urgent matters this form is not complied with in the first instance, the proceeding being by a petition and affidavit.

2d. With regard to the *judicial* injunction. This process issues subsequent to a decree made in a suit where all the parties are regularly and formally before the court: it is, in fact, an order directing the defendant or other party to the suit to deliver up possession, or to continue in possession of lands, &c., and is in the nature of a writ of execution: the first injunction enjoining a party not to do such a thing, the second enjoining that such a thing be done.

This process is also made subservient to the courts of equity, as a means to compel a specific performance of any act covenanted to be done, either by restraining a person from breaking his covenant or compelling him to perform it. The compelling a party to specifically perform his agreement or covenant is upon the principle, that a man might suffer more damage from the violation of an agreement than he could recover readily compensation at law; and therefore, to a certain extent, might sustain an irreparable injury, unless the benefit of equitable interference was granted him.

Great caution, however, has always been exercised in granting injunctions at the commencement of a suit, (for a suit in most cases is to be commenced,) because, if the preliminary decision is erroneous, a defendant suffers a great loss, which, like the plaintiff's alleged damage, may not admit of reparation.

Injunctions as *preventive* processes do not restrict the plaintiff from prosecuting his legal remedy; they rather act in concurrence with other remedies, and afford the complaining party his full measure of relief.

The court generally exercises its discretion as to costs, which, however, ordinarily follow the event of the application.

INLAND BILLS. Bills of exchange drawn upon persons in this country, in contradistinction to foreign or outland bills, as they used formerly to be termed.

INNINGS. Lands recovered from the sea in Romney Marsh, Kent.

INNOCENCE. As the law always presumes the best, it presumes a man's character is good until the contrary be shown, or that he is not guilty of an offence until it be shown that he is; therefore no person is presumed cognisant of any particular fact, the knowledge of which imputes the commission of an offence; as, if a woman marries again in her husband's lifetime, her innocence of knowledge of his being alive is presumed.

INNS AND ALEHOUSES. Inns are places of resort and accommodation for travellers; but every inn is not an alehouse, nor every alehouse an inn. If an inn uses the common selling of ale it is then an alehouse, and subject to the statutes concerning alehouses; and if an alehouse lodges or entertains travellers it is an inn.

The keeping an inn is a trade which is to be exercised for the public accommodation of travellers at all times; and the refusal of lodging or refreshment to a traveller or guest, upon tender of a reasonable sum, is indictable as a misdemeanor, or may subject the innkeeper to an action on the case for damages.

An innkeeper is liable for the goods of his guest, if lost during his stay in the inn, and moreover he is compellable to receive them; but he is not bound to keep them longer than his guest remains with him; and if he does receive them he is not responsible, for his profit ceases on the guest's departure.

But an innkeeper is not chargeable but upon some default or want of care in him or his servants; for if the goods are lost through the guest's own negligence, as by not availing himself of the means of safe custody afforded by his host, it would be unreasonable.

An innkeeper may limit his responsibility by express agreement or actual notice, which it will be incumbent on him to prove clearly, as, *primâ facie*, he is liable at law.

Innkeepers are to charge reasonable prices (in the strictest sense of the word) for their hay, oats, &c., without taking anything for litter, and this without regarding the prices of the markets, under the penalties of fine, at the discretion of the justices, for the first offence; a month's imprisonment for the second; and some punishment equivalent to pillory (now disused) for the third. Yet this is not to prevent the innkeeper charging a reasonable compensation to his guests for his trouble in attending and waiting upon them, and taking care of their property; indeed the regulations for hay, oats, &c., are based upon two very old statutes, and not meant to apply to charges for meat, and drink, and lodging. The remedy for overcharges being by indictment (upon conviction the landlord will be fined), or by action, a tender of a reasonable sum being first made.

A house of public entertainment where provisions and bed are furnished for all persons applying, is an inn.

The remedy which an innkeeper has beyond his action, (his right to which is not affected by any steps he takes to secure himself by his guest's horse or goods,) is by detaining the goods, horse, or even the person of his guest till he is paid his just reckoning. If an innkeeper give a guest credit, he loses his right of detaining his guest's horse or goods.

It seems now doubtful, notwithstanding an ancient authority, how far the innkeeper might detain the person of his guest.

If an innkeeper detains a horse, he may charge for the keep, and, if he eat out his head, he may sell him at a reasonable price, upon proper appraisement; but this rule does not extend to a chaise or other goods left by a traveller, or detained for charges; for the host will be liable in an action of trover to restore the value of the things left, *minus* his charge, and without any allowance for warehouse room, for which he has a distinct remedy by action against the owner.

A livery-stable keeper cannot detain a horse for his keep: he must sue his action against the owner upon the contract. If an agreement, mutual and acknowledged, on both sides can be shown, viz., that the horse was to remain till the keep was paid for, of course it would be otherwise; the law only giving this right to detention to innkeepers in their character of hosts.

By the 24 *G.* 2. *c.* 40. *s.* 12. (the tippling act), no person shall recover any debt on account of spirituous liquors, unless *bonâ fide* contracted at one time to the amount of 20*s.* or upwards. Therefore an innkeeper cannot recover charges for spirits, unless each item is for spirits furnished to the amount of 20*s.*, although forming items in a dinner bill: and where a bill of exchange is given in part for spirits furnished in small quantities (under 20*s.*), although the rest of the consideration is good, the innkeeper cannot recover.

If several persons meet at an inn or tavern, and dine there, without a special agreement with the innkeeper, each is liable for the whole expense of the dinner, unless the inn or tavern-keeper has previous notice that they came by invitation of others, in which case they are not liable for even their own share, for the credit was given to others. And in the case of a regimental mess, and a public dinner, each person is liable for his own share; for their manner of dining is notice to him who provides the dinner.

Where any part of an innkeeper's bill is for ale or beer, he must furnish the items; and, if he refuse, he is refused his remedy against his guest's goods. Innkeepers are also required by the licensing act (*s.* 19.) to use the standard measure in the sale of liquors.

Licensing Alehouses.—The licensing of alehouses is regulated by an act, 9 *G.* 4. *c.* 61., which enacts, that in every division and liberty, city, and town corporate, there shall be annually holden a special session of justices of the peace, to be called "the general annual licensing meeting," for the purpose of granting licences to persons keeping, or about to keep inns, alehouses, and victualling houses, to sell exciseable liquors by retail, to be consumed in such inns, &c.: such meetings to be holden, in Middlesex and Surrey, within the first ten days in March, and, in every other place, between the 20th of August and the 14th of September inclusive; of which meeting the justices at a petty sessions are to give twenty-one days notice to all innkeepers and applicants for licences, in addition to a notice thereof on the church door. At an adjournment of this meeting, which must be held in the said months, eight special sessions, at equidistant periods, are to be appointed for *transferring licences.*

Justices in any way concerned (except as trustees for strangers) as brewers or maltsters, &c., or as owners of any house licensed, or for which a license is sought, are prohibited from being present or interfering with such meetings, under a penalty of 100*l.*

Sheriffs' officers or bailiffs executing legal process cannot be licensed.

No licence for the sale of exciseable liquors by retail, to be drunk on the premises of the person licensed, is to be granted by the excise officer to any person not licensed to keep an inn, alehouse, and victualling house under this act. (But see the act licensing the sale of beer, tit. Ale and Beer.) And the penalty inflicted for a sale of exciseable liquors by retail, to be drunk on the premises, is 20*l.* to 25*l.*, on conviction before a single justice.

In the Ale and Beer Act, 1 *W.* 4. *c.* 51., regulations are imposed as to the sale of *ale and beer*, which are noticed under that title.

INNS OF COURT. Societies of law which are governed by masters and benchers, and of which all barristers are fellows, they being called to the bar by these societies, which are four in number, viz. the Inner Temple, the Middle Temple, Lincoln's Inn, and Gray's Inn. Subject to these are lesser inns, called

Inns of Chancery, which appertain to some of the inns of court, and are governed by principals, and ancients, or pensioners. They consist of attorneys, solicitors, and clerks in chancery. Clifford's Inn, Clement's Inn, and Lyon's Inn belong to the Inner Temple; New Inn to the Middle Temple: Furnival's Inn and Thavie's Inn (which has lost its exclusiveness,) to Lincoln's Inn; and Staple Inn and Barnard's Inn to Gray's Inn.

INNUENDO. A word formerly used in Latin pleadings, and now in the present English forms, to point out the person or thing meant; as to say "he," (*innuendo, i. e.,*) "*meaning* the plaintiff," did so and so, or such a thing was meant, when there was previous mention made of another person or thing. An *innuendo* will not enlarge the sense of words, or supply any thing where the words themselves are not slanderous or illegal. In slander and libel both the person and the scandalous words should be certain, and not want the *innuendo* to make them out or explain them, so that the jury may be convinced with what intent the words were spoken, without the assistance, and independent of the explanation, by an *innuendo*.

INQUEST. An inquiry by a jury of twelve men, impanelled by the sheriff, which is the means of trying or ascertaining any fact in a cause civil or criminal; but the term is usually confined to inquiries before grand juries, which consist of more than twelve and not exceeding twenty-four, and is always used on the queen's behalf in criminal, or presumed criminal, matters, offences, &c.; as the grand jury who are sworn at assizes, and sessions, and commissions of the peace, or *oyer* and *terminer*, to inquire into bills presented to them of indictment and other matters, which they may *present* or notify to the court, the coroner's jury, and the leet jury.

INQUISITION is the verdict of twelve men impanelled by the sheriff (a petty jury) to inquire of damages in civil actions, where the defendant has suffered judgment by default, and the damages are required to be assessed: also of various other matters, where the court requires a particular fact certified, or requires the sheriff to do certain acts in furtherance of its judgment; as to extend and appraise goods of outlaws, lands of debtors by *elegit* (which see); goods and lands of persons found indebted to the revenue, property of persons dying intestate, and without lawful heir, to which the crown is entitled by escheat, and in numerous other instances.

Inquisition is also synonymous with inquest, though the latter is more frequently applied to coroners', leet, and grand juries. See Jury.

INROLMENT. The registering or recording of any deed or recognisance, or other instrument, on the rolls of the court of chancery, queen's bench, or common pleas; which cannot be done till the deed is acknowledged by the party before a judge or master in chancery, or oath made of its due execution.

Memorials of deeds, judgments, and acts, concerning land or terms of years, exceeding twenty-one, in Middlesex and Yorkshire, are required to be inrolled.

Also, memorials of all grants of annuity are to be inrolled in chancery.

The certificate of inrolment, indorsed by the registering officer, is generally deemed good evidence of the inrolment.

INSOLVENT, in the general acceptation of the word, is a term applied to designate any one who is unable to perform his engagements with his creditors, and a declaration of this fact made by any trader so circumstanced, and published in the London Gazette, is an act of bankruptcy as will be seen on reference to that article; but in its more restricted and legal sense, it means, a person under actual imprisonment for any species of debt, *and for that only*, and who being unable to obtain his discharge, or (as is very often the case) is willing to yield up his estate to his creditors without preference or collusion, petitions the court for relief of insolvent debtors for his *discharge, i. e.* that his person may be freed, upon the performance of the conditions imposed by law.*

The insolvent laws, notwithstanding the multitudes subjected to their operation, seem to be but little understood; but the motives which actuated the legistature in passing and continuing the present Insolvent Act are plainly perceivable, and are forcibly illustrated by Mr. Cooke in his "Treatise upon the Law and Practice of the Court for Relief of Insolvent Debtors," in the following words:—"The legislature has wisely provided that unless fraud be proved against a debtor, his person shall not continue liable to the power of his creditors, when he shall have divested himself of all his property, and shall have satisfied a court of competent jurisdiction that he no longer possesses the means of discharging his debts. The legislature has guarded (as far as human foresight can do) against the possibility of using its benevolent provisions as instruments of fraud" (viz. by collusive or *friendly* arrests, concealment of property, fraudulent preference, &c.), or as the means of inflicting injuries upon creditors. If debts have been fraudulently, or even improvidently contracted, if property be concealed or fraudulently made away with, the offender is liable to be visited with the most serious consequences: punishments of various kinds await him; and, although he may eventually obtain the enlargement of his person, even then he is not relieved from the absolute necessity of paying his debts, should he *at any time* in after life obtain the means of discharging them. If creditors be watchful, and attentive to their own interests, they will find the laws sufficiently powerful to prevent and punish guilt, and to make them full satisfaction for the injuries they may have sustained. The future industry or good fortune of their debtor remains for ever

* The editor has thought it necessary to explain very fully the law and practice of insolvency to the unprofessional reader, as though the law of debtor and creditor will in all probability be altered, yet a compulsory *cessio bonorum* will be substituted for the arrest of the debtor's person; and that proceeding will be assimilated to the present Insolvent Act, which is in fact nothing else, only the *cession* is voluntary on the part of the debtor, and imprisonment must necessarily precede it.

subject to their just claims; and some hundreds of instances have occurred when the debts of persons discharged as insolvents have in consequence of the assiduity of the creditors, or the honesty of the parties themselves, been subsequently paid to the uttermost farthing."

The bankrupt laws only assist *traders* presumedly capable of affording a dividend upon their estates; but the insolvent laws, in their operation, relieve not only the trader, and even bankrupt whose imprisonment may be prolonged by the not obtaining his certificate, but also persons in every class of society, whether traders or not, or whether labouring under any legal disabilities or incapacities, as minors, married women, and persons of unsound mind.

The petition by an insolvent debtor is a voluntary act on his part: there is a compulsory insolvency which will be presently mentioned.

Another species of insolvency and mode of procuring a discharge from imprisonment is called "taking the benefit of the Lords' Act:" but the operation of this act is limited not to the description of person, for all debtors come under its provisions, but to the sum of 300*l.*; and, moreover, cannot be taken advantage of by the debtor but at particular times of the year, and after some previous imprisonment of an uncertain period; and is suspended during the continuance of the present insolvent act, as far as regards the right of the debtor to petition: yet, on the other hand, the creditor can by the process under this act compel, under the penalty of transportation upon refusal, an obstinate debtor to assign his property for the benefit of his creditors generally. This "compulsory" process, however, is not much used, it being like the debtor's process, only available at certain times of the year, and surrounded with technical difficulties, owing to the imperfect construction of the act. See LORDS' ACT.

The provisions of the present Insolvent Act, 7 *G.* 4. *c.* 57., are very numerous; more especially from their being assimilated to those of the bankrupt acts, in regard to the disposition of property passing to or recoverable by the assignees, fraudulent transfers, &c., in addition to those clauses which were rendered necessary to afford creditors summary assistance in recovering *future* property, the most formidable obstacle insolvent laws have to grapple with.

The subject of insolvency law, as administered under the present act, may be considered with reference to — 1. The constitution and practice of the court, and its mode of dealing with the debtor's *person;* the only gage the creditors have for his conformity with the act: 2. As to the distribution of his estate and means of recovering his future property.

1. "The Court for Relief of Insolvent Debtors" in England and Wales, is by the act declared to be a court of record, and, consequently, invested with the power of inflicting fine and imprisonment; consisting of a chief commissioner, and three other commissioners, who are barristers of at least ten years' standing. The principal officers of the court being the chief clerk and the *provisional assignee.* The court usually sits at the court-house, in Portugal Street, Lincoln's Inn Fields; and with the exception of the *long vacation,* wherein the commissioners may regulate their sittings, so as they do not adjourn longer than six weeks, they are required to sit *at least* twice a week throughout the year. The commissioners are also required *severally* to make circuits through England and Wales thrice a year, if necessary; the time and manner resting with themselves, subject to the approval of the secretary of state.

Petition of an Insolvent.—When any debtor is imprisoned for any species of debt, except a crown debt solely, he is at liberty within fourteen days after the commencement of his detainer in prison, to apply in a summary way by petition; which must state the time and place of his first arrest, and the time of his first and any subsequent commitment to prison, together with the names of his creditors at whose suit he is detained, with the amount of their debts, and whether he has before been insolvent or bankrupt; and, if the latter, whether he has or has not obtained his certificate. These facts are stated in a precise form, from which no material deviation is allowed. To this petition are annexed various official documents, verifying the facts stated, and also a paper signed by the debtor briefly setting forth in gross an account of all the real and personal property then in his possession or control: this is technically called an *estate paper*.

Should the insolvent not present his petition within the fourteen days, an application must be made to the court for leave so to do, which the court usually grants upon being satisfied that the delay was *reasonable*, *i. e.* that it arose by the insolvent's endeavouring to effect a compromise, or that he was too poor, or in other respects unable to comply with the rule: indeed, almost any statement upon affidavit which demonstrates that the delay was not for the purpose of making away with property, or creating an unnecessary expenditure, will suffice, but if the delay exceeds three calendar months, the court always requires very explicit and precise information as to the cause of delay, and the detaining creditor must have notice of the application in order that he may have an opportunity of detecting any error in the accounts the insolvent is on this occasion obliged to furnish in order to satisfy the court of the *reasonableness* of this further delay; and if the creditor can detect any error or mis-statement in the insolvent's application (which is either by motion of counsel, or by a petition subscribed by the insolvent, and read to the court by the chief clerk) it will not be entertained; as the object of these regulations is to prevent persons staying in prison, and thus gaining time to commit fraud and undue preference to favoured creditors, and certainly dissipating in prison that property which should be distributed among their creditors.

All persons may petition for their discharge; but they must be in actual imprisonment within the walls of some prison, not enjoying any rules or liberties, or even what are termed day-rules, and not *solely* charged at the suit of the crown (the court of exchequer alone having the power to discharge these debtors). Prisoners for actual contempt, or *for not performing certain acts* (not being payment of money); and persons confined under sentence of any court of criminal jurisdiction, no matter whether they are *also* detained for a debt; are unable to petition.

At the time of signing the petition, which is done in the presence of the provisional assignee, who attends in the prison for that purpose, the debtor assigns to him all his present and *future* property; and the provisional assignee thereupon takes possession of what is mentioned in the paper specifying generally what that is, and sells it, bringing the produce into court, in order that it should be paid to the assignees chosen by the court at the hearing, or by the creditors at a meeting; or if the insolvent should compound or abandon his petition, that it should be paid or restored to him. From this universal assignment necessaries and wearing apparel are excepted to the value of 20*l.*, and no more.

The act of signing the petition, and executing the assignment, is called "filing the petition," and is an act of bankruptcy, if the insolvent's creditors can or choose to avail themselves of it, which is sometimes done where the amount of debts and value of property will fairly warrant such a proceeding; especially, as the insolvent may abandon his petition at any stage, and, by compounding with those who actually detain him elude further detention at the suit of the less vigilant.

The Schedule.—The petition being filed, it is next requisite that the insolvent should within fourteen days after the *date* of his petition, or before the expiration of such further time as the court may think reasonable, file a *schedule* which is to contain, according to the terms of the act, "a full and fair description of the insolvent as to his or her name, trade, profession, last usual place of abode, and the places where he or she has resided during the time of contracting the debts specified therein; also, a full and true description of all debts due or growing due from the prisoner *at the time of filing* his or her petition; and of all persons to whom he or she is indebted, or who to his or her knowledge or belief claims to be his or her creditors, together with the nature and amount of such debts, and claims respectively, distinguishing such as shall be *admitted* from such as shall be *disputed* by the prisoner; and also a perfect account of all the estate and effects of the prisoner, real or personal in possession, reversion, remainder or expectancy, and of all places of benefit or advantage held by the prisoner; of all pensions or allowances; and of all rights and powers which shall in any way belong to the prisoner, with the names and abodes of the persons so indebted; and also the nature of the evidence by which such debts or claims may be proved, so far as the prisoner is able to set it forth:" *In* this schedule, to the whole of which the insolvent is sworn, and to the truth of which he makes oath at the time of his hearing, is contained a *special* balance sheet.

By the 70th section of this act, an insolvent wilfully and fraudulently omitting from his *schedule* (which comprises his special balance sheet), as finally (*i.e.* on hearing after the termination of the examination) sworn to by him any property *whatsoever*, or wilfully, or fraudulently retaining property beyond the amount of 20*l.* allowed by the act; and every person aiding and assisting in the fraud may be indicted for a misdemeanor, and if convicted may be imprisoned, and kept to hard labour for any period not exceeding three years. It matters not how *small* the amount may be: if it is above the 20*l.* allowed and accepted by the act, the offence is complete, and an indictment may *also* be preferred for the perjury.

The schedule being filed, which is done by the insolvent's attorney, the same being first carefully read over to, and signed by the insolvent, an order of the court is delivered to the insolvent's attorney, appointing a certain day for the insolvent to be heard upon the matters of his petition; and of which all creditors of the amount of 5*l.* are to have notice by a service or delivery, by post paid, of a copy of such order, if to creditors within ten miles of London, twenty-one clear days, if to creditors resident elsewhere twenty-five clear days previous to such day appointed for hearing: forms whereof, as they contain matter of practical information are here given, the first being an order for hearing in London; the second, for hearing on the circuit.

40,348.

Pursuant to the Act for the Relief of Insolvent Debtors in England.

The Court for Relief of Insolvent Debtors, —— on the *twenty-eighth* day of *July* 1835.

Upon the filing of the petition and schedule of *S. W., formerly of the cloisters, Windsor Castle, widow; then of Gloucester Place, King's Road, both in the town of Windsor and in the county of Berks, widow and boarding-house keeper; afterwards of No. 42. Upper Gower Street, Bedford Square, Middlesex, boarding-house keeper; then of No. 6. East Place, Walcot Place, Lambeth, and lastly of No. 24. Webb's County Terrace, New Kent Road, both in Surrey, widow; out of business*, a prisoner in the *King's Bench Prison*, in the *county* of *Surrey*.

It is ordered and appointed that the matters of the said petition and schedule shall be heard by the court at the court-house in Portugal Street, Lincoln's Inn Fields, on the *eighteenth* day of *September* next, at the hour of ten in the morning precisely; of which all creditors and persons claiming to be creditors of the said insolvent for the sum of five pounds, or more, shall have notice, by service of a copy of this order, made within such time and in such manner as is prescribed by the rule of court in that behalf.

By the Court.

Take Notice.

1. If any creditor intends to oppose the said prisoner's discharge, notice of such intention must be given by entry thereof in the proper page and column of the book kept for that purpose at the office of the court, between the hours of ten in the forenoon and four in the afternoon, three clear days before the day of hearing above-mentioned, exclusive of Sunday, and exclusive both of the days of entering such notice and of the said day of hearing. Notice to produce at the hearing any books or papers filed with the schedule must be given to the officer having the custody thereof, within the same hours on any day previous to the said day of hearing.

N. B. Entrance to the office in Portugal Street.

2. The petition and schedule, and all books, papers, and writings filed therewith, will be produced by the proper officer for inspection and examination on Mondays, Wednesdays, and Fridays, until the last day for entering opposition inclusive, on this notice being exhibited:— and copies of the petition and schedule, or such, part thereof as shall be required, will be provided by the proper officer according to the act 7 *G.* 4. *c.* 57. *s.* 76.

3. Opposition at the hearing can only be made by the creditor in person, or by counsel appearing for him.

41,239.

Pursuant to the Act for the Relief of Insolvent Debtors in England.

The Court for Relief of Insolvent Debtors, —— on the *twenty-seventh* day of *January*, 1836.

Upon the filing of the petition and schedule of *F. P. formerly of Sheffield and late, of Doncaster, both in the West Riding of the county of York, Surgeon*, a prisoner in the gaol *of York Castle*, in the *county* of *York*.

It is ordered and appointed that the matters of the said petition and schedule shall be heard by William John Law, esquire, or one other of her majesty's commissioners for the relief of insolvent debtors proceeding on his circuit, at the court-house, at *Wakefield*, in the said county, on the twenty-fifth day of February next, at the hour of ten in the morning precisely; of which all creditors, and persons claiming to be creditors of the said insolvent for the sum of five pounds or more, shall have notice by service of a copy of this order, made within such time and in such manner as is prescribed by the rule of court in that behalf. It is likewise ordered that the said prisoner shall, within ten days after the issuing hereof, cause the duplicate of the said petition and schedule, and all books, papers, and writings relating thereto in his possession or power, to be lodged with the clerk of the peace, at his office, at *Wakefield*, in the said county.

By the Court.

TAKE NOTICE.

1. If any creditor intends to oppose the said prisoner's discharge, notice of such intention must be given to the said prisoner in writing, three clear days before the day of hearing above-mentioned, exclusive of Sunday, and exclusive both of the day of giving such notice and of the said day of hearing.

2. The petition and schedule will be produced by the proper officer for inspection and examination at the office of the court in London, on Mondays, Wednesdays, and Fridays, between the hours of ten and four, on this notice being exhibited:—and copies of the petition and schedule, or such part thereof as shall be required, will be provided by the proper officer according to the act *7 G. 4. c. 57. s. 76.*

N. B. Entrance to the office in Portugal Street, Lincoln's Inn Fields.

3. The duplicate of the petition and schedule, and all books, papers, and writings filed therewith, will be produced by the said clerk of the peace, for inspection and examination, at his office above-mentioned; and copies of the petition and schedule, or such part thereof as shall be required, will be provided according to the act 7 *G. 4. c. 57. s. 77.*

In all cases notice is given in the London Gazette; and, if the insolvent is to be heard in the country, or if the *last* residence of the insolvent was in some county or place, except in London, Middlesex, and Surrey, an advertisement must be inserted in some provincial newspaper, most usually circulated in the county or place where the hearing is to take place, or, in the latter case, in the neighbourhood of such last usual place of residence.

The Hearing.—Should a creditor think proper to oppose the insolvent's discharge, he may (having given previous notice to the insolvent according to the instructions at the foot of the notice which is served upon him) make his opposition either by himself in person, or by a barrister who is instructed by some attorney. The court, in admitting evidence, hold themselves bound by the same rules of law in that respect, as the superior courts, with some trifling exceptions arising out of the constitution of the court; and that in some cases, distant creditors need not personally appear, but may send affidavits, an advantage an insolvent does not possess in regard to his defence.

In giving their judgment the commissioners consider the charges of impropriety in contracting debts, or other conduct injurious to creditors; which have been urged against the insolvent; which charges, Mr. Cooke in his treatise observes, are distinguished by the act into two classes.—1. Those which affect *the whole body* of creditors. 2. Those which affect only *individual* creditors.

The first class comprehends the act by an insolvent of having *fraudulently, and with intent to conceal* the state of his affairs or *to defeat the objects of the act,* destroyed or otherwise wilfully prevented, or purposely withheld the production of any books, papers, or writings, relating to such of his affairs as are subject to investigation under this act; or kept, or caused to be kept, false books; or made false entries in, or withheld entries from, or wilfully altered or falsified any such books, papers, or writings; or if the insolvent has *fraudulently, with intent of diminishing the sum* to be divided among his creditors, or of giving an *undue preference* to any of his creditors, discharged or concealed any debt due *to or from* him, or made away with, mortgaged, or concealed any part of his property, either before or after his imprisonment; in both these cases, the court or commissioner may adjudge the insolvent to be discharged out of custody, and entitled to the benefit of the act, so soon as he shall be in custody at the suit of *some one or more* of his creditors for any period not exceeding, in the whole, three years.

The second class of cases which are considered to affect *individual* creditors, are stated concisely by Mr. Cooke to be as follows:—That he has contracted the debt of the opposing creditor fraudulently; or by false pretences; or by breach of trust; or without having had any reasonable or probable expectation at the time when the debt was contracted, of paying the same; or shall have fraudulently, or by false pretences, obtained the forbearance of a debt; or shall have put the opposing creditor to any unnecessary expense, by a frivolous or vexatious defence or delay to any suit for recovering a debt; or shall be indebted for damages on account of criminal conversation with opposing creditor's wife; seduction, malicious prosecution, libel or slander; or any injury, wrong, or trespass, which may appear to the court to have been maliciously effected. In all these cases, the court is empowered to order the discharge of the prisoner, when, or so soon as the prisoner shall be in custody at the suit *of the opposing creditor*, for any period not exceeding two years, which is to be computed, as in the last instance, from the date of the insolvent's petition.

If the insolvent is not opposed, the court inquires into the matters of his petition and schedule for the purpose of ascertaining that he is duly entitled to avail himself of the provisions of the act; and if the answers are not satisfactory, or the facts are not sufficiently explained, has power to *adjourn* the hearing of the insolvent till the conscience of the court is satisfied, or pronounces him entitled to his discharge forthwith, or at the expiration of any time not exceeding three years from the date of filing the petition; or it may exercise its discretion, as by dismissing the order for hearing, *i. e.* ordering the insolvent not only to be brought up again, but to give fresh notices to all his creditors; or by dismissing his petition, in effect, compelling him to apply *de novo* for his discharge, if the court will, on his future application, permit him so to do.

When the court adjudges or declares that the insolvent shall not be discharged forthwith, but at the expiration of some future period, he is liable to be detained in prison, at the suit of some creditor, in pursuance of the terms of the adjudication until such expiration shall arrive; and in practice, such creditor detains him, if his debt is 20*l.*; otherwise the insolvent may, and frequently does, compound with his first or other detaining creditor, and obtains his discharge; for after the time specified in the adjudication has elapsed, he cannot be retaken, although he may not have remained in custody a day subsequent to the adjudication. So where an insolvent is ordered to be detained at the suit of particular or individual creditors, it is incumbent upon such creditors to lodge detainers against the insolvent, if they have not so done before; it being an erroneous notion that a *remand* by the judgment of this court operates as a criminal punishmemt for an offence. The judgment which the court is empowered to give only states, "that the insolvent shall not be entitled to his discharge until he shall have been in custody *at the suit* of individual creditors [*naming them*], or at the suit of some one or more of his creditors, for the space of ———," &c.; thereby leaving it a matter of consideration for the individual creditor, or the general body of creditors, to accept a composition; or for each of the creditors at large who have not detained him, to proceed in separate suits in the ordinary manner to judgment and execution, which they may do at any time before the period specified by the court arrives; and if at large, take him and confine him for the remainder of the time which shall not have elapsed, to be calculated from the date of the petition; for, after the lapse of the period specified in the adjudication, the insolvent's person is absolutely discharged.

The effect of a discharge under this act, is to perpetually free the insolvent's person from arrest, on account of any debt or costs arising upon any debt contained in the schedule; and if a discharged insolvent is arrested, he is at liberty to apply summarily to a judge at chambers, who is *bound* to release the insolvent on his entering a common appearance; and to order such costs to be paid by the arresting creditor as he shall think fit. The insolvent, also, is in like manner, absolutely protected from any new contract into which he may have entered for the payment of a debt mentioned in his schedule. The object of this provision is to protect insolvents from undue importunities by rapacious creditors, who may by this device obtain a preference over other creditors; for it must always be borne in mind that the *future* property of the insolvent is as much the property of his creditors as the property he surrenders, subject to his maintenance and ordinary engagements.

The law discountenances the application for relief, if the debtor shall have been previously discharged under this or any other insolvent act, or having been a bankrupt, shall not have obtained his certificate within five years; and, therefore, it is incumbent upon any debtor petitioning for relief under these circumstances, to be prepared with the consent of three fourths in number and value of his creditors, or to prove that he has by industry and frugality endeavoured to pay all just demands; that he has incurred no unnecessary debts, and that his insolvency has arisen from misfortune alone: and the court is very particular in requiring accounts respecting his subsequent transactions, in order to ascertain how far the insolvent's case is within the object and spirit of this provision.

II. The practice of the appointment of an assignee or assignees of an insolvent's estate, when none are appointed before the hearing (which is seldom done), is declared by the following rules of court: viz.

"They may be appointed by the court or commissioner at the hearing.

"They may be appointed by the court, if approved after nomination.

"1. By the justices in Wales, or Berwick-upon-Tweed, at the hearing by them.

"2. By a majority in value of creditors, whose debts shall be admitted in the schedule.

"3. By a majority in value of creditors who shall meet in pursuance of such notice given by advertisement or otherwise, as shall be in each case directed by the court or the proper officer for that purpose.

"When the court has decided that a party shall be removed from the office of assignee, a new assignee not being as yet appointed, the creditor or creditors may proceed to a choice of new assignees, as above pointed out.

"Persons so nominated, as aforesaid, may apply to be appointed assignees by petition to be filed at the office of the court; the nomination of and acceptances by such persons, together with all notices, proceedings, and necessary signatures, being duly proved by affidavit: every such person must also state by affidavit, whether he has been appointed in any other case, and, if so, whether he has filed his account in such case.

"No person can be appointed who is not a creditor:—and no person will be appointed, who, as assignee in any other case, has failed in any of the duties required of him; nor will any female be appointed.

"That the provisional assignee shall, in every case of a prisoner who has petitioned the court and duly executed a conveyance and assignment to the said provisional assignee, sell all goods, chattels, and personal estate of such prisoner of which the said provisional assignee shall take possession according to the statute; and out of the proceeds thereof shall defray in the first place all such costs and expenses of taking possession of and selling the same as shall be allowed by the court; and shall account for the produce of such sale to the court.

"That in every case to be heard by a commissioner on circuit, in which there shall have been any property in the possession or under the control of the prisoner to be given up to the provisional assignee, there shall be obtained and produced at the hearing, a certificate from the provisional assignee, or other sufficient voucher, that such property has been duly given up or accounted for."

The property which passes to the provisional assignee, and consequently to the subsequently appointed assignees, is precisely the same as in bankruptcy, with the exception that the *future* property passes to the assignees, placing the insolvent in precisely the same condition as a bankrupt who has not paid 15*s*. in the pound upon his second bankruptcy, or bankruptcy after a previous composition.

Therefore the act has invested the court with powers of sequestering benefices or curacies, and to recommend that a portion of the salary of officers in the army or navy, or East India Company's service, or government officials, should be paid to the assignee for the benefit of the creditors; but this does not extend to the pensions of widows, or of persons who have not been actually employed.

The court also are invested with ample powers for the seizure and appropriation of property, of whatever kind or nature, and particularly reserve to themselves a discretion in the sale of any estate or interest which has been claimed or taken possession of by the assignee.

In all other cases respecting the property, or reputed property of the insolvent, subject, however, to the immediate control of the court, the assignees may generally be governed by the provisions of the Bankrupt Act, and rules in bankruptcy, as detailed under the title BANKRUPT.

It must, however, be noticed, that if an insolvent is possessed of a lease, and his assignees or the landlord refuse to take it, he will be liable to the future rent and performance of the covenants.

No warrant of attorney or cognovit, although the various rules provided by the act regulating these securities have been complied with, can be acted upon for the benefit of the holder, at any time after the imprisonment of the insolvent, which imprisonment is termed the "act of insolvency," with the same meaning and intent, and with relation to the same acts which are influenced by an "act of bankruptcy."

It scarcely need be added, that all fraudulent preferences and conveyances by an insolvent are equally voidable with those committed by a bankrupt. See also WARRANTS OF ATTORNEY.

The future Property of the Insolvent.—The course that is taken to secure the future property of a discharged insolvent, is by requiring the insolvent to confess a judgment at the suit of the provisional assignee for the amount, and for the purpose of securing the debts named in the schedule; upon which, previous leave of the court being first obtained, execution may be issued and levied, if the ability to pay such debts or any part thereof be apparent. In any application that is made to the court for this purpose, the insolvent has notice, and is at liberty to show that the extent of his subsequently acquired property is not more than sufficient to maintain himself and family, and (as Mr. Cooke continues) to carry on his business without reducing him to the necessity of again contracting debts which would subject him to arrest; or any equitable or special matter may be shown to the court, who never use this power of causing execution to be issued, but in cases where a surplus evidently is available for the benefit of the creditors, without interfering with the claims of those, who *bonâ fide* have lent money, or are otherwise entitled to be satisfied out of such subsequently acquired property.

The court also has a special jurisdiction in respect to the seizure of immovable property, and of such a nature that it cannot be taken in execution by process of law, and will on a similar application take possession thereof. The application of a creditor, and the counter statement of the discharged insolvent must always be supported by the most conclusive and satisfactory affidavits.

Dividend.—The mode of dividing the insolvent's estate is a very simple process, as full instructions are given in the printed form of acceptance of the assignment, which is signed by the assignee on his appointment, and printed forms which may be filled up without professional assistance, can be purchased at a law stationer's, opposite the court-house. The primary duties of an assignee, being to file an account of his receipts and expenditures, verified by affidavit (the form of which may be bought as before) within three calendar months; and if he have received or expended nothing, still a statement upon oath must be made, certifying that fact. The form of a productive account is required to be in the following form:—

An Account of all Monies received and paid by C. D., Assignee of the Estate of A. B., an Insolvent Debtor, to the Day of 1837, *inclusive.*

1837	Dr.	£	s.	d.	1837	Cr.	£	s.	d.
	By cash, received of provisional assignee					To paid Mr. A. B., solicitor, his costs as annexed			
	By cash, received from sale of ——					To paid auctioneer his expenses on sale of——, as by bill and receipt annexed			
	By cash, received from debtor to insolvent, No. —— in schedule					To paid E. F., as by receipt annexed, for ——			
						To paid G. H.			
						To do. I. K.			
						Balance due to estate			
	Total £					Total £			
	Balance in hand £								

This is the account referred to in the affidavit of C. D. sworn before me this —— day of —— 1837.

FORM OF AFFIDAVIT TO BE MADE BY ASSIGNEE.

In the Court for Relief of Insolvent Debtors.

In the matter of the petition of A. B., late of , in the county of an insolvent debtor, who hath been discharged from the custody of the keeper of her majesty's gaol of , in the county of , under and by virtue of an act of parliament made and passed for the relief of insolvent debtors in England.

C. D. of in the county of , assignee of the estate and effects of the said insolvent, maketh oath and saith, [that the account hereunto annexed contains a fair and just account of all monies received by this deponent as assignee of the estate of the said insolvent, and of all payments made in respect thereof, and that all payments in the said account charged are truly and *bonâ fide* made and paid by this deponent.*]

Sworn at ——, in the county of ——, this — day of ——, 1837, Before me } C. D.
G. H. a commissioner.

The assignee is required to give a notice of dividend to his fellow creditors by an advertisement, the form of which can be purchased, which form also gives ample directions for the publication of such advertisement, thirty days before the making the dividend in the Gazette, and in a newspaper which circulates in the neighbourhood of the insolvent's last place of abode, previous to his imprisonment. The court expects that assignees *themselves* shall perform these ordinary duties, which they have taken care shall be sufficiently specified and explained in the printed forms published under their directions; but in cases where legal assistance is *absolutely* necessary, there the assignees are allowed to debit the estate with reasonable costs, *but not otherwise.*

If the insolvent's estate, whether given up to the assignees on his imprisonment, or realised out of future property, renders 20*s.* in the pound, after all charges of the assignees; or if the insolvent compounds, or in any way satisfies all his creditors; the warrant of attorney which he gave on his adjudication may be cancelled, and the re-assignment must be executed by the assignees of all the insolvent's estate and effects; and they are bound to deliver up to him (which can be enforced in a summary manner by application to the court upon affidavit) all surplus or property of his, remaining in their hands.

Notwithstanding the discharge of an insolvent, whether in the first instance, or even after a remand at the suit of any creditors, the court still has a power reserved to it, to *rehear* the insolvent; upon which *rehearing* the former discharge may be revoked, and, consequently, the insolvent remanded to his former custody. This power is only exerted in cases where the discharge was obtained by fraud or false evidence, or where property was concealed by the insolvent.

A rehearing may also be applied for by the assignee (and none but him) for the purpose of compelling the insolvent to make out and adjust his accounts, manage his affairs, and do any reasonable and proper act for facilitating the getting in and arrangement of his property; this course is only necessary where the schedule is not sufficiently explicit, or the insolvent refuses reasonable assistance to the assignee in winding up his affairs.

If an insolvent is lunatic, or of unsound mind, after a certificate to that effect from one or more justices of the peace, and on the petition

* If the account is unproductive, state *that no money hath been received by this deponent as assignee of the estate of the said insolvent.*

of any person on the behalf of the insolvent, to apply to the court for his discharge, upon which the court will grant a day for hearing, at which time the creditors can oppose the lunatic's discharge, by showing that his case does not come within the meaning of the act; but the soundness or unsoundness of the insolvent's mind cannot be gone into, and the question of fraud or criminality cannot be agitated; for, after the commissioners have inquired whether the arrest was *bonâ fide* made, &c., and examined witnesses concerning the property, they are bound to discharge him.

The property of a lunatic thus discharged, is divisible amongst the creditors in the ordinary manner.

INSTALMENT. The giving possession of an ecclesiastical dignity, and is correlative to a rector or vicar's induction to a benefice.

It also signifies the payment, or the time appointed for payment, of different portions of a sum of money.

INSTANCE COURT, is a technical or practical name given to the court of admiralty, which has jurisdiction in respect to private rights or private injuries, connected with maritime transactions at sea. See ADMIRALTY.

INSTANTER. Instantly, forthwith.

INSTITUTION, is a writing or *faculty* made by the bishop, whereby a clergyman is approved to be inducted to a rectory or parsonage; *i.e.*, the bishop, having upon examination found the *clerk* presented capable of the benefice, admits and *institutes* him. On such institution, the clerk or clergyman, who is then called the *parson*, has a right to enter on the parsonage-house and glebe, and to take the tithes, but he cannot grant, let, or do any act to charge them till he is *inducted* into the living. By the institution he is only admitted to pray and preach, and upon formal induction he is entitled to the freehold and profits of the rectory or cure. See INDUCTION.

Taking a reward for institution incurs a forfeiture of double value of one year's profit of the benefice, and makes the living void.

INSURANCE or ASSURANCE, is an agreement or contract of indemnity, whereby a person, who is termed the *insurer* or *underwriter*, in consideration of a specified sum, denominated a *premium*, undertakes to secure another, who is called the *assured*, from certain risks or perils (*i. e.* casualties) to which he is or may be exposed. This contract is termed a *policy;* and as it is only signed by the insurer or insurers, who subscribe their names and the amount for which they become liable, they are usually distinguished as *underwriters.* There are but three companies or public societies in London who *underwrite* policies of insurance, but any person or number of persons may be insurers without restriction.

Marine Insurance, is the term used for the insurance on ships, goods, &c., and the freight and hire of ships; and, incidental to this insurance, *bottomry* and *respondentia* are insurable, if expressed in the policy, unless by usage of the trade otherwise understood: *Fire insurance*, houses, warehouses, and goods therein from fire: *Life insurance*, for the assuring the payment of a particular sum to another on the death of an individual, or to the executors or assignees of that individual on his own decease.

In marine insurance, the policy may be effected in the name of any person who has an interest in the thing insured: and trustees and consignees may insure while the ship is on her passage. But insurance on seamen's wages, money payable to a captain out of freight, on the property of enemies, and upon slaves, or in any respect relating to the slave trade, are void and illegal.

Policies in marine insurance are either valued or open; valued, *i. e.* where a *value* has been set upon the goods or ships insured: this value is the prime cost at the time of effecting the policy: this amount, therefore, is considered as *agreed*, or as proved. An open policy is where the value is not mentioned: the standard for ascertaining the value of the goods is the invoice price at the port of lading, together with the premium on insurance and commission.

A policy must be made out within three days after the insurance is effected, under a penalty of 100*l*. These contracts are negotiated and arranged by brokers or agents, who for a certain *per centage* obtain the signature or subscription of one or more underwriters, who frequent a room in the Royal Exchange, called Lloyd's Coffee House, where all matters relating to individual insurance are adjusted. The three companies who insure transact their affairs in their own offices. Their (or at least two of their) insurances are *sealed;* but, though this formality is recognised at law, yet in commercial usage those that are signed by individuals are of the same credit.

Policies cannot be altered after signature, unless it can be shown by some *written* document that the intent of the parties was mistaken, or unless the *consent* to such alteration can be clearly shown.

Law and usage jointly require that in a policy be expressed, 1st. The name of the person insured, or the name or firm of one or more of the parties interested, or the consignor or consignee, or of the person receiving the order for, or effecting, or giving directions to effect, the same. 2d. The names of the ship and master, unless the insurance be general, or any ship or ships. 3dly. Whether the assurance be made upon ships or goods. 4thly. The place at which the goods are laden, and to which they are bound. It is advisable, though not absolutely requisite, to state the places at which the ship may touch. 5thly. The commencement and determination of the risk. On the goods it usually begins from the lading on board, and continues till the landing; on the ship, from her beginning to lade at the port of lading, and continues till she arrives at the port of destination, and be there moored in safety twenty-four hours. 6thly. The various "perils" or casualties against or to cover which the insurance is effected. These "perils" are comprehensively enough stated in the policy, the form of which is very ancient. "Lost or not lost" means, that even though it turn out that the ship was lost at the time of the insurance, yet that the insurer shall be liable if no fraud. 7thly. The premium. 8thly. The precise date, *i. e. day of the month*, and *year*. Lastly, the proper stamp must be impressed.

Policies, being contracts of great credit, are construed liberally, and for the benefit of the party assured; and doubtful expressions will be referred to the practice of the trade, the law regarding commercial usage and custom in the construction of a policy.

Every assurance on alien property by a British subject must be understood with this implied exception, that it shall not extend to cover any loss happening during hostilities between the countries of the assured and assurer.

The conditions in a policy are termed *warranties*, and are, like all other contracts, express or implied. The latter assume in this transaction that the ship is seaworthy; and, indeed, any fact, the nonperformance of which would amount to a fraud. The former warranties which are *express* are of great importance, as upon their *literal* and strict performance the validity of the policy as a beneficial contract depends. A warranty, therefore, is a separate condition or contingency that a certain thing shall be done or happen, and, unless that is performed, the contract is not valid; it is immaterial for what end the warranty is inserted in the contract, but, being inserted, it becomes a binding condition upon the insured, and he must show a literal compliance with it: the law making a distinction, not readily discernible at first sight, between an express *warranty* and a *representation;* for, if the *substance* of a representation be performed, the contract is effective, *i.e.* if the representation turn out not to be false in a material point; but a warranty must be complied with strictly, no matter whether the non-compliance is of moral consequence or not: for instance, if a warranty is to sail on or before a certain day, and the ship be prevented from unmooring by stress of weather, although quite ready in other respects to sail, yet the policy will be invalid, on account of this involuntary non-compliance.

But in order to make warranties binding as warranties they must be in the policy, not annexed to or wafered; for then they are but representations, which demand not such a strict compliance.

A warranty "to depart" before a certain day, which is used by the Royal Exchange Assurance Company in their policies, does not mean merely to break ground, but fairly to set forward upon the voyage.

The obligation to depart with *convoy* is a warranty imposed by act of parliament, or by the express terms of the policy; therefore if from any cause, no matter what, the ship depart without *convoy*, the underwriters are not responsible.

But an unforeseen separation from convoy is a *peril* to which the underwriters are liable.

Neutrality is a warranty that the ship and goods insured are neutral property. If this warranty be not complied with, the policy is absolutely, and from the beginning, void for fraud; but if the ship be neutral at the time of the commencement of the risk, the underwriter takes upon himself the chance of war and peace during the continuance of the policy.

The remedy which the insured has against the insurer is an action at law; and even if the parties, by a clause in the policy, should agree to refer any dispute to arbitration, that will not be a sufficient bar to an action at law, unless a *reference* is in fact made or really depending. Courts of equity have no jurisdiction to compel payment; the demand being provable by witnesses, as any other species of damage arising on contract. Separate actions brought against underwriters are *consolidated*, *i. e.* the proceedings in all but one action are stayed, and the others abiding the event of the action upon which the insured proceeds to trial. The insured, in case of loss, having a separate demand, can of course bring separate actions, though he cannot continue them: he can, consequently, choose to bring his action against any one underwriter, who must call on his brother insurers for *contribution*, *i. e.* to pay their proportion.

The questions of partial and total *loss* being considered under the titles Abandonment and Average, it is sufficient to notice in this place that the loss must always be a direct and immediate consequence of the peril insured, and not a remote one, in order to entitle the assured to recover.

The general rule being, as to "perils of the sea," that every accident happening by the force of wind or waves, by thunder and lightning, by driving against rocks, or by the stranding of the ship, or any other violence that human caution could not provide against, or human strength resist, is to be considered as a "peril of the sea," and for such losses the underwriter or insurer is liable, legal decisions have rather extended than narrowed the principle, by laying it down that all losses *immediately* arising from the perils of the sea, such as wind and waves, are to be compensated by the insurers, although the *remote* cause was negligence of the master or crew, or of other persons. A ship which is never heard of after her departure is presumed to have perished at sea. In England no time seems absolutely fixed within which payment may be demanded from the underwriter, in case the ship is not heard of: but a practice prevails among merchants, that a ship shall be deemed lost, if not heard of within six months after her departure for any part of Europe, or within twelve months, if for a greater distance. This latter term, however, seems short with respect to India voyages, and is extended in Spain to a year and a half, and formerly in France to two years; and in case of an adjustment of such supposed loss, if the ship arrives, the underwriter may recover back the money paid by him. (*Park on Insurance.*)

A *capture* is a loss, and is a taking of the ship or goods belonging to the subjects of this country by those of another, when in a state of public war; and, if retaken, the underwriter must pay salvage, and indeed all loss or expenses sustained in consequence, such as a compromise. The salvage payable to a recaptor is from one eighth to one half of the value. But it is unlawful to ransom ships or goods which shall be captured by the subjects of any state at war with her majesty, or by any persons committing hostilities against her subjects, under a penalty of 500*l.*

A *detention* by foreign powers is also a loss, which the insurers must make good as a *total* loss; but, notwithstanding, all costs are recoverable from the insurers arising from a partial or limited detention (although the object of such detention be only to search for enemies' goods, &c.): yet any detaining for non-payment of customs, or any violation of the law of nations, shall not be made good; but, with this exception, the general principle is that all charges consequent upon a detention are to be borne by the underwriters.

The underwriters expressly, by the terms of the policy, undertake the risk arising from the barratry, or *wilful misconduct*, of the master or crew. See BARRATRY.

The contribution called general average, or average loss, falls also upon the insurer, but petty average does not. See AVERAGE.

Having drawn the reader's attention to those circumstances or risks against which the policy mainly provides, and to those losses for which the insurer is liable, it remains only to notice what it is incumbent upon the assured to bear in mind in respect to the preservation of his assurance, and its validity.

Policies are annulled by any fraud or undue concealment of facts, either by the insurer or the assured.

Several cases have determined that the policy shall be void where goods, &c., are insured as the property of an ally, or as *neutral* property, when, in fact, they are the goods of an enemy: and such false assertions in a policy will vitiate the contract, though the loss happen in a mode not affected by that falsity.

Concealment of circumstances vitiates all contracts of insurance, as the underwriter relies upon the insured for all necessary information; and must trust to him that he will conceal nothing, so as to make him form a wrong estimate: but there are many matters as to which the insured may be innocently silent: 1st, As to what the insurer knows, however he came by the knowledge; 2d, As to what he ought to know; 3d, As to what lessens the risk; and here it may be remarked, that an underwriter is bound to no political perils, as to the state of war or peace: he also ought to be acquainted with the nature and danger of every voyage, which may be called natural perils: if he insure a privateer, it is understood that he is not to be informed of its destination. In short, the question, in cases of concealment, must always be, "whether there was, under all the circumstances, at the time the policy was underwritten, a fair statement or concealment; fraudulent, if designed, or, if not designed, varying *materially* the object of the policy, and changing the risk understood to be run.

A *representation*, we have already found, is not embodied, nor does it form part of the policy as a *warranty* does; therefore, if the assured represent facts which, though not true, do not *materially* affect the terms or the risk of the policy, he will be entitled to the benefit of it; but if he make a representation *materially* varying the object of the policy, even through mistake, the policy is invalidated; for if one represent facts without knowing them to be true, he takes the risk upon himself. If a warranty is not literally correct, or is not performed according to the strictest interpretation, inasmuch as such warranty forms part of the policy, and is expressed on the face of it, its falsity or breach of performance, whether material or immaterial, practicable or impracticable, nullifies the transaction, whether negotiated by the merchant or his broker.

The concealment of any circumstances or facts must be of something having a positive existence, not founded on a mere speculation or expectation of the assured.

As the object of inserting the name of the vessel or master is for the preventing a substituted vessel being palmed upon the insurers for the one actually insured, such substitution, or similar act, would be deemed a fraud upon the insurers; so the goods insured cannot, without permission from the insurers, or by the express allowance of the policy, be removed from one ship to another, or without an *unavoidable necessity*, under which every thing possible must be done for the benefit of all parties concerned: nor can what is termed a *deviation* take place without express allowance by the terms of the policy, or by *absolute necessity*, which, except in the cases of absolute warranty, before noticed, excuses the assured.

Deviation is understood to mean a voluntary departure, without necessity or any reasonable cause, from the regular and usual course of the specific voyage insured: whenever this happens, the voyage is determined, and the insurers are discharged from any responsibility; because the ship goes upon a different voyage from that which the insurer undertook to indemnify. And it is not material in this case whether the loss be or be not an actual consequence of the deviation; for the insurers are in no case answerable for a subsequent loss, in whatever place it happen, or to whatever cause it may be attributed: neither does it make any difference whether the assured was or was not consenting to the deviation. If, therefore, the master of a vessel put into a port not usual, or stay an unusual time, it is a deviation ; and if the *deviation* be but for a single night, or for an hour, it is fatal : but if a merchant ship carry *letters of marque* she may *chase* an enemy, though she may not *cruise* without being deemed guilty of a deviation. But wherever the deviation is occasioned by absolute necessity, as where the crew force the captain or master to deviate (a barratry), the insurers continue liable. The justifications for a deviation seem to be these : to repair the vessel, to avoid an impending storm, to escape from an enemy, or to seek for convoy.

In all cases of deviation, it may be laid down as a general rule, that wherever a ship does that which is for the general benefit of all parties concerned, the act is as much within the spirit of the policy as if it had been expressed : and, in order to say whether a deviation be justifiable or not, it will be proper to attend to the motives, end, and consequence of the act, as the true ground of judgment ; but to avoid as much as possible any additional risk in case of a deviation from necessity, the ship must pursue such *voyage of necessity*, in the direct course, and in the shortest time possible, as nothing more must be done than the necessity requires, otherwise the underwriters will be discharged.

If a ship mean to go to more than one of the places named in a policy, she must visit them in the order in which they stand in such policy.

A deviation *merely intended*, but never carried into effect, does not discharge the insurers ; and whatever loss happens before actual deviation, or the dividing point of the voyage, falls upon the underwriters. But if it can be shown that the parties never intended to sail upon the voyage insured, if all the ship's papers be made out from a different place from that described in the policy, the insurer is discharged, though the loss should happen before the dividing point of the two voyages.

Seaworthiness.—This is a warranty, whether expressed or implied; and it is incumbent upon the assured to know how far the ship is able to perform the voyage or not, *at the time of the insurance effected*, for a latent defect unknown to all parties will vitiate the policy. But if the decay, to which the loss of the ship is attributable, occur at a period subsequent to the date of the policy, the insurers or underwriters are liable, though the loss take place a few days after her departure.

Unless underwriters call for particular information upon the subject, it is not incumbent upon the assured to disclose every minute matter of which the seaworthiness is supposed to consist, or relative thereto ; but if special information is required, there the assured is bound to disclose all that has come to his knowledge : the principle being, that an assured is not bound, without request, to state every special circumstance, even though it would enhance the premium if disclosed : it seems sufficient that general facts are stated, into which the insurers may inquire, and, thereupon, either require special information or decline the policy.

The assured cannot in any case recover unless the ship be fully equipped ; consequently, if no pilot be on board, the insurers are exonerated.

Gambling policies, or, as they were commercially termed, "interest or no interest," are void by statute. By the terms of the statute forbidding such insurances, it seems to be incumbent upon every assured *to prove* his interest, whether it be disputed or not, else he will not recover. In fact, any policy which has for its object to make gain, rather than indemnify the assurer from an actual loss, is within the strict rule of the statute. Where property has been insured to a larger amount than the real value, the overplus premium shall be returned, or the assured can only claim to the real extent of his loss.

Where a *double* assurance is effected (*i. e.* where the same man is to receive two sums instead of one, or the same sum twice over, by reason of his having made *two* insurances on the same property), it is not void, but is simply considered as made by the assured to increase his security; for the assured shall only receive *one* satisfaction to the real amount of his loss, and no more, which he may recover from which set of underwriters he pleases; and with respect to the underwriters themselves, they, in their turn, after payment, may call upon the other underwriters to contribute in proportion to the sums they have insured.

Valued policies do not come under the description of wager policies. *Valued* policies originate from the circumstance of its being sometimes troublesome for the assured to prove the exact amount or *value* of his interest, or to ascertain the extent of his loss: the assured, in this case, gives the insurer a higher premium to agree to estimate his interest at a sum certain. Therefore, if the assured is able to prove some interest, he need not prove the full value. But, if such a policy could be shown to have been used as a cover for wagering or gambling, then it would come under the rule with respect to such policies, and be voided accordingly.

In an action on a valued policy, effected by double assurance, it is no defence to prove that the assured has received the amount of one policy from the underwriters of that policy; for, if the assured can show that the goods or ship insured were equal in value to the sums upon *both* insurances, he will be entitled to recover.

Insurances may be effected upon profits, whether real or imaginary, so that the thing upon which the profit is to accrue be in existence. The word "profits" is sufficient description. A mariner cannot insure his wages, but a master, it seems, may; and several interests may be included in one policy, by specifying the number or the nature of such interests.

Insurances made on prohibited voyages, or upon goods, the importation or exportation of which is prohibited, are void, and the underwriter may retain the premium, whether he was aware of the fact or not; for no court of law or equity can substantiate an illegal contract.

Reassurance, a contract, which the first underwriter or set of underwriters enter into, in order to relieve or indemnify themselves from the risks attendant upon the first or original assurance, is prohibited by the laws of this country, though allowed in other countries. The statute, however, excepts reassurances, if the original underwriters should be insolvent, bankrupt, or dead; and it must be stated in such policy that it is a reassurance, so careful is the legislature to confine beneficial contracts to the principles upon which they were originally established.

The return of premium by the underwriters to the assured, in case the policy is vacated by reason of any act done by the assured, or by breach of the terms or warranties of the policy, is sometimes a matter upon which the courts of law (courts of equity act more as arbitrators in this contract) find a difficulty in coming to a decision. The broadest rule laid down with respect to return of premium is, that, if the underwriter has been guilty of fraud, an action lies against him to recover the premium: on the other hand, if the fraud be on the part of the assured, and is notoriously gross and palpable, the courts of law will order that the underwriter retain the premium. In equity, where the underwriters have claimed relief on account of fraud, it has been decreed that the premium shall be returned. The great question being, in cases of *fraudulent* insurance, where the underwriter has *run no risk*, whether he shall be liable to return the premium. The courts, indeed, have laid down two or three rules, but they are subject to the finding of an express commercial usage by the jury; and the question of return of premium is clearly a commercial matter, and depends upon mercantile custom. However, in all cases of gross fraud and illegal assurances, the underwriter may retain the premium. *Morally* speaking, and the editor believes that it is in accordance with merchant law, where the underwriter's risk has not commenced, a return of premium can be called for reasonably. After the commencement of the risk, upon an infraction of the terms of the policy, the underwriter may retain.

INSURANCE UPON LIFE, is a contract by which the insurers, for a certain sum, proportioned to the age, health, and profession of the person whose life is the subject of the insurance, engage that, if that person die within a time limited in the policy, they will pay a sum of money to the executors or administrators of the person himself (if he effects the insurance), or to those in whose favour the policy is granted.

These contracts have been found to be attended with so many advantages, to persons whose incomes might otherwise determine with their own lives or those of others, that many companies have been incorporated and subsist for this purpose.

To avoid the iniquitous gambling which had begun to take place upon this as well as on other insurances, the stat. 14 *G.* 3. *c.* 48. provides, that "no insurance shall be made on the life or lives of any person or persons, wherein the person for whose use the policy is made shall have no interest, or by way of gaming or wagering, but such insurance shall be null and void." And in order more effectually to guard against any imposition or fraud, and to be the better able to ascertain what the interest of the person entitled to the benefit of the insurance really is, it is further enacted, by the same statute, "that it shall not be lawful to make any policy or policies on the life or lives of any person or persons, or other event or events, without inserting in such policy or policies the person's name interested therein, or for whose use or benefit, or on whose account, such policy is so made or underwritten. And that in all cases where the insured has an interest in such life or lives, event or events, no greater sum shall be recovered or received from the insurer than the amount or value of the interest of the insured in such life or other event."

A creditor has such an interest in the life of his debtor, that he may insure it and recover upon the policy, provided that the debt be in its nature and essence legal, *i. e.*, not a gambling debt, &c.; and provided that the debt be unpaid at the death of the party whose life is insured. A pecuniary or *money* interest is also necessary; for, where a father insured the life of his son in which he had no such interest, the policy was held void. But a wife making an insurance on her husband's life, need not prove that she was interested therein.

In a life insurance, the insurers undertake to answer for all those accidents to which the life of man is exposed (except suicide or the hands of justice.* The death must happen within the time limited by the policy, otherwise the insurers are discharged; but where a party whose life was insured went to sea, and the ship in which he sailed had not been heard of, in an action on the policy, it was necessarily a question peculiarly for the jury to decide whether, from the circumstances, the party might not be presumed to have died within the time limited by the policy.

To prevent disputes, it is usual to insert in the policy words limiting the continuance of the policy to 12 o'clock at night of the day of the month on which the policy bears date; as, "from the day of the date" would exclude the day on which the policy bears date.

Fraud equally vitiates policies on lives, as it does those in marine insurances. But where there is a warranty that the party is in good health, it is sufficient that he is in a reasonable good state of health. And even, if the party whose life was insured, laboured under any particular infirmity, if it be proved by medical men that, in their judgment, it did not contribute to his death, the warranty of health has been fully complied with, and the insurers are liable.

Insurance against fire, is a contract by which the insurers undertake, in consideration of the premium, to indemnify the party insuring, against *all* losses which he may sustain in his house or goods, by means of fire, within the time limited in the policy. The rules by which the insurance companies are established by their own managers, and a copy given to every person at the time he insures, or printed at the back of the policy, so that by the party's acquiescence, he submits and accedes to their proposals, and is fully apprized of their rules, upon the strict compliance or non-compliance with which he will or will not be entitled to an indemnity.

Most insurance companies insert clauses in their proposals, by which they declare that they will not hold themselves liable for any damage by fire, occasioned by any *invasion, foreign enemy, military or usurped power, or civil commotion* whatever. Under this proviso, it has been held that the insurers are not liable to satisfy losses occasioned by rioters or mobs.

When a loss happens (and these losses are generally considered as *total losses*), the party insuring is bound in all cases to give immediate notice of the loss, and make a declaration in the nature of an oath before a magistrate of the district in which the loss happened; and in such declaration, as in the account or statement delivered to the insurers, give as particular an account of the value, &c., as the nature of the case will admit. He is generally required to produce a certificate of the minister and churchwardens as to his character, and their belief of the loss sustained, and the truth of what he advances, the doing which is a condition precedent to the right of the assured to recover on the policy; and if the minister, &c., wrongfully refuse to sign the certificate, the party insuring, is without remedy, so that every *assured* should carefully inspect and consider the *proposals* before he pays the premium, as he may be, by such stipulations, practically deprived of

* When an assured commits a felony for which he is afterwards executed, his representatives are precluded from claiming payment, as, by the general policy of the law, the insurance became void in consequence of his own criminal act: so it seems the policy would become void in case an assured commits suicide, and a verdict is returned of *felo de se*. Some insurance offices undertake to indemnify against these risks; and some specially except or otherwise notice them.

the advantage of his insurance. Some insurance offices are more strict than others in this respect.

In these insurances against fire, the offices expressly undertake to allow all reasonable charges attending the removal of goods in case of fire, and to pay the assured's loss, whether the goods are destroyed, lost, or damaged. See ABANDONMENT.

These policies are not in their nature transferable, without the consent of the office, contrary to what has been expressly determined in the case of marine insurance. It is provided, however, that when any person dies, the interest shall remain to his heirs, executors, or administrators respectively, to whom the property, the subject of insurance, belongs, if they will procure their right to be indorsed on the policy, or the premium be paid in their name.

It is necessary that the assured should have an interest or property in the house or goods insured, at the time the policy is made out, *and at the time the fire happens;* and, therefore, after the lease of the house is expired, the insured's assigning the policy does not oblige the insurers to make good the loss to the assigned.

A duty is payable to government upon the insurances, except those upon public hospitals; and persons signing policies not duly stamped, are subjected to a penalty, and the policy vitiated, unless a penalty of 5*l.* be paid over and above the unpaid duties. The same principles as to fraud and the return of premium, apply to cases of insurance against fire as to other contracts of insurance.

A party insured is not precluded from bringing his action against the insurers in the first instance, in case of refusal to pay a loss, by reason of the usual clause in the proposals requiring an arbitration. A demand of payment ought, in prudence, to be made before suit.

Marine Insurance: — Form of Policy.

IN THE NAME OF GOD, AMEN.— W. P. Litt and Bushby, or as agents, as well in their own name, as for and in the name and names of all and every other person or persons to whom the same doth, may, or shall appertain in part or in all, doth make assurance, and cause themselves and them, and every of them, to be insured, lost or not lost, at and from *Burin to any port or ports, place or places of trade on the coast of Africa, during the ship's stay, and trade there; and until her arrival back to any port or ports of the United Kingdom, with liberty to touch, stay, trade and barter at all ports and places whatsoever and wheresoever, backwards and forwards on the coast of Africa, and for any purpose whatsoever, and including all risk of craft to and from the ship,* upon any kind of goods and merchandises, and also upon the body, tackle, apparel, ordnance, munition, artillery, boat, and other furniture, of and in the good ship or vessel called the *Wilberforce,* whereof is master under God, for this present voyage, *Thomas Jones,* or whosoever else shall go for master in the said ship, or by whatsoever other name or names the same ship or the master thereof, is or shall be named or called; beginning the adventure upon the said goods and merchandises, from the loading thereof aboard the said ship, [*as above*] upon the said ship, &c., and so shall continue and endure, during her abode there, upon the said ship, &c. And further, until the said ship, with all her ordnance, tackle, apparel, &c., and goods and merchandises whatsoever, shall be arrived at [*as above*], upon the said ship, &c., until she hath moored at anchor twenty-four hours in good safety; and upon the goods and merchandises, until the same be there discharged and safely landed. And it shall be lawful for the said ship, &c., in this voyage, to proceed and sail to, and touch and stay at, any ports or places whatsoever, *and wheresoever, with leave to discharge, unload, reload, sell, and barter (all or either) goods and property upon the said coast of Africa and African Islands, and with any vessel, boat, or boats, factories, and canoes, in port or at sea, and to transfer interest from this to any other vessel or vessels, or from any other vessel or vessels to this vessel, all or any in port, or at sea, or any port or places she may call at and proceed to without being considered any deviation* without prejudice to this insurance. The said ship, &c., goods and merchandises, &c., for so much as concerns the assured, by agreement between the assured and assurers in this policy, are and shall be valued at [*as under*].

Touching the adventures and perils which we the assurers are contented to bear, and do take upon us in this voyage; they are of the seas, men of war, fire, enemies, pirates, rovers, thieves, jettisons, letters of mart and countermart, surprisals, takings at sea, arrests, restraints, and detainments of all kings, princes, and people, of what nation, condition, or quality soever, barratry of the master and mariners, and of all other perils, losses, and misfortunes that have or shall come to the hurt, detriment, or damage of the said goods and merchandises, and ship, &c., or any part thereof. And in case of any loss or misfortune, it shall be lawful to the assured, their factors, servants and assigns, to sue, labour, and travel for, in and about the defence, safeguard and recovery of the said goods, and merchandises, and ship, &c., or any part thereof, without prejudice to this insurance; to the charges whereof, we the assurers will contribute, each one according to the rate and quantity of his sum herein assured. And it is agreed by us, the insurers, that this writing or policy of assurance shall be of as much force and effect as the surest writing or policy of insurance heretofore made in Lombard Street, or in the Royal Exchange, or elsewhere in London. And so we, the assurers are contented, and do hereby promise and bind ourselves, each one for his own part, our heirs, executors, and goods to the assured, their executors, administrators, and assigns, for the true performance of the premises, confessing ourselves paid the consideration due unto us for this assurance, by the assured, at and after the rate of *six guineas per cent.*

In witness whereof, we the assurers have subscribed our names and sums assured in London.

N. B. — Corn, fish, salt, fruit, flour and seeds, are warranted free from average unless general, or the ship be stranded; sugar, tobacco, hemp, flax, hides, and skins are warranted free from average, under five pounds per cent., and all other goods; also the ship and freight are warranted free of average under three pounds per cent. unless general, or the ship be stranded.

On cargo valued at 6,000*l.*

		£	
(Underwriters' names.)	Jacob Adams,	2,000.	12 June, 1837.
	T. Williams,	2,000.	13 June, 1837.
	Walter Peake,	2,000.	13 June, 1837.

Obs. If the name of the broker, effecting the policy of insurance, be inserted in the policy as *agent* generally, without saying *for whom*, it is a sufficient compliance with the statutes which require the names of the parties interested to be inserted in the policy.

Form of Policy upon the Life of another for Years.

Term *seven years.*

	£	*s.*	*d.*	
Number 8596.				
Sum insured,	1	13	2	annual premium.
100*l.*	1	0	0	stamp.
	£ 2	13	2	

*** No receipts are to be taken for premiums of insurance but those printed, signed by three of the directors, issued from the office in London, and witnessed by the clerk or agent to whom the money is paid.

This Instrument, or Policy of Insurance, witnesseth that whereas A. B. of —— in the county of —— gentleman, has paid the sum of one pound thirteen shillings and twopence of lawful money of Great Britain, into the capital joint stock of the Westminster society for insurance of lives and survivorships, and for granting annuities; and has agreed to pay or cause to be paid into the capital joint stock of the said society, at their office in the city of Westminster, on the twenty-eighth day of July in every subsequent year, during the continuance of this policy, the like yearly sum of one pound, thirteen shillings, and twopence, for *insurance of the life of C. D.* of —— in the county of —— gentleman, now warranted in good health, and not exceeding the age of twenty-seven years, and of the description set forth in a certificate or declaration signed by the said A. B., and dated the twenty-eighth day of July instant, and lodged with the said society. And whereas the said A. B. has signed a declaration of his acceptance of the said joint stock as his security for the said insurance; Now know ye, that from the date of these presents, and in case the said A. B., his executors, administrators, or assigns, do, and shall during the continuance of this policy, pay, or cause to be paid, the said yearly sum of 1*l.* 13*s.* 2*d.* at the times and place aforesaid, the stock and fund of the said society shall be subject and liable to pay unto the said A. B., his executors, administrators, or assigns, the sum of 100*l.* of lawful money of Great Britain within three calendar months after good and sufficient proof shall be made upon oath, or otherwise, as shall be required to the [reasonable] satisfaction of the said society, of the death of the said *C. D., should such death happen on or before twelve o'clock at night of the twenty-eighth day of July, in the year of our Lord* 1838: provided that if the said C. D. shall at any time or times before the expiration of this policy depart beyond the limits of Europe, or shall die upon the seas (except during peace in passing from Dover to Calais or Boulogne, and returning from Calais or Boulogne to Dover; or from any part of the United Kingdom to any other part thereof, in vessels fitted up for carrying passengers) or enter into or engage in any military or naval service whatsoever; or if the declaration above-mentioned contains any untrue averment; that then, and in every such case, this policy and every thing herein contained shall cease, determine, and be void and of none effect; in witness whereof, we (three of the directors of the said society), have hereunto set our hands and seals this twenty-eighth day of July, in the year of our Lord one thousand eight hundred and thirty-one.

Signed, sealed, &c. E. F. (the place of the seal).
G. H. (the place of the seal).
J. K. (the place of the seal).

Obs. This form with trifling variations will apply to a policy on the life of the assured himself, and by simply expressing that the premium is paid "for insurance of the life *of him the said A. B.*"

INTENDMENT OF LAW. The understanding, intention, and true meaning of law; and by which judges ought to give judgment.

Intendment will sometimes supply that which is not fully expressed or apparent, and when a thing is doubtful in some cases *intendment* may make it out; also many things will be intended after verdict in a cause, to make a good judgment: but intendment cannot supply the want of certainty in a charge in an indictment for any crime, &c. Sometimes a thing is necessarily *intended* by what follows or precedes it; and where an indifferent construction may have two intendments, the general rule is to take it most strongly against the plaintiff.

The intent of parties in deeds, contracts, &c., is much regarded by the law, though it cannot take effect against the direct rules of law.

Usury will not be intended unless expressly found by the jury. Fraud also will not be presumed in law unless expressly averred. So every rector is presumed to be resident on his benefice until the contrary be proved.

INTENDMENT OF CRIMES. The law generally does not punish *intendments* or intentions to do ill, if the intent be not executed, except in case of treason, where intention proved by circumstances shall be punished as if put in execution.

The intent is a material ingredient in an offence; indeed, in respect of most offences the *intent* must be stated in the indictment, and consequently proved; *i. e.* such circumstances must be adduced which demonstrate that the prisoner could have no other object in view than the commission of the felonious act: in burglary for instance, the *intent* is stated "to steal, take, and carry away," or do any other act in itself felonious; and if the evidence do not warrant the conclusion that the party broke open the house with the particular intent as *laid* or stated in the indictment, an acquittal must take place. For instance, where the intent *laid* was to kill a horse (a felonious act), and the intent proved was merely to lame him (a misdemeanor), in order to prevent him from running a race, the party was acquitted. Intent is the essence or main ingredient of particular offences. So an apparent crime may upon explanation turn out to be but a mere trespass.

It is the intention of force and violence which makes riots criminal; the law inferring or *intending* that every man contemplates the probable consequences of his own act; as, if the intention is only to beat a person and the party kill him, he is punishable for the murder or manslaughter, whichever it happens to be.

INTENT or INTENTION. The words of deeds, &c., are construed according to the meaning of the parties, and not otherwise; but the law does not in conveyances or deeds under seal, which are made with due consideration, imply intents not very apparent upon the face of them; though in wills a milder course is pursued, and property bequeathed will pass by intendment or implication.

In every contract the intent is the thing to be considered; and if by unforeseen accident, or other means not arising from the party himself, the agreement cannot be performed according to the words, yet the party must perform it as near to the intent as he may.

Common usage and reputation frequently govern the subject-matter of an agreement, and direct the intention of the parties; yet in equity, which follows the law, the intent is not to be pursued against law: as if a man settles a term of years (which is a chattel, and consequently a personalty,) upon another and his *heirs*, yet it shall go to the executor.

In an act of parliament the intention appearing in the preamble, controls the letter of the law.

INTERCOMMONING, is where the commons of two manors lie together, and the inhabitants of both have time out of mind depastured their cattle promiscuously in each.

INTEREST. A legal term applied to any inferior estate in land, or connected with it as a lease, or mortgage; it is mentioned in contradistinction to "estate" which is significative of the entirety. It is a redundancy of expression to repeat in deeds "all the estate, right, title, *interest*, claim, &c.," as the greater interest would of course include the lesser.

INTEREST OF MONEY. The profit on loans of money, which is always recoverable on bonds, bills, and notes, and upon express promises made for that purpose, or where such a promise can be implied from the custom or usage of the parties, or trade; but does not attach upon money lent or paid, or upon the balance of an account stated, or ordinary debts; and chancery will not allow interest on book debts, unless upon debts which are by law liable to interest, although it will on purchase money not paid at the appointed time, on stated accounts, and in many other cases; and executors and trustees are also chargeable in equity on witholding money, or calling it in unadvisedly when out on good security. The question of interest being allowed or not, is generally raised in carrying devises and trusts for payment of debts into execution, and passing executors' accounts in chancery or equity side of the exchequer.

Interest is also payable on legacies charged or payable out of land or funded property, because land yields an immediate profit, and so do the funds; but if a legacy is charged on personal estate, which cannot be immediately got in, it shall only carry interest from the end of the year after the testator's death.

"Lawful interest" is *5l. per cent., per annum*, and in England cannot exceed that limit.

The act 3 & 4 *W.* 4. *c.* 42. provides that upon all debts or sums certain, the jury on a trial, or inquiry, may allow interest at 5 *per cent.*, from the time when the sum was payable, or from the time of demand and notice in writing that the interest will be required. Therefore a creditor, to avail himself of the provisions of the act in respect of his book debt, should either obtain an express contract for interest, or give a written notice as soon as the debt is payable, requiring the prospective payment of such interest.

Such demand of interest may be made in the following form:—

" Sir,

" You being indebted to me in 48*l.* 2*s.* 6*d.* for groceries sold you as per account delivered, I beg to inform you of my claim and demand of lawful interest upon the same at 5*l.* per cent. from this day until your payment of the above debt.

" Sir, your obedient Servant,
" JAMES SCHOFIELD."

INTEREST upon Interest, or Compound Interest, is when the interest instead of being paid, is added to the principal sum, and becomes an increased capital bearing interest. This is not allowed by law, though it can be practised without infringing any statute, by renewing the bond or instrument, and comprising the whole in it, or by lending the interest separately. See Usury.

INTERPLEADER is the trying a point incidentally happening, before the principal cause can be determined; and occurs where two or more persons claim the thing in dispute, of a third party in whose hands it is, but who claims no interest, and desires to be relieved by way of indemnity at the hands of a court of law or equity, which will adjudge to whom the thing belongs; as if I am a stakeholder, or depositary of property, and two persons severally claim this of me, I can interplead, *i. e.* call upon the court to adjudge to whom the money shall be paid, or goods delivered. Till very lately, relief in these cases could only be had by applying to the courts of equity; but a late statute has facilitated the adjudication of disputed rights, where the party sued or fearing suit has no interest, but is merely stakeholder, depositary, trustee, or sheriff levying goods, the property wherein is disputed, warehouseman, wharfinger, &c., by directing an issue to be tried, just the same as if an action had been commenced, which puts the fact of the ownership before a jury in the same manner as upon the trial of any other cause.

INTERROGATORIES. Particular questions in writing, to which witnesses are to give answers singly, as they are read over to them. These interrogatories are administered by commissioners, or officers named by the court out of which they issue. As the court of chancery and equity side of the exchequer proceed chiefly by deposition, this proceeding is more common there than in the courts of law, which only use them to examine *witnesses* abroad, sick, aged, &c., and on a few other occasions. Interrogatories administered by courts of equity are presented in writing, and answered by an answer in writing, called "an examination," the truth of which is sworn to; the object generally being the development of accounts, in which the *parties to the suit* are examined: a course of proceeding peculiar to the courts of equity, for at law plaintiffs or defendants are never examined.

INVENTORY. A list, containing a true description together with the values of goods and chattels, made on various occasions, as on the sale of goods, or transfer of movables for pecuniary consideration; sometimes it signifies a mere list of things taken or seized, as an inventory taken on a distress for rent. Inventories generally state for what purpose they are made, so that they are not unfrequently evidences of title, when actual possession of the things inventoried accompanies the inventory. Inventories are also in common parlance termed *appraisements*, when a gross sum is named by the appraiser as the total value; a very imperfect mode of information, as the appraiser's valuation is not governed by the intrinsic value of the things appraised, and the single values are omitted. See APPRAISEMENT.

By the 21 *H.* 8. *c.* 5., an executor or administrator is bound to make an inventory of the deceased's *personal* estate and effects, in the presence of two creditors, or legatees, or next of kin, or in their absence of two other honest persons (there is generally no necessity for an appraiser); and to cause it to be delivered to the ordinary (*i. e.* the bishop or archdeacon having jurisdiction to prove the will,) upon oath, who is under a penalty of 10*l.* not to refuse it: a transcript of it must be kept by the executor, &c. It should be fairly written, and must contain a perfect description and estimate of *all* the deceased's personal estate, distinguishing the debts as good, bad, or doubtful.

In practice however, executors or administrators do not according to the tenor of their oath and bond on taking out administration, exhibit their inventory within the six months, or till cited, or warned so to do; a very improvident act, and often exposing the executor to the effect of a presumption the law entertains in this case, viz., that the executor has enough to pay all debts and legacies, which presumption he may have to repel at his own cost.

Any two credible persons of sufficient capacity may make the inventory or appraisement, which it should be noticed is required to contain an account of the property as it was at the deceased's death, and not as it was at the date of the inventory.

If there be goods to the amount of 5*l.* in any other diocese or jurisdiction, there should be a separate inventory for each.

A stamp duty is payable upon the inventory or appraisement.

The inventory and appraisement may be made in the following form:—

" A true and perfect inventory of all the goods, chattels, wares, and merchandises, and all other the personal estate and effects of A. B., late of the parish of —— in the county of ——, and in the diocese of ——, yeoman, deceased, made by us whose names are hereunder written, the —— day of —— 1837.

	£	s.	d.
The money of the deceased in his house - - - -			
The money at the bankers - - - - . -			
His wearing apparel - - - - - -			
One bay mare - - - - - -			
Six cart horses - - - - - -			
Cattle, viz. (enumerating them) - - - -			
Wool - - - - - - - -			
Swine and poultry - - - - - - -			
Standing corn and growing crops, at the time of his decease viz. ——— - - - - - -			
Corn in stack, and in the granary - - - -			
Hay - - - - - - - -			
Malt - - - - - - - - -			
Farming implements, viz. - - - - - -			
Plate, household goods, china, linen, and furniture - -			
A lease of two cottages and an outhouse - - -			

A lease of the Great Hill Field, for 21 years from 1835, 107 acres, at £ —— *per annum* - - - -			
Ale and liquors - - - - - -			
Stock in the funds, £69 Long Annuity - - -			
Debts due to the deceased, viz. (specify same) - -	1678	17	6
Debts believed to be irrecoverable (to be deducted) - -	457	14	3
	£		

	£.	s.	d.
Deduct debts owing by deceased, at his death, and since paid, (viz.) - - - -			
A. B., butcher, for meat - - -			
C. D. apothecary, for medicine - -			
Rent and taxes due in respect of land -			
Debts not yet paid: (*viz.*			
E. F., tailor - - - - - -			
G. H., carpenter - - - - -			
Undertakers' bill - - - - -			

"ABRAHAM BROWN.
THOMAS WILSON." Total balance £

IPSO FACTO, *by the very act.* This expression is used where any forfeiture or invalidity is incurred; and the meaning of it is, that it shall not be necessary to declare such forfeiture or invalidity in a court of law, but that by *the very doing of the act* prohibited the penalty shall be thereby instantly and completely incurred. When a condition is broken the estate is said to be *ipso facto* void, *i. e.*, the defect is irremediable, unless cured by confirmation or waiver. See VOID.

ISSUE is taken for children born in wedlock; and in that sense is applied to the issue of a marriage, as children to be begotten between A. and B. his wife particularly named, or by A. with any other woman.

It also signifies the profits of lands or tenements.

It is also used to signify the point of matter. When in the course of pleading the parties in a cause come to a point, which is affirmed on one side and denied on the other, they are then said to be *at issue*.

Issue is also a term applied to the sum levied, which the sheriff is directed to take by a writ of *distringas*, in order to compel the appearance of a party in court.

JOINT STOCK COMPANIES. See COMPANY.

JOINT TENANTS. An estate in joint tenancy is where two or more persons hold by grant or will from another any lands or tenements, or even personalty. As such possession can never arise by means of descent or by other operation of law, it follows that the creation of a joint tenancy can only arise by the act of the parties themselves, as by will, deed, &c.; and this object is effected by merely giving or granting the estate to a number of persons and their heirs or executors, without adding any words restricting or explaining the grant: for, as the grantor has united their names, so the law gives them a union in respect of possession.

The essential difference between joint tenants and tenants in common, is, that joint tenants have the lands by one *joint* title, and in one right, and tenants in common by *several* titles, or by one title and *several* rights.

The essential requisites of *a joint tenancy* are, that the parties must have, 1st, one and the same interest; 2dly, an unity of title; 3dly, there must also be an unity of time at the commencement of their estates; and, 4thly, an unity of possession.

There is a peculiar and important incident to this estate, that the right, upon the death of one of the parties, increases or accumulates, or, as the law terms it, *survives* to the longer liver; and this, with an exception in respect to the queen, and a corporation, who cannot be joint tenants with others is the distinguishing principle governing this species of right. For if lands or interests in land are devised or given to A. B. and C., or more, the survivor of them will ultimately take the whole.

A joint-tenancy may be dissolved by act of the parties, as by their making a voluntary partition or allotment between themselves; or they may destroy any one of the requisites before noticed by selling their interest, which will turn the joint tenancy into a tenancy in common; and by law a compulsory partition can be enforced, so that this inconvenient and uncertain possession is not of very frequent occurrence, or in practice, of very long duration.

Under the Reform Act joint tenants may *each* vote in respect of the same property, if of sufficient value.

This estate may exist in goods and chattels, and its incident of *survivorship* applies; but where parties take at different times, or any act is done to divide the possession, there the parties take as tenants in common and have several interests.

The rule of survivorship however by merchant law, recognised by the common law, does not permit the surviving partner in trade to take his deceased partner's share of stock or debts; though, with respect to the liabilities of the partnership, the deceased partner's executor is not at *law* liable.

An estate in joint tenancy in old books is sometimes styled an *estate in jointure;* but the word "jointure" applies in ordinary construction to that joint-tenancy which was formerly created on a marriage settlement of lands, because the husband and wife *jointly* occupied.

JOINTURE. See Married Women.

JUDGES. Chief magistrates appointed by the queen to try civil and criminal causes and punish offences. The usual number of the judges of the law was twelve, but it has varied, and at present there are sixteen. A late statute having empowered the queen to appoint an additional *puisne* judge in each court, they are thus: the Lord Chief Justices of the courts of queen's bench and common pleas; the Lord Chief Baron; the four puisne (*i. e.* younger or inferior) judges of the two former courts; and the four puisne barons of the latter: but no more than four sit on the bench together, one of the puisne judges or barons sitting at his chambers to decide on ordinary matters of practice.

To these may be added the judges in equity, the lord chancellor, master of the rolls, and vice chancellor; as also

The ecclesiastical judges, judge of the admiralty court, judges of the court of bankruptcy, and the judges of the insolvent court.

The chief justice of the queen's bench has the title of *Lord* while he hold his office, his title being "Lord Chief Justice of England."

The chief justice of the common pleas has also the title of Lord whilst he is in office, and is called Lord Chief Justice of the Common Pleas. The chief justices are installed or placed on the bench by the lord chancellor; and the other judges by the lord chancellor, and the lord chief justices.

Besides the lords chief justices, and the other judges of the courts at Westminster, there are many other justices commissioned by the queen to execute the laws: as justices of assize, of *nisi prius*, *oyer*, and *terminer*, justices of the peace, &c.

The judges of the court of queen's bench are sovereign justices of *oyer* and *terminer*, gaol delivery, conservators of the peace, and sovereign coroners of the land.

JUDGMENT. The sentence of the law pronounced by the court or awarded by the judges.

In civil cases, Judgments are said to be of four sorts: 1st, where the facts are admitted by the parties, but the law arising from the pleadings is disputed, and consequently determined by the judges, this is termed judgment on demurrer; 2dly, where only the facts are disputed, as in judgment upon verdict; 3dly, where the defendant admits the law and facts as laid in the declaration: this occurs in judgments by *confession* or *default*, or in judgments *acknowledged for debts;* 4thly, where the plaintiff abandons his suit either at the last or at any previous proceeding, whereby the defendant has what is termed judgment of *nonsuit* or *non pros.*

These judgments are not delivered in court, except the judgment upon demurrer; but as all judgments are rather the consequence and determination of law, they are merely entered by the proper officer, technically *signed* at a convenient time after verdict or nonsuit, and immediately upon default, confession, non pros., and demurrer. The time that is allowed for entering or signing the judgment after verdict or nonsuit, is for the purpose of giving the party time to move for a new trial, or in arrest of judgment to make any proper application to the judges in full court, on the law or merits of the case.

In many cases upon *default of pleading*, judgments consequent thereon, are what are termed interlocutory or *incomplete*, whereby the right of the plaintiff is indeed established, but the precise amount of damages is not ascertained, as it is supposed to be in actions of debt, brought for a certain and precise demand; therefore the assistance of a jury is requisite, which is obtained by what is termed a *writ of inquiry;* a process which directs the sheriff of the county to inform the court above, by the oath of twelve men, what damages the plaintiff hath sustained, the sheriff sitting as judge, and trying by a jury subject to the same law and conditions as a judge of the superior courts sitting for the purpose of trying causes, or, as it is termed, "nisi prius;" and, after the verdict has been returned, the judgment is entered or signed in the court from whence the writ of inquiry issued, being that in which the action commenced; and, thus, the interlocutory judgment is made *final* or complete. All other judgments not interlocutory may be termed *final*, that is complete, and such whereupon execution may forthwith issue.

Judgments acknowledged for debts, are noticed under the title WARRANTS OF ATTORNEY and COGNOVITS.

If there is any error apparent upon the judgment as it appears upon the records of the court (every judgment is, or ought to be, entered at full length upon a long scroll of parchment, in a fair hand) a writ of error may be brought, or the party may move in arrest of judgment; but these proceedings, generally speaking, can only be had in respect of material objections, not in respect of mere clerical errors. In some cases the unsuccessful defendant may move for judgment (*i. e. that judgment may be entered for him*), non obstante veredicto (*notwithstanding the verdict*). These applications to the court arise from the matters of *law* arising upon the pleadings alone; matters concerning the *merits* of an action being the subject of a *motion for a new trial.*

In criminal cases. When upon a capital charge, the jury have brought in their verdict *guilty*, in the presence of the prisoner, he is either immediately, or at a convenient time soon after, asked by the court if he has any thing to offer why judgment should not be awarded against him. And in case the defendant be found guilty of a misdemeanor (the trial of which may happen in his absence, after he has once appeared, *i. e.* put in bail and pleaded), a *capias* is issued to bring him in to receive his judgment; and if he absconds he may be prosecuted even to outlawry. But whenever he appears in person, upon either a capital or inferior conviction, he may at this period, as well as at his arraignment, offer any exceptions to the indictment, in arrest or stay of judgment; as for want of sufficient certainty in setting forth either the person, the time (when essentially necessary), or the offence; and if the objections be valid the whole proceedings shall be set aside; but the party may be indicted again. If these objections are found untenable the court must pronounce that judgment which the law has annexed to the crime; some being capital, some consisting in transportation or imprisonment; and both sometimes extend to forfeiture of lands either absolutely or during life, and of moveable property absolutely, and create various disabilities; and some are merely pecuniary, by stated or discretionary fines; and lastly, there are others which are deemed ignominious, as whipping if a male, imprisonment in a house of correction *and* hard labour, and any punishment inflicted in cases of perjury.

With respect to the giving judgment for offences adjudged capital, which was formerly passed, whether intended to be put in execution or not, a statute passed in 1824, authorises the court to abstain passing the sentence of death upon offenders whom it shall think proper objects for mercy, except in cases of murder; and in the place thereof, order the judgment to be recorded in the usual form, the effect of this judgment having the same effect as if the judgment or sentence were actually pronounced and the party reprieved.

JUDGMENT BY NIL DICIT. A judgment by default. The words *nil dicit* signifying, when all the proceedings of the courts were in the Latin language, "says nothing," which words are now the words used in the record of a judgment by default. Judgments acknowledged by means of a warrant of attorney state that the judgment thereupon is to be entered up by *nil dicit*, or "otherwise;" so that the judgment when entered up appears as a judgment by default in a common action, although no previous process has been issued.

JURATS. Officers in nature of aldermen, sworn for the government of many corporations.

JURISDICTION. An authority or power which a man hath to do justice in causes of complaint brought before him.

JURY. A certain number of men sworn to inquire of, and try a matter of fact, and declare the truth, upon such evidence as shall be delivered them in a cause; and they are sworn judges upon evidence in matter of fact.

In *Magna Charta* it is more than once insisted on, as the principal bulwark of our liberties, but especially by chapter 29., that no freeman shall be hurt in either his person or property unless by the judgment of his peers (*i. e.* his legally presumed equals *), or by the law of the land. If a coroner inquire how a person killed, came by his death, he does it by a jury; and the justices of peace in their quarter sessions, the sheriff, in his county court, the steward of a court leet or court baron &c., if they inquire of any offence, or decide any cause between party and party, do it in like manner.

* In law, all persons under the degree of a peer of the realm are equal.

When an issue is joined between the parties to a suit, the court awards a writ of *venire facias* upon the roll or record, commanding the sheriff, "that he cause to come here, on such a day, twelve men of the body of his county, qualified according to law, by whom the truth of the matter may be better known; and who are neither of kin to the plaintiff nor the defendant, to recognise the truth of the issue between the parties." And such writ is accordingly issued to the sheriff; but in practice, it is not issued for the purpose of being obeyed, except where cases are to be tried at bar, *i. e.* before a full court in Westminster Hall; therefore another subsequent writ is delivered to the sheriff, commanding him that he cause the jurors to come to Westminster on a particular day in a following term, or any other day, *nisi prius, unless before* that day the judges assigned to take assizes shall come into his county by virtue of which the sheriff returns his jury to the judges of assize, or the judge who takes the sittings in London or Middlesex.

The sheriff returns a jury in criminal cases, according to the jury act.

When a case, civil or criminal, is ready for trial, the jury is called and sworn. The jurors contained in the panel are either special or common jurors.

Special juries are used when the causes are of too great nicety for the discretion of ordinary juries.

The 6 *G.* 4. *c.* 50. *s.* 30. declares it lawful for the judges of the supreme court at Westminster, &c., on motion made on behalf of the queen, or of any prosecutor, plaintiff, or defendant, in any case whatsoever, whether civil or criminal, or on any penal statute (excepting only on indictments for treason or felony) to order and appoint special juries to be struck before the proper officer of each respective court, for the trial of any issue joined in any of the said cases, and triable by a jury in such manner as the said courts have usually ordered the same; and that every jury so struck shall be the jury returned for the trial of such issue.

By *s.* 31. every man described in the juror's book as an esquire, or persons of higher degree, or as banker or merchant, is qualified and liable to serve on special juries; and his name is to be inserted in a separate list to be subjoined to the jurors' book, such list to be called "the Special Jurors' List."

By *s.* 32. the officer of the court is to appoint the time and place for nominating the special jury, where the under-sheriff or his agent is to attend with the special jurors' list. The officer is to draw 48 out of a box, any of which may be objected to by the parties on each side, by showing the officer they are incapacitated; and a list of 48 names is to be delivered to each party, to be reduced as theretofore, namely, by each party striking off 12, whereupon the remaining 24 are to be returned upon the panel.

A common jury is one returned by the sheriff, according to the directions of the 6 *G.* 4. *c.* 50. *s.* 15. to 26., which appoints that the sheriff or officer shall return one and the same panel for every cause to be tried at the same assizes, containing not less than 48, nor more than 72 jurors; and (*s.* 26.) that their names being written on a card, shall be put into a box or glass; and when each cause is called, 12 of these persons, whose names shall be first drawn out of the box, shall be sworn upon the jury, unless absent, challenged, or excused; or unless a previous view of the messuages, lands, or place in question, shall have been thought necessary by the court; in which case it is provided by *s.* 23. of the same act, that six or more of the jurors returned, to be agreed on by the parties, or named by a judge or other proper officer of the court, shall be appointed by special writ of *habeas corpora*, or *distringas*, to have the matters in question shown to them by two persons named in the writ; and then (*s.* 24.) such of the jury as have had the view, or so many of them as appear shall be sworn on the inquest previous to any other jurors. See this Dict. tit. VIEW.

The first section of the above statute, defines the qualification of jurors in England in the superior courts, assizes, and sessions of the peace; and allows persons in Wales, being there qualified to the extent of three-fifths of the qualification required in England, to serve on juries in Wales: viz., every man between 21 and 60 years of age (if not expressly excepted) who shall have 10*l.* *per annum* above reprises in lands or tenements, freehold, copyhold, customary, or of ancient demesne; or in rents issuing out of such lands, tenements, and rents taken together in fee simple, fee tail, or for the life of himself or any other; or 20*l.* in land or tenements held by lease for 21 years or longer, absolutely, or for any term determinable on life; or who, being an householder, sholl be rated or assessed to the poor rates (or to the inhabited house duty) in Middlesex upon a value of not less than 30*l.*, and in any other county not less than 20*l.*; or who shall occupy a house not containing less than fifteen windows. All such persons are declared to be qualified, and liable to serve on juries, for the trial of all such issues in the courts of record in Westminster, and in the superior courts, both civil and criminal, of the three counties palatine, Chester (now abolished), Durham, and Lancashire, and in all courts of assize, *nisi prius*, *oyer*, and *terminer*, and gaol delivery; such assizes being respectively triable in the county in which every man so qualified shall reside; and on grand juries in courts of session of the peace; and on petty juries for the trial of all issues joined in such courts of session of the peace, and triable in the county, riding, or division, where the person so qualified resides. Section 2. The following persons are exempted:—peers, judges of the courts of Westminster, &c., clergymen, Roman catholic priests, protestant dissenters, and preachers duly registered, &c., and not following any secular occupation, except that of schoolmaster; practising serjeants, barristers, doctors, and advocates of the civil law, attorneys, solicitors, and proctors; officers of all courts of justice, coroners, gaolers, physicians, and licentiates; surgeons of the royal colleges of London, Edinburgh, and Dublin; apothecaries; officers in the navy or army on full pay, licensed pilots, &c.; the queen's household servants; officers of custom and excise, sheriff's officers, high constables, and parish clerks. All these are absolutely freed and exempted from being returned, and from serving upon any juries or inquests whatever, and are not to be inserted in the lists required by the act.

Proviso is also made for all persons exempted by any prescription, charter, grant, or writ.

By *s.* 48. no justices of peace are to be summoned as jurors at sessions; nor, by *s.* 49., any inhabitants of Westminster at the Middlesex sessions.

The mode of summoning aliens, in case of the trial of any alien, indicted, or impeached of any felony or misdemeanor, is directed by *s.* 47. of this act, which provides that such aliens shall not be challenged for want of freehold or qualification, required by the act, but they may for any other crime.

The act contains a multiplicity of directions as to the making out yearly lists of persons qualified to serve on juries by the churchwardens, &c., of every parish, under the warrant of the clerk of the peace and the precept of the high constable.

These lists are to be kept by the clerk of the peace in a book, called the jurors' book, from which the juries are to be returned by the sheriff. Power is reserved to the court of queen's bench, and all other courts of criminal jurisdiction, to call a jury, or to amend or enlarge the panel returned by the sheriff. In certain cases of treason, a copy of the panel is to be delivered to the parties indicted; but this does not extend to treason, in conspiring the queen's death, nor to offences relating to counterfeiting the coins. Special reservations are made as to qualification of jurors in London and other cities and liberties, and as to inquests before sheriffs and coroners.

By *s*. 22. the justices of assize, &c., may direct the sheriff to summon the same panel not exceeding 144 jurors, for the criminal and civil side, and order two sets of jurors to be summoned; one to serve during the former part (usually the first week) of the assizes, and the other for the residue of the time.

By the 18 *Eliz. c.* 5. *s.* 2. (which is not repealed by the act 6 *G.* 4.) no jury is to appear at Westminster for a trial, when the offence was committed thirty miles off, except the attorney general require it.

The jury for the trial of prisoners is returned by this act which applies equally to criminal as to civil causes.

Any one of the jury may be *challenged*, *i. e.* objected to by either party as interested, or partial; but the most usual cause of challenge is for want of qualification. When jurors are singly challenged, it is termed a *challenge to the polls;* but the whole twelve may be challenged (termed *challenging the array*) if it is presumed that the jury are *packed*, or irregularly returned, or that the sheriff is a party, or interested; but this cause is usually obviated or prevented, by the coroner being required to return the panel, or list of jurors.

If a sufficient number of jurors do not appear, the judges may appoint some of the standers by (being also qualified) called a *tales*, or in criminal cases, order the sheriff instantly to prepare a new panel.

The jury, after the proofs in a cause are summed up, unless the case be very clear, withdraw from the bar to consider of their verdict; and, in order to avoid intemperance and causeless delay, are to be kept without meat, drink, fire, or candle, unless by permission of the judge, till they are all unanimously agreed. If they eat or drink at all, or have any eatables about them without consent of the court, and before verdict, it is fineable; and if they do so at his charge for whom they afterwards find, it will set aside the verdict. Also if they speak with either of the parties, or their agents, after they are gone from the bar, or if they receive any fresh evidence in private; or if, to prevent disputes, they cast lots for whom they shall find; any of these circumstances will entirely vitiate the verdict. And it has been held, that if the jurors do not agree in their verdict before the judges are about to leave the town, though they are not to be threatened or imprisoned, the judges are not bound to wait for them, but may carry them round the circuit from town to town in a cart, and discharge them, if they do not agree, at the bounds of the county.*

After a juror is sworn, he may not go from the bar until the evidence is given, for any cause whatsoever, until leave of the court; and with leave, he must have a keeper with him.

* The presiding judge has the power to discharge a jury who cannot agree in a civil or criminal case, and in a criminal case may discharge the jury where a material witness is absent. "Carting" the jury has been long obsolete

A VERDICT is either privy or public. A privy verdict is when the judge hath left or adjourned the court, and the jury being agreed, in order to be delivered from their confinement, obtain leave (in civil cases) to give their verdict privily to the judge out of court; which privy verdict is of no force, unless afterwards affirmed by a public verdict given openly in court; wherein the jury may, if they please, vary from their privy verdict. So that the privy verdict, is, indeed, a mere nullity, and it cannot be given in treason or felony. But the only effectual and legal verdict is the public verdict, in which the jury openly declare to have found the issue for the plaintiff or for the defendant; and, if for the plaintiff, they assess the damages also sustained by him. Sometimes, if there arises in the case any difficult matter of law, the jury, for the sake of better information, state the naked facts as they find them proved, and pray the advice of the court thereon; concluding, conditionally, that if upon the whole matter the court shall be of opinion that the plaintiff had cause of action, they then find for him; if otherwise, then for the defendant. This is entered at length on the record, and afterwards argued and determined in the court at Westminster, from whence the issue came to be tried. Another method of finding a species of special verdict, is where the jury find a verdict generally for the plaintiff, but subject, nevertheless, to the opinion of the judge, or the court above, on a special case stated by the counsel on both sides, with regard to a matter of law; but, in both these instances, the jury may, if they think proper, take upon themselves to determine, at their own hazard, the complicated question of fact and law; and without either special case or special verdict, may find a verdict absolutely either for the plaintiff or the defendant. It may be sufficient in this place to remark that, in case the jury find against law, the court will repeatedly grant a new trial, till what they consider to be a proper verdict is found. This might alone be an answer to juries who claim to be judges of law in civil cases.

In criminal cases a prisoner may peremptorily challenge (*i. e.* object to), without assigning any reason, to the number of 20, and in treason to the number of 35.

Foreigners are tried by a jury of half foreigners, except in cases of treason.

In cases, strictly criminal, the prosecutor cannot withdraw a juror, or postpone the indictment because he is not prepared with his evidence; for, after the jury are once sworn they can only be discharged by giving a verdict.

In criminal cases the jury consider the evidence, and deliver their verdict, as in civil cases, but they cannot return a *privy* verdict; the practice is for the judges to adjourn while the jury are withdrawn, and return to receive the verdict in open court.

If a juryman is taken ill, the remaining 11 may be sworn with a new juror, and the prisoner is entitled to challenge them again.

If the prisoner is too ill to remain at the bar, the jury may be discharged from the trial of that indictment, and the prisoner on his recovery tried by another jury.

The jury, as in civil cases, may give a general or special verdict; in the latter case, the verdict states the facts as found, and prays the judgment of the court to decide whether it be the crime stated in the indictment or no crime at all.

JUSTICES. Officers deputed by the queen, who is the supreme executive power to administer justice, and to *do right by way of judgment*, as the books emphatically say. Of these *justices* there are various sorts. See JUDGES, and the following titles.

Justices of *assize* and *nisi prius*, are composed of two or more commissioners, who are sent twice in every year, by the queen's special commission, all round the kingdom, viz. England and Wales (except London and Middlesex, where courts of *nisi prius* are holden in and after every term, called *sittings*, before the chief or other judge of the several superior courts) to try by a jury of the respective counties the truth of such matters of fact as are then under dispute in the courts of Queen's Bench, Common Pleas, and Exchequer of Pleas.

Justices of gaol-delivery are those who are sent with commission to hear and determine all causes relating to those who for any offence are committed to gaol.

Justices of *nisi prius* are the same with justices of *assize;* for the form of the record in all the courts adjourns the trial of the cause to a future day at Westminster; in the old Latin form, *nisi prius justiciarii venerint, &c. i. e. unless* the justices shall *first* come to a place named to take the assizes, which they are sure to do.

Justices of *oyer* and *terminer* are justices especially deputed to try prisoners upon extraordinary occasions, and for the dealing with offences which stand in need of immediate inquiry and punishment; but a *general* commission of *oyer* and *terminer* is given to the queen's commissioners, among whom are, usually, two judges of the courts at Westminster, to try prisoners at what is called *the assizes* twice every year in every county of England and Wales, for treasons, felonies, and misdemeanours.

The judges sit at the assizes by virtue of five commissions: the commission of assize and the commission of *nisi prius;* a commission of the peace; of gaol-delivery and of *oyer* and *terminer*, which last is directed to the judges and several others; but the judges, or serjeants at law, only are of the *quorum*, so that the rest cannot act without the presence of one of them. As the words of the commission are, "to inquire, hear, and determine," by virtue of this commission they can only proceed upon an indictment found at the same assizes; for, they must *inquire* by means of the grand jury or inquest, before they are empowered to *hear and determine* by the assistance of the petty jury. And the *gaol-delivery* empowers them to deliver the gaol of every prisoner therein, for whatever cause indicted. See ASSIZE.

JUSTICES OF THE PEACE. Judges appointed by the queen's commission to be justices in certain limits, generally within the counties wherein they are resident. There are many persons who are justices by virtue of their offices, as the mayors and aldermen of cities or towns and liberties, and the chancellor or keeper. The judges of the queen's bench are justices by *prescription.* There are also justices of the peace paid or appointed by government. See POLICE.

The ordinary or county justices are appointed by the queen's special commission. The power of constituting them is only in the queen, though they are generally made at the discretion of the chancellor or keeper by the queen's leave, who may appoint as many as she thinks fit; their commission appoints them all jointly and severally to keep the peace, and any two or more of them to inquire of and determine felonies and other misdemeanours: in which number some particular justices, or one of them, are directed to be always included, and no business to be done without their presence; the words of the commission running thus, "*quorum* (of whom) *aliquem vestrum*, A. B. C. D. &c. *unum esse volumus*, any one of you the aforesaid A. B. C. D. &c. we will shall be one;" whence the persons so named are usually called justices of the *quorum*. And formerly it was customary to appoint only a select number of justices, eminent for their skill and discretion, to be of the *quorum;* but now the practice is to advance almost all of them to that dignity, naming them all over again in the *quorum* clause, excepting, perhaps, only some one person for the sake of conformity. When any justice intends to act under this commission, he sues out a writ of *dedimus* from the clerk of the crown in chancery, empowering certain persons therein named to administer the usual oaths to him; which done, he is at liberty to act, but not before.

The office of these justices may be determined by the death of the queen, by tbe issuing a new commission, and by the chancellor's recalling the *dedimus*, or rather discharging the justices by writ; and the office may be suspended, if the justice is appointed sheriff. Misconduct, non-residence in the county, or ceasing to be possessed of the qualification, will be cause of discharging the justice.

The *qualification* of a justice, in addition to character and fitness, is the being possessed of 100*l. per annum*, freehold or inheritance, or 21 years' leasehold in possession, or the being entitled in immediate reversion to 300*l. per annum* in freehold or copyhold of inheritance, or 21 years' leasehold; but this does not extend to corporation justices, or the eldest sons of peers and of gentlemen qualified to be knights of shires, the officers of the board of green-cloth, principal officers of the navy, under secretaries of state, heads of colleges, or to the mayors of Oxford and Cambridge; all of whom may act without any qualification by estate.

The *power*, *office*, and *duty* of a justice of the peace depend on his commission, and on the several statutes which have created objects of his jurisdiction. His commission, first, empowers him singly to conserve the peace; and thereby gives him all the power of the ancient conservators at the common law, in suppressing riots and affrays, in taking securities for the peace, and in apprehending and committing felons, and inferior criminals. It also empowers any two or more to determine all felonies and other offences, which is the ground of their jurisdiction at the sessions. If a well-meaning justice makes any undesigned slip in his practice, great lenity and indulgence are shown to him in the courts of law; and there are many statutes made to protect him in the upright discharge of his office; which, among other privileges, prohibit such justices from being sued for any oversights, without notice beforehand; and stop all suits begun, on tender made of sufficient amends. But, on the other hand, any malicious or tyrannical abuse of their office is usually severely punished; and all persons who recover a verdict against a justice, for any wilful or malicious injury, are entitled to double costs. See *Blackstone's Commentaries*, 350—354.

Justices of the peace are to hold their sessions four times in the year. See QUARTER SESSIONS.

Justices act either at quarter sessions, at special, or petty sessions, or singly.

The acts done at quarter sessions, or, as they are termed, *the sessions of the year*, are treated of under the tit. QUARTER SESSIONS.

Petty sessions, or special sessions, are holden by two or more justices for the purpose of executing some particular business, or branch of their authority, such as licensing, &c.; or at small intervals in populous districts for the adjudication of those matters which can only be determined by two justices. To a certain extent, petty sessions are voluntary meetings or appointments of the justices, and are a great convenience to the public, for two justices cannot always be brought promptly to act without the chance of inconvenience or delay to some party or other.

The acts to be done *singly*, *i. e.* by *one* justice, are extremely numerous, and extend to a great multiplicity of cases, justices sometimes acting in a *ministerial* and sometimes in a *judicial* capacity; and their acts and forms of proceedings are regulated by such a vast number of statutes that uniformity of practice is scarcely possible; therefore the reader must be content with the following summary of a justice's duty, and derive more special information from *Burn's Justice of the Peace*, or some concise treatise on this very voluminous subject.

The proceedings of justices, *individually* or *plurally*, independent of acting in relation to the poor, vagrants, highways, rates, taxes, and the repression of outrages, trespasses, indecencies, and all things tending directly or indirectly to a breach of the peace, may be shortly considered.

1st. As to their committal of suspected offenders; and

2dly. As to the exercise of their *summary* jurisdiction under several statutes.

1. It is the duty of every justice or magistrate to grant a warrant for the apprehension of a party suspected of *felony* upon receiving information on oath; or if he *see* a felonious act done, the suspected party being apprehended, the justice proceeds to hear and to reduce into writing (called a deposition) the more full particulars of the charge against the prisoner, and if he feels convinced that the charge is sustainable, or violent suspicions are entertained of the prisoner's guilt, he commits him for trial, either to the next quarter sessions if only a larceny or felonious offence not of a very high nature, otherwise to the assizes. If the offence took place within the jurisdiction of the central criminal court, the commitment for trial is made out for that court. The duty of a magistrate as to bailing a prisoner is set forth in the following extract from a late statute which provides, "That where any person shall be taken on a charge of felony, or suspicion of felony, before one or more justice or justices of the peace, and the charge shall be supported by positive and credible evidence of the fact, or by such evidence as, if not explained or contradicted, shall in the opinion of the justice or justices raise a strong presumption of the guilt of the person charged, such person shall be committed to prison by such justice or justices, in the manner hereinafter mentioned; but if there shall be only one justice present, and the whole evidence given before him shall be such as neither to raise a strong presumption of guilt, nor to warrant the dismissal of the charge, such justice shall order the person charged to be detained in custody, until he or she shall be taken before *two* justices at the least; and where any person so taken, or any person in the first instance taken before two justices of the peace, shall be charged with felony, or on suspicion of felony, and the evidence given in support of the charge shall, in their opinion, not be such as to raise a strong presumption of the guilt of the person charged, and to require his or her committal; or such evidence shall be adduced on behalf of the person charged as shall in their opinion weaken the presumption of

his or her guilt; but there shall notwithstanding appear to them, in either of such cases, to be sufficient ground for judicial inquiry into his or her guilt, the person charged shall be admitted to bail by such two justices. Provided always, that nothing shall be construed to require any such justice or justices to hear evidence on behalf of any person so charged as aforesaid, unless it shall appear to him or them to be meet and conducive to the ends of justice to hear the same."

"That the two justices, before they shall admit to bail, and the justice or justices, before he or they shall commit to prison any person arrested for felony, or on suspicion of felony, shall take the examination of such person, and the information upon oath of those who shall know the facts and circumstances of the case, and shall put the same, or as much thereof as shall be material, into writing; and the two justices shall certify such bailment in writing; and every such justice shall have authority to bind by recognisance all such persons as know or declare any thing material touching any such felony, or suspicion of felony, to appear at the next court of *oyer* and *terminer*, or gaol-delivery, or superior criminal court of a county palatine, or great sessions, or sessions of the peace, at which the trial thereof is intended to be, then and there to prosecute or give evidence against the party accused; and such justices and justice, respectively, shall subscribe all such examinations, informations, bailments, and recognisances, and deliver, or cause the same to be delivered, to the proper officer of the court, in which the trial is to be, before, or at the opening of the court."

When the magistrates have, in a case of *felony*, resolved to admit the party to bail, they settle the amount (seldom under 40*l.*) of the bail, and the notice to be given to the prosecutor, in order that he may inquire into their sufficiency. The amount is discretionary in the magistrate; it is presumed he takes the condition in life of the party, and all other circumstances, into his consideration.

A refusal of bail by the magistrate, or magistrates, will not prevent the party accused from being bailed by the court of queen's bench.

In cases of *misdemeanour*, unless the case be gross and enormous, and the offender is taken in the act, it is not usual or regular to cause a party to be apprehended, unless it is supposed the party intends to abscond; but, after the information has been taken, the justice summons the party to appear before him on a particular day and time, when the examination of all parties is taken as in a case of felony: another section of the statute before mentioned, in relation to the magistrate's duty as to bailing on this occasion, is as follows:—

"That every justice of the peace before whom any person shall be taken on a charge of misdemeanour, or suspicion thereof, shall take the examination of the person charged, and the information upon oath of those who shall know the facts and circumstances of the case, and shall put the same, or as much thereof as shall be material, into writing, *before* he shall commit to prison, or require bail from the person so charged; and, in every case of bailment, shall certify the bailment in writing; and shall have authority to bind all persons by recognisance to appear to prosecute, or give evidence against the party accused, in like manner as in cases of felony; and shall subscribe all examinations, informations, bailments, and recognisances, deliver, or cause the same to be delivered to the proper officer of the court in which the trial is to be, before, or at the opening of the court, in like manner as in cases of felony."

In *misdemeanours* it is the *right* of the party to be admitted to bail; the justice, however, still has the power of fixing the amount, in doing which, although he is morally bound to take all circumstances into his consideration, as in cases of felony, he must not demand *excessive bail:* this, in fact, being a denial of bail, which is against the bill of rights, is an indictable offence, and also subjects the magistrate to an action on the case for damages at the suit of the party. After committal to prison the party may be bailed by a judge at chambers, the committal being, *for want of sureties, or until he be discharged by due course of law.*

2. Mr. Chitty observes *, that anciently the functions and jurisdiction of one or more justices of the peace, when not assembled at general or quarter sessions, were almost entirely *ministerial;* viz., to preserve and prevent breaches of the peace, and to cause malefactors to be apprehended, and their appearance secured to take their trial for alleged offences before a higher tribunal, either at the assizes or sessions. In more modern times the increase of population, and still more, the increase of legislation, has rendered it essential to delegate jurisdiction over small matters of police to justices; and, in numerous cases, whether for prevention or punishment of breaches of some police regulations, small offenders were subjected to *pecuniary penalties,* and to imprisonment for a short time if they did not pay them; frequently *one* justice, and, in cases of more importance, *two* justices had power to decide summarily, subject sometimes to an appeal to sessions, but very frequently final without any appeal, and even without the power of the superior court of queen's bench to review their formal proceedings upon *certiorari.*

The jurisdiction of justices at length became extended to cases of contract, as in enabling them to decide between masters and servants in certain trades.

The next step (Mr. Chitty proceeds to observe) was to afford compensation by the decision of a justice for *verbal abuse* by stage-coachmen to passengers; but there were no regulations affording general compensation or punishment for small private injuries until the three principal statutes were recently passed, viz. the 7 *&* 8 *G.* 4. *c.* 29. relative to small *illegal takings* of property, whether strictly personal, or in part connected with the freehold, not exceeding 5*l.* in value; the 7 *&* 8 *G.* 4. *c.* 30. relative to small wilful or malicious injuries to personal or real property, whether public or private, not exceeding 5*l.*; and the 9 *G.* 4. *c.* 31. relative to common assaults and batteries not causing injury exceeding 5*l.* The former two acts enabling one justice summarily to hear and determine the complaint of the party aggrieved, and award him compensation to the extent of 5*l.*, unless *when he has given evidence,* and then to be paid in aid of the county rate; and the latter act requiring two justices to hear and determine, and convict in a penalty not exceeding 5*l.* to be paid in aid of the county rate. These statutes being enacted with a view to prevent expensive actions in the superior courts for trifling assaults and trespasses.

The game act, 1 *&* 2 *W.* 4. *c.* 32., empowers *two* justices to inflict penalties upon the occupier for sporting, or permitting others to sport, on his land, while the right is reserved to his landlord or any one else; and also the penalties of 5*l.* for destroying eggs; and 10*l.* for laying

* Practice of the Law, *Summary Proceedings before Justices of the Peace,* vol. ii. part i. 128.

poison for game; and *one* justice is empowered to deal with trespassers in pursuit of game, having regard to the exceptions in the act in favour of persons coursing who started the game on their own or other lands.

The mode of commencing a prosecution for payment of penalties, either before one or two justices, is for the complainant to attend before one justice and lay his information, which is a memorandum either prepared by the complainant or informer, or more usually by the justice or his clerk, stating the commission of the act, or offence, in precise language, to the truth of which the complainant is sworn. An information may be by word of mouth, but almost always it is reduced into writing, in order that the magistrate may embody the substance of the information in his summons; but if the statute inflicting the penalty require an *information* thereupon to be in writing, it is imperative. In this *information* should be stated the name, and description, and place of abode, of the informer or complainant, or the name of the *witness*, if the information is laid by one person, and supported by the testimony of another; the time and place of exhibiting the information; the magistrate's name, and the name, &c., of the offender; the time and place of committing the alleged offence, and the offence itself. It may contain, like a *declaration* or *indictment*, various counts, or statements, for different offences committed on the same or other days, or in the nature of special counts, stating the same offence in a varied language, where the nature of the offence requires extreme particularity in the statement, so that if one should prove defective in law the other may not be open to the same objection.

Upon the information being sworn to, in almost all cases an indispensable requisite, the single justice grants a summons, which fully sets forth the charge as stated in the information, signed by the justice calling upon the accused to appear before him, on a particular day, at a *certain* hour, a few days intervening; but if it is supposed that the party will elude pursuit, the magistrate may issue his warrant for the supposed offender's apprehension, after the information has been sworn to; on the *return* of the summons, either before one (the same) justice, or two justices, the party either attends by being compulsorily brought before them, or voluntarily attends upon the summons, or makes default. At which time the summons may be adjourned if the defendant request it, or state adequate excuse for his not being prepared to answer the charge; but, if it is proceeded with, the information is read over to him, the witnesses sworn, and the examination entered into, the justices, or their clerk, taking exact minutes in writing of the whole evidence, termed *depositions*, and convict or acquit accordingly; if the former, a memorandum is signed of the conclusion or adjudication, termed *the conviction*, from which the party may sometimes appeal; if the latter, they sign a certificate of acquittal.

If the party summoned does not appear, the information may be proceeded with, as it is termed, *ex parte*, *i. e.*, the complainant proves his case, and the magistrate or magistrates sign the conviction. And unless an express power is given to the magistrate to apprehend before conviction, a justice, or justices, is not warranted in issuing a warrant to imprison the accused party or compel him to attend; all that he can do in that case is to hear the case *ex parte*.

Justices of the peace refusing to interfere in the execution of the law, are compellable to act by a writ of *mandamus*, and if they behave corruptly or illegally, they can be proceeded against by a criminal information, or by attachment, on the motion of the attorney-general, or, by action on the case, they may be punished in damages; but a party aggrieved cannot have more than *one* of these remedies.

The law provides for their protection against litigious persons, as well as to prevent their being too severely visited, where *error*, and not *malice* or tyrannical feelings, have rendered them amenable to damages ; for, by stat. 7 James I., if any action shall be brought against a justice for any thing done by virtue of his office, he may plead the general issue, and give the special matter in evidence ; and if he recover a verdict, he shall have double costs.

The stat. 24 *G.* 2. *c.* 44. particularly provides, that no writ shall be sued out against any justice of peace for any thing done by him in the execution of his office, until a notice in writing shall be delivered to him one month before the suing out the same, containing the cause of action, &c. within which month he may tender amends, and if the tender be found sufficient, he shall have a verdict. No such plaintiff shall recover against the justice, unless such notice shall be proved at the trial. If the justice shall neglect to make such tender, he may, before issue joined, pay into court such sum as he shall think fit. Where an action is against a justice and constable, if there be a verdict against the justice, and the constable be acquitted, the plaintiff shall recover such costs against the justice, as to include the costs the plaintiff shall be obliged to pay the constable. And this statute enacts, that if the plaintiff in any such action shall recover against a justice, *and the judge shall certify that the injury was wilfully and maliciously done*, the plaintiff shall recover double costs. No action shall be brought against a justice for any thing done in the execution of his office, unless commenced within six months after the act committed.

This act is by very many subsequent acts extended to justices of various descriptions, and on several occasions, as militia, &c.

By 43 *G.* 3. *c.* 141. it is provided, that in all actions against justices on account of any conviction, &c. by them, the plaintiff (besides any penalty levied) shall recover only *two-pence* damages; unless notice and want of probable cause be expressly alleged in the declaration, and which shall be in an action upon the case only. And if on the trial of any such action it shall be proved that the plaintiff was guilty of the offence whereof he was convicted, and that he underwent no greater punishment than was by law assigned thereto, he shall not be entitled to recover any penalty levied, or any costs or damages against the justice.

JUSTICIES. A writ directed to the sheriff, directing him to do justice to the plaintiff: it is the process by which suits to any amount may be commenced in the sheriff's county court, where the damages are above 40*s*. As the sheriff cannot, by this process, or the judgment to be obtained thereupon, arrest the defendant's person, but only take his goods, and as the cause may be removed at the defendant's pleasure into the superior courts, this process is not very much in use.

JUSTIFICATION is a special plea in bar, *i. e.* in answer to a plaintiff's action, as in actions of assault and battery ; viz. that the plaintiff first, with force and arms, assaulted the defendant, and he defended himself, or gently laid hands on plaintiff (as the case may be) ; and, therefore, if any damage happened to plaintiff, it was owing to the assault he made on defendant, and in his necessary defence;—in other actions of trespass, that the defendant did the thing complained of in right of some office or right which warranted him so to do ;—or, in an action of slander, that the plaintiff was guilty of such or such a crime, and therefore he, the defendant, spoke the words.

KEEPER OF THE GREAT SEAL. See CHANCELLOR, LORD KEEPER OF THE PRIVY SEAL, PRIVY SEAL.

KINDRED. Persons of kin, or related to each other by descent through the father or mother. There are two degrees of either kindred; the one in the right or direct line ascending or descending, and the other in the collateral line.

The line *descending* is from the father to the son, and so on to his children in the male and female line; and if no son, then to the daughter and to her children in the male and female line *ad infinitum.*

The line *ascending* is directly upwards, as from the son to the father or mother; and if neither father nor mother, to the grandfather or grandmother; and if no grandfather or grandmother, to the great grandfather or great grandmother; if neither great grandfather nor great grandmother, to the father of the great grandfather or the mother of the great grandmother; and if neither of them then to the great grandfather's grandfather, or the great grandmother's grandmother; and if none of them to the great grandfather's great grandfather, or great grandmother's great grandmother; and so on *ad infinitum.*

The *collateral* line is either descending by the brother and his children downwards, or by the uncle upwards, and downwards to the nephew and his children; and, if none of them, to the niece and her children; if neither nephew nor niece, nor any of their children, then to the grandson or grand-daughter of the nephew; and if neither of them, to the grandson or grand-daughter of the niece; and if none of them, then to the great grandson or great grand-daughter of the nephew and of the niece; and so *ad infinitum,* the *collateral* line being between brothers and sisters, and to uncles and aunts, and the rest of the kindred, upwards and downwards, across and amongst themselves.

If there are no kindred in the right descending line, the inheritance of lands goes to the ascending line. The right of representation of kindred (for the purposes of distribution of personalty) in the descending line reaches beyond the great grandchildren of the same parents; but in the collateral line it is not by law allowed to reach beyond brothers' and sisters' children.

In the direct or right ascending line, the father or mother are always in the first degree of kindred. See DESCENT.

There are several rules to know the degrees of kindred; in the ascending line, take the son and add the father, and it is one degree ascending; then add the grandfather, and it is a second degree, a person added to a person in the line of consanguinity making a degree: and if there are many persons, take away one and you have the number of degrees: as if there are four persons, it is the third degree; if five, the fourth, &c.; so that the father, son, and grandchild, in the descending line, though three persons, make but two degrees. To know in what degree of kindred the sons of two brothers stand, begin from the grandfather and descend to one brother, the father of one of the sons, which is one degree, then descend to his son the ancestor's grandson, which is a second degree: and then descend again from the grandfather to the other brother, father of the other of the sons, which is one degree, and descend to his son, &c., and it is a second degree: thus reckoning the person from whom the computation is made, it appears there are two degrees, and that the sons of two brothers are distant from each other two degrees: for, in what degree either of them is distant from the common stock, the person from whom the computation is made, they are distant between themselves in the same degree; and in every line the person must be reckoned from whom the computation is made. If the kindred are not equally distant from the common stock, then in what degree the most remote is distant, in the same degree they are distant between themselves, and so the kin of the most remote maketh the degree; by which rule, I and the grandchild of my uncle are distant in the third degree, such grandchild being distant three degrees from my grandfather, the nearest common stock.

Our law agrees in its computation with the civil and ecclesiastical law, as to the right line, and with the civil law as to collaterals, in computing who are entitled to administration and distribution of the personal property of intestates.

The reckoning of degrees according to our law, showing the degrees within which persons must not intermarry (Leviticus, cap. 18.) are attempted to be more fully explained by the following diagrams :—

Terah.

Abraham — Nahor

Nahor — Bethuel 2.

Bethuel — Rebecca 3., Laban 1.

I. Isaac = Rebecca 3.

II. Jacob 4. = Rachel.

The reckoning of lineal degrees of kindred or relationship is either of 1. Consanguinity, or, 2. Affinity.

1. Consanguinity:
   1. Ascending — Father, Mother, Grandfather, Grandmother.
   2. Descending — Father, Mother. Sons, Daughters.

   So many generations upwards or downwards so many degrees: therefore there is *one* between the father and son, as Abraham and Isaac, and one between Isaac and Jacob, who is in the second degree.

2. Affinity:
   1. Ascending — Father-in-law, Mother-in-law. Step-Father, Step-Mother.
   2. Descending — Son-in-law, Daughter-in-law.

The nearest *collateral* degrees of *consanguinity* are—brother, sister; brother's and sister's children; uncle and aunt: but *collateral affinity* comprises the brother's wife, the sister's husband, the uncle's wife, the aunt's husband, &c.

The *direct* line of consanguinity is thus exemplified :—

Abraham	(*not counted*)
I. Isaac	1 degree
II. Jacob.	2 degrees.

In the *collateral* line,

Bethuel 2.

Rebecca 3. Laban 1.

Jacob 4. = Rachel.

In the direct and collateral degrees of consanguinity by the common and civil law, it is settled that in so many generations (except the first, which is the stock *from* which the computation proceeds,) there are so many degrees: therefore, Jacob is in the second degree from Abraham, and Jacob is in the fourth degree from Rachel: Rachel being the first, Laban the second, Rebecca the third, and Jacob the fourth, or, according to the technical mode of computation, *from* Rachel to her father Laban 1, from Laban to Bethuel (the grandfather of both) 2, then downwards to Rebecca the aunt 3, from aunt to cousin Jacob, 4 degrees.

In regard to the prohibition of marriage, the following rules are to be observed:—

In the right or direct line ascending or descending all degrees are forbidden.

In collateral *consanguinity*, the prohibition reaches to the third degree, so that it is not lawful to marry the uncle or aunt who are in the third degree from the nephew or niece; but marriages with cousins are not prohibited, they being in the fourth degree.

In collateral *affinity*, the prohibition is extended to the fourth degree, for affinity is always beyond that of consanguinity. The consequence is, that it is unlawful to marry the uncle's wife, who is in the fourth degree from the nephew, being one degree beyond her husband, who is uncle, and consequently in the third degree: as a corollary to this proposition,- there can be no affinity in the first or second degree, but the nearest is the third, as the wife's or husband's father, brother, or daughter, which are all in the third degree: as the husband is the first, the wife the second, and they in the third.

KING. The supreme executive power of these kingdoms is by law vested in a single person, the king, or queen, for it matters not to which sex the crown descends, according to hereditary right; which, however, may be defeated or qualified by the supreme legislative authority of this kingdom, viz. the king and both houses of parliament, or by the latter alone, if the throne be declared vacant, or necessity dictate the alteration of the course of succession.

KING'S BENCH, COURT OF, is so called, because the king used formerly to sit there in person. During the reign of a queen it is called the queen's bench.

This court consists of a chief justice and four puisne judges, though in practice seldom more than four sit on the bench, and they are by their office the sovereign conservators of the peace, and supreme coroners of the land.

The jurisdiction of this court is very high, and claims precedence of the court of chancery. It keeps all inferior jurisdictions within the bounds of their authority, and may either remove their proceedings to be determined here, or prohibit their progress below. It superintends all civil corporations in the kingdom. It commands magistrates and others to do what their duty requires, in every case where no particular remedy is appointed. It protects the liberty of the subject, by liberating persons unjustly imprisoned or restrained of their liberty, by *habeas corpus* or bail. It takes cognisance both of criminal and civil causes (the common pleas and exchequer are confined to civil actions); the former in what is called the crown side or crown office, the latter in the plea side of the court.

On the crown side, that is, in the *crown office*, this court takes cognisance of all criminal causes, from high treason down to the most trivial misdemeanor or breach of the peace. Into this court, also, indictments from all inferior courts may be removed, by writ of *certiorari*, and tried, either *at bar*, that is, at the bar of the court, while sitting in term time, or at *nisi prius*, by a jury of the county out of which the indictment is brought; the court itself being the principal court of criminal jurisdiction known to the law.

In the county where the *king's bench* sits (Middlesex, unless in time of plague or internal commotion, as in 1642 and 1665), there is every *term* a grand inquest or jury sworn to present all criminal matters arising within that county, and then the court proceeds upon the indictments so taken; or if in *vacation*, when the court is not sitting, any indictments are found within the county before the justices of *oyer* and *terminer*, or gaol-delivery there sitting, they may be removed by *certiorari* into this court.

This court awards execution against persons attainted in parliament, or convicted and condemned in any other court, the record of their attainder or conviction, or a transcript of the same, being removed into this court, together with the persons of the parties, by *habeas corpus*; the marshal of the king's bench being the officer who is to perform the execution *, although the sheriff of the county may be ordered to assist him therein.

The *king's bench* is likewise a court of appeal, into which may be removed, by writ of error, all determinations of inferior courts of record.

The court also grants writs of *habeas corpus* to relieve persons wrongfully imprisoned, and may bail any person whatever. (See Bail.) Writs of *mandamus* are also granted by this court to restore officers in corporations, colleges, corporate cities, &c., unjustly turned out, and freemen wrongfully disfranchised; also writs and informations in the nature of *quo warranto* (which see) against individuals or corporations usurping franchises and liberties against the king, and on misuse of privileges to seize the privileges, &c. In this court the king's letters patent may be repealed by writ of *scire facias* (which see). Writs of *prohibition* are also issued from this court to keep inferior courts within their proper jurisdiction.

KING'S STORES. See Naval and Military Stores.

KNIGHTS OF THE SHIRE. Knights or gentlemen of worth, chosen by the freeholders of a county or other electors qualified to sit in parliament for a county or division of a county.

LABOURERS, or servants in husbandry, are placed by several statutes under the control of magistrates, both as to the regulation of their hours of work and the amount of wages. By several acts magistrates have the power to regulate or make a rate of wages, and to compel payment (in money and not in goods) in a summary manner; but many trades and classes of labourers or workmen are excluded, or rather not

* The place of execution is at the Marshal's discretion; formerly at Saint Thomas a watering in the Old Kent Road, beyond the boundary line of the jurisdiction of the city of London and borough of Southwark; latterly at the County Jail for Surrey.

included in the beneficial provisions which secure the workman his wages; although by a general act the labourer is punishable for misconduct or wilful breach of contract.

Domestic or menial servants are not subject to the control of a justice of the peace. See SERVANT.

LAMMAS-DAY. The first of August. The inhabitants and parishioners of many places exercise or claim a right of common in various plots or fields of open pasture and arable land, from this day to Candlemas Day in respect of the former, and to All Souls Day in respect of the latter. Notwithstanding the claim in fact exercised by many, it is settled that no allotment under the Inclosure Act can be awarded to any one on the ground of inhabitancy, as the right is confined to those who claim by prescription in respect of an ancient messuage *and* lands. By an act passed 20th August, 1836, for the object of facilitating the inclosure of common fields, this right to "Lammas land" will soon be extinguished.

LANDLORD AND TENANT. The editor has found it impossible to compress a connected statement of the law upon this legal relation, within the limits of a work of this nature. The reader will, however, find some information upon questions of ordinary occurrence under the title TENANT. Also see LEASE, PARTY-WALLS.

LAND TAX. A tax assessed upon land made perpetual, but subject to redemption or purchase by the act 38 *G.* 3. *c.* 60. It is levied under the authority of the land tax commissioners of every county.

This is a landlord's tax, payable by the tenant, who may deduct it from the rent of the *current* year, otherwise it cannot be recovered back from the landlord at any future time.

LARCENY. The legal term for stealing or theft. The law defines a stealing or larceny to be the taking and carrying away with a felonious intent (*i. e.* with the intention of unlawful appropriation) the goods of another. It is distinguished as simple and compound; simple, when the stealing is unaccompanied with aggravating circumstances; compound, when the theft is committed upon the person, or consists in stealing from a dwelling-house. Stealing under particular circumstances is a crime of another denomination; for instance, taking from the person in a violent manner is *robbery*, and stealing in a dwelling-house after having broken therein, is *burglary*.

Larceny is now extended to stealings of almost every possible denomination; and many offences which savour of larceny or partake of its character are, by one of Mr. Peel's acts (7 *&* 8 *G* 4. *c.* 29.), which consolidated the criminal law, punishable as such.

The intent is the material ingredient in this offence. The *taking* must be actual or constructive: *actual*, where the offender takes the goods away without the owner's consent; *constructive*, where the owner, although he has parted with the possession of the goods, has not divested himself of the right of such possession, or where a fraud has been practised with an intent to steal them.

An actual taking and carrying away, or leading away of an animal, scarcely needs any illustration, further than to notice, that the slightest act of removal is sufficient to support a larceny; but the doctrine of constructive *takings* gives rise to very nice distinctions; for instance, whatever may have been the intent of the party, when a person has sold goods upon credit, the taking or converting such goods to his own use can never amount to a larceny, nor will any case, however gross the fraud may be, support an indictment, where the prosecutor has parted with the legal possession of his property by treating the transaction as a matter of contract. On the other hand, if a cheat is practised, as to *whom* the goods shall be delivered, and the party contrives to get the goods in his possession, or where from circumstances it can be shown that it was not the intent to part with the goods but upon previous terms or conditions, such as payment of money, &c., there the transaction is one which is a larceny, for the possession gotten by the party was not voluntarily obtained. Another instance: a man hires a chaise in his own name for a given period, and never returns it: this is no larceny; otherwise it would be if he hire it, and afterwards sell it, or converts it to his own use; for here the intent of stealing is apparent, and the delivery by the owner will not neutralise the constructive taking and carrying away, for the owner's consent can never be presumed. So where a defendant by artifice got possession of a permit whereby he obtained a chest of tea, this was held to be a larceny; and similar acts whereby goods have been obtained, have been decided to be larcenies. These distinctions approach the line which divides larceny from obtaining goods under false pretences, and as the punishment of this offence is nearly the same as larceny, and as the law is now framed, the defendant can be convicted of the larceny if the false pretences be not made out, it may oftener be more expedient to prosecute for the cheat.

Violations of trust, where the possession of the goods have been previously obtained without any fraudulent intention, are not larcenies.

Embezzlements by clerks or servants are larcenies, if the money or goods were actually received by the clerk or servant by virtue of his employment.

Larceny cannot be committed of animals that are wild by nature and at large, as deer in a chase or forest, hares, rabbits in a warren, or wild fowls, rooks for instance; but deer in an inclosed part of a forest or park, fish in a trunk, or pheasants in a mew, as well as swans marked, and all valuable domestic animals, are subjects of larceny. Dogs, birds, pigeons, not kept inclosed, and other animals kept for pleasure, not being subjects of larceny, are protected by summary proceedings before justices, who may inflict fine, imprisonment and whipping.

The punishment of larceny is transportation for 7 years, or imprisonment not exceeding 2 years (with or without hard labour, and with or without solitary confinement, for the whole or any part of the imprisonment), and, if a male, to be once, twice, or thrice publicly or privately whipped, in addition to the imprisonment, if the court shall think fit. If the defendant be previously under sentence of transportation or imprisonment for another crime, the court may award the transportation or imprisonment for every subsequent felony, to commence at the expiration of the transportation or imprisonment to which the prisoner was previously sentenced.

Petty-stealings and illegal-takings are also punishable summarily, by a single justice of the peace. *7 & 8 G. 4. c. 29.*

LEASE. A letting of lands, tenements, or hereditaments, to another for term of life or years, for a rent reserved. Any letting, however short, is termed in law a lease—as lessee at will, for tenant at will.

A lease for more than 3 years must be made a lease in writing, called a lease by indenture; it may be also made by deed poll; but leases not exceeding 3 years may be made by words of mouth; verbal agreement to lease lands for four years creates a tenancy from year to year.

The law reckons an estate for years inferior in interest, as compared to an estate for life; for, an estate for life, even if it be *pur auter vie*, is a freehold: but an estate for a thousand years is only a chattel, and reckoned part of the personal estate.

Generally to the making of a good lease several things necessarily concur; there must be a lessor not restrained from making a lease; a lessee not disabled to receive: a thing demised which is demisable, and a sufficient description of the thing demised, &c. If it be for years, it must have a certain commencement and determination: it is to have all the usual ceremonies, as sealing, delivery, &c., and there must be an acceptance of the thing demised. Whether any rent be reserved upon a lease for life, years, or at will, or not, is not material, except only in the cases of leases made by tenant in tail, husband and wife, and ecclesiastical persons, and leases under powers which usually require a rack-rent to be obtained.

A paper containing words of present contract, with an agreement that the lessee should take possession immediately, and that a lease should be executed in future, operates only as an agreement of a lease, and not as a lease itself. This however is a question of intention upon the construction of the words of each individual case.

An instrument on an agreement stamp, reciting that in case he should be entitled to certain copyhold premises on the death of B. would immediately demise the same to C. declaring, that he did thereby agree to demise and let the same, with a subsequent covenant to procure a license to let, from the lord, operates as an agreement for a lease, and not as an absolute lease.

By various acts of parliament, and also by private settlements, a power is granted for making leases to take effect in possession, but not in reversion, for a certain time; the object being that the estate may not be incumbered by the act of the party, beyond a specific time.

Of all kinds of powers in wills or settlements the most frequent is that to make leases. In the making such leases all the requisites particularly specified in the power, must be strictly observed; and such leases must contain all such beneficial clauses and reservations as ought to be, for the benefit of the remainderman; the principle being, that the estate must come to him in as beneficial a manner as the ancient owners held it.

Infants, lunatics, and femes covert, may apply to the courts of chancery or exchequer, by petition or motion in a summary way; and by the order of those courts respectively, such persons may, by deed only, surrender leases for lives or years of the premises comprised therein.

Lessees are bound to repair their tenements, except it be mentioned in the lease to the contrary. Though a lessee for years is not obliged to repair the house let to him, which is burnt by accident, if there be not a special covenant in the lease that he shall leave the house in good repair at the end of the term, yet, if the house be burnt by negligence, the lessee shall repair it, although there be no such covenant. See ACCIDENTS. A tenant at will is not bound to sustain or repair, as tenant for years is bound. If the house of such a tenant is burnt down by negligence, no action lies against the tenant.

A lessee who covenants to pay rent and to repair, with an exception of casualties by fire, is liable upon the covenant for rent, though the premises are burnt down and not rebuilt by the lessor after notice;

but the tenant will be relieved in equity, when the landlord recovers the value against the insurer.

A proviso in a lease for 21 years, that the landlord shall re-enter, on the tenants committing any act of bankruptcy whereon a fiat shall issue, is good.

As to the bankruptcy of the lessee, see BANKRUPT.

As to the bankruptcy of the lessee being no bar to an action of covenant. See titles RENT, DISTRESS.

If a lease contain a covenant that the lessee, his executors, &c., shall not set, let, or assign over, the whole or part of the premises without leave in writing, on pain of forfeiting the lease, the administratrix of the lessee cannot under-let without incurring a forfeiture, though for less time than the whole term: a verbal licence to let *part* of the premises does not discharge the lessee from the restriction of such a proviso.

In leases of tenements, especially in towns, a covenant is frequently inserted to restrain the lessee from carrying on or assigning the houses to persons carrying on obnoxious trades, and also from having or permitting any sale of furniture in the house.

Where the tenant of a house and garden covenanted not to use or exercise any trade or business whatever without the licence of the landlord, and afterwards without licence assigned the lease to a schoolmaster, who carried on his business in the house, the assignment was held to be a breach of the covenant. The same has been held in respect of the converting a private house into a lunatic asylum.

A landlord cannot maintain an action of covenant for rent against an under tenant, who holds for a term *less* than the time granted in the original lease. But if the *whole* of a term is made over by the lessee, although in the deed he reserves the rent, and a power of entry for non payment to himself and not to the original lessor, and although he introduce new covenants, the person to whom it is made over may sue the original lessor or his assignee of the reversion, or be sued by them as assignee of the term, on the respective covenants in the original lease; such a lease being in fact an assignment.

Proprietors who take the reversion have the same remedy, the original lessees, their executors, &c., as grantors had.

Persons for whose lives estates are held by lease, &c., remaining beyond sea, or being absent seven years, if no proof be made of their being alive, shall be accounted dead, 19 *Car.* 2. *c.* 6.; also see 6 *Ann. c.* 18.

Where the term of a lease is to end on a precise day, there is no occasion for a notice to quit: unless the parties come to a fresh agreement. In the case of a tenancy from year to year, there must be half a year's notice to quit, ending at the expiration of the year. Six calendar months' notice is not sufficient, and there is no distinction between houses and lands as to the time of giving notice to quit.

LEASE AND RELEASE. A conveyance of the inheritance in land, the lease giving *first* * the possession, and the release, the right and

* One of the legal operations of a release of land is to enlarge or extend the estate of a person who is in possession of it; and, therefore, he who has the inheritance, or reversion of land, may, by a release of all his interest, *enlarge* the estate of one who has a possession of such land, which possession is created by what is termed the "lease for a year." This lease, which gives the possession, must necessarily precede the release, and bears date the day previous to the date of the release, though in practice both are executed at the same time. As the release has express reference to the lease, nothing passes by the release which is not comprised in the "lease for a year."

interest. This mode or form of conveyance, which is almost universally adopted, was originally framed to avoid the necessity of a bargain and sale enrolled, which is quite as applicable to the purpose, and has, the advantages of being registered at full length, thereby preventing the consequences of loss or accident to the writing. A feoffment is also a deed answering the same purpose, as an absolute conveyance; but, though not inrolled, a species of publicity is necessary for the effectuating this conveyance, for corporeal and formal possession must be given in the presence of witnesses, and this cause operates against the frequent adoption of this conveyance. Corporations, however, for technical reasons, cannot convey their lands by lease and release, and, therefore they must take by a feoffment, or bargain and sale enrolled when they purchase land.

LECTURES, DEBATING SOCIETIES, READING-ROOMS, &c. Any house or other place in which any lecture is delivered, or debate had, or which is open for reading books, pamphlets, newspapers, or other publications, and to which admission is obtained by payment of money upon any pretence whatever (such house, &c. not being previously licensed), shall be deemed a disorderly house, and the proprietor thereof shall forfeit 100*l.*, and the lecturer or president, on such occasion, shall forfeit 20*l.* 39 *G.* 3. *c.* 79. *s.* 15.

LECTURES, COPYRIGHT IN. A person delivering lectures has a legal title to the copyright, whether they are *orally* delivered, or read from a written composition, the first being a case where there is no *MS.*; the other is where there is an undue publication of *MS.* unpublished by the author.

In the first instance, although an injunction cannot be obtained to restrain the publication of lectures *orally*, delivered where no *MS.* exists, yet persons attending such lectures will subject themselves to an action upon an implied contract if they publish them for profit; and courts of equity will grant an injunction against third persons publishing lectures *orally* delivered, who must have procured the means of publishing those lectures from persons who attended the oral delivery of them, and were bound by the implied contract.

In the other instance, the court will grant an injunction upon the plaintiff producing his *MS.* to show that the lecture pirated was substantially reduced into writing.

Lord Eldon in one of his judgments in the litigation between the late *Mr. Abernethy*, and the editors of the *Lancet*, said, "that it never was understood that lectures were capable of being published by any of the persons who heard them." See LITERARY PROPERTY.

LECTURERS. Assistants to rectors of parishes chosen by the vestry or parishioners: they are usually afternoon preachers, they are to be licensed by the bishop or archbishop, and must subscribe the thirty-nine articles.

The rector, it seems, has a power of thwarting the wishes of his parishioners who choose a lecturer, even if they pay him themselves, unless an immemorial consent to elect without such consent can be shown.

LEGACY is a bequest of a sum of money, or any *personal* effects of a testator, and these are to be paid by his executors or those who administer the will, after all the debts of the deceased are discharged as far as the assets will extend.

All the goods and chattels of the deceased are by law vested in the representative, who is bound to see whether there is left a sufficient fund to pay the testator's debts, and the legacies specifically bequeathed, which take priority next after the debts are paid; and if the fund for general legacies prove inadequate, they must proportionally *abate*, *i. e.* a deduction must be made from each. Specific legacies, *i. e.* gifts of particular chattels, as "my bay mare," "my silver cup," my "long annuity," "the mortgage debt due to me from A. B.," do not suffer this deduction or abatement unless there is a default of assets to pay debts.

If the legatee die before the testator, the legacy will fall into the residue or *lapse;* and although from the general import of the will it may be collected that the legacy was not to lapse, yet the representatives of the deceased legatee will not take it, unless the lapse is expressly provided for; the words "executors and administrators" being deemed words of surplusage. As many nice questions have arisen on this point, in all well-penned wills the contingency of a *lapse* is expressly provided for, more especially as if where money is given to one for life, remainder to other persons, the death of the party first entitled in the lifetime of the testator will destroy the subsequent limitations.

Legacies may be given upon any terms that the testator may choose to impose (except those which have been considered unfavourable to the good order of society); testators have not been behindhand in availing themselves of this liberty; but in a great multitude of cases the testator's intent is so obscurely expressed that the courts of equity are mostly employed in administering their estates, and declaring the intents of their wills, or rather supplying their defects for the indemnity of the executors. The numerous rules of construction in reference to vesting of legacies, *i. e.* where the legacy is to be paid at a future time, or on the happening of a future event, their ademption, (*i. e.* implied revocation), conditions upon which the legatees are to take legacies in performance of covenants, substitution and accumulation are sufficient to justify those executors who have a distribution of a large estate, to seek the relief and indemnity of a court of equity.

A year from the death of the testator is, generally speaking, the period fixed for the payment of a legacy, upon the presumption that by such time the property has been got in and is making interest; this will be the case, though the fund out of which it is to be paid is making interest, the court having adopted the year as a rule of convenience: there are, however, cases in which interest will be allowed from the death of the testator.

Interest is payable upon legacies given out of personal estate from the completion of a year from the death of the testator, unless some other period is fixed by the will: at that time the right to payment exists, and carries with it the right to interest until actual payment.

Where there is a charge upon the personal estate, though it is not immediately payable, yet the person entitled may come into a court of equity, and pray that a sufficient sum may be set apart to answer the legacy when it shall become due.

An executor, however, may relieve himself from all responsibility by paying a legacy into the Bank of England, pursuant to the direction of the stat. 36 *G.* 3. *c.* 52. *s.* 32.

No legacy can be recovered in any court after twenty years next after a present right to receive it accrued to some persons capable of giving a discharge or release for the same, unless some principal or interest be paid thereon, or an acknowledgment in writing, signed by the party liable to pay, or his agent, and then only within twenty years after the last of such payments or acknowledgment; and the recovery of interest is in like manner limited to the last six years.

LETTERS, THREATENING. See THREATS.

LETTER-MISSIVE. A letter from the queen to a dean and chapter containing the name of the person whom she gives them leave to elect (*congé d'elire*) as bishop. Also the letter addressed to a peer by the chancellor, when a bill is filed against him in chancery, requiring him to appear; the writ of *subpœna* not being considered in its form sufficiently respectful.

LETTER OF ATTORNEY. A writing, authorising another person, who in such case is called the "attorney" of the party, appointing him to do any lawful act in the stead of another; as to receive debts or dividends; sue a third person; transfer stock, or give possession upon a deed of feoffment. It is either general or special; *i. e. general* in respect of the conduct of all a person's affairs, as where he leaves the country: special, in respect of any one or more named matters, as to receive money. This instrument gives the "attorney" authority to act in his name, exactly as the party giving it would himself do, *until revocation.* Letters of attorney which authorise the receipt of money payable, and are intended to operate as assignments thereof, are irrevocable, and will enable the "attorney" or assignee to receive the money for his own use.

LETTER OF CREDIT is where a merchant or correspondent writes to another, requesting him to credit another with a sum of money on the account of the writer. See BILL OF CREDIT.

LETTER OF LICENCE. A writing signed by creditors allowing a debtor longer time for the payment of his debts, and protecting him from the suits of those who sign it. It must be duly stamped.

LETTERS OF MARQUE and REPRISAL are commissions granted by the commissioners of the admiralty in war time, empowering owners of ships called privateers, to make *reprisals* upon the enemy, *i. e.* take their ships; the *prizes* captured, being divided between the owners, captain, and crew of the privateer. Security is given by the owners to the admiralty, to make compensation for any violation of treaties between those foreign powers with whom the nation is at peace, and against smuggling. Prize acts are passed on the breaking out of a war, or the king may authorise the admiralty by proclamation, to grant and regulate these *letters* or commissions.

LEVANT AND COUCHANT, is a law term denoting that cattle have been a day and night upon land.

LEVARI FACIAS. A writ of execution executed by the sheriff, for *levying* money upon the goods and lands of another. It issues from the county court and other inferior courts, but is also used for the levying money due for taxes, upon recognisances, &c., and in the latter case is issued from the exchequer.

LEVY. To collect or exact by seizure or distress.

LEWDNESS is an indictable offence, and, like all indecencies and offences against religion or morality, punishable in the court of queen's bench. Ecclesiastical courts also take cognisance of many offences against morality, as fornication, adultery, &c.

LIBEL is the term used for written scandal; slander being used to denote verbal scandal or defamation: there is an important distinction between words written and words spoken; for many words which would render another ridiculous, or lower him in the estimation of the world, are not remediable at law unless they are written; for instance, reflections upon a lady's chastity are actionable if printed or written, otherwise not, unless followed by actual damage. An action for a libel also differs from an action for words in this particular; that the former may be brought at any time within six years, and *any* damages will entitle the plaintiff to full costs.

Every *written* calumny is actionable, and punishable, although it do not impute any indictable offence, but merely tend to disgrace or ridicule, or bring into contempt the party calumniated, even by imputing hypocrisy and want of proper feeling, and still more if it impute fornication, swindling, or any other deviation from moral rectitude or principle.

No indictment or criminal information will lie for mere words, not deduced into *writing*, unless they be seditious, blasphemous, grossly immoral, or uttered to a magistrate in the execution of his office, or uttered as a challenge to fight a duel, or with an intention to provoke the other party to send a challenge.

Words Spoken.—An action will lie (without proving special damage) for all words spoken of another, which impute to him the commission of some crime *punishable by law*, such as high treason, murder, or other felony, forgery, perjury, subornation of perjury, or other misdemeanor; or even an offence punishable merely by the custom of some particular place, if the words be uttered there. But words imputing to a man an act, which (however immoral) is not punishable criminally by law, cannot be made the subject of an action, without proof of special damage.

Words spoken of another tending to exclude him from society are actionable; as, for instance, to charge him with having any particular disease, otherwise if charging him with *having had* such disease, for as this relates to a time past, it is no reason why his society should be avoided *at present.*

Also action may be sustained for words spoken of a man, which may hurt his trade or livelihood.

Writings, &c.—An action will lie (without proving special damage) for writing and publishing any thing of a man, which renders him ridiculous or contemptible.

Writings, vilifying the characters of persons deceased, are libels, and may properly be made the subject of an indictment or information, on the prosecution of the relatives of the deceased. So with respect to writings which tend to degrade or revile persons in high office in foreign countries, when they have a tendency to interrupt the pacific relations between the two countries. Also writings reflecting upon public or corporate bodies, if such writings have a manifest tendency to stir up public hatred against them, are libels.

It is not an excuse in law to repeat in writing what has been previously spoken or written by others; and in cases of verbal slander, it seems no excuse to repeat what another has said, though the party at the time of speaking the words names the person who told him what he relates.

Those who indulge in scandalising others cannot shelter themselves from the punishment that ought to await such a mean propensity by using indirect modes of expression; for it is a matter for the jury to consider whether in their minds the hint or mode of expression conveyed the idea imputed.

The punishment of libel or written scandal is by fine or imprisonment, or both, in the discretion of the court; it is immaterial on a criminal prosecution whether the libel be true or false, because it equally tends to a breach of the peace; though the court will consider all circumstances of aggravation and mitigation: in a civil action, a libel must not only appear to be scandalous, but false, for if the charge be true, the plaintiff has received no private injury.

The court of queen's bench is now in the practice of granting a criminal information for every species of written scandal; but inasmuch as the truth of a libel may, in moral consideration, extenuate the offence, it has laid down this general rule, viz. that it will not grant an information for a libel, unless the prosecutor who applies for it makes an affidavit, asserting, directly and pointedly, that he is innocent of the charge imputed to him. But this rule may be dispensed with, if the person libelled resides abroad; or if the imputations of a libel are general and indefinite; or if it is a charge against the prosecutor for language which he has held in parliament.

The court of queen's bench does not grant an information unless the libel is very gross or enormous.

Booksellers, printers, publishers, and even the venders of newspapers are liable for the contents of the books and papers they circulate. The stat. 1 *W.* 4. *c.* 73., by requiring proprietors of newspapers to find sureties, affords some protection against the libel therein.

Written statements, however disadvantageous the contents may be to another, may be what is termed *privileged*, as a fair and impartial account of a trial or proceeding in court (not an *ex parte* proceeding); also written letters confidentially addressed to others upon lawful occasions: it is, however, a matter for the jury to consider whether the statements or communications were actually and *bonâ fide* confidential, *i. e.* written upon sufficient occasion, for the word "confidential" will not privilege writing evidently written with malice, and not reasonably called for by the occasion.

No one is punishable for writing a libel unless he actually publishes it to the world; but the communication of the libel to any one person is a publication. Upon this principle, the writing an abusive letter to a person is as much a libel as if openly printed, and punishable by information.

We have seen that damages for libels carry costs, however small such damages may be, but for slanders which are *verbal*, costs are not recoverable unless the jury give damages to forty shillings.

As to libels against estate, see SEDITION.

LIEN is a right in one man to retain that which is in his possession belonging to another, till certain demands of him, the person in possession, are satisfied.

The possession must be lawful; a creditor cannot seize his debtor's goods and then retain them by virtue of a lien.

There are two kinds of lien: 1. General. 2. Particular.

1. A general lien is a right to hold not only for demands arising out of the thing retained, but for a general balance of accounts relating to dealings of the like character: this lien is regarded strictly by the law; therefore can only be established by an express contract, or by that which is evidence of contract, usage of trade, or previous dealings between the same parties, wherein such a right has been allowed.

An attorney has a lien for his general balance on papers that come professionally to his hands; so a factor has a lien upon goods for his general balance, as well for the charges, &c. due upon those particular goods. Bankers likewise upon all bills for their general account, but not on securities pledged for specific sums, or on deeds casually left in their shops after a refusal to advance money on them. Wharfingers, dyers, and calico-printers have general liens; but in other similar trades something like a *usage* should be shown, or the manner of dealing between the parties should be such as to warrant the conclusion that the lien was general. Carriers, it seems, have no common law right to a general lien.

2. Particular liens are charges made in the respect of the labour, expense, skill, &c. bestowed upon a particular or specific thing; as a tailor for mending a coat, a farrier for training a horse, a miller upon the corn ground. Innkeepers have a lien upon the horse or goods of a traveller, but a livery-stable keeper has no lien for the keep of a horse. The master of a ship has no lien for money expended on the ship. In the two last cases the law has provided adequate remedies—action against the owner, and attachment or arrest of the ship.

A lien is in effect a pledge, which pledge may be forfeited, by the party having the lien pledging the goods to others, or by other improper conduct, or by claiming to retain them on some other ground, or by entering into some contract inconsistent with the right of lien, as by stipulating for a particular mode of payment, or taking a security for its satisfaction.

Persons improperly retaining goods under pretence of debts, or where there is a debt which does not constitute a lien, are subject to an action of trover or detinue. A mere deposit of goods creates no further lien than the actual costs of warehouse room: a special agreement must warrant the detention for any other real or pretended claim; for a person retaining goods cannot plead as a set-off any debt the owner owes him.

LIFE ESTATES. See Leases.

LIGHTS. A right to the enjoyment of light and air may commence by mere occupancy. Every man on his own land has a right to all the light and air which will come to him; and he may erect, even on the extremity of his land, buildings with as many windows as he pleases, without any consent from the owner of the adjoining lands. After he has erected his building, the owner of the adjoining land may, within 20 years, build upon his own land, and so obstruct the light which would otherwise pass to the building of his neighbour; but after that time it will be presumed that the owner of the adjoining land has consented that the light may be enjoyed without obstruction. Therefore the enjoyment of light for 20 years is absolutely acquired by the permission or consent of others after that period, or rather, if the enjoyment has been exercised during that period; but this right of ancient light may be lost by shutting up the windows with brick and mortar for above 20 years.

When a party has acquired the right to the use of light, an action on the case lies for obstructing it, and the court of chancery will grant a injunction for that purpose. Reversioners and remaindermen may also bring an action or obtain an injunction; for if they were restrained from so doing during the continuance of their leases, they might not be able to prove their rights when they came into possession.

LIMITATION. A certain time assigned by the statute law within which a civil action must be brought; for felonies are punishable at any lapse of time, though in many statutes concerning penal offences, a time is limited for the bringing action thereupon, varying from three months to two years.

By the Statute of Limitations (21 *James* 1. *c.* 16.), all actions of trespass, detinue, trover, replevin, account and case (*open* accounts between traders excepted), debt upon simple contract (*i. e.* not upon bond or deed under seal), or for arrears of rent, are limited to six years after the cause of action commenced.

Actions of assault, menace, battery, mayhem, and imprisonment, must be brought within four years.

Actions for slander (*words*) must be brought within two years after the injury committed.

Suits in the ecclesiastical courts for defamatory words must be commenced within six months.

Suits, indictments, and informations upon *penal* statutes, where the forfeiture is to the crown alone, must be sued within two years, and where the forfeiture accrues to the subject, or the crown and a subject, one year, unless any other time is limited by the statute.

A late statute of limitations (3 & 4 *W.* 4. *c.* 27.) has settled the time (previously uncertain in law, though settled by the courts) within which, actions upon bonds, deeds, judgments, recognisances, or other specialties, must be brought, viz. within twenty years from the cause of suit.

Actions of debt upon award, where the submission is *not* made by deed or bond, fines due upon copyholds, or for an *escape*, or for money levied on *fieri facias*, within six years. And all actions for penalties, damages, or sums of money due to any party grieved by statute, not penal, must be brought within two years from the cause of action. Most penal statutes, however, specially limit suit for damages to a shorter period.

No memorandum or indorsement of payment written on the bill or security, shall be deemed sufficient proof of payment, so as to take the case *out of* the operation of the statute.

To bring a case of the above description *within* the operation of the statute, so as not to be excluded from suit, a written acknowledgment of the party must be obtained, or a suit must be commenced within the time.

The law with respect to claims or suits in respect of *real* property has been by a statute of the same session, 1833, very much altered; and the general time to recover is limited to 20 years, with a saving of 10 years for persons abroad, women married, minors and lunatics, but not in any case to exceed 40 years although the 10 years have not expired.

LIMITATION OF ESTATE. A modification or settlement of an estate, determining how long it shall continue; or a qualification of a precedent estate.

LINEAL CONSANGUINITY is that which subsists between persons of whom one is descended in a direct line from the other. See DESCENT, KINDRED.

LINEAL DESCENT. The descent of estates from ancestor to heir, *i. e.* from one to another, in a right or direct line. See title DESCENT.

LITERARY PROPERTY or COPYRIGHT, is the interest or property which an author has in his book or *copy* (which word *copy* means the MS. itself*), after publication, by means of printing, engraving, or lithographing. The etymology of the word *copyright* sufficiently

* "Copy, the autograph, the original, the archetype; that from which any thing is copied." *Johnson.*

explains this, as the *copy* or MS. is the symbol of possession, as well as the evidence of the author's identity.

The crown, at a very early period after the invention of printing, assumed not only a right to control the press, but claimed a monopoly in respect of the publication and sale of all books relating to law, religion, and state, the remains of which exist in the patent rights, or *special* copyrights of the two universities to publish Bibles: the printing of acts of parliament by the king's printer's patent, and the privilege till lately enjoyed by the company of stationers, in respect of their *almanack*-patent, which in 1778 was declared illegal.

Although an author had a right of action against those who pirated his work, yet in respect of the *property* which an author had in his book, the law, in early times, appears not to have been expressly declared; and it is remarkable, that the question, as to the duration of an author's right, as distinct from a title by royal patent, proclamation, or grant of privilege, was never determined till many years after 1710, in which year an act was passed (8 *Ann. c.* 19.), specifying the term for which an author was to enjoy his interest or property. One cause of which was the restrictive system of licensing and registering all publications*; for he who published a book without a licence, was punishable in the star chamber by the heavy penalties of that arbitrary court; and, moreover, no person was able to obtain a licence for printing a book already registered. By this preventive remedy against literary piracy, authors were relieved from the necessity of prosecuting, either for damages at common law, or in the star-chamber, for infraction of the licensing edict, or breach of prerogative, if the author's interest was acknowledged or preserved by patent, or grant of privilege from the king, as will be shown hereafter.

These circumstances probably caused the opinion to grow up, that every author's interest in his work was as perpetual and unlimited *after its publication*, as while it was a simple MS. or copy (which the reader must understand, always was, and is now, the subject of sale, as any chattel or moveable goods, to any extent, either as regards duration of time, or number of owners); the multiplication of copies by

* In 1556, by a decree of the star-chamber, it was forbidden to print against the force of any ordinance, &c. in any of the statutes or laws of the realm.

By another decree, in 1585, every book, &c. is to be *licensed*: nor shall any one print any book, &c. against the form or meaning of any restraint contained in any statute or laws of the realm — or contrary to any allowed ordinance set down for the good government of the Stationers' Company.

In 1623, a proclamation sets forth that the above decree had been evaded "by printing beyond sea such allowed books, &c. as have been imprinted with-"in the realm, by such to whom the sole printing thereof, by letters patent, or "lawful ordinance or authority, doth appertain;" and then the proclamation enforces the decree.

Again, in 1637, by another decree, no person is to print or import any book or copy which the company of stationers, or any other person, hath or shall by any letters patent, order or entrance in their register-book, or otherwise, have the right, privilege, authority, or allowance solely to print.

An ordinance of parliament, June 14. 1643, enforces the registry of every book in the registry-book of the Stationers' Company, and prohibits the importation of books from abroad formerly printed here, upon pain of forfeiture of the books to the author, and such other punishment as shall be thought fit.

Ordinances, in 1647 and 1649, enforced the licensing of books; and the licensing act of *C.* 2., 1662, controlled the liberty of the press by instituting a licensing officer: but at the same time it prohibited literary piracy, by heavy penalties besides forfeiture of the book and 6*s.* 8*d.* fine for each book, besides bodily punishment at the discretion of the judge.

printing, engraving, or lithographing, altering the property and converting it to a copyright.

However, whatever was the notion entertained of an author's perpetuity, the right of publishing a book for an unlimited duration of time, in any manner exercised, appears to have been regarded at the beginning of the 17th century, and to the year 1666, in no other light than a *private* monopoly, and consequently, to require royal confirmation, or approbation, as is very evident from grants of privilege conceded to authors and publishers of popular or expensive books, by the crown (particularly James I.), whose patent, proclamation, or grant of privilege*, as

* The following is a *Grant of Privilege*, copied from the back of the title-page of one of Matthew L'Obel's works.—"Licensed" and "Imprimatur" subsequently appeared on the backs of title-pages, till the licensing system fell into disuse, or was repealed.

"PRIVILEGIUM REGIVM.

"Jacobi, Dei gratiâ, Magnæ Britanniæ, Franciæ, et Hyberniæ "Regis authoritate et privilegio sancitum est, (perpensis assi-

The author's name and motives for granting the privilege.

"duis laboribus et magnis expensis *Matthiæ L'Obelii* Botano-"graphi nostri, tàm operum, jamdiu in lucem editorum, quàm "novissimè in Reipublicæ utilitatem excudendorum), ne quis "*Plantarum Historiæ ejus illustrationes, Rariorum Stirpium* "*Appendices, et cum Simplicium Medicamentorum, Materiæve*

The works protected.

"*Medicæ Balsami, Opo-balsami, Hylo-balsami, Cinnamomi,* "*Casiæ, Hylo-Cassiæ et cæterorum explicationes; tum composi-*"*torum Medicamentorum enodationes, Animadversionesque in* "*Pharmaceuticam Rondelletianam Officinam et Censuras bene-*"*volas in Antidotaria vulgaria,* necnon *Collectanea* sua, intra

Translation and importation forbidden.

"*viginti* annos, ipso inscio, invitoque, aut hæredibus suis, im-"primat, aut plantarum Icones suas, sive integrâ, sive aliquâ "ex parte, imitetur; aut alibi impressa, in ditionis nostræ "Regiones deferat, distrahatque vernaculove idiomate, (ut "sordidâ Typographorum authoritate, plerumque fieri solet) "pervertat, vertat, depersatque, præter præfati *L'Obelii* aut suo-

Forfeiture of the books and an arbitrary penalty.

"rum hæredum voluntatem. Qui secus fecerit, confiscatione "Librorum et summâ pecuniariâ ex *arbitrio nostro*[1] mulctabitur. "Datum in Aula Regia nostra, Grynwich, secunda Junii "1605.

"Signatum,

"JACOBUS REX."

A similar privilege for 14 years, in terms quite as peremptory, was, by Charles the Second, granted to the dean of Peterborough, the king's chaplain, for the protection of a Greek paraphrase of the Psalms. It is quite as comprehensive as the preceding, after a similar preamble, concluding thus:—

"Regio etiam Nostro Diplomate sancitum ac provisum est, ne quis Bibliopola aut typographus, aut alius quicumque, infra quatuor-decim annos dictæ, *Metaphraseos* exemplaria citra voluntatem ac consensum autoris hìc infra ditiones nostras imprimere aut imprimi facere, aut in exteris regionibus impressa hùc importare aut divendere præsumat; sub pœna confiscationis et amissionis eorundem librorum, et mulctæ prætereà secundùm *Leges nostras*[1] infligendæ.

"Dat' in Palatio nostro de Whitehall, 20 die Februarii, 1666, Regniq: nostri decimo nono.

"Ad mandatum sacræ Regiæ Majestatis,

"GUILIELMUS MORICE."

The publishers of the *Biographia Britannica*, in 1741, obtained a grant of privilege from George II., which is in much the same form as the preceding, and contained a similar *in terrorem* inhibition. The curious reader will find it at the commencement of the first volume.

---

[1] *Leges nostras* is not more constitutional than "*arbitrio nostro*," and quite as uncertain, and shows the absence of any express declaration of the law of copyright.

the law then stood, not only protected the author from every species of *piracy*, but inflicted an arbitrary fine (to be assessed in the star-chamber, which took cognisance of breaches of prerogative) upon those committing the piracy, and superadded the forfeiture of the books so unduly published, without affecting the author's right to his remedy at law for damages; which, by the by, has always been deemed unsatisfactory, and comparatively worthless when compared with the amount of injury actually sustained. In fact, these grants of privilege, which closely follow the tenor of licences granted by the pope to the printers in the Italian states, at and previous to that period, operated as an assertion of the royal prerogative in regard to the book, and thereby seemed to secure to the author a perpetuity in his copyright interest; and are the sole foundation of the opinion that prevailed till 1774 (notwithstanding the act passed in 1710), that every author's interest, whether secured by patent, grant or licence from the crown, or not, was of an unlimited duration, and assignable by him or his executors, to others, *ad infinitum*.

When the prerogative of creating monopolies, by means of letters patent, was questioned and complained of, these grants of privilege for a time ceased; but they seem not to have been considered as being within the stat. 21 *Jac.* 1. *c.* 3., which excepted from the monopolies declared void by that statute, letters patent, or grants of privilege for 14 years, of the sole working or making of the same. See Patent.

As Charles II. gave similar grants of privilege, the effect of the statute of James respecting patents appears to have suggested to the framers of the statute of 8 *Ann.* c. 19. the term and duration of literary property, which is after all, like a patent, a private monopoly in a benign sense of the word, and consequently to be governed by rules analogous to patents for inventions. For, the limitation of a specific term in literary property, and the restriction of a right of patent in a manufacture or invention to 14 years, are evidently created upon the same principle, and to the intent, that as the author or inventor is sufficiently recompensed for his book or invention, by the enjoyment of a temporary monopoly, or privilege of selling it, or using it, therefore, on the expiration of the times limited by law, the public are to acquire an interest therein.

After royal monopolies were destroyed or restrained, there only remained the licensing system, which had more for its object the control of the press, than any thing else, though it certainly tended to preserve the copyright from piracy; but the licensing system, after the abolition of the star-chamber, did not prevent needy and unprincipled persons from republishing and importing from abroad copies of works originally printed here, to the great detriment of authors in general, who now began to find that actions against worthless people only verified a coarse adage. The stationers' company, whose charter was very ample, and the universities who had acquired valid patent rights, appear to have been the only persons uninjured. Therefore the statute of 1710, before alluded to, was passed; which, amongst other provisions, re-enacted in the last copyright act), particularly enacted that the author of any book, and his assigns, should have the sole liberty of printing it for 14 years; and for a further term of 14 years, if the author were living at the end of the first 14 [now 28 years absolute, and to the end of the author's life]. A similar statute was passed on the union with Ireland, which is now on the same footing as England, with regard to copyright.

The importation of books reprinted abroad, was also prohibited by another act passed in 1739. Notwithstanding the terms of that statute an opinion still prevailed, that copyright was unlimited, and this fallacy was not exposed till 1774, when the act judicially received its proper construction and interpretation; viz. that after the expiration of the time mentioned in the act, any person might republish a copy.

This decision overturned the claim of unlimited copyright, which had existed previously to 1710, and (in opinion) from that time to 1774; and therefore, the universities sought the security of an act of parliament for securing the copyright which they had acquired by bequest, which in 1775, was passed, and enabled the two universities in England, the four universities in Scotland, and the several colleges of Eton, Westminster, and Winchester, to hold *in perpetuity*, their copyright in books, given or bequeathed to the said universities and colleges, for the advancement of useful learning, and other purposes of education; such books to be printed at the presses of the universities or colleges respectively.

The stationers' company, whose charter seems expressly framed for the securing to them a great number of purchased copyrights, of course lost all their property of this nature; and, some individual bringing the legality of their patent for the exclusive printing of almanacs in question, the same patent was in 1778 declared to have been granted against law.

The act now governing literary property is the stat. 54 *G*. 3. *c*. 156. which contains all the enactments affecting copyright, after reciting the previous acts which gave the author of a book and his assigns the liberty of printing his book for 14 years; and for another 14 years, if living at the end of the first 14 years, enacts that the author of any books composed, and not printed and published, or which thereafter should be composed and be printed and published, and his assignee or assigns, shall have the sole liberty of printing and reprinting such book for 28 years, to commence from the day of first publishing the same; and also, if the author shall be living at the end of that period, for the remainder of his natural life.

The act then goes on to provide, that if any bookseller, or printer, or other person in the United Kingdom, or in the Isles of Man, Jersey, or Guernsey, *or in any other part of the British dominions*, shall within the times and terms limited by the act, print, reprint, or import, or cause the same to be done without the consent *in writing*, of the author, or other proprietors of the copyright; or knowingly, and without such written consent, shall sell, publish, or expose to sale, or cause the same to be done, or shall have in his or their possession, for sale, such books without consent in *writing*, then the author or proprietors may, by a special action on the case, recover damages with double costs of suit. And the offenders shall forfeit such books, and every sheet being part of such books, and are upon order of any court of record made upon motion or petition, to deliver the same to the author or proprietors, who are to *damask* and *waste* the same; and the offenders are also to forfeit the sum of 3*d*. for every sheet printed, or printing, or exposed to sale, contrary to the meaning of the act, one moiety to the king, and the other moiety to the informer, recoverable in any court of record.

All books are required to be entered (within one month if published in London, and three months if published elsewhere) at Stationers' Hall; and one copy, on the best paper, to be then delivered for the

British Museum: 2*s*. to be paid for each entry; penalty for neglect of entry 5*l*. and eleven times the price of the book. § 5. The warehouse keeper at Stationers' Hall is to transmit lists of all publications to the librarians of the libraries entitled to copies, and to demand the copies of the publishers when required, but who may deliver the books at the several libraries if they please. § 6, 7.*

A failure in making the entry shall not affect the copyright, but only subject the publisher to the penalty imposed. § 5.

This act secured to the representatives of the authors of books, the benefits they might have derived from the second 14 years, under the act of 1710, if they were living at the time of the act, and died before the expiration of the first 14 years, but without prejudicing the rights of the assignees or proprietors. § 8. And the authors of books published at the passing of the act, had secured to them the copyright for the remainder of their lives, if they survived the term of 28 years, but without affecting the right of any assignee or proprietor. § 9.

Legal proceedings under this act are limited to 12 months after the commission of the act. § 10.

The remedies for infringing an author's or proprietor's copyright are now very complete; for under the statute, he can have an action for penalties, he can maintain an action on the case for damages, and recover double costs; and what is the better remedy, he can file a bill in equity (upon which an injunction can be obtained as a provisional step) for restraining the publication, and compelling the party to account for the profits of his piracy. But the author of an immoral or libellous work has no legal property in such a production; and consequently, cannot proceed with effect against those who pirate his book; and this doctrine extends to prints, &c.

A fair and *bonâ fide* abridgment of any book is considered as a new work; and however it may injure the sale of the original, yet it is not deemed in law to be a piracy; and *after the time limited by law has expired*, the author, or any other person, may reprint the book with original notes, or additions; for these are, in fact, new works.

A translation of a work, either from the ancient classic authors, or of a work written in Latin by an Englishman, or of papers in any of the modern languages, as French or German are protected by the act.

By a liberal interpretation of the law, musical compositions are protected, even though upon a single side or sheet of paper; for the word *book* applies to any writing.

Every distinct and independent part of a work is also a book within the meaning of the act, as a tale or piece of music bound up with other tales or pieces of music.

As the law intends that all intellectual labour should be protected, it is settled that lectures either *read*, or orally delivered, may not be published for profit.

Many persons have thought, that as the MS. of a work is the symbol and the evidence of possession in the author's or proprietor's hands, it may have the same operation when in theirs; but this notion has long been repudiated; for though an individual may possess a MS., even by

* The libraries to which copies of *books* (for maps and prints *without* letter-press are not liable) are to be delivered, are—1. The British Museum (the best paper copy); 2. The Bodleian Library at Oxford; 3. The Public Library at Cambridge; 4. The Library of the Faculty of Advocates at Edinburgh; and, 5. Trinity College Library at Dublin.

the gift of the writer, yet *the profit of multiplying copies by printing or otherwise* is prohibited; and the court of chancery will interfere, to restrain the publication of MS. of a deceased person; and the letters of a deceased, are also either the subject of copyright in the representatives, or their publication is calculated to wound private feelings, in both which cases, injunctions can be obtained. Indeed, the intelligent reader can easily draw the distinction between the possession of sheets of written paper, as a mere chattel, and the publication and infinite multiplication of those sheets by means of printing. A manuscript has been peviously noticed as a mere chattel before publication even in the author's hands, and consequently, not subject to any limitation as to time; but when published, its duration is limited, and subject to that restriction, like a patent invention, it will eventually become public property. The consent to print a work must be in writing, so that to make any other use of a MS. than to read it, is an infraction of the author's right.

Prints and engravings have received the protection of the legislature since 1735, and three acts relate to this species of literary property. The following are the principal distinctions of these statutes: an exclusive privilege of publishing is given to those who invent the design, or make a print from another's design or picture, for 28 years; and those who copy such prints within that time, forfeit all their copies, to be destroyed, and *5s.* for each copy: maps, charts, and plans, are among the prints enumerated; and the proprietor has an action on the case, to recover damages and double costs, for any violation of his right without any particular limitation.

The assignee of a print may therefore have the same remedy at law, or in equity, for piracy, as an author or proprietor; and the mere seller or publisher of a pirated copy of a print is liable to an action, although it is not an exact copy of the original, and although the seller did not know it to be a copy.

It is no piracy of one engraving to make another from the original picture.

It may here be remarked, that the copies, maps, charts, and plans, while unaccompanied with letter press, are not demandable by the libraries.

Copyright may be bequeathed for the unexpired term; but as the custom is for an author to transfer his interest to the publisher, and as the available duration of copyright is short and precarious, instances rarely occur of a bequest of copyright.

Copyright, *i. e.* the interest in a MS. after publication, will pass to creditors like any other distinct right or property; but before publication, in nowise can it be taken in execution or seized, even if the author be bankrupt or insolvent.

The courts of judicature exercise the power of restraining the publication of their proceedings until judgment is given; and though, generally speaking, the true representation and narration of a judicial proceeding is justifiable, yet that doctrine is subject to various qualifications.

The transfer or assignment of a copyright in books must be evidenced by some writing, signed by the author or proprietor; and it is not absolutely requisite that it should be attested by any witness. But the transfer of copyright in prints, engravings, maps, and charts, must not only be signed by the proprietor, but the transfer or deed *must* be attested by two credible witnesses at the least.

Copyright in prints and engravings is extended to Ireland by an act passed on 13th August, 1836.

As to copyright in plays, see Dramatic Literary Property.

LIVERY. Used for a suit of clothes, cloak, hat, &c., which a nobleman or gentleman gives to his servants with a badge, or without. Formerly, great men gave liveries to several who were not of their family, to engage them in their quarrels for that year; but afterwards it was enacted, that no man should give any livery, but to his domestics, his officers, or counsel learned in the law.

Livery, in another signification, means a delivery of possession of lands and tenements to a purchaser, being a ceremony in the law formerly used in all conveyances of lands, where an estate of fee-simple, fee-tail, or other freehold passed; but now it is confined to a feoffment to complete which, the ceremony of livery of seisin is very material to be performed, for without this the feoffee has but a mere estate at will. This livery, which is termed livery of seisin, is the remains of the pure feodal investiture or delivery of corporeal possession of the land or tenement, which was held absolutely necessary to complete the donation. See Livery of Seisin.

LIVERY OF SEISIN, is the putting a person in corporal possession of a freehold, by giving him the ring, latch, or key of the door; or, if land, by delivering him a turf or twig; or in either case, doing any act before witnesses, which clearly places the party in possession. It formerly accompanied all conveyances of land, but is now confined to that conveyance called a feoffment: it is necessary that no other person should be in possession at the time this formal delivery of possession takes place, except by necessity. See Feoffment.

LIVERYMEN OF LONDON. So called because they anciently wore liveries or badges peculiar to each company. In the companies of London liverymen are chosen out of the freemen, as assistants to the masters and wardens in matters of council, and for government, a select number generally acting as a court of assistants, *i. e. assisting* the master and wardens. If any one refuse to take upon him the office, he may be fined, and an action of debt will lie against him for the amount in the lord mayor's court. It seems questionable how far these fines, or rather the by-laws, which assume the power of inflicting them, are supported or countenanced by the superior courts to which they can be removed by *certiorari;* certainly an unreasonable fine would not be enforced as against law, notwithstanding any by-law or charter to the contrary.

LOBSTERS may be imported by natives or foreigners, and in any vessels. Lobsters are not to be taken on the sea-coast of Scotland, from the 1st of June to the 1st of September, yearly, under a penalty of 5*l.*, recoverable before two justices.

LOCAL ACTION, is that action which must be tried in the county where the subject-matter takes place. An action for recovery of land, viz. ejectment, is local, and must therefore be tried in the county where the lands lie. Actions of another nature, called *transitory*, may or may not be brought in the county where the subject arises. The courts will always interfere to prevent this liberty being oppressively, or improperly, used, as if plaintiff brings his action in a distant county to which the witnesses must travel at a great expense, or in a county where strong prejudice may be supposed to exist in favour of the claim.

LOCUS IN QUO. The place where any thing is alleged to be done.

LODGINGS. When part of a messuage or house is let to another, it is called a lodging or lodgings.

Lodgings may be let in the same manner as lands and tenements; in general, however, they are let either by agreement in writing between the landlord and tenant, or by verbal agreement.

A verbal agreement to take lodgings *from a future day*, is an agreement relating to an interest in land, and may be abandoned where there has been no part execution of the contract by entering on the premises, although the lessor, before the time is arrived for taking possession, has, at the request of the lessee, removed the advertisement of lodgings from his windows.

With respect to the general rule, that, in the case of a yearly tenancy, notice to quit must be half a year before the expiration of the year; the case of lodgings depends upon a particular contract, and is an exception to that rule.

The whole question depends upon the nature of the first contract; so that if the parties have agreed that the tenant shall hold for a term certain, no notice of course can be necessary; but if the tenant hold for no particular period, reasonable notice must be given, which is regulated generally, if not always, by the local custom of the particular place or district, which, for the most part, requires the same space of time for notice as the period for which the lodgings are taken; as, a week's notice when taken for a week, a month's where taken for a month, and so forth: but this is not always the case, for it is not always necessary (it is presumed) that a quarter's notice should be given where the rent is paid quarterly, and it is understood to be a quarterly taking; for a month's notice is sometimes customary.

A tenant from week to week, continuing in possession after the expiration of a notice to quit, and demand made, is not liable to an action on the stat. 4 *G.* 2. *c.* 28. for double value.

If the lodgings be furnished, it may be as well to have a schedule of the goods they contain affixed to the agreement, if there be one in writing; in the same manner as in the case of a lease of a house with goods. See *Woodfall's Landlord and Tenant.*

LONDON. The metropolis of this kingdom, which is a county of itself. It is divided into 26 wards, over each of which there is an alderman, and is governed by a lord mayor, who is chosen yearly, and presented to the barons of the exchequer at Westminster.

The lord mayor of London for the time being, is a justice of gaol delivery, escheator within the liberties, and bailiff of the river Thames; therefore returns writs of escheat, holds courts of conservancy for the river, and is the first person named as one of the judges of the central criminal court. He is also a high officer in the city, having all courts for distribution of justice under his jurisdiction, viz. the court of hustings, sheriff's court, mayor's court (of which the recorder is the judge), and court of common council. He is likewise coroner of the city; but this office is generally delegated to a deputy.

No person, not being a freeman of London, shall keep any shop or other place to put to sale by retail any goods or wares, or use any handicraft, trade for hire, gain, or sale within the city, upon pain of forfeiting 5*l.*—*Charter of Charles I.*

London is a *market overt*, every day in the week, save Sunday.

There are three ways to be a freeman of London. 1. By servitude or apprenticeship; 2. By birth-right or patrimony, *i. e.* the being born after the father became free; 3. By redemption or purchase by leave of the court of aldermen.

The estates of freemen of London are distributable (in case of intestacy) by a special custom (see EXECUTORS and ADMINISTRATORS); but the child of a freeman may, when of age, in consideration of a present fortune, bar herself of her customary share. It has also been held, that an agreement on marriage that the husband shall take up the freedom of London, in equity binds the distribution of his effects.

The city of London is entitled to a fine imposed by the courts at Westminster, for a misdemeanour committed within the city.

The customs of London are various, all confirmed by act of parliament: they relate to the distribution of freemen's assets, the *attaching* money or goods, and in various particulars relate to trade; as that a married woman may be a sole trader; or commerce, as duties payable, &c.

There is a court of requests for the recovery of debts not exceeding 10*l.* [It would be a convenience that such courts existed in all places for *debts* to this amount; for the costs of an action of law, though scarcely remunerating the attorney, yet are very grievous to a defendant when compared with the *amount* of the debt, which this court can order to be paid by instalments; whereas debt and costs recovered in the superior courts are payable forthwith, so that an improvident debtor may be ruined by a number of small suits.]

The gaol delivery for London and Middlesex was, until recently, held at the sessions-house in the Old Bailey eight times in the year; but now a "Central Criminal Court" is established, to which the king may direct commissions of oyer and terminer to inquire of all felonies and misdemeanours committed within the city of London and county of Middlesex, and those parts of Essex, Kent, and Surrey about 10 miles round London, in the same manner as commissions of oyer and terminer used formerly to be addressed to the lord mayor and judges for London and Middlesex; such sessions to be holden at least 12 times in every year, or oftener if need be.

The rates of tonnage imposed on ships frequenting the port of London are stated in and regulated by the stat. 4 *&* 5 *W.* 4. *c.* 32.

The city of London has the appointment of its own police; and numerous acts have been passed from very early periods regulating the sale of goods, manufactures, markets, trades, and other matters affecting the commercial relations of this great city.

LORDS' ACT. Debtors charged in execution for a sum not exceeding 300*l.* exclusive of costs, and who shall not within three months after their committal satisfy the same, may be required by any creditor, upon 20 days' written notice, to give in a true account in writing, signed by him, of all his real and personal estate, and incumbrances affecting the same; the other detaining creditors are also to have notice.

The prisoner is to be brought up to the court wherein he is committed, and is bound, under penalty of transportation for seven years, to deliver in open court a full account of his property, excepting necessary articles, not exceeding 10*l.*

Upon the prisoner's being brought up, the court will make an assignment to a particular person, and he is thereupon discharged.

This proceeding is not much used, as these proceedings are often expensive and surrounded with petty technicalities, and have in the first instance to be borne by the creditor. See act 32 *G.* 2. *c.* 28.

LOST and STOLEN BILLS or NOTES. Bills and notes being negotiable when lost or stolen, may be transferred to innocent holders, who, if timely notice be not given of the circumstance, may discount or cash them, and resort to the acceptor on their becoming due; and bank notes or securities transferable by mere delivery, may be utterly lost to the owner, if such notice be not given.

The ancient practice was for the possessor of the bill, losing it, to cause a memorandum of the fact to be made by a notary public before witnesses, and protested before the acceptor; and there is no reason why this practice should not be continued as far as regards notice to him.

The effect of such notice, which should be published in such a manner that all persons may reasonably be supposed to have an intimation of the facts, will be to stop the negotiability of the bill in the hands of the wrongful holders, or those who discount it with notice, and to give the loser his action of trover for the recovery. The question always is, has the discounter or holder of the bill or changer of a bank note used ordinary and proper caution in receiving the subject of the action, and has he had sufficient notice (if direct fraud against the holder, &c., cannot be proved) of the circumstances under which the bill, note, or security was obtained? if so, the plaintiff's right of action to recover back the same is complete; otherwise, not.

By stat. 9 *&* 10 *W.* 3. *c.* 17., if any *inland* bill of exchange for 5*l.* or upwards shall be lost, the drawer of the bill shall give another bill of the same tenor, security being given to indemnify him in case the bill so lost be found again.

Against the person who finds a bill, the real owner may maintain an action of trover.

Persons who obtain bills from others on a *written* order for appropriation of the proceeds, are guilty of a felony in embezzling the same; or if the party entrusting them with the bill has not given a written order or direction, he may bring his action of trover against them for the bill, and may publish notice to restrain the future negotiability of the bill, and no person discounting it after public and *sufficient* notice can recover upon it. See Agents.

LOTTERIES. See Nuisances.

LUNATIC, or **Non Compos Mentis,** is the term applied to a person who has had a sound mind or understanding, but which is subsequently impaired or lost: a lunatic, indeed, is generally said to be a person mad, but alternately enjoying lucid intervals; while *non compos mentis*, or *of unsound mind*, is applied to those who lose their intellects by disease, imbecility, great age, or are deaf and dumb — in short, not capable of managing their own affairs. Idiots, we have seen, are persons born under incurable defects of understanding. The legal, as well as physiological distinction being, that the idiot has a defective brain, and the lunatic a diseased brain, and therefore the law always assumes the possibility of the return of understanding to the latter.

The term "of unsound mind," is very comprehensive: it embraces not only the condition of idiots and lunatics, but also all cases of imbecility of mind, extending to absolute incapacity, arising from disease, age, or other causes.

The king is guardian, by virtue of his prerogative, to all lunatics, &c., and delegates his trust to the lord keeper or chancellor, who administers their estates, and appoints a committee of the person as well as of the estate, which should be preserved for the lunatic on his recovery, or his heir if he die insane.

The inquiry whether a person is idiot or lunatic is by a commission directed to a commissioner, who, by the verdict of 12 men summoned by the sheriff, and upon view of the lunatic himself, decides the question.

In case of the lunatic's recovery, he may petition the chancellor to supersede the commission, upon the hearing of which the lunatic must attend in person, that he may be inspected by the chancellor: it is also requisite that the physician should attend, and make affidavit that he is perfectly recovered.

Idiots and lunatics, &c., may inherit, but of course they are disqualified for the performance of public duties; and if trustees or mortgagees, their committee may convey, under direction of the court of chancery: they are incapable of being executors or administrators.

The marriage of a lunatic is valid, if previous to the date or time at which his lunacy has been found by a jury to have commenced; but though he may have lucid intervals between the commencement of his lunacy and his subsequent marriage, yet by statute it is rendered void; for it would be extremely difficult to prove the exact state of a party's mind at the celebration of the marriage. The marriage of an idiot is always void, for as he never had any understanding, so he never was able to consent, consent being purely an act of the understanding.

Acts done by a lunatic during a lucid interval are valid; but the proof of their being so done is thrown on the party seeking to recover against the lunatic, if a general lunacy from a previous date has been established.

The lunatic's *name*, not the *committee's*, must be used in actions of trespass and ejectment, in respect of the lunatic's possession; and in all other actions he sues, pleads, and defends, as an ordinary person, except in chancery, where he defends by his committee. A lunatic is liable to actions for debts accrued before his lunacy, and for acts of trespass to the persons or property of others *after* his lunacy; and a lunatic cannot avoid an arrest on account of his being *non compos;* but the Insolvent Act declares how a lunatic insolvent shall be discharged.

Idiots, as persons permanently insane, also lunatics whose alienation of mind is unequivocal, are not chargeable with criminal acts of any nature whatever; but he who incites an insane person to commit an offence, is as much punishable as if he had done it himself.

Insane persons acquitted on the ground of insanity are kept in custody, and remain at the disposal of the queen.

The restraint of insane persons is warranted by law, but under certain restrictions, to prevent its abuse; and by late statutes* various provisions have been made for the reception and care of lunatics and insane persons in licensed mad-houses; and the maintenance of pauper and criminal lunatics in *county lunatic asylums* is, by particular statutes, chiefly vested in the justices at quarter sessions, who may appoint a committee for the erection of *asylums*, also visitors, in the manner directed by the acts; and are empowered to order the conveyance of pauper lunatics to an asylum, &c.

* The care and treatment of lunatics is regulated by 2 *&* 3 *W*. 4. *c*. 107., amended by 3 *&* 4 *W*. 4. *c*. 64. The regulation of county lunatic asylums, and the care of pauper and criminal lunatics, in *England*, is provided for by 9 *G*. 4. *c*. 40., and 1 *W*. 4. *c*. 1., which repeal all previous acts for that purpose; and with regard to the committal of *any* insane person likely to commit crime or a misdemeanor, and the disposal of insane criminals, provision is made by 39 *&* 40 *G*. 3. *c*. 94. *ss*. 1, 2, 3., and 9 *G*. 4. *c*. 40. *ss*. 54, 55.

By another late statute, the lord chancellor may appoint visitors to superintend and report to him upon the care and treatment of idiots, lunatics, and persons of unsound mind, found such by inquisition, who are to be visited once a year. — 3 *&* 4 *W.* 4. *c.* 36.

MAGISTRATE, is in effect the same as justice; justices and magistrates being correlative terms.

MAGNA CHARTA. The great charter of liberties granted in the 9th year of king Henry III. King John had previously granted a similar one, but he broke it. The laws contained therein are the earliest written declaration of the liberty of the subject, as opposed to the then overweening power of the crown.

MAIMING. See WOUNDING.

MAINPRIZE. A term used for bail in criminal cases.

MAINTENANCE and CHAMPERTY. An agreement, which gives a stranger the benefit of a suit, on condition of his conducting it and prosecuting it. This is an indictable offence, and punishable by fine and imprisonment. See BARRATRY.

It is an invidious inquiry, but suggested by the practice of a peculiar class of lawyers, how far an attorney may be guilty of this offence. An attorney, it seems, ought not to undertake a suit upon an understanding that he would bear all the costs out of his own pocket, and that his client should be indemnified from all loss. Also, if an attorney take up a doubtful claim, and inform the party of it, and offer to recover the same for him upon terms of future profit and advantage to himself, derivable from the fruits of such suit, he is, according to general received opinion, guilty of *maintenance,* and in the second instance barratry.

The bare solicitation by an attorney to conduct a suit is not barratry or maintenance; though a pure honourable feeling would restrain the tender of professional services till they were sought for by the client.

The simple advancing of money for a suit, however poor the client may be, cannot be deemed maintenance while the attorney has any expectation of being repaid; and, indeed, such an act is a charitable office, where the motives are upright and correct.

Suits or actions being evidently frivolous or vexatious, and instituted only for the purpose of exacting money from the defendants, coupled with the fact of a guarantee being given by the attorney or solicitor for the plaintiff against the expenses of the suit to the defendant, will, upon motion, be dismissed by the court.

It has been stated upon good authority, that any legitimate common interest will justify the uniting of parties in subscribing to bear expenses even of a third party, where the subscribers have an interest; but subscriptions for supporting the *suit* of *another* are certainly within the scope of the law.

MALICIOUS MISCHIEF. See MISCHIEF.

MANDAMUS. [Lat. we command.] Is a high writ issuing in the queen's name out of the court of queen's bench, and directed to any person, corporation (public or incorporated by act of parliament), or inferior court of judicature, *commanding* them to do some particular thing therein specified, as appertaining to their *public* office and duty.

This writ generally issues upon *public* considerations, although upon *private* complaint; for if the matter of complaint be *wholly* private, as to compel a trading corporation to account with one of its members, in fact, to settle partnership accounts, the court will not interfere, for the writ ought only to issue where the remedy is inadequate, and where the refusal by a party in office to do justice, though at the application of a private party, creates a public wrong. This writ is *remedial*, and generally is used for the purpose of compelling the admission or restoration to an office; for the production of books and writings; to compel inferior courts to do particular acts, the delay or refusal of which may tend to interrupt the course of law and justice; to compel lords of manors to permit inspection of court rolls, churchwardens to deliver up books to their successors in office, and an infinite number of other purposes, which, though apparently injuring an individual, yet, as matters of public consideration, should be summarily remedied, even though an indictment might lie; for an indictment cannot compel a party to do a particular act, but can only be the means of inflicting a punishment for non-performance.

MANOR. The jurisdiction and rights upon a certain district or site of land, with the perquisites belonging to it. The origin of manors was the granting by the king to some great person a tract of ground, rendering certain military services; he in his turn granted and parcelled out the same to inferior tenants, who rendered to him similar and sometimes pecuniary services, the better to enable him to perform his tenure in chief, and they regranted *ad infinitum*. But the subdivision of tenures was soon stopped by an act of parliament, which provided that in granting of land, the party who aliened should not reserve or stipulate for other services than those he himself was bound to perform; so that no new manor can be created at this day, for no man can grant lands to be holden of himself by services; and this sufficiently explains the reason why some manors are so large and some so small and inconsiderable.

Lords of manors formerly granted large parcels of land, which became manors themselves; the chief manor then was called an honour, of which there very few now remaining.

Lords of manors, by founding a church, assumed the filling it up, or *presenting* to it, by the right of foundation. See ADVOWSON.

Although the lords of manors let out or re-granted their land to others, yet they reserved some land for tillage and for their own support these were occupied by those who were called *villeins*, in plain English, slaves or serfs. They held *at the will of the lord*, and they having, by long usage or by indulgence, commuted their servitude and tenancy at will into a tenancy which was only subject to pecuniary payments or fines, at last obtained a permanent interest against their lord: this is the origin of copyholders and copyhold tenants, who yet are *said* to hold at the will of the lord, though subject to the payment of their fines and heriots, and have as permanent an estate as any other class of landed proprietors.

The persons who held of a manor as grantees of the lord, only doing him homage, and performing the services he enjoined them by his grant, which, as we have noticed, were in aid of those he himself had to perform for the king or other superior lord, were termed *barons*, and now are represented by the *freeholders* of a manor, who pay quit rents, but no fines.

Freemen, or those who held of lords by plough-service, afterwards commuted into a pecuniary payment, were called tenants in socage; these tenants held all the land that was not occupied or holden by the military tenants and *villeins*. Tenants in *ancient demesne* had their origin in a similar manner, though, as they held the private or *demesne* land of the king, they obtained greater privileges, and were made quit of many duties others had to perform. See SOCAGE—TENURE.

At this day a manor rather represents the perquisites or dues from the copyholders, who hold by custom at the will of the lord (the representatives of the ancient villeins or serfs), and the quit rents of the freeholders and socage tenants, than the land itself, which, in nine cases out of ten, does not, one inch of it, belong to the lord; save as waste, which he cannot alien, and can only enclose under restriction of allowing commonage.

The right of presentation to the church is sometimes *appendant* to the manor, and is sold or descends with it as part thereof, or is detached by having been previously sold; then it is termed *in gross.*

A manor is a freehold estate.

MANUFACTURES, and MANUFACTURERS. Persons employed in working up goods embezzling or destroying the same are punishable before justices of the peace, who may commit them to the house of correction and cause them to be whipped.

Receivers are liable to forfeit from 20*l.* to 40*l.*, or to be whipped; for a second offence, from 50*l.* to 100*l.* or be whipped.

By the 7 *&* 8 G. 4. *c.* 29. *s.* 16., stealing, to the value of ten shillings, goods of silk, woollen, linen or cotton, or of such materials mixed, laid or exposed during any stage, process, &c. of manufacture, subjects the offender to transportation for life, &c.

Machinery or machines used in the woollen, cotton, calico, linen, or silk manufactures of this kingdom, are prohibited to be exported under the penalty of forfeiture.

The wilful destruction of machinery is a felony punishable by transportation or imprisonment, and, if a male, whipping. See MISCHIEF—MALICIOUS.

MAPS, CHARTS, and PRINTS. See LITERARY PROPERTY.

MARINE STORES, DEALERS IN, are bound to keep books, in which they are to enter the name and address of all persons with whom they deal, together with the price of the article purchased by them. Also see NAVAL AND MILITARY STORES.

MARKET. The liberty by grant or prescription, whereby a town is enabled to *set up and open shops*, &c., at a certain place therein, for buying and selling, and better provision of such victuals as the subject wanteth: it is less than a fair; and usually kept once or twice a week.

The establishment of public marts, or places of buying and selling, such as markets and fairs, with the tolls thereunto belonging, is enumerated by Blackstone as one of the king's prerogatives. These can only be set up by virtue of the king's grant, or by long and immemorial usage and prescription, which presupposes such a grant.

All fairs are markets, and there may be a market without an owner; though where there is an owner, a butcher cannot prescribe to sell meat in his own house upon a market-day; for the market must be in an open place, where the owner may have the benefit of it.

The general rule of law is, that all sales and contracts of any thing vendible in fairs or markets overt (that is, open), shall not only be good between the parties, but also binding on all those that have any right or property therein.

Markets overt are only held on the special days provided for particular towns, by charter or prescription; but in London, every day except Sunday is market-day. The market-place or spot of ground set apart by custom for the sale of particular goods, is also in the country the only *market overt;* but in London, every shop in which goods are exposed publicly to sale is a market-overt for such things as the owner professes to trade in. If goods are stolen from one, and sold out of market overt, the property is not altered, and the owner may take them wherever he finds them. If the buyer knows the property not to be in the seller, or there be any other fraud in the transaction; if he knows the seller to be an infant, or feme covert not usually trading for herself; or if the sale be not originally and wholly made in the fair or market, or not at the usual hours; the true owner's property is not bound thereby. If a man buys his own goods in a fair or market, the contract of sale shall not bind him, so that he shall render the price, unless the property had been previously altered by a former sale: and notwithstanding any number of intervening sales, if the original vendor, who sold without having the right of property, comes again into possession of the goods, the original owner may take them, when found in his hands who was guilty of the first breach of justice

Every one that hath a market, shall have toll for things sold, which is to be paid by the buyer, and by ancient custom may be paid for standing of things in the market, though nothing be sold, but not otherwise. A piepowder court is incident as well to a market as a fair.

MARRIAGE. A civil contract, to which may be superadded a religious ceremony, whereby a man is united to a woman, for the purposes of civilised society.

Marriages may be solemnized—1. According to the rites and ceremonies of the church of England; or, 2. According to the provisions of the act 6 & 7 *W.* 4. *c.* 85. amended by 1 *Vict. c.* 22.

1. Marriages according to the rites of the church of England are celebrated or solemnized by banns, notice in lieu of banns, or licence from the bishop.

By banns.—According to the Marriage Act, 4 *G.* 4. *c.* 16.* all banns of matrimony are to be published in an audible manner, in the parish church, or in some public chapel in which banns may now or hereafter be lawfully published, of the parish or chapelry wherein the persons to be married shall dwell, according to the form of words contained in the Book of Common Prayer, upon three Sundays preceding the solemnization of marriage, during morning service, or evening service (if there shall be no morning service in the church or chapel on the day of publication), immediately after the second lesson; and if the persons to be married shall dwell in different parishes or chapelries, the banns shall be published in the church or chapel of the parish or chapelry wherein each person shall dwell; and in all cases where banns have been published, the marriage shall be solemnized in one of the parish churches or chapels where the banns have been published.

Banns may also be published and marriages solemnized in such chapels licensed for that purpose by the bishop of the diocese, pursuant to 6 & 7 *W.* 4. *c.* 22. *s.* 26., amended by 1 *Vict. c.* 22. *s.* 33. These chapels, in lieu of the notice which is required by the 6 & 7 *W.* 4. *c.* 22. in respect of chapels licensed for the *solemnization only* of marriage† are required to have the words "*Banns may be published and* marriages

* This statute is, in many of its provisions, a re-enactment of the Marriage Act, 26 *G.* 2. *c.* 33.

† Chapels licensed for the solemnization only of marriage, are required to have the words "Marriages may be solemnized in this chapel" placed in some conspicuous part in the interior. *Sect.* 29.

may be solemnized in this chapel," placed in some conspicuous part of the interior.

Marriages are also authorised to be solemnized in these last-mentioned chapels between parties, when only *one* of them is resident within the district specified in the chapel licence; the publication of banns where the parties reside in two different districts being made not only in the chapel where the marriage is intended to be solemnized, but also in the licensed chapel for the district in which the *other* party is non-resident; or if there should be no such licensed chapel, then in the church or chapel in which banns may be lawfully published.—1 *Vict. c.* 22. *s.* 34.*

No clergyman is *obliged* to publish the banns of matrimony unless the persons to be married shall, seven days at least before the first publication, deliver or cause to be delivered to him a notice in writing of their true Christian and surnames, of their respective residences, and of the time during which they have occupied such residences.

If the marriage be not solemnized within three months, a complete republication of banns is necessary.—26 *G.* 2. *c.* 33.

The marriages of persons who *knowingly and wilfully* intermarry without due publication of banns (by licence excepted) are void; but any misrepresentation of residence will not affect the validity of the marriage *after* solemnization; and though false names are given, if it can be shown that it was not with the consent of *both*, the marriage will yet stand good.

If *at* the publication of banns a dissent of parents or guardians is *publicly* declared, the banns are void; and if *after* publication the clergyman marry the parties, he is subject to ecclesiastical punishment.†

Ministers are not liable to ecclesiastical censure for marrying persons under age, provided banns have been published and no dissent declared, although under suspicious circumstances.

By notice in lieu of banns.— According to the act 6 & 7 *W.* 4. *c.* 85. *s.* 4., a notice in lieu of banns, according to the form given in the schedule to that act (A.), may be given by one of the parties to the superintendent registrar of the district in which the parties shall have dwelt for not less than seven days next preceding; or if they dwell in different districts, to the superintendent registrars of both districts, which notice is entered in a book kept for that purpose, and to which every one may have access without fee; but such marriage cannot be solemnized until 21 days after such notice given or entered. This notice continues in force for no longer than three months, in analogy to the law respecting publication by banns: at and *before* the expiration of this time, the superintendent registrar, on application from either party, grants a certificate, according to the form in the act, schedule (B.), which sets forth a copy of the notice, and states that the period has elapsed, and that the marriage has not been forbidden, provided that such is the fact, and that no lawful impediment has been shown to his satisfaction why such certificate should not issue.

This certificate, for which and the notice fees of 1*s.* each are payable, is then delivered to either of the applicants, who both deliver the same to the minister, which is his authority for performing the ceremony.

* Parties have the option, notwithstanding the terms of the licence authorise marriage at the licensed chapel, to have their marriages solemnized in the parish church in which the licensed chapel is situate.

† That is, he incurs no legal penalty, but may be visited with ecclesiastical censure, viz. suspension for three years.

The certificate authorising a marriage by notice, in lieu of bans, is in black ink.

The following are the forms of the notice and certificate:—

NOTICE OF MARRIAGE.

To the registrar of the district of *Hendon* in the county of *Middlesex.*

I hereby give you notice, that a marriage is intended to be had, within three calendar months from the date hereof, between me and the other party herein named and described; (that is to say,)

Name.	Condition.	Rank or Profession.	Age.	Dwelling Place.	Length of Residence.	Church or Building in which Marriage is to be solemnised.	District and County in which the other Party resides, when the Parties dwell in different Districts.
James Smith	*Widower*	*Carpenter*	*Of full Age*	*26, High Street*	*23 Days*	*Sion Chapel, West Street, Hendon, Middlesex*	*Tonbridge, Kent.*
Martha Green	*Spinster*	- -	*Minor*	*Grove Farm*	*More than a Month*		

Witness my hand this Sixth day of May, 1838.

(Signed) *James Smith.**

* The *italics* in this Schedule to be filled up as the case may be.

REGISTRAR'S CERTIFICATE.

"I *John Cox*, registrar of the district of Stepney in the county of *Middlesex*, do hereby certify, that on the sixth day of May notice was duly entered in the Marriage Notice Book of the said district of the marriage intended between the parties therein named and described, delivered under the hand of *James Smith*, one of the parties; (that is to say,)

Name.	Condition.	Rank or Profession,	Age.	Dwelling Place.	Length of Residence.	Church or Building in which Marriage is to be solemnized.	District and County in which the other Party dwells, where the Parties dwell in different Districts.
James Smith	*Widower*	*Carpenter*	*Of full Age.*	*16, High Street*	*23 Days*	*Sion Chapel, West Street, Stepney, Middlesex*	*Tonbridge, Kent.*
Martha Green	*Spinster*	- -	*Minor*	*Grove Farm*	*More than a Month*		

Date of Notice entered 6th May, 1838.
Date of Certificate given 27th May 1838.
} The issue of this certificate has not been forbidden by any person authorised to forbid the issue thereof.

Witness my hand this *twenty-seventh* day of *May, one thousand eight hundred and thirty-eight.*

(Signed) *John Cox*, Registrar.†

This certificate will be void unless the marriage is solemnised on or before the *Sixth* day of *August* 1838.

* The *italics* in the above form to be filled up as the case may be.

Publicity is given to the notice, in lieu of bans, by the superintendent-registrar's book being rendered accessible to all persons without fee, and by the same being read over at three weekly meetings of the guardians of any poor-law union, parish, or district, or by being suspended in the superintendent-registrar's office (in case there should be no guardians) for the space of 21 days; and if any person, who, as parent or guardian, would have been entitled to forbid bans, forbids the notice, by entering the word "forbidden" opposite the entry in the superintendent-registrar's book, and by subscribing his or her name and place of abode, and his or her character in respect to either of the parties, by reason of which he or she is so authorised, *before the issue of the certificate*, the notice is utterly void. *ss.* 9.

By License. Bishops have power to grant licenses or dispensations, which authorise the marriage of persons without publication of bans or notice in lieu thereof, termed "ordinary licenses," in contradistinction to those licenses which are termed "special licenses," and which are granted by the Archbishop of Canterbury, to persons of quality, which licenses frequently allow the solemnisation of matrimony in their own houses, out of canonical hours, in the evening, and in other churches of the parish, &c., than where one of the parties lives.

Application for a license is made by means of a proctor, grounded upon the applicant's affidavit, stating "that there is no impediment of kindred or alliance, or of any other lawful cause, nor any suit commenced in any ecclesiastical court, to bar or hinder the proceeding of the said matrimony, according to the tenor of the said license, &c.; that one of the parties hath, for the space of 15 days immediately preceding such license, had his or her usual place of abode within the parish or chapelry within which such marriage is to be solemnised;" also, where either of the parties (not being a widower or widow) is a minor, that the consent of the father, or if he be dead, of one of the guardians of such minor, lawfully appointed; and if there be no such guardian, then of the mother, if unmarried; and should there be no mother unmarried, then of the guardians appointed by the court of chancery, if consenting in fact, hath been obtained to the marriage. But if there be no person authorised to give consent, then upon oath to that effect, by the party requiring the license, it may be granted, although the consent be wanting. 4 *G.* 4. *c.* 76. *s.* 14. 16.

A *caveat* may be entered against the grant of a license, such caveat being duly signed by or on behalf of the person who enters the same, with his place of residence and the ground of objection, and thereupon no license can issue till the matter shall have been examined by the judge. *S.* 11.

The language of this 14th section of the "old marriage act," merely *requires* consent, but it does not make the marriage void or voidable if no consent be had, for the 21st section declares that certain marriages shall be null and void, and a marriage by license without consent is not specified as one of them; by consequence therefore, if a minor marries by license without consent of parent or guardians, the marriage is still good. It may here be noticed, though not exactly in its place, that this principle of the old marriage act is extended to the new marriage act, 6 *&* 7 *W.* 4. *c.* 85., in regard to the licenses granted by the superintendent-registrar, to Jews, Quakers, Roman Catholics, Dissenters, or others declining the offices of the Established Church, as hereafter mentioned.

In cases of difficulty or unreasonable conduct, a person desirous of marrying may petition the lord chancellor, who will judicially declare whether the marriage is proper or not; if in the affirmative, the order is held as a valid consent by the terms of the marriage act, 4 *G*. 4. *c*. 76. *s*. 17.

In marriages of persons under guardianship of the court of chancery, it is a "contempt" of that court to marry a "ward" without a judicial consent, and the court will, in case of a clandestine marriage, imprison the party and all parties concerned therein, save the "ward," and restrict the transfer or disposal of the ward's property until a proper settlement be made thereof, in preparing which, the master in chancery will take into consideration all the circumstances of the case.

The marriage ceremony is to be performed (except when time or place are dispensed with by a *special* license) in a church or chapel, or at any licensed episcopal chapel, or chapel licensed by the bishop, pursuant to the act, 6 & 7 *W*. 4. *c*. 85. (amended by 1 *Vict*. *c*. 22.), as before mentioned, where divine service according to the Church of England is performed, or wherein the bans have been published, or specified in the *bishop*'s license (for no superintendent-registrar's license can authorise a marriage in any such church or chapel) by a priest in holy orders, and in the presence of two witnesses, who, with the minister and parties themselves, are to subscribe a certificate, pursuant to the parochial registry act, 6 & 7 *W*. 4. *c*. 86. See PAROCHIAL REGISTRIES.

2. Jews, Quakers, and Roman Catholics, have always been permitted to solemnise their marriages in such manner as the ceremonies of their persuasions direct, where *both* parties were of the same persuasion; but it was not till very lately that the marriages of Roman Catholics were deemed legal, for the purposes of entitling the husband to curtesy, or the wife to dower. Mere dissenters from the Church of England, however, have had to complain of an apparent intolerance on the part of the legislature, in not legalising marriages solemnised in the chapels or places appropriated to their peculiar forms of worship. This source of complaint is now removed by the act above alluded to, and marriages of dissenters, as of Jews, Quakers, Roman Catholics, and other sects and persuasions, may be legally and adequately solemnised in their own synagogues, tabernacles, chapels, or meeting-houses, subject to a few necessary restrictions.

The above act, 6 & 7 *W*. 4. *c*. 85. (amended by 1 *Vict*. *c*. 22.), which came into force on the 1st of March, but was suspended in its operation till the 1st of July, 1837, provides, that in addition to churches and licensed episcopal chapels, which last are registered with the bishop of the diocese, marriages may be solemnised at places of worship registered according to the 52 *G*. 3. *c*. 155., in the presence of some registrar or his deputy, and two credible witnesses, or at the office of a superintendent-registrar in his presence, in the presence of some registrar of the district, or his deputy, and of two credible witnesses.

The parties solemnising marriage in a registered building, may adopt any form or ceremony they may think fit, provided that in some part of the ceremony *and in the presence of such registrar and witnesses*, each of the parties shall declare as follows: —

'I do solemnly declare, That I know not of any lawful impediment why I, 'A. B. may not be joined in matrimony to C. D.'

And each of the parties shall say to the other,

'I call upon these persons here present to witness that I, A. B. do take 'thee C. D. to be my lawful wedded wife [or husband].'

In order to celebrate a marriage as before mentioned, which may be done by notice or licence from the superintendent-registrar, the parties proceed as follows:—

The building or place of worship in which the marriage is intended to be had, having been duly certified according to the 52 *G.* 3. *c.* 155., or duly registered as a Roman Catholic chapel, and the proprietors or trustees having delivered a certificate from twenty housekeepers, that the place has been used for worship one year, and of their desire that such place should be registered, to the superintendent-registrar who causes the same to be entered with the registrar-general, one of the parties delivers a notice to the superintendent-registrar of the district within which the parties shall have dwelt for 7 days next preceding (as in the case of a notice in lieu of bans), stating both their names, condition, dwelling, and the building in which the marriage is to be solemnised, which last may be described by its usual name, in the proper column, as "Ebenezer Chapel," "Baptists' Meeting-house," "the Jewish Synagogue, Duke's Place, near Aldgate, London," "the Meeting-house of the people called Quakers, at Wandsworth, in the county of Surrey," or "the Office of the Superintendent-registrar for the district of ——."

This notice is entered in the book kept for that purpose, but such marriage cannot be solemnised until 21 days after the entering the notice (*unless by license*, and then not till after 7 days); this notice continues in force for no longer than 3 months. At the expiration of either time, and *within* the 3 months, the superintendent-registrar on application from either party, grants a certificate as before mentioned, which sets forth the notice, and states that either period (as the case may be) has elapsed, and that the marriage has not been "forbidden:" in case of *caveat* having been entered against a license, he examines the objection or refers it to the registrar-general for decision, as hereafter mentioned, but if no such *caveat* has been entered, or if entered, the same shall be declared frivolous, the certificate mentioned in the schedule to the act (B), is delivered to either of the applicants, who both give notice to the priest or minister, and to the registrar to attend, at which time the certificate, or license and certificate (as the case may be) is delivered to the registering office of the Quakers and Jews, if solemnised according to their usages, and in other cases to the registrar or his deputy present at the marriage, when the ceremony takes place in the usual manner, the necessary declaration mentioned in the statute being made.

The certificate authorising a marriage by notice, in lieu of bans, is in black ink; the "license certificate" is in red ink, and also has the word "license" in the water mark, so that the minister or priest can discern when to require a license in addition to the certificate, and when not.

There must not be any lawful impediment to the marriage of the parties, and the registrar present is empowered to examine the parties touching the same.

Marriages before the superintendent-registrar at his office, must be contracted and solemnised with open doors.

All marriages, whether according to the form of this act or according to the old marriage act, must be solemnised between the hours of 8 and 12 in the forenoon, those being the canonical hours.

Licenses, it has been noticed, are granted by the superintendent-registrar, after a notice entered, and no *caveat* or cause shown at the expiration of 7 days, when he grants a certificate, as before mentioned, and gives the license in the form following:—

LICENSE OF MARRIAGE.

"A. B., Superintendent Registrar of , to C. D. of and E. F. of sendeth greeting.

"Whereas ye are minded, as it is said, to enter into a contract of marriage under the provisions of an act made in the seventh year of the reign of his Majesty King William the Fourth, intituled [*here insert the title of this act*], and are desirous that the same may be speedily and publicly solemnised: And whereas you C. D. [*or* you E. F.] have made and subscribed a declaration under your hand that you believe there is no impediment of kindred or alliance or other lawful hindrance to the said marriage, and that you C. D. [*or* E. F.] have [*or* has] had your [*or* his *or* her] usual place of abode for the space of fifteen days last past within the district of [ ], and that you C. D. [*or* E. F.], not being a widower [*or* widow, are [*or* is] under the age of twenty-one years, and that the consent of G. H., whose consent to your [*or* his *or* her] marriage is required by law, has been obtained thereto [*or* that there is no person having authority to give such consent]: I do hereby grant unto you full licence, according to the authority in that behalf given to me by the said act, to proceed to solemnise such marriage, and to the registrar of the district of [*here insert the name of the district in which the marriage is to be solemnised*] to register such marriage according to law; provided that the said marriage be publicly solemnised in the presence of the said registrar and of two witnesses within three calendar months from the [*here insert the date of the entry in the notice book of the superintendent-registrar*], in the [*here describe the building in which the marriage is to be solemnised*], between the hours of eight and twelve in the forenoon. Given under my hand this day of one thousand eight hundred and .

(Signed) A. B., Superintendent Registrar."

This license is, in every respect, assimilated to licenses granted by the bishop; and therefore the consent of the father is requisite, if living; if he is dead, one of the guardians; if no guardian, the mother, if unmarried; otherwise a guardian appointed by the court of chancery, or by the order of that court.

Caveat.—Persons authorised as parents or guardians may forbid the issuing of the superintendent-registrar's certificate, by writing the word "forbidden," and their name and address, with the character and right in which this *caveat* or warning is entered; the superintendent-registrar examines the objection, and if doubtful, refers it to the registrar-general, or the registrar-general may be appealed to.

If the *caveat* be declared frivolous, the party entering the same is liable for costs and damages in an action, the case of which the registrar-general's certificate shall be evidence. 1 *Vict. c.* 22. *s.* 5.

All marriages, whether under the old marriage act, or the new act, must be solemnised in the presence of two witnesses, in addition to the registrar, and with open doors.

The registry of a marriage must be in the form prescribed by "an act for registering births, deaths, and marriages, in England," which, with this latter act of 6 & 7 *W.* 4. *c.* 85., came into force on the 1st of March, but was delayed in its operation till the 1st of July, 1837.*

* The fees payable under the act 6 & 7 *W.* 4. *c.* 85., are the following; *viz.*:—

	£.	s.	d.
To the superintendent registrar with the notice of marriage - -	0	1	0
For his certificate of due notice at the end of twenty-one days -	0	1	0
For license, besides the stamps - - - - - -	3	0	0
On a *caveat* against a certificate or license - - -	0	5	0
For registering buildings as a place for solemnising marriages, and every transfer of registry - - - - - -	3	0	0
To the registrar for attending at, and registering a marriage without license - - - - - - - -	0	5	0
When by license - - - - - - - -	0	10	0

With regard to marriages under the old and new marriage acts, it seems that if the forms have been apparently complied with, it is no matter how false they may have been, as regards the legal validity of the marriage, for that will not be affected unless *both* parties were cognisant of the fraud; the same rule also applies, with respect to the validity of the marriages under the new act *after* solemnisation, as to the want of consent of guardian, or misrepresentation of residence. The only effect of a false notice or declaration being the punishment of the offender, not the invalidity of the marriage. By this act also, the provisions of an act of 4 *G.* 4. *c.* 76., by which a party who obtains property by a wilfully false certificate, declaration, or notice, forfeits the same, is extended to marriages under the present act, and the attorney general will, upon information, sue for the forfeiture.

It must be borne in mind, that the omission of or non-compliance in the matters of fact required by the new act, such as there being no notice or certificate at all, or no solemnisation in a registered building, or at the office of the superintendent-registrar, or the omission of the words required by the new act, will vacate the marriage, and render it null and void, from the beginning, thereby basterdizing the issue, if it can be shown that such omission or non-compliance took place with the knowledge of both parties, or such knowledge can be reasonably inferred from the conduct of both parties. *ss.* 42, 43.

False declarations and notices are punishable as perjury. The undue solemnisation of any marriage is a felony. The making false entries in the register books or giving false certificates is also declared a felony in the superintendent-registrar, but the prosecution of offences under this new marriage act is limited to three years. *ss.* 38—41.

Independent and exclusive of the *wilful* non-compliance with the provisions of the old and new marriage acts, marriages may be annulled, by reason of the parties being within the prohibited degrees: (see KINDRED) either party being insane, or being married to another person who is alive at the time of the second marriage. Impotency, and either of the parties being under marriageable age, which is generally twelve in females and fourteen in males, are causes of avoiding or annulling the marriage.

The decision of the validity or invalidity of a marriage is a matter generally cognisable by the ecclesiastical courts, but the fact which often incidentally arises, viz. whether a woman is married, or a man is the husband of such a woman, or a woman the wife of such a man, is triable by a jury, the question of the lawfulness of the marriage being decided in the ecclesiastical court, and the fact of the marriage as a collateral question in order to establish a defect or right of action being determinable by a jury.

The law casts an invidious eye upon conditions in restraint of marriage generally, and will only limit the restraint to twenty-one, or any other reasonable age (perhaps twenty-five in a male), but no farther. Legacies are often bequeathed upon condition that the consent of particular persons shall be obtained previous to marriage, but this condition can only be enforced as a restraint upon an early or improvident marriage, and when a legacy is bequeathed upon condition of marriage with consent of particular persons, and there is no bequest or devise over to other persons upon breach of the condition, such condition is void, *i. e.* the legatee will take the money or estate without the restraint.

If parties promise to marry each other, an action will lie for the non-performance of such promise if not performed within a reasonable time, or if either marry so that the performance is rendered impossible. An "infant" may be sued upon this promise.

The statute of frauds provides that all promises upon consideration or agreement of marriage shall be in writing; but this provision it need scarcely be remarked does not extend to a mutual promise of marriage which is a different contract, the former being simply transactions concerning the furtherance of or carrying into effect the marriage such as a settlement, articles &c., and very often made and conducted by the parents and relatives of the parties, the latter being a contract between the parties to marry each other.

MARRIED WOMEN. The provisions that are made for securing to married women an income on the decease of their husbands have been mentioned under the title of HUSBAND AND WIFE, and the "*Separate Estate*" or equitable provision of the wife is also noticed under the same title. It only remains to state the interests a married woman may acquire in *real* estate or estates of inheritance, and how she may bar her interest therein, in less technical language how she may join with her husband in parting with the same.

A married woman may just as if she was single, take freehold or copyhold estates, or what is in equity the same, money to be laid out in real estates, and the inheritance will on the decease of her husband, if he survive her, go to her heir-at-law, her eldest son, and, if no son, daughters as tenants in common; if no children, then to her father, and if he is dead, then her eldest brother or his children, according to the rules of descent.

The married woman, however, has no power to alien such estates without the concurrence of her husband, he being entitled to the rents during his life, but if she will do so, she must extinguish her interest as if she was sole, by deeds to be acknowledged by her before judges, masters in chancery, or two commissioners, she being at the same time examined by the judge, master, or commissioners, as to her free will and consent; and the same with copyhold, the acknowledgment being made before the steward, according to the custom of the manor.

The court of common pleas in the case of the husband being lunatic, his residence unknown, living apart from his wife by consent or by reason of a divorce, or in consequence of transportation, or from any other cause, may dispense with his concurrence.

If the husband desires to mortgage or sell his real estate, and the wife should by reason of her being married before the 1st of January, 1834, be entitled to dower, his wife must concur in the deed, and make the necessary acknowledgment.

Money directed to be laid out in the purchase of land is considered by the courts of equity as converted into real estate; and where in pursuance of such direction an estate has been actually purchased, the wife must extinguish her interest in the above form, but by the late act for abolishing fines and recoveries, which substitutes an ordinary conveyance and acknowledgment to bar the estate of a married woman, it is not now necessary to have such money actually invested in land, but a court of equity on a petition of the party entitled will order the money to be paid to her, she being separately examined, in fact treating the money as personal estate, and treating such personalty as a separate estate or not, at the will of the married woman. These deeds are all to be enrolled. See RECOVERIES.

MARSHAL. There are several officers of this name, the chief whereof is hereditary, earl marshal of England (the Duke of Norfolk). The office originally was "to marshal the king's host." There is the marshal or knight marshal of the queen's house: he holds a court for determining offences and suits within the verge of the court, but his criminal jurisdiction is not now used.

The Marshal of the queen's bench has the custody of the queen's bench prison, and executes the judgment of that court upon those who receive judgment at the bar of the court; he, as well as the deputy marshal, ought to reside within the prison or its rules.

There is also a marshal of the exchequer, but his office is merely nominal, as the warden of the Fleet has the custody of the prisoners committed to his charge.

There is also a marshal, or provost marshal, of the admiralty, whose duty it is to act ministerially, under the orders of the court of admiralty, in securing prizes, executing warrants for these and other purposes, arresting and attending the execution of criminals, &c.

MASTER and SERVANT. The relation between master and servant will be considered under the title SERVANT.

MASTER IN CHANCERY. In the chancery there are masters who are assistants to the lord chancellor, or lord keeper, and master of the rolls. Of these there are some ordinary, and some extraordinary: the masters in ordinary are twelve in number, of whom the master of the rolls is chief; they have referred to them orders for taking accounts, &c.; they also administer oaths, take affidavits, and acknowledgments of deeds and recognisances; they also examine, on reference, the propiety of bills in chancery. The extraordinary masters are appointed to act in the country, in the several counties of England, beyond ten miles distance from London, by taking affidavits, recognisances, acknowledgments of deeds, &c.

The masters in ordinary sit at a building called the public office, in Southampton-buildings, Chancery-lane.

There are masters on the equity side of the exchequer, who perform similar acts; they sit at their office under the exchequer office in the Temple.

MASTER OF THE QUEEN'S BENCH. A chief clerk or prothonotary of that court; to him the court refer when they wish to be informed of any matter. He taxes or assesses all bills of costs; he records all civil actions, has the custody of the recognisances, and does various important acts.

MASTER OF A SHIP, in law, is defined to be any "person having the charge or command of any ship." No person is qualified to be master of a "*British*" ship, except he be a natural born subject of her majesty, or naturalised by act of parliament, or made a denizen, or except he has become a *British* subject by virtue of conquest, or cession of some newly acquired country, and who shall have taken the oath of allegiance, or the oath of fidelity required by the treaty of capitulation, or except he shall have served in the navy in time of war for the space of three years.

MAYOR. The chief governor or magistrate of a city or town corporate; as the lord mayor of London, the lord mayor of Dublin, the lord mayor of York, the mayor of Southampton, &c. King Richard I., anno 1189, changed the bailiffs of London into a mayor.

Mayors of corporations are justices of peace.

The powers and duties of a mayor, or other head officer of a corporation, depend in general on the provisions of the charters, or prescriptive usages of the corporation, or the express provisions of the act of parliament regulating municipal corporations.

Where the mayor's presence is necessary at a corporate assembly, his departure before a business regularly begun be concluded, will not invalidate that particular business; but the assembly cannot proceed to any thing else. And on the death of the mayor, or during the vacation of the office, the corporation can do no corporate act but that of choosing a new mayor. See CORPORATIONS.

MEASURE. A certain quantity or proportion of any thing sold. See WEIGHTS AND MEASURES.

MESNE PROCESS. Such process as issues pending the suit upon some collateral interlocutory matter, as to summon juries, witnesses, and the like; distinguished from the original process which is the writ. Mesne process is also sometimes put in contradistinction to *final process*, or process of execution; and then it signifies all such process as intervenes between the beginning and end of a suit.

MESSENGER is a carrier of messages, particularly employed by the secretaries of state, commissioners of bankrupt, &c.; and to these commitments may be made of prisoners, but persons committed to a messenger by a commissioner of bankrupt must, within two days afterwards, be brought before the subdivision court. See BANKRUPTCY.

MESSUAGE. A dwelling-house; but a shop and almost any other building may pass in a conveyance under that name.

MILITARY OFFENCES. By the annual acts for punishing mutiny and desertion, if any officer or soldier shall excite or join any mutiny, or, knowing of it, shall not give notice to the commanding officer, or shall desert or list in any other regiment, or sleep upon his post, or leave it before he is relieved, or hold correspondence with a rebel or enemy, or strike or use violence to his superior officer, or shall disobey his lawful commands; such offender shall suffer such punishment as a court martial (established by the act) shall inflict, though it extend to death itself.

MILITIA. The object of the militia laws is to discipline a certain number of the inhabitants of every county chosen by lot. The operation of the militia laws, as far as regards the 28 days' training, is at present suspended.

MILL. A house or engine to grind corn, and is either a water mill, wind mill, horse mill, hand mill, &c.; and besides corn and grist mills, there are paper mills, fulling or tucking mills, iron mills, oil mills, &c.

MINES. Quarries or places whereout any thing is dug. Persons maliciously setting on fire any mine or pit of coal, are guilty of felony. See MISCHIEF, MALICIOUS.

To steal from mines is a larceny, and punishable as such. See LARCENY.

MINUTE TITHES, or SMALL TITHES. Such as usually belong to the vicar, as of wool, lambs, pigs, butter, cheese, herbs, seeds, eggs, honey, wax, &c. See title TITHES.

MISADVENTURE. The killing a man, partly by negligence and partly by chance is in fact excusable homicide. See MURDER.

MISCHIEF, MALICIOUS, is the committing an injury to public or private property, not for the purposes of theft, but from sheer wantonness or malice. This offence is punishable with great severity, as such injuries are seldom inflicted without great disturbance and terror of the public peace. Statutes have been passed at different times for the purpose of punishing and repressing injuries of this nature, but they have been lately repealed to make way for an enactment consolidating the statute law on this subject.

Intent is the material ingredient in offences of this nature, but as the law presumes malice in the very commission of the act, it lies on the party indicted to rebut the presumption of malice or sufficiently explain the act.

The following are the injuries which the *7 & 8 G. 4. c.* 30., in very comprehensive terms renders punishable (with some few exceptions) as felonies: —

† Cutting silk and goods in the loom, or in *any* process of manufacture of the value of *5l.*

† Cutting or destroying warps of silk, &c. in the loom, or any loom, machine or instrument for preparing the same, to the value of *5l.*

† Entering by force into a house, with intent to commit the two previous offences.

‡ Destroying threshing-machines.

‡ Drowning, obstructing or pulling down airways, or destroying engines, staiths, buildings, waggonways or trunks of a mine.

* Destroying a ship, with intent to set fire to, cast away, or destroy a ship, with intent to damage underwriters or others.

‡ The damaging a ship *otherwise than by fire.*

* Exhibiting false signals to bring a ship into danger.

* Doing any act tending to the immediate loss of a ship in distress.

* Destroying part of a ship in distress, wrecked or stranded.

§ Cutting away, casting adrift, or doing any act with intent to cut away, &c. any buoy, buoy-rope, or mark belonging to any vessel.

† Cutting down river or sea-banks.

† Throwing down locks, sluices, &c. on rivers, or canals.

‡ Cutting or removing piles, &c. used for securing a bank or sea wall, or bank or wall of a river, canal, &c.

‡ Opening flood-gates.

† Pulling down a public bridge, or injuring the same.

§§ Destroying a turnpike. (*Misdemeanor.*)

‡ Breaking down the dam of a fish-pond. (*Misdemeanor.*)

§§ Putting lime, or any noxious material into a fish-pond. (*Misdemeanor.*)

‡ Breaking down a mill-dam. (*Misdemeanor.*)

† Killing or maiming cattle.

† Destroying hop-binds.

‡ Cutting and destroying, barking or damaging any tree, sapling, shrub, or underwood growing in any park, pleasure-ground, garden, orchard, avenue, or grounds adjoining or belonging to a dwelling-house, above 1*l.* value. *a*

a The destroying, rooting up, or committing any similar injury to trees, shrubs, &c., with *intent to steal*, is larceny under the act *7 & 8 G. 4. c.* 29.; but when the theft or injury amounts to one shilling at the least, and does not amount to more than one pound, summary punishment may be imposed before a single justice by fine not exceeding *5l.* as a recompence beyond the amount of injury done, upon the *first* conviction. On the *second* conviction by imprisonment with hard labour, for not more than twelve months, and (if

‡ Cutting and destroying, barking or damaging any tree, sapling, shrub, or underwood growing elsewhere, (for instance, in a close,) above *5l.* value.

‡ Cutting and damaging trees, *wheresoever growing*, of the value of 1*s.* after two previous convictions for that offence. (This offence is summarily punishable before a single justice on the first conviction, by a fine not exceeding *5l.*, and payment of the value of the tree, &c., and imprisonment, with hard labour, for not exceeding 6 months, in default of payment. On the second conviction, by imprisonment with hard labour, for not exceeding 12 months, and if the conviction is made before *two* justices, by whipping.)

‡ Destroying or damaging, with that intent, any plant, root, fruit, or vegetable production growing in any garden, orchard, nursery-ground, hothouse, greenhouse, or conservatory, after a previous conviction for that offence. *a* (This offence is summarily punishable on the first conviction before a single justice, by imprisonment and hard labour, for not exceeding 6 months, or forfeiture of any sum not exceeding 20*l.* beyond the damage done, at the discretion of the justice.)

Punishments.—* Death.

† Transportation for life, or for not less than 7 years, or imprisonment, (with or without hard labour, and with or without solitary confinement, for the whole or any part of the imprisonment,) not exceeding *four* years; and if a male, to be once, twice, or thrice publicly whipped, in addition to the imprisonment, if the court shall think fit.

‡ The same punishment, except that the imprisonment is not to exceed *two* years.

§ Transportation for seven years, or imprisonment for any number of years, in the discretion of the court.

§ § Fine, or imprisonment, or both. See TRANSPORTATION.

Small malicious mischiefs or injuries to property, are summarily cognisable before a single justice of the peace, if the injury does not exceed *5l.* in value, and on nonpayment of a penalty not exceeding that sum *and* making recompense, the offenders may be committed to the house of correction, and kept to hard labour therein for three months.

MISDEMEANOR. A crime less than felony. The term misdemeanor is generally used in contradistinction to felony, and comprehends all *indictable offences*, which do not amount to felony, as *perjury*, *libels*, *conspiracies*, *assaults*, &c. The refusal to do a thing enjoined by law is a misdemeanor, although no penalty for disobedience be named.

The punishment for misdemeanor is fine or imprisonment, or both, some particular offences of violence, such as destroying turnpikes, &c., are expressly punishable by transportation, although the statute may declare the offence to be a misdemeanor.

MISNOMER. The using one name for another; a mis-naming. A defendant may avoid an outlawry, by pleading a misnomer of name of baptism, or surname; but in pleadings or indictments, in civil or criminal cases, misnomers do not abate the proceedings.

---

the conviction is made by two magistrates) whipping. The *third* offence after two previous convictions is a felony, and punishable as a simple larceny,

a The words "any plant, root, fruit or vegetable production," do not apply to young trees or saplings, and therefore two previous convictions for stealing plants or vegetables will not support a conviction for cutting, damaging, or destroying trees wheresoever growing, of the value of one shilling after two previous convictions for that offence.

MISPRISION. A neglect, oversight, or contempt: as for example, misprision of treason is a negligence in not revealing treason to the king, his council, or a magistrate, where a person knows it to be committed: so of felony.

MITTIMUS. A writ by which records are transferred from one court to another. This word is also used for the precept directed to a gaoler, under the hand and seal of a justice of the peace, for the receiving and safe keeping a felon, or other offender, by him committed to gaol.

MIXED TITHES are those of cheese, milk, &c., and of the young of beasts. See TITHES.

MODELS. See SCULPTURE.

MODUS DECIMANDI is when either land, a sum of money, or yearly pension is given to the parson, &c., by composition or custom, as satisfaction for his tithes in kind. See TITHES.

MOLLITER MANUS IMPOSUIT. Several justifications in trespass, *i. e.* actions of assault, are called by this name, from the words *gently laid his hands upon him*, used in the plea: as where the defendant justifies an assault, by showing that the plaintiff was unlawfully in the house of defendant, making a disturbance, and being requested to cease such disturbance and depart, he refused, and continued therein, making such disturbance, he the defendant, *gently laid his hands on the plaintiff*, and removed him out of the house.

MONOPOLY was an allowance by the king, by his grant, commission, or otherwise, to any persons, for the sole buying, selling, making, working, or using any thing whereby any persons were restrained of any freedom or liberty they had before.

It seems that the queen's charter, empowering particular persons to trade to and from such place is void, so far as it gives such persons an exclusive right of trading, and debarring all others; and it seems now agreed, that nothing can exclude a subject from trade but an act of parliament.

MONOPOLIES were abolished by a statute passed in the reign of James I., which excepted letters patent and grants of privilege for the term of 14 years to the inventors of a new manufacture, since extended to 7 years more; by a late statute, perpetual and even limited copyrights were considered as like objects of the prerogative, at different times in the 17th century, from 1600 to 1666. See LITERARY PROPERTY; PATENTS.

MONTH. A space of time, containing 28 days; if a calendar month, sometimes 30 and sometimes 31 days. By the common law (and generally by the statute law also, unless the contrary be directed,) a month is but 28 days. But where the statute reckons by the year, half year, or quarter of a year, it is to be reckoned agreeably to the calendar.

A MONTH is either lunar, 28 days, or calendar, according to the number of days mentioned in the almanack. In law, a month means the lunar month, unless specially expressed to the contrary.

MORTGAGE. A pledging or pawning of freehold or leasehold or any other property of a nature not susceptible of personal delivery. The form of a mortgage of land is, by a conveyance of the inheritance or estate to another, on condition that if the borrower do not by a certain day repay the money, the lender may enter and enjoy the land, or, in technical language, *that the lender's estate shall be absolute in the premises*; equity, however, intervenes and compels the lender or mortgagee to account to the borrower or mortgagor for the true value; and if the mortgagee is in possession, by virtue of an ejectment brought at law, equity will make him render an account of the profits received: and this account may be opened at any time during twenty years, in favour of heirs, infants, and other parties entitled. This rule also extends to cases where the conveyance has *apparently* been an absolute conveyance, but the transaction has been treated as a mortgage, by the payment and receipt of interest or other similar acts.

The right which a mortgager has to redeem his property, is termed his *equity of redemption.*

Sometimes a mortgage is effected by granting a lease at a peppercorn rent, or some petty nominal sum for 999 years, or some long term, which is to void or cease on payment of the money borrowed. And of personalty, the conveyance is not strictly a mortgage, but an assignment *by way of mortgage;* but generally the mortgagor has the same rights of surplus, or of redemption, as in the mortgage of *real* property.

When a mortgagee wants to bar or deprive the mortagor of his equitable rights, or rather have the mortgagor's equitable rights ascertained, he files a bill of foreclosure, *i. e.* he prays to have a decree for the purpose of having the accounts taken, and that his mortgage-money be repaid, which is either done by the mortgagee's retaining the estate, if the value be swallowed up with principal interest and charges, or by a sale being made, and the surplus rendered to the mortgagor, or by the mortgagee's paying any sum (if the balance be but small) to the mortgagee in full, for an absolute right.

Many times a mortgage is effected by a simple deposit of deeds, and if a memorandum in writing accompanies the deposit, equity will consider it as a mortgage, and decree payment or a sale of the estate or property mortgaged, &c. If no memorandum accompanies the deposit, the court will not readily interfere, and the lender generally has to go to a court of law for his money, retaining the deeds till he is paid.

As the mortgagee's interest *at law* becomes absolute on nonpayment by a particular day, it is usual to make special stipulations as to the time the money shall lay out, and to prevent the lender suffering by this accommodation, in some cases a sale is stipulated for, in case of nonpayment *, at the expiration of the period named. In mortgages, many devices are used by lenders for *attempting* to bar mortgagors from seeking account, and by the intervention of trustees, raising powers and trusts which are often oppressively executed, and not always with the desired effect, for the doors of equity are always open to cases of hardship and account, so that the common mortgage conveyance, which is concise and simple, and has its attendant equities, is more advantageous for borrower and lender than deeds scrivened up to several skins of parchment, containing trusts to be executed by attorneys and auctioneers at a great expense.

Mortgagors of real property who were married *before* 1st January, 1834, must procure their wives' consent, by deed acknowledged and inrolled, in order to bar them of their dower, unless previously barred by jointure or trust, raised for that purpose. See Dower, Married Women.

Mortgagors, while in possession, may vote as long as the interest due

* A power of sale is deemed a hard condition, and should only be insisted upon, when the mortgage is a second or subsequent mortgage, or the money lent is nearly the value of the premises mortgaged

does not reduce the beneficial interest below 40*s*.; but after a mortgagee is in possession, his right ceases: mortgagees in possession of the premises mortgaged may vote, otherwise not.

MORTMAIN. The holding of land by corporations, whether aggregate, as companies, &c., or sole, as parsons, vicars, &c. The giving or devising land to such bodies who never die, but are perpetually renewed, is against the policy of the law. A bequest of land to charities is the same, and within the intent of the prohibition. See CHARITIES.

MOTION IN COURT. An occasional application to a court of justice, by the parties or their counsel, in order to obtain some rule or order of court, which becomes necessary in the progress of a cause.

A MOTION is either for a *rule absolute* in the first instance, which is sometimes moved for in open court; and sometimes merely drawn up on a motion-paper, signed by counsel, and delivered to the clerk of the rules; or it is only for a *rule to show cause*, or, as it is commonly called, *a rule nisi*, i. e. *unless* cause be shown to the contrary; which is afterwards moved to be made absolute.

MOTIONS are of a *civil* or *criminal* nature. Of the latter kind is the motion for an attachment, which may be moved for on account of contemptuous words spoken of the court, or its process; for a rescue, or disobedience to a subpœna, or other process; against a sheriff, for not returning the writ, or bringing in the body of a defendant; against an attorney, for not performing his undertaking, or otherwise misbehaving himself; against other persons for nonpayment of costs, on the master's allocatur; for the nonpayment of money generally, or not performing an award, &c.

An attachment for misbehaviour is commonly preceded by a motion for a rule to answer the matters of the affidavit; and the party being taken on the attachment, either remains in custody, or puts in bail before a judge (for he is not bailable before the sheriff), to answer interrogatories to be exhibited against him.

MOTIONS of a civil nature are made on behalf of the plaintiff or of the defendant.

A MOTION is in general accompanied with an affidavit, and sometimes preceded by a notice. The affidavit should contain a full statement of all the circumstances necessary to support the application; and the rather, as it is a rule not to receive any supplementary affidavit on showing cause.

On the day appointed for that purpose, the counsel for the party called upon by the rule, may show cause against it, either upon or without an affidavit, as circumstances require.

On showing cause against the rule, the court either make it absolute, or discharge it, and that either with or without the costs of the application; or such costs are directed to abide the event of the suit, according to the discretion of the court under all the circumstances of the case.

MUTE. A prisoner is said to *stand mute* when being arraigned for treason or felony, he either makes no answer at all, or answers foreign to the purpose, or with such matter as is not allowable, and will not answer otherwise; or upon having pleaded *not guilty*, refuses to put himself upon the country.

Standing mute, in all cases, amounts to a constructive confession.

To advise a prisoner to stand mute, is a contempt of the court, and punishable by fine and imprisonment.

MURDER is homicide, or the slaying of another with malice, aforethought, either express or implied. Malice is *presumed* from the very fact of killing or homicide; but the party charged may rebut that presumption, by proving that the homicide was justifiable or excusable, or that at most it amounted to manslaughter and not to murder.

Justifiable homicide is, where a person kills another in self-defence, or in the performance of a particular duty. Homicide is said to be excusable when the killing takes place by mere accident.

Manslaughter is the unlawful and felonious killing of another, without any malice, either express or implied: it is, 1. Involuntary manslaughter where a man doing an *unlawful act*, not amounting to felony (for if it did it would be murder), by accident kills another. 2. Voluntary manslaughter, where upon a sudden quarrel two persons fight and one of them kills the other, or where a man greatly provokes another by some personal violence, &c., and the other immediately kills him.

Malice and intent are the peculiar ingredients of *murder*; and the indications of malice can only appear from the facts proved, though in many cases where no malice is expressly or openly indicated, the law will imply it, such as poisoning another because the act is deliberate, firing a loaded gun amongst a concourse of people, because every man must contemplate the probable consequences of his own acts, or if a man drive over a man deliberately and kill him; but where these acts were simply the result of great incaution, as if poison was laid for rats and a man eat it, or the gun was supposed not to be loaded, or the driving of the cart was heedless and without intention, then the act of killing would be but manslaughter.

Murder is a felony punishable by death. Manslaughter is also a felony punishable with transportation for life, or for not less than seven years, or with imprisonment, with or without hard labour, not exceeding four years, or with fine.

Duel. If two persons deliberately fight a duel and one of them be killed, the other and his second are guilty of murder, no matter how grievous the provocation, or by which party it was given: the second of the deceased also, is deemed guilty of murder, as being present, aiding and abetting.

Fighting. Persons who quarrel and afterwards fight, whereby one kills the other, are guilty of murder or manslaughter, according to the facts; for if there intervened between the quarrel and the fight, a sufficient cooling time for passion to subside, and reason to interpose, the killing would be murder, otherwise not; for if the parties on the quarrel went out and fought in a field (this being deemed a continued act of passion), the killing in such a case would be manslaughter only.

Negligence. Any act lawful in itself, but which by want of precaution in the performance occasions the death of another, may be deemed murder or manslaughter, according to the circumstances and the degree of caution used: if every reasonable caution was used, it will be *homicide by misadventure,* i. e. excusable homicide.

MUSLINS, PRINTED. See PRINTED LINEN, &c.

NATURALISATION. The making an *alien*, or rather putting an *alien* in the situation of a natural-born subject; this can only be done by act of parliament. In practice, aliens club together to pay the expenses of a private bill, which includes them all. See ALIENS.

NAVAL, or MILITARY STORES. The stealing or embezzlement of naval stores, is an offence which is punishable where the value of the stores is above 20*s*., with transportation for life, or for not less than seven years, or imprisonment, with or without hard labour, not exceeding seven years.

The having the manifest possession of naval stores, subjects the party to 200*l*. fine, together with the costs of the prosecution, one half to the queen and the other to the informer, and imprisonment until the fine be paid ; and also whipping or imprisonment, or both, at the discretion of the court. The penalty, however, may be mitigated: but for a second offence, the defendant is liable to be transported for seven years. The penalty can, in this case, be mitigated. It behoves every one, therefore, to be very cautious how they purchase queen's stores, even at sales; though, in cases where the purchase took place under circumstances tending to lull suspicion, the party will be acquitted, as well as in cases where the acquisition of the stores came by gift or bequest, or in any similar manner. As the commissioners of the navy, ordnance, or victualling office, grant certificates to parties having possession of the stores, by purchase or otherwise, there is little excuse for purchasers dispensing with the caution of requiring the production of such certificate or evidence of the seller being a contractor or manufacturer of such stores.

NAVIGATION ACTS. Those acts which regulate the commercial intercourse with this kingdom, and its colonies with other countries, particularly as regards the carrying of goods in British vessels. These are now consolidated by the act 3 & 4 *W.* 4. *c.* 54, which defines a vessel to be a British ship, which is duly registered and navigated as such, *i. e.* when the master and three fourths of the crew are British, and if employed in coasting, or between the British islands, the whole crew must be British. In all cases, however, in which the whole crew is to be British, the ship is duly navigated if she have one British seaman for every 20 tons, though the other seamen may exceed in number one fourth of the crew. The act states, that master and seamen are considered British, if natural-born subjects, or denizens, or naturalised, &c.; and having taken the oath of allegiance, or persons who have served on board a queen's ship for three years, (or in war time, two, by proclamation); and exceptions are allowed as to ships trading eastward of the Cape of Good Hope, and provides, in case of an unavoidable deficiency of British seamen.

The act expresses the ships in which what are termed "enumerated articles," shall be imported into Great Britain or her colonies; *viz.*, whether in British ships, or in ships of the country whereof the goods are the produce, or in ships of the country from which the goods are imported, and generally secures the privilege of carrying goods coastwise, the importation from the British possessions to England, and between one British possession and another, to British-built ships, with an exception in favour of ships of the country where the goods are the produce or manufacture.

The "*enumerated* articles" are, timber, grain, tea, hemp and flax, potashes, wines, spirits, sugar, fruits, and seeds, and other articles of general commerce.

NAVY. Late acts, 11 *G.* 4. and 1 *W.* 4. *c.* 20. and 3 & 4 *W.* 4. *c.* 25., provide for the pay of the royal navy, and amongst other things, regulate—

1. The advances made to volunteers and others, and the time of payment of their wages, &c.

2. Allotments of wages by seamen, for the maintenance of their wives and families, &c.

3. Remittances of wages by seamen, for the benefit of their wives and families, &c.

4. Advances and other payments to officers, &c.

5. Wills, &c., and letters of attorney, made by seamen.

6. Provisions for the passage home, and maintenance of unserviceable or shipwrecked sailors.

And 7. Forgeries, &c. under the act.

The discipline of the navy, and the punishment of offences, are regulated by the Articles of War, which are executed by courts martial.

NE EXEAT REGNO. A writ to restrain a person from going out of the kingdom without the king's licence. It is directed to the sheriff to make the party find surety that he will not depart the realm; and, on his refusal, to commit him to prison: it is, however, now used for private purposes; and is granted by the chancellor, on the application of a creditor who fears that his debtor may leave the kingdom. It seems an uncertificated bankrupt may be detained, by this process, even at the suit of a party who has proved under his estate.

NISI PRIUS. See JUSTICES OF ASSIZE.

NEWSPAPERS. The proprietors of, are bound to find sureties by the act 1 *Will.* 4. *c.* 73., to which the reader is referred.

NOLLE PROSEQUI (unwilling to prosecute), is a term used in the law, where a plaintiff in any action will not proceed any further. *Non prosequi* has a similar signification. In common parlance, these words are abbreviated, as *nolle pros.* and *non pros.* A defendant is entitled to his costs when a plaintiff abandons his action.

NON ASSUMPSIT (that he did not undertake), is a plea to an action on promises.

NON EST FACTUM. The general issue, in an action on bond or other deed, whereby the defendant *denies that to be his deed*, whereon he is sued.

NON OBSTANTE (notwithstanding), was a clause heretofore frequent in statutes and letters patent, and was a licence from the king to do a thing which, as the common law, might be lawfully done; but which, being restrained by act of parliament, could not be done without such licence. But this doctrine of *non obstante's*, which sets the prerogative above the laws, was effectually demolished by the Bill of Rights at the revolution, and abandoned Westminster Hall when king James abdicated the kingdom.

NONSUIT. A renunciation of a suit by the plaintiff, most commonly upon the discovery of some error or defect, when the matter is so far proceeded in that the jury is ready to deliver their verdict.

Before the jury gave their verdict on a trial, it was formerly usual to call or demand the plaintiff, in order to answer the amercement, to which by the old law he was liable, in case he failed in his suit. And it is now usual to call him, whenever he is unable to make out his case, either by reason of his not adducing any evidence in support of it, or any evidence ariising in the proper county.

It is settled that the king, being in supposition of law always present in court, cannot be nonsuit in any information or action wherein he is sole plaintiff; but it is held, that any informer *qui tam*, or plaintiff in a popular action, may be nonsuit, as well in respect of the king as of himself.

NOTARY, OR NOTARY PUBLIC, is one who publicly attests deeds or writings, to make authentic in another country; but their principal business in London and elsewhere is to protest foreign bills of exchange, and inland bills and notes; which latter are, if protested, to be at the charge of the holder, if paid on the day of protest, as it is not imperative on holders of inland bills to cause them to be protested. Notaries are regulated by an act, 41 *Geo.* 3. *c.* 79., which imposes a 7 years' apprenticeship to a notary, and an admission in the civil law courts, under a penalty. Notaries are prohibited from permitting others to act in their names; and in London they must be free of the Scriveners' Company.

NUISANCE. Nuisances are of two kinds: *public or common*, which affect the public, and are an annoyance to all the king's subjects; and *private nuisances*, which may be defined to be any thing done to the hurt or annoyance of the lands, tenements, or hereditaments of another. *Common nuisances* are a species of offences against the public order and economical regimen of the state: of this nature are, annoyances in *highways*, *bridges*, and the *public* rivers, by rendering the same inconvenient or dangerous to pass, either positively by actual obstructions, or negatively by want of reparations.

All those kind of nuisances (such as offensive trades and manufactures) which, when injurious to a private man, are actionable, are, when detrimental to the public, punishable by public prosecution, and subject to a fine according to the quantity of the misdemeanor.

All disorderly *inns*, or *alehouses*, *bawdy houses*, *gaming houses*, *stage plays* unlicensed, booths and stages for *rope dancers*, *mountebanks*, and the like, are public nuisances, and may, upon indictment, be suppressed and fined. Inns in particular, being intended for the lodging and receipt of travellers, may be indicted, suppressed, and the innkeepers fined, if they refuse to entertain a traveller, without a very sufficient cause; for thus to frustrate the end of their institution is held to be disorderly behaviour.

All *lotteries* are declared to be public nuisances; and all grants, patents, or licences for the same to be contrary to law.

The making and selling of *fire-works* and *squibs*, or throwing them about in any street, is, on account of the danger that may ensue to any thatched or timber buildings, declared to be a common nuisance, and therefore is punishable by fine. To this head also may be referred (though not declared a common nuisance) the making, keeping, or carriage of too large a quantity of *gunpowder* at one time, or in one place, or vehicle, which is prohibited under heavy penalties and forfeiture.

If a man build a house so close to mine that his roof overhangs my roof, and throws the water off his roof upon mine, this is a private nuisance, for which an action will lie. Likewise to erect a house or other building so near to mine that it obstructs my ancient lights and windows. Also if a person keeps his hogs, or other noisome animals, so near the house of another that the stench of them incommodes him, and makes the air unwholesome, or renders the enjoyment of life or property uncomfortable, this is an injurious nuisance, as it tends to deprive him of the use and benefit of his house. A like injury is, if one's neighbour sets up and exercises any offensive trade, as a tanner's, a tallow-chandler's, or the like: for, though these are lawful and necessary trades, yet they should be exercised in remote places. But depriving one of a mere matter of pleasure, as of a fine prospect, by building a wall, or the like; this, as it abridges nothing really convenient or necessary, is no injury to the sufferer, and is therefore not an actionable nuisance.

OATH. An affirmation or denial of any thing before one or more persons who have authority to administer the same, for the discovery and advancement of truth and right, calling God to witness that the testimony is true; it is called a *corporal* oath, because the witness, when he swears, lays his right hand on the Holy Evangelists, or New Testament.

There are several sorts of oaths in our law, viz. *juramentum promissionis*, where oath is made either to do, or not to do, such a thing; *juramentum purgationis*, where any one is produced as a witness, to prove or disprove a thing; and *juramentum triationis*, when any persons are sworn to try an issue, &c.

All oaths must be lawful, allowed by the common law, or some statute: if they are administered by persons in a private capacity, or not duly authorised, they are void; and those administering them are guilty of a high contempt, for doing it without a warrant of law, and punishable by fine and imprisonment.

If oath be made against oath in a cause, it is not apparent to the court which oath is true; and in such case the court will take that oath to be true, which is to affirm a verdict, judgment, &c., as it would be absurd to set aside a verdict or judgment upon conflicting testimony. See AFFIDAVIT.

OBLATIONS. Offerings to the church.

Oblations are in the nature of tithes, and may be sued for in the ecclesiastical courts; and it is said, are included in the act 7 *&* 8 *W.* 3. *c.* 6., for recovery of small tithes under 40*s.* by the determination of justices of peace, &c.

OBLIGATION. A bond, containing a penalty, with a condition annexed for payment of money, performance of covenants, or the like. A bond is styled a writing obligatory.

OBLIGOR. He who enters into an obligation; as obligee is the person with whom it is entered into.

OBSCENITIES and INDECENCIES, in whatever manner committed, are punishable by fine and imprisonment, being misdemeanors. The selling or exhibition of obscene or scandalous prints or books, is only a variation in the mode of committing such offences, which is punishable in like manner. See EXPOSURE OF PERSON.

OBVENTIONS. Offerings or tithes, and oblations. Obventions and offerings are generally the same thing, though obvention has been esteemed the most comprehensive.

OFFENCES. An "offence" is the general term for an injury inflicted either against the public peace in the person or property of an individual, against the laws of religion or decency, or against those laws of constitution and state recognised and allowed for the preservation of society. Those acts which involve wrongs against individuals in respect of their property or persons, may be termed "offences against property," and "offences against the person;" distinctions pretty well understood by all. These wrongs or offences may be also termed "private" (although "public" in regard to their evil example), to distinguish them from injuries of a more public nature, and which peculiarly and directly affect the peace and welfare of the community at large; such as offences against the queen and her government, public justice, trade, policy, and internal government.

In a strict legal sense and understanding, the word "offence" signifies a mere breach of a penal statute, *not indictable*, but by which a forfeiture accrues to some one, which may be summarily inflicted by one or two magistrates, and is below a "misdemeanor," — a term which includes every offence or misconduct inferior to felony, punishable by indictment or information on the prosecution of the crown; but the word "offence" is here used in a more unrestricted sense, and according to its generally received interpretation.

Offences against property, may be classed as those acts which are termed malicious mischief, larceny, embezzlement, cheats, forgery, and such like.

Offences against the person, may be stated to be, assault, abduction, murder, rape, wounding, and those felonious acts specifically so termed, and included in the 1 *Vict. c.* 65.*

Some offences may be of a mixed nature, and involve injuries against

* This act, which came into operation on October 1. 1837, repeals the 9 *Geo.* 4. c. 31., which consolidated the law relative to offences *against the person*, and declares the following offences to be felonies, and punishable as follows:—

To administer to or cause to be taken by any person any poison or other destructive thing, or to stab, cut, or wound any person, or by any means whatsoever to cause any person any bodily injury dangerous to life, with intent to commit murder. *Death.* — § 2.

The attempt to administer to any person any poison or other destructive thing, or to shoot at any person, or by drawing a trigger or in any other manner to attempt to discharge any kind of loaded arms at any person, or to attempt to drown, suffocate, or strangle any person, with intent in any of the cases aforesaid to commit the crime of murder, *although no bodily injury be effected. Transportation, (at the discretion of the court) for life, or for any term not less than fifteen years, or imprisonment for any term not exceeding three years.* — § 3.

To unlawfully and maliciously shoot at any person, or by drawing a trigger or in any other manner to attempt to discharge any kind of loaded arms at any person, or to stab, cut, or wound any person, with intent in any of the cases aforesaid to maim, disfigure, or disable such person, or to do some other grievous bodily harm, or with intent to resist or prevent the lawful apprehension or detainer of any person. *Transportation (at the discretion of the court) for life, or for any term not less than fifteen years,* or imprisonment *for any term not exceeding three years.* — § 4.

To unlawfully and maliciously send or deliver to or cause to be taken or received by any person any explosive substance, or any other dangerous or noxious thing, or cast or throw upon or otherwise apply to any person any corrosive fluid or other destructive matter, with intent in any of the cases aforesaid to burn, maim, disfigure, or disable any person, or to do some other grievous bodily harm, and whereby in any of the cases aforesaid any person shall be burnt, maimed, disfigured, or disabled, or receive some other grievous bodily harm. *Transportation (at the discretion of the court) for life, or for any term not less than fifteen years, or imprisonment for any term not exceeding three years.* — § 5.

To administer unlawfully and with intent to procure the miscarriage of any woman, or to cause to be taken by her any poison or other noxious thing, or unlawfully to use any instrument or other means whatsoever with the like intent. *Transportation (at the discretion of the court) for life, or for any term not less than fifteen years, or imprisonment for any term not exceeding three years.* — § 6.

Principals in the second degree, and accessories before the fact, are punishable with *Death, or in the same manner as the principal in the first degree is by this act punishable:* accessories after the fact are, on conviction, liable to *Imprisonment for not exceeding two years.*—§ 7.

Where the crime charged includes an assault against the person, the jury are empowered to acquit of the felony, and may find a verdict of Guilty, for the assault, *if the evidence will warrant such finding*, upon which the court have power to award *Imprisonment for any term not exceeding three years.*—§ 11.

both person and property; as riotous destruction of houses or machinery *, arson, and burglary.

Public offences, are those which tend to the destruction of the queen or subversion of her government, and may be chiefly enumerated as high treason, offences against the coin, sedition, blasphemy (an offence involving an offence against God and the laws of morality), and administering unlawful oaths.

Those offences which militate against the administration of *public justice*, are bribery, extortion and misconduct of officers of justice, compounding felonies, libels reflecting unduly on judges and juries or public functionaries.

Offences which endanger the *public peace*, arrange themselves as riots, affrays, challenges, libels, and threatening letters, &c.

Offences against *public* trade and commerce, are smuggling and infractions of the various revenue laws.

Lastly, Those offences which are contrary to *public* policy as subversive of good government, may be classed thus: bigamy, common nuisance (see BAWDY HOUSE, and NUISANCE), open lewdness and obscenities, blasphemous libels, gaming, offences against the game laws, disturbances of public worship, disinterment of dead bodies, refusal to execute a public office, &c.

Of these various offences, the reader will perceive, on referring to the proper titles, some few are capital felonies; some are simple felonies, punishable with transportation for life or lesser punishment; and many (especially those which endanger the administration of public justice, public peace, trade, or policy) are mere misdemeanors, the punishment of which is in some cases allotted by particular statutes, or, where the offence is punishable " at common law," left to the discretion of the presiding judge.

OFFERINGS, are reckoned among parsons' tithes, payable by custom to the parson or vicar of the parish, either occasionally, as at sacraments, marriage, christenings, churching of women, burials, &c., or at constant times, as at Easter or Christmas. The law enforces the payment of offerings according to the custom and place where they grow due.

The four offering days are, Christmas, Easter, Whitsuntide, and the feast of the dedication of the parish church. It seems that 1*s*. is all that need be given, or less, according to the state in life of the parishioner.

OFFICES, are either judicial or ministerial: the first, relating to the administration of justice, or the actual exercise thereof, must be executed by persons of sufficient capacity, and by the persons themselves to whom they are granted; ministerial, are merely matters of employment, and may be executed by deputy.

A man may have an estate in offices, either to him and his heirs, or for life, or for a term of years, or during pleasure only; save only that offices of *public* trust cannot be granted for a term of years, especially if they concern the administration of justice; neither can any *judicial* office be granted in reversion; but ministerial offices may be so granted, for these may be executed by deputy.

The grant of an office generally may be made to any person the queen pleases, even to a woman. So an office of inheritance may descend to a woman.

* Which is a felony now punishable by *Transportation for life, or for a lesser term, at the discretion of the judge.*

By statute 5 *&* 6 *Ed.* 6. *c.* 16., it is enacted, "that if any person bargain or sell any office, or deputation of any office, or any part of any of them, or receive any money, fee, &c., directly or indirectly, or take any promise, &c. to receive any money, &c., directly or indirectly, for any office, or for the deputation of any office, or any part of any of them; or to the intent that any person should have, exercise, or enjoy any office, or the deputation of any office, or any part of any of them, which shall in anywise concern the administration or execution of justice, or the receipt, &c. of any of the king's treasure, &c., or the keeping of any of the king's towns, &c., being for a place of strength and defence; or which shall concern or touch any clerkship to be occupied in any manner of court of record wherein justice is to be ministered; that then every person that shall so offend shall not only lose and forfeit all his and their right, interest, and estate in or to any of the said office or offices, &c., but also persons who shall give or pay any sum of money, &c., or shall make any promise, &c., shall immediately be adjudged a disabled person in the law to all intents and purposes to have, &c. the said office, &c."

"Provided always, that this act shall not extend to any office whereof any person is seised of any estate of inheritance, nor to any office of parkership, or of the keeping of any park-house, manor, garden, chase, or forest, or to any of them."

By 49 *Geo.* 3. *c.* 126., "For the further Prevention of the Sale and Brokerage of Offices," the said statute 5 *&* 6 *Ed.* 6. is extended to Scotland and Ireland, and to all offices in the gift of the crown, or of any office appointed by the crown, and to all offices under the East India Company; the buying, selling, or the bargaining, or soliciting for such offices, by means of money, is declared a *misdemeanor*. The purchase of military commissions at the regulated prices, and lawful deputations and payments to the principal out of the fees received, are excepted from the operation of the act.

ORDINARY. A term applied to a bishop, or other person having peculiar or original ecclesiastical jurisdiction in a diocese in contradistinction to extraordinary or delegated jurisdiction. This term is derived from the imperial or civil law.

OUTLAWRY. The being put out of the law.

Outlawry is a punishment inflicted for a contempt, in refusing to be amenable to the justice of a court.

And as to forfeitures for refusing to appear, the law distinguishes between outlaws in capital cases, and those of an inferior nature; for as to outlawries in treason and felony, the law interprets the party's absence a sufficient evidence of his guilt, and without requiring further proof, accounts him guilty of the fact, on which ensues corruption of blood, and forfeiture of his personal estate.

Outlawry, in civil actions, is putting a man out of the protection of the law, so that he is not only incapable of sueing for the redress of injuries, but may be imprisoned, and forfeits all his goods and chattels, and the profits of his lands; his *personal* chattels *immediately* upon the outlawry, and his chattels real, and the profits of his lands, when found by inquisition, which are afterwards granted by the queen to satisfy the plaintiff's debt.

Outlawry, in civil actions, is used where the defendant is abroad, or keeps out of the way, so that he cannot be arrested or served with process; if there be several defendants in a joint action, and one of them be abroad, or keep out of the way, the plaintiff must proceed to outlawry against him before he can go on against the others.

OVERSEERS OF THE POOR. Public officers created by the 43 *Eliz.* *c.* 2., to provide for the poor in every parish. Churchwardens, by this statute, are called "overseers of the poor," and they join with the overseers in making a poor-rate. This statute requires that the overseers of parishes shall be four, three, or two substantial householders; and that they shall be nominated yearly in Easter week, or within one month after Easter; and that their appointment shall be under the hand and seal of two or more justices of the peace in the same county, whereof one to be of the *quorum*, dwelling in or near the same parish: and by the same statute, the same authority is given to the mayor's bailiffs, or other head officers of every town and place corporate and city within the realm, being a justice or justices of the peace, as is conferred on county magistrates; and where a parish shall extend into more jurisdictions than one, each set of magistrates are to respectively nominate overseers within their respective jurisdictions, who shall execute the office through the entire parish. Another act provides, that there shall be two or more overseers for towns and villages. A further act directs the appointment to be made annually on the 25th of March, or *within* 14 days afterwards. Another statute enables the justices, in petty sessions, to appoint as overseer, upon the nomination of the parishioners assembled in vestry, any person rated in the parish, though not resident, provided he is a householder resident within 2 miles of the parish church, and consents to accept the office, but not otherwise. The 17 *Geo.* 2. *c.* 38. enacts, "that if any overseer shall die or remove from the place for which he is appointed, or become insolvent before the expiration of his office, two justices may appoint an overseer in his stead for the remainder of the year.

The exemptions mentioned in respect to churchwardens, apply to this office. See CHURCHWARDENS.

A person disputing the validity of his appointment, by reason of privilege or exemption, may appeal to the sessions, or may remove the order of justices by writ of *certiorari* to the queen's bench, who will quash it, if any defect appear on the face of it, or if it is erroneously or improperly made.

The principal duties of the overseers are, to collect a poor-rate, and to do various acts in relation thereto, as, to remove such persons as the parish or place is not liable to support, and other acts incidental to the management of the poor under the directions of the poor-law commissioners, or their assistant commissioner, or according to the provisions of any local act for that purpose; also, to enter in the rate-books, the names of the owners or their proxies, who wish to avail themselves of the privilege of voting for guardians: they are to give publicity to rules of commissioners; and to account quarterly, and when going out of office; and they are liable to various penalties if they refuse or neglect to pay the balance, or if they disobey the *legal* or reasonable orders of justices or guardians, or purloin the property of the parish.

Overseers and guardians of the poor are expressly prohibited from furnishing goods, &c. for the use of the poor, under a penalty of 100*l.*, unless two justices certify that there is no person competent to supply the articles to be found within a convenient distance from the workhouse.

A pertinacious neglect or refusal to obey the rules and regulations of the poor-law commissioners, subjects an overseer or other officer of the parish or union, to penalties; *viz.* 5*l.* for the first offence; 20*l.* for the second offence; and, for the third, he may be indicted for a misdemeanor, and is liable to pay a fine not less than 20*l.*, in addition to imprisonment.

If an overseer does not find *immediate* relief for a pauper, in case of *urgent* necessity, he may be indicted; in ordinary cases he is not indictable, unless a magistrate's order has been given; and if he relieves where there is no necessity, he is also indictable. See POOR, and POOR-RATE.

OVERT ACT. An open act, which by law must be manifestly proved. Some overt act is to be alleged in every indictment for high treason; and *no evidence* shall be admitted of any overt act that is not expressly laid in the indictment.

OYES, corrupted from the French oyez, *hear ye*, is an expression used by the crier of a court, in order to enjoin silence when any proclamation is made.

OYSTERS. The stealing or taking of oysters or oyster brood from any oyster bed, laying, or fishery, being the property of any other person, is a larceny, punishable as such. See LARCENY.

Dredging for oysters within the limits of an oyster bed belonging to another, is a misdemeanor, punishable by fine not exceeding 20*l.*, or imprisonment not exceeding 3 months (with or without hard labour, and with or without solitary confinement, for the whole or any part of the imprisonment).

PANEL. The *pane* or square piece of parchment on which the names of the jury are written.

PARCENERS, or CO-PARCENERS, as they are sometimes called, are tenants in common, by operation of law or custom. By common law, as where a person *seised* in fee simple or fee tail dies, and his next heirs are two or more females, his daughters, sisters, aunts, cousins, or their representatives, whether male or female, in this case they shall all inherit. These co-heirs are then called parceners. Parceners by custom, are where land descends to all the males in equal degree; *viz.* in *gavelkind*, as in Kent, or by the custom of particular manors, as at Islington, Hackney, or in other manors, as sons, brothers, uncles. In contemplation of law, these parceners make but one heir, *i. e.* they represent but one estate.

Partition may be compelled between parceners at law, if they cannot agree by deed or private arrangement, by a writ of partition in the common pleas, or in chancery or exchequer by bill. Advowsons may be presented to in turns, the eldest presenting first.

Coparcenary estates may vest ultimately in the survivor, by descent; and this will bring it to an estate in *severalty*, as distinguished from an estate in common. See JOINT TENANTS; TENANTS IN COMMON.

PARDON. The effect of a pardon is, to make the offender a new man,—to acquit him of all forfeitures; but nothing but an act of parliament can restore the party after actual attainder.

A pardon is either under the queen's seal, or by general act of parliament.

Pardons may be conditional, or upon terms.

A person convicted, and having undergone his sentence, is restored to legal competence as a witness, &c.; but it seems, a person convicted of perjury can never be restored to competence as a credible person.

PARENT AND CHILD. This legal as well as moral relation is

comprised within a narrow compass. The father is entitled to the custody and care of his children, and may re-take them if taken from his custody; and the courts will grant a *habeas corpus* to restore them, as well as entertain actions of trespass brought by him against the parties taking them away. The parent has a right to direct the education of his children, and may correct them in a proper manner, and delegate that authority to a schoolmaster or tutor, who must exercise his delegated authority in a careful and temperate manner.

Courts of equity, especially the chancery, exercise a power of restraint upon parents in matters tending to the detriment of children who have property within their jurisdiction; and the parent's power may be controlled, in cases wherein the chancellor thinks fit to interpose his wholesome jurisdiction; the courts of law will interfere in cases of personal ill usage; and courts of equity, upon motives involving pecuniary interests, will interpose, and impose regulations tending for the benefit of children, and their future interests and station in life, without interfering materially with parental rights.

A parent withholding maintenance from a child unable to support itself, is indictable at law; and in other cases magistrates are bound to interfere, where proper sustenance is not afforded. The court of chancery will interfere on behalf of a child entitled to property, where proper maintenance and education are withheld. The parent, while able to maintain his children, cannot charge them with or be allowed for their maintenance and education, out of property they are entitled to; but the court of chancery will, in its discretion, allow the parent for maintenance, where he is not in circumstances to maintain and educate his infant children, out of funds to which they are absolutely not (*contingently* or *conditionally*) entitled. See WARD.

PARLIAMENT. The great council of the realm; the *legislative* branch (the king, the executive) of the supreme power of Great Britain; consisting of the king, the lords spiritual and temporal, and the knights, citizens, and burgesses, representatives of the commons of the realm, in parliament assembled.

The constituent parts of a parliament are, the king's majesty sitting there in his royal political capacity; and the three estates of the realm, the lords spiritual, the lords temporal, (who sit together with the king in one house,) and the commons, who sit by themselves in another. Others, however, more consonantly with the common understanding of the nature and powers of parliament, consider the three states of the realm to be king, lords, and commons, who form the great body politic or corporation of the kingdom, of which the king is the head, beginning, and end; for, upon their being convened, the king meets them, either in person or by representation, *i. e.* by commission, without which there can be no beginning of a parliament; and he alone has the power of dissolving them.

Blackstone, in his *Commentaries*, vol. i. p. 153—155., shows how necessary it is, for preserving the balance of the constitution, that the executive power should be a branch, not the whole of the legislative, and how each branch of our civil polity supports and is supported, regulates and is regulated by, the rest.

A parliament may be holden at any place the king shall assign. The constituent parts of parliament next in order, are the spiritual lords, who hold, or are supposed to hold, certain ancient baronies under the king. Bishops sat in the great council under the Anglo-

Saxon monarchs; so that custom and the laws of tenure seem to concur in demonstrating their right to sit in the upper house, and no rational or ancient principle can be suggested to deprive them of the same legislative functions as the other peers of parliament.

The lords temporal are the next part of the constituency, consisting of all the peers of the realm, (a style opposed to that of "lords of parliament," which belongs to the bishops, and formerly did to the mitred abbots,) by whatever title they are distinguished,—dukes, marquesses, earls, viscounts, or barons,—some of whom sit by descent, as do all ancient peers; some by creation, as new made peers; or some by election, as the 16 Scotch representative peers, for one parliament; and the 28 temporal peers elected for life by the peers of Ireland. The number of lords temporal is indefinite.

The commons are the remaining part of the constituency, and, in common parlance, consist of all such men of property in the kingdom who have not seats in the house of lords: the counties being represented by knights elected by the proprietors and occupiers of lands; the cities and boroughs by citizens and burgesses chosen, or supposed to be chosen, by the mercantile part or trading interest of the kingdom.

Every member, though chosen by one particular district, when elected and returned, serves for the whole realm; therefore it is a great absurdity in electors to demand a moral pledge of a candidate that he will advocate or support particular measures.

The powers and jurisdiction of parliament, *i. e.* the three estates, are very high, and, as old writers term them, "transcendent," and are so large that they are indefinite; which, indeed, is the chief cause of its independence and dignity, as some observe, though others seem to think that clearness and certainty are essentially necessary to the liberty of England: however, the two houses are governed very much by usage and precedents; and their privileges, ordinary and extraordinary, are displayed in their journals and records.

The ordinary privileges of members of parliament, particularly of members of the house of commons, are those of speech and person; which privilege not only includes privilege from illegal violence (which is punished by the house of commons with the utmost severity), but from legal arrests and seizures by process from the courts of law; for no member can be taken into custody, unless by order of the house, for *actual* contempt of the courts of law or equity, or for some indictable offence, without a breach of the privilege of parliament.

All other privileges which derogate from the law in matters of right are now at an end, save as to the freedom of the member's person, which in a peer (by the privilege of peerage) is for ever sacred and inviolable, and in a commoner (by the privilege of parliament) for 40 days after every prorogation, and 40 days before the next appointed meeting, which is in effect as long as the parliament subsists, it seldom being prorogued for more than 80 days at a time. The privilege from arrest extends only to a *convenient* time after the dissolution. The law provides a process for a member of either house to be served withal, and the stat. 6 *Geo.* 4. *c.* 16. provides, that any trader, having privilege of parliament, may be served with legal process for any just debt, to such amount as will support a fiat of bankruptcy, and unless he make satisfaction within one month, it shall be deemed an act of bankruptcy, and a fiat of bankruptcy may be issued against such privileged trader in like manner as against any other. And any such trader disobeying any decree or order for the payment of money made in equity, bankruptcy, or lunacy, and after being served with a peremptory order, naming a day for payment, and not paying the same, shall be deemed to have committed an act of bankruptcy. And upon a fiat being issued, he is, during 12 months, declared incapable of sitting, unless within that time the fiat be superseded or the creditors paid, or, in case of dispute, secured by the bond of the bankrupt and two sureties; if that is not done, the speaker issues his warrant for the election of a new member.

In respect of the privilege of franking, no member can send more than 10, or receive above 15 letters, free from postage, in one day.

The house of peers is the supreme court of judicature in the kingdom, being a court of appeal, in respect of appeals and writs of error from the courts below; and is the last resort for litigants, who are finally bound by its decision.

The practice of parliament, in regard to making acts of parliament, which when introduced are termed *bills,* is much as follows: —

The persons who have obtained leave to bring in the bill (if leave be necessary), or who have made it their business to bring it in, present it to the house drawn out on paper, with a variety of blanks, for dates, sums, and other unsettled or dubious matters, being little else than a skeleton of the bill. In the house of lords, if the bill begins the e (which it does when of a private nature), it is referred to two of the judges to examine and report the state of the facts alleged, to see that all necessary parties consent, and to settle all points of technical propriety. This is read a first time, and at a convenient distance a second time; and after each reading, the speaker opens to the house the substance of the bill, and puts the question whether it shall proceed any further: the introducing of the bill may be originally opposed, as the bill itself may at either of the readings; and if the opposition succeeds, the bill must be dropped for that session, as it must also be if opposed with success in any of the subsequent stages. But it is not unusual to introduce a rejected bill under a new form and title.

After the second reading it is *committed, i. e.* referred to a committee, which is either selected by the house in matters of small importance, or else upon a bill of consequence the house resolves itself into a committee of the whole house.

A committee of the whole house is composed or every member, and to form it the speaker quits the chair (another member being appointed chairman), and may sit and debate as a private member. In these committees, the bill is debated clause by clause, amendments made, the blanks filled up, and sometimes the bill entirely new modelled.

After it has gone through the committee, the chairman reports it to the house with such amendments as the committee have made, and then the house reconsiders the whole bill again, and the question is repeatedly put upon each clause and amendment. When the house has agreed or disagreed to the amendments of the committee, and sometimes added new amendments of its own, the bill is then ordered to be engrossed, or written in a strong *engrossing* hand, on long rolls (or, as they are termed, *presses*) of parchment, sewed together at the end, making one long roll. This being finished, it is read the third time; and even then amendments are sometimes made to it; and if a new clause be added, it is done by tacking a separate piece of parchment on the bill, which is called a *rider*. The speaker then again opens the contents, or uses a form of language explanatory of the bill and the amendments, and, holding it up, puts the question, That the bill do pass. If this is agreed to, the title is then settled.

The bill thus being passed in the house of commons, one of the members is directed to carry it to the lords, and desire their concurrence, who, attended by seven or more, carries it to the bar of the house of lords, and there delivers it to their speaker (usually the chancellor), who, on the house being formally apprised of the presence of the members, comes down from his woolsack to the bar to receive the bill. It there passes through the same forms as in the lower house (except engrossing, which is already done), and if rejected, no more notice is taken, to prevent unbecoming altercations. But if it is agreed to, the lords send a message by two masters in chancery, or sometimes, upon matters of great importance, by the judges, saying that they have agreed to the bill; and the bill remains with the lords, if they have made no amendment to it. But if any amendments are made, such amendments are sent down with the bill, to receive the concurrence of the commons. If the commons disagree to the amendments, a conference usually follows between members deputed from each house, whose place of meeting was usually in a room called *The Painted Chamber*, at present forming the house of lords, but now in a committee-room, and there debate the matter by a *conference*, and either settle the difference, or remain inflexible; in which latter case the bill is dropped. If the commons agree to the amendments, the bill is sent back to the lords by one of the members, with a formal message to acquaint them therewith.

The same forms are observed, *mutatis mutandis*, when the bill begins in the house of lords. But when an act of grace or pardon is passed, it is first engrossed and signed by her majesty, and then read once only in each of the houses, without any new engrossment or amendment; and when both houses have done with any bill, it is always deposited in the house of peers, to await the royal assent, except in the case of a bill of supply, which, after receiving the concurrence of the lords, is sent back to the house of commons.

If any debate happen on the first reading of a bill, the speaker puts the question whether the same shall have a second reading; and sometimes, upon motion, appoints a day for it; for public bills, unless upon extraordinary occasions, are seldom read more than once a day, the members being allowed convenient time to consider of them. If nothing be said against a bill, the ordinary course is to proceed without a question; but if the bill be generally disliked, a question is sometimes put, whether the bill shall be rejected? If it be rejected, it cannot be proposed any more that session: when a bill has been read a second time, any member may move to have the same amended; but no member of the house is admitted to speak more than once in a debate, except the bill be read more than once that day, or the whole house is turned into a committee; and after some time spent in debates, the speaker, collecting the sense of the house, reduces the same to a question, which he submits to the house, and is put to the vote; and a question is to be put, after the bill is so read a second time, whether it shall be committed? The chairman of the committee makes his report of a bill at the side bar of the house, reading all the alterations made, and then delivers the same to the clerk of the parliament; who likewise reads all the amendments, and the speaker puts the question, whether they shall be read a second time? And if that be agreed unto, he reads the amendments himself, and puts the question, whether the bill so amended shall be engrossed, and read a third time some other day? In the house of lords, if a bill be not committed, then it is to be read a third time, and the next question to be for its passing; and on the third reading of the bill, any member may speak against the whole bill, to throw out the same, or for amendment of any clause.

In cases of private bills, when the petition is read, and leave given to bring in the bill, the persons concerned and affected by it may be heard by themselves or counsel at the bar, or before the committee to whom such bill is referred; and in case of a peer, he shall be admitted to come within the bar of the house of commons, and sit covered on a stool whilst the same is debating. And after counsel are heard on both sides, and the house is satisfied with the contents of the bill, it goes through the several forms.

The *royal assent* may be given in two ways.—1. In person; when the king comes to the house of peers, in his crown and royal robes, and sending for the commons to the bar, the titles of all the bills that have passed both houses are read; and the king's answer is declared by the clerk of the parliament in Norman French. If the king consents to a public bill, the clerk usually declares, "*Le Roy* (or if a queen regnant, *la Reine*) *le veut*—The king (or *queen*) wills it so to be:" if to a private bill, "*Soit fait comme il est désiré*—Be it as it is desired." If the king refuses his assent, it is in the gentle language of "*Le Roy* (or *la Reine*) *s'avisera*—The king (or *queen*) will advise upon it." When a bill of supply is passed, it is carried up and presented to the king, by the speaker of the house of commons; and the royal assent is thus expressed: "*Le Roy* (or *la Reine*) *remercie ses loyal subjects, accepte leur benevolence, et ainsi le veut*—The king (or *queen*) thanks his (*her*) loyal subjects, accepts their benevolence, and wills it so to be." In case of an act of grace, which originally proceeds from the crown, and has the royal assent in the first stage of it, the clerk of the parliament thus pronounces the gratitude of the subject: "*Les prelats, seigneurs, et commons, en ce present parliament assemblés, au nom de touts vos autres subjects, remercient très humblement votre majesté, et prient à Dieu vous donner en santé bonne vie et longue*—The prelates, lords, and commons, in this present parliament assembled, in the name of all your other subjects, most humbly thank your majesty, and pray to God to grant you in health long to live."

2. By commission, *i. e.* by the king's letters patent under his great seal, signed with his hand, and notified in his absence to both houses assembled together in the lords' house, which is of the same force as if given by the king in person.

When the bill has received the royal assent in either of these ways, it is then, and not before, a statute or act of parliament, and being inrolled in chancery, is placed among the records of the chancery; and being printed by the king's printer, copies are distributed among the several courts of justice and magistracy throughout the kingdom, at the public expense, and at a cheap rate to those who will purchase them.

An act of parliament, thus made, binds every subject in the land, and even the king himself, if particularly named therein. And it cannot be altered, amended, dispensed with, suspended, or repealed, but in the same forms and by the same authority of parliament: for it is a maxim in law, that it requires the same strength to dissolve, as to create an obligation. Nor can the king, by proclamation or otherwise, dispense with penal statutes, or suspend their operation.

For dispatch of business, each house of parliament has its speaker. The speaker of the house of lords, whose office it is to preside there, and manage the formality of business, is the lord chancellor, or keeper of the king's great seal, or any other appointed by the king's commission: and if none be so appointed, the house of lords elect one *pro tempore*. The speaker of the house of commons is chosen by the house; but must be approved by the king. And herein the usage of the two houses differs, — that the speaker of the house of commons cannot give his opinion or argue any question in the house, unless the house is in a committee, or when the house is equally divided, and the casting vote of the speaker is requisite to determine a question; but the speaker of the house of lords, if a lord of parliament, may, in all cases speak and argue.

The salary of the speaker of the house of commons is now settled at 5000*l*. a year, and he is prohibited from holding any office under the crown during pleasure.

In each house the act of the majority binds the whole; and this majority is declared by votes openly and publicly given.

In the house of commons the speaker never votes (unless in committee), except when there is an equality without his casting vote, which in that case creates a majority of the house; but the speaker of the house of lords has no casting vote, his vote being connected with the rest of the house; and in the case of an equality, the *non contents*, or negative voices, have the same effect and operation as if they were in fact a majority. Hence the order in putting the question, on appeals and writs of error, is this; "Is it your lordships' pleasure, that this decree or judgment should be reversed?" for if the votes are equal, the judgment of the court below is affirmed.

With respect to other formalities in the two houses, it may be observed, there are no places of precedency in the house of commons, as there are in the house of lords; only the speaker has a chair or seat fixed towards the upper end, in the middle of the house; and the clerk, with his assistant, sits near him at the table, just below the chair.

No knight of the shire, citizen, or burgess of the house of commons, can depart from the parliament without leave of the speaker and commons.

"Calling the house" is to discover what members are absent, without leave of the house, or just cause; in which cases fines have been often imposed.

Forty members are requisite to make a house of commons for despatch of business. The speaker of the house of commons, according to the duty of his office, as a servant to the house, may publish such proceedings as he shall be ordered, by the commons assembled; and he cannot be liable for what he does that way by the command of others.

The speaker of the house of commons is not allowed to persuade or dissuade in passing a bill, only to make a short narrative of it; opening the parts of the bill, so that all may understand it: if any question be upon the bill, he is to explain, but not enter into argument or dispute.

When Mr. Speaker desires to speak, he ought to be heard without interruption; and when the speaker stands up, the member standing up is to sit down: if two stand up to speak to a bill, he who would speak against the bill, if it be known, is to be first heard; otherwise he who was first up, which is to be determined by the speaker *; and whosoever hisses or disturbs any person in his speech, is liable to answer it at the bar of the house.

In enacting laws, and other proceedings in parliament, the lords give their voices in their house, from the puisne lord, *seriatim*, by the word *content* or *not content;* the manner of voting in the house of commons, is by *yea* and *no;* and if it be difficult to determine which are the greater number, the house divides, and four tellers are appointed by the speaker, two of each side, to number them, one party going out of the house, and the other staying in; and thereof report is made to the house.

An *adjournment* is a continuance of the sessions from one day to another, as the word itself signifies; and this is done by the authority of each house separately every day; and sometimes for a fortnight or month together. But the adjournment of one house is no adjournment of the other. It is, however, usual, when his majesty hath signified his pleasure that both or either of the houses should adjourn themselves to a certain day, to obey the king's pleasure so signified, and to adjourn accordingly.

A *prorogation* is the continuance of the parliament from one session to another, as an adjournment is a continuation of the session from day to day. This is done by the royal authority, expressed either by the lord chancellor in his majesty's presence, or by commission from the crown, or frequently by proclamation.

At the beginning of a new parliament, when it is not intended that the parliament should meet, at the return of the writ of summons, for dispatch of business, the practice is to prorogue it, by a writ of prorogation.

Both houses are necessarily prorogued at the same time, it not being a prorogation of the house of lords, or commons, but of the parliament. The session is never understood to be at an end until a prorogation. Formerly the usage was, for the king to give the royal assent to all such bills as he approved, at the end of every session, and then to prorogue the parliament.

By prorogation all orders of parliament determine: and one taken by order of the parliament, after their prorogation, may be discharged on an *habeas corpus*, as well as after a dissolution; but it is determined, that the dissolution of a parliament does not alter the state of impeachments, brought up by the commons in a preceding parliament. Cases of appeals and writs of error continue, and are to be proceeded on, *in statu quo*, as they stood at the dissolution of the last parliament.

By 37 *Geo.* 3. *c.* 127., whenever the king shall be pleased, by advice of the privy council, to issue a proclamation that parliament shall meet and be holden for dispatch of business, on any day not less than 14 days from the date of such proclamation, the same shall be sufficient notice to all persons, and that the parliament shall stand prorogued to the day and place therein declared, notwithstanding any former prorogation, or any law or usage to the contrary. And by 39 & 40 *Geo.* 3.

* In practice, the member who first "catches the speaker's eye" has the precedence of speech.

c. 14., this provision is extended to the case of an adjournment of parliament, as well as a prorogation.

A *dissolution* is the civil death of the parliament; and this may be effected in three ways: — *First*, By the king's will, expressed either in person or by representation by his commissioners. For, as the king has the sole right of convening the parliament, so also it is a branch of the royal prerogative, that he may (whenever he pleases) prorogue the parliament for a time, or put a final period to its existence.

Secondly, A parliament may be dissolved by the demise of the crown. This dissolution formerly happened immediately upon the death of the reigning sovereign: for he being considered in law as the head of the parliament, that failing, the whole body was held to be extinct. But the calling a new parliament immediately on the inauguration of the successor being found inconvenient, and dangers being apprehended from having no parliament in being, in case of a disputed succession, it was enacted by stat. 7 *&* 8 *W.* 3. *c.* 15., that the parliament in being should, if sitting, continue for six months after the demise of the crown, unless sooner dissolved, &c. by the successor: and if not sitting, should meet on the day of prorogation; and that in case no parliament was in being, the last preceding parliament should convene and sit. By stat. 6 *Ann. c.* 7. *s.* 4., it is more explicitly enacted, that parliament shall not be determined or dissolved by demise of the crown; but shall continue, and if sitting at the time of such demise, immediately proceed to act for six months and no longer, unless sooner prorogued or dissolved by the successor: and if prorogued, shall meet on the day of the prorogation, and sit for the remainder of the said six months, unless sooner dissolved. The same statute also provides, that if there be a parliament in being at the time of the demise, *but adjourned or prorogued*, it should proceed immediately to act for six months and no longer.

To summon, prorogue, and dissolve the parliament, is undoubtedly the prerogative of the crown; and when it is to be summoned, a warrant, or letter, signed by the king, is sent to the chancellor of Great Britain and Ireland, by the advice of that part of the privy council, styled "the Cabinet," commanding the said chancellor to issue, under the great seal, writs for that purpose, which writs are made out by the clerk of the crown in chancery, and returnable after the election, in his office, called the Crown Office in chancery, and 50 days generally intervene between the date of their being issued (called the *teste*), and the time of their being returnable.

If, after a parliament has assembled, a vacancy occur, the house of commons exercises the power of filling it up, which is done by an order from the speaker to the clerk of the crown of either Great Britain or Ireland, directing a new writ to be made and issued for the election of a new member. These vacancies, it may here be observed, occur ordinarily on the death, promotion to the peerage, acceptance of office, or bankruptcy of a member; in which last case, if the member (being a trader) does not pay his debts in a limited time, the speaker causes a notice thereof to be inserted in the "Gazette."

The writs, when issued, are delivered by the messenger to the great seal to the sheriffs of London and Middlesex, and to those officers or sheriffs who have offices in London or Westminster, or within 5 miles thereof, and the remaining writs are forwarded by the general post to the sheriffs of counties, and returning officers of boroughs and towns in the country, and the election is forthwith proceeded in.

The place of election in *counties*, is at the most usual place for the last 40 years, of which the sheriff is to make proclamation within two days after receipt of the writ; but in those counties which are divided by the reform act *, proclamation is to be made of the day of election for each respective division, at the places fixed by the boundary act (2 *W*. 4. *c*. 45. *s*. 61. 64. sched. N.).

In *boroughs and towns*, the returning officer gives public notice of the time and place of election; this notice is given in the most usual place.

On the day nominated for the election, between 8 and 11 in the morning, the returning officer opens the proceedings by reading the writ of summons, if the election be for a county, or city, or town, which is a county of itself; or the precept, if it be in a borough, and the election takes place by virtue of a precept from the sheriff, in conformity to the writ delivered to him. The returning officer then takes and subscribes the bribery oath, and reads the bribery act (2 *Geo*. 2. *c*. 24. *s*. 9.). The candidates are then nominated, which is done by calling upon the electors to name them, and these candidates may be generally called upon to take the qualification oaths.

If no more candidates are named than the legal number of representatives, the returning officer must return those nominated as duly elected; but when more are proposed than the number to be returned, a poll is demanded, which for *counties* commences the next day but two after the day of nomination, at 9 o'clock in the morning, and continues for two successive days only, for 7 hours the first day, and 8 the second, closing at 4 o'clock on the second day (in Ireland, the poll lasts 5 days); and for boroughs, on the day after the nomination, at 8 in the morning, and continues open for that day only till 4 o'clock.

The only inquiries to be made of the voter when he comes to the poll, are three. The 1st is, " Are you the same person whose name appears as A. B. on the register of voters, &c.?" 2d. " Have you already voted at this election, &c.?" 3d. " Have you the same qualification for which your name was originally inserted, &c.?"

Persons are entitled to a copy of the poll on payment of a reasonable charge. On the second day from that on which the poll closes for counties, and on the same day or the day after for boroughs, the returning officer must, not later than 2 o'clock, fairly and publicly proclaim the names of those who have been chosen, and forthwith make a return, except Sunday or a Fast-day intervene. The sheriff is generally the returning officer for counties, and the bailiff, or customary returning officer, or those nominated by the reform act, in boroughs or towns.

Registration of Electors.—To prevent any dispute at the time of election, as to the right of an elector to vote, the reform act has constituted annual courts to be holden for the discussion of disputed rights

---

* SCHEDULE (F.)

COUNTIES TO BE DIVIDED.

Cheshire	Hampshire	Somersetshire
Cornwall	Lancashire	Staffordshire
Cumberland	Leicestershire	Suffolk
Derbyshire	Norfolk	Surrey
Devonshire	Northumberland	Sussex
Durham	Northamptonshire	Warwickshire
Essex	Nottinghamshire	Wiltshire
Gloucestershire	Shropshire	Worcestershire
Kent		

of voting, commonly called "courts for revising the lists of electors," the judges of which are barristers annually appointed by the senior judge of each circuit, and their duty is to revise and settle the lists of voters and claimants to vote, furnished to them by the overseers and officers of boroughs, &c., which when settled become the registers of voters, and which the sheriff or returning officer has furnished him previous to the election. The only control of these lists, as finally settled, (for they cannot be impugned at the election,) is a committee of the House of Commons. We will now see what these lists are, and how framed.

With respect to the registration of county voters, the overseers of parishes are directed, by the reform act, every year to make out an alphabetical list of persons entitled to vote in respect of property within their parishes. In order to obtain the means of making out such lists correctly, they are on the 20th June to give a public notice [see Form, No. 1.], requiring persons claiming to vote to deliver a notice of their claim as such voters [see Form, No. 2.] on or before the 20th July; persons once on the register not being required to make a fresh claim. The alphabetical list of county voters being made out from these notices, [see Form, No. 3.], containing the names of those already on the list or register, and including those who claim to be inserted, containing the christian and surname, and abode of every person, with the nature of his qualification, are, after having been published the two next Sundays after the last day of July, on the doors of the churches and chapels within the parish, to be delivered to the high constable of the hundred or district in which the parish is situate, by whom they are to be transmitted to the clerk of the peace (the overseers signing the original lists, and keeping the copies of same for perusal, without fee or reward, during the two first weeks after such list shall have been made). With regard to objections to votes, the overseers may mark any person in the list whose claim to vote they consider doubtful as "objected to," which will compel the party objected to to prove his claim before the revising barrister; persons also who are in the lists of electors, or who claim insertion therein, may object to the retention of the name of any person on the list, by giving notice in writing to the overseers as well as to the party objected to, on or before the 25th day of August [see Form, No. 5]. The overseers then make out lists of the parties objected to [see Form, No. 6.], which are to be affixed for the two Sundays preceding the 15th September, on the doors of the churches and chapels within their parish; and, for 10 days immediately previous to the 15th September, the overseers shall keep a copy of such list for perusal, without fee.

A written statement of the parties objected to is handed by the overseers to the high constable, and by him to the clerk of the peace, who makes out an abstract of the persons objected to in each parish, and transmits it to the revising barrister. The revising barristers make a circuit of the county, &c., for which they are named, between the 15th September and the 25th October, of which three days' notice is given by advertisement.

In *Boroughs*.—The overseers are to prepare a similar list of persons having a right to vote under the reform act as 10*l*. occupiers (see Form, No. 7.), and another list of persons (other than freemen, who will be noticed presently,) entitled to vote under any other right (see Form, No. 8.) on or before the last day of July. (Places having no overseers being deemed to be within the least populous of the adjoining parishes, and to be inserted by the overseers of such parish accordingly.) The lists of freemen in cities and boroughs are to be prepared and published by the town clerks on the same day, and they are to affix copies of such freemen's lists on some public place (usually the Town-hall), and they are to keep copies for general perusal without fee during the first two weeks that such lists are made. They are to receive claims from freemen claimants, also notices of objections, to fix up copies of such lists on the Town-hall, or some public place, and to keep others for general perusal without fee in a manner strictly analogous to the regulations concerning county lists, and at precisely the same periods. (See Forms, No. 9. to 19.)

Lists of the liverymen of London are made out by the clerks of the several companies, and the notices to be given of omissions and objections, and the times of preparing lists of freemen, are strictly analogous to the preceding rules; and, as to the periods of time, precisely the same.

The christian name of an objector should be at full length.

The proof of the qualification of a borough voter, freeman or liveryman of London, stands upon different grounds from that of a county voter; the latter is bound to send in his claim to the overseer, and to specify in that claim his qualification. The borough voter freeman or liveryman has his name and qualification inserted by the overseer, town-clerk, or clerk of his company; therefore, should not be held to proof of his qualification as *stated in the* list; for if he proves himself qualified in any other manner, his name is to be retained, the revising barrister amending the list.

Claimants must pay 1*s*., or their names will not be inserted in the list; and registered voters are liable to pay 1*s*. as an addition to the poor-rate, and leviable accordingly. County voters pay the 1*s*. before registry, but borough voters afterwards.

Qualifications of Electors. — The next consideration seems to be the voter's qualification, and the method of proceeding in the court for revision of the lists of electors before the revising barristers.

The elective franchise does not extend to minors, nor women, aliens (unless endenisened or naturalised), idiots, and persons not in a sound state of mind at the time of voting. Imbecile and deaf and dumb persons are qualified to vote, if it can be shown that the voter understands what he is doing. Outlawry in a civil action, it seems, does not disqualify for a seat in parliament, therefore not to be objected against a voter. Officers under government are disqualified; paid agents at the election, persons in receipt of parochial relief within 12 months of the 31st of July in the year of registration, persons convicted of perjury or bribery, and persons *fraudulently* qualified, are disabled from voting.

Votes for counties.— By the reform act the electors for *counties* now consist of four classes, viz.—

1. *Freeholders.* — All freeholders of *inheritance* of the value of 40*s*. clear annual value.

But as regards freeholders *for life*, the franchise is narrowed; for by *s*. 18. of the reform act, no freeholder for life (except when he is in actual or *bonâ fide* occupation, or where the lands or tenements come to him by marriage, marriage-settlement, devise or promotion to a benefice or office,) shall have a right of voting, unless the property be worth 10*l*. *per ann*. free from all rents and charges. (These words do not include taxes.)

This restriction is only prospective, as the rights of 40*s*. freeholders for life, created before the reform act (7th June 1832), are saved.

Formerly in cities and towns that *were* counties of themselves (Caermarthen, Canterbury, Chester, Coventry, Gloucester, Kingston-upon-Hull, Lincoln, London, Newcastle-upon-Tyne, Poole, Worcester, York and Ainsty, Southampton,) freeholders had no vote, but now such cities and towns are included in the adjoining counties. For instance, a person may claim to vote in respect of a freehold house in London for the county of Middlesex, but it must not be occupied by the owner in London if above 10*l.*, for then the occupation qualifies for a vote in London; but if *under* 10*l.*, it gives a vote for the county, whether the owner occupy or not. *S.* 17. of the Reform Act; also *s.* 24.

2. *Copyholders and tenants in ancient demesne.*—Every male person of full age (notwithstanding by the custom of some manors he may be admitted before 21) seised at law or in equity of copyhold lands or tenements, or any other tenure (except freehold for life), or larger estate of not less than 10*l.* clear yearly value, is entitled to vote for *counties.* But a copyhold house or building situate in a borough, will not, if of sufficient value to give a borough vote, confer a *county* vote, whether in the occupation of the owner or tenant.

3. *Leaseholders.*— Leaseholders of full age entitled to any term, originally created for at least 60 years (whether for lives or not), where the land or tenement is worth 10*l. per annum*, or for any term originally granted for 20 years where the yearly value is 50*l.*, are entitled to vote for counties; but the lessee or assignee of a lease must be in actual occupation to entitle him to vote.

4. *Tenants or occupiers.*—Persons occupying lands or tenements for which they are liable to a *bonâ fide* rent of 50*l.* a year are likewise entitled to vote for counties.

Note.—All persons must be registered, and freeholders or copyholders must have been in possession of the property for which they claim to vote six calendar months, and leaseholders twelve calendar months, before the last day of July, in the year in which they seek to be registered. There is an exception, in case the property comes to them within the six or twelve months by descent, succession, marriage, marriage-settlement, devise or promotion to any office or benefice.

County voters need not be assessed to the land tax.

Persons cannot vote for any freehold office unless it is coupled with an interest in *land.*

Persons claiming to be registered as freeholders in respect of an annuity or rent-charge issuing out of freehold, must register the same with the clerk of the peace 12 calendar months before; unless it accrues or devolves by descent, marriage, &c., within a year before the election, when a certificate of it to be entered with the clerk of the peace before the first day of election is all that is requisite.

Voters in cities and boroughs.— The electors for *cities* and *boroughs* now consist partly of the old voters, and of a new class of householders created by the reform act, freeholders. In cities and towns *being counties of themselves*, (Bristol, Exeter, Haverford-west, Lichfield, Norwich and Nottingham), the right of voting consists of a 40*s.* freehold as in counties; in freeholds, not of inheritance, 10*l. per annum* as before; and actual possession of the profits for 12 months before the 31st July in the year in which he claims to be registered, except it came to him by descent or operation of law. This right is extended to the *new* boundaries, and 6 months' residence within the borough, or within 7 miles of the polling place, next before 31st July is now required: in cities and boroughs *not being counties of themselves*, no person is entitled in respect of a burgage or freehold tenement, acquired since the 1st March 1831. unless acquired between that time and 7th June 1832, by descent, &c. This is applicable to the boroughs of Shoreham, Cricklade, Aylesbury and East Retford, and the adjacent districts included in them.

The old franchise is in 40*s.* freeholders in Shoreham, but it ceases with those who came into possession before the passing of the reform act 7th June 1832.

Leaseholders in several boroughs possess the right of voting, and in one borough, Cricklade, common copyholders occupying 40 days before the election have a right of voting.

Burgage-holders. — Those who hold in an ancient borough a tenement in fee paying an *undivided* rent to the lord; the tenement, or the site of it, must be ancient and entire as it hath been beyond memory.

In cities and towns *not* counties of themselves, the voter must have acquired possession before 1st March 1831, or have come to it between that time and 7th June 1832, by descent, &c.

If the burgage tenement is in a city or town *being a county of itself*, the voter must have had possession of the profits for 12 months before the last day of July, except he has acquired the same by descent, &c.

Occupation of a house, &c. — Persons occupying either as owner or tenant, any house, warehouse, counting-house, shop, or other building, either separately or jointly with any land within the limits of the borough occupied therewith of the clear yearly value of 10*l.*, are entitled to vote as electors for the borough, and the occupation need not be actual *i. e.* the voter need not sleep or have his meals in the house, &c.

Chambers in the inns of Court or Chancery confer the right of voting.

The occupation must be 12 months immediately previous to the 31st July in the year wherein the party claims to be registered; and he must also have been rated, and have paid or at least tendered his rate.*

Freemen. — By the reform act all freemen created since the 1st March 1831, *other than those admitted by birth or servitude*, are excluded from voting, and the freemen who vote under their former or present right must be resident 6 months immediately previous to the last day of July; indeed, must be qualified to vote on that day as if it were the day of election, which applies to all qualifications whatever.

The former rights are those to which burgesses were entitled as inhabitants paying scot and lot (termed familiarly *pot-wallopers*). Burgage-tenants, &c., are continued in cities and boroughs *not* counties of themselves, according to the usages of the borough, under the condition of residence and registration, but under the previous exception as to freemen, who can only be admitted by birth or servitude.

The right of election in boroughs being various, is determined by a committee of the House of Commons, who by statute can by their decision bind the right of election. And burgage tenants in the few places where they still exist must comply with the conditions of the reform act.

The different qualifications of electors having been noticed, the practice of the court of revision of the lists and the mode of substantiating objections before the revising barristers require some observation.

The barristers' court is an open court, but counsel are not to attend, attornies and agents being employed; the clerk of the peace is to produce the lists of voters, and overseers are to attend and to deliver to the barrister copies of the list of persons objected to in each parish, and to

* By the reform act *s.* 27., the occupier of a 10*l.* house, &c., must not only have been rated to all poor's-rates made during his year's occupation next before the last day of July, but *must have paid* on or before the 20th of July *all poor's-rates and assessed taxes* "which shall have become *payable* from him in respect to such premises previously to the 6th day of April."

The rate is *payable* as soon as it is made and allowed, and the voter is bound to take notice of it, and pay or tender the same, furnish him on oath with all the information in their power in order to enable him to revise the lists; and, for the like purpose, collectors and officers having the custody of tax-assessments and rate-books, are, on being required, to produce them before him.

The barrister is to retain on the lists all names to which no objection is made by electors or claimants, or which are not marked, "objected to" by the overseers themselves, as well as those who are objected to, if the persons giving notice of such objection do not attend by themselves or agents to support them. Persons objected to must appear to prove their qualification, else their name will be expunged.

Where a person fails to prove that he was entitled to be inserted in the list on the last of July preceding, his name will be expunged; the objection is thus proceeded with: viz.,

The party appearing to an overseer's objection, in the first place gives evidence of his qualification by his own oath or by the oath of others and if no sufficient reasons are urged, the revising barrister strikes out, the word "objected to."

Where a person on the register or a claimant for insertion, has given the notice in the form No. 4. *post*, to the overseers, and the notice No. 5. *post*, to the party objected to, he must attend and produce exact duplicates or counterparts of the notices of objection served on the person objected to, as on the overseers, also a copy of the list of voters containing the name of the party signing the notice of objection, who is called the objector, and he must be identified as the same person. The objector having established his own identity and consequent right to object, is then called upon to prove the service upon the overseers and the party objected to, by calling the person who served the notices, who for that purpose should carefully compare them before service, so that he can conscientiously swear that the copies served are true copies of the notices then produced before the barrister, and were served personally upon or left at the abode of the party objected to, or served upon the tenants *personally*, or in case of an annuity, upon the party objected to *personally* or left at his place of abode. The party objected to must then prove to the satisfaction of the barrister that he is entitled to have his name inserted in the list of voters, by his witnesses, to rebut whose statement the objector may produce other witnesses.

If the incapacity or disqualification should be personal, *i. e.* that the party objected to or claiming, is a minor, alien, has been convicted of perjury, bribery, &c., the objector must enter into his case first, and so should the overseers, if they rest their "objected to" upon such an alleged incapacity.

The rules of evidence are adhered to and the investigation is pursued, similar to an investigation of the same fact in a court of law; for instance, to prove a conviction for bribery or perjury, an examined office copy should be produced which can be proved to be a true copy; to prove a person an alien, the registry of aliens, &c., &c.

The objector having in cases of supposed disqualification (not of a *personal* nature) put his antagonist the party objected to, to the necessity of supporting his claim, may rest his case, if it be a legal point, upon the cross-examination of the witnesses examined in favour of the claim, which will raise a case upon which the revising barristers will give their judgment.

The lists as finally revised are controllable only by a committee of the House of Commons, which is the only jurisdiction competent to try disputed elections; the forms and proceedings in which are regulated by various acts or facts relative to elections.

I.

SCHEDULE (H.)

Forms of Lists and Notices applicable to *Counties.*

No. 1.—*Notice of the making out of the Lists to be given by the Overseers.*

We hereby give notice, that we shall, on or before the last day of July in this year, make out a list of all persons entitled to vote in the election of a knight or knights of the shire for the county of [*or* for the riding, parts, or division of the county of *as the case may be*], in respect of property situate wholly or in part within this parish [*or* township]; and all persons so entitled are hereby required to deliver or transmit to us, on or before the twentieth day of July in this year, a claim in writing, containing their christian name and surname, their place of abode, the nature of their qualification, and the name of the street, lane, or other like place, wherein the property in respect of which they claim to vote is situated; and if the property be not situated in any street, lane, or other like place, then such claim must describe the property by the name by which it is usually known, or by the name of the tenant occupying the same; and each of such persons so claiming must also at the same time pay to us the sum of one shilling. Persons omitting to deliver or transmit such claim or to make such payment will be excluded from the register of voters for this county [*or* riding, parts, or division, *as the case may be*]. [*In subsequent years after one thousand eight hundred and thirty-two, add the following words,* " but persons whose names are now on the register are not required to make a fresh claim so long as they retain the same qualification and continue in the same place of abode as described in the register."]

(*Signed*) A. B. } C. D. } E. F. } Overseers of the Parish [*or* Township] of

No. 2.—*Notice of Claim to be given to the Overseers.*

I hereby give you notice, that I claim to be inserted in the list of voters for the county of [*or* for the riding, parts, *or* division of the county of *as the case may be,*] and that the particulars of my place of abode and qualification are stated below. Dated the day of in the year

(*Signed*) John Adams.

Place of abode, Cheapside, London.

Nature of qualification, freehold house, [*or* warehouse, stable, land, field, annuity, rent-charge, &c. *as the case may be, giving such a description of the property as may serve to identify it*].

Where situate in this parish [*or* township], King Street. [*If the property be not situate in any street, lane, or other like place, then say,* " name of the property Highfield Farm," *or,* " name of the occupying tenant, John Edwards."]

No. 3.

County of to wit, [*or* riding, parts, or division of the county of *as the case may be.*] } The Lists of Persons entitled to vote in the election of a knight [*or* knights] of the shire [*or* for the riding, parts, *or* division of the county of *as the case may be*], in respect of property situate within the parish of [*or* township, *as the case may be*].

Christian name and surname of each voter at full length.	Place of abode.	Nature of qualification.	Street, Lane, or other like place in this parish [or township] where the property is situate, or name of the property or name of the tenant.
Adams, John	Cheapside, London -	Freehold House - -	King Street.
Alley, James	Long Lane, in this Parish	Copyhold Field - -	J. Edwards, tent.
Ball, William	Market Street, Lancaster -	Lease of warehouse for years	Duke Street.
Boyce, Henry	Church Street, in this Parish	50 Acres of Land as occupier	Highfield Farm.

(*Signed*) A. B. } C. D. } E. F. } Overseers of the said parish [*or* township].

No. 4.—*Notice of Objection to be given to the Overseers.*

To the overseers of the parish of [*or*, township, *as the case may be*]. I hereby give you notice, that I object to the name of William Ball being retained in the list of voters for the county of [*or* for the riding, parts, *or* division of the county of]. Dated the day in the year

(*Signed*) A. B. of [*Place of abode*].

No. 5.—*Notice of Objections to Parties inserted in the List.*

To Mr. William Ball.—I hereby give you notice, that I do object to your name being retained in the list of voters for the county of [*or* for the riding, parts, *or* division of the county of], and that you will be required to prove your qualification at the time of the revising of the said list. Dated the day of in the year

(*Signed*) A. B. of [*Place of abode*].

No. 6.—*List of Persons objected to, to be published by the Overseers.*

The following persons have been objected to as not being entitled to have their names retained in the list of voters for the county of [*or* for the riding, parts, *or* division of the county of].

Christian name and surname of each person objected to.	Place of abode.	Nature of the supposed qualification.	Street, Lane, or other like place in this parish [or township] where the property is situate, or name of the property, or name of the tenant.
Alley, James	Long Lane in this Parish	Copyhold Field .	John Edwards, Tenant.
Ball, William	Market Street, Lancaster	Lease of Warehouse for years .	Duke Street.

(*Signed*) A. B., C. D., E. F. Overseers of the parish [*or* township], *as the case may be*].

II.

SCHEDULE (I.)

Forms of Lists and Notices applicable to *Cities* and *Boroughs.*

No. 1.

The List of Persons entitled to vote in the election of a member [*or* members] for the city [*or* borough] of in respect of property occupied within the parish [*or* township] of by virtue of an act passed in the second year of the reign of King William the Fourth, intituled "An Act to amend the representation of the people in England and Wales."

Christian name and surname of each voter at full length.	Nature of qualification.	Street, lane, or other place in this parish where the property is situate.
Ashton, John	House - -	Church Street.
Atkinson, William	Warehouse - -	Bolt Court, Fleet Street.
Bates, Thomas	Shop - -	Castle Street.
Bull, Thomas	Counting-house -	Lord Street

(*Signed*) A. B., C. D., E. F. Overseers of the said parish [*or* township].

No. 2.

The List of all Persons (not being freemen) entitled to vote in the election of a member [*or* members] for the city [*or* borough] of in respect of any rights other than those conferred by an act passed in the second year of the reign of King William the Fourth, intituled "An Act to amend the representation of the people in England and Wales."

Christian name and surname of each voter at full length.	Nature of qualification.	Street, lane, or other place, in this parish where the property is situate. *If the right of voting does not depend on property, then state the place of abode.*

(*Signed*) A. B. C. D. E. F. } Overseers of the parish of [*or* township] within the said city [*or* borough].

No. 3.

The List of the Freemen of the city [*or* borough of , *or* of being a place sharing in the election with the city, *or* borough, of] entitled to vote in the election of a member [*or* members] for the said city [*or* borough.]

Christian name and surname of each freeman at full length.	Place of his abode.

(*Signed*) A. B. { Town Clerk of the said city [*or* borough, or place].

No. 4.

Notice of Claim.

To the Overseers of the parish [*or* township] of [*or* to the town clerk of the city [*or* borough] of *or otherwise, as the case may be.*]

I hereby give you notice, that I claim to have my name inserted in the list made by you of persons entitled to vote in the election of a member [*or* members] for the city [*or* borough] of , and that my qualification consists of a house in Duke Street in your parish, [*or otherwise, as the case may be*]; [*and in the case of a freeman, say,* and that my qualification is as a freeman of , and that I reside in Lord Street in this city *or* borough]. Dated the day of one thousand eight hundred and thirty

(*Signed*) John Allen of [*Place of abode.*]

No. 5.

Notice of Objection.

To the Overseers of the parish [*or* township] of [*or* to the town clerk of the city [*or* borough] of *or otherwise, as the case may be*].

I hereby give you notice, that I object to the name of Thomas Bates being retained in the list of persons entitled to vote in the election of a member [*or* members] for the city [*or* borough] of , and that I shall bring forward such objection at the time of the revising of such list. Dated the day of in the year

(*Signed*) A. B. of [*Place of abode.*]

No. 6.

List of Claimants, to be published by the Overseers.

The following persons claim to have their names inserted in the list of persons entitled to vote in the election of a member [*or* members] for the city [or borough] of

Christian name and surname of each claimant at full length.	Nature of qualification.	Street, lane, or other place in this parish where the property is situate. *If the right does not depend on property, state the place of abode.*
Allan, John	House.	Duke Street.

(*Signed*) A. B. } C. D. } Overseers of, &c. E. F. }

No. 7.

List of persons objected to, to be published by the Overseers.

The following persons have been objected to as not being entitled to have their names retained in the list of persons qualified to vote in the election of a member [*or* members] for the city [*or* borough] of

Christian name and surname of each person objected to.	Nature of the supposed qualification.	Street, lane, or other place in this parish where the property is situate. *If the right does not depend on property, state the place of abode.*
Bates, Thomas	Shop.	Castle Street.

(*Signed*) A. B. } C. D. } Overseers of, &c. E. F. }

No. 8.

List of Claimants, to be published by the Town Clerks.

The following persons claim to have their names inserted in the list of the freemen of the city [*or* borough] of [*or* of being a place sharing in the election with the city [*or* borough] of], entitled to vote in the election of a member [*or* members] for the said city [*or* borough].

Christian name and surname of each claimant at full length.	Place of his abode.

(*Signed*) A. B. { Town Clerk of the said city [*or* borough *or* place].

No. 9.

The list of persons objected to, to be published by the Town Clerks.

The following persons have been objected to as having no right to be retained on the list of the freemen of the city [*or* borough] of [*or* of being a place sharing in the election with the city, *or* borough, of], entitled to vote in the election of a member [*or* members] for the said city [*or* borough].

Christian and surname of each person objected to.	Place of his abode.

(*Signed*) A. B. { Town Clerk of the said city [*or* borough *or* place].

III.

SCHEDULE (K.)

A List of such of the Freemen of London as are Liverymen of the Company of entitled to vote in the election of members for the city of London.

Christian name and surname of the voter at full length.	Street, lane, or other description of his place of abode.

(*Signed*) A. B. Clerk.

No. I.

Notice of Claim to be given to the Returning Officer or Officers of the City of London, and to the Clerks of the respective Livery Companies.

To the returning officer or officers of the City of London [*or* to the clerk of the company of].

I hereby give you notice, that I claim to have my name inserted in the list made by the clerk of the company of [*or, in case of notice to the clerk, say,* made by you] of the liverymen of the said company [*or, in case of notice to the clerk, say,* of the liverymen of the company of] entitled to vote in the election of members for the city of London. Dated the day of

(*Signed*) A. B. { [*Place of abode. Name of company.*]

No. 2.

List of Claimants, to be published by the Returning Officer or Officers of the City of London.

The following persons claim to have their names inserted in the list of persons entitled to vote as freemen of the city of London and liverymen of the several companies herein specified, in the election of members for the city of London.

Christian name and surname of claimants at full length.	Place of abode.

No. 3.

Notice of Objection to Parties inserted in the List of the Livery.

To Mr. William Baker.

I hereby give you notice, that I object to your name being retained in the list of persons entitled to vote as freemen of the city of London and liverymen of the company of in the election of members for the said city, and that I shall bring forward such objection at the time of revising the said list. Dated the day of

(*Signed*) A. B. [*Place of abode.*]

PAROCHIAL REGISTRIES. In early times the monks registered the ecclesisastical ceremonies of baptism, marriage, and burial. On the dissolution of the monasteries, Thomas Lord Cromwell, in 1538, caused a proclamation to be issued, directing every parson, vicar, and curate, under a penalty, to keep a register for every church, and on each Sunday to enter therein, in the presence of the wardens, all the weddings, christenings, and burials of the preceding week. Similar injunctions followed from *Ed.* 6. and *Q. Eliz.;* and in 1597, the clergy consented that a copy of each parochial register should be sent yearly to the registrar of the diocese, which is the origin of the existing custom of transmitting the registers yearly to the bishop's registrar. This arrangement was suggested by themselves, on successfully opposing a measure then introduced for a general register office. In 1652, a civil register of these transactions was established; but on the restoration the clergy resumed their office of parochial registrars, and up to the present century, 1813, they remained a remarkable monument of carelessness and irregularity. In that year a very defective act was passed, to effectuate the purposes of acts passed early in the last century, for the purpose of registering the baptism, marriage, and burial of parishioners and others; but this last act, while it preserved the custom of continuing the clergy as registrars, proved ineffectual for the important purposes intended. The entry of marriages having been most carefully provided for by the marriage acts, appears to have answered the purpose intended; indeed, as the registry required the signature of the parties married, no clergyman, however careless, could omit it; and therefore the legislature, in framing the following act for registering births, deaths, and marriages, has not interfered with the registry of the clergy, of marriages solemnised by them, further than by prescribing a new form, and subjecting them to a penalty for any deviation therefrom.

This act, which was passed on the 17th of August, 1836, and came into operation on the 1st of March, but suspended till the 1st of July, 1837, provides for the creation of a "General Register Office" in London, for the above purpose, and a registrar-general, and of district registrars, and superintendent-registrars who are to be appointed by the guardians of the poor, who are to divide the *union* or parish into districts; to each district, they are to appoint a superintendent-registrar, who holds office during the pleasure of the registrar-general. Deputy-registrars may be appointed in each district; and in parishes in which guardians are not yet appointed, the poor-law commissioners have power to appoint temporary registrars. The duties of these officials are enumerated under the title Registrars.

The district-registrar having been furnished by the superintendent with a sufficient number of books and forms, is to receive the information of births and deaths, in the following manner:—

The parents of children, or the occupiers of houses in which any birth or death shall happen, after the 1st of July, 1837, *may*, within 42 days (six weeks), give notice thereof to the district-registrar; and *are* (upon request) * to give the particulars required by the registrar, (one of which is, the *cause* of death).

Some person present at the death, or in attendance during the last illness of persons dying in England, or the occupier, or some inmate, is to give information to the registrar, on request of the necessary particulars; and it is the duty of a coroner to inform the registrar of the finding, upon an inquest, who makes the entry accordingly.

The registry of persons dying at sea on board a British vessel, is effected by the commanding officer making a minute of the particulars required to be registered, and the name of the vessel, and by sending, on the first opportunity, a certificate of the minute, through the post-office, to the registrar-general, who is to file it, and enter a copy in the marine register-book, to be kept along with the other register-books.

All persons informing the district-registrar of any particulars, are required to sign the entry that is made thereof.

The registrar on his entering information of a death, gives a certificate to the undertaker, who will be the medium of communication of these facts, and delivers the certificate to the minister at the time of burial.

The coroner, after the holding an inquest, when he orders the body to be buried in the usual manner, gives a certificate, and to bury without it subjects the party to a penalty of not less than 10*l.*; but every person who shall bury or perform any religious service for the burial of a dead person, without a certificate of the registrar or coroner, and who shall not within 7 days give notice thereof to the registrar, is subject to a penalty of 10*l.*; *i. e.* he may bury without a certificate, but he must give notice within 7 days.

The *birth* of an infant may be registered within 42 days, by the notice being given to the district-registrar, but as the *name* is given at the time of baptism, it may be subsequently inserted in the blank column, in the form in which the occurrence is entered by the district-registrar, provided that such baptism takes place within 6 months from the registration of the birth, and the minister's certificate thereof, within 7 days, is to be delivered to the superintendent-registrar.

No birth can be registered after the expiration of 6 months, except of children born at sea; and no register can be given in evidence where 6 months have elapsed between the birth and the registration.

A mode of registration of the birth of an infant is yet provided *after* the 42 days allowed for sending the notice to the district-registrar has elapsed, and *before* 6 months have intervened from the date of birth, (beyond which time no registry can ever take place); viz.:—

Any person present at the birth of such unregistered child, or for the father or guardian (*i. e.* mother, or testamentary guardian, or nearest

* The reader is particularly required to notice that the information required by the act may be either given *voluntarily* within the 42 days by the parents or occupier, &c., or *compulsorily*, upon a request made by the registrar of the district. No penalty is specified in case of refusal, but the wilful non-performance of any act required to be done by law or statute is a misdemeanour, and consequently punishable by fine or imprisonment, or both. The Editor has thought it right to be thus explicit upon this head, as the "Companion for the Almanac for 1837," p. 70. broadly asserts that "the parents may, if they choose, refuse information." A very serious error.

of kin,) may make a solemn declaration of the particulars required to be known, touching the birth of such child, according to the best of the informant's belief, upon which the district-registrar, in the presence of the superintendent-registrar, who is also to sign the entry (else it never can be received in evidence), make the entry according to the information; for the register can never be given in evidence to prove the birth of the child when 42 days have intervened between birth and registration, unless such entry be also signed by the superintendent, as well as the district-registrar, and this mode of registry is only available for 6 months from the birth of the child.

The Registry of Marriages. — The ministers of churches and chapels, and the registering secretaries of the Quakers or Jews, being furnished with duplicate register-books, enter in duplicate, the registry of marriage in the following form, both of which are to be signed by the minister officiating, the registering-officers or secretaries of the Quakers and Jews, the parties married, and by two witnesses.

Certificates of Registries. — Rectors, vicars, curates, and registering-officers, are at all reasonable times to allow searches, and give certified copies; and certified copies from the office of the registrar-general, to which all registries are transmitted, stamped with the seal of office, are to be received in evidence of birth, death, or marriage.

Penalties. — The following penalties are recoverable from rectors, registering-officers, and persons in general, viz.: —

	£	s.	d.
Registering births or deaths unduly, or not in accordance with the act, or for losing or injuring the register books - -	50	0	0
Burial without certificate and not giving notice thereof to superintendent registrar - - - - - - -	10	0	0

Which may be recovered before two justices of the peace, and recovered by imprisonment or seizure of the party's goods; but if the sum exceed 5*l.*, a right of appeal is granted if notice thereof is given within 3 days after conviction, but *certiorari* is taken away.

The giving false information to the registrar, *knowingly*, is punishable as a perjury.

The destruction or falsification of the register-books (accidental errors are to be corrected in the presence of the superintendent-registrar) is a felony.

FEES.

	£	s.	d.
To the minister baptizing a child, for his certificate thereof -	0	1	0
To the registrar or superintendent registrar, for entry thereof, and sending same to registrar general - - - - - -	0	1	0
To the registrar for entering special information of birth after 6 weeks 5*s*., and his ordinary fee 1*s*. - - - - - -	0	6	0
To the superintendent registrar on the same occasion - -	0	2	6
For a search with the rector &c., or registering officer of Jews and Quakers, for not more than a year - - - - - -	0	1	0
For every additional year - - - - - -	0	0	6
For every single certificate - - - - - - - -	0	2	6
For a search with the superintendent registrar, if *general* - -	0	5	0
If *particular* - - - - - - - -	0	1	0
For a certified copy* - - - - - - - - -	0	2	6
For a search with the registrar general, at the general register office, if *general* - - - - - - - - - -	1	0	0
If *particular* - - - - - - - -	0	1	0
For a certified copy, *stamped with the seal of office* - - -	0	2	6

* N. B. — Only the stamped certified copies from the general registrar office are receivable in evidence.

FORMS OF NOTICES, REGISTRIES, AND CERTIFICATES.

1836. — BIRTHS in the *District* of *Mary-le-bone, North,* in the County of *Middlesex.*

N	When born.	Name, if any.	Sex.	Name and Surname of Father.	Name and Maiden Surname of Mother.	Rank or Profession of Father.	Signature, Description, and Residence of Informant.	When registered.	Signature of Register.	Baptismal Name, if added after Registration of Birth.
1.	*7th January.*	*James.*	*Boy.*	*William Green.*	*Rebecca Green, formerly Jennings.*	*Carpenter.*	*William Green, Father, Carpenter,* 17. *North Street, Marylebone.*	*9th January.*	*John Cox, Registrar.*	

1836. — DEATHS in the *District* of *Mary-le-bone, North,* in the County of *Middlesex.*

No.	When died.	Name and Surname.	Sex.	Age.	Rank or Profession.	Cause of Death.	Signature, Description and Residence of Informant.	When registered.	Signature of Registrar.
17.	*4th February.*	*William Green.*	*Male.*	43	*Carpenter.*		*Rebecca Green, Widow,* 17. *North Street, Marylebone.*	*5th February.*	*John Cox, Registrar.*

In cases of foundlings, or exposed dead bodies, the overseers or coroner are to give this notice; and the keepers of workhouses, lunatic asylums, gaols, hospitals, or public institutions, are to give notice of these occurrences: the act considering such persons as occupiers, who, in default of parent or relative, may give notice, and upon request are required so to do.

1836. — Marriages solemnised *at the Parish Church* in the *Parish* of *Mary-le-bone*, in the county of *Middlesex*.

No.	When married.	Name and Surname.	Age.	Condition.	Rank or Profession.	Residence at the Time of Marriage.	Father's Name and Surname.	Rank or Profession of Father.
1.	*17th March*, 1836.	*William Hastings.*	*Of full Age.*	*Bachelor.*	*Carpenter.*	3. *South Street.*	*Peter Hastings.*	*Upholsterer.*
		Sophia Anne Mitchell.	*Minor.*	*Spinster.*	- -	17. *High Street.*	*Geoffry Mitchell.*	*Butcher.*

Married in the *Parish Church*, according to the rites and ceremonies of the *Established Church*, *by Licence*, or *after Banns*, by me,

James Hollingshead, Vicar.

This marriage was solemnised between us, { *William Hastings*, *Sophia Anne Mitchell*, } In the Presence of us, { *John Hastings.* *Geoffry Mitchell.*

I *Gilbert Elliott*, *Vicar* of *Barming*, in the county of *Kent*, do hereby certify, That I have this day baptised by the name of *Thomas* a *male* child, produced to me by *William Green*, as the *son* of *William Green* and *Rebecca Green*, and declared by the said *William Green* to have been born at *Mary-le-bone*, in the county of *Middlesex*, on the *seventh* day of *January*, 1836. Witness my hand this *first* day of *December*, 1838.

Gilbert Elliott, Vicar.

[The figures and words in *italics* in the above Schedules to be filled in as the case may be.]

It may not unfrequently happen that parents, from various accidents, will omit to register within the specified periods, or to deliver the minister's certificate of baptism to the superintendent-registrar, thereby invalidating the evidence of birth derivable from the register; a circumstance which may produce injury, litigation, and at least confusion. In such a case, it is incumbent on the parents to do what might have been done before this act, and the necessity of which this act, in nowise, supersedes, viz. make an entry in the family Bible, or other book used for the noting of these occurrences; as entries or memoranda by a parent, relation, or other competent person, in family Bibles or Prayer-books, when spontaneously made at or near the time of their occurrence, and of facts within the parties' own personal knowledge, are deemed good evidence of such occurrences at a future period. Indeed, the neglect of a registry cannot be remedied by any less cautious act than a memorandum of that nature, it being just as important that the facts of birth and death should be duly testified, as that any deed, will, or transaction regarding the disposition of property, should be properly completed or evidenced.

It may finally be noticed that the wilful noncompliance with any act *required* by the statute, subjects the party to punishment, as for a misdemeanor, viz. fine and imprisonment, proportioned to the circumstances of the case.

PARTNERS AND PARTNERSHIP. When two or more agree to come into any trade, bargain, or speculation, in the nature of a trading concern, in equal proportions or as agreed on, they are partners. A partnership, then, is a voluntary contract, by words, bare consent, or writing, by two or more persons, for joining together their money, goods, labour, skill, or all or either of them, upon an agreement that the gain or loss shall be divided in certain proportions amongst them. In general, all the partners appear ostensibly to the world, and constitute what is called the *house* or *firm*. It is, however, by no means uncommon for monied men to embark considerable sums in trade, without taking any part in the management of the concern or suffering their names to appear; such persons are called *dormant* or *sleeping* partners, and when discovered, are liable, in common with the rest, to the creditors of the firm.

There are also *special* partnerships, formed for a single adventure, and the consequences and liabilities of these are confined to the transactions thence arising.

The legal distinction of joint tenancy does not exist in regard to mercantile property, whether it be mere personalty or freeholds, &c., so that it be purchased with the partnership funds, or forming part thereof; therefore, each partner holds his share in severalty, and individually, according to his due proportion.

The general rule is, that one partner may, by his own acts, bind his copartners in all transactions relating to the partnership, but this only extends to engagements not under seal; for a partner cannot bind his copartners by deed, unless by express or implied authority, though he may by drawing or accepting bills of exchange. In all cases of this sort, the liability seems to attach on the partners held forth in the transaction; as if a partnership firm consist of A. B. C. and D., if either draw, accept, or indorse, as A. and Co., or in words comprehending the firm, they are of course bound, whatever become of the money obtained by such transactions; but if C. or more partners borrow money on their own names, even if the proceeds are applied to the partnership purposes, the firm, *i. e.* all the partners, are not liable. A single partner may, by *implied* authority, bind his copartners, as where the dealing had been carried on in that manner, or under similar or analogous circumstances, but a notice from the other partner may exonerate them, even if such a course of signature or liability had been previously adopted.

The liabilities of partners, although extended to almost every transaction which it may be inferred that the firm assented to or authorised, yet are restricted or neutralised in particular instances, and where it is obvious that credit was given to the individual partner, and not to the firm at large; as where several persons *horsed*, with horses, their *several* property, the several stages of a coach, in the general profits of which they are partners, they are not all jointly liable for goods furnished to one partner for the use of the horses drawing the coach along his part of the road.

If a partner make a bargain for himself with others for his own advantage, although in the name of the partnership, he is individually liable, and cannot plead that the contract was made with him and his partners.

Public partnerships are associations, consisting of a great number of persons, called companies or societies; many of whom are incorporated by act of parliament, or by letters-patent-royal, and others not.

Those who are not incorporated, are in fact partnerships, and subject to the liabilities of such contracts; many insurance companies are of this description, or are only incorporated for the limited purposes of being sued or suing by their clerk, or any particular members, pursuant to a late act, which authorises the crown to grant such letters or charters of incorporation which do not confer upon the company so incorporated, the benefits of incorporations as they exist under the old charters, but leave the liabilities to the operation of law, restricting the plaintiffs as to their mode of proceeding against individual members. The old or perfect corporators, or those now *incorporated by act of parliament*, are not individually liable for the engagements of the company, unless it is so expressed, which perhaps may be so declared in respect of the new schemes.

Partners Bankrupt.—*Fiats* against some or one of the partners in a firm vary little in effect from *fiats* issued against individual traders, the reader bearing in mind what are *joint* and what *separate* debts; the first, being those which are legally recoverable from all the partners; the latter, from the individual partner who contracted them: and also, regarding what is joint property and what is separate property or *estate*. *Joint estate* being that which consists of the effects applicable for the purposes of the partnership (whether it stands in one partner's name or not), and *separate estate* being the private acquisitions of each partner not blended with the partnership funds.

None but a joint creditor can sue out a *fiat* against one or more of a firm, such creditor possessing the option of suing out a fiat against a single member of the firm, or against those who have actually committed acts of bankruptcy; but where a joint fiat is issued against some of the partners of a firm, and another is issued against one or more of the remaining partners, the two fiats are directed to be consolidated after adjudication, and the commissioner or commissioners (if in the country) convey the estate to the assignees named under the first *fiat*. This proceeding operates only as an annexation of the second fiat to the first, not to annul it, the second fiat being directed to the commissioners under the first fiat,

Where a separate *fiat* issues against one partner, and a joint fiat is afterwards issued against him and his copartners, as the joint fiat is deemed more advantageous for the creditors, the court of review will annul the separate *fiat* at the cost of the joint estate.

The property passing under a joint fiat is not only the partnership property, but the private or separate estate of each individual found to have committed an act of bankruptcy. To prevent confusion, distinct accounts are kept of each estate, and the same if bankrupts carry on several trades under distinct firms.

Under a *fiat* against one individual of a firm, it is often beneficial that the estates should be consolidated, and that the joint and separate creditors should share equally; the court will, therefore, confirm an agreement made to effect that purpose, upon being satisfied by a report of the commissioners that this arrangement is for the benefit of both classes of the creditors generally.

Separate creditors, under a joint estate, may assent to or dissent from the certificate, and *vice versâ*. Joint creditors under a separate estate may prove for the purpose of voting, and of assenting to or dissenting from the certificate. The effect of a certificate, under a joint-fiat, is to bar both private and partnership debts.

PARTY WALLS, *reimbursement to owner part of expense for building of.*—By the Building Act, 14 *G.* 3. *c.* 78. *s.* 41., the person at whose expense any party-wall shall be built, shall be reimbursed a part of the same by that owner of the adjoining building or ground who is entitled to the improved rent, and who shall at any time cut into, or make use of such wall.

The act expresses in what proportions such reimbursement shall be made, the rates at which the building the same shall be estimated, and in case double costs are sought for, a three months' notice must be given, but not else.

The following is the 41st section :—

"That the person or persons at whose expense any party-wall or party-arch shall be built agreeably to the directions of this act, shall be reimbursed by the owner or owners who shall be entitled to the *improved* rent of the adjoining building or ground, and who shall at any time make use of such party-wall or party-arch, a part of the expense of building the same, in the proportion after mentioned, (that is to say); if the adjoining building then erected or afterwards to be erected be of the same rate or class of building as, or superior to, the building belonging to the person or persons at whose expense the said party-wall was built, then the owner or occupier of such adjoining building or ground shall pay one moiety of the expense of building so much of the said party-wall or party-arch as such owner or occupier shall make use of; and if the adjoining building then erected or afterwards to be erected be of an inferior rate or class of building, then the owner or occupier of such adjoining building or ground shall pay a sum of money equal to one moiety of the expense of building a party-wall or party-arch of the thickness by this act required for the rate or class of building whereof such adjoining building shall be, and of the height and breadth of so much of the said party-wall or party-arch as such owner or occupier shall make use of; and in the mean time and until such moiety or other proportional part of the expense of building such party-wall or party-arch be so paid, the sole property of such whole party-wall or party-arch, and of the whole ground whereon the said party-wall shall stand, shall be vested entirely in the person or persons at whose expense the same shall be built: and such moiety or other proportional part of the expense of building such party-wall or party-arch shall be so paid to the person or persons at whose expense the same shall be built, or in whom the property thereof shall be vested, at the times hereinafter mentioned; (that is to say), in respect of every such party-wall to any house or building whereunto, at the time of building the same, no other house or building was adjoining, so soon as such party-wall shall be first cut into or made use of; and in respect of every such party-wall or party-arch as shall be built against or adjoining to any other house or building, so soon as such party-wall or party-arch shall be completely built and finished: and in respect of such last-mentioned party-wall or party-arch, the owner or occupier of such adjoining house or building shall, together with such proportional part of the expense of building such party-wall or party-arch, also pay a like proportional part of all other expenses which shall be necessary to the pulling down the old party-wall, or timber or wood partition, and the whole of all the reasonable expenses of shoring up such adjoining house or building, and of removing any goods, furniture, or other things, and of pulling down any wainscot or partition, and also all such costs, if any, as may have been awarded by the said court of mayor and aldermen, or court of sessions as aforesaid: but not any part of the expense of pulling down and clearing away any such old party-wall or party-arch or old partition, if any such there was: and it is hereby directed, that the expense of building such party-wall or party-arch shall be estimated after the rate of 7*l.* 15*s.* by the rod for the new brickwork, deducting thereout after the rate of 1*l.* 8*s.* by the rod for the materials (if any) of so much of the old wall or arch as did belong to such adjoining building or ground, and also after the rate of *two-pence* by the cubical foot for the materials (if any) of so much of the old timber partition as did belong to such adjoining building or ground: and that *within* ten days after such party-wall or party-arch shall be so built, or so soon after as conveniently may be, such first builder or builders shall leave at such adjoining house or building a true account in writing of the number of rods in such party-wall or party-arch for which the owner or owners of such adjoining building or ground shall be liable to pay, and of the deduction which such owner or owners shall be entitled to make thereout on account of such materials, and also an account of such other expenses and costs as aforesaid: whereupon it shall be lawful for the tenant or occupier of such adjoining building or ground to pay one moiety, or such proportional part as aforesaid, to such first builder or builders for the same, and also for shoring and supporting such adjoining building as aforesaid, and for all such other expenses as are hereinbefore directed to be paid by the owner or owners of such adjoining building or ground, and to deduct the same out of the rent which shall become due from him or her to such owner or owners, under whom he or she holds the same respectively, until he or she shall be reimbursed the same: and in case the same be not paid within twenty-one days next after demand thereof, then the same shall and may be recovered, together with full costs of suit, of and from such owner or owners, by action of debt or on the case, in any of his majesty's courts of record at Westminster, wherein no essoign, protection, or wager of law, or more than one imparlance, shall be allowed: And if the plaintiff or plaintiffs in any such action shall, three calendar months at the least before

Rates for building party walls.

Tenants or occupiers *may* pay and deduct for same.

Remedy for recovery.

Double costs may be recovered if 3 months notice given (*not else*).

the commencement thereof, give notice in writing to the person or persons against whom such action is intended to be brought, of his, her, or their intention to bring the same, or leave the same at his, her, or their last or usual place of abode, and shall in such notice specify the sum for which it is to be brought, and also annex to such notice a bill of the just and true particulars of the expenses and charges with which the intended defendant or defendants is or are to be charged; then such plaintiff or plaintiffs, if he, she, or they recover the full sum specified in such notice, shall also recover and be entitled to double costs of suit, and shall have and be entitled to the like remedies for recovery thereof, as are usually given for costs in other cases of costs at law."

It is now settled that the lessee who has the improved or rack rent, or who hath (as in a building lease) taken the premises or ground with a view to underlet at an improved rent, is the party liable to pay the half or proportional reimbursement to the builder of a party-wall. If there is no such person, then the lessor at a rack rent is liable although his tenant has increased the value by improvements; so if he has received a consideration in money or building, and grants a lease at a low rent, he is liable—but the moment such lessee underlets at a profit, then he is the party chargeable. Also, where a lessee has absolutely *assigned*, not *underlet*, his term the lessor is liable.*

Where there are several improved rents, the owner of the highest must bear the expense, although his interest has nearly expired, for there is no provision in the act for dividing the burden between the owners of the different improved rents.

A general covenant to repair will not render the tenant liable unless it is stipulated that party-walls are to be repaired; and as this is not an "usual" covenant, intended tenants should oppose the insertion of any words tending to fix them with this liability in leases or agreements for leases.

It seems that no more than the statutable compensation can be recovered, whatever the price of brickwork may be.

The sum due for a party wall may be paid by a tenant, who may deduct it from his landlord's rent.

There is a three months' notice required by sect. 38. of the act, which is only requisite where the person, who at the time when it is necessary to build, &c. is liable to pay, cannot agree with the owner of the adjoining house.

The following is a form of notice to be left at the house, in respect of which the reimbursement is claimed, and may be addressed to the owner of the rack rent. There must also be a formal demand of the money (viz. by the claimant in the presence of a witness) 21 days before action brought.

"In pursuance of a certain act of parliament, made and passed in the 14th year of the reign of his late Majesty King George III., intituled, 'An Act for the further and better regulation of buildings and party-walls, and for the more effectually preventing mischief by fire, within the cities of London and Westminster and the liberties thereof, and other the parishes, precincts, and places within the weekly bills of mortality, the parishes of St. Mary-le-bone, Paddington, St. Pancras, and St. Luke at Chelsea, in the county of Middlesex, and for indemnifying, under certain conditions, builders and other

* Mr. Elmes, in his Treatise on Dilapidations, p. 225. *3d edit.*, has laid down a contrary rule. His doctrine is evidently based upon *dicta* ascribed to Lord Kenyon, and Chief Justice Gibbs, and which Mr. Chitty, in his collection of Statutes, 1829, vol. i. p. 128., *in n.*, observes, seem not law.

persons against the penalties to which they are or may be liable, for erecting buildings within the limits aforesaid contrary to law,' I, *James Collins*, of &c., do hereby demand of you payment of the annexed account, being an account of a moiety of the expense of building a certain party-wall, built by me or by my order, at my expense, and being parcel of the messuage or dwelling-house now occupied by me, situate and being at &c., and which said party-wall has been cut into and made use of by you, by your building against the said messuage or dwelling-house, a certain other messuage or dwelling-house, of the same rate or class of buildings. Dated, &c."

N. B. *This notice should be delivered within the time specified, but if there should be no adjoining house, the builder of the wall must wait until the vacant ground is built on, and give the notice within a reasonable time afterwards.*

PATENTS, or LETTERS PATENT ROYAL. Grants from the king under the great seal, so called, from their being *open* (*patentes*) in contradistinction to those acts of the king which were sealed up and called *close*, such as grants of privilege, protections, &c. The term is used in common parlance for

PATENTS FOR INVENTIONS. Previous to the stat. 21 *James* 1. *c.* 3. letters patent were granted by virtue of the royal prerogative as it then stood, for an infinity of monopolies (see that title), or granting power to one or more persons alone to sell particular articles of merchandise. This power or prerogative, being against the fundamental laws of the realm, and tending to impoverish artisans, created great discontent, to remedy which, in that year was passed an act, the 6th section of which excepts from the monopolies, declared void by that statute, letters patent or grants of privilege for 14 years "of the sole working or making of *new manufactures* within the realm, to the *true and first inventor* and inventors of such manufactures, which others at the time shall not use, so as also they be not contrary to the law, nor mischievous to the state, by raising prices of commodities at home, or hurt of trade, or generally inconvenient."

A statute has lately passed (the 5 *&* 6 *Will.* 4. *c.* 83.) which empowers the judicial committee of the privy council to prolong the term of an existing patent right, under the statute of James I., for not exceeding seven years.

The statute of James declares who is an *inventor*, and what is the subject of an *invention*, viz. a manufacture, which is a *thing made*, or the application of a particular principle in mechanics, chemistry, or the like, to, or essentially connected with, corporeal and existing substances; these new *manufactures* must not have been previously used in the kingdom, but may be imported from abroad. Additions and improvements to existing patents are subjects of patent-right, but the second patentee will have no right to manufacture such subjects of patent-right; he must make and sell his own invention separately.

A patent is obtained as almost a matter of course, by a petition to the crown, and persons soliciting patents are entitled to notice of other applications to the crown for subjects interfering with their inventions, upon entering a *caveat*. *Caveats* also may be entered against the prolongation of a patent, which entitles the party to notice of the application in order that he may oppose the same.

All patents granted since the reign of Queen Anne, contain a clause peremptorily requiring a particular description of the invention to be enrolled in Chancery, which is termed the *specification*. The patent is void if this be not done, or if the specification does not make a complete disclosure of the invention, or the title of the patent does not agree with the specification, or, as it is termed, if the specification does not support the title of the patent, so as to indicate one and the same thing, the patent will be declared void.

In the specification of a substance, the thing itself should be accurately ascertained, the materials of which it is composed, the method by which it is made, and the use to which it is to be applied, correctly developed, and particularly described. The main object of this precision is, that as the invention becomes the property of the public at the expiration of the term, it is but reasonable that the public should know how to use it.

Patents must be taken out for things totally new, they must not attempt to incorporate an old and known invention under cover of, or joined with a new invention.

The late act permits patentees to amend the titles of their patents in certain cases.

Where a patent is invalid, the *repeal* or quashing the patent is by a writ of *scire facias*, a process calling upon the patentee to show cause why the letters patent should not be repealed : any person may do this.

The remedies which a patentee has for the infringement of his patent, are, injunction against the party pirating the invention, the bill requiring him to keep an account of the profits he derived by using it, until the patentee is able to try his right at law; but as the courts of equity grant injunctions but cautiously, the injunction for this purpose will not be granted without stipulating that the patentee shall establish his right in an action at law, if the possession be recent or the right appear at all doubtful.

The remedies for infringement of a patent, either at law or in equity are provided for in the 8th section of the late act, viz.—

"That if any action at law or any suit in equity, for an account, shall be brought in respect of any infringement of such letters patent heretofore or hereafter granted, or any *scire facias* to repeal such letters patent, and if a verdict shall pass for the patentee or his assigns, or if a final decree or decretal order shall be made for him or them, upon the merits of the suit, it shall be lawful for the judge before whom such action shall be tried to certify on the record, or the judge who shall make such decree or order to give a certificate under his hand, that the validity of the patent came in question before him; which record or certificate being given in evidence in any other suit or action whatever touching such patent, if a verdict shall pass, or decree or decretal order be made, in favour of such patentee or his assigns, he or they shall receive treble costs in such suit or action, to be taxed at three times the taxed costs, unless the judge making such second or other decree or order, or trying such second or other action, shall certify that he ought not to have such treble costs"

"That in any action brought against any person for infringing any letters patent, the defendant on pleading thereto, shall give to the plaintiff, and in any *scire facias* to repeal such letters patent, the plaintiff shall file with his declaration a notice of any objections on which he means to rely at the trial of such action, and no objection shall be allowed to be made in behalf of such defendant or plaintiff respectively at such trial, unless he prove the objections stated in such notice: provided always that it shall and may be lawful for any judge at chambers, on summons served by such defendant or plaintiff on such plaintiff or defendant respectively to show cause why he should not be allowed to offer other objections whereof notice shall not be given as aforesaid, to give leave to offer such objections, on such terms as to such judge shall seem fit."

"That in any action brought for infringing the right granted by any letters patent, in taxing the costs thereof, regard shall be had to the part of such case which has been proved at the trial, which shall be certified by the judge before whom the same shall be had, and the costs of each part of the case shall be given according as either party has succeeded or failed therein, regard being had to the notice of objections, as well as the counts in the declaration, and without regard to the general result of the trial."

"That if any person shall write, paint, or print, or mould, cast or carve, or engrave, or stamp upon any thing made, used, or sold by him, for the sole making or selling of which he hath not or shall not have obtained letters patent, the name or any imitation of the name of any other person who hath or shall have obtained letters patent for the sole making and vending of such thing, without leave in writing of such patentee or his assigns, or if any person shall upon such thing, not having been purchased from the patentee or some person who purchased it from or under such patentee, or not having had the license or consent in writing of such patentee or his assigns, write, paint, print, mould, cast, carve, engrave, stamp, or otherwise mark the word, 'patent,' the words, 'letters patent,' or the words, 'by the king's patent,' or any words of the like kind, meaning or import, with a view of imitating or counterfeiting the stamp, mark, or other device of the patentee, or shall in any other manner imitate or counterfeit the stamp or mark or other device of the patentee, he shall for every such offence be liable to a penalty of fifty pounds, to be recovered by action of debt, bill, plaint, process, or information in any of his majesty's courts of record at *Westminster* or in *Ireland,* or in the court of session in *Scotland,* one half to his majesty, his heirs and successors, and the other to any person who shall sue for the same: provided always, that nothing herein contained shall be construed to extend to subject any person to any penalty in respect of stamping or in any way marking the word 'patent,' upon any thing made, for the sole making or vending of which a patent before obtained shall have expired."

PAWN, or PLEDGE, is a bailment or delivery of valuables to another as a gage for the payment of money. The following abstract of cases may be useful to the reader, as though the business of pledging is carried on by pawnbrokers, the law respecting which is known, yet much misunderstanding prevails on the powers of a pawnee or depositary of goods on a loan of money. The borrower is termed the pawnor.

The law as hereinafter declared applies to *all* cases of pawning not noticed by the pawnbrokers' act; for that act does not deprive the pawner of any remedy he had by law.

The party who pawns goods hath a general property in them; they cannot be forfeited by the pawnee or party who hath them in pawn, for any offence of his; nor be taken in execution for his debt; neither may they otherwise be put in execution till the debt for which they are pawned is satisfied.

The pawnee of goods hath a special property in them, to detain them for his security, &c., and he may assign the pawn over to another, subject to the same conditions; and if the pawnee die before redeemed, his executors shall have it upon the like terms as he had it. Where goods are pawned for money borrowed, without a day set for redemption, they are redeemable at any time.

If goods are lost, *after the tender of money,* the pawnee is liable to make them good to the owner, for after tender it is a wrongful detainer; and he who keeps goods wrongfully must answer for them at all events, his wrongful detainer being the occasion of the loss.

If a pawnee keeps the pawn without making any use of it, he is not liable for its loss, through robbery, fire, or unavoidable accident, but if the pawn is of such a nature that the keeping is a charge to the pawnee, as a cow, or a horse, &c., he may milk the one or ride the other; and this shall go in recompense for his keeping. Things which will grow the worse for usage, as apparel, &c., he may not use.

Negligence in keeping the goods will render the pawnee liable. In cases of *negligence* the question is confined to this point: did the pawnee keep the goods as a prudent person would keep his own goods?

Where money is lent on a pledge, the borrower is personally liable to the payment; unless there be an agreement to the contrary.

It was always illegal for a pawnee to pawn the pledge, and the pawnbrokers' act renders it expressly punishable.

Factors formerly had no power to pledge or deposit warrants for the delivery of goods, bills of lading, &c., or more properly speaking, persons making advances to a factor, even though the factor had a lien on the goods, could not bind them; but a late statute has protected transactions of this nature, as far as the interest or lien of such factor or agent extends; and a later statute has provided that if any factor or agent shall for his own benefit, and in violation of good faith, deposit or pledge any goods, bill of lading, certificate, warrant or order for delivery of goods, he shall be guilty of a misdemeanor, and be liable to 14 years transportation.

PAWNBROKERS. All persons who receive by way of pawn, pledge, or exchange any goods for the repayment of money lent thereon, and taking a greater profit for the loan thereof than 5 per cent. per annum.

Pawnbrokers are licensed by the commissioners of stamps, and only one house can be kept by such licence; persons in partnership taking out one licence for one house, which, if within the limits of the two-penny post, costs 15*l.*, in any other place 7*l.* 10*s.*, payable yearly, extending from the 1st of August to the 31st of July. A *plate* licence (5*l.* 15*s.*) must be taken out by those pawnbrokers who take pawns upon gold or silver plate.

The rate of interest to be taken by a pawnbroker and the general conduct of this business, is regulated by a well-known statute, the 39 *& 40 G. 3. c.* 99.

	£	*s.*	*d.*	Interest.	*d.*
For any sum per month (calendar) not exceeding	0	2	6	the sum of	0½
If there shall have been lent - - - - -	0	5	0	- - -	1
If	0	7	6	- . -	1½
If	0	10	0	- - -	2
If	0	12	6	- - -	2½
If	0	15	0	- - -	3
If	0	17	6	- - -	3½
If	1	0	0	- - -	4
If	1	2	6	- - -	4½
If	1	5	0	- - -	5
If	1	7	6	- - -	5½
If	1	10	0	- - -	6
If	1	12	6	- - -	6½
If	1	15	0	- - -	7
If	1	17	6	- - -	7½
If	2	0	0	& not exceeding	8
If	2	2	0	- - -	8

And where the sum lent shall exceed 2*l.* 2*s.*, and shall not exceed 10*l.*, 3*d.* and no more, for every 20*s.* by the month, including the current month, and so in proportion for any fractional sum. The party applying for the redemption of goods pawned, within 7 days after the expiration of the first month, may redeem the same *without paying anything* for such 7 days, and where he applies *after* the expiration of such first 7 days and before the end of the first 14 days of the second month, he may redeem the goods upon paying for one month and a half only, but, *after* such 14 days, the pawnbroker is entitled to take the profit for the whole second month; and this regulation takes place in every subsequent full or calendar month which does not include the day of pawning, so that if a pledge be taken on the 5th of any month, the month does not expire till after the closing of the house on the 5th of the next month; and the year is computed in like manner, the party having all the 5th of the 12th month to redeem or to claim his stay of sale, as hereafter mentioned.

Intermediate Sums.—Where fractional sums lent upon pawns, exceed 2*s.* 6*d.*, and do not exceed 40*s.*, the pawnbroker may take 4*d.* for 20*s.* by the month, or ¼*d.* on every 1*s.* 3*d.*, which is equal to 4*d.* on 20*s.*; *e. g.* 3*s.* 9*d.* is an intermediate sum between 2*s.* 6*d.* and 5*s.*, and the interest on 3*s.* 9*d.* will be ¾ *d.*, which is the intermediate interest between ½*d.* and 1*d.*

The following table of interest is calculated according to the preceding scale, at the rate of 4*d.* for every 20*s.*; with respect to the fractional parts of a farthing, it seems that the pawnbroker claims the farthing, but the principle of the act allows no more than 4*d.* for 20*s.* by the *calendar* month, either on the named or on the intermediate sum.

Pawnbrokers must always give an odd farthing in exchange, or abate it if they have not one, in cases where the farthing accrues either as principal or interest.—*s.* 4.

Table of Interest at the Rate of 4*d. in the Pound, from* 2*s.* 6*d. to* 42*s.*

Interest from one calendar month to six months.

Sum Lent.		1 Month and 7 Days.		1 Month and 14 Days.		Two months.		Three months.		Four months.		Five months.		Six months.	
s.	*d.*	*s.*	*d.*	*s.*	*d.*	*s.*	*d.*	*s.*	*d.*	*s.*	*d.*	*s.*	*d.*	*s.*	*d.*
2	6	0	0½	0	0¾	0	1	0	1½	0	2	0	2½	0	3
5	0	0	1	0	1½	0	2	0	3	0	4	0	5	0	6
7	6	0	1½	0	2¼	0	3	0	4½	0	6	0	7½	0	9
10	0	0	2	0	3	0	4	0	6	0	8	0	10	1	0
12	6	0	2½	0	3¾	0	5	0	7½	0	10	1	0½	1	3
15	0	0	3	0	4½	0	6	0	9	1	0	1	3	1	6
17	6	0	3½	0	5¼	0	7	0	10½	1	2	1	5½	1	9
20	0	0	4	0	6	0	8	1	0	1	4	1	8	2	0
22	6	0	4½	0	6¾	0	9	1	1½	1	6	1	10½	2	3
25	0	0	5	0	7½	0	10	1	3	1	8	2	1	2	6
27	6	0	5½	0	8¼	0	11	1	4½	1	10	2	3½	2	9
30	0	0	6	0	9	1	0	1	6	2	0	2	6	3	0
32	6	0	6½	0	9¾	1	1	1	7½	2	2	2	8½	3	3
35	0	0	7	0	10½	1	2	1	9	2	4	2	11	3	6
37	6	0	7½	0	11¼	1	3	1	10½	2	6	3	1½	3	9
40	0	0	8	1	0	1	4	2	0	2	8	3	4	4	0
42	0	0	8	1	0	1	4	2	0	2	8	3	4	4	0

These and progressive sums for loans not exceeding 10*l.*, (the greatest sum to which the act extends), are to be taken as a full satisfaction for interest and warehouse-room. The pawnbroker being liable, *notwithstanding any notice to the contrary*, for damage arising from exposure to damp, &c., &c.

Every pawnbroker, when he shall take any goods by way of pawn, whereon shall be lent *above* 5*s.* shall, *before he advance any money thereon*, enter in a book to be kept for that purpose, a description of such goods, and the sum lent thereon, with the day and year, the name of the person by whom pawned, the name of the street, and number of the house [if numbered] where such person shall reside, and whether he be a lodger or housekeeper, by using the letter L, if a lodger, and the letter H, if a housekeeper; and also the name and place of abode of the owner; and if the sum lent shall not exceed 5*s.*, such entry shall be made within four hours; and every pledge upon which shall be lent above 10*s.* shall be entered in a book separate from all other pledges, and numbered progressively, as they are pawned, in the following manner, viz. — the first pawn that shall be received in the month, No. 1. ; the second, No. 2 ; and so on progressively until the end of the month; and so on in every succeeding month ; and upon every note respecting such pledge shall be written the number of the entry aforesaid ; and at the time of taking every pawn, a note or memorandum (commonly called a *duplicate*) shall be given by the pawnbroker to the person pawning the same ; containing a description of the goods, the money advanced, the day and year, the name and place of abode of the party, whether L, or H, (that is, lodger or housekeeper) and the name of the pawnbroker; otherwise the pawnbroker shall not retain the pledge.— *s.* 6.

Where the sum lent is *under 5s.*, the duplicate or note is to be delivered *gratis*.

Where it is	5*s*. and under 10*s*. the pawnbroker may charge -	½*d*.
	10*s*. and under 20*s*. - - - -	1*d*.
	20*s*. and under 5*l*. - - -	2*d*.
	5*l*. and upwards - - - -	4*d*.

which note (or duplicate) must be produced to the pawnbroker before he is compellable to deliver the goods, as the act declares that the persons producing the notes are to be deemed the owners, unless notice to the contrary of the same having been procured fraudulently or unjustly from the real owner has been given to the pawnbroker. Upon the loss of a duplicate, or if the same has been feloniously or fraudulently taken or detained, the proper course is for the pawner to go to the pawnbroker, or what is more safe, to make a memorandum in writing, by way of notice, addressed to the pawnbroker, stating the circumstance of the loss, &c., and requesting a fresh duplicate; this notice should be signed by the applicant, or some person authorised by him, wherein he should state his name, place of abode, and business, or quality. This proceeding will secure the goods in the hands of the pawnbroker, but the pawnbroker (if the goods are unredeemed) is bound to deliver (as by the words of the act),—

A copy of the duplicate so lost, or fraudulently obtained, with the form of declaration of the particular circumstances attending the case, as the same shall be stated to him by the party applying as aforesaid, for which copy of such duplicate and form of affidavit, if the money lent shall not exceed 5*s.* the pawnbroker is to receive one halfpenny; and if the money lent shall not exceed 10*s.* one penny; and if the money lent shall exceed 10*s*. the like sum of money as the original duplicate cost, such money to be paid by the party applying for the same at the time of making the said application ; and the person having so obtained such copy of the duplicate, and form of affidavit, shall thereupon prove his right to such goods, to the satisfaction of some justice of the peace for the place where the said goods shall have been pledged or exchanged, and shall also verify on oath or affirmation, as the case may be, before the said justice, the truth of the particular circumstances attending the case mentioned in such declaration or affirmation to be made, the caption of such oath or affirmation to be authenticated by the handwriting of the justice before whom the same shall be made, and who shall authenticate the same ; whereupon the pawnbroker shall suffer the person proving such property, and making such affidavit or affirmation as aforesaid, on leaving such copy of the said duplicate, and the said declaration or affirmation, with the said pawnbroker to redeem such goods, for which no fee is payable.

Any person fraudulently pawning the goods of another, and convicted before a justice, shall forfeit from 5*l.* to 20*s.* and also the value of the goods pawned, &c. to be ascertained by the justice ; and on failure of payment, may be committed to the house of correction, for not more than three months, and be publicly whipped : the forfeitures, when paid, to be applied towards making satisfaction to the party injured, and defraying the costs ; the overplus, if any, to the poor of the parish.— *s.* 8.

A magistrate has no power under this section unless the party be charged with having knowingly and designedly pawned, pledged, or exchanged, or unlawfully disposed of the goods of another person; and an information that the complainant *believed* the goods to have been illegally pawned is not a sufficient charge. It is also a matter of some doubt whether a magistrate has a *power to remand for further examination.*

Any person counterfeiting or altering a duplicate, may be seized and taken before a justice, who is to commit the party to the house of correction, for not more than three months, nor less than one.— *s.* 9.

If any person shall offer to pawn any goods, refusing to give a satisfactory account of himself and the goods; or if there shall be reason to suspect that such goods are stolen; or if any person not entitled, shall attempt to redeem goods pawned; they may be taken before a justice, who shall commit them for further examination; and if it appears that the goods were stolen, or illegally obtained, or that the person offering to redeem the same has no title or pretence to them, the justice is to commit him to be dealt with according to law, where the nature of the offence shall authorise such commitment by any other law; or otherwise, for not more than three months.— *s.* 10.

Persons buying or taking in pledge unfinished goods, or any linen, &c. entrusted to be washed, shall forfeit double the sum lent, and restore the goods; and a justice may grant a search warrant *for the purpose of restoring such goods, as for restoring any other goods which are suspected to be unlawfully pawned, and and concerning which complaint shall be made by the owner on oath before such justice;* in executing which, a peace officer may break open doors, and the goods, if found, shall be restored to the owner.— *s.* 11, 12, 13.

Pawnbrokers, refusing to deliver up goods pledged within one year, on tender of the money lent, and interest, on conviction, a justice is empowered to commit the offender till the goods be delivered up, or reasonable satisfaction made.— *s.* 14.

Goods to be sold by public auction after the expiration of one year; being exposed to public view, and catalogues thereof published, and two advertisements of sale by the pawnbroker to be inserted in some newspaper two days at least before the first day's sale under penalty of 10*l.* to 40*s.* to the owner.—*s.* 17.*

All pictures, prints, books, bronzes, statues, busts, carvings in ivory and marble, cameos, intaglios, musical, mathematical, and philosophical instruments, and china, which shall be sold by public auction as aforesaid, shall be sold by themselves, and without other goods being sold at such sale, four times only in every year, (that is to say,) on the first Monday in the months of *January, April, July,* and *October,* in every year, and on the following day, or days, if the sale shall exceed one day, and at no other time; and the person who shall be employed to sell the same by auction, shall cause the same to be exposed to public view, and catalogues thereof to be published, and an advertisement, giving notice of such sale, and containing the name or names of the pawnbroker or pawnbrokers with whom the said goods are in pledge, to be inserted two several days in some public newspaper three days at the least

* Under this section 17. it has been decided that a pawnbroker has no right to sell unredeemed pledges at the expiration of the year and day, or further time of three months, as the case may be, if while they are in his possession and *before a sale actually take place* the owner of the goods or *bonâ fide* holder of the duplicate tender the principal and interest and expenses (if any) incurred; the power of sale being intended more as a method of securing the repayment of the money advanced, than as a means of affording a bonus to the pawnbroker.

It may here be noticed that pawnbrokers are not compellable, nor is it usual with them to insure against fire. The hazard attaches on the party pledging the articles, who is at liberty to insure for their value.

Pawnbrokers, as *bailees* of goods, cannot discharge themselves of responsibility as to damages or loss in respect of the articles pledged, even by notice written or printed. Indeed, the remedies afforded by the statute, which are very summary, do not deprive any person of his right to an action of trover to recover goods illegally pawned, which he may bring without applying to a magistrate, nor does the act affect the legal remedies or incidents of a pawn, the act only superadds a cheaper and more summary remedy for those who prefer adopting it.

before the first day of sale, upon pain of forfeiting to the owner or owners of the said goods for every offence in the premises, any sum not exceeding *5l.* nor less than *40s.*— *s.* 18.

Pawnbrokers receiving notice from the owners of goods before the expiration of a year, shall not dispose of them, until after the expiration of three months from the end of the said year.— *s.* 19.

No fee is payable to the pawnbroker upon this occasion, but as the notice must be either given in writing, or in the presence of one witness, *i. e.* verbal; persons prefer the pawnbrokers' method of indorsing on the duplicate, which on such occasions must be produced, "3 months," called "backing," for which they illegally demand a fee, but to avoid this contention, the act should be complied with. The written notice, which is equivalent to a witness, may be in this form: "To Mr. A. B., Pawnbroker," (as in the duplicate) "I hereby give you notice not to sell the undermentioned pledge until after the expiration of 3 calendar months." [*Here copy the articles, and the sum lent, as in the duplicate.*] "Yours, &c." (To be signed by the owner or lawful holder of the duplicate, with name, address, and date.)

This is *all* that is required.—*s.* 19.

Pawnbrokers are to enter an account of sales in their books of all goods pawned for upwards of ten shillings; and in case of any overplus by the sale, upon demand within 3 years, it shall be paid to the owner, the necessary costs, principal and interest, being deducted; persons possessing duplicates entitled to the inspecting of the book; and in case the goods shall have sold for more than the sum entered, or the farther entries not made, or the overplus is refused to be paid, the offender shall forfeit *10l.* and treble the sum lent, to be levied by distress.—*s.* 20.

Pawnbrokers shall not purchase goods whilst in their custody, or suffer them to be redeemed for that purpose; nor lend money to any person appearing to be under twelve years of age, or intoxicated, or purchase duplicates of other pawnbrokers, or buy any goods before eight in the forenoon, and after seven in the evening; nor receive any goods in pawn before eight in the forenoon, or after eight at night, between Michaelmas and Lady-day; and before seven o'clock in the forenoon, and after nine at night, during the remainder of the year; except till eleven o'clock on the evenings of Saturday, and that preceding Good Friday and Christmas Day; nor carry on the trade on any Sunday, Good Friday, or Christmas Day, or any fast or thanksgiving-day.— *s.* 21.

Pawnbrokers are to place in their shops a table of rates allowed by this act. — *s.* 22.

Pawnbroker's christian and surname, and business, to be written over the door; under a penalty of *10l.*: half to the informer and half to the poor.—*s.* 23.

Pawnbrokers having sold goods illegally, or having embezzled or injured goods, justices may award reasonable satisfaction to the owners, in case the same shall not amount to the principal and profit; or if it does, the goods shall be delivered to the owner, without paying any thing, under a penalty of *10l.*— *s.* 24.

Pawnbrokers to produce their books before any justice, if required, on a penalty of *10l.* to *5l.* (This provision is a very necessary one, as magistrates will not in many cases convict, except upon some other evidence than the complainants' own testimony,— a rule which, however just, might be productive of wrong, except the power of producing the books could be enforced.)— *s.* 25.

Penalty on pawnbrokers neglecting to make entry, *10l.*, and for every offence against this act, where no penalty is provided, *40s.* to *10l.*: half to the informer, the remainder to the poor.— *s.* 26.

Complaint shall, in all cases, be made within twelve months.— *s.* 27.

No person convicted of a fraud or felony may be an informer under this act. — *s.* 29.

Churchwardens to prosecute for every offence at the expense of the parish, on notice from a justice. (But the complainant is the necessary party to lay the information, and must attend with his witness at the time appointed for the pawnbroker's appearance.)— *s.* 28.

[This act does not extend to persons lending money upon goods at 5 per cent. interest.]

This act to extend to the executors, &c. of pawnbrokers and pawners.—*s.* 31.

Persons sued for any thing done in pursuance of this act, are entitled, in case of a verdict, or the plaintiff be non-suit, to double costs.

The following is a form of information against a pawnbroker for taking higher interest than allowed by the act, which must be fairly copied by the complainant in words at length, without figures, and taken to the police office or magistrate, at the time of making his oath — more special informations are drawn by the clerks or by an attorney.

MIDDLESEX, to wit. } BE IT REMEMBERED, that on the —— day of ———, in the year of our Lord, ———, A. B., of ——— street, in the parish of ———, in the county of Middlesex, weaver, came before me, [*here insert the name of the magistrate*] one of his Majesty's justices of the peace, in and for the said county, and made complaint, and informeth me, that [*here insert the pawnbroker's name*] using and exercising the trade and business of a pawnbroker, in —— street, in the parish of ——, in the said county, on ——— the ——— day of ——, in the year of our Lord ——, did demand, receive, and take, of and from one A. B., on redeeming the pledge hereinafter mentioned, the sum of ten shillings, as and for, and by way of profit, for the loan of two pounds for twelve calendar months, thentofore (to wit) on ———, the ——— day of ———, in the year aforesaid, in the parish and county last aforesaid, lent and advanced to the said A. B., in the name of A. B., upon a certain pledge, (that is to say) twelve silver table spoons, the same not having remained in pawn exceeding twelve calendar months. The said sum of ten shillings so demanded, received, and taken as aforesaid, being more than at and after the rate allowed by Act of Parliament, and contrary to the statute made in the thirty-ninth and fortieth years of the reign of King George the Third, intitled "An Act for better regulating the business of pawnbrokers;" which has imposed a forfeiture of such sum of money, as to the justice or justices before and by whom any information thereon shall be heard and determined, in his or their discretion shall seem reasonable and fit, not less than forty shillings, nor more than ten pounds.

I ——— receive this information, this —— day of —— one thousand eight hundred and ———. }

PECULIAR. A particular parish or church that has jurisdiction within itself, and power to grant administration or probate of wills, &c., exempt from the bishop or other ecclesiastical authority exercising ordinary jurisdiction. Some of these peculiar jurisdictions belong to deans and chapters, some to the king, thence called *royal* peculiars, some to the archbishop, called archbishop's peculiars. The king's chapel is a peculiar or exempt jurisdiction.

Some lords of manors have a peculiar jurisdiction of proving the wills of the tenants. This unequal distribution of jurisdictions for probate, is felt as a great evil.

PEERS. All persons under the degree of a peer are commoners, and subject to the common tribunals and ordinary jurisdiction of the kingdom, and in a legal sense are "peers" of each other, *i. e.* equal to each other, for the law knows no distinction between them. But peers of parliament are judges of each other, and exempt from the common and ordinary jurisdiction, and are distinguished as "peers" of the realm.

PERJURY. The taking a false oath or making a false declaration before a magistrate in writing, or if a Quaker, Moravian, or Separatist, making a false affirmation knowingly, so that a thing material to the question before a competent and judicial authority be falsely and wittingly denied or intentionally concealed. Voluntary and corrupt perjury must be proved, for mistake or inadvertence, however reprehensible, will not subject a party to an indictment for this offence.

The allegation of a falsehood as well as the suppression of a truth are equally perjuries, especially when a witness is sworn in open court to tell *the truth, the whole truth, and nothing but the truth;* many persons imagine that when they are called upon to give evidence, they may conscientiously suppress circumstances disadvantageous for the party who summons them, but all wilful suppressions are perjuries, and punishable accordingly.

In proceedings by motion before the courts at Westminster, persons who make affidavits have a practice of only telling one side of a story, instead of stating *all* facts; a wicked and most corrupt mode of proceeding, and equally punishable. The difficulty of procuring evidence to ensure a conviction for this offence, renders it comparatively secure in its commission, for two witnesses at least must prove the falsity of the thing sworn, and that it was done knowingly.

The punishment for perjury, is fine, imprisonment (hard labour) and pillory at the discretion of the court, and the judge may order the party to be transported or imprisoned, and kept to hard labour in the house of correction for not exceeding 7 years.

It seems that a conviction for perjury renders the party incapable of giving testimony again, notwithstanding the rule that a party who has undergone his punishment is restored to legal competence.

Where perjury is committed on a trial in court, the judge may commit the party, and order him to be prosecuted, and such prosecution is to be carried on without payment of fees.

The soliciting or procuring perjury to be committed is punishable as perjury: but it must be proved that the perjury *was* committed.

The punishment for perjury is annexed to offences of swearing to false affidavits, and making false written declarations before persons not strictly judicial, as registers, &c.

The punishment of perjury, though very severe, is scarcely, in the ideas of many, proportioned to the heinousness of the offence.

PEW. A place or seat in a parish church. An exclusive title to pews and seats in the body of the church may be maintained in virtue of an ecclesiastical licence termed a faculty, or by prescription, which last is founded on the presumption that a faculty had been long previously granted. All other pews and seats in the body of the church are the property of the parish, and the churchwardens as the officers of the ordinary (viz. the bishop or other person having supreme ecclesiastical jurisdiction), and subject to his control, have authority to place the parishioners therein; no precise rules are prescribed for the government of churchwardens in the use of this power, for its due exercise must depend on a sound judgment and discretion applied to the circumstances of the parish.

By the general law and of common right, all the pews in a parish church are the common property of the parish; they are for the use in common of the parishioners, who are all entitled to be seated orderly and conveniently, so as best to provide for the accommodation of all; and it has been lately solemnly adjudged, that a parishioner paying church or vicar-rates, can demand a seat free of expense in the church, more particularly as the expenses of the church are to be raised by a church-rate. The distribution of seats rests with the churchwardens, as the officers subject to the control of the ordinary. Neither the minister nor the vestry have any right whatever to interfere with the churchwardens in seating and arranging the parishioners, as often erroneously supposed; at the same time, the advice of the minister, and even sometimes the opinions and wishes of the vestry may be fitly appealed to by the churchwardens, and to a certain extent referred to in this matter. The general duty of the churchwardens is to look to the general accommodation of the parish, consulting as far as may be, that of all the inhabitants. The parishioners, indeed, have a claim to be seated according to their rank and station, but the churchwardens are not, in providing for this, to overlook the claims of all the parishioners to be seated, if sittings can be afforded them. Accordingly, they are bound in particular not to accommodate the higher classes beyond their real wants, to the exclusion of their poorer neighbours, who are equally entitled to accommodation, with the rest, though they are not entitled to quite as commodious accommodation, supposing the seats to be not all equally convenient.

The general right therefore is in the parish and the ordinary, but a party in possession has such a right as to maintain an action against an intruder, and the person in possession is not to be turned out at the mere will of the churchwarden or ordinary.

A right superior to the churchwardens can be obtained by procuring a faculty, by which the ordinary parts with the right, or, if there be no proof of a faculty. there may be proof of prescription, and such immemorial usage as presumes the grant of a faculty; — for instance, a long and uninterrupted possession.

The possession must be ancient and going beyond living memory. Extra-parochial persons cannot under any circumstances establish a claim to seats in the body of a parish church, even by a faculty.

A pew annexed by prescription to a certain messuage, cannot, as is often erroneously conceived, be separated from the occupancy of the house, but passes with the messuage, the tenant of which, for the time being, has for the time being the prescriptive right to the pew, which cannot be sold or let without a special act of parliament. Where an occupier of a pew ceases to be an inhabitant of the parish, he cannot let the pew with, and thus annex it to his house, but it reverts to the disposal of the churchwardens.

The foregoing remarks cannot relate to new churches belonging to any district or part of a parish, the appropriation or letting the seats whereof are regulated by particular acts of parliament passed for the express purpose of settling these rights and conveniences, and of affording a certain number of "free sittings."

PER STIRPES. A distribution *in* or *per stirpes* is when, by a fiction of law, a family comes by representation into the place of the person deceased, and so divide that share amongst themselves which the deceased would have received if he had been living: as where one of four children dies before the father, and leaves children behind him, those children represent their father, and have his part, viz. a fourth part, amongst them all. *In* or *per capita* is when the fund is to be divided according to the number of persons who are to succeed, as where the personalty of the father is divided amongst his four children.

PIGEONS. The killing and taking pigeons when *at large,* subjects the offender to a penalty of 2*l.*; when in a state of confinement they are the subjects of larceny.

PIRACY. A robbery on the high seas, and within the jurisdiction of the admiralty, which does not extend to any creek or arm of the sea, or sea flowing between two points of land, such, in contemplation of law, being within a county. The piracy or robbery must be upon persons not at enmity with this country, and must be without authority of any state. Intent is an ingredient in this offence (as with almost all offences); for a person accused of piracy may show that he captured the vessel, or took the goods, under an impression that the ship belonged to a state at war with England. See PIRATES.

PIRATES. Common sea rovers, without any fixed place of residence, who acknowledge no law, and support themselves by pillage and depredation on the high seas in ships or vessels. Many statutes, the earliest of which is in the reign of H. 8., define what is piracy, but these are repealed, as far as relates to punishment of the offence, by the *Stat.* 1. *Vict. c.* 88., which declares that the act of assaulting (on the occasion of committing piracy) with intent to murder, or stabbing, cutting, or wounding any person on board the vessel, in respect of which the piracy is committed, or doing any act whereby the life of such person shall be endangered, is a capital felony.

The punishment of simple piracy is transportation for life, at the discretion of the court, or for not less than 15 years, or imprisonment not exceeding 3 years, with or without hard labour, and solitary confinement.

Principals in the second degree, and accessories before the fact, are punishable as the principal; and accessories after the fact are punishable by imprisonment for not exceeding 2 years, with or without hard labour and solitary confinement.

The offence of piracy is generally stated to consist in committing those acts of robbery and depredation upon the high seas which, if committed on land, would have there amounted to felony. It has been by various statutes more closely defined to be the boarding of a merchant vessel, though without carrying her off, or seizing any of her goods. The assisting or combining with known pirates is also deemed piracy, and such accessories are deemed principal pirates.

Pirates are also those who, owing allegiance to the crown of Great Britain, during war commit hostilities on the sea against her majesty's subjects, by colour of any commission from the enemy, or adhere or give aid to the enemy upon the sea. 18. *Geo.* 2. *c.* 30.

Piracies are triable at the central criminal court, or by commission directed to the lord admiral, and other persons named by the chancellor, to be executed in any county in England.

PLEADING, in a large sense, contains all the proceedings in a trial or action, from the declaration until the issue is joined (see ISSUE); but in its immediate or direct sense is taken for the defendant's answer to the *declaration.* Pleadings are the mutual altercations between the plaintiff and defendant in a suit, which are delivered between the attorneys on each side. There is —

1. The *declaration*, setting forth the plaintiff's complaint.

2. The *Plea*, or answer to it, (if negative *Issue* can be taken upon it, as is usually the case).

3. The *Replication.* The exception or answer made by the plaintiff to the defendant's plea.

4. The *Rejoinder.* The answer of the defendant to the plaintiff's replication.

5. The *Surrejoinder*,
6. The *Rebutter*, } See these titles.
7. The *Surrebutter.*

When, in the course of these *special* pleadings, the plaintiff and defendant have agreed upon a point, they are said to be at *issue*, which is often done at the replication or the surrejoinder, and not so frequently carried through the whole course of pleading.

POACHING. Poaching in the daytime is subject to various penalties under the Game Act, 1 & 2 *W*. 4. *c*. 32.; but, with respect to *night poaching*, the 9 *G*. 4. *c*. 69. *s*. 1. enacts,—

"That if any person by *night* (that is, between an hour after sunset and an hour before sunrise,) unlawfully take or destroy any game, or any rabbit, in any lands, whether open or inclosed, or shall, by night, unlawfully enter or be upon the land, whether open or inclosed, with any gun, net, engine, or other instrument, for the purpose of taking or destroying game, such offender shall, upon conviction thereof before two justices of the peace, be committed for the *first* offence to the common gaol or house of correction, for any period not exceeding *three calendar months*, there to be kept to hard labour, and, at the expiration of such period, shall find securities by recognizance, or in Scotland by bond of caution, of himself in 10*l*. and two securities in 5*l*. each, or one surety in 10*l*., for his not so offending again for the space of one year next following; and, in case of not finding such sureties, shall be further imprisoned and kept to hard labour for the space of *six* calendar months, unless such sureties are sooner found. The punishment of a *second* offence is six months' imprisonment, and to be kept to hard labour, and to find sureties; and for a *third* offence the offender is liable to transportation. The 2d section, where any person shall be *found* upon any land, committing any such offence, authorizes the owner or occupier of such land, and other specified persons, to seize and apprehend such offender upon such land, or, in case of pursuit being made, in any other place to which he may have escaped therefrom, and to deliver him as soon as may be into the custody of a peace officer, in order to his being conveyed before two justices of the peace; and in case such offender shall assault or offer any violence with any gun, cross-bow, fire-arms, bludgeon, stick, club, or any other *offensive* weapon whatsoever, towards any person thereby authorized to seize and apprehend him, he shall, whether it be his first, second, or any other offence, be guilty of a *misdemeanor*, and shall be liable, at the discretion of the court, to be transported for seven years, or to be imprisoned and kept to hard labour, in the common gaol or house of correction, for any term not exceeding two years. The 4th section limits the summary proceeding to six, and indictment to twelve, calendar months; and the 5th, 6th, and 7th sections give the form of conviction and proceedings on appeal, and take away any removal by *certiorari*.

Upon this act it will be observed, that the omission of the words "forest, chase, park," &c. which were in the prior [repealed] act, is immaterial, as they would unquestionably be included under the comprehensive words "open or inclosed grounds." The word "*found*," in this act, means "having been seen or discovered;" and if game-keepers attempt to apprehend persons armed with offensive weapons, who are poaching in the night, and one of the game-keepers be shot by one of the poachers, this will be murder in all, unless it be shown that either of the poachers separated himself from the rest, so as to establish that he did not join in the act; and where game-keepers had seized two persons who were poaching in the night, and they, having surrendered, called to a third, who came up, and he killed one of the keepers, this was held to be murder in all, though the two struck no blow, and though the keepers had not announced in what capacity they had apprehended them."—*Chitty's Practice of the Law*, vol. i. p. 403.

The same act, *s*. 9., enacts,

"*That if any persons, to the number* of three or more together, shall, by *night*, unlawfully enter or be in any land, whether open or inclosed, for the purpose of taking or destroying *game* or rabbits, any such persons being armed with any gun, cross-bow, fire-arms, bludgeon, or any other offensive weapon, each and every of such persons shall be guilty of a *misdemeanor*, and, being convicted thereof, shall be liable, at the discretion of the court, to be transported beyond seas for any term not exceeding fourteen years, nor less than seven years, or to be imprisoned and kept to hard labour for any term not exceeding three years."

POISONING is murder, and punishable accordingly. The law implies malice in this offence, although no particular enmity be proved. The burden of proof, therefore, is on the prisoner, to show that the poison was administered with an innocent intent. Persons, whether apothecaries, &c. or not, administering medicine or drugs, or any other thing with a criminal disregard of human life, are punishable as for manslaughter; such homicide being not justifiable. The administering poison with intent to murder is a capital felony. Evidence of administering at different times may be given to show the intent. See the title OFFENCES; and therein of *Offences against the Person.*

POISONING WATER, by putting in lime or any noxious material, is a *malicious mischief.* See that title.

POISONING, OR ATTEMPTING TO POISON, GAME is punishable summarily before two justices with a penalty not exceeding 10*l.*

POISONING FOWLS is also punishable summarily by a fine, not exceeding 5*l.*

POLICE. The municipal regulations of a city, as far as regards the prevention of crime, public convenience and cleanliness, the prompt and efficacious administration of those summary remedies administered by magistrates, and the disposal of offenders, by committing them to prison till duly delivered. The system of the London police is regulated by the acts 10 *G.* 4. *c.* 44. (the Middlesex Police Act), and the 3 *&* 4 *W.* 4. *c.* 9. (the Police Magistrates' Act), and the 3 *G.* 4. *c.* 55. and 6 *G.* 4. *c.* 21., for the purpose of adding to public security,

POOR. Compulsory charity was first introduced in the reign of king Henry VIII.; and the object of the statute which established the system had in view the support of the impotent, *i. e.* indigent, and the setting to work the able-bodied poor, creating thereby a distinction between *indigence* and *poverty;* the one being the state of a person unable to labour, or unable to obtain in return for his labour the means of subsistence, the other being the state of one who, in order to obtain a mere subsistence, is forced to have recourse to labour. This distinction was evidently the basis of subsequent enactments for the relief of the poor of both classes; the oldest unrepealed statute being the act 43 *Eliz. c.* 2., on which the present legislative relief is founded; that act appointing overseers of the poor in every parish, whose office and duty are principally these:—1. To raise competent relief for the first class of poor, and to provide work for the second class; also empowering a justice of the peace to commit to the house of correction any such persons as shall not employ themselves to work, being appointed thereto.

From several causes, not necessary to be here noticed, these principles of action were departed from, and a variety of acts have been passed, the construction of which has rendered the law intricate and confused, and a variety of evils engendered, which it is the object of the late act (4 *&* 5 *W.* 4. *c.* 76.) to suppress, the greatest of which appeared to be *out-door relief to the able-bodied*, persons never *originally* considered or recognised as objects of compulsory *charity.* As the present Poor Law Amendment Act materially varies the practice of relief, the Editor intends to confine himself to an analysis of that act, noticing those statutes that are totally or partially unrepealed, in order that the operation of that act may be more fully understood. This statute is intituled "An Act for the Amendment and better Administration of the Laws relating to the Poor in England and Wales," and was passed in the month of August, 1834.

It authorises the appointment of commissioners (who form a central board of control), and assistant commissioners, to carry the act into effect. The commissioners are appointed by the crown, and removable at pleasure. They, by summons under their hands and seal, may require the attendance of all such persons as they may think fit to call before them, upon any question or matter connected with the administration of the laws for the relief of the poor, and also make any inquiries, and require any answer or returns as to any such question or matter; and also may administer oaths, and examine all such persons upon oath, and enforce the production, upon oath, of books and writings; or may require such person to subscribe a declaration of the truth of the matters respecting which he shall have been examined; but no person shall be required to travel more than ten miles from the place of his abode.

The commissioners cannot act as a court of record, or require the production of the title of lands, &c. not being the property of any parish or union.

They are to make a record of their proceedings, to be submitted to one of the principal secretaries of state once, or oftener (if required), in the year; also, to submit a general report of their proceedings to both houses of parliament, within six weeks after their meeting; and also to give to the principal secretary of state any information he may require concerning their proceedings.

Assistant commissioners are appointed to act at such places, and in such manner, as the chief commissioners may direct. They are not to exeeed 9 in number, and, as well as the chief commissioners, they are not to sit in parliament.

The commissioners are empowered to appoint a secretary, assistant secretaries, clerks, messengers, and officers, removable at their discretion, whose salaries are to be regulated by government; their appointment is also limited to five years.

The commissioners have power to delegate to the assistant commissioners their powers; and various provisions are made for securing the attendance of witnesses, and payment of their expenses, subject to the restriction of not compelling any one to travel more than 10 miles from his abode.

The limitation or restriction of five years extends to every commissioner and person appointed under the act.

The giving false evidence, or subscribing a false declaration, subjects the party to the penalties of perjury; and wilful neglect of a commissioner's summons, or suppressing evidence, is a misdemeanor. The expenses of witnesses, in all cases, are allowable, and chargeable as incidental expenses, under the act.

In the report of the commissioners of inquiry, upon the existing poor-laws and their defects, it was recommended that a central board be appointed to control the administration of the poor-laws, with requisite assistant commissioners; and that the commissioners should be empowered and directed to frame and enforce regulations for the government of workhouses (an object previously the subject of a statute), and as to the nature of the amount of the relief to be given, and the labour to be exacted in them, and that such regulations be uniform throughout the country.

Therefore, from the 14th of August, 1834, it is provided, that the administration of relief to the poor, according to the existing laws (which clearly recognise the classification above-mentioned), shall be subject to the control of the commissioners; and, for executing the powers of the act, they are authorised and required to issue rules, orders, and regulations for the management of the poor — for the government of workhouses — the education of children therein — the management of poor children under the act 7 *G.* 3. *c.* 39. — superintending, inspecting, and regulating houses wherein such children are kept — apprenticing children — the guidance of all guardians, vestries, and parish officers — the keeping and auditing accounts — making contracts — and, generally, carrying the act into effect, subject to the approval of the secretary of state, who is to lay the same before parliament. The orders of assistant commissioners not to be in force till sealed with the seal of commissioners, and with respect to guardians, overseers, &c. not till after 14 days have elapsed from the sending a copy to such guardians, overseers, &c. (except orders made in answer to reports of overseers or guardians.)

Workhouses. — By the principal act of 43 *Eliz.* it is provided, "to the intent that necessary places of habitation may more conveniently be provided for poor impotent (*i. e.* indigent) people," that the churchwardens and overseers, or the greater part of them, by the leave of the lord of the manor, whereof any waste or common within their parish is parcel, to erect, build, and set up, in fit and convenient places of habitation, in such waste or common, at the general charge of the parish, or otherwise of the hundred or county, to be taxed, rated, and gathered, in manner as therein expressed, convenient houses of dwelling for the impotent poor, and also to place inmates, or more families than one, in one cottage or house.

By the 9 *G.* 1. *c.* 7., the churchwardens and overseers of parishes, or of two or more parishes united, may purchase or hire a house for the poor; and contract with persons, or with the overseers of another parish, for the lodging, keeping, maintaining, and employing the poor.

Under these acts it is not absolutely necessary for parishes to provide a workhouse for the poor, but they may relieve them at their own houses.

The *majority* of churchwardens *and* overseers may contract for maintaining the poor.

Guardians of the poor have the same authority as overseers, except the collection of the rate, which, by the act first appointing them (22 *G.* 3. *c.* 83.), and regulating their election, was to be collected by the overseers, who handed over sufficient to the guardians for maintenance of the poor; but the election of guardians is now to be made according to the provisions of the present act, as hereafter mentioned.

By another act (30 *G.* 3. *c.* 49.), justices were authorised to visit workhouses or poorhouses, and they were to certify to the quarter-sessions the state and condition of the poor.

By a subsequent act, churchwardens and overseers were empowered to build, enlarge, or sell workhouses, and to buy one in an adjoining parish.

Birth or residence in a poorhouse does not confer a settlement.

The rules for the regulation of workhouses or poorhouses are contained in the schedule to the 22 *G.* 3. *c.* 83.; and punishments for misconduct therein are declared by the 55 *G.* 3. *c.* 137.; and by the 50 *G.* 3. *c.* 50. justices had the power of directing the regulations in the schedule to the 22 *G.* 3. to be observed in workhouses where there was no master or mistress, and they might also alter such regulations.

But now, these rules of 22 *G.* 3. are placed under the control of the commissioners, no magistrate having power to make any alteration without their consent.

The building, hiring, enlarging, or altering workhouses is vested in the persons now legally authorised, subject, however, to the orders of the commissioners; and the commissioners, or assistant commissioners, are empowered to attend at every parochial or local board and vestry, &c. to take part in the discussions, but not to vote thereat.

In parishes or unions *not having a workhouse*, the consent of a majority of the guardians, or the consent of the majority of the rate-payers, is necessary previous to the commissioners purchasing a workhouse; but no such consent is necessary where a workhouse already built is required to be altered or enlarged.

Unions of Parishes.— Unions can be formed by the commissioners, who may declare so many parishes as they think fit to be *united* for the administration of the laws for the relief of the poor, and such parishes are deemed by the act a union for that purpose; and thereupon the workhouses of such parishes are for their common use; and, when a union is proposed, the commissioners are to calculate the average expense of each parish, the parishes united contributing to a common fund; and these unions can be dissolved or added to at the discretion of the commissioners. And so much of an act (22 *G.* 3. *c.* 83.) as restrains parishes from contributing to workhouses at a greater distance than 10 miles, or as limits the class or description of persons to be sent to workhouses, and so much of another act (56 *G.* 3. *c.* 129.) as repeals the provisions in any acts, whereby any parish at a greater distance than 10 miles from any house of industry or workhouse shall be authorised to contribute to, or take the benefit of, such house are repealed; and

No union or incorporation of parishes shall be formed under an act 22 *G.* 3. without consent of commissioners.

Guardians of the Poor.—The first appointment of guardians is contained in the 22 *G.* 3. *c.* 83., which authorised parishes to elect guardians under certain regulations, who should receive salaries, and be invested with all the powers and authorities given to overseers (except the making and collecting rates), and be subject to the same liabilities. Subsequent statutes contained particular provisions respecting their election, which is to be made according to the provisions of the present act, which enacts

That, where a union of parishes shall take place, a board of guardians shall be chosen for administering the relief of the poor of such union; and the commissioners are to determine the numbers and prescribe the duties of such guardians, and also fix a qualification, without which no person shall be eligible; such qualification to consist in being rated to the poor's-rate of some parish in such union, but not so as to require a qualification exceeding the annual rental of 40*l.* Guardians may also be elected for a single parish.

The election to take place on or about the 25th of March in every year; and justices resident within the parish, and acting for the county, are, *ex officio*, declared members of such board.

The guardians are elected by rate-payers and owners of property in the parish or union: *rate-payers* under 200*l.* to have a single vote; if rated at 200*l.* or more, but under 400*l.*, to have two votes; if rated at 400*l.* or more, to have three votes. *Owners* to vote according to the scale laid down in an act (58 *G.* 3. *c.* 69.) for inhabitants and other persons, that is, to have one vote for the first 50*l.*, and one vote for every 25*l.* above that sum, but so that no owner can have more than six votes. An owner may vote by proxy; and, if he shall be *bonâ fide* occupier of any such property, he may vote in respect of his occupation as well as of his ownership, the amount of the assessment to determine the annual value of the ownership. As the votes are to be taken in writing, and collected in such manner as the commissioners may direct, it is not requisite that the votes should be taken in vestry.

Guardians of the poor have but little responsibility beyond administering the poor-laws according to the rules laid down by the commissioners; and make the necessary appointments, under the control of the commissioners. Their consent is requisite for building workhouses (where no workhouse is already built), to dissolve, add to, or take from, a union, and subject to the approbation of the commissioners. United parishes may be one for the purposes of settlement and of rating, in which last case the guardians have to assess the property in the several parishes for that purpose.

They are liable to the same penalties as overseers, and subject to a penalty of 100*l.* for contracting to supply the poor with provisions.

Regulation of Workhouses.—The schedule in the act of 22 *G.* 3., before referred to, sets forth the following rules and orders, which the commissioners may suspend, alter, vary, amend, or rescind, or make new or other rules or orders at their discretion; and it is particularly provided that the commissioners' rules are to be observed, as if the same were specifically embodied in the act.

Dangerous lunatics, insane persons, or idiots are not to be detained in any workhouse longer than 14 days.

Justices of the peace have power to visit workhouses in the same manner as they are authorised by another act (30 *G.* 3.); and persons disobeying the rules can be convicted before *two* justices, and are punishable as parties who wilfully neglect or disobey the rules of the commissioners; and, where no rules have been made by the commissioners, any justice, physician, surgeon, or apothecary, or the officiating clergyman of any parish, may examine and certify the state of the same, in the same manner as they are authorised by the last mentioned act. The rules and orders before alluded to are as follows:—

First. — That the several persons who shall be sent to any such poor-houses who are capable of doing any work, shall be employed by the governor in some labour which may be best suited to their strength or capacity.

Second. — That the governor shall take particular care to keep the said house and the several apartments therein, and also the several persons who shall inhabit the same, clean and wholesome; and for that purpose he shall employ such of the said poor persons who shall be sent thither, whom he shall think most able and best qualified for the offices, to assist him therein, and also in providing and dressing victuals for the use of such poor persons; and if any poor person shall refuse or neglect to perform the work or labour in which he or she shall be so employed, or shall be directed to do, by the governor, every such person shall be punished by confinement, or alteration of diet, in such manner as the governor shall direct; and for a second offence of the like sort complaint thereof shall be made to some justice of the peace for the limit, who, on conviction, shall commit such person to the house of correction for any time not exceeding two calendar months, nor less than one calendar month.

Third.— That the apartments in the house or houses, to be provided as aforesaid, shall be adapted so as to accommodate the poor who shall be sent thither in the best manner they are capable. That the governor shall place in the best apartments such poor persons who, having been creditable housekeepers, are reduced by misfortune, in preference to those who are become poor by vice and idleness; and that separate apartments shall be provided for the reception of the sick and distempered poor, and an apothecary or surgeon to be sent to attend them, when there shall appear necessity for it, at the expense of the parish or place to which such poor persons belong.

Fourth. — That such poor persons who are able to work shall be called up by ring of bell, and set to work by six in the morning, from Lady-day to Michaelmas, and by eight from Michaelmas to Lady-day; and continue until four in the afternoon from Michaelmas to Lady-day, and from Lady-day to Michaelmas till six in the afternoon (meet time and times for reasonable recreation excepted); and if any such poor person shall refuse or neglect to do such work as shall be allotted him or her, or wilfully spoil the same, or depart from such house without leave from the governor, or shall be guilty of disorder or disobedience to these rules and orders, the governor shall reprove such person for the same, and punish him or her by confinement, or alteration of diet, as the said governor shall think fit; and, if such person shall be guilty of the like offence a second time, the governor shall complain to the visitor of such house, who is hereby authorised to order the punishment of confinement to be increased to such degree as he shall think fit.

Fifth. — That the governor shall enter in a book, to be kept by him, an account of the household goods, linen, furniture, and utensils provided for the said house, and also an account of the materials bought for manufacture, and of the goods manufactured there, which shall be laid before the guardians at their monthly meeting, and before the visitor whenever he comes to such house.

Sixth. — That the governor shall visit the several persons maintained in such house or houses, and their apartments, once at least in every day; and shall take care that there is no waste of fire, candles, or provisions; and shall see that the fires and candles are put out at the hours fixed for such persons going to bed, which shall be at eight of the clock between Michaelmas and Lady-day, and nine between Lady-day and Michaelmas.

Seventh. — That, when any person shall die in the house, the governor shall take care that the body of such person be immediately removed into some separate apartment, and be decently buried, as soon as conveniently may be; and also take care of the clothes and goods of such person, and deliver them to the guardian of the poor of the parish or place to which such person did belong, who is to pay the charges of the funeral of such poor person.

Eighth. — That no poor person be permitted to go out of the poorhouse, nor any person permitted to come into such house or houses, except the persons maintained or employed there, without the permission of the governor; and that no spirituous liquors be permitted to be drank in such house or houses; and that no other liquors shall be brought thither without the permission of the said governor.

Ninth. — That the rules, orders, and bye-laws shall be publicly read by the governor to all the poor persons kept in such house or houses, once at least in every month.

Tenth. — That all poor persons, able to go to church, shall attend divine service every Sunday.*

Eleventh. — That the governor shall dismiss from the poorhouse or work-

---

* But, by the present act, no inmate of a workhouse is compellable, by these or any rules to be made by the commissioners, to attend any religious service contrary to his religious principles; nor is the education of any child authorised contrary to the religious creed of his parent or guardian; and any licensed minister is permitted to attend any inmate for the purpose of affording religious assistance, and also for the purpose of instructing his child or children in the principles of their religion; *s.* 19.

house every person who shall, in the opinion of the guardian or guardians, be thought improper to continue longer there, and upon an order from him or them for that purpose.

The following rules have been suggested in the first report of the poor-law commissioners, for the regulation of the inmates of workhouses.

First. — To separate the men and women.

Second. — To prevent any from going out or seeing visitors, and to make them keep regular hours.

Third. — To prevent smoking.

Fourth. — To disallow beer.

Fifth. — To find them work.

Sixth. — To treat them with proper attention.

Parochial Offices.—The control of all officers under the overseers or guardians is vested in the commissioners, who may direct them to appoint such paid officers, with such qualifications as the commissioners may think necessary for superintending or assisting in the relief and employment of the poor, and for the examining and auditing, allowing or disallowing, of accounts in the parish or union. The duties of such officers, and the limits within which they are to be performed, their mode of appointment and dismissal, the continuance in office and the amount or nature of the security given, are also specially within the directions and power of the commissioners.

Overseers, treasurers, or, in fact, any person having the collection or distribution of the monies assessed for relief of the poor, are required, not less than once in every quarter, *and in addition to the annual account, now by law required*, to render their accounts to the guardians or auditors, &c.; and, if there should be no guardian or auditor, then to the justices of the peace at their petty session for the division, and, if required, verify on oath, or subscribe a declaration, to the truth thereof.

Balances due from any guardian, &c. may be recovered in the same manner as penalties under the act are recoverable.

Masters of workhouses, assistant overseers, or other paid officers, are removable by the commissioners, upon the suggestion or complaint of the overseers or guardians, or by the commissioners themselves; and any person removed is not competent to be appointed to any *paid* office connected with the relief of the poor, except with the consent of commissioners.

Persons convicted of felony, fraud, or perjury are ineligible to hold any parish office, or have the management of the poor in any way whatever.

Mode of administering Relief, and to whom. — The 43 *Eliz.* enacts, that the churchwardens of every parish, and four, three, or two substantial householders there, as shall be thought meet, having respect to the proportion and greatness of the same parish and parishes, to be nominated yearly in Easter week, or within one month after Easter, under the hand and seal of two or more justices of the peace, in the same county, whereof one to be of the quorum, dwelling in or near the same parish or division where the same parish doth lie, shall be called overseers of the poor of the same parish; and they, or the greater part of them, shall take order from time to time, by and with the consent of two or more such justices of the peace as is aforesaid, for setting to work the children of all such whose parents shall not, by the said churchwardens and overseers, or the greater part of them, be thought able to keep and maintain their children; and also for setting to work all such persons, married or unmarried, having no means to maintain them, and using no ordinary and daily trade of life to get their living by; and also to raise weekly or otherwise (by taxation of every inhabitant, parson, vicar, and others, and of every occupier of lands, houses, tithes appropriate, propriations of tithes, coal mines, or saleable underwoods, in the said parish, in such competent sum and sums of money as they shall think fit,) a convenient stock of flax, hemp, wool, thread, iron, and other ware and stuff, to set the poor (*i. e.* the able-bodied, unable to get work,) on work; and also competent sums of money for and towards the necessary relief of the lame, impotent, old, blind, and such other among them being poor *and unable to work;* and also for the putting out of poor children to be apprentices, to be gathered out of the same parish, according to the ability of the same parish; and to do and execute all other things, as well for the disposing of the said stock as otherwise concerning the premises, as to them shall seem convenient.

And the said justices of peace, or any one of them, are to send to the house of correction, or common gaol, such as shall not employ themselves to work, being appointed thereunto as aforesaid.

It is also provided, that the father and grandfather, and the mother and grandmother, and the children, of every poor, old, blind, lame, and impotent person, or other poor person not able to work, being of a sufficient ability, shall at their own charges relieve and maintain every such poor person in that manner, and according to that rate, as by the justices of peace of that county, where such sufficient persons dwell, or the greater number of them, at their general quarter-sessions, shall be assessed, upon pain that every one of them shall forfeit 20*s.* for every month which they shall fail therein.

Under the 9 *G.* 1. persons refusing to go into the workhouse are not to be relieved, unless in circumstances of *temporary* illness or distress, or in cases respecting the situation, health, or condition of the poorhouse, in which cases they might, under another act (36 *G.* 3.), be relieved at their own houses.

Upon these statutes, it has been held that overseers are bound to relieve the necessities of all poor persons in the parish, whether those wants are the ordinary necessaries of life, or necessary care, and medical and surgical attendance during illness, when such poor persons are unable to provide for themselves or families, whether they be *settled* inhabitants or *casual* poor; that is, persons who, having come casually into the parish upon temporary business or otherwise, and not with any intention of settling there, have sustained some sudden injury, or fallen suddenly ill, so as to render it dangerous or improper to remove them; or persons who, having fallen ill or been injured near the boundaries of the parish, have been without fraud taken to any place in their parish as the most convenient. They are also bound to relieve the necessities of a bastard child in their parish; and for the amount of such relief they are entitled to sue the sureties on a bond of indemnity given them.

It has been decided that a man who has more children than he can maintain, or who cannot obtain work, is entitled to relief as an impotent person; though, as hath been remarked already, the term "impotent" means actual disability to work, and as such, under the present act, out-door relief would not be afforded him.

The overseers are also chargeable for medical attendance, nurses, &c. afforded to the poor *within* their parish, whether casual poor or settled inhabitants.

The present act vests the administration of relief absolutely in the commissioners; for after reciting that a practice had obtained of giving relief to persons or their families, who at the time of applying for or receiving such relief were wholly or partially in the employment of individuals, and after repealing all former enactments authorising justices to order relief to poor persons at their own houses, and in other cases, being extensions of that practice, and deviations from the principle of the 43 *Eliz.*, (the system of out-door relief remaining chiefly on the enactments of the present statute, and the power of justices thereunder,) it provides, that the commissioners, by such rules or regulations as they may think fit, may declare to what extent and for what period the relief to be given to *able-bodied* persons or their families, in any particular parish or union, may be administered out of the workhouse of such parish or union, by payments in money, or with food or clothing in kind, or partly in kind and partly in money, and in what proportions, to what persons or class of persons, at what times and places, on what conditions, and in what manner such out-door relief may be afforded; and all other relief is declared unlawful, and consequently will be disallowed, with an exception in favour of special circumstances, upon which the overseers or guardians may make a report to the commissioners within 20 days, and whereof a special report shall be laid by the commissioners before one of the principal secretaries of state.

The rules promulgated by the commissioners in consequence of this enactment are very simple, nothing more or less in effect than that no able-bodied person, except in cases of sickness, accident, or infirmity, (in all which, as being exceptions from the general rule, the guardians have the power of assisting him with money, medicine, or food, and clothing,) will receive any pecuniary relief in aid of his wages from the poor's-rates, or any relief at all, without entering into the workhouse with his family.

By whom Relief is to be administered.—Relief to the poor of a parish, in *unions formed under the present act*, may be directed to be given by two justices usually acting for the district, who, at their just and proper discretion, may direct relief to be given to any adult person who shall, from old age or infirmity of body, *be wholly unable to work*, without requiring such person to reside in any workhouse, one of such justices also certifying of his own knowledge that such person is wholly unable to work; *s.* 27. But the giving or ordering relief to the poor generally in all cases belongs exclusively to the guardians of the poor, or select vestry, according to the provisions of those acts under which they have been appointed.

No overseer of the poor to give any further or other relief or allowance from the poor's-rate than such as shall be ordered by such guardians or select vestry, *except in cases of sudden and urgent necessity*, in which cases he is required to give such temporary relief as each case shall require, in articles of absolute necessity, *but not in money*, and whether the applicant for relief be settled in the parish where he shall apply for relief or not.

If such overseer neglect to give such necessary relief to poor persons not settled nor usually residing in the parish, any justice of the peace may order the overseer to give such temporary relief in articles of absolute necessity as the case shall require, *but not in money;* and in case such overseer shall disobey such order he shall, on conviction before two justices, forfeit any sum not exceeding *5l.* Any justice of the peace may also give a similar order for medical relief (only) to any parishioner as well as out-parishioner, where any case of sudden and dangerous illness may require it; and any overseer shall be liable to the same penalties for disobeying such order. But no justice shall order relief to any person except as herein provided; *s. 54.*

The present act also directs that relief in or at the workhouse be registered, as well as out-door relief, by the master of the workhouse or similar officer, and by the overseers; *s.* 55.

The act declares that the husband is liable for relief given to his wife, and the father is liable for relief given to any child under 16, not blind, or deaf and dumb; and a widow is in like manner liable, *i. e.* the relief is considered as being given to the husband, father, or widow.

The act also confirms the liability of parents to relieve and maintain their children not able to work, and children to maintain their parents in like manner, as before noticed.

A clause of a former *poor act* enabled parish officers to relieve any one, who, but for his extravagance or neglect, might have been able to maintain his family, by an advancement of a loan weekly or otherwise: the present act directs the commissioners to make such advancements, which, if given to any person above 21, or to his wife, or any part of his family under 16, is to be considered as a loan, whether any engagement of repayment shall be taken or not; and the wages of such person receiving relief, or to whom such relief shall be *considered* to have been paid, can be attached in the hands of his employer, under the 59th section of the present act.

So much of an act of 43 *G.* for the relief of militia-men, as enacted that relief should be given to the family of a militia-man in actual service, at a certain rate, is also by this act repealed; the effect of that provision familiarising magistrates and parish officers with the *allowance system* (the eradication of which is one of the great objects attained by the present act), and diminishing the shame of applications for parochial relief, is now repealed.

Apprentices.—By the original poor act of 43 *Eliz.*, the churchwardens and overseers (with consent of two justices) were enabled to bind poor children apprentices, till 24 if a male, and 21 or day of marriage if a female, and a variety of provisions have been made by subsequent acts in regard to these compulsory contracts. The present act now requires, that justices who approve and allow of such bindings do certify that the rules which the commissioners are at liberty to promulgate have been fully complied with, else such binding shall be void. The certificate is to be made *at the foot* of every such indenture.

Emigration.—The 62d and 63d sections provide for the facilitating the emigration of poor persons *having settlements* (of which next hereafter) in a parish.

Settlement is generally defined to be a right to demand relief in any parish or district which provides for its own poor, to which persons are removable, for the purpose of obtaining such relief by the order of justices. But no settlement can be obtained in a place having no overseers (such as the Inns of Court), nor can a poor person be removed from or to such a place. Therefore, every person born in England or Wales (except it be in an extra-parochial place, for which no overseers have been appointed,) is entitled to a settlement by birth or parentage.

The methods whereby a settlement can *now* be acquired are—1. Birth; 2. Parentage; 3. Marriage; 4. Apprenticeship; 5. Renting a tenement and paying a year's rate; 6. Estate; and 7. Payment of rates. Before the passing of the present act, there were two other methods of acquiring a settlement, viz. by hiring and service, and by serving office.

1. *Birth.*—The settlement by birth of legitimate children follows the settlement of the father, if it is known, if not, that of the mother: but, if the settlement of neither can be ascertained, the settlement of the child will be its birthplace; and, if that cannot be discovered, it must

be provided for in the place where it may happen to be, as casual poor.

The settlement of an illegitimate child follows that of its mother, until it shall attain the age of 16, or acquire a settlement in its own right, as by marriage.

By the present act, "any man marrying a woman having children, whether legitimate or illegitimate, is liable to maintain such children as part of his family until they attain 16, or until the death of the mother.

2. *Parentage.*—We have seen that the settlement of a child derived from its father changes with his, and that a setttlement derived from the mother also shifts with hers, while acquired by her own right; but this settlement is not communicable after the child has attained 21, or married, or by contracting some other relation which wholly excludes parental control; therefore, a minor cannot be in technical language "*emancipated,*" unless by marriage, or by acquiring a settlement in his own right.

3. *Marriage.*—If a woman marry a man who hath a known settlement she thereby acquires it as her settlement, whether she had a settlement before or not; and the same as to any new settlement he may have acquired until his death, and this whether she have ever lived with him in his settlement or not. During the marriage she cannot acquire any settlement in her own right distinct from his; or if the husband has none her's is suspended: after his death her settlement revives, *i. e.* she retains her previous settlement until she acquires a new one.

4. *Apprenticeship.*—If a person is bound an apprentice, and inhabit in any town or parish, such binding *and* inhabitation is a good settlement by various statutes; the settlement to be in the parish in which the apprentice resided during the last 40 days of the service; unless the binding be to a certificate-man, or the apprentice be a certificate-man in that parish, *i. e.* a certificate or acknowledgment from the parish from which a party likely to become chargeable removes, acknowledging that the party and his family are their legally settled inhabitants, which of course indemnifies the parish to which the certificated party removes from any burden he may bring upon it by reason of his removal thither.

5. *Renting a tenement, &c.*—The tenement (house, land, &c.,) must be rented or held of other persons, and not be the party's own freehold (see the next qualification): it should be a separate and distinct building, not lodgings or a portion of a house, and the party must be the sole occupier; but it is no objection if the tenement consist of several parcels, rented of different persons at different times, so that the total rents amount to 10*l.* and the whole be within the parish.

It must be rented and actually held or occupied, *not underlet,* by the party for 10*l.* a year for one whole year, and the rent actually paid; and there must also be a residence for 40 days in the parish, but not necessarily on the tenement or holding.

In addition to these requisites, the 60th section of the present act enacts, that *in future* no settlement shall be acquired or completed by occupying a tenement, unless the person occupying the same shall have been assessed to the poor's-rate, and shall have paid the same in respect of such tenement for one year.

6. *Estate.* — The estate may be freehold or copyhold, and holden by any tenure recognised by law. It may come to the party by descent, by conveyance, by marriage, or in any other manner than by buying it. The estate may consist of house or land; but an annuity, or a mere unexercised right of common in gross, will not confer a settlement; the value of the estate is immaterial.

To acquire a settlement thus by estate, it is not sufficient that he have an estate in the parish, but he must also reside upon it, or in the parish in which it is situate, during 40 days : the residence must be personal, *i. e.* by himself; for a residence by wife and children will not be sufficient. The residence may either be consecutive or at different times. It is not necessary, however, that he should occupy it himself: that may be done by his tenant; but the residence must then be within the parish wherein the estate is situate.

The 68th section of the present act, which, it should be remembered, is not retrospective, and does not affect settlements already obtained, provides that no person shall be deemed to retain any settlement gained by virtue of any estate, in any parish, for any longer or further time than he shall inhabit within ten miles thereof; and in case such person shall cease to inhabit within such distance, and thereafter become chargeable, such person shall be liable to be removed to the parish wherein previously to such inhabitancy he may have been legally settled, or in case he may have, subsequently to such inhabitancy, gained a legal settlement in some other parish then to such other parish.

The heir at law of an estate cannot acquire a settlement until he reduce it into possession.

7. *Payment of Rates.*—In order to gain a settlement, the party must be rated, and pay the rate. Where the landlord is rated, and the tenant pays, the latter does not gain a settlement: so that the rates be paid in the name of the tenant, it is sufficient; the payment need not actually be paid by him. The rates within the meaning of the statutes are the poor's-rate, church-rate, land-tax, and every public tax which is payable within a parochial limit. By statute, payment of the scavengers'-rate, highway-rate, house-duty, window-duty, or any of the assessed taxes, will not confer a settlement.

Maintenance of Bastards.— It has already been noticed that a bastard follows the settlement of the mother until it attain 16, or acquire a settlement in its own right; and that such mother, so long as she shall be unmarried or a widow, is bound to maintain such child as part of her family, until it shall attain 16, or until the marriage of such child, if a female.

The present act, after repealing the acts which render the father liable to be committed, &c., or the mother removable, punishable, &c., goes on to provide "that if, by reason of the inability of the mother to maintain such child, it becomes chargeable to the parish the overseers or guardians may apply to the next *general* quarter-sessions, after such child shall become chargeable, for an order upon the person whom they shall charge with being the putative father of such child to reimburse such parish or union for its maintenance."

The court (fourteen days' notice of the application having been given to the father) shall proceed to hear evidence thereon; and if it shall be satisfied, after hearing both parties, that the person so charged is really and in truth the father of such child it shall make such order in that respect as shall appear to be just.

But no such order shall be made unless the evidence of the mother of such bastard child shall be corroborated in some material particular by other testimony to the satisfaction of such court; and such order shall in no case exceed the actual expense incurred for the maintenance of such bastard child, and shall continue in force only until such child shall attain the age of 7 years; and no part of the monies paid by such putative father shall be paid to the mother of such bastard child, nor in any way be applied to the maintenance and support of such mother.

On the hearing of such application, the costs of the maintenance of such bastard child shall, in case the court shall think fit, be calculated from the birth of such bastard child, if such birth shall have taken place within six calendar months previous to such application being heard; but if such birth shall have taken place more than six calendar months then from the day of the commencement of six calendar months next preceding.

If the court shall not think fit to make any order, the full costs and charges incurred by the person so intended to be charged in resisting such application shall be paid by such overseers or guardians; *s.* 73.

On default of appearance of the person so intended to be charged, or his attorney, at the time when such application shall come on to be heard, the court shall nevertheless proceed to hear the same, unless such overseers or guardians shall produce an agreement under the hand of such person to abide by such order as such court shall make, without the hearing of evidence. But the court may, notwithstanding such agreement, require that evidence shall be given in support of such application.

A single justice has the power of summoning a putative father; and, if such justice shall be satisfied that he has any intention to abscond, he may be compelled to enter into a recognizance, and may be committed, in case of refusal, to the house of correction, till his compliance or till the hearing of the application.

The recovery of arrears one month due, in respect of an order for maintenance, is obtained by a single justice causing him to be brought before two justices, who, upon refusal or neglect, may proceed to recover the sum due and costs by distress and sale of his goods, or by attaching his wages in the hands of his employer.

Removal of a poor person. — As the law stood before the present act, when poor persons came into a parish to settle in a tenement under the yearly value of 10*l.* they might be removed to the place of their last legal settlement as soon as they became actually chargeable; in fact, no person could or can now be removed by an order of removal until they shall become actually chargeable. Rogues, vagabonds, and convicts are deemed actually chargeable, and liable to be removed.

To authorise a removal (where, as in the last instance, persons are not *ipso facto* chargeable) the poor person must not only ask for relief, but obtain it from one of the parish officers; but persons residing on their own estate are irremovable, however small the estate may be; and there are some relations which prevent a removal — thus, a married woman cannot be separated from her husband, though he be a foreigner having no settlement of his own, without their consent, otherwise, if she live apart from her husband; and a child within the age of nurture is not separable from the mother; and it seems that in many cases servants and apprentices cannot be removed from their masters without *mutual* consent; persons in extra-parochial places, or who have no place of settlement, are not removable. The practice is, when a pauper becomes chargeable, the officers of the parish or township should apply to the magistrates for an order to remove him; but, before the order is made, the pauper or other persons cognizant of the facts should be examined as to his settlement; whereupon, the justices, when satisfied by the evidence adduced before them that the pauper is become chargeable there, being legally settled in another place, ought to make their order for removal thither.

But no poor person shall be removed, under any order of removal from any parish or workhouse by reason of his being chargeable therein, until twenty-one days after a notice in writing of his being so chargeable or relieved, accompanied by a copy of the order of removal, and a copy of the examination upon which such order was made, shall have been sent, by post or otherwise, by the overseers or guardians, to the overseers of the parish to whom such order shall be directed. If such overseers or guardians as last aforesaid shall agree to submit to such order, such poor person, according to the tenor of such order, may be removed, although the period of twenty-one days may not have elapsed.

Provided, that if notice of appeal against such order of removal shall be received by the overseers or guardians of the parish, from which such poor person is directed in such order to be removed, within the said period of twenty-one days, it shall not be lawful to remove such poor person until after the time for prosecuting such appeal shall have expired, or, in case such appeal shall be duly prosecuted, until after the final determination of such appeal; *s.* 19.

Against this order of removal an appeal may be had to the next quarter-sessions either by the pauper, or, what is more commonly the case, by the parish officers, or any person who may think himself aggrieved; of which appeal 14 days' notice must be given, containing the motives and grounds of appeal, signed by the majority of the churchwardens and overseers, or by three guardians at least; and, at the trial of the appeal at the quarter-sessions, the appellants will not be allowed to give evidence of, or insist on any other grounds, except those stated in their notice.

The practice of these appeals against an order of removal does not always terminate at the quarter-sessions; for, if the court of quarter-sessions entertain a doubt of the legality of their decisions, it is their duty to grant a case for the opinion of the court of queen's bench, if requested to do so by counsel for the defeated party; *i. e.* a case to be settled by the counsel, which is argued in court the following term, or as soon after as can be; or, if the sessions do not grant a case, the original order made by the justices, and also the order of sessions on the appeal, may be removed by *certiorari* into the court of queen's bench, where they may be quashed, for defects appearing on the face of them; but 6 days' notice must be given to the justice or two of the justices who made the order, to the end that they may show cause, if they think fit, against the issuing thereof; and such notice is necessary even when a special case is granted. The application for the *certiorari* must be made within 6 months after the date of the order which it is intended to impugn.

When a final decision is made, the parish in which the pauper is adjudged to be settled is compellable to pay to the parish relieving the pauper all the expenses of relief administered by the latter, after the former had notice of the pauper becoming chargeable; and now, as the removing parish is bound to maintain the pauper until the appeal be decided, if notice of such appeal be given within 21 days after the order is made, and a copy thereof sent, it seems that, if the appellant parish be successful, neither party will have to pay costs of maintenance. The present act, however, gives the justices no authority respecting costs of maintenance; for such costs are recoverable as penalties and forfeitures, whether the appeal be tried or not.

The costs of appeal are allowable at the discretion of the justices; and, though the appellants do not appear, the justices may determine the appeal, and allow the respondent parish costs, or they may award costs incurred in consequence of frivolous or vexatious statements, without general costs of the appeal.

Penalties.—The present act prohibits the introduction of any spirituous or fermented liquor improperly into the workhouse, either by strangers or by the master of the workhouse, by a penalty of not less than 10*l.* payable by a stranger, and 20*l.* by the master of the workhouse, which latter person is subjected to a similar penalty for punishing corporally any adult, or confining any poor person longer than 24 hours, or any further space of time than is necessary for his being carried before a justice of the peace, and, in default of payment, imprisonment for not less than 6 months. Also, the act enjoins that the two clauses inflicting these penalties be printed or fairly written, and hung up in one of the most public places in the workhouse, on pain of forfeiting 10*l.*

Penalties are also inflicted upon overseers, masters of workhouses, and other officers, for disobeying rules or purloining goods. It also inflicts penalties upon persons wilfully neglecting or disobeying rules of the commissioners, or assistant-commissioners, or being guilty of a contempt of the commissioners sitting as a board; viz. for the first offence, a sum not exceeding 5*l.*; for the second offence, 20*l.*; and the third and subsequent offence is to be deemed a misdemeanor, and punishable with a fine not less than 20*l.*, and imprisonment with or without hard labour, at the discretion of the court.

All sums payable by parents and children, under the statute of 43 *Eliz.*, and other sums, are recoverable as penalties: it therefore behoves the reader to notice that these penalties and sums are recoverable before two justices of the peace, the party being first summoned thither by any commissioner, assistant-commissioner, or one justice of the peace, which justices are empowered to determine the matter or complaint, and to order the fines, penalties, and sums to be levied, with the costs, by distress and sale of the party's goods; also, if the sum is not forthcoming upon conviction, the justices can order a detention of the party until a return can be made of the distress warrant, unless security is given; and, if there should be no sufficient distress, then the party is to be committed to the common gaol or house of correction for not exceeding three calendar months.

An appeal is given to the quarter-sessions upon any conviction for a penalty or order for payment of a sum above 5*l.*, or in respect of any bastard child; and 14 days' notice is to be given, and a recognizance to be entered into within 5 days after notice, with sufficient securities to try the appeal, and abide by the order; upon which the justices may order costs; and their decision is to be deemed conclusive.

POOR-RATE. That rate or tax, which in the preceding article is noticed, to be raised by the statute 43 *Eliz.*, for the purpose of purchasing materials to set the poor on work, and to relieve the lame, blind, impotent, and unable to work, and for putting out poor children apprentices, and for other purposes relating thereto.

This rate is made by the churchwardens and overseers, with the consent of two justices, and must be published, the next Sunday after its allowance by the justices, in the church. To secure impartiality, the churchwardens and overseers are to permit every inhabitant to inspect the rate-book signed by them, at reasonable times, paying 1*s.*, and to give a copy at the rate of 6*d.* for every twenty-four names, under a penalty of 20*l.* to the party aggrieved, recoverable by action.

Overseers, where there are no churchwardens, may do all necessary acts relating to the poor and poor-rate.

The rate which the churchwardens and overseers are authorised to make must be assessed only on the visible property, both real and personal, which the occupier or owner may have within the parish, and not upon that which a person may have out of the parish. The general rule seems to be, that every species of property lying within the parish, and from which an *annual* profit arises, is rateable to the poor.

By a particular statute, provisions are made for rating the owners of houses let at rents from 6*l.* to 20*l.* *per annum* for less than a year, or at rents payable at a shorter period than 3 months; the goods of the occupier being made liable to the rate, which, if levied, may be deducted by the tenant from the rent.

The rate, when made, should be in equal proportion on all the parties assessed, in considering which, the overseers should take former assessments as their best guide; and, if any inequality arises, the justices in petty-sessions, and, ultimately, the quarter-sessions will correct it: the justices at sessions being the ultimate judges of the equality and due proportion. A pound rate upon the moiety of the yearly value of houses, and a rate upon three fourths of the yearly value of land, has been established as not disproportionate or unequal.

By an act which came into operation on 21st March 1837, being the 6 & 7 *W.* 4. *c.* 96., an uniform mode of making a rate for the relief of the poor is intended to be established. The poor-rate is to be made upon an estimate of the net annual value of property rateable, that is to say, of the rent at which the same might reasonably be expected to let from year to year, free of all usual tenants' rates and taxes, and tithe commutation rent-charge (if any), and deducting therefrom the probable average annual cost of the repairs, insurance, and other expenses necessary to maintain them in a state to command such rent; but the principles upon which property has hitherto been rateable are not altered.

The poor-law commissioners may, by their order, direct when this mode of estimate is to take effect; and with them it lies to cause surveys and valuations to be made for the purposes of the act.

Persons rated may take copies or extracts of rates gratis.

Appeals against parochial assessments, by those who state that they are improperly assessed to the poor-rate, are heard at a special sessions held by the justices for every petty sessions division, and appointed by them, notice being affixed at or near to the church door 28 days previous. An appeal is given from their decision to the quarter-sessions, the appellant, within 14 days after the decision, giving notice of appeal, and entering into a recognisance, with securities conditioned to try the same at the next sessions, and also giving 7 clear days notice previous to the session to the collector, overseers, or other persons making the rate.

In these appeals, the justices at quarter-sessions may award costs; but defects in mere form may be amended without costs; for the justices are to determine an appeal upon the merits of the case.

Parishes may be rated in aid, *i. e.* in assistance, of other parishes, unable to raise sufficient for the purposes of the poor.

A person not paying the rate assessed upon him must be summoned before 2 justices, who may, by their warrant, levy the arrears, and in default commit the defaulter till payment.

The following is the form of rate according to the act: —

An assessment for the relief of the poor of the parish of *Merton*, in the county of *Surrey*, and for other purposes chargeable thereon according to law, made this *thirtieth* day of *March*, in the year of our Lord, one thousand eight hundred and *thirty-seven*, after the rate of *sixpence* in the pound.

No.	Arrears due, or if excused.	Name of Occupier.	Name of Owner.	Description of Property rated.	Name or Situation of Property.	Estimated Extent.	Gross estimated Rental.	Rate-able Value.	Rate at 6*d*. in the Pound.
	£ s. d.					A. R. P.	£ s. d.	£ s. d.	£ s. d.
1	- - -	James Smith	John Green	Land and Buildings	Whiteacre Farm	40 0 0	60 0 0	55 0 0	1 7 6
2	- - -	Ditto	Ditto	House and Garden	In West Street	0 1 0	30 0 0	25 0 0	0 12 6
3	- - 7½ Excused	John Poor	Ditto	House -	In Brick Lane	- - -	1 10 0	1 5 0	0 0 7½
&c.	&c.	&c.	&c.	&c.	&c.	&c.	&c.	&c.	&c.

We, *Thomas Jones, John Thomas, and William Atkins* do declare the several particulars specified in the respective columns of the above rate to be true and correct, so far as we have been able to ascertain them, to which end we have used our best endeavours.

Thomas Jones, Overseer.
John Thomas, } Churchwardens.
William Atkins, }

POPULAR ACTION. An action given by statute to any one who will sue for the penalty.

PORTERS AND PORTERAGE. Porters are persons employed to carry messages and parcels. In London they are divided into different classes.

The 39 *Geo.* 3. *c.* 58. enacts, that the following rates shall be the maximum charge upon all parcels not exceeding 56 lbs. weight, in London and the suburbs; viz.—

		s.	d.
For any distance not exceeding	¼ of a mile -	0	3
	½ a mile -	0	4
	1 mile -	0	6
	1½ mile -	0	8
	2 miles -	0	10

And the additional sum of 3*d.* for every further ½ mile.

Tickets are to be made out at the inns and given to the porters, who are to deliver them with the parcels; and any innkeeper not making out such tickets to forfeit not exceeding 40*s.* nor less than 5*s.* The non-delivery or defacing the ticket subjects the porter to a fine of 40*s.* Porters overcharging forfeit 20*s.*

Parcels brought by coach are to be delivered within 6 hours, if brought by wagon, within 24 hours, under a penalty of 20*s.*, reducible to 10*s.*; and if parcels are directed to be left till called for they are to be delivered accordingly, with only 2*d.* charge for warehouse-room, and 1*d.* for every week after the first, or fractional time may also be charged; misbehaviour, and non-delivery of parcels, to be punished by a fine, which one justice may inflict, of 20*s.*, reducible to 5*s.*, and of 20*s.*, reducible to 10*s.*, for non-delivery of a parcel to the person calling for it.*

* As the act gives special remedies in favour of the porter, in case of non-payment of the porterage, it seems he cannot retain the parcel or luggage as a lien for his charges.

Tackle-house porters have the privilege of unshipping the produce of the plantations and Ireland, and goods coastwise. They give bond for 500*l*., and are regulated by the corporation of London.

Ticket-porters also have a similar privilege of unshipping goods brought from what is termed the East country, which the tackle-house porters are not privileged to exclusively perform, as well as all other goods brought to London, save lead. They are freemen of London, have a metal or silver badge, and give 100*l*. bond for good behaviour.

Any person may bring goods to London, but the porters of London are the only persons who may take and carry them within the city; and this privilege is protected by a fine.

The ticket-porters are second to the tackle-house porters, who, if there be no ticket-porters in attendance, may employ other labourers.

POSSE COMITATUS. The power of the county, which includes the aid and attendance of all persons of the degree or wealth of a knight (the *title*, in its legal sense, is dispensed with), including all persons of lower quality, and men above 15, within the county; and this *posse* the sheriff may raise to the assistance of the justices, upon apprehension or happening of any riot or breach of the peace.

Justices may also raise the *posse*.

Persons refusing to attend, when charged by the sheriff or a justice, are indictable for a misdemeanor.

POSTEA. Afterwards: the return of the judge's associate, indorsed on the transcript or *record* of the pleadings taken down to the assizes, or to the sittings in London or Middlesex, stating the verdict, or nonsuit, as the case may be, commencing "afterwards, on such a day, &c." When the proceedings were in Latin, the word "Postea" was the initial word, from whence this return has its name. It is upon sight of this "postea" that the master or prothonotary taxes the costs of the plaintiff or defendant; the damages, if any, being mentioned in the *postea;* and he makes a memorandum thereof, with his signature upon or at the foot of the *postea*, thus—

	£	s.	d.
Damages - - -	30	10	0
Costs - - -	2	0	0
Increase costs - -	38	0	0
In all £	70	10	0

POST-OFFICE. By the Act of the 1 *Vict. c.* 36. *s.* 2., every person who despatches or sends, or causes to be sent, or tenders or delivers in order to be sent, otherwise than by post, a letter not exempted from the exclusive privilege of the postmaster-general (hereafter named), forfeits *for every letter five pounds.*

Every person who receives, takes up, or collects any letter not exempted from the exclusive privilege of the postmaster-general forfeits *for every letter five pounds.*

Every person who conveys otherwise than by post, or delivers a letter not exempted from the exclusive privilege of the postmaster-general, forfeits *for every letter five pounds.*

Every person who makes a collection of exempted letters, for the purpose of conveying or sending them otherwise than by post, *or even by the post*, forfeits *for every letter five pounds.* And every person who is in the *practice* of committing *any* of the above mentioned acts forfeits for *every week* during which the practice is continued *one hundred pounds.*

By the 13th section, pecuniary penalties incurred under the Post Office Acts, not exceeding 20*l.*, may be recovered in a summary way before a justice of the peace, by *any person* who will sue for the same; one moiety whereof will belong to the crown, and the other moiety, *with full costs of suit*, to the person who informs and prosecutes.

Magistrates, clerks of the peace, and town-clerks, are to pay over and remit the crown's share of the penalties, in strict conformity to the directions of the 16th section.

The following letters are exempted from the exclusive privilege of the postmaster-general; viz., letters sent by a private friend in his way, journey, or travel, if delivered by such friend to the party to whom they shall be directed; letters sent by a messenger on purpose; commissions or returns thereof, and affidavits and writs, process or proceedings, or returns thereof, issuing out of a court of justice; letters sent out of the United Kingdom by a private vessel; letters of merchants, owners of vessels of merchandise, or of the cargo or loading therein sent by such vessels, or in charge of any person employed by such owners for the carriage of such letters, according to their respective directions, and delivered to the respective persons to whom they shall be directed, without paying or receiving hire or reward, or other advantage or profit for the same; letters concerning goods or merchandise sent by common known carriers to be delivered with the goods, without hire or reward, or other profit or advantage, for receiving or delivering such letters.

But the following persons are expressly forbidden to carry a letter, or to receive, or collect, or deliver a letter, although they shall not receive hire or reward for the same; viz., common known carriers, their servants or agents, except a letter concerning goods in their carts or wagons, or on their packhorses; and owners, drivers, or guards of stage-coaches.

POUND. A place of strength, inclosed, wherein to keep cattle, distrained for rent or for damage feasant, until they are redeemed or replevied. Common pounds are termed pounds *overt, i. e.* open: any place where cattle or goods are kept, being part of a dwelling-house or outhouse, barn, or stable are called pounds *covert, i. e.* close. If cattle are put in a pound overt the owner is bound to feed them; if in a pound covert the distrainer. If cattle are put into a common pound no notice is necessary; but otherwise, if the impounding be in a pound-covert: any person distraining goods or cattle can use any secure place, even part of the premises where the things are taken, as a pound for securing the distress.

Pound-breach, or rescuing cattle from the pound, and goods distrained, subjects the parties to an action and treble costs; it is also an indictable offence, being a misdemeanor, punishable by fine or imprisonment, or both, according to the circumstances.

A pound-keeper is bound to receive every thing offered to his custody, and is not answerable for the legality of the impounding.

POWER. An authority which one man gives another to act for him: it is also a term commonly applied to reservations made in a conveyance for persons to do some certain acts, as to make leases, raise portions, create a jointure, charge, sell, or exchange, which are chiefly inserted in marriage-settlements and wills, and technically distinguished as "powers of revocation and appointment," all of them postponing, abridging, or defeating, in a greater or less degree, the previous uses and estates, and appointing new uses in their stead. Also a man may by deed or will give an estate to such persons as another shall appoint or direct.

By a *general* power of appointment is legally understood that kind of power which enables the party to appoint the estate to any person he thinks proper; and in this sense it is opposed to a qualified or *particular* power, which enables the party to appoint to or among particular objects only; as a power of appointing to his children, or the children of any other person. The former has been termed a power of Ownership,—the latter, a power of Selection. *Butler's Notes on Co. Lytt.* s. 463., 472. n. Estates created by powers, and estates created by conveyances, are after their creation the same. The deed expressing the operation of a power is termed an "appointment," and such deed of appointment has relation to the will or deed creating the power, and such *execution* of a power should conform to the words of the power; equity, however, will in many cases relieve the *defective* execution of a power, though not the *non-execution* of a power.

Contingent or future uses or trusts, which depend upon the designation of the party having the power of appointment, are termed simply "powers" while they are in suspense, though afterwards, upon the operation of the power, they become "estates."

The doctrine of powers is connected with some of the most abstruse learning in the law of property. It would be extremely difficult in a work of this nature to fully illustrate their general principles and application.

PRACTICE is the form and manner of conducting and carrying on suits at law, or in equity, or in criminal procedure, according to the principles of law and the rules of the courts.

As suits are prosecuted and defended chiefly by the attorneys and solicitors of the courts, the public are but little acquainted with the practice of the courts, except as to those things that are *visible*, such as trial by jury, or the jurisdiction the courts exercise upon applications made to them by motion, or, in equity, by petition or motion, which are proceedings of a summary nature, and particularly referable to that head. See Motion to the Court.

The proceedings in criminal matters, or crown causes, are simple, and are partially treated of under the titles Justices of the peace, Information, Indictment, as well as in this article.

The practice of the courts, therefore, may be divided into three divisions; viz. 1. The practice of the courts of law. 2. The practice of the courts of equity. 3. Proceedings at assizes or sessions, on indictments for felony or misdemeanor.

1. The process which brings a party into court in an action at law is either bailable or non-bailable, being the *capias* and the *writ of summons*. The capias causes the conditional or provisional arrest of the party: the writ of summons compels a party to enter an appearance in the books of the court, within 8 days after service upon him personally, or, in his default, the plaintiff may do it for him, and proceed as if he had appeared. If a defendant cannot be found, so as to be arrested on the capias, the writ must be renewed every 4 months till he is taken; and the same method may be observed with respect to a writ of summons, if the plaintiff chooses; but another process can be had recourse to, called a writ of *distringas*, to obtain which, every endeavour must be previously made to effect personal service; and the judge or court who grants it must be convinced that the defendant purposely avoids personal service: by this writ the goods of the defendant can be distrained

upon to the value of 40*s.*; and after this has been done, or in case the sheriff returns that the defendant has no goods, and the defendant does not *appear*, the plaintiff may enter an appearance for him, and proceed to execution. When a party who is arrested has *put in* bail to the action, he is considered as having appeared, and the action proceeds by filing a *declaration*, stating his cause of action according to the rules and course of pleading, which must be done in a certain time, else the defendant may, after a short notice, put the plaintiff out of court, technically called "entering judgment of *non pros.*," and recover his costs. The declaration being delivered, and the plaintiff's attorney having demanded a plea, the defendant pleads to the action, demurs, or lets judgment go against him by default.

Demurring is where the defendant admits the facts, but asks the opinion of the court as to the validity of the pleading, either in form or substance; and this may be done at any stage of the proceedings upon each pleading, as causes of *demurrer* arise, by plaintiff or defendant. The judges either allow the demurrer, and give the defendant his costs, or permit the plaintiff to amend (if the error be in form only), with or without payment of costs, at their discretion.

If the defendant lets judgment go by default, he (unless the action is in *debt* or *detinue*) thereby admits a claim to a certain extent; but, as the claim in the declaration is stated at a gross or nominal sum as damages, it is referred to the sheriff to inquire, by means of a jury, what damages the plaintiff has sustained, which he does by virtue of the writ of inquiry which issues after an *interlocutory* judgment has been signed for want of plea. When the jury have assessed the damages, a *final* judgment is obtained, upon which execution issues against the defendant's goods or person.

In actions of debt and detinue, which are actions brought to recover a sum or thing certain, if the defendant does not plead, *final* judgment is obtainable immediately; but this distinction, though based on the distinction that a debt is certain, and damages uncertain, is practically bad, as the plaintiff can issue execution without the intervention of a jury, and the debt is stated at a formal and gross sum, as in actions *on promises*, on the *case*, &c.; but, if the plaintiff takes more than he is actually entitled to under his writ of execution, he is amenable in damages.

If the defendant pleads, by his attorney delivering his plea to the plaintiff's attorney, the plaintiff either replies, *i. e.* delivers a *replication*, or draws and delivers his *issue*, which is done when, at any stage of the pleadings after plea, certain facts, material, and arising from the declaration, appear as expressly alleged or denied, technically termed *at issue:* upon this a transcript of the whole pleadings is made out, and the cause is tried before a judge at assizes, or before a judge at the sittings in London or Middlesex, the sheriff having been warned by writs called *venire facias juratores*, and *habeas* or *distringas corpora juratorum*, to produce a common or special jury to try the issue, viz. the material facts, between the parties, which are in artificial and legal language put upon record, and witnesses are summoned by writs of subpœna to give evidence accordingly.

It must be observed, however, if the debt be under 20*l.*, and the claim does not involve any difficult point of law, the issue is tried by an analogous process, termed a "Writ of Trial," before the sheriff of the county, who returns the process (which authorises him to try the issue before a jury) in the same manner as a writ of inquiry to assess damages upon a judgment by default; and judgment is signed, and execution issued, accordingly.

2. The proceedings in a suit in the *courts of equity* are commenced by filing a bill, which is carefully and artificially drawn, stating all circumstances of the plaintiff's case, with times, dates, and other incidents, in which are contained interrogatories or questions, which the defendant must answer: and this bill, which is drawn as a petition to the chancellor, or lord-keeper, or chancellor of the exchequer, prays relief thereupon.

There are a variety of *bills*, suitable for various cases. The *original* bill, or common bill, praying a remedy upon an ordinary subject for relief: bill of *interpleader*, where two or more seeking the same thing require the adjudication of the court, or a third party claims indemnity against various claimants: *certiorari* bill, to remove a cause from an inferior court of equity, such as the chancery of the duchy of Lancaster, or Durham, &c.: bill *to perpetuate testimony of witnesses*, when witnesses are aged, sick, or likely to die, or are going abroad, so that their testimony, to be taken upon interrogatories, may be preserved: bill of *discovery*, for discovery of deeds, facts, &c. in the knowledge of a defendant: this is used for the purpose of producing the defendant's answer in another court, or to assist the interference of another court: *amended* bill, is an addition of some new matter subsequently discovered in an *original* bill, or the bill where the amendments are numerous is engrossed *de novo*: *supplemental* bill is when the suit has progressed, and new matter must be stated in aid of the original or amended bill: bill of *revivor* is for the purpose of continuing a pending suit by or against the representatives of a deceased party: *cross* bill is for a plaintiff in another suit to be examined on behalf of a defendant who seeks to be heard or relieved in that suit: these are mostly heard together if practicable: bill of *review* is for the purpose of reversing a previous decree: bill *to carry a decree into execution* is for the purpose of carrying a previous decree into execution, where, by the terms of the decree, it is impracticable to do so without further directions or assistance. There is also the bill *of information*, filed by the attorney-general in respect to rights of the crown, and for the carrying public charities, &c., into execution.

The bill being filed, a writ of subpœna is issued; upon which the defendant must enter an appearance; for, if he do not appear and put in his answer, an *attachment* will be issued against him for the contempt; upon which he will be committed to the Fleet till he put in his answer; and, if he still refuse, the decree will be made according to the prayer of the bill; but the defendant must first have appeared or been in custody.

The defendant's answer is analogous to the plea in an action at law; for the defendant may either simply deny or confess the contents of the bill; or he may *disclaim*, *i. e.* deny all title or interest to the thing in demand; or he may *demur*, *i. e.* shew that the plaintiff has not equity, *i. e.* that the facts stated in the bill are insufficient for the purpose of compelling an answer. There are also *pleas* in equity, which are in the nature of pleas in *abatement* or *in bar* at law, the defendant either insisting that the court has no jurisdiction, or showing matter in bar of the plaintiff's suit, outlawry of the plaintiff, or any disability he is under from seeking the relief of a court of equity.

The plaintiff, having obtained the defendant's answer, enters a formal *replication*, which in effect puts the suit at issue; and thereupon the examination of witnesses on behalf of each party takes place by examiners of the court, or by commissioners, if the witnesses live in the country, who are compellable to attend, as in the case of actions and trials at law. The evidence of the witnesses is taken down in writing by the examiners or commissioners, and the questions and answers are given out to the opposite parties, who do the like on their side. The cause is set down for a *hearing;* upon which the court makes a *decree,* which generally refers all matters to the consideration of a master of the court, who is to make his report, or the court will, if the question arise upon a matter of fact, direct an issue to be tried by a jury, for the event of which the court reserves its judgment.

In the master's office the matters are investigated according to the terms of the decree, which are very often matters of account and law mixed; as to inquire how much a testator died worth, to ascertain his debts and incumbrances, and to marshal the assets, to make inquiry for the next of kin, &c.; in partnership suits, to take accounts; in foreclosure suits, to compute principal and interest, &c. When the master has come to a decision, he certifies or reports to the court how the matters referred to him generally appear, or he otherwise informs the court of special matters; the one is styled a *general report,* the other a *special report:* upon this (if neither party *except* to, *i. e.* call in question, the master's report for insufficiency or other reason,) the cause is again set down for what is termed *further directions,* whereupon the report is confirmed, and a final reference is awarded to the master to tax all parties their costs, &c.; and this is generally the conclusion of the suit, which, it should be remembered, is not extinguished, as the court, having the funds under its control, as in trusts, &c., will have afterwards to make orders in reference to matters springing out of the suit, till the funds are completely distributed, so that a suit may be in existence for many years, though practically the court awarded the direction of the money or estates forming the subject of the suit in a very short period.

It may be observed, that (besides the above) there are numerous interlocutory proceedings and orders made; for the court is called upon frequently to make special orders on particular matters consequent upon the suit, which cannot be further noticed in a summary like the present.

3. In most cases of felony and misdemeanor, the prisoner has been committed by a magistrate, and the prosecutor bound over to prosecute; or the prisoner may have been bailed, or under recognisance to appear at the next sessions or assizes, or, if within 10 miles of London, at the central criminal court: but it is not absolutely necessary that the party should first be in custody; for a prosecutor may, if he choose, commence his prosecution by preferring an indictment without any other preliminary. However, in common cases of felony and misdemeanor, where the prisoner has been committed, the clerk of indictments prepares the proper indictment, he looking at the depositions which have been returned to the court by the committing magistrates: on the back of the indictment the names of the witnesses are written: sometimes the indictment is framed by some barrister or crown-draftsman, in which case the clerk of indictments only *passes* it, and takes his fee, just as if he had drawn it.

The indictment or bill, fairly engrossed, is taken before the grand jury; and they, having heard the evidence of the witnesses (indorsed on the bill), settle amongst themselves how far a *primâ facie* case is made out, sufficient to call upon the prisoner to answer it: if they think the charge is primarily substantiated, it is their duty to *find the bill*, or to return *a true bill;* otherwise to *ignore* it, or throw it out.

If the prisoner is in custody, he will be arraigned and put upon his trial directly; if not in custody, a *bench-warrant* can be obtained for his apprehension.

A prisoner indicted for felony at some former session or assizes must give the prosecutor four clear days' notice of his intention to take his trial, such notice to expire before the session or assizes; at which time, if the prosecutor and his witnesses do not appear, the prisoner will be acquitted.

The pleading of the prisoner is by word of mouth, and "not guilty*;" an issue which puts the prosecutor to the proof of the matters as laid in the indictment.

Persons indicted for felony, and committed a very short time before the session or assizes, may postpone their trial, by showing that the absence of a material witness, to whom notice could not be given, impedes the course of their defence.

And in cases of *misdemeanor* (except for keeping bawdy, gaming, or disorderly houses), if a party, who has not been committed or bailed 20 days before the session or assizes, does not choose to be tried the next session or assizes, he may *traverse* the indictment till the next session or assizes; but if he requires to be liberated from custody, he must, on *traversing*, appear in court with his sureties, who, if found sufficient, sign the recognisance, and the defendant, having pleaded "not guilty," departs; and

At the next sessions the *traverse* is tried.

The trial for felony is commenced by the clerk of the court calling over the names of the persons to be sworn as jurors, in the prisoner's presence, asking the prisoner whether he objects to any of them, (for he is at liberty to challenge or reject 20 without giving any reason, or more with sufficient cause allowed;) and when 12 jurymen are sworn the trial proceeds. In cases of misdemeanor, the prisoner can only *challenge* for cause shown.

The case against the accused is stated by the prosecutor's counsel, who proceeds to examine the witnesses in support of the same, and these are cross-examined by the accused or his counsel. When the case for the prosecution is closed, the prisoner or his counsel addresses the jury, and examines witnesses for the defence; to which the prosecutor's counsel has the right of addressing the jury in reply, if witnesses have been called for the defence, except for the purpose of proving the prisoner's character; for, if the defence rests entirely on cross-examination and character, the prisoner or his counsel has the last word. The judge then sums up, and the jury return a verdict. If the verdict be "guilty," the court pronounces its sentence.

If the proceedings are erroneous upon the face of them, the convict may have a writ of error, and obtain thereby a reversal of his conviction. If he is convicted upon false evidence, or a misdirection of the judge, the secretary of state must be informed of it, as it is only by grace that a pardon can be obtained.

* If the prisoner has been previously tried and acquitted for the same offence, or has been tried and found guilty or acquitted on a former ocsasion, he must plead those facts, and prove them by the record of the former indictments. The plea of the acquittal is termed *autrefois acquit*.

PRÆMUNIRE. Whenever it is said that a person by any act incurs a *præmunire*, it is meant to express that he thereby incurs the penalty "of being out of the king's protection; and his lands and tenements, goods and chattels, are forfeited to the king, and that his body shall remain in prison during the king's pleasure;" but these forfeitures never denoted a felony, though the party was in effect outlawed. This penalty attached in former times upon the offences of asserting the jurisdiction of the pope, denying the king's supremacy, and, latterly, to enormous offences or acts which required a severe or discretionary punishment; such as for setting up a bubble (since repealed), transgressing the statute of *habeas corpus*, refusing the oath of allegiance, &c. A prosecution on the part of the crown for the severe penalties of a *præmunire* has not been heard of for upwards of a century; and upon a criminal information against a party for setting up a bubble, it was determined that the court was not bound by the bubble-act to give the whole judgment, but only such part as to them seemed proper; therefore the defendant was fined 5*l.*, and remained in prison at the king's pleasure: and, as the king by his prerogative may remit the whole, it is not likely that this process will be again used, except any public officer transgress the *habeas corpus* act, in which case the king cannot use his prerogative and remit the penalty, which, in that case, would extend to imprisonment during life.

On an indictment of præmunire, a peer of the realm shall not be tried by his peers.

PRE-AUDIENCE, or precedence of serjeants and barristers, is of some practical importance. It is settled as follows:—

1. The King's Advocate-General.
2. The King's Attorney-General.
3. The Lord Advocate of Scotland.
4. The King's Solicitor-General.
5. The King's Premier Serjeant.
6. The King's Ancient Serjeant, or the eldest of the King's Serjeants.
7. The King's Serjeants.
8. The King's Counsel, and counsel having patents of precedence before the 24th of April, 1834, according to seniority, with the Queen's Attorney and Solicitor.
9. Serjeants named in a royal warrant of 24th of April, 1834, which comprised all the Serjeants at law at present in practice.
10. Two Serjeants at law not practising at the bar, (and therefore not named in the royal warrant of 1834,) and Serjeants who may hereafter be created.
11. The Recorder of London.
12. The Common Serjeant of London.
13. The Advocates of the Civil Law.
14. The Barristers at large, according to the dates of their call to the bar.

In the court of exchequer, two barristers called the *post-man* and the *tub-man* (from the places where they sit) have a precedence in motions. See MOTION IN COURT.

PREBEND AND PREBENDARY. A prebend is a benefice appropriated for the maintenance of a *clerk*, or member of a collegiate or cathedral church. This benefice is land, or a manor, and is called after the name of the possession: as the prebend of Cantellows, prebend of Iseldon, &c. Prebendary is the *clerk* or clergyman, who is one of the chapter or council of the dean who enjoys this benefice.

PRECEDENCE. Degrees of superiority amongst the nobility, who are all peers, *i. e.* equal, as being of the greater nobility; and amongst the commoners, of whose lesser nobility the law takes no notice, they being all peers, *i. e.* equals, in the eye of the law. Many of the following degrees are established by ancient usage, some by letters patent or statute:—

TABLE OF PRECEDENCE.

The King's children and grandchildren.
——— brethren.
——— uncles.
——— nephews.
Archbishop of Canterbury.
Lord Chancellor or Keeper, if a Baron.
Archbishop of York.
Lord Treasurer. } if Barons.
Lord Pres. of the Council. } if Barons.
Lord Privy Seal. } if Barons.
Lord Great Chamberlain. But see private act 1 *G.* 1. c. 3. } Above all peers of their own degree.
Lord High Constable. } Above all peers of their own degree.
Lord Marshal. } Above all peers of their own degree.
Lord Admiral. } Above all peers of their own degree.
Lord Steward of the Household. } Above all peers of their own degree.
Lord Chamberlain of the Household. } Above all peers of their own degree.
Dukes.
Marquesses.
Dukes' eldest sons.
Earls.
Marquisses' eldest sons.
Dukes' younger sons.
Viscounts.
Earls' eldest sons.
Marquisses' younger sons.
Secretary of State, if a Bishop.
Bishop of London.
——— Durham.
——— Winchester.
Bishops.
Secretary of State, if a Baron.
Barons.
Speaker of the House of Commons.
Lords Commissioners of the Great Seal.
Viscounts' eldest sons.
Earls' younger sons.
Barons' eldest sons.
Knights of the Garter.
Privy Counsellors.
Chancellor of the Exchequer.
Chancellor of the Duchy of Lancaster.
Chief Justice of the King's Bench.
Master of the Rolls.
Chief Justice of the Common Pleas.
Chief Baron of the Exchequer.
Judges, and Barons of the Coif.
Knights Bannerets, Royal.
Viscounts' younger sons.
Barons' younger sons.
Baronets.
Knights Bannerets.
Knights of the Bath. Enlarged in 1815, and distinguished as Knights Grand Crosses, and Knights Commanders; thus abbreviated: K.G. C.B. and K.C.B.
Knights Bachelors.
Baronets' eldest sons.
Knights' eldest sons.
Baronets' younger sons.
Knights' younger sons.
Colonels.
Serjeants at Law.
Doctors: — With whom, it is said, rank Barristers at Law: as to whose precedence among each other, see PRE-AUDIENCE.
Esquires (of whom Companions of the Bath rank first).
Gentlemen.
Yeomen.
Tradesmen.
Artificers.
Labourers.

Married women and widows are entitled to the same rank among each other, as their husbands would respectively have borne between themselves; except such rank is merely professional or official: — and unmarried women to the same rank as their eldest brothers would bear among men, during the lives of their fathers. 3 *Blackst. Comm.* c. 21. p. 405. in note.

PRECEDENTS. Authorities to follow in determinations in courts of justice.

PREDIAL TITHES. Tithes paid of things arising and growing from the ground only, as corn, hay, fruit of trees, and such like. See TITHES.

PREFERENCE. A fraudulent preference in law is a transfer of money or other subject of value to a creditor, with the intention in the mind of the debtor of preventing the law of bankruptcy operating over his effects, in the distribution of them for the equal benefit of all his creditors. Such act, however *moral* in intention, and notwithstanding the creditor is in the highest degree meritorious, in law is a fraud. To amount to a fraudulent transfer, it must be made in contemplation of bankruptcy or insolvency, *and* voluntary or spontaneous, or *not in the usual course of business;* which, after all, is the chief point for jurymen to consider, when they have to consider a verdict involving this consideration.

PREGNANCY (PLEA OF). Where a woman is capitally convicted, and pleads her pregnancy, though this is no cause to stay the judgment, yet it is to respite the execution, till she is delivered.

PREMISES. That part, in the beginning of a deed, the office of which is to express the grantor and grantee, and the land or thing granted or conveyed.

PREMIUM (*Præmium*). A reward. Among merchants it is used for the money the insured gives the insurer for insuring the safe return of any ship or merchandise. See INSURANCE.

PREPENSED. Forethought: as prepensed malice is, which makes killing murder; and when a man is slain on a sudden quarrel, if there were malice prepensed previously between the parties, it is prepensed murder. See HOMICIDE.

PREROGATIVE, from *præ* and *rogo*, to ask or demand before or above others. A word of large extent, including all the rights which, by law, the king has as chief of the kingdom, and as entrusted with the execution of the laws.

PREROGATIVE COURT. The court in which all wills are proved and administrations taken out, where the testator or intestate had goods in *divers dioceses;* the archbishop of the province having the *prerogative* of proving the will and granting administration. The two *prerogative* courts are those of the archbishops of Canterbury and York.

PRESCRIPTION is a title or right to a thing, existing substantially from usage and time by the authority of the law. In contemplation of law, every prescription supposes a grant once made and afterwards lost.

Rights by prescription are often confounded with *custom;* prescription being annexed to a particular person, and custom being a local usage not annexed to the person: such as a custom that all the copyholders of a manor should have common of pasture upon a particular waste. Prescription being annexed to a particular person is of two sorts; either a personal right, used and enjoyed by a man and his ancestors, or a right attached to the ownership, and going along with particular prescription lands.

By the act 2 & 3 *W.* 4. *c.* 71., a period of limitation for bringing actions and suits for the establishment of "incorporeal rights" (the usual subjects of prescriptive title), in which are not included rents or tithes, has been settled.

1. By making the enjoyment of any right of common, or other profit or benefit from or upon land (except tithes and rent), without interruption for 30 years, *primâ facie* evidence of a right, liable to be rebutted by proof, that during that time the owner of the land was under what is termed "disability," (*i. e.* minority; being married, if a woman; being out of the kingdom, and lunacy, &c.); and by making such enjoyment for 60 years *conclusive* evidence of a right, unless it appear to have been with some consent *in writing.*

2. By making the enjoyment of any way, or other easement or watercourse, or the use of water, without interruption for 20 years, *primâ facie* evidence of a right, liable to be rebutted by proof that the owner of the land was under legal "disability;" and by making such enjoyment for 40 years *conclusive* evidence of the right, unless it appear to have been with some consent in writing.

3. By making the enjoyment of lights for 20 years *conclusive* evidence of a right, unless it appear to have been had by some consent or agreement in writing.

The most known and frequent subjects of *prescription* are the following rights annexed to land, styled "incorporeal" hereditaments: (viz.) right of common, or other profit out of land, and those rights without profit which are called *easements*, viz. right of way, watercourses, pews, and lights, being conveniences possessed by one man, to be enjoyed in the land of another. These annexations to land being the subject of grant are either held by grant or deed under seal, or by virtue of a prescription, which after the 60, 40, and 20 years, in the first, second, and third instances above noticed, is *conclusive* evidence of a grant and the loss of it. The rights to waifs, strays, wreck, warren, park, treasure-trove, royal fishes, fairs, markets, franchises, and tolls are also incorporeal hereditaments, but being manorial rights, generally speaking, are pretty well evidenced by rolls and records; but these, as well as all prescriptive rights, will be lost by non-user, or by suffering any interruption of right to intervene by the possession or user of adverse parties. Prescriptions in favour of *moduses* for tithes have been settled by another act.* See TITHES.

In all conveyances, surveys, terriers, &c., all rights or *easements* should be carefully noticed, and acknowledgments of right obtained.

PRESENTMENT. An information made by the jury in a court, before a judge who hath authority to punish an offence. 2 *Inst.* 739.

The presentment is drawn up in English by the jury, in a short note, for instructions to draw the indictment by; and differs from an indictment in that an indictment is drawn up at large, and brought ingrossed to the grand jury to find. 2 *Lill. Abr.* 353.

There are also presentments of justices of peace in their sessions, of offences against statutes, in order to their punishment in superior courts; and presentments taken before commissioners of sewers, &c. Presentments are made in courts-leet and courts-baron, before stewards; and, in the latter, of surrenders, grants, &c.: also, by constables, churchwardens, surveyors of the highways, &c. of things belonging to their offices.

A presentment, generally taken, is a very comprehensive term; including not only presentments, properly so called, but also inquisitions of office, and indictments by a grand jury. A presentment, properly speaking, is the notice taken by a grand jury of any offence from their own knowledge or observation, without any bill of indictment laid before them at the suit of the king. *Lamb. Eiren.* l. 4. c. 5. — As the presentment of a nuisance, a libel, and the like; upon which the officer of the court must afterwards frame an indictment, before the party presented can be put to answer it. 2 *Inst.* 739. An inquisition of office is the act of a jury, summoned by the proper officer to inquire of matters relating to the crown, upon evidence laid before them. Some of these are in themselves convictions, and cannot afterwards be traversed or denied; and therefore the inquest or jury ought to hear all that can be alleged on both sides. Of this nature are all inquisitions of *felo de se*, of deodands, and the like; and presentments of petty officers in the sheriff's-tourn or court-leet, whereupon the presiding officer may set a fine. Other inquisitions may be after-

* The stat. 2 & 3 *W.* 4. *c.* 71. *s.* 4. expressly declares that an interruption shall be deemed immaterial, unless acquiesced in for a year after the party interrupted shall have had notice of the interruption, and of the person making the same. This act came into operation on 2d Nov., 1833.

wards traversed or examined; as particularly the coroner's inquisition of the death of a man, when he finds any one guilty of homicide.

PRESENTMENT OF A BILL OR NOTE. See BILL OF EXCHANGE.

PRESENTATION TO A LIVING. See ADVOWSON.

PRINCIPAL AND ACCESSORY. The relation of principal and accessory is noticed under the title ACCESSORY. Principals are either in the first or second degree. Principals in the first degree being those who are the actors or actual perpetrators of the offence, and principals in the second degree being those who are *present*, aiding, and abetting at the commission of the act. Presence may be, and often is, constructive —as if a party is sufficiently near to give assistance when a felony is committed, and participates in the act with a felonious design. Accessories before the fact, in felonies, are chiefly punishable by specific enactments, and according to the terms of the statute which applies to the offence; but where no statutory punishment is provided, then they may be transported for 7 years, or imprisoned, and, if a male, whipped.

By the statutes passed 1 *Vict.* for amending the criminal law, accessories before the fact, and principals in the second degree, of the felonies there enumerated, are treated as principals in the first degree, as far as *punishment* is concerned. Principals in the second degree are punishable by transportation or imprisonment, with or without hard labour, part of which may be in solitary confinement, not exceeding one month at any one time, and not exceeding two months in one year.

PRINCIPAL AND AGENT. There are several acts which, being done by an agent, will be equally effectual and advantageous as if done by the principal or master himself. Hence, it has been always held that the principal shall have advantage of his agent's acts in the same manner as he is by law declared to be bound by them, provided they come within the scope and compass of the agent's authority; with this qualification, a promise made to an agent is available for the principal, and a contract made by an agent binds the principal. The relations to which this doctrine chiefly applies are those of master and servant, attorney and client, merchant and factor.

PRINTED LINEN, &c. In analogy to the doctrine of literary property, the 34 *G.* 3. *c.* 23. gives to the proprietors of new patterns in printed linens, cottons, muslins, &c., the sole right of printing them for 3 months, and gives the proprietor injured his remedy by an action on the case for damages; and the proprietor can also have relief by bill in chancery and injunction.

PRINTERS. Every person having any printing-press or types for printing must deliver a notice, signed and attested by one witness, to the clerk of the peace of the town or place where it is intended the same shall be used; and such clerk of the peace is required to deliver a certificate to the printer on the payment of 1*s*. The penalty for keeping presses or types without giving notice, or using them in any place not expressed in the notice, is 20*l*. But this does not extend to the queen's printers, or to presses belonging to the Universities of Oxford and Cambridge.

Under the like penalty of 20*l*., letter-founders and printing-press makers, or sellers of types and printing-presses, are required to give notice to the clerk of the peace, and receive a certificate.

Sellers of types or printing-presses are directed to keep an account to whom sold, and produce the same to any justice requiring it, in writing, under penalty of 20*l*.

The printer of any book or paper meant to be published, whether sold or given away, is required to print on the front of every paper, if printed on one side only, and on the first and last leaves of every paper or book containing more than one leaf, his name and address; the penalty for omission, or on any person distributing any paper without the printer's name and abode, 20*l.* for every copy; (but not more than 25 penalties can be levied.)

Papers printed by authority, or for the use of either house of parliament, and also visiting cards, and papers relative to auctions, stock-receipts, &c., are exempt.

Printers are required to preserve a copy for six calendar months of every paper they print for hire or profit, with the name and abode of the persons by whom employed written or printed thereon, under a penalty of 20*l.* for neglect, or refusing to produce such copy when required by a justice.

Persons publishing, distributing, or placarding any paper without the printer's name and abode may be seized by any person and carried before a magistrate. See *Stat.* 39 *G.* 3. *c.* 79.

These severe penalties are seldom enforced, as justices of the peace have the power to mitigate them. The information must be laid within 3 months after the commission of the offence.

Printers are not entitled to recover for printing, unless they have complied with this act.

The printers of newspapers are subject to various statutory regulations, which have for their object the securing payment of the stamp duties, and the better guaranteeing damages in actions of libel.

The printing of advertisements is subject to the regulations of the stamp acts; and with respect to certain advertisements, declared illegal, such as advertising a reward for a thing lost or stolen, with "no questions asked," or containing any similar intimation; advertising any meeting or entertainment on a Sunday; advertising horse-races, where the plate or prize is of less value than 50*l.*; advertising the sale of any place under government, or in the East India Company's service, or advertising schemes for lotteries, they are subject to penalties, under various acts, from 50*l.* to 500*l.*

PRINTS AND ENGRAVINGS. See LITERARY PROPERTY.

PRIVILEGED COMMUNICATIONS are communications and correspondence privately and confidentially made upon the ordinary occurrences of life, which, if made and continued without malice or injury to another, are protected from being taken advantage of by third parties; for instance, if one man for proper purposes inquire the character or responsibility of another, and the party addressed answer unfavourably, such letter or statement cannot be the object of an action or prosecution against the individual making it; — otherwise, if the statement were malicious, or the writer exceeded the bounds of ordinary communication.

Communications made by clients to their attorneys or counsel, or their clerks, are privileged, *i. e.* the persons to whom they were made are forbidden to disclose them, or, if they are disclosed, they are not receivable as evidence. This *privilege* is, like other *privileges* of attorneys, not so much belonging to them as to their clients.

PRIVY COUNCIL. The principal council of the queen, styled, *par excellence*, the council: the members are constituted at the pleasure of the queen; from these are selected the ministers of state who form the "cabinet."

Privy councillors hold their offices for life, but are subject to removal at the queen's pleasure.

The power of the privy council is to inquire into all offences against the government, and to commit the offenders to prison to be dealt with according to law. They have an appellate jurisdiction in colonial or admiralty prize causes, and in matters of lunacy or idiotcy, as concerning the queen's prerogative, and also East India appeals. The powers of the high court of delegates in ecclesiastical and maritime causes have lately been added to its jurisdiction, and a judicial committee formed, who, being conversant with legal principles, preserve an uniformity of judgment, adding greatly to the dignity of this tribunal; the members of which are, 1. the president of the council; 2. the lord chancellor, or lord keeper, or first lord commissioner of the great seal; 3. the chief justice of the queen's bench; 4. the master of the rolls; 5. the vice chancellor; 6. the chief justice of the common pleas; 7. the lord chief baron; 8. the judge of the prerogative court; 9. the judge of the high court of admiralty; 10. the chief judge in bankruptcy; 11. the members of the privy council who shall have held any of the offices before mentioned; 12. two other privy councillors appointed by her majesty, who shall have held the office of judge in the East Indies, or any of the queen's dominions beyond seas. 13. The queen may summon *any other* members of the privy council. Four members constitute a *quorum*.

PROCHEIN AMI. *The next friend;* a term used for the next of kin who sues for an infant in any suit respecting the infant's rights; any other person may be *prochein ami*. *Prochein amis* are liable for costs. Infants defend suits by their guardians, either *natural*, as father, mother, &c., or at *law* by a guardian specially appointed. A married woman suing in equity in respect of her separate estate, may sue by *prochein ami*.

PROCTOR. An attorney in a *civil* or ecclesiastical court, or admiralty, which is governed by the rules and practice of the Roman or civil law.

PROHIBITION. A writ which lies from the queen's bench to *prohibit* inferior courts, either ecclesiastical or temporal, as courts of request, &c., from taking cognisance of suits that do not belong to them, or are not comprehended within the jurisdiction. Very lately, where commissioners of a 5*l.* court took cognisance of a cause of action which was only remediable by a special form of action, to which their jurisdiction did not apply, they were prohibited from proceeding therein, and were compelled to pay the costs of their injudicious proceedings.

PROOF. The showing any matter alleged by witnesses. See EVIDENCE.

PROTHONOTARY. A chief officer. In the queen's bench the master is the prothonotary. In the common pleas there are four who are termed "masters." They enter and enrol declarations, judgments, and other proceedings, tax costs, and hear matters which the court may refer to them for their report, &c. Many other courts style their first clerks (proto-notarius) prothonotaries; viz. the Marshalsea, court of record at Stepney, &c.

PROTECTOR. The person who, upon the settling or limiting of an estate in tail, is actually in possession of a prior estate of freehold or for lives: his consent is requisite, if the tenant in tail wishes to alien. If the tenant in tail is in possession he may alien by deed inrolled: for instance, if land be settled on A. for life, remainder to B. and his heirs male, which is an estate in tail, B. cannot during the life of A., and without his consent, alien, A. being the protector to the settlement. A power is also given by the act for abolishing fines and recoveries, for a settlor to appoint three protectors in lieu of the protector by operation of law, who may be perpetuated as they may happen to die or relinquish their protectorship. The number is not to exceed three, and aliens are incapable. The person who would be at law, protector, as having a prior estate for life, may also be protector with those appointed, unless otherwise directed. The protectorship appointments are to be inrolled in chancery. Protectors are rather *consenting* than *conveying* parties. See RECOVERIES AND FINES.

PROTEST, has two meanings or applications; one by way of caution, to call witnesses (as it were), or openly affirm that the party either doth not at all, or but conditionally, yield his consent to any act, or to answer any thing further than he is lawfully bound, the other is by way of complaint, as to protest a man's bill, which is done upon refusal of the acceptor to pay, or the drawee to accept.

Inland bills are not so frequently *protested* as outland or foreign bills, but a memorandum is simply made thereof by the notary, or those who present the bill with the intent of protest, which memorandum is called "*noting*," and this affords sufficient instructions for a formal protest to be made out when wanted, as the notary keeps a copy of the bill.

Foreign bills returned for non-payment, or for non-acceptance, are always protested.

Although protests are usually made in London, and in other great towns, by persons of acknowledged credence, termed "notaries," yet a protest may be made by any other substantial person of the city, town, or place, in the presence of two or more credible witnesses, refusal or neglect being made of due payment of the same, which protest shall be made, and written under a fair copy of the said bill of exchange, in the words or form following:—

Know all men that I [the person presenting], *on the —— day of —— at the usual place of abode of the said* [acceptor], *have demanded the payment of the bill of which this is a copy, which the said* [acceptor] *did not pay, wherefore I the said* [party presenting] *do hereby protest the said bill, dated at* Croydon, *this —— day of* —— 1838.

The form of a protest made by a notary, it is not necessary here to insert.

Bills are generally noted or protested on the evening of the day on which they become due. A tender of the amount of the bill, *and no more*, on that day, will save the charge; for, if the notary or his clerk refuse to deliver up the bill without such charges, the tender may be pleaded in bar of an action, if the holder be foolish enough to commence one. The tender of the money under such circumstances should not be accompanied with any condition; it should be a mere offer. See TENDER.

PROTEST FOR BETTER SECURITY. The custom of merchants is stated to be, that, if the *drawee* of a bill of exchange abscond before the day when the bill is due, the holder may protest it, in order to have better security for the payment, and should give notice to the drawer and indorsers of the absconding of the drawee; and, if the acceptor of a foreign bill *become* bankrupt before it is due, it seems that the holder may also, in such case, protest for better security; but the acceptor is not, on account of the bankruptcyof the *drawer*, compellable to give this security. The neglect to make this protest will not affect the holder's remedy against the drawer and indorsers; and its principal use appears to be, that, by giving notice to the drawers and indorsers of the situation of the acceptor, by which it is become improbable that payment will be made, they are enabled by other means to provide for the payment of the bill when due, and thereby prevent the loss of re-exchange, &c. occasioned by the return of the bill. It may be collected that, though the drawer or indorsers refuse to give better security, the holder must, nevertheless, wait till the bill be due before he can sue either of those parties. (*Chitty on Bills*, chap. vii. § 2.)

PURCHASE. The buying or other acquisition of lands of inheritance with money, or by deed, gift, or agreement, as distinct from the obtaining them by descent or hereditary right, and the course of descent is somewhat varied accordingly. See DESCENT.

QUAKERS are now admissible to serve on juries, and as members of parliament, and are eligible to places of profit in the government; and they and Moravians are enabled to make affirmation, or declaration, in the nature of an oath, in *all* cases where oaths are requisite.

Quakers refusing to pay tithes or church-rates, justices of peace are to determine the information, and order costs; and Quakers, as well as others, may be committed to prison for non-payment of tithes in London. (7 & 8 *W.* 3. *c.* 34.; 1 *Geo.* 1. *c.* 6.; also 21 *H.* 8. *c.* 20.)

Quakers are exempted from serving in the militia.

QUARANTINE. The 40 days which a widow of a deceased proprietor of land may claim to remain in the chief house till her dower is assigned her.

QUARANTINE. A regulation by which all communication with individuals, ships, or goods, arriving from places infected with the plague, or other contagious disease, or supposed to be peculiarly liable to such infection, is interdicted for a certain definite period. The term is derived from the Italian *quaranta*, forty; it being generally supposed that, if no infectious disease break out within 40 days, or 6 weeks, no danger need be apprehended from the free admission of the individual under quarantine. During this period, too, all the goods, clothes, &c. that might be supposed capable of retaining the infection, are subject to a process of purification. The period of quarantine varies, as respects ships coming from the same place, according to the nature of their bills of health. These are documents, or certificates, signed by the consul or other competent authority in the place which the ship has left, describing its state of health at the time of her clearing out. A *clean* bill imports that, at the time of her sailing, no infectious disorder was known to exist: a *suspected*, or, as it is more commonly called, a *touched* bill, imports that rumours were afloat of an infectious disorder, but that it had not actually appeared. A *foul* bill, or the absence of clean bills, imports that the place was infected when the vessel sailed. The existing quarantine regulations are embodied in the act 6 *G.* 4. *c.* 78., and the different orders in council issued under its authority. These orders specify what vessels are liable to perform quarantine, the places at which it is to be performed, and the various formalities and regulations to be complied with. The publication in the Gazette of any order in council with respect to quarantine is deemed sufficient notice to all concerned, and no excuse of ignorance is admitted for any infringement of the regulations. To obviate, as far as possible, any foundation for such plea, it is ordered that vessels clearing out for any port or place, with respect to which there shall be at the time any order in council subjecting vessels from it to quarantine, are to be *furnished* with an abstract of the quarantine regulations; and are *to furnish themselves* with quarantine signal flags and lanterns, and with materials and instruments for fumigating and immersing goods. (*M'Culloch's Commercial Dictionary.*)

QUARE IMPEDIT (wherefore he hinders). The name of a writ and suit which lies for the recovery of an advowson, or right of presentation.

QUARRELLING IN A CHURCH or CHURCHYARD, is an offence punishable by the ecclesiastical court.

QUARTER-SESSIONS. See SESSIONS OF THE PEACE.

QUASH. To annul for insufficiency or for other cause. The court of queen's bench will *quash* an indictment for informality, or an order of sessions for irregularity.

QUEEN. The wife of the king. The queen of England is either queen-regent, regnant, or sovereign holding the crown in her own right; queen-consort, the wife of the reigning king, or queen-dowager, the wife of the late king. The queen-regnant, in all respects, has the powers and authorities of a king; and the queen-consort is, by the law, deemed a single woman, for the purpose of purchasing property, or enjoying her own revenues, and of devising them by will. She has many exemptions; but, unless expressly exempted, is upon the same footing as other subjects, being the king's subject, not his equal.

QUI TAM (who as well). The plaintiff, in an action to recover a penalty, describes himself as suing as well for the king as for himself; *i. e.* where any part is given to the king, and any proportion to the informer, a penal action is therefore vulgarly called a *qui tam* action.

QUO WARRANTO (by what warrant or authority). A writ that lies against any person that usurps the office or franchise of another: the writ itself is fallen into disuse; but the same end is attained by the attorney-general filing an information in the nature of a *quo warranto.* This proceeding is applied to the decision of corporation disputes, in respect of offices held under acts of parliament or at common law, as for deciding the right to a stewardship of a court leet, a ferry, a fair or market, a toll, &c.

RAPE, is a felony, and punishable by death; but sentence may be recorded. So the abusing girls under 10 years (whether they consent or not) is a felony punishable in the same manner. The abusing girls above 10 and under 12 years of age is a misdemeanor (whether they consent or not). The punishment is imprisonment, with or without hard labour, at the discretion of the court.

Assault with intent to commit a rape is a misdemeanor, punishable by imprisonment, with or without hard labour, for not more than two years, or fine, or both, and to find, if required, sureties to keep the peace.

RAPE. A division of a county, similar to that of a hundred, but sometimes containing in it more hundreds than one. Sussex is divided into six rapes.

RASURE of a deed in a material part, if not evidenced to be made before sealing and delivery, will render such deed void. An indorsement or memorandum is usually made at the time of the execution of any deed that is rased or interlined in material parts. If put in suit, the defendant can plead that it is not his deed.

READING-ROOMS. See LECTURES.

REAL PROPERTY, is legally distinguished from *personalty*, principally in two respects: first, its permanent, fixed, and immoveable quality; and, secondly, that the interest therein must be not less than the term of the life of the owner, or of another person or persons; whereas personalty is either moveable, or readily capable of being so, or, as in the case of a lease for years, is considered as of so inferior a nature that it is not allowed the incidents and privileges of *real* property. (*Blackst. Comm.* vol. ii. p. 386.)

Even a long term of years perpetually renewable is not real, but only personal, property.

REBUTTER. The answer of a defendant to a plaintiff's surrejoinder, *i. e.* the defendant *rebuts* the assertion stated in the plaintiff's previous pleading. See PLEADING.

RECEIPT, is an acquittance for a sum of money. It is not demandable of right, or, rather, by law; so that if a man offer to pay money to another, provided he will give him a receipt, this is not a sufficient tender, for the party tendering has attached a condition which vitiates the *tender*. See TENDER.

As a stamp-duty is payable on all payments above 40*s*., the commissioners of stamps might proceed against the party for a breach of revenue law, but no further. A person paying money should take a witness to the payment, or evidence it in some other manner.

Receipts not stamped, or improperly stamped, cannot be given in evidence, nor can they be re-stamped to render them valid as evidence of payment.

RECEIVER. A person appointed by the court of chancery to receive the rents of lands, &c. in its custody or direction: he gives sureties for his due payment of the rents, &c., and is chargeable with interest if he delay payment.

RECEIVING STOLEN GOODS. The receiving "any chattels, money, valuable securities, and other property whatsoever," knowing the same to have been stolen, is a felony, and punishable with transportation for not more than 14 nor less than 7 years, or imprisonment not exceeding three years (with or without hard labour, and with or without solitary confinement, for the whole or any part of the imprisonment), and, if a male, to be once, twice, or thrice publicly or privately whipped, in addition to the imprisonment, if the court shall think fit.

The receiver may either be indicted as an accessory after the fact, or for the offence of receiving, whether the *stealer* be convicted or not.

The buying or receiving anchors, goods, &c. weighed up, is a misdemeanor, punishable as such, or by transportation for 7 years. (*1 & 2 G. 4. c. 75. s. 11.; 1 & 2 G. 4. c. 76.*)

Persons prosecuting are entitled to have their goods restored; otherwise, if the thing stolen was a negotiable security, and in the hands of an innocent holder for good consideration.

RECOVERIES AND FINES, were proceedings by which persons were enabled to bar estates tail, and, with the concurrence of their wives, to bar them of dower, and to exclude remainder-men. As all men's titles to their real estates must, for a few years, depend upon the law of fines and recoveries, it may be useful to notice, in the words of the commissioners of real property, their intent and operation, and to show briefly how their abolition by a late act is beneficial; which act, to check the alienation by a tenant in tail with remainder, has introduced a "protector," without whose consent this alienation cannot be effected — a measure which may have the operation of confining improvident alienations of entailed property within a narrower compass: —

"A fine in its origin was an amicable composition, by leave of the king or his justices, of an actual suit, whereby the lands were acknowledged to be the right of one of the parties; and, at common law, all persons were barred by it who did not claim within a year and a day. The safe title acquired by this process led, it is supposed, to the practice of transfering lands, by means of a fictitious suit of the same nature as the real suit above alluded to. This is the origin of the fines of the present day, which, subject to certain modifications made from time to time by statutes, have been in use for centuries. The statutes 1 *Ric.* 3. *c.* 7., and 4 *H.* 7. *c.* 24., have declared, that a fine proclaimed in four successive terms, the first proclamation being made in the term in which the fine is engrossed, shall operate as a bar by non-claim, at the end of five years after the last proclamation; but with a certain limited extension of time in the cases of infancy, coverture, lunacy, and absence beyond seas: and by the latter statute, and the statute 32 *H.* 8. *c.* 36., the further effect of barring estates tail was given to fines levied with proclamations.

"The three principal uses to which fines are applied are to bar estates tail, and enable a tenant in tail to acquire or pass a base (or conditional) fee, determinable on the failure of the issue in tail, to gain a title by non-claim, and to pass the estates and bar the rights of married women.

"A common recovery is a judgment in a fictitious suit, in the nature of a real action, brought by the demandant against the tenant of the freehold, who vouches some person to warrant the lands, and judgment is given for the demandant to recover them against the tenant in consequence of the person vouched, or the person last vouched, if there should be more than one vouchee making default to the title to the lands, which title he has supposed to have warranted. In a recovery, the regular process of a real action is pursued throughout, and no compromise takes place as in a fine.

"The principal use of a recovery is to enable a tenant in tail to bar not only his estate tail, but also all remainders, reversions, conditions, collateral limitations, and charges, not prior to the estate tail, and to acquire or pass a fee-simple, or an estate commensurate with the estate of the settler; but a reversion vested in the crown cannot, as it is generally understood, be barred by a recovery.

"Although it is not usual to suffer a recovery, except when it is necessary to bar entails and remainders over, yet, when resorted to for those purposes, it is not unfrequently made use of, at the same time, to convey, release, bar, or extinguish the estates, rights, powers, and interests of married women and others."

Fines and recoveries, the report stated, had other effects; viz. to operate to bar or shut out persons who had contingent or expectant interests, and sometimes expectant heirs; and they also extinguished contingent remainders, and a variety of other floating interests and claims.

The artificial devices which these fictitious proceedings gave rise to, and the expense with which they were attended, independent of the inconvenience, *viz.* that they could only be transacted at particular times of the year, rendered it necessary that the legislature should provide a certain remedy; and, while it restrained the improvident power of alienation which the eldest son of a tenant in tail or fee-simple has during the life of his father, should facilitate the conveyance of land for prudent and legitimate purposes. Therefore the statute 3 & 4 *W.* 4. *c.* 74. abolishes fines and feigned recoveries — enables tenants in tail to make an effectual alienation by any deed to be inrolled in chancery, by which a tenant in fee can convey — creates a *protector* to the estate, by requiring that the owner of a beneficial and prior estate for life should first give his concurrence (see PROTECTOR) — provides new methods for barring estates tail and expectant interests, and enables married women to dispose of their lands and money subject to be invested in lands with the concurrence of their husbands (see MARRIED WOMEN), independent of many other subsidiary provisions. This act extends to freehold as well as copyhold estates, and money subjected to be invested in lands, which, in equity, is equivalent to a real estate. The forms of simple conveyances are not materially altered; and their *real* intents are now more easily understood by the party conveying, who previously was obliged to sign whatever was presented to him for signature by his solicitor, without comprehending the abstruse technicalities of these exploded fictions. See TAIL.

REGISTERS, or REGISTRARS. Officers in the chancery who enter all decrees and orders made by the chancellor, vice-chancellor, and master of the rolls: they are experienced barristers. Similar officers are appointed in other courts of equity; and in other courts, where no such officer is appointed by name, the burden of the office lies on the chief clerk. In the court of bankruptcy registrars are appointed to assist the commissioners.

There are no registries of deeds in England, properly so called, although there are some conveyances that are required to be inrolled, a general registry of all deeds relating to land being opposed to the habits and associations of the landed proprietors: however, the dread of secret incumbrances, which can be effected in a thousand ways so as to deceive the most vigilant purchasers, induced the legislature to pass acts, about a century since, whereby memorials or minutes of deeds, conveyances, judgments, &c., affecting lands in Yorkshire and Middlesex are to be registered, upon the penalty of forfeiting the priority against conveyances or judgments subsequently memorialised.

Bargains and sales (now little used), deeds regulating companies, deeds acknowledged by married women, deeds appointing protectors of entails, and continuing them, and annuity deeds, and any deed a party is willing to have inrolled for perpetuity, or in regard to its future production, may be inrolled in chancery, or in any other court; but these registries, being partial and compulsory, do not generally assist those who seek a full knowledge of the incumbrances, &c. of an estate.

REGISTRARS. The officers for carrying into effect the statutes 6 & 7 *W.* 4. *caps.* 85, 86. being the "Act for Marriages in England," and the "Act for Registering Births, Deaths, and Marriages in England," are, 1. the registrar-general; 2. the superintendent registrar; and, 3. the registrar and his deputy. Their duties are regulated by the latter statute; and their functions, and the practice of registration as to marriages, are noticed under title MARRIAGE: with regard to *births* and *deaths*, their duties are fully explained by the following

NOTICES FURNISHED BY THE REGISTRAR-GENERAL, UNDER THE PROVISIONS OF THE ACT FOR REGISTERING BIRTHS, DEATHS, AND MARRIAGES IN ENGLAND.

Acts required to be done after the 1st Day of July, 1837, in all Cases of Birth.

The father or mother of any child born after the 1st day of March, 1837, or the occupier * of any house or tenement in which any such birth shall happen, may give notice of such birth to the registrar of the district in which the birth happens, within forty-two days next after the day of such birth; and the father or mother, or (in case of their death, illness, absence, or inability) the occupier of the house or tenement must, within the said forty-two days, give information to the registrar, on being requested to do so, according to the best of his or her knowledge and belief, of the following particulars; namely,

The day of birth of the child.
The name (if any be given).
The sex.
The name and surname of the father.
The name, and maiden surname of the mother.
The rank, profession, trade, or calling, of the father.

The person giving such information must also state and sign in the register his or her name, description, and residence; and unless this be done no register can be given in evidence. No fee or payment can be lawfully required of the person so giving information respecting any birth; and the entry in the register, which the registrar will thereupon be obliged to make, being signed as aforesaid, will be evidence of such birth in any court of law or equity.

No birth may be registered after forty-two days from the time of such birth, unless the father or guardian of the child, or some person present at the birth, make a solemn declaration of the foregoing particulars, according to the best of his or her knowledge and belief, and the registrar shall register the birth accordingly, in the presence of the superintendent registrar: and the person requiring the birth to be so registered shall pay to the superintendant registrar 2*s.* 6*d.*, and to the registrar (unless the delay shall have been occasioned by his default) 5*s.*

No person shall knowingly cause any birth to be registered, otherwise than as herein-before mentioned, after forty-days, under a penalty of 50*l.*; and no person shall knowingly cause any birth to be registered at all after six calendar months from after the day of birth (except in the case of children born at sea,) under the like penalty.

No register of births made after six calendar months from the day of birth (except in the case of children born at sea) will be received as legal evidence in any court of law or equity.

Acts required to be done after the 1st Day of July, 1837, in all Cases of Death.

Some person present at a death, or in attendance during the last illness, or (in case of the inability of such person) the occupier, or (if the occupier be the person that has died) some inmate of the house or tenement in which a death shall have happened, may, within five days after the death, give notice thereof to the registrar of the district; and must within eight days give information to the said registrar, on being requested to do so, according to the best of his or her knowledge or belief, of the following particulars; namely,

The day of death.
The name and surname of the person who has died.
The sex.
The age.
The rank, profession, trade, or calling.
The cause of death.

The person giving information must also state and sign in the register his or her name, description, and residence; and unless this be done no register can be given in evidence. No fee or payment can be lawfully required of the person so giving information respecting any death; and the entry in the register,

* For the purposes of this act, the master or keeper of every gaol, prison, or house of correction, or workhouse, hospital, or lunatic asylum, or public or charitable institution, shall be deemed the occupier thereof.

which the registrar will thereupon be obliged to make, being signed as aforesaid, will be evidence of such death in any court of law or equity.

Every person who shall bury, or perform any funeral or any religious service for the burial of, any dead body, for which no certificate shall have been made and delivered, either by the registrar or (in cases of inquest) by the coroner, and who shall not within seven days give notice thereof to the registrar, will forfeit 10*l*. And no certificate can be given (except by the coroner when an inquest has been held) unless the death has been registered by the registrar of the district. It is, therefore, of the greatest importance that persons directed as above shall, without delay, give information respecting a death to the registrar of the district within which the death has taken place, that he may register the same, and thereupon deliver a certificate to the undertaker, or other person having charge of the funeral.

Caution. — Every person wilfully making or causing to be made any false statement touching any of the particulars required to be known and registered, for the purpose of such statement being inserted in any register of birth, death, or marriage, will be subject to the same pains and penalties as if guilty of perjury.

N. B. Persons failing to do that which is by an act of parliament enjoined are indictable for a misdemeanor, although no specific penalty is imposed by the act which they have disobeyed.

Acts required to be done by Persons who may be desirous of solemnizing Marriage after the 1st Day of July, 1837, under the Provisions of the Acts of the 6th and 7th of William IV. caps. 85. and 86.

1. Persons desirous of solemnizing marriage, according to the rites and ceremonies of the church of England, may be so married after publication of bans, or by license, or by special license, as heretofore; or they may be married (without publication of bans, or by license, or special license,) according to the rites and ceremonies of the church of England, on production of a certificate from the superintendent registrar of the district, to be obtained in the following manner; namely, —

One of the parties intending marriage must give notice under his or her hand to the superintendent registrar of the district, within which the parties shall have dwelt for not less than seven days then next preceding; or, if they dwell in different districts, they must give the like notice to the superintendent registrar of each district. The notice must be in the form of a schedule, which the superintendent registrar will furnish on being applied to, and must be filled up with the following particulars: —

The name and surname of each of the parties.

Whether bachelor or widower, spinster or widow.

Their respective rank, profession, or calling.

Whether minors, or of full age.

Their respective dwelling-places.

Whether they have resided within the district more than one calendar month, or, if not, how long.

In what church or building the marriage is to be solemnized.

The district and county in which the other party resides, when they dwell in different districts.

A copy of such notice will be entered by the superintendent registrar in a book called "The Marriage Notice Book," which will be open at all reasonable times, without fee, to all persons desirous of inspecting the same.

The notice must be read by the superintendent registrar, or by the clerk to the guardians, at three weekly meetings of the guardians, or, if such meetings are not held weekly, at any meeting of the guardians within twenty-one days from the day of the notice being entered in the marriage notice book. And after the expiration of twenty-one days after the entry of the notice, if no impediment has been shown, the superintendent registrar may be required to issue a certificate.

2. Persons (except Quakers and Jews) desirous of solemnizing marriage, not according to the rites and ceremonies of the church of England, may be married according to other rites and ceremonies, on production of a certificate obtained as above-mentioned, in a registered place of worship, provided that every such marriage shall be solemnized with open doors, between the hours of eight and twelve in the forenoon, in the presence of some registrar of the district in

which such registered building is situate, and of two or more credible witnesses; provided also that in some part of the ceremony, and in the presence of such registrar and witnesses, each of the parties shall declare as follows:— "I do solemnly declare that I know not of any lawful impediment why I, A. B., may not be joined in matrimony to C. D." And each of the parties shall say to the other, "I call upon these persons here present to witness that I, A. B., do take thee, C. D., to be my lawful wedded [wife or husband]." Provided also, that there be no lawful impediment to the marriage of such parties.

Persons may be married after seven days from the entry of the notice, if by license, and after twenty-one days, if without license. A license may be granted by the superintendent registrar; but only for marriage in a registered building within his district, or in his office; but, before any license can be granted by him, one of the parties intending marriage must appear personally before him, and, in case he shall not be the superintendent registrar to whom notice of such intended marriage was given, shall deliver to him the certificate of the superintendent registrar, or superintendent registrars, to whom such notice shall have been given; and such party shall make oath, or shall make his or her solemn affirmation or declaration, instead of taking an oath, that he or she believeth that there is not any impediment of kindred or alliance, or other lawful hindrance, to the said marriage; and that one of the said parties hath, for the space of fifteen days immediately before the day of the grant of such license, had his or her usual place of abode within the district within which such marriage is to be solemnized; and, where either of the parties (not being a widower or widow) shall be under the age of twenty-one years, that the consent of the person or persons whose consent to such marriage is required by law has been obtained thereto, or that there is no person having authority to give such consent, as the case may be.

3. Persons objecting to be married, either according to the rites and ceremonies of the church of England, or in any such registered building, may, after notice and certificates as aforesaid, solemnize marriage at the office of the superintendent registrar, with open doors, between the hours of eight and twelve in the forenoon, in the presence of the superintendent registrar and some registrar of the district, and in the presence of two witnesses, making the declaration, and using the form of words, required in the case of marriage in a registered building.

Quakers may contract and solemnize marriage according to the usages of their society, provided both parties are of that society, and that notice shall have been given to the superintendent registrar, and a certificate shall have been issued as before mentioned.

Jews may likewise contract and solemnize marriage according to the usages of the Jewish religion, under similar provisions.

Every marriage of which notice has been entered as aforesaid must be solemnized within three calendar months after such entry, or the notice must be renewed.

Every marriage solemnized after the 1st of July, 1837, under the provisions of this act for marriages in England, in any other manner than as hereinbefore directed, will be null and void.

Be it also particularly observed, that, if any valid marriage shall be had under the provisions of the act for marriages in England by means of any wilfully false notice, certificate, or declaration made by either party to such marriage, as to any matter to which a notice, certificate, or declaration is therein required, her majesty's attorney-general or solicitor-general may sue for a forfeiture of all estate and interest in any property accruing to the offending party by such marriage; and the proceedings and the consequences will be the same as are provided in the like case with regard to marriages by license before the passing of these acts.

All births and deaths which occur after June, 1837, may be registered by the registrar of the district within which they occur, without any payment being required from the persons applying to have them registered, provided that, in the case of a birth, it is registered within six weeks after the day of the birth.

A birth cannot be registered more than six weeks after the day of the birth, without payment of *7s. 6d.*; nor can it be registered at all more than six months after the day of the birth.

All persons, therefore, should have the births of their children registered without delay.

The time at which a death, happening after June, 1837, may be registered, is not limited; but it is very desirable that it should always be done as soon as possible.

The registrar may be compelled to register a birth or death, if notice is given him of the birth within six weeks after it, and of the death within five days after it, by persons duly authorised.

Notice may be given to the registrar either by word or by writing.

All persons may give notice; and it is to be desired that whosoever has an opportunity should do so.

The name and dwelling-house of the registrar of each district may be seen in a list which the superintendent registrar is required to publish.

Any person applying to have a birth or death registered will be told by the registrar what kind of information is required.

No birth or death which occurs before July, 1837, can be registered.

Births.—It is very useful to persons in all stations, and to the poor as well as to the rich, to be able to obtain legal evidence of their age. In this point of view, entries of birth made in the new register book, by the registrar of births and deaths, will be of great importance.

All persons may have the births of their children, born after June, 1837, registered, without any payment being required, at any time within six weeks after the birth.

The church register is not a register of births, but only of baptisms; and is evidence only of the time of baptism, which sometimes does not take place till many years after birth. All members of the established church ought to take their children to be baptised: but baptism is to be regarded as a sacred rite, and not merely as a means of registration, for which purpose, indeed, it is no longer requisite.

Parents causing the births of their children to be registered before baptism, are recommended to state the name by which they intend they shall be called when baptised. The statement of the name in the first instance, in order that it may be registered, will save parties the trouble and expense of having the baptismal name added afterwards.

Deaths.—It may be of great importance to persons in all stations, and to the poor as well as to the rich, that they should be able to obtain legal evidence of the time of any death. The right to a legacy sometimes cannot be established without proving the exact day of a person's death. For this purpose the church register of burials is, in general, of no use. It is not a register of deaths; and is evidence, not of the day of the death, but only of the day of the burial, which sometimes does not take place till several weeks after the death.

But the entry of the death in the new register book, by the registrar of births and deaths, is legal evidence of the day of the death; and this entry may be made at any time, without any payment being required.

Though a death may be registered at any time, it ought, if possible, to be registered before burial, and a certificate of registry obtained from the registrar, to be shown to the clergyman officiating at the funeral. If this is not done, the clergyman will be liable to a fine, unless within seven days he gives notice to the registrar.

The new register books used by the secular registrar, for the registration of births and deaths, are the only register books provided by law for that purpose; and registration in those books is equally applicable, useful, and obligatory for persons of all religious persuasions, both churchmen and dissenters.

Certified copies of the entries of all births and deaths, registered by the registrar, may be obtained from him, or from the superintendent registrar. Certified copies will also be sent four times a year to the General Register Office in London, where any person will be able, on application, to obtain a copy of any entry made in any part of England and Wales; and every such copy, whether obtained from the registrar, the superintendent registrar, or at the general register office, will be receivable as evidence of a birth or death in any court of law; and the parties concerned will be thereby saved much trouble and expense.

General Register Office, July, 1837.

REGISTRIES, PAROCHIAL. See Parochial Registries.

REGISTRIES OF WILLS. Wills, when proved, are entered or recorded in the books of the ecclesiastical court belonging to each bishop or peculiar.

REGISTRY OF SHIPS. A ship is a personal chattel, and is acquired by building, purchase, mortgage, or capture; the evidence of the owner's title being a certificate of registry from the collector and controller of the customs at the port where registered, or similar functionaries in other parts of the world, being British possessions.

As no vessel can be entitled to the privileges of a *British* registered ship until registry, and as forfeiture accrues in case a ship exercises any such privileges before registry, all merchant and trading vessels are registered under the provisions of the 3 *&* 4 *W.* 4., which commenced on the 1st of September, 1833, and consolidated and amended a previous act, *viz.* the 6 *G.* 4. *c.* 110.

The registry of vessels takes place at the port to which they belong, unless the commissioners of customs think fit to permit a registry at another port. A vessel is deemed to belong to that port at or near to which those owners or that managing owner resides who subscribes the declaration required by the act before registry be made: and a new registry is required if the managing owner change his residence to another port.

As the provisions of this act are numerous, it will suffice, for the purposes of general information, to quote the following clauses of the act which particularly relate to the transfer or mortgage of this valuable property:—

When the property in any ship or vessel, or any part thereof, belonging to any of her majesty's subjects, shall, after registry thereof, be sold to any other of her majesty's subjects, the same is to be transfered by bill of sale or other instruments in writing, containing a recital of the certificate of registry, or the principal contents thereof; but no error that does not invalidate the evidence of identity will vitiate the transfer. — § 31.

A bill of sale is not effectual until produced to the officers of customs, and entered in the register book. — § 34.

The property in ships and vessels, of which there is more than one owner, shall be taken and considered to be divided into sixty-four equal parts or shares, and the proportion held by each owner shall be described in the registry as being a certain number of sixty-fourth parts or shares; and that no person shall be entitled to be registered as an owner of any ship or vessel, in respect of any proportion of such ship or vessel which shall not be an integral sixty-fourth part or share of the same; and, upon the first registry of any ship or vessel, the owner or owners, who shall take and subscribe the declaration required by this act before registry be made, shall also declare the number of such parts or shares then held by each owner, and the same shall be so registered accordingly. Provided that, if it shall at any time happen that the property of any owner or owners in any ship or vessel cannot be reduced by division into any number of integral sixty-fourth parts or shares, it shall and may be lawful for the owner or owners of such fractional parts as shall be over and above such number of integral sixty-fourth parts or shares, into which such property in any ship or vessel can be reduced by division, to transfer the same one to another, or jointly to any new owner by memorandum, upon their respective bills of sale, or by fresh bill of sale, without such transfer being liable to any stamp duty; provided also, that the owner or owners to any such fractional parts shall not be affected by reason of the same not having been registered; and that it shall be lawful for any number of such owners, named and described in such registry, being partners in any house or co-partnership actually carrying on trade in any part of her majesty's dominions, to hold any ship or vessel, or any share or shares of any ship or vessel, in the name of such house or co-partnership as joint owners thereof, without distinguishing the proportionate interest of each of such owners; and that such ship or vessel, or the share or shares thereof so held in co-partnership, shall be deemed and taken to be partnership property to all intents and purposes, and shall be governed by the same rules both in law and equity as relate to and govern all other partnership property in any other goods, chattels, and effects whatsoever. — § 32.

No greater number than thirty-two persons shall be entitled to be legal owners at one and the same time of any ship or vessel, as tenants in common, or to be registered as such. Provided, that nothing herein shall affect the equitable title of minors, heirs, legatees, creditors, or others, exceeding that number duly represented by or holding from any of the persons within the said number, registered as legal owners of any share or shares of such ship or vessel; — also, that if it shall be proved to the satisfaction of the commissioners of the customs that any number of persons have associated themselves as a joint-stock company, for the purpose of owning any ship or vessel, or any number of ships or vessels, as the joint property of such company, and that such company have duly elected or appointed any number, not less than three of the members of the same, to be trustees of the property in such ship or vessel, or ships or vessels, so owned by such company, it shall be lawful for such trustees, or any three of them, with the permission of such commissioners, to make and subscribe the declaration required by this act before registry be made, except that, instead of stating therein the names and descriptions of the other owners, they shall state the name and descriptions of the company to which such ship or vessel, or ships or vessels, shall in such manner belong. — § 33.

Where any transfer of a ship or vessel, or of any share or shares thereof, shall be made only as a security for the payment of a debt or debts, either by way of mortgage or of assignment to a trustee or trustees for the purpose of selling the same for the payment of any debt or debts, then, and in every such case, the collector and controller of the port where the ship or vessel is registered shall, in the entry in the book of registry, and also in the endorsement on the certificate of registry, in manner hereinbefore directed, state and express that such transfer was made only as a security for the payment of a debt or debts, or by way of mortgage, or to that effect; and the person or persons to whom such transfer shall be made, or any other person or persons claiming under him or them as a mortgagee or mortgagees, or a trustee or trustees only, shall not by reason thereof be deemed to be owner or owners of such ship or vessel, share or shares thereof; nor shall the person or persons making such transfer be deemed by reason thereof to have ceased to be an owner or owners of such ship or vessel, any more than if no such transfer had been made; except so far as the same may be necessary for the purpose of rendering the ship or vessel, share or shares, so transfered available, by sale or otherwise, for the payment of the debt or debts for securing the payment of which such transfer shall have been made. — § 42.

A provision is made by this act, that the rights of mortgagees of registered ships shall not be effected by the circumstance of the mortgagor having the reputed ownership or disposition of the ship; and this corresponds with a clause in the bankrupt act which provides for this case.

In respect of acquisition by capture.—In time of war, king's ships, vessels having letters of marque, commonly called privateers, and merchant vessels fighting in their own defence, have a right by the law of nations to capture prizes, which prizes, when adjudicated upon by the admiralty, vice-admiralty, or prize court, become the possession of the captors, and are dealt with pursuant to the "instructions to privateers" issued in council at the commencement of the war.

For information respecting ships and shipping, the reader is referred to "Steel's Ship-master's Assistant," and "M'Culloch's Commercial Dictionary," which comprise all the knowledge upon this subject, legislative, legal, and commercial.

REMAINDER, is an estate limited in lands, tenements, or rents, to be enjoyed after the expiration of another intervening, or, as it is technically termed, "particular" estate.

An estate in remainder is an estate limited to take effect, and be enjoyed, after another estate is determined. As if a man, seised in fee-simple, grants lands to one for twenty years, and, after the determination of the said term, then to another and his heirs for ever; here the former is tenant for years, remainder to the latter in fee. In the first place, an estate for years is created or carved out of the fee, and given to the former, and the residue and remainder of it is given to the latter. Both their interests are, in fact, only one estate; the present term of years, and the remainder afterwards, when added together, being equal only to one estate in fee. (2 *Black. C.* 11.) Remainders are either vested or contingent. Vested remainders, or remainders executed, are those by which a present interest passes to the party, though to be enjoyed in future, and by which the estate is invariably fixed to remain to a determinate person after the particular estate is spent; as if A. be tenant for years, remainder to B. in fee; hereby B.'s remainder is vested, which nothing can defeat or set aside. So, where an estate is conveyed to A. for life, remainder to B. in tail, remainder to C. in tail, with any indefinite number of other remainders over in tail to persons *in esse*, all these remainders are vested. The person entitled to a vested remainder has an immediate fixed right of future enjoyment, that is, an estate *in præsenti*, though it is not to take effect in possession, with primary profits, till a future period; and such an estate may be transfered, aliened, and charged, much in the same manner as an estate in possession. It is not the uncertainty of ever taking effect in possession that makes a remainder contingent, for to that every remainder for life or in tail is and must be liable, as the remainder-man may die, or die without issue, before the death of the tenant for life. The *present capacity* of taking effect in possession, if the possession were to become vacant, and not the certainty that the possession will become vacant before the estate limited in remainder determines, universally *distinguishes a vested remainder* from one that is contingent. (*Fearne*, 215.)

RENT, or RENDER, is the compensation or return given for the possession of some corporeal possession.

Rent-charge is where the owner of the rent has no future interest in the land or reversion therein; as if a person assigns all his estate with a rent payable thereout, and secures it by a covenant of distress, the land is said to be *charged* with it. Where such a rent is reserved without distress, the rent is said to be *seck*, or barren. A clear rent-charge must be free from the land-tax.

Rents of *assize* are the quit-rents of freeholders and copyholders of a manor: they are called *quit* rents, because, on payment of the rent, the holder was *quit* for all other services then existing, but now abolished. A fee-farm rent is a grant from the crown in perpetuity of land, reserving a rent equal to its presumed value, as it stands in the king's books, but practically of a very inconsiderable rent, compared with the present value.

The most common rent known to the *law* (for, in common parlance, there are many terms used to denote rents, such as "ground-rent," "improved-rent," &c.) is rack-rent, being the full value of the land at the time it was let, which may be subsequently improved by buildings, &c., when for many purposes it will be called improved rent, as in the "Building Act," and other acts.

The reservation of rent should be certain, and not be part of the possession let, and should be reserved or made payable to the lessor or landlord himself, and not to a third party, for it should be made to him from whom the land passes. The clearest and safest way is to reserve the rent generally, *i. e.* without naming any one, during the term, and leave it to be distributed at law.

If the reservation be only to the lessor, and the lease or deed do not say "to his heirs, executors," &c., this reservation will only continue for the lifetime of the lessor, and will determine and cease with his death.

Reservation of 5*l.* per acre during the last twenty years of the term for every acre of meadow thereby demised, which the tenant should plough, dig, break up, or convert into tillage during the last twenty years of the term, and so, after that rate, for any greater or less quantity than an acre, or less term than a year. The rent is due in the last twenty years, if the land is then ploughed, whether it was first ploughed within the last twenty years or before; and the rent continues payable during the last twenty years, though the land be again laid down to permanent grass.

With respect to the time when the rents are payable, it is either by the particular appointment of the parties in the deed, or else by appointment of law; but the law never controls the express appointment of the parties, when such appointment will answer their intention.

If rent be payable yearly, without saying "during the said term," yet the payment must be made every year during the continuance of the lease.

If a lease be made, rendering rent at the two usual feasts of the year, without specifying what feasts, the law construes such payments to be made at *Michaelmas* and *Lady-day*, because those are the usual days appointed in contracts of this nature for payments. So, if a man grants a rent of 10*l.* to another, payable at the two usual feasts of the year, this shall be intended by equal portions, though not so mentioned in the deed; because, where there are two several days appointed for payment, it is the most equal construction that a moiety of the rent shall be paid at each day.

In a question between landlord and tenant, whether the rent was payable quarterly or half-yearly, evidence of the mode in which other tenants pay is not admissible.

If a man make a lease, the 1st of May, reserving rent payable quarterly, this shall be intended quarterly from the making of the lease; for, if the beginning of the quarter should be construed to be any other day than the date of the lease, the lessor would lose the profits of his land for some time, and, consequently, not have quarterly payment made during the continuance of the lease. Under an agreement to let a house for a year, the rent to commence at *Michaelmas*, and to be paid three months in advance, such advance to be paid on taking possession; — it seems this stipulation relates to the first quarter's rent only.

As to apportionment of rent, see APPORTIONMENT.

Rent is demandable at sunset of the day on which it becomes due, although not due till midnight; and a forfeiture may accrue by non-payment at sunset.

REPLEVIN, is a proceeding upon which the right of a distress for rent rent-charge, or rent-service is tried. When a party is distrained upon for any cause whatever, and wishes to dispute the right of the distrainor, application must be forthwith made to the sheriff or one of his deputies, who, by law, are required to be within twelve miles of each other, to *replevy them*, *i. e.* to restore the goods or cattle taken to the owner, which the sheriff or his deputy does, as a matter of course, upon the owner with two sufficient sureties, giving a bond, called a replevin bond (which the deputy or officer prepares), with a penalty in double the value of the goods, and conditioned for the owner's prosecuting a suit or plaint in the county court against the distrainor without delay, and for a return of the goods, if a return of them should be ultimately adjudged. The party distrained upon, therefore, gives to the deputy the names of two solvent persons of the county or city wherein the distress was made; and, upon their execution of the bond, the deputy will authorise his officer to cause a restoration of the goods, in doing which the sheriff's officer may break open an outer door, if admittance be refused.

If the distress be for rent, or for any thing in the nature of rent, the *replevy* must be made within five days; in other cases no particular time is limited by law.

The party distrained upon, in this stage of the proceeding, called "the plaintiff in replevin," must prosecute his suit for the complete restoration of his goods without delay in the county court; but this suit or action "in replevin" is, for many purposes, more conveniently removed to one of the superior courts by a process called a *re*cordari *fa*cias *lo*quelam (in practice called a *re. fa. lo.*), or by writ of *accedas ad curiam*, and in the superior courts the cause is determined.

It must be remembered that the sureties to the replevin bond have to make good the restoration of the things distrained, with costs of suit, if the plaintiff, or party distrained upon, does not proceed to try the right of distress, or, having caused it to be tried, it is determined against him, and he does not perform the condition of the bond. The sureties cannot render their principal to prison as in other cases. See DISTRESS.

RESCUE. The freeing or rescuing a distress after distraint made. If such distraint is made unlawfully, the owner may rescue before impounding, but not after, for then the goods are in the custody of the law. It is a misdemeanor, and punishable as such.

Rescuing any person in custody of a sheriff's officer on his way to gaol is punishable as a misdemeanor, or summarily by attachment by the court from whence the process issued.

The rescuing of a felon from the constable is a misdemeanor, simply punishable as such, if the party in custody is not convicted; but, if he has been convicted, the rescue is treason, felony, or mere misdemeanor, according to the conviction of the party rescued, and punishable accordingly.

RESIDUARY LEGATEES. Those to whom is given the residue of a testator's estate, after payment of debts and prior legacies, or who have a legacy payable out of the residue.

RESPONDENTIA. The borrowing money upon goods and merchandise which are to be sold or exchanged in the course of a voyage. The borrower upon this contract is liable, unless the goods be lost. It differs not much from bottomry, except that in a loan of money upon *bottomry* the lender runs no risk, though the goods be lost; and on *respondentia* the lender must be paid his principal and interest, although the ship perish, provided the goods are safe.

RETURN, is the certificate of a sheriff to whom a writ, warrant, or precept is directed, setting forth what has been done by virtue of such writ, precept, or warrant. It is generally indorsed on the writ, or is contained in a parchment annexed to the writ, called a schedule. Writs, &c., directed to private persons, such as writs of summons, summonses, &c., are said to be returnable when the limited time for the parties' appearance has expired: some writs are returnable immediately, as writs of *habeas corpus;* which means that the party to whom the writ is directed is to do the thing immediately, *i. e.* within twenty-four hours. Some writs are returnable immediately after the execution of them; *i. e.* the *return* should be forthwith made. Sheriffs or other persons have, in cases where the writ is returnable on a day certain, all that day to make the return. Sheriffs who have the execution of process should *return* the same duly; but for the convenience of their bailiffs they do not do so till called upon by the court from which process issues, which is a species of oppression upon the subject and suitor, who is put to delay and expense in defiance of the rules of the courts and acts expressly prohibiting such a practice.

REVERSION, signifies the expectant interest which will accrue on the expiration of an estate or tenancy to the party creating such estate. A proprietor has the reversion of land after the determination of the leases. A mortgagor who grants a leasefor securing the money borrowed, has a reversion expectant on its determination, by payment of the money or otherwise, though this is more properly an equity of redemption. A person who grants a lease for another's life has a reversion expectant on the lessee's death; in fact, that interest which will revert to the owner or his heirs, on the falling in of the estate parted with, or incumbered for a particular period, is a reversion. A remainder may be made to any third person after a partial grant or temporary parting with an estate; but a reversion can only be to the grantor, or those who represent him, being his heirs or assigns, &c.

RIOTS, ROUTS, AND UNLAWFUL ASSEMBLIES. Lord Holt thought the law on this subject uncertain in its definition, and many law writers have quoted cases in favour of a particular illustration of this branch of law. A *Manual of the Law, with regard to Public Meetings**, concisely and clearly states the law on this subject from Blackstone and Hawkins.

A riot seems to be a tumultuous disturbance of the peace, by three or more persons assembling together of their own authority, with an intent mutually to assist one another against any who shall oppose them in the execution of some enterprise of a private nature, and afterwards actually executing the same in a violent and turbulent manner, to the terror of the people, whether the act intended were of itself lawful or unlawful.

If the parties assembled use force or violence in the execution of their design, whatever that design may be, they are guilty of a riot, unless in cases where the law allows of such force or violence; as for a sheriff, or a constable, or perhaps even a private person, to assemble a competent number of people, in order to suppress rebels or enemies or actual rioters.

If the original intention of meeting be lawful, as at a fair or market, and a sudden quarrel and combat arise, this is not a riot, but an *affray.* But if, being innocently assembled, a dispute arise, and the parties arrange themselves into sides, and then commence a combat, it will amount to a riot, by reason of their confederating with an intention to break the peace: so, if parties, lawfully assembled, on a sudden propose to do an act of violence, and actually execute it, because they

* By T. J. Arnold, Esq. of Lincoln's Inn. 12mo. 1832.

have associated themselves for a different purpose from that on which they at first met.

The grievance complained of must relate to some private quarrel only, or the interests or disputes of particular persons, and not concerning the public at large; for if the intention of a meeting be to redress public grievances, such as to remove evil counsellors from the king, &c., and they attempt to execute it with force, it amounts to treason.

To constitute a riot, the enterprise must be attended, either with circumstances of actual force or violence, or with such as have an apparent tendency thereto, and are apt to strike a terror into the people; such as the show of armour, threatening speeches, or turbulent gestures. Hence, it follows, that parties may assemble with the intention of executing an illegal act, and actually execute it, without being guilty of a riot.

As an unlawful act may be performed without committing a riot, so, on the other hand, a lawful act may be executed with such circumstances of violence as to render the parties executing it rioters; as if three, in a violent and tumultuous manner, join together in removing a nuisance which may lawfully be done in a peaceful manner, they are as properly rioters as if the act intended to be done by them were ever so unlawful. The justice of a cause, however, in which such an assembly is engaged, is to be considered as a great mitigation of the offence.

All persons concerned in riot are principals; so that if any one encourages, or promotes, or takes part in riots, whether by words, signs, or gestures, or by wearing the badge or ensign of the rioters, he is himself considered a rioter.

A simple riot is a misdemeanor, punishable by fine and imprisonment, with hard labour.

But there are some particular species of riots and assemblies, which, by acts of parliament, have been declared more highly criminal, and the actors in which are subjected to a severe penalty.

Persons riotously assembled, demolishing a church, chapel, house, or certain other buildings, or any machinery in any manufactory, or mine, are guilty of a capital felony.

Persons unlawfully and riotously assembled, to the number of twelve at least, and not dispersing within an hour after being commanded by proclamation by one justice, &c., are guilty of a felony, punishable by transportation for life, or for a lesser term.

Military training is prohibited under the penalty of transportation for not more than seven, or of imprisonment for not more than two, years.

Meetings of more than fifty persons, within a mile of Westminster Hall, on any day on which either of the houses of parliament, or of the courts of law, shall sit there, are prohibited as unlawful assemblies.

Repairing to the king or parliament to present a petition with a company of more than ten persons, is forbidden, under 100*l.* penalty, and three months' imprisonment.

By the common law, any sheriff, under-sheriff, peace-officer, or even a private person, may suppress *riots*, *routs*, or *affrays*.

Riotous or unlawful meetings may be suppressed by justices, or any persons called to their aid: the offenders may be apprehended either on the spot or by warrant afterwards. Any justice, &c., may read a proclamation, at a *riotous* meeting, commanding the rioters to disperse; that if, after this proclamation, they remain rioting on the ground, they become felons, and, as such, may be seized; and if any such felons should resist, and in consequence thereof be killed or hurt, the peace-officers and their assistants are to be indemnified.

Killing of constables in the execution of their office is murder.

The same of peace-officers, and persons interposing of their own accord to prevent mischief in an affray, or endeavouring to apprehend felons; but peace-officers and others are bound in some manner or other to notify their authority and their intent in interposing, such as the ordinary method of exhibiting their staff of office. And if the peace-officer, or those assisting him, misbehave themselves in the discharge of their duty, it is not deemed murder if they are killed.

All societies, for whatever purpose constituted, are declared unlawful;

1. Where the members are required to take or subscribe any unlawful oath or declaration.

2. Where the committee, or any of the officers, or other members, are kept secret from the society at large.

3. Where there are different divisions or branches.

4. Where committees, delegates, representatives, or missionaries are elected or appointed to communicate with any other society, or with any committee, &c. of such other society.

Any one being a member of any such society, or holding correspondence with any member thereof, is guilty of an unlawful confederacy, and punishable by fine and imprisonment.

ROBBERY, is an aggravated larceny or stealing, and is defined to be the forcible taking from the person of another, or in his presence, against his will, of any "chattel, money, or valuable security," to any value, by violence, or putting him in fear.

The "fear" need not be proved further, than that the circumstances of the taking were such as to induce a prosecutor to part with his property, or were calculated to create fear also. See THREATS.

Snatching property from another unawares is not robbery, unless some injury be done to the person, or there is a struggle for the property, or some force be used to obtain it.

The taking must be with a "felonious intent;" for if a man use menaces in order to obtain property, imagining or believing it to be his own, this is a trespass, not a robbery. The punishment for this felony, in some cases, is death. See STEALING FROM THE PERSON.

ROGUES AND VAGABONDS. See VAGRANTS.

ROLLS, are parchments which may be turned up with the hand in the form of a pipe. All the acts and records of courts are entered on rolls, and bound up with files.

ROUT. An assembly of persons going forcibly to commit an illegal act, though they do not actually commit it.

SACRILEGE. The breaking and entering a church or chapel, and stealing therein, is a felony; so of stealing in and breaking out of a church or chapel. See BURGLARY.

Burning or riotously demolishing a church or chapel, is also a capital felony. See BURNING.

SCAN. MAG. Scandalum magnatum (libelling of great men), a criminal proceeding against those who speak scandalous or derogatory words of peers, judges, "great men of the realm," and some high officers, seldom resorted to. It is founded upon an ancient statute against "devisers of false news and horrible lies of prelates, dukes, earls, barons, &c.," and compels the offender to produce his authority; and in default punishes him at the discretion of the council.

Scan. Mag., or scandalising peers, &c., is very often committed; but the punishment or remedy seems unconstitutional; and though words which would not support an action in the case of a commoner, are punishable as *scan. mag.* in the case of a peer, the proceeding is in disuse. A peeress is not within the statute, or any woman noble by birth. Words imputing corruption to a judge, are *scan. mag.;* but punishment by information or indictment is the more usual course.

SCIRE FACIAS. A writ which lies to enforce the execution of judgments, patents, or matters of record, or to vacate, quash, or annul them. A judgment upon which execution has not issued within a year and a day, is revived by this writ. A recognisance, which is matter of record, is enforced by this process; and a patent is repealed by its operation. The writ calls upon the party to make known to the court why such and such thing should not be done, and calling upon him to show sufficient cause to the contrary.

SCULPTURE. By the stat. 54 *G.* 3., called the *Copyright Act,* every person who shall make any new and original sculpture or model, or copy, or cast of the human figure, or of any bust or part of the human figure, clothed in drapery or otherwise, or of any animal or part of any animal combined with the human figure or otherwise, or any subject being matter of invention in sculpture, or of any alto or basso rilievo, or any cast from nature, of man or animals, whether separate or combined, &c., shall have the sole right and property of the whole of such new and original sculpture, &c. for fourteen years, putting their name and date thereon.

Persons (not having purchased the property in the original) making, importing, or selling pirated copies or casts of such sculptures, are made liable to damages in an action on the case. An additional term of 14 years is given to the proprietor, if living, and not having assigned his property.

The transfer of sculpture or models, &c., must be by *deed* signed and sealed, and attested by two credible witnesses.

SEAMEN IN MERCHANT VESSELS. By the Merchant Seamen's Act, 5 *&* 6 *W.* 4. *c.* 19., the legislature has provided, "that no seaman (apprentices excepted) be taken to sea without a written agreement," copies of which are to be deposited with the comptroller of customs at the ports of destination, or ports to which they belong, pursuant to the forms stated in the schedule to the act.

This agreement is to be carefully read over to each seaman; and with respect to the agreement itself, it is provided, that the seamen are not bound to produce it, in any action or suit; that its tenor shall not affect their lien on the ship; that the agreement itself shall not contain any agreement inconsistent with the provisions of the act, or make the seamen forego the right which the maritime law gives him to wages, in the case of freight earned by ships subsequently ost.

Punishments and forfeitures are inflicted on seamen for desertion or temporary absence from duty, and the 8th section sets forth the mode of ascertaining the amount of forfeiture, when the seamen contract for the voyage; and absolute desertion causes a forfeiture of his clothes and effects; and the increased wages payable to another to supply the deserted place, is summarily recoverable.

The secreting seamen who have signed the agreement, subjects the party to a penalty of *5l.* for every seaman. No debt exceeding *5s.* is recoverable from them, until the voyage is ended; and lodging-house-keepers cannot detain seamen's chests, &c.

Wages are payable within ten days after the seaman's discharge, or within three days after delivery of the cargo, whichever shall first happen; but if the ship is a coast trader, then, in two days from the termination of the agreement, or at the time of his discharge, whichever shall first happen.

Justices of the peace may adjudge summarily upon claims for wages not exceeding *20l.*; which provision supersedes the necessity of an admiralty suit, the justices being empowered to cause the tackle to be seized, in case the owner of the ship or master cannot be found, or sufficient distress cannot be had.

The registry of British merchant seamen is also effected; and the binding of apprentices is regulated.

The forcing on shore, or leaving behind, any person belonging to the crew, is made a misdemeanor, triable in *any part* of her majesty's dominions; and a seaman cannot be discharged abroad without the consent of consuls, &c.

Where assaults and batteries take place on board of ships, two justices of the peace are empowered summarily to decide thereon, and inflict a fine, as by the Petty Assault Act. See Assaults.

The produce of deceased seamen's effects is to be remitted to the corporation for relief of merchant seamen.

Penalties are inflicted on masters and owners, for not conforming to the regulations with regard to the signing and reading over the agreement; and in this act (here very imperfectly abstracted) the legislature has provided fully against the improvidence and ignorance of common sailors.

SEAMEN'S WAGES are recoverable in the admiralty court, by proceeding against the ship, or the master or owners; but if the wages due are under *20l.*, the plaintiff will not be allowed costs; for the Merchant Seamen's Act has provided a remedy, without depriving the seaman of his claim upon the tackle of the ship, or the ship itself, by referring all complaints for nonpayment of wages to two justices, who may summon master or owners, &c.; and, if he or they are not to be found, may seize and sell the tackle of the ship.

The pay of petty officers, seamen, and marines is regulated by the act 11 *G.* 4. *c.* 20., which amended and consolidated the laws relating to the pay of the royal navy, by which seamen are protected from various frauds by means of their giving powers of attorney, and making wills in respect of their pay, &c., and the distribution of their effects fully provided for. See Wills.

SEAWORTHINESS. A term applied to a ship, signifying that she is in every respect equipped for her voyage. In war-time a ship is not deemed seaworthy unless she be provided with all the papers necessary for the manifestation of the ship and cargo, or supplied with the sails required to facilitate her escape from an enemy.

SECONDARIES. Officers who are next or second to the chief officers, as the *secondaries* to the prothonotaries of the court of common pleas, the *secondaries* of the sheriffs of London, &c.

SEDITION. The uttering political writings and words which intemperately or indecently criticise the public measures of the king and his ministers, by imputing to them corrupt and improper motives, are, in law, *seditions;* for though temperate observations on such measures are allowable, yet the attempting to possess the people with an ill opinion of the government must necessarily be considered as an offence of a serious nature, whether the expedient resorted to be obloquy or ridicule. Verbal sedition chiefly consists in uttering intemperate words against the king, as by wishing him ill, repeating scandalous stories concerning him, cursing him, or denying his right to the throne; in fact, advisedly and deliberately saying any thing to bring the government into dis-esteem. Libels of this nature are misdemeanors, punishable by fine and imprisonment proportioned to the heinousness of the offence and the circumstances attendant upon it, at the discretion of the court.

The "uttering" may also be by printing and publishing or circulating in any manner whatever, with knowledge of its contents, the alleged libel; newspaper-publishers, booksellers, and venders of newspapers are answerable for the publications they print, publish, sell, or let to hire.

The defendant can never give in evidence the truth of any seditious libel: he may *justify*, that the publication is not libellous, or that he was not the author, or the circulator of the seditious libel was without knowledge of its contents, (but this line of defence cannot avail newspaper-printers, &c., and booksellers,) and all matters within the rules of evidence may be offered as tending to exonerate the party.

SEISIN, signifies the possession of freehold or copyhold estate or property. The word "possession" applies in strictness to personal property. A man is said to be *seised* of freehold, &c., *possessed* of leasehold or other personalty.

SERJEANT-AT-LAW. The highest degree in the law (excepting the judges, who are chosen from the serjeants), corresponding to that of "Doctor" in the civil law. See PRE-AUDIENCE.

SERVANTS are of various descriptions. They are either servants in husbandry and labourers, artisans and workmen in particular trades, and menial or domestic servants. The two first are controllable and regulated by various acts. (See LABOURERS.) But domestic servants are not. The acts chiefly relating to the two former classes of servants are the 20 *G*. 2. *c*. 19., and the 4 *G*. 4. *c*. 34. Several decisions have rather restricted than enlarged the powers apparently exerciseable by the act in respect of both master and workman; it is not unlikely that some general law will be soon promulgated, extending to every description of servants, giving two magistrates summary jurisdiction in all cases.

The hirings of agricultural servants are generally from Michaelmas to Michaelmas; but the hiring of a domestic servant is a continuing service from month to month, or, as it is termed, "a month's wages or month's warning," which agreement is reciprocal. Such agreement is seldom reduced into writing, the understanding is so commonly referred to.*

Servants may be dismissed instanter for improper or immoral conduct; and, on the other hand, if a master misconducts himself to his servant, he or she may leave. Where a dismissal takes place for misconduct, the current wages are forfeited.

Clerks are a superior sort of servants, and the doctrine of a month's

* This depends upon custom entirely. It is no general rule of law.

wages or month's warning does not apply to them. It does not appear settled what warning they are entitled to: a service of two or more years would raise the inference that the service was from year to year, and that half a year's warning would be mutually required. A quarter's notice on either side would probably, as Mr. Chitty suggests, be deemed sufficient.

The sudden dismissal of a clerk may be justified in cases of misconduct, open and palpable: mere suspicion, or trifling doubts of honesty, or capability, will not suffice, more especially as these matters, it may fairly be presumed, have been carefully considered or inquired into before the service commenced.

As to bonds for indemnifying a master from his clerk's embezzlement, see BOND.

Masters are liable for the faults as well as for the general negligence of their servants, but not for wilful misconduct, or, as the term is, *misfeazance*. The master being only made liable by virtue of an *implied* authority given to his servant, if that authority can be fairly presumed not to have existed, which it may, in cases of wilful fault, the master is exonerated; and it is always left to the jury to consider whether the servant acted under the *implied* authority of the master or not, or committed the act wilfully and of his own head or inclination, or only negligently or injudiciously; in which latter case the master is liable.

Masters cannot inflict corporal punishment, or strike their servants or clerks.

Apprentices, — a class of servants whose situation has been noticed under another title, — may be moderately punished, as their master stands in the place of a parent, and the waywardness of youth may require coercion; but manual correction is not, even in those cases, favoured by law.

SESSIONS OF THE PEACE. There are three different kinds of sessions holden by justices of the peace.—1. General sessions, which may be held at any time of the year, for the general execution of the authority of the justices. 2. The general quarter sessions, holden at four stated times in the year, pursuant to statute. 3. A special or petty sessions, which is holden upon particular occasions or settled times, as every market day, and is rather a voluntary arrangement of the justices to decide matters which should belong to the jurisdiction of two justices, a single justice having previously granted a summons compelling the party summoned to appear before the petty sessions.

In most corporate towns there are quarter sessions, &c.; and the king is empowered to grant a court of quarter sessions to those municipal corporations who shall petition for the same under particular circumstances.

There are sessions of constables of hundreds, or high constables, held at particular times, generally in the autumn, for regulating the hiring of servants, who go thither for the purpose of being hired: these are called statute sessions, or a statute fair.

SET-OFF. Where there are mutual debts due between plaintiff and defendant, the debts may be set-off, or allowed one against the other; but such matter must be pleaded; and where the debt due to the defendant is less than that due to the plaintiff, he must, on pleading such set-off, pay the remaining balance into court. It is only in actions for the non-payment of money that set-offs are allowable; set-offs not being allowed against unliquidated damages, penalties of bonds for the performance of covenants, &c.

SHERIFF. A conservator of the peace, appointed by the king, for the purpose of executing process, and preserving the peace, and assisting justices and others therein. He is, during his office, which is for a year, the first man in the county, and superior to any nobleman: he sits, or is entitled to sit, on the bench with the justices of assize.

The sheriffs of London and Middlesex are chosen by the citizens of London, who have the inheritance of that office by charter; and no one is excused from *fining* (paying 600*l.*), unless he swears he is not worth 15,000*l.*

Barristers and attorneys are exempted from being chosen sheriffs.

No person that has been sheriff, shall be chosen again within 2 years.

A sheriff cannot exercise the office of a justice of the peace.

Under-sheriffs must be appointed without fee, under a penalty of 500*l.*

The duties of a sheriff are very numerous: he executes all writs directed to him; also all precepts, warrants from justices of the peace, upon extraordinary occasions, to apprehend felons, traitors, and notorious delinquents: he executes all sentences of the law; and, in many instances, acts in a judicial capacity, as by executing writs of trial for debts under 20*l.*, administering justice in the county court, &c. All fines due to the king are receivable by him, and he is accountable for them; he makes and returns all inquisitions upon interlocutory judgments, writs of *ad quod damnum*, *extents*, *elegit*, &c. &c. The gaol of the county is under his government; the houses of correction being under that of the justices.

The under-sheriff performs most of the duties of the office. The under-sheriff is not to be an attorney or sheriff's officer, or continue in his office above a year.

SHIP, in law, signifies any description of vessel navigating on the sea, and includes all steam and other vessels employed in carrying passengers or goods.

If a ship is not duly registered, and exercises the privileges of a British-built ship, she is forfeited. Registry, although in every case adopted, is not material but for this purpose; though the omission might occasion inconvenience, as the certificate of registry evidences the title, and demonstrates its identity. See Registry of Ships.

The navigation of ships is regulated by the Navigation Acts.

The transfer of a ship or share in a ship is by a bill of sale, reciting the certificate of registry; and the same is not effectual until produced to the officers of customs, and entered in the Registry Book.

Upon a change of ownership, a new registry may be granted, if required; but is not necessary.

Registers of ships, if lost, may be granted anew; and persons wilfully detaining a ship's register, or certificate of registry, forfeit 100*l.*, on conviction before a justice, who is to certify the detainer; upon which certificate, a new registry can be had, or certificate granted.

The name of a vessel once registered, cannot be altered, and must be painted over the stern, in white or yellow letters on a black ground, under a penalty of 100*l.* See further the act *3 & 4 G. 4. c.* 55.

Ships declared unseaworthy, to be deemed lost or broken up, and never after entitled to the privileges of a British-built ship, for trade or navigation. *Ibid.*

Offences committed on board of ship, and malicious mischiefs committed to the destruction of a ship, or tending to its loss, or plundering it when cast ashore or in distress, are provided for by the statutes which punish offences against property.* And all felonies, robberies, and offences committed on the high seas, are triable before the judge of the admiralty court, and two of the judges of the common law courts, under a commission of oyer and terminer.

SHIP'S PAPERS. The papers or documents required for the manifestation of the property of the ship and cargo, &c. They are of two sorts; *viz.* 1st, Those required by the law of a particular country, as the certificate of registry, licence, charterparty, bills of lading, bill of health, &c. (see these titles), required by the law of England to be on board British ships; and, 2dly, Those required by the law of nations to be on board neutral ships, to vindicate their title to that character. Mr. Serjeant Marshall, following Mr. Hubner, has given the following description of the latter class of documents:—

1. The Passport, Sea Brief, or Sea Letter.—This is a permission from the neutral state, to the captain or master of the ship, to proceed on the voyage proposed, and usually contains his name and residence; the name, property, description, tonnage, and destination of the ship; the nature and quantity of the cargo the place whence it comes, and its destination; with such other matters as the practice of the place requires. This document is indispensably necessary for the safety of every neutral ship. Hubner says that it is the only paper rigorously insisted on by the Barbary corsairs; by the production of which alone their friends are protected from insult.

2. The Proofs of Property.—These ought to show that the ship really belongs to the subjects of a neutral state. If she appear to either belligerent to have been built in the enemy's country, proof is generally required that she was purchased by the neutral before, or captured and legally condemned and sold to the neutral after, the declaration of war; and in the latter case, the *Bill of Sale*, properly authenticated, ought to be produced. Mr. Hubner admits that these proofs are so essential to every neutral vessel, for the prevention of frauds, that such as sail without them have no reason to complain if they be interrupted in their voyages, and their neutrality disputed.

3. The Muster Roll.—This, which the French call *rôle d'équipage*, contains the names, ages, quality, place of residence, and, above all, place *of birth*, of every person of the ship's company. This document is of great use in ascertaining a ship's neutrality. It must naturally excite a strong suspicion if the majority of the crew be found to consist of foreigners, still more if they be natives of the enemy's country. (See Seamen.)

4. The Charterparty.—Where the ship is chartered, this instrument serves to authenticate many of the facts on which the truth of her neutrality must rest, and should therefore be always found on board chartered ships.

5. The Bills of Lading.—By these the captain acknowledges the receipt of the goods specified therein, and promises to deliver them to the consignee or his order. Of these there are usually several duplicates, one of which is kept by the captain, one by the shipper of the goods, and one transmitted to the consignee. This instrument, being only the evidence of a private transaction between the owner of the goods and the captain, does not carry with it the same degree of authenticity as the charterparty.

6. The Invoices.—These contain the particulars and prices of each parcel of goods, with the amount of the freight, duties, and other charges thereon, which are usually transmitted from the shippers to their factors or consignees. These invoices prove by whom the goods were shipped, and to whom consigned. They carry with them, however, but little authenticity, being easily fabricated where fraud is intended.

* The destruction of a ship or vessel, with the intent to murder or endanger the life of any one, and the doing of any act tending to the *immediate* loss of a vessel, are declared capital felonies by stat. 1 *Vict. c.* 89. *ss.* 4, 5. The setting fire to a ship or vessel is a felony punishable by transportation for life, or for not less than 15 years, or imprisonment for not exceeding 3 years; *s.* 6. These acts must be proved to have been done maliciously, *i. e.* advisedly or deliberately.

7. The Log Book, or Ship's Journal.—This contains a minute account of the ship's course, with a short history of every occurrence during the voyage. If this be faithfully kept, it will throw great light on the question of neutrality; if it be in any respect fabricated, the fraud may in general be easily detected.

8. The Bill of Health.—This is a certificate, properly authenticated, that the ship comes from a place where no contagious distemper prevails; and that none of the crew, at the time of her departure, were infected with any such disorder. It is generally found on board ships coming from the Levant, or from the coast of Barbary, where the plague so frequently prevails.

A ship using false or simulated papers is liable to confiscation.

SIMONY, is a corrupt presentation of any one to an ecclesiastical benefice, for money, gift, or reward: the right of presentation to a living is forfeited, and vested, *pro hâc vice*, for the turn, in the crown. By the statute 31 *Eliz. c.* 6., it is, for avoiding simony, enacted, that if any person shall, for any sum of money, reward, gift, profit, or benefit, present or collate any person to an ecclesiastical benefit or dignity, such presentation shall be void, and the presentee be rendered incapable of ever enjoying the same benefice, and the crown shall present it for that turn only. But if the presentee dies without being convicted of such simony in his lifetime, it is enacted by stat. 1 *W. & M. c.* 16., that the simoniacal contract shall not prejudice any other innocent patron, on pretence of lapse to the crown or otherwise. Also by the stat. 12 *Anne*, *stat.* 2. *c.* 12., if any person, for money or profit, shall procure, in his own name, or the name of any other, the next presentation to any living ecclesiastical, and shall be presented thereupon, this is declared to be a simoniacal contract, and the party is subject to all the ecclesiastical penalties of simony, is disabled from holding the benefice, and the presentation devolves to the crown.

Where a clerk, who had been presented corruptly, continued incumbent until his death above 30 years after, it was held that the king's right of presenting was not gone. And it has been lately decided, that where a clerk was simoniacally presented, instituted, and inducted, and the king, on the ground of simony, presented another clerk, who was instituted and inducted the king's presentee might maintain ejectment for the benefice against the other clerk, since the church was void by reason of his simoniacal presentation; although it had been held in an early case, that the king could not take advantage of the corrupt presentation, until the clerk had been removed by *quare impedit*.

General bonds, to resign at the patron's request, were held by the house of lords to be simoniacal and illegal. But it was afterwards considered that a bond to resign in favour of a *particular* person was valid, until a recent case in the house of lords, in which it was decided that there was no distinction between a bond conditioned for resigning generally on the request of the patron, and a bond conditioned to resign in favour of a particular relation of the patron, and therefore a bond for resigning in favour of one or two brothers of the patron was held simoniacal and void.

In consequence of that decision, two statutes have been passed on the subject, rendering such bonds valid to a certain extent and under certain regulations.

SIMPLE CONTRACT, DEBT BY. Debts by simple contract are those where the contract upon which the obligation arises is neither ascertained by matter of record, nor yet by deed or special instrument, but by mere oral evidence, the most simple of any; or by notes unsealed, which are capable of a more easy proof, and (therefore only) better than a verbal promise.

SINECURE, is where a rector of a parish hath a vicar under him, endowed and charged with the cure, so that the rector is not obliged either to duty or residence. And when a church is fallen down, and the parish becomes destitute of parishioners, it is said to be a *sinecure*.

SIX CLERKS IN CHANCERY. Officers in chancery, who transact and file all proceedings by bill and answer; and also issue some patents that pass the great seal, as pardons of men for chance-medley, patents for ambassadors, sheriffs' patents, and some others. They likewise sign all office copies of bills and answers to be read in court, and also certificates of their being filed; and are required to attend upon the court in term, by two at a time, at Westminster, and there read the pleadings. (See titles CHANCELLOR, CHANCERY.) Each six clerk has 10 clerks, and these 10 clerks (commonly called "clerks in court,") are the attorneys in chancery, attorneys at law, practising, or, as it is termed, *soliciting* suits through their intervention. Hence the term *solicitor*, which is a title inferior to that of attorney.

SMALL DEBTORS. All persons in execution upon any judgment, in whatsoever court the same may have been obtained, for any debt or damages not exceeding the sum of 20*l*. *exclusive of costs*, and who shall have lain in prison for the space of 12 successive calendar months next before the time of their application, shall, upon application for that purpose in term time, made to some one of her majesty's courts at Westminster, to the satisfaction of such court, be forthwith discharged out of custody, as to such execution, by the rule or order of such court. These 12 months are reckoned inclusive of the day the party were charged in execution.

SPIRITUAL COURTS. Courts having jurisdiction over matters appertaining or annexed to ecclesiastical affairs; such as, the probate of wills; suits for "brawling" or "smiting" in a church or churchyard; slander imputing incontinence, as well as the offence itself; the validity of marriages; the restitution of conjugal rights; subtraction of tithes; and some others, which are termed *spiritual* causes (although some of them are of a secular nature); because the interference of these courts is suggested to be for the "soul's health" of the party cited.

SPRING GUN. The setting a spring gun, excepting within a dwelling house from sunset to sunrise, is declared by statute to be illegal, and will subject the offender to an indictment, although no actual injury has ensued. The same of man-traps, or other engines calculated to destroy human life or inflict grievous bodily harm. A trespasser in grounds, hurt by these inhuman contrivances at night, might even indict the offender; and certainly, if hurt in the daytime, bring his action for the injury he had sustained, notwithstanding notice given; for it is a misdemeanor to set them at all, except, as before stated, in a dwelling-house at night.

SOCAGE. Service of the plough; from *soc*, a plough. An inferior free-tenant's service on a grant of land from his superior lord. The tenure was not base, as that of villenage, which is the foundation of copyhold; nor was it honourable, as the service was not a military tenure, as knight's service or its subordinate tenures, escuage, serjeanty, &c.: but the circumstance of its being certain in its render, and as all those who held not by knight's service, &c., or in villenage, held by this service, it gradually became commuted into a money payment, or render of a thing certain. As certainty of rent was the distinguishing mark of socage, it fell out, when military service was on the decline, that the military tenures were discharged in like manner by a small rent; so that by degrees all land was holden by certain services or ancient rents, which the tenants bought off or extinguished, and became socage by reason of the certainty of render. On the abolition of military tenures, in the reign of Charles II., all land (except copyhold) became socage, or, in legal phrase, "holden of our sovereign lord the king in free and common socage," with the exception of copyholders, who hold according to their ancient tenure, "at the will of the lord." See MANOR.

Tenants in ancient demesne were, in fact, nothing more than socage or agricultural tenants upon those lands which, as being those formerly of Edward the Confessor, became the *demesne* or private lands of William the Conqueror, and enjoyed various privileges; such as to have their own courts, where the steward is the judge together with the freehold tenants, to be free of tolls, &c. They were anciently termed *soc-men*. The manors which are ancient demesne are only those noted in Domesday Book as *terræ regis Edwardi*.

SOLICITATIONS TO COMMIT CRIME. To incite or solicit another to commit an offence is a misdemeanor, although no crime be perfected.

STABBING. See WOUNDING.

STEALING IN A DWELLING-HOUSE. This offence is a larceny, and punishable as such. (See LARCENY.) But stealing in a dwelling-house to the value of 5*l*. is, by statute, punishable by transportation for life; and, if the court shall think fit, imprisonment before transportation, with or without hard labour, in the common gaol or house of correction, or confinement in the penitentiary, for not more than four years, nor less than one year.

If a man steal the goods of another in his own house, or a woman steal the goods of a stranger in the house of her husband, it is not within the statute, which was not intended to protect property which might be in a house from the owner of the house, but from the depredations of others. So, if the goods be under the protection of the person of the prosecutor at the time they are stolen, the case will not be within the statute. For a case to be within the meaning of the statute, it is necessary that the goods should be under the protection of the house, and be deposited in it for safe custody. It is a question for the court, not the jury, to decide, whether goods are under the protection of the dwelling-house, or in the personal care of the owner. —(*Archbold's Crim. Pleading*.)

The stealing in a dwelling-house, with menace or threat, some person therein being put in fear, is punishable, by 1 *Vict. c.* 86. *s.* 5., with transportation for not exceeding fifteen years, nor less than ten years, or imprisonment for not exceeding three years.

For the punishment of accessories, see PRINCIPAL and ACCESSORY.

STEALING FROM THE PERSON. By the stat. 1 *Vict. c.* 87., repealing part of the act 7 *&* 8 *Geo.* 4. *c.* 29., relative to larceny and other offences against property, and obtaining money by means of threats, the robbing of any person, attended with stabbing, cutting, or wounding is a capital felony; *ss.* 1, 2. Robbery, attended with personal violence, as well as an assault with that intent, the offender being armed with any offensive weapon or instrument, is a felony, punishable by transportation for the offender's life, or for not less than fifteen years, or imprisonment for not less than three years; *s.* 3.

Simple robbery, or stealing from the person, is punishable at the discretion of the court, by transportation for not exceeding fifteen years, nor less than ten years, or imprisonment for not exceeding three years; *s.* 5.

A simple assault, with intent to rob, is a felony, and (except in the cases where a greater punishment is provided by this act) punishable by imprisonment for not exceeding three years; *s.* 6.

Accessories before the fact are punishable as principals. Accessories after the fact (except a receiver of stolen property) being punishable with imprisonment for not exceeding two years.

To constitute the offence of robbery, there must be a taking from the person, or in the presence of the prosecutor, with violence, or with such force, or by such gestures or acts, as to excite the apprehension of danger; putting in fear being that criterion that distinguishes robbery from other larcenies. A *previous* putting in fear is also necessary to complete this offence; for a *subsequent* aggression is only a simple assault. See THREATS.

STOCK IN TRADE, appears to be rateable to the poor-rate, if it be productive, and is the property of the person in possession. Custom and long usage appear to be in favour of its rateability; and, if it can be shown that stock in trade has once been rated, it will warrant the justices at sessions in confirming the rate, if appealed from.

A farmer cannot be rated for the stock absolutely necessary for his farming and paying his rent, but for his stock in hand he is liable to be rated.

However, the cases on this subject are numerous, and, like all particular instances, depend upon the peculiarity of the facts.

A late act has passed, the operation of which will settle all doubts on this subject. See POOR-RATES.

STOCK-BROKERS, or STOCK-JOBBERS. Stock-brokers are those who conclude contracts or bargains for the sale or transfer of government or South-sea stocks. They are admitted, as other brokers are, by the lord mayor and aldermen. Stock-jobbers are generally members of an association called "The Stock Exchange," and accommodate the buyers and sellers of stock with the exact sums they want. A jobber is generally possessed of considerable property in the funds, and declares a price at which he will either sell or buy. Thus he declares he is ready to buy 3 per cent. consols at 85½, or to sell at 85⅝; so that, in this way, a person willing to buy or sell any sum, however small, has never any difficulty in finding an individual with whom to deal. The jobber's profit is generally ⅛ per cent., or 2*s.* 6*d.* for the 100*l.*, for which he transacts both a sale and a purchase: he frequently confines himself entirely to this and similar sort of business, and engages in no other sort of stock speculations. — (*M'Culloch's Comm. Dict.*)

Time bargains are prohibited under heavy penalties, on account of the pernicious nature of such contracts; and money lent for the purpose of paying differences (whatever be the security given to the lender) cannot be recovered by him. It seems, however, by a late decision, that the act prohibiting speculations by way of time bargains, &c., does not extend to dealings in foreign funds.

STOPPAGE IN TRANSITU, is the term applied to the right a seller of goods has to stop them in their *transit* or passage to the buyer, in case of his bankruptcy or insolvency.

SUMMARY APPLICATION, means redress by means of a

motion in court, which is applicable to cases respecting annuities, attorneys, warrants of attorney, &c., and to those matters which by law or statute are placed within the immediate and peculiar jurisdiction of the courts of law; so that the party complaining may state his grievance, and have ample redress, without the delay or hindrance of a suit, in which he could not be a witness.

The term is also used to denote penal inflictions by one or two justices, under the Game Acts, and many other acts, giving magistrates summary jurisdiction, with or without right of appeal. In summary applications, the courts and magistrates are bound to take the *sum* or all the circumstances into consideration.

SUNDAY. The stat. 29 *C.* 2. *c.* 7. prohibits the exercise of any man's "ordinary calling" on a Sunday: therefore any contract *in pursuance of a man's ordinary calling**, entered into on that day, knowingly, is void; but if a party buy goods, *and keep them*, the price may be recovered, as upon an account subsequently stated.

Various penalties are inflicted upon persons exercising their trades on this day, but they are only subject to one penalty, for the whole is but one offence, though the trading be carried on during the whole day.

Law processes cannot be executed on a Sunday; but bail may take their principal, and felons may be apprehended, on this day.

SUPERCARGOES, are persons employed by commercial companies or private merchants to take charge of the cargoes they export to foreign countries, to sell them there to the best advantage, and to purchase returning cargoes of the most advantageous kind. The supercargoes generally go out and return with the ships on board of which they embarked; and therein differ from factors, who reside abroad at the settlements of the companies for which they act. The East India Company send out supercargoes only to the places where they have no factories; and sometimes the chief supercargo remains at the place of the ship's destination some time, waiting the arrival or return of other ships, and acting as factor for the company. The contracts of a supercargo are equally binding as those of a master, within the scope of his authority.—(*Steel's Ship-master's Assistant.*)

SURGEONS AND APOTHECARIES. The business of an apothecary is to prepare and administer the prescription of the physician, pursuant to his directions; or they practise physic on their own account, and administer medicines upon their own responsibility or discretion. Surgeons are said to deal in the mechanical part of physic, by performing cures, or operating with the hand, and must not, *in that capacity*, administer inward medicine. The apothecaries are under the control of the Apothecaries' Company, who, by virtue of an act, 55 *Geo.* 3. *c.* 194., are to examine persons intending to practise; and the College of Surgeons regulate the admission of surgeons, by their examiners, under the 32 *Hen.* 8.

By the 55 *Geo.* 3. *c.* 194. *s.* 20., it is enacted, "That no person (except such as be then [1st of August, 1816] actually practising as such) shall act or practise as an *apothecary*, in any part of England, without having obtained a certificate as therein described, under a penalty of 20*l.* for every offence;" therefore, a person having a certificate from the College of Surgeons cannot charge for attending a

* It has been determined that contracts, *not* in pursuance of a man's ordinary calling, are valid, though made on a Sunday.

patient in a fever, unless he also have a certificate from the Apothecaries' Company. But it seems that a surgeon may charge for medicine administered in a surgical case, when the medicine was subservient and subordinate to the discharge of his duty as a surgeon.

It is now settled that an apothecary may recover a compensation for his attendance as well as for medicine furnished; but, on the other hand, it has been in another case decided, that an apothecary who charges for his attendance is not entitled to remuneration for the medicine he supplies, and *vice versâ*. These decisions, apparently so opposite, but which depended upon particular circumstances, are reconciled by a subsequent decision, which held, that where one is both apothecary *and* surgeon, he may, besides his charges for medicine, recover reasonable charges for attendance.

Action on the case lies against surgeons and apothecaries for gross ignorance and want of skill in their profession; and any conduct that manifests a criminal disregard of human life is a misdemeanor, if not manslaughter, according to the event. Gross inattention or ignorance in a non-medical or not regular practitioner, followed by loss of life, seems to have been considered as manslaughter, while the same act in a regular practitioner was a *misdemeanor;* however, at this day it may be deemed invidious to pursue this inquiry, as no profession is better supplied with intelligent and learned men than the medical.

Neither surgeons nor apothecaries are liable to serve on juries.

SURPLUSAGE. A superfluity or redundancy of expression in the mode of statement: useless additions the courts reject, but retain the material part of the plea, writing, &c.

SUR-REBUTTER. (In pleading.) The replication or answer of the plaintiff to the defendant's *rebutter*. See REBUTTER.

SUR-REJOINDER. A second defence (as the replication is the first) of the plaintiff's declaration in a cause. As a rejoinder is the defendant's answer to the *replication* of the plaintiff, so a sur-rejoinder is the plaintiff's answer to the defendant's rejoinder. See REJOINDER; PLEADING.

SURRENDER, is a yielding up of an estate for life or years to him that has the immediate estate in reversion or remainder, and is either in fact or in law. Surrenders in fact must be made by deed, which is the allowable evidence: a surrender in law is one which may be implied, and generally has reference to estates or tenancies from year to year, &c.; as where a landlord receives the key or accepts possession of the tenement let, or does any act so inconsistent with the subsisting relation of landlord and tenant, as to imply an intention that the landlord should be in the same situation as if an express surrender had been made. Estates or tenancies created by any writing should be surrendered by writing; and the cancelling a lease will not of itself operate as a surrender.

TAIL, or FEE-TAIL. A conveyance of lands (not copyhold, unless by special custom of the manor,) to a man and the heirs of his body, or the heirs of the bodies of him and A. his wife: the first is called tail general, the latter tail special; or such estate in tail may be diversified by the distinction of sexes, for both of them may be either tail-male or tail-female: for if the lands be given or conveyed to a man and the heirs *male* of his body this is tail-male general; but if to a man and the heirs female of his body, on his present wife begotten, tail-female special. This estate may arise in wills by implication.

This estate is a freehold in law, and the tenant or party entitled, although his interest is but for life, may commit waste and cut timber; and as to dower, curtesy, or the like, it is subject to the same incidents as freehold. As limitations of estates, in this manner, are constantly made for perpetuating the possession of landed property, either by will or settlement, it has been the object of the legislature, for many years, to facilitate their alienation, and to render them subject to the debts and contracts of the possessor: this is completely effected with regard to bankrupt tenants in tail; and with respect to other persons entitled, they can, where the limitation does not extend beyond their own issue, bar the entail, and either dispose of the land, or resettle it. This process was effected by fictitious suits, termed "fines and recoveries," now superseded by an ordinary conveyance enrolled, and, if married women are parties, acknowledged before a judge, master in chancery, or two commissioners, with the consent of the person called the "protector," if he is not in possession, or has not the prior estate; but those in immediate expectancy cannot bar such their interests or expectancies; for instance, an eldest son of a tenant in tail cannot sell his interest during his father's life, who is the tenant in tail; nor can the father himself do it, if a kind of trustee, called a "protector," has been appointed, whose consent must be obtained before any alienation can be perfected. See PROTECTOR; RECOVERIES.

Leases made by tenants in tail, which do not tend to the prejudice of the issue in tail, being for three lives, or 21 years, and reserving the usual rents, are good, but will not bar the reversioners or remaindermen, although they will the issue; such leases not being granted to take effect at a future time. And if a husband is possessed, in right of his wife, of an entailed estate, he may, with her concurrence, grant similar leases, which will bind the issue.

TENANT. One that holds or possesses lands or tenements by any kind of title, either in fee, for life, years, or at will. The word in law is used with divers additions: thus, Tenant in dower, is she that possesses land by virtue of her dower; Tenant by the curtesy, he that holds for his life, by reason of a child begotten of him by his wife, being an heiress; Tenant in mortgage, that holds by means of a mortgage; Tenant by the verge in ancient demesne, who is admitted by the rod in the court of ancient demesne; Tenant by copy of court roll, who is admitted tenant of any lands, &c. within a manor; Tenant in fee simple; Tenant in fee tail; Tenant at the will of the lord, according to the custom of the manor; Tenant at will by the common law; Tenant from year to year; Tenant by lease; and Tenant upon sufferance.

So there are also joint tenants, that have equal right in lands and tenements by virtue of one title; tenants in common, that have equal right, but hold by divers titles; particular tenant, as tenant for years, for life, &c., that holds only for his term; sole tenant, he that hath no other joined with him; several tenant, as opposite to joint tenant, or tenant in common.

TENANTS IN COMMON, are such as hold by several and distinct titles, but by unity of *possession* only.

For instance, one may hold his part in fee simple, the other may hold in tail, or for life; so that there is no necessary unity of *interest*. One may hold by descent, the other by purchase; or the one by purchase from A., the other by purchase from B.; so that there is no unity of title. The estate of one may have been vested 50 years, the estate of the other but yesterday; so there is no unity of time. The only unity there is is that of possession.

Tenancy in common may be created either by the destruction of two estates, in joint-tenancy and coparcenry, or by special limitation in a deed. By the destruction of the two estates last mentioned is intended such destruction as does not sever the unity of possession, but only the unity of title or interest: as, if one of two joint tenants in fee aliens his estate for the life of the alienee, the alienee and the other joint tenant are tenants in common; for they now have several titles,—the other joint tenant by the original grant, the alienee by the new alienation; and they also have several interests,—the former joint tenant in fee simple, the alienee for his own life only. In short, whenever an estate in joint-tenancy or coparcenry is dissolved, so that there be no partition made, but the unity of possession continues, it is turned into a tenancy in common. — (*Black's Comm.*)

A tenancy in common may also be created by express limitation in a deed: but here care must be taken not to insert words which imply a joint estate; and then, if lands be given to two or more, and it be not joint tenancy, it must be a tenancy in common. Land given to two, to be holden, the one moiety to one, and the other moiety to the other, is an estate in common; and, if one grants to another half his land, the grantor and grantee are also tenants in common.

The words, *equally to be divided*, make a tenancy in common, in surrenders of copyholds.

Tenants in common (like joint tenants), are compellable to make partition of their lands. See title JOINT TENANTS.

TENANTS, in the most ordinary acceptation of the word, mean those who hold land or houses at stipulated rents, or at rack rent, or, as in case of tenants at sufferance, at a reasonable rent to be recovered by action; *viz.*—

TENANT AT WILL. Tenant at will is where lands or tenements are let by one man to another, to have and to hold to him at the will of the party letting, by force of which letting the lessee is in possession. In this case, the lessee is called tenant at will, because he hath no certain nor sure estate, for the lessor may put him out at what time it pleaseth him. But every lease at will must be at the will of both parties.—(*Litt. Tenures.*)

If an agreement be made to let premises so long as both parties like, and reserving a compensation accruing daily, and not referable to a year, or any aliquot part of a year, it does not create a holding from year to year, but a tenancy at will, strictly so called. And though the tenant has expended money in improving the premises, that does not give him a term to hold until he is indemnified.

A man who enters and enjoys under a void lease, and pays rent, is tenant at will.

A mortgagor is in some respects strictly tenant at will, and in many cases is like a tenant at will.

If a tenant whose lease is expired, is permitted to continue in possession, pending a treaty for a further lease, he is not a tenant from year to year, but so strictly at will, that he may be turned out of possession without notice.

Where a letting is at will, rent being paid quarterly, the tenant, after a quarter of a year is commenced, may determine his will, but then he must pay that quarter's rent; and if the landlord determine his will after the commencement of a quarter, he shall lose his rent for that quarter. So, if half-yearly.

Tenant at will may be ousted also by express words, or by implication; as, if the landlord come upon the land, and say that the tenant shall not continue over, he may determine his will, though in the absence of the tenant. But words *off* the land will not, till notice to the tenant.

A tenancy at will is generally determined by the death of either party; but an interest from year to year is transmissable to representatives beneficially, or as trustees.

Tenants from year to year, and Notices to quit.—Tenants from year to year are where one lets lands or tenements to another without limiting any certain or determinate estate; especially if an *annual* rent be reserved.

But, if an agreement be made to let premises so long as both parties like, and reserving a compensation accruing from day to day, and not referrible to a year, or any aliquot part of a year, it does not create a holding from year to year, but a tenancy at will, strictly so called.

Where the parties are silent as to the length of the notice required, the law requires that in case of a tenancy from year to year, it should be at least *half a year* (not merely six lunar months); so that it may be laid down as a general rule, that, in order to put an end to a tenancy from year to year, there must be half a year's notice to quit, ending at the period of the year when the tenancy commenced: a rule that extends equally to houses, lands, tithes, &c.

If there be a tenancy for a year, and by consent of both parties the tenant continue in possession afterwards, the law implies a tacit renovation of the contract; for where a tenant holds over after the expiration of his term, without having entered into any new contract, he holds upon the former terms; they are therefore supposed to have renewed the old agreement, which was to hold for a year. But then it is necessary for the sake of convenience, that, if either party should be inclined to change his mind, he should give the other half a year's notice befor the expiration of the next or following year.

A party verbally agreed to rent a house as tenant from year to year, for the residue of a term which was three years and three quarters; the court determined, that though perhaps he might have quitted without notice at the end of three years, yet the remaining longer implied a contract to pay rent for the residue of the term.

In tenancies from year to year, there must always be six months' notice to quit on either side, according to the ancient law, except where any special agreement, or the custom of particular places, intervenes.

By special custom, three months' notice, or twelve months', will be the proper notice. As by the custom of London, where a tenant, under the yearly rent of forty shillings, is only entitled to a quarterly notice.

A tenancy from year to year cannot be determined so as to bar the interest of the tenant's creditors, unless there be either a legal notice to quit, or a surrender in writing.

An agreement, by which "the tenant is always to be subject to quit at three months' notice," constitutes a tenancy which may be determined by a three months' notice to quit, expiring at the same time of the year it commenced, or at any corresponding quarter-day.

But although the tenant, under such an agreement, enters in the middle of one of the usual quarters, if there appear to be no agreement to the contrary, he will be presumed to hold from the day he enters, and the tenancy can only be determined by a notice expiring that day of the year, or some other quarter-day calculated from thence.

A tenancy commenced on the 21st of November, and the tenant, after settling for the fraction of the quarter, continued to pay his rent half-yearly, — at Midsummer and Christmas. The holding is to be computed, not from the middle of the quarter, but from the succeeding quarter-day. A notice to quit therefore, expiring at Christmas, is in such case good.

But where premises are let *from year to year*, upon an agreement that either party may determine the tenancy by a *quarter's* notice, this notice must expire at the period of the year when the tenancy commenced.

A quarterly reservation of rent is not of itself sufficient to dispense with the necessity of a regular six months' notice to quit.

Tenancies from year to year, if the tenant dies, do not determine; but the same notice must be given, and the executor must pay the rent.

Tenant from year to year, also, *before* a mortgage or grant of the reversion, is entitled to six months' notice to quit before the end of the year, from the mortgagee or grantee; but if the tenancy commence after the mortgage or grant, notice is not necessary, for the mortgagee and grantee have a superior title. A lease would be voidable under the same circumstances.

There is no distinction between houses and lands, as to the time of giving notice to quit; they are both governed by one rule.

Tithes, in this respect, are assimilated to land. If, therefore, a composition for tithes be made by A., as proprietor, and he leases them to B., whose interest is afterwards put an end to by A., before any alteration is made in the composition, A. cannot determine it without six months' notice.

Where a house, land, and tithes are held under a verbal letting at a joint rent, a notice to quit "*the house, lands, and premises, with the appurtenances,*" includes the tithes, and is sufficient to put an end to the tenancy.

A notice to quit has reference, in all cases, to the letting; therefore, where a house was taken by the month, it was held that a month's notice was sufficient to entitle the landlord to recover possession.

A tenant sometimes enters upon different parts of the land at different periods of the year, although all are contained in one letting. When this happens, the notice to quit must be given with reference to the time of entry upon the substantial parts of the demised premises, without regard to the other parts, which are auxiliaries only, though the tenant will be obliged to quit them at the respective times of his entry thereon.

Difficulties frequently arise as to the period of the commencement of a tenancy; and, when a regular notice to quit on any particular day is given, and the time when the term began is unknown, the effect of such notice, as to its being evidence or not of the time of the commencement of the tenancy, will depend upon the particular circumstances attending its delivery, for the tenant may assent to it by promising to quit; but mere angry words will not bind the tenant to quit; it must be a deliberate assent.

When the landlord is ignorant of the time when the term of his tenant commenced, a notice to quit is sometimes given, not specifying any particular day, but ordering the tenant in general terms to quit, and deliver up possession of the premises "at the end and expiration of the current year of his tenancy thereof, which shall expire next after the end of one half-year from the date of the notice;" and such general notice is sufficient to support an ejectment.

Where a tenant, by lease, continues to hold after the expiration of it, as tenant at will, and assigns to another, the tenancy of the assignee shall be held to commence at the day on which it commenced under the lease; and a notice to quit on that day only is good, notwithstanding the assignee came in on a different day.

A notice desiring the defendant to "quit the premises which you hold under me, your term therein having long since expired," does not recognise a subsisting tenancy from year to year subsequent to the term, but is a mere demand of possession.

Where a notice to quit is given at *Lady-Day* or *Michaelmas* generally, it shall be *prima facie* held to mean *New Lady-Day* or *New Michaelmas;* but it is open to explanation, that *Old Michaelmas* or *Old Lady-Day* was intended.

A notice dated 27th, and served on the 28th September, requiring a tenant to quit "at Lady-Day next, or at the end of this current year," must be understood to mean a six months', and not a two days' notice to quit.

Where a power is given to a party to determine a lease, on giving a notice in *writing*, he cannot determine it by giving a verbal notice.

A parol notice would be sufficient under a verbal letting: in other cases it should be in writing. Yet a lease of tithes cannot be without deed; yet a parol agreement for retaining tithes must be determined by a written notice, with analogy to the notice given in a holding of land.

A receiver appointed by the court of chancery, with a general authority to let the lands to tenants from year to year, has also authority to determine such tenancies by a regular notice to quit.

In the case of a tenancy from year to year, a notice to quit given by a person acting as steward of the corporation is sufficient, without evidence that he had an authority under seal from the corporation for that purpose.

Where there are three joint trustees of an estate, notice to quit or to discontinue the possession given by two is bad, even though given in the name of the third, and the third trustee afterwards adopts it, and joins in an ejectment.

To entitle joint tenants to recover in ejectment against a tenant from year to year, the notice to quit must be signed by all the joint tenants at the time it is served; but if the notice be given by an agent, it is sufficient if his authority be subsequently recognised.

Notice to quit served upon one of two tenants upon the premises, who hold under a joint demise, is evidence that the notice reached the other who lived elsewhere,

It is not necessary that a notice to quit should be directed to the tenant in possession, if proved to be delivered to him at the proper time.

If a notice to quit is directed to the tenant by a wrong Christian name, and he keeps it, it is a waiver of the misdirection; and the lessor may recover on it, if there was no other tenant of the name.

A misdescription of the premises, in a notice to quit, is immaterial, if they are otherwise sufficiently designated, so that the party to whom notice has been given has not been misled by it.

When a notice to quit is signed by the party, and attested by a witness, such witness must be called to prove the handwriting of the party, or his absence be accounted for, although he was not the person who served it upon the tenant: proof that it was served upon the tenant, that he read it, and did not object to it, is not, in such case, sufficient.

The delivery of the notice to quit to the servant of the tenant, at his dwelling-house, to whom the nature of it was explained, though such dwelling-house was not situated on the premises, and it did not appear to have come to the tenant's hands, is strong presumptive evidence that it reached him, which may be rebutted by the evidence of the servant; but the mere leaving a notice to quit at the tenant's house, without further proof of its being delivered to a servant, and explained, or that it came to the tenant's hands, is not sufficient to support an ejectment.

If a landlord receive rent, due after the expiration of a notice to quit, it is a waiver of that notice; otherwise, if the money had not been received as rent, but as a satisfaction for the injury done by the tenant, in continuing on his late landlord's premises as a trespasser: but a notice to quit is, in general, waived by the receipt of rent due subsequent to such notice, yet the mere acceptance of rent by a landlord, subsequent to the time when the tenant ought to have quitted, according to the notice given him for that purpose, is not itself a waiver on the part of the landlord of such notice, but matter of evidence only, to be left to the jury under the circumstances of the case: for the landlord might possibly have accepted the rent under terms, or made an express declaration that he did not mean to waive the notice; and that, notwithstanding his acceptance or receipt of the rent, he should still insist upon the possession; or fraud, or contrivance might have been practised on the part of the tenant on paying it. The question, therefore, in such cases is, with what intention the rent was *received*, and what the real intention of both parties was.

A tenant who holds over after the expiration of his lease is not entitled to notice, unless the occupation has continued for a year, or rent has been paid.

Where rent is usually paid at a banker's, if the banker, without any special authority, receive rent accruing after the expiration of a notice to quit, the notice is not thereby waived.

A notice to the tenant, that if he do not quit in fourteen days, he will be required to pay double rent, given after the expiration of a regular notice to quit, is no waiver of such notice.

So, if a landlord give notice to his tenant to quit at the expiration of the lease, and the tenant hold over, the landlord is entitled to double rent; and a second notice delivered to the tenant, after the expiration of such notice, "to quit on a subsequent day, or pay double rent," is no waiver of the first notice, or of the double rent which has accrued under it.

If at the end of the year (where there has been a tenancy from year to year) the landlord accepts another as his tenant, without any surrender in writing, such acceptance shall be a dispensation of the notice to quit.

Notice to quit, however, is not necessary in every case. Thus, where a lease is determinable on a certain event, or at a particular period, no notice to quit is necessary, because both parties are equally apprised of the determination of the term.

So, if the tenant has paid rent, or "attorned," *i. e.* acknowledged himself by such payment or otherwise, tenant to some other person, or done some other act, disclaiming to hold as tenant to the landlord, in that case, no notice is necessary. Indeed, if a tenant put his landlord at defiance, his landlord may either consider him as his tenant or a trespasser, and, in the latter case, need not give him a notice to quit before he brings his ejectment; but a refusal, however, to pay rent to a devisee in a will which was contested, is not such a disavowal of the title, as to entitle such devisee to maintain an ejectment without giving a previous notice.

A mortgagee may recover possession against the mortgagor, or a tenant under a lease from the mortgagor, posterior to the mortgage, without notice to quit; for, when the mortgagor is left in possession, the true inference to be drawn is an agreement that he shall possess the premises at will in the strictest sense, and therefore no notice is ever given him to quit.

Tenants holding from year to year under the receiver for a mortgagee, are entitled to notice to quit.

It may again be observed, that where the estate or lease is *ipso facto* void by reason of the condition or limitation, no acceptance of the rent after can make it to have a continuance; otherwise it is of an estate or lease voidable by entry. And this distinction is, because the acceptance of rent in the one case cannot make a new lease, and the old one was determined; but the acceptance of the rent in the other is a sufficient declaration that it is the lessor's will to continue the lease, for he is not entitled to the rent but by the lease.

As if a man get into possession of a house to be let, without the privity of the landlord, and they afterwards enter into a negotiation for a lease, but differ upon the terms, the landlord may maintain ejectment to recover possession of the premises, without giving any notice to quit.

A tenant from year to year underlet part of the premises, and then gave up to his landlord the part remaining in his own possession, without either receiving a regular notice to quit the whole, or giving notice to quit to his sub-tenant, or even surrendering that part in the name of the whole. The landlord cannot entitle himself to recover against the sub-tenant (there being no privity of contract between them), upon giving half a year's notice to quit, in his own name, and not in the name of the first tenant; for as to the part so underlet, the original tenancy still continued undetermined.

The landlord's remedy for his rent is distress, or by action for use and occupation, or upon special promises, if the holding commenced by a particular agreement in writing; it seems that those who occupy under a mere agreement for a lease, are not distrainable till they have done some act to create the presumption of a yearly tenancy, such as by payment of rent. Leaseholders can be sued in debt or covenant for their rent, or non-performance of the covenants. With respect to tenants at sufferance, or those who hold over, it seems no distress can be had: all that the landlord can do is to give them a notice, and compel them to pay double rent, sue them in an action for use and occupation, or eject them.

Tenants at Sufferance. — Tenant at sufferance is he who enters by lawful letting or title, and afterwards wrongfully continues in possession.

There is a great difference, therefore, between a tenant at will and a tenant at sufferance; for tenant at will is always by right, whereas tenant by sufference entereth by a lawful letting, and holdeth over by wrong.

Mortgagee covenants that mortgagor shall quietly enjoy till default of payment, and assigns; after assignment, mortgagor is only tenant at sufferance; for his continuing in possession does not turn the term to a right.

Tenants holding over, are generally expelled by process of an ejectment; and where premises are deserted, and a half year's rent due, two justices will put the landlord in possession; but where the value of the mises, or the extreme poverty of the tenant, or particular circumstances present a serious moral objection to these procedures, the landlord may in a qualified degree take the law into his own hands, by obtaining possession in any manner, without using violence, or by gently removing the goods in the absence of the tenant, to the nearest place of convenient and proper shelter. It seems most expedient that this should be done in the absence of the tenant or his family; for it would be difficult to obtain possession, *in case of resistance by the tenant*, without committing that force which it is the object of law to prevent. Certain it is that, in an action of trespass to be brought by a tenant holding over, after notice to quit against his landlord, for an entry in the tenant's absence, by pulling down a wall, or breaking open the door, the landlord could plead the fact, that the premises were his, that the tenant's term had expired in them, after due notice to quit; but that the tenant, insisting on his right to continue therein, he, the landlord, had entered for the purpose of *amoving* him. It must, however, be admitted that *experiments* of this nature are not favoured by law, more especially as it is somewhat difficult in these cases for a jury to distinguish between the commencement of an act negatively lawful, or rather not declared unlawful, and the precise point where positive illegality or violence begins. The judges have been extremely cautious in dealing with these cases, leaving it for the jury to consider as to the necessity of the act, or the quantum of violence used to dispossess before or after resistance made by the tenant, not giving any opinion as to the legality of the dispossession itself: but any dispossession by stratagem without force, is perfectly justifiable.

Tenants whose terms, according to *any* written agreement, expire at a certain term, and from whom possession has been demanded in writing, after an action of ejectment has been commenced, can be called upon to put in bail to answer costs and damages.

Where a tenant suffers judgment by default in ejectment, the costs are not immediately recoverable of the tenant, they can be added to the *mesne* profits which a jury will give in an action brought for the rent accrued during the holding over.

The case of a tenant holding over with menaces, or what is termed "forcibly detaining," has been remedied by a very old statute (8 *H.* 6.) which gives justices of the peace power to put out persons *forcibly, and with strong hand detaining* premises, after an *un*lawful entry; therefore this remedy cannot be applied to the general case of landlord and tenant holding over, even with violence, for the entry by the refractory tenant must be admitted to have been lawful in its commencement.

Forms of Notices to Quit, &c.

1. *Notice to quit by the Landlord, to a Tenant from Year to Year.*

Sir,

I hereby give you notice to quit and deliver up on the ——— of ——— next, the possession of the messuage or dwelling-house, (or "rooms and apartments, or farms, lands and premises,") with the appurtenances, which you now hold of me, situate in the parish of ——, in the county of ——. Dated the —— day of ——, 18 .

To Mr. *C. D.* (*the tenant in possession:* Your's, &c. *A. B.*

Or, if it be doubtful who is tenant,)

To Mr. *C. D.*, or whom else it may concern,

2. *The like by an Agent for the Landlord.*

Sir,

I do hereby, as the agent for and on behalf of your landlord *A. B.* of —— give you notice to quit and deliver up on the —— day of —— next, the possession of the messuage, &c. (*as above*) which you now hold of the said *A. B.* situate, &c. (*as above.*) Dated, &c. (*as above.*)

To Mr. *C. D.* &c. (*as above.*) Yours, &c. *E. F.*

Agent for the said *A. B.*

3. *The like by the Landlord where the Commencement of the Tenancy is doubtful.*

Sir,

I hereby give you notice, &c. (*as in sect.* 1. *to the date*) provided your tenancy originally commenced at that time of the year; or otherwise, that you quit and deliver up possession of the said messuage, &c. (*as above*) at the end of the year of your tenancy, which will expire next after the end of half a year, from the time of your being served with this notice. Dated, &c. (*as above.*)

To Mr. *C. D.* (*as above.*) Yours, &c. *A. B.*

4. *The like more general.*

Sir,

I hereby give you notice to quit and deliver up the possession, &c. (*as above*) which you now hold of me, situate, &c., at the end of the year of your tenancy, which will expire next after the end of half a year from the time of your being served with this notice. Dated, &c.

To Mr. *C. D.* &c. (*as above.*) Your's, &c. *A. B.*

5. *Notice by a Joint-tenant, or Tenant in Common, to determine Tenancy of a Moiety, &c.*

Sir,

I hereby give you notice of my intention to determine on the —— day of —— next, the tenancy under which you now hold of me, one undivided moiety or half part, (*or whatever part or share the landlord may have*) of and in a certain messuage, &c. (*as in sect.* 1. situated, &c. Dated, &c.

To Mr. *C. D.* &c. (*as in sect.* 1.) Yours, &c. *A. B.*

6. *The like by a Tenant from Year to Year of his Intention to quit.*

Sir,

I hereby give you notice of my intention to quit, and that I shall on the —— day —— next, quit and deliver up the possession of the messuage, &c. (*as in sect.* 1.) which I now hold of you, situate, &c. (*as in sect.* 1.) Dated, &c.

To Mr. *A. B.* Yours, &c. *C. D.*

7. *The like by an Agent for the Landlord to determine a Tenancy of, or Composition for Tithes.*

Sir,

I do hereby as the agent for and on behalf of *A. B.* of —— give you notice of his intention to determine, and that he will accordingly determine on the —— day of —— next, the agreement under which you hold (*or* "the composition payable by you, for and in respect of") all and singular the tithes of corn, &c. (*describing them*) arising, growing, increasing, renewing and happening in, upon, from, or out of all and every the several and respective farms, lands and premises, (*or* "in, upon, from and out of certain lands and premises in your occupation,") situate in the parish of ——, in the county of ——, and within the bounds, limits, and titheable places thereof, and that the said tithes will, from and after the said —— day of ——next, be taken in kind. Dated, &c.

To Mr. *C. D.*

Yours, &c. *E. F.*

Agent for the said *A. B.*

8. *Notice to Tenant to quit Lodgings.*

Sir,

I hereby give you notice to quit and deliver up on or before —— next, the rooms or apartments and other tenements which you now hold of me in this house (*as the case may be.*) Witness my hand this —— day of ——, in the year *A. B.*

To Mr. *C. D.*

9. *Notice to Tenant to quit or pay double Value.*

Sir,

I hereby give you notice to quit and yield up on the —— day of —— next, possession of the messuage lands, tenements and hereditaments, which you now hold of me, situate at——, in the parish of——, and the county of——; in failure whereof, I shall require and insist upon double the value of the said premises, according to the statute in such case made and provided. Dated this —— day of ————.

To *C. D.* Yours, &c. *A. B.*

10. *Notice by Tenant to quit Lodgings.*

Sir,

This is to give you notice, that on the —— day of —— next, I shall quit and deliver up possession of the rooms and apartments and other tenements which I now hold of you in this house.

Witness my hand this —— day of ————, 18

To *A. B.* *C. D.*

11. *Notice to Tenant to repair.*

Sir,

You are hereby required to put in good and tenantable repair, all and singular the messuage or tenement, and the premises which you now hold of me, situate at, &c.; particularly the servants' hall in the said messuage or tenement, and the tiling or roof at the northern end thereof (*as the case may be*).

Witness my hand this —— day of ————.

To *C. D.* *A. B.*

12. *Notice to Tenant to pay Rent, or a Claim of Forfeiture.*

Sir,

This is to warn you, that unless you pay or cause to be paid unto me, on or before the —— day of —— next, the sum of——, being—— year's rent, due on the ——day of——, for the messuage or tenement, and premises which you now hold of me, at the yearly rent of——, situated, &c., I shall claim and insist upon such forfeiture thereof, as I may be by law entitled to.

Witness my hand *A. B.*

To *C. D.*

TENDER. The producing and offering to pay money in satisfaction or payment of a claim or covenant. The effect of this is, that if a creditor refuse the sum tendered, and commences an action, the tender accompanied by a payment of the sum tendered into court will be a good defence, unless the creditor can prove that more is due, or can prove a prior or subsequent demand and refusal; or, in other language, wherever a person admits that he is indebted to another to some extent, he is at liberty to tender him a certain sum, *before any action is commenced*, and by this tender to throw upon his adversary the burthen of proving that more was due, at the risk of costs in case of failure. After an action commenced, the defendant, in a similar situation, may pay that sum of money into court which he admits to be due, with costs up to that time, and by this payment may throw the risk of further costs upon the plaintiff. This privilege is extended to all cases in all actions termed "personal," where damages are recoverable, uncertain in their nature, or for a wrong done, except assault, false imprisonment, libel, slander, malicious arrest or prosecution, crim. con., or seduction.

Where goods or specific things are demanded, they may be tendered before action brought, or a sum of money only, if the defendant have not the goods; and after action brought, the defendant may pay money into court, or apply to a judge at chambers, for liberty to restore the goods under certain regulations.

In making a tender (which should be done by the party or some person properly authorised by him, *and in the presence of a credible witness*,) the exact amount of what is admitted to be recoverable should be produced, and counted in English gold and silver (the latter not exceeding 40*s*.), or in foreign coin made current by proclamation; such amount should be named to the claimant or his attorney or agent, and if practicable, be laid down and counted in his presence, (though that may be dispensed with, if the claimant says he will not take the sum named). The tender must be unconditional and unqualified, for any stipulation or proposition will vitiate the tender, even demanding a receipt; for if the claimant were to accept it, his claim for any residue or balance would be prejudiced. The legal tender is so simple, being an offer to pay the money *without more*, that to state further what a party tendering may *not* do, may induce him to forget what he *is* to do.

A tenant who fears a forfeiture from a sudden and capricious demand from his landlord, whom he cannot find out (for the debtor is to go to the creditor), may prevent it thus: he should, on the day when the rent falls due, produce the sum then accruing due, and in the presence of witnesses, who should count the amount, declare that he produces the same ready to pay, and as a tender of his rent to his landlord; and this suffices, although neither the landlord, nor any person on his behalf, be upon or near the land.

Persons wrongfully distraining, may tender amends; and so of distresses for poor-rates; so in actions against justices, excise and custom-house officers, by virtue of various statutes, amends may be tendered.

TENURE. The manner whereby lands or tenements are holden. A tenure may be of houses, and land, or tenements; but not of a rent, common, &c., these being incident to tenure.

Under the word tenure, is included every holding of an inheritance; but the signification of this word, which is a very extensive one, is usually restrained by coupling other words with it: this is sometimes done by words, which denote the duration of the tenant's estate; as, if a man holds to himself and his heirs, it is called tenure in fee-simple; if to him and his heirs male, tenancy or tenure in tail, &c.

At other times, the tenure is coupled with words pointing out the instrument by which an inheritance is held: thus, if the holding is by copy of court-roll, it is called tenure by copy of court-roll. At other times, this word is coupled with words that shew the principal service by which an inheritance is held; as, where a man held by knight-service, it was called tenure by knight-service.

Almost all the real property of the kingdom is, by the policy of our laws, supposed to be granted by, dependent upon, and holden of, some superior lord; by and in consideration of certain services to be rendered to the lord by the tenant or possessor of this property.

The thing holden is styled a tenement; the possessors thereof, tenants; and the manner of their possession, a tenure: thus, all the land in the kingdom is supposed to be holden directly or indirectly of the king, who is styled the lord paramount, or above all.

The above maxim, and the whole of the doctrine of tenures, are founded on the feudal system, "feud," "fief," or "fee," signifying land held as a feud or military tenure, which subsisted in England by the name of knight-service; but in process of time, many feuds were bartered for services of a certain nature, such as payment of rent, and gradually assimilated themselves to the service called *socage*, a free service very inferior, consisting in plough-service, afterwards existing as a rent; and therefore, all *freehold* lands at the time of Charles the 2nd, consisted of land held or presumed to be held by knight-service, or by socage. Knight-service, and its subordinate military tenures, being abolished by an act of parliament in that reign, all freehold tenures (copyhold tenures being expressly excepted) became socage; consequently, to hold land in fee-simple, or as a feud of the king, as superior lord, is tenure in free and common socage. See SOCAGE.

Copyhold or "base" tenure is explained under the title, *Manor*.

THREATS. The sending or delivering a letter demanding money, with menaces, and without reasonable or probable cause, is a felony, and punishable by transportation for life, or for not less than seven years, or imprisonment (with or without hard labour, and with or without solitary confinement, for the whole or any part of the imprisonment,) not exceeding four years; and if a male, to be whipped, at the discretion of the court. 7 & 8 *G.* 4. *c.* 29.

The accusing or threatening to accuse a man *of any crime punishable by law with death, transportation, or pillory; or of any assault, with intent to commit a rape, or attempt or endeavour to commit any rape, or of any infamous crime,* with a view to extort money, or valuable security, is a felony, and punishable as the preceding offence. So the sending a letter for the like purpose of extortion, is punishable in like manner. *Ibid.*

The sending a letter threatening to kill or burn, is a felony, punishable with transportation for life, or not less than seven years, or imprisonment, or imprisonment and hard labour, not exceeding seven years. 4 *G.* 4. *c.* 54.

The accusing or threatening to accuse another of any unnatural offence, or extorting any property by the intimidation or threat of such accusation, is a felony, punishable by transportation for life, or for not less than 15 years, or imprisonment for not exceeding 3 years. 1 *Vict. c.* 87, *s.* 4.

The attempting to obtain by menaces or force any property, with intent to steal the same, is a felony punishable by imprisonment for not exceeding three years. *s.* 7. See also STEALING FROM THE PERSON.

TIMBER. Oak, ash, and elm are timber trees in all places; and in countries where timber is scanty, beech and any other trees that are used for building are accounted timber. The oldest houses in London are built of beech wood, which when old is not readily distinguishable from oak.

The injuring timber is a malicious mischief.

To cut timber is waste in a lessee. A tenant for life will also be restrained by injunction from cutting timber improvidently, and ornamental timber he cannot cut at all. A tenant or lessee is not entitled to a tree felled by the wind.

TIME-BARGAIN. An illegal contract between two stockholders, generally members of an association, called "The Stock Exchange," who agree that on a specified future day, the difference in value of a nominal sum in some particular stock, as may be agreed upon, shall be paid over to the individual in whose favour the rise may be determined; accordingly, when what is termed the "settling day" arrives, the amount of the wager is paid to the winner. High penalties are incurred by both parties in these transactions, and the person who cannot "settle" or pay his difference, is expelled the "House," *i. e.* The Stock Exchange, which is governed by a committee, who regulate these illegalities. See STOCK-BROKERS OR STOCK-JOBBERS.

TIPPLING. The act 24 *G.* 2. passed to prevent tippling, enacts that no person shall be entitled to sue for or on account of any spirituous liquors, unless such debt shall have been *bonâ fide* contracted for at one time to the amount of 20*s*. or upwards; nor shall any particular item or article in any account, or demand for distilled spirituous liquors, be allowed and maintained, where the liquors delivered at one time, and mentioned in such article or item, shall not amount to 20*s*. at the least, and that without fraud.

This act does not apply to liquor sold for the purpose of a re-sale.

Where parties having cross demands settle and balance their accounts, it is no defence to an action brought for the balance, that a great part of the amount was for spirituous liquors delivered in quantities under 20*s*. value.

TITHES are the tenth part of the increase arising from the produce of lands, payable to the rector, vicar, or perpetual curate, by endowment or prescription. They are said to be predial, mixt, and personal. Predial are such as are derived immediately from the earth by culture or tillage, as corn, grass, wood, fruit, &c. Mixt tithes arise from the product of nature, improved by the care of man, as the young of cattle, wool, milk, cheese, eggs. Personal tithes are payable in respect of the profit arising from labour, confined to fish and corn mills, not in existence before 1315. Of the two first the tithe is payable of the actual produce; of the last, a tenth part of the actual gains. In general (as Blackstone observes) tithes are payable for everything that yields an annual increase, but not of any thing that is of the substance of the earth, or is not of annual increase; as stone, lime, chalk, and the like; nor for creatures that are of a wild nature, as deer, hawks, swarms of bees, &c. whose increase so as to benefit the owner, is not annual but casual, though for deer and rabbits, tithes may by special custom be payable.

Tithes are divided into great and small: great tithes consist of all species of corn and grain, hay and wood; all other tithes are accounted small. The rector is entitled to all the tithes, both great and small, except they are by endowment or by prescription receivable by the vicar or perpetual curate; or except there is a special exemption by prescription, custom, composition, modus or act of parliament. The small tithes usually belong to the vicar, and in some parishes some of the great tithes also, being included in the original endowment; usage and custom may also govern the payment of tithe. Small tithes comprehend *all* seeds, tares, and vetches, cut green for cattle, garden herbs and vegetables, hops, and all things not included under the description of grain, hay and wood; together with what is called *agistment* tithe, being the pasturage of barren cattle.

Tithes are due at the times when they severally accrue, that is, *predial* tithes, on their being gathered; mixt, according to the reasonableness thereof, as the young of cattle when weaned, wool at the time of shearing, eggs, honey, and wax, when they are taken; and land that has paid tithe on its *annual* crop is not titheable the same year, but clover-grass and lucern pay an aftermath tithe.

The tithe should be set out, *i.e.* separated from the nine parts, in the presence of the parson or his bailiff, in such a manner and at such a time, that the just and fair quantity can be discerned. Those occupiers of land who interpose difficulties to the getting in of the tithe, by a hasty removal or short notice, will find themselves in the wrong; for as the parson cannot tithe the crop himself, the law sets its face against any precipitate or wrongful gatherings or removals of crops. Corn and grain is set out by being sheafed, and the tithe-owner takes the tenth sheaf or shock, which has a bough stuck in it, or is otherwise marked. Barley and oats, though often swathed, should be set out in *sheaf*, at least in *cock;* peas are generally set out in *swathe*, but *cocking* them is the proper mode; beans are sheafed and set up in *shocks*, the tenth of which is given to the parson, though where corn and beans, or other grain, are set up in shocks, it is more regular to show the tithe-bailiff the tenth sheaf, as the tenth *shock* might be made up of damaged or defective sheaves. Peas gathered *green* for home consumption are not titheable.

Wood under 20 years' growth, is set out by the bavin or faggot: timber trees of above 20 years' growth, are not titheable unless when lopped under that age, in which case the toppings and loppings always afterwards pay tithe.

Fruit grown in gardens and orchards is set out by the measure.

Hot-house fruit it seems is not titheable.

Agistment-tithe for the pasturage of cattle unprofitable to the parson or tithe owner, must be rendered in money, being a tenth part of the value of the food which they eat, or of the money paid for their re-pasturing. The occupier of the land pays it not to the owner, except when fed on commons or wastes.

The tithe of milk is the tenth *meal, i. e.* the milk yielded every tenth day.

Fish is only titheable by custom.

As to mills, they are, if they can be shown to have been built since 1315 (but not otherwise, except the scite is altered), liable to pay tithes if they grind meal, not being the corn which the miller grows or for his own consumption: *viz.* the tenth part of the profits of grinding.

Ancient mills not liable to pay tithes will render themselves liable to pay a tithe if the power of the mill is increased, and then tithe is payable for such increased power. A mill is presumed to be ancient, *i. e.* had existence before 1315, till the contrary be shewn by the parson or tithe-owner of the parish wherein the mill is situate, claiming tithe.

Dogs and animals kept for amusement, protection, or curiosity, do not pay tithes. Head-lands being only large enough to turn the plough upon, do not pay tithes unless grain be grown upon them.

Barren ground, having never previously paid tithes by reason of its barrenness, but afterwards converted into arable or meadow land, pays no tithes for seven years; the seven years run from the doing some act, having a tendency to render the land productive.

The exemptions from tithes are, composition, a *modus decimandi*, prescription, or act of parliament. These require but little explanation beyond the term modus, which is a presumed agreement entered into by the parson, patron, and ordinary, with the parishioners, beyond the time of memory; and therefore, like prescription, is presumed to have existed from time immemorial, having its origin from a legal instrument executed by all the above parties, which has been lost from lapse of time. *Moduses* are various in their nature; but mostly a small pecuniary payment, which may very well be supposed to have been an adequate payment for the tithes, considering the value of money at the time of the commencement of legal memory; viz. 1. June, 1189, as compared at the present time: therefore if the present payment is too large to bear that comparison it is termed *rank*, and therefore void. These ancient compositions in *reality* could never be proved to have existed so long, and therefore a late statute has done much to establish moduses, by enacting that a modus paid, or nothing rendered in respect of tithes for 30 years, will be a *primâ facie* bar, and for 60 years, a complete bar to any demand made by a layman for tithes in kind, unless such modus or exemption has arisen by some deed or writing; and proof of the payment of a modus, or non-payment of tithes during the lives of two successive incumbents, and three years after the induction of a third incumbent, will be a bar of a demand made by a parson, if 60 years have not elapsed during the two first incumbencies, unless (as in the previous case of claim) such modus or exemption has arisen by some deed or writing; in less technical language, unless the *commencement* of the payment can be shown by any writing in *actual* existence, not presumedly in existence, which is the origin of prescription.

Another late statute provides that where no tithes have been paid to a lay impropriator (the king seems excepted) and he has been in a situation to enforce or recover them, the lands will from thenceforth be tithe-free.

Allotments of common are by inclosure-acts rendered tithe free.

And lands may be discharged by an ancient composition made between the rector or vicar, and the landowners; or by any other arrangement confirmed by a decree of a court of equity, or any transaction by deed between competent parties.

A late act of parliament has been passed for effecting a commutation of tithes (6 & 7 *W.* 4. *c.* 71.) which has for its object the establishment of a corn-rent, payable in money, and chargeable on the land. The execution of the act is vested in commissioners and assistant-commissioners, who, having ascertained the value of the tithes of any parish in the manner directed by the act, make an award of the rent-charge payable in lieu of the tithe, and are to deposit such award at some place in the parish for inspection, and give twenty-one days' notice of their holding a meeting to hear objections against it, when it may be amended if they think fit.

The award may either be compulsory, or till 1 October, 1838, voluntary if two thirds of land-owners, and two thirds of tithe-owners in a parish consent, such agreement to be confirmed by the commissioners.

When an agreement or award has been confirmed, an even number of persons are to be appointed to apportion such rent-charge, which is estimated in gross, according to the quality and produce of the lands in the parish, or as the parishioners, at a meeting, may agree. The apportionment may be objected to, and the commissioners are to hear such objections, and, if need be, alter the apportionment. Then the instrument of apportionment is to be confirmed by the commissioners, and one copy to be deposited in the registry of the diocese, and the other with the incumbent or churchwardens.

The apportionment, or rather apportioned rent-charge, is to be calculated according to the septennial average of the value of wheat, barley, and oats, as published in the gazette on the Thursday next before Christmas-day in every year; and therefore this rent charge will fluctuate accordingly, and is payable on the 1st of January and July, yearly.

A tenant at rack-rent, *at the time of the apportionment*, may within a month of its being confirmed by the commissioners, give notice to his landlord of his dissent, and then the landlord must pay the rent and take the *tithe* from his tenant.

In all subsequent leases and agreements, the landlord is liable to pay the rent-charge, not the tenant, which is payable whether the land be in culture or not, but not if destroyed by accident.

The remedy for the rent-charge is by distress on the land, in the same manner as a landlord is empowered to distrain for rent; but ten days' notice must be given to the tenant, and the rent must be twenty-one days in arrear, and no more than two years' rent can be distrained for; or,

If the rent is in arrear for forty days, a writ may be sued out, directed to the sheriff, and possession of the lands may be given to the owner of the rent-charge, until the arrears of the rent and costs are satisfied; but, as in the last remedy, no more than two years' rent-charge are recoverable.

The rent-charge can be shifted, or compounded for by a grant of *land*, or, in the case of lay owners of tithes or rent-charge, may be extinguished by payment of a sum of money, in much the same manner as land-tax is redeemable.

The remedies for tithes generally, are—

1. By suit in the ecclesiastical courts for *subtraction of tithes*, in cases where the right to the tithe itself is not disputed, a fact which the ecclesiastical courts have not jurisdiction to try.

2. The courts of law lend their assistance to the tithe-owner, who can bring his action of *debt* for them, as for any other claim, and by a statute of Edward VI., can recover treble the value of the tithes subtracted or withdrawn.

3. The courts of equity take cognisance of suits for tithes, and will compel the defendant to discover what tithes he has subtracted; but, on the other hand, the plaintiff must satisfactorily show his right, and if a *modus*, or any matter of fact is urged as a defence, the court will direct an issue to be tried by a court of law, matters of fact being peculiarly the subject of trial by a jury.

In cases where the tithes do not exceed 10*l*., and (in cases of quakers) 50*l*., two justices are empowered to make an order, and enforce the payment by distress, and if there are no goods, by committal to gaol; a single magistrate having power to summon the party to appear before the two justices.

The tithes of houses in London, which are regulated by a well-known statute (37 *H*. 8. *c*. 12.), may also be recovered in the court of exchequer: but a better remedy is provided by a statute of 22 & 23 *C*. 2. *c*. 15. The tithes of all the parishes in London, injured by the fire in 1666, are settled to be levied by an equal rate; and, on non-payment, the lord mayor is to grant a warrant of distress for the same, or, on his refusal, the lord chancellor, or two barons of the exchequer. (The remedy through any other courts is taken away by this statute.) These tithes are a rent-charge upon the houses, payable although they are empty, and leviable on the goods of the succeeding occupier. Persons may appeal from the lord mayor's decision to the chnncellor.

The method of trying the *inheritance* to tithes is by ejectment.

TITLE. The legal term signifying the means by which a man becomes seised of real property or possessed of personal property. As title by descent, title by purchase, title by administration, title by bankruptcy, title by marriage, &c.

This term is also used to signify, generally, a right to land, and the buying or selling of "titles" is prohibited by statute, as Maintenance. — See that title.

TITLE-DEEDS. The writings evidencing a man's right or title to property. The stealing of such documents is a misdemeanor, and subjects the offender to transportation for seven years, or fine and imprisonment.

TOBACCO. The growth of this plant (except in physic-gardens, &c.), is prohibited. Persons having tobacco in their possession exceeding one pound in weight, not having paid duty, or without a permit, forfeit 100*l*. The duties on the importation and manufacture of tobacco are regulated by the 3 & 4 *W*. 4. *c*. 56.

TOD of WOOL. Twenty-eight pounds, or two stone.

TOFT. A messuage, or rather the scite of a messuage, or place where a messuage formerly stood, being decayed or burnt, and not rebuilt; it is a word getting into disuse.

TRANSPORTATION, RETURNING FROM; is a capital felony, but sentence of death may be recorded. Almost all the felonies which were before the 1st Oct. 1837 capital offences, are by the statutes passed 1 *Vict.* for the amendment of the criminal law, punishable by transportation for not exceeding 15 years nor less than 10 years, or imprisonment for not exceeding three years. See CAPITAL OFFENCES.

TRAVERSE is the denying or disputing any matter of record, such as an inquisition or presentment; and in this sense it is used when a party indicted of a misdemeanor, pleads and *traverses, i. e.* denies the indictment, so that it stands over till the ensuing sessions. — See PRACTICE (Div. 3.)

Traverse also means any denial of a fact alleged in pleading.

TREASON. An overt (open) act of compassing or devising the death of the king. Every thing wilfully or deliberately done or attempted, whereby the king's life may be endangered, is an *overt* act of compassing his death. Conspiring to depose him, or attempts to usurp the powers of government, are also overt acts; so inciting foreigners to invade the kingdom, or openly adhering to the king's enemies, are deemed *overt* acts.

Writings which import such compassings or devices, attempts or intentions, if *published* or shown to third persons, or words of advice or persuasion, importing deliberation and design, are deemed *overt* acts.

Levying war against the king is an open act of treason; and this may be actual or constructive: actual, as rebellion, or concerting with others in open rebellion; constructive, where armed force is adopted for the purpose of effecting any particular political object, as to obtain the repea of a statute, or even to enhance the price of wages; but local outrages having reference to peculiar petty grievances, as pulling down inclosures, or delivering a party from prison (if not imprisoned for treason), are not treasons, but acts indictable under various statutes, as misdemeanors.

There are no accessories to treason, all are principals.

There are many other treasons of a special nature, such as killing the judges, &c., or to violate the queen, or eldest daughter, unmarried, or his eldest son's wife.

The punishment for treason is, that the offender be drawn upon a hurdle to the place of execution, and there hanged; that his head be cut off, and the body divided into four quarters; but the king, by warrant, may dispense with all the immaterial parts of the punishment.

The consequence of a conviction for treason is, that the party is attainted, and forfeits all lands and property, and his blood being corrupted, his heirs cannot take by any descent through him. — See FORFEITURE.

Treason used to be styled *high* treason, in contradistinction to what was termed *petty* treason, which was the killing of a master by his servant, a husband by his wife, &c.

TRESPASS is a term applied to those wrongs which are committed with actual or implied force, and the action that lies to redress those wrongs are termed actions of trespass.

Any injuries, or adverse contacts, committed against real property, *i. e.* land or buildings, are, in the most ordinary sense of the word, "trespasses;" as entering another's house without permission, or suffering any cattle to stray upon another's field, undermining, or even piling earth against a wall, or any detrimental act, or any practice which damages in the slightest degree the property, or interferes with the owner's or occupier's right of possession.

A person trespassing upon another's land can be turned off at a moment's notice; and if he enter again after notice, it is actionable. Cattle may be distrained if they do damage, and detained in the pound till the same be paid, together with the charges of impounding.

Compensation to the extent of 5*l.* for small, wilful, or malicious trespasses, occasioning actual damage, and not mere trespasses by walking over land, may be obtained by summary proceeding before a single justice.

Trespasses against game are provided against by the *game act*, which authorises the owner or his agent to apprehend and detain, for even twelve hours, a trespasser who refuses to tell his true name and place of abode, and to take him before a justice; and such justice may convict in the penalties for trespassing in pursuit of game, or doing any injury thereto.

The action for trespasses against the person, goods, or land is restrained by statutes, providing that the plaintiff, whenever he recovers a verdict for less than 40*s.*, shall have no more costs than damages, unless the judge certify, in cases of trespass to land or buildings, that the trespass was wilful, or that the freehold came in question; or in cases of trespass and assault, a beating be proved, or a tearing of clothes; in all other cases the damages must exceed 40*s.* or the plaintiff will not recover costs: hence the necessity of not proceeding but for malicious trespasses, or trespasses after full notice given (by writing, board, verbal to the party, or otherwise), or where, from the circumstance of the case in regard to other trespasses and this, it is a moral probability that more than 40*s.* will be recovered.

TRIAL. The trial of an action at law is very simple. After the jury are sworn, the plaintiff's counsel, who generally has to prove the affirmative issue or fact in dispute, opens the pleadings by stating them briefly to the jury, and upon what point the issue is to be determined; and he, or his senior, address the jury on the nature of the case, and the evidence intended to be produced. Witnesses for the plaintiff are then examined, which the defendant's counsel cross-examines, and that concludes the plaintiff's *case.* Then the defendant's counsel addresses the jury, stating the cause and reasonableness of the defendant's defence, calls his witnesses, which are singly cross-examined by the plaintiff's counsel, and there ends his client the defendant's case. The plaintiff's counsel then addresses the jury in reply to the evidence for the defence. The judge, who has taken notes of the whole proceedings, then *sums* up, *i. e.* states to the jury all the facts and circumstances as detailed in evidence, interposing such observations as are likely to assist the jury, or to explain the law to them, and explains the point upon which they are to decide. The jury then consider of their verdict, and deliver it by their foreman to the court; the associate, or his clerk, asking the jury who they find for? and, if for the plaintiff, what damages? the jury naming the sum, and what costs. The associate makes a minute of it on the back of the record, as instructions for a more complete entry, which is called the *postea*, and delivered to the successful party's attorney, who taxes his costs thereupon, and issues execution.

It not unfrequently happens that a defendant has to prove the affirmative issue, in which his counsel opens the case.

Very often, after a plaintiff has closed his case, the defendant's counsel does not think it advisable to examine witnesses for the defendant, but simply addresses the jury on the case as presented by the plaintiff's evidence and their cross-examination. In this case the plaintiff's counsel is not generally entitled to a reply, unless new matter has been laid before the jury; but this is rather a favour or concession from the judge than a plaintiff's right.

Also, after the speech and evidence of the defendant's counsel, and before he replies, the plaintiff may produce evidence to disprove the defence set up by defendant, but not merely evidence to strengthen his case as originally put. On this fresh evidence, the defendant's counsel has a right again to address the jury, but his observations must be confined to the evidence last given, and the reply of the plaintiff's counsel closes the case.

The form of a trial in criminal cases is narrated under the title PRACTICE (Div. 2.).

TROVER. A form of action which lies in general against a defendant for the conversion, or appropriation to his own use of any personal property in which the plaintiff has a general property as owner, or special property as carrier, depositary, trustee, &c.

It will lie for deeds, unstamped agreements, bills unlawfully withheld under a verbal promise of being discounted, for goods *wrongfully* distrained, money deposited, or any other chattel-personal.

But it will not lie for fixtures, money had and received, goods *irregularly* sold under a distress where rent was due, nor for goods purchased, unless the purchaser first pay the price.

A demand must be made before an action of trover can be brought; for the denial, refusal, or neglect, is legal evidence of the wrongful conversion or appropriation of the goods, &c., by the defendant.

The action in trover is brought to recover the specific chattels themselves, or damages for their conversion: in giving damages, the jury are not limited to find as damages the mere value of the property at the time of the *conversion*, but they are, at their discretion, to find the value at a subsequent time as damages.

In trover upon a bill of exchange, the damages are to be calculated according to the amount of the principal and interest due upon the bill at the time of the conversion.

Nominal damages are only given where the defendant restores the specific chattel, such as a deed, &c.

A person may be held to bail, upon a judge's order, in an action of trover, but not without.

TRUCK-SYSTEM. The practice of paying workmen in goods instead of money. This mode of payment is prohibited by the statute 1 & 2 *W.* 4. *c.* 32., which inflicts penalties recoverable before two justices. The advocates for the non-abolition of this practice stated, that the wives and families of the workmen were well supplied with meat and clothing, and that the compulsory supply of those necessaries left but little for the purposes of drinking and idleness. However, the system was susceptible of an infinite abuse.

TRUSTS. See Uses and Trusts.

TRUSTEE, is a person who holds lands or tenements, or other property, upon the *trust*, or confidence that he will apply the same for the benefit of those who are entitled, according to an expressed intention, either by the parties themselves, or by the deed, will, settlement, or arrangement of another.

All trusts must be expressed or declared in writing; when the trust is not declared by a will or settlement, the deed expressing the purposes of the trust is termed "a declaration of trust."

There are, however, trusts which are *implied* in law, and which need not be in writing, as, where a man has land or other things conveyed to him, he having purchased the same with the money of another, and for his benefit, or where the owner of property makes a voluntary conveyance to another, and declares the trust of part of it, but is silent as to the disposal of the remainder; in these cases a trust is implied, and, in technical language, *results* for his own benefit.

The courts of equity only, can take cognisance of trusts, whether expressed, or implied and resulting. The constitution of the courts of law are not framed for any remedy, so that the person in whom or in whose name the land or property is vested, has what is termed the *legal* estate, *i.e.* the law considers him the owner, as the estate is vested in him. The person for whose benefit the trust is created, is said to have the *equitable* estate, because his rights are morally defined and relievable in equity.

The persons for whose benefit a trust is created or declared are termed the "cestuique trusts."

Acts of parliament have provided for the conveyance or assignment of trust-estates, where the trustees become bankrupt, insolvent, or are of unsound mind, or where they are out of the jurisdiction of the courts of equity; and there are scarcely any cases where the court of chancery cannot interpose its jurisdiction, as the property of married women, infants, and persons of unsound mind, are peculiar objects of its jurisdiction.

Where personal property is bequeathed to executors, the probate of the will is an acceptance of the trust.

If a person is appointed a trustee, and, by a deed, the property is vested in him, and he refuses to execute such deed, he may disclaim or renounce the trust, or be discharged in equity; therefore, to avoid such an inconvenience, no person should be appointed a trustee, whose concurrence or *acceptance* of the trust is not previously obtained. Executors renouncing probate in fact disclaim the trust.

Sir George Hampson, in his "Treatise on the Liabilities of Trustees," premises that, as the office of trustee is purely honorary, he being required to execute his trust diligently and providently, as well as gratuitously, trustees are not (unless express provision has been made in the deed or will for that purpose) entitled to any remuneration for managing the trust-funds; but, he observes, the rule has been modified in equity, and mentions a case where remuneration was allowed to a trustee whose services had been very beneficial, and who would not continue to act without such remuneration.

The doing any thing that is not in conformity with their trust, unless their discretion is enlarged, will render them liable to the deficiencies that may arise thereby, or the replacement of monies lent out on securities, the nature of which are not in conformity with the powers of investment. On the other hand, trustees are not liable for any accident or unavoidable loss, or by any depreciation of funded property.

A distinction is noticed by the learned author in reference to the duties of trustees who act for creditors, and those who act for charities; the former being authorised to do those acts most for the immediate advantage of the creditors, the latter being rather bound to consider the future prosperity of the estate.

A trustee who assigns his trust without the knowledge of his cestuique trusts, thereby makes himself answerable to them for any breach of trust committed by his assignee.

In cases of breach of trust (a term which does not include moral breaches of trust, but that negligence or deviation which is supposed, directly or indirectly, to deteriorate the fund), the only remedy is in equity, *i. e.* by bill in chancery, or on the equity side of the exchequer; for no action at law or other proceeding will lie against trustees for any abuse of their trust, however gross.

The estates of trustees deceased, who have not acted in conformity with the trust, are liable for the consequences.

Cestuique trusts concurring or assenting in any act which equity may declare or construe to be a breach of trust, preclude themselves from any relief; therefore, on any disposition of a trust fund, the consent of all parties (being of age, and unmarried, or, if married, the consent of their husbands) must in prudence be obtained.

Grossly negligent, mistaken, or improper conduct in the administration of a trust, is all that trustees have to guard against; and, where trustees have notice or information of prior deviations from the trust instrument, they are bound to do their utmost to repair the breaches the former managers of the trust had created or committed.

Trustees are generally indemnified by the terms of the trust instrument from the expenses necessarily attaching on the performance of the trust; but if that should not be the case, equity will relieve by ordering the payment of costs in suits and proceedings necessary for administering the trust, that is, the costs and charges of solicitors and others, reasonable and suitable to the occasion.

The statute of 3 & 4 *W.* 4. *c.* 27., limiting the time within which actions at law or suits in equity may be brought, does not operate as a bar to suits commenced in equity, in respect of concealed frauds (§ 26.); yet claims brought at a distant period, technically styled *stale* suits, require more precise and distinct proof to support them than if they had been made earlier; and innocent purchasers of land are protected.

Courts of equity will cause trustees, upon their application, to be released, if upon inquiry it be found that they have done nothing to render themselves accountable at a future period; and trust instruments and well-penned wills provide for the removal of trustees who decline, or refuse to act; and the court will interfere to remove bankrupts, insolvents, or persons the court may deem improper to be trusted with large funds. The renewal or "continuing" of trustees in the room of others dying or removed, is either provided for by the trust instrument, or referable to the jurisdiction of equity.

The executors or administrators of a surviving trustee or his assignee, are the persons in whom the trust fund vests; therefore, trustees should always be appointed in succession to prevent the necessity of such trustees being supplied by means of a suit.*

Trustees *in possession* are entitled to vote.

The following are notes of a few cases decided with respect to the liabilities of trustees and executors :—

If a trustee empowered to put money to interest let the money lie idle, he shall be accountable for interest; and if a trustee trade or job with the money, he shall be accountable, not for the interest only, but for the profit of the trade, because he acts at his own peril, without applying to the court of chancery for direction in disposing of the money. And if a trustee or executor retain money in his hands for any length of time which he might, by application to the court, or by investing in the funds, have made productive, he shall be charged with interest thereon.

An executor being directed by will to sell houses, and invest the proceeds, paid the produce of a sale into his bankers, mixing it with his own money: it was held that he was liable to pay the money to the legatees with interest, on failure of the banker.

If an executor pay over part of the testator's effects in any other way than his trust authorises or requires, the loss which accrues must be borne by himself, and the gain (if any) will be for the benefit of the *cestuique trust*. A distinction has been taken between negligence and corruption in executors; but there are many cases in which executors have been adjudged responsible for *gross* negligence; therefore executors and trustees are chargeable with the amount of debts they had taken no pains to recover.

Executors should lay out balances not wanted for the exigency of the testator's affairs in the 3 per cent *consols*.

Executors joining in receipts.—An executor who is a trustee, joining in a receipt and re-conveyance of a mortgaged estate, though he does not receive the money, is liable. The receipt being in evidence, no enquiry will be made as to the fact.

It is a general rule that executors joining in a receipt, are all chargeable. Executors *may* act independently (and, therefore, the receipt of one will be a discharge); but administrators *must* act jointly; but it seems that though one executor has joined in a receipt, yet, whether he is liable shall depend upon his acting. And if a trustee be privy to the embezzlement of the trust fund by his co-trustee, he will be chargeable with the amount.

There is a difference between the responsibility of trustees and executors, for trustees have all equal powers, interest, and authority, and cannot act separately as executors may, but must both join in conveyances and receipts; for one cannot sell without the other, or desire to receive more of the consideration money, or to be more a trustee than his partner: and therefore it is against natural justice to charge them for each other's receipts, unless in case of necessity, where they so join in a receipt, that it cannot be distinguished what has been received by one, and what by the other: there, from their own neglect or default, both shall be charged with the whole; as, if a man should blend his money with mine, so as to render my property uncertain, he loses his own.

* Under the Bankrupt Act, 6 *Geo.* 4. *c.* 16. *s.* 79., the Lord Chancellor has the power of appointing new trustees in the room of a trustee who becomes bankrupt.

Executors have each an absolute power over the whole, and therefore, if they join, they trust one another. Under a will, *containing the usual indemnity clause*, one of the executors allowed a debt due to the testator from the other executor, who afterwards became insolvent, to continue unpaid. The vice-chancellor, Sir John Leach, decreed the solvent executor to pay the legacy with interest, which decree was, on appeal, confirmed by Lord Eldon, who observed, that if a man took upon himself to be executor, he was to do all that the testator intended his executors to do, and that it was the testator's intention that the persons taking out probate should take upon themselves all the trusts. (*Worthington on Wills*, p. 468-9., *in note*.)

USE and OCCUPATION. In cases where a house, &c. is not let by any deed or lease under seal, the proper remedy is an action on premises for use and occupation. This action is founded either upon a contract, express or implied, between the plaintiff and defendant: it will not serve to try a right to premises. It is also settled, that the defendant's use and occupation of the premises should be beneficial and advantageous to him; and, in one case, where it appeared that the house was not fit for comfortable occupation, it was held the plaintiff could not recover; so it would be held if the premises are unwholesome, and cannot be rendered otherwise by any care the tenant may exercise: but a landlord of premises carelessly burnt may recover in an action for use and occupation, although no longer inhabited by the tenant.

This action will not lie where premises are let for an illegal or immoral purpose, such as prostitution, &c.

USES and TRUSTS are akin to each other; a use being in law the profit of lands and tenements, upon a trust and confidence reposed in another, that he to whose use the trust is made, shall take the profits thereof.

All modern conveyances are, directly or indirectly, founded on the doctrine of uses and trusts, which has been deemed the most intricate part of our property-law. Uses and trusts, being acts of confidence reposed, are cognizable in equity, when coupled with the performance of any act tending to the benefit of the party for whose enjoyment the use or trust was created. Uses, as a term, are applied to lands of inheritance; and the party *to whose use* they are conveyed has the absolute possession; as, if land is conveyed to A to the use of B, B has by law the possession vested in him; but, if land be conveyed to A, to the use of B in trust, to permit C to enjoy and receive the profits of the land, B has the *legal*, C the *equitable* estate; the law transferring the use into possession; or, as is the more common mode, land is conveyed to A, to the use of A, in trust for B and his heirs, or to permit B to occupy, &c. See TRUSTEE.

The person to whose use a conveyance is made, is termed the *cestuique use*.

Uses only apply to land of inheritance: the trust, being a creature of equity, only attaches on the profits or personalty. Therefore, no use can subsist of leaseholds; the conveyance being made to A *in trust* for B.

Uses and trusts do not practically interfere with the purchaser's possession of land: they are only used when estates are settled, or it is requisite to vest the property in third persons, without interfering with the temporary possession, which may be vested in A in trust for B for life, remainder to C for life, remainder to D and his heirs, and the like of trusts.

Persons, also, whose estates are in trust, can sell their estates independent of their trustees, though it is safer to obtain their concurrence, as they may have had notice of claims affecting the *cestuique trust* property, and, of course, would be considered as trustees for those claimants in equity. — See Trustee.

The reader is referred to the second volume of Blackstone's Commentaries, chap. xx., for more regular and perspicuous information on this head.

USURY. The offence of *taking* (not simply stipulating for) a greater interest than 5*l.* per cent. *per annum*, which is punishable by a forfeiture of treble the money borrowed, one half to the prosecutor, the other half to the king. By an old statute, the repurchase of goods (with knowledge of their being the same) at a lesser price, of the party originally selling the same, subjects the party to the same penalty.

It seems any transaction, whereby to secure by indirect means the repayment of a loan with more than lawful interest, is usurious, and therefore not good in law. And, in some particular instances, the actual advance of *money* is not necessary to constitute usury, for *goods* may be delivered. The question of usury, or whether a contract is a colour and pretence for an usurious loan, or is a fair and honest transaction, must, under all its circumstances, be determined by a jury.

Usurious bargains, or, rather, loans *morally* usurious, are often protected by lending the money upon contingency, as annuities, or making the repayment to depend upon certain lives being in existence at a particular time; but these last can be set aside upon terms, if outrageously oppressive.

By a late act, bills of exchange and promissory notes not exceeding a year's date, or not having more than that time to run, may be discounted at any rate of interest.

VAGRANTS are classed by the law as — 1. Idle and disorderly persons; 2. Rogues and vagabonds; 3. Incorrigible rogues.

The following analysis of the Vagrant Act, 5 *G.* 4. *c.* 83., is taken from "*Burn's Justice*" (26th ed.): —

"Every person being able wholly or in part to maintain himself or herself, or his or her family, by work or by other means, and wilfully refusing or neglecting so to do, by which refusal or neglect he or she, or any of his or her family, whom he or she may be bound to maintain, shall have become chargeable to any parish, township, or place;"

2. "Every person returning to and becoming chargeable in any parish, township, or place, from whence he or she shall have been legally removed by order of two justices of the peace, unless he or she shall produce a certificate of the churchwardens and overseers of the poor of some other parish, township, or place, thereby acknowledging him or her to be settled in such other parish, township, or place;"

3. "Every petty chapman or pedlar wandering abroad, and trading, without being duly licensed, or otherwise authorised by law;"

4. "Every common prostitute wandering in the public streets or public highways, or in any place of public resort, and behaving in a riotous or indecent manner;"

5. "And every person wandering abroad, or placing himself or herself in any public place, street, highway, court, or passage, to beg or gather alms, or causing, or procuring, or encouraging any child or children so to do,"

"Shall be deemed an *idle and disorderly person*, within the true intent and meaning of this act; and it shall be lawful for any justice of the peace to commit such offender (being thereof convicted before him by his own view, or by the confession of such offender, or by the evidence on oath of one or more credible witness or witnesses) to the house of correction, there to be kept to hard labour for any time not exceeding one calendar month."

By the 5 *Geo.* 4. c. 83. § 4. it is enacted, "that every person committing any of the offences hereinbefore mentioned, after having been convicted as an idle and disorderly person;"

2. "Every person pretending or professing to tell fortunes, or using any subtle craft, means, or device, by palmistry or otherwise, to deceive and impose on any of his majesty's subjects;"

3. "Every person wandering abroad and lodging in any barn or outhouse, or in any deserted or unoccupied building, or in the open air, or under a tent, or in a cart or waggon, not having any visible means of subsistence, and not giving a good account of himself or herself;"

4. "Every person wilfully exposing to view, in any street, road, highway, or public place, any obscene print, picture, or other indecent exhibition;"

5. "Every person wilfully, openly, lewdly, and obscenely exposing his person in any street, road, or public highway, or in the view thereof, or in any place of public resort, with intent to insult any female;"

6. "Every person wandering abroad, and endeavouring, by the exposure of wounds or deformities, to obtain or gather alms;"

7. "Every person going about as a gatherer or collector of alms, or endeavouring to procure charitable contributions of any nature or kind, under any false or fraudulent pretence;"

8. "Every person running away and leaving his wife, or his or her child or children, chargeable, or whereby she or they, or any of them, shall become chargeable to any parish township, or place;"

9. "Every person playing or betting in any street, road, highway, or other open and public place, at or with any table or instrument of gaming, at any game, or pretended game of chance;"

10. "Every person having in his or her custody or possession any picklock key, crow, jack, bit, or other implement, with intent feloniously to break into any dwelling-house, warehouse, coach-house, stable, or outbuilding, or being armed with any gun, pistol, hanger, cutlass, bludgeon, or other offensive weapon, or having upon him or her any instrument with intent to commit any felonious act;"

11. "Every person being found in or upon any dwelling-house, warehouse, coach-house, stable, or outhouse, or in any inclosed yard, garden, or area, for any unlawful purpose;"

12. "Every suspected person or reputed thief, frequenting any river, canal, or navigable stream, dock, or basin, or any quay, wharf, or warehouse, near or adjoining thereto, or any street, highway, or avenue leading thereto, or any street, highway, or place adjacent, with intent to commit felony;"

13. "And every person apprehended as an idle and disorderly person, and violently resisting any constable or other peace officer so apprehending him or her, and being subsequently convicted of the offence for which he shall have been so apprehended;"

"Shall be deemed *a rogue and vagabond*, within the true intent and meaning of this act: and it shall be lawful for any justice of the peace to commit such offender (being thereof convicted before him by the confession of such offender, or by the evidence on oath of one or more credible witness or witnesses) to the house of correction, there to be kept to hard labour for any time not exceeding three calendar months; and every such picklock key, crow, jack, bit, and other implement, and every such gun, pistol, hanger, cutlass, bludgeon, or other offensive weapon, and every such instrument as aforesaid, shall, by the conviction of the offender, become forfeited to the king's majesty."

By the 5 *Geo.* 4. *c.* 83. *s.* 5. it is enacted, 1. "That every person breaking or escaping out of any place of legal confinement before the expiration of the term for which he or she shall have been committed or ordered to be confined by virtue of this act;"

2. "Every person committing any offence against this act, which shall subject him or her to be dealt with as a rogue and vagabond, such person having been at some former time adjudged so to be, and duly convicted thereof;"

3. "And every person apprehended as a rogue and vagabond, and violently resisting any constable or other peace officer so apprehending him or her, and being subsequently convicted of the offence for which he or she shall have been so apprehended;"

"Shall be deemed an *incorrigible rogue*, within the true intent and meaning of this act; and it shall be lawful for any justice of the peace to commit such offender (being thereof convicted before him, by the confession of such offender, or by the evidence, on oath, of one or more credible witness or witnesses) to the house of correction, there to remain until the next general or quarter sessions of the peace; and every such offender, who shall be so committed to the house of correction, shall be there kept to hard labour during the period of his or her imprisonment."

VERGE, a rod. Tenants by the rod or verge are copyholders, who, upon receiving admittance by the lord or his steward, hold a small rod which gives, or is symbolical of, possession; for the terms of admission are, "to hold by *the rod* at the will of the lord, according to the custom of the manor."

VESTRIES are meetings in the "vestry," which is a place or room adjoining to a church, where the *vestments* of the minister are kept.

The minister, churchwardens, and chief men of a parish, do generally constitute a vestry, and they appoint a clerk, styled a "vestry clerk," who draws up and enters their acts in a book, of which he generally has the custody. The office of a vestry clerk is not fixed, but temporary, and at will.

The Sunday before a vestry is to meet, notice is to be given by affixing a notice thereof, previous to the commencement of divine service, on the church door, so as three days' notice be given. If the rector, vicar, or perpetual curate is not present at the vestry, a chairman is to be elected by the persons present: in cases of equality of votes, the chairman shall have the casting vote in addition to his vote as a vestryman. Votes are to be proportioned to the amount of the poor's-rate upon the parties voting, not exceeding six votes; the parties not having neglected or refused to pay the rates when called on. The minutes of the proceedings are to be entered in the parish books, and signed by the chairman and such vestrymen as choose so to do, and such books are to be carefully kept, &c. Provision is made for vestries regulated by special acts, &c.: persons rated to the poor, though not inhabitants, and the clerks, &c. of corporations, are allowed to attend and vote. (58 *G.* 3. *c.* 69., amended by 59 *G.* 3. *c.* 85. and 1 *Vict. c.* 45.)

Vestries for church matters are to be regularly called by the "churchwardens, with the consent of the minister:" for the statute law has not altered the general authority under which, or the persons by whom, vestries are to be called.

The persons who are ordinarily entitled to be admitted to a vestry generally are, parishioners paying *scot and lot*, and all persons occupying land in the parish, although "foreigners" or out-dwellers. And the rector, vicar, or curate also has a right to be admitted into the vestry, and to vote, although not assessed to the church rates; and the minister has a right to preside over the meeting, whether rector, vicar, or perpetual curate, and, indeed, the minister is entitled to preside.

The majority of the vestrymen present bind the absent parishioners in the matters which properly and legally are cognizable by a vestry, which are the investigation into, and restraining the expenditure of the parish funds, and the enlarging or alteration of the churches or chapels within the parish. The appointment of many of the parish officers rests also with the vestry, and certainly in all weighty matters the vestry has a superintending and controlling authority.

The ordinary vestry is called an *open* vestry; but some large and populous parishes, especially near London, by custom, or under the directions of various acts of parliament, choose *select* vestries; and, in particular, the stat. 10 *Anne, c.* 11. *s.* 20., for building fifty new churches, gives certain commissioners power to appoint a convenient number of vestrymen, and to fill up vacancies; and, in other *local* or *personal* acts, the legislature has described the persons of whom a select vestry shall consist.

By the 59 *G.* 3. *c.* 12. *s.* 1., the inhabitants of any parish, in vestry assembled, may appoint no more than 20, nor less than 5, householders to be a select vestry; and the rector, vicar, or other minister of the parish, and, in his absence, the curate (such curate being resident and rated), and the churchwardens and overseers, with the inhabitants elected as aforesaid (such inhabitants being first appointed by writing under the hand and seal of a justice of the peace), shall constitute a select vestry for the management of the poor; and any three (two of whom shall neither be churchwardens or overseers), shall be a quorum. Magistrates are bound to appoint persons elected by the parishioners under the above act, and have no discretion to reject any person elected. A magistrate acting within the parish may, if an inhabitant, be a select vestryman, and an overseer may be a member by election, though he be also a member by virtue of his office. Wherever a select vestry is appointed under this act, the right of the common law vestry has always, in practice, been considered as superseded: it is optional with the parishioners whether they will or will not proceed upon the old law or upon the statutes, by appointing a select vestry; but if they pursue the latter course, they delegate their authority to that body.

The poor-law act of 4 & 5 *W.* 4. *c.* 76. *s.* 54. enacts, that after the passing of that act, the giving of any relief to the poor of any parish, which, according to the provisions of any of the acts therein recited, or of the 1 & 2 *W.* 4. *c.* 60., or of that act, or of any local acts, shall be under the government of any guardians of the poor, or of any select vestry, and whether forming part of any union or incorporation or not, (but subject in all cases to the powers of the said commissioners appointed under that act,) shall appertain exclusively to such guardians of the poor or select vestry, according to the respective provisions of the acts under which they shall be appointed; and no overseer of the poor shall give any further or other relief or allowance from the poor-rate than such as shall be ordered by such guardians or select vestry, except in cases of urgent necessity, &c.

The acts of one vestry may be rescinded by another and subsequent vestry; but there is never any necessity for the subsequent vestry to confirm what the former has done.

The following act of parliament, which is only applicable (see § 43.) to cities and towns, and to parishes having eight hundred or more rate-payers, and which may or may not be adopted, as the parishioners think fit, will put the reader in possession of all the editor conceives he can advantageously present upon this subject.

1 & 2 Gul. 4. *c.* 60.

An Act for the better Regulation of Vestries, and for the Appointment of Auditors of Accounts, in certain Parishes of England and Wales.

Whereas it is expedient to provide for the election of vestries, and of auditors of parish accounts, in certain parishes of England and Wales; be it therefore enacted by the king's most excellent majesty, by and with the advice and consent of the lords spiritual and temporal, and commons, in this present parliament assembled, and by the authority of the same, that this act and the several provisions thereof shall apply to and may be adopted, under and subject to the regulations herein contained, by any parish or parishes in England and Wales.

2. And be it further enacted, that when in any parish certain of the rate-payers thereof may desire that the said parish should come under the operation of this act, then and in that case any number of rate-payers amounting at least to one fifth of the rate-payers of such parish, or any number of rate-payers amounting at least to fifty parishioners, may, on some day between the first day of December and the first day of March, deliver a requisition, by them signed, and describing their places of residence, to the churchwardens, or to one of them, serving for the said parish, requiring of the said churchwardens to ascertain according to the manner herein-after mentioned whether or not a majority of the rate-payers of the said parish do wish and require that this act and the provisions thereof should be adopted therein; and which requisition may be in the form or to the tenor and effect following; (that is to say,)

"To the churchwardens of the parish of [*insert here the name of the parish*].

"We, whose names are hereunto subscribed, being rate-payers resident in the said parish, and respectively rated or assessed to the relief of the poor thereof, do hereby require you the said churchwardens to ascertain and determine the adoption or non-adoption of an act of the second year of the reign of King William the Fourth, chapter 60., intituled an act [*here insert the title of the act*].

"Dated this day of in the year of our Lord,

3. And be it further enacted, that the said churchwardens of the said parish shall on the first Sunday in the month of March next after the receipt of such requisition affix or cause to be affixed a notice to the principal doors of every church and chapel within the said parish, specifying some day not earlier than ten days and not later than twenty-one days after such Sunday, and at what place or places within the said parish, the rate-payers are required to signify their votes for or against the adoption of this act; which votes shall be received on three successive days, commencing at eight of the clock in the forenoon and ending at four of the clock in the afternoon of each day; and the said notice shall be to the following effect:—

"The churchwardens of this parish [*insert here the name of the parish*] having received a requisition duly signed according to the provisions of an act of the second year of the reign of William the Fourth, chapter 60., for the better regulation of vestries, the rate-payers of this parish of [*insert here the name of the parish*] are hereby required, all and each of them, on the day of next, and the two following days, to signify to the said churchwardens by a declaration, either printed or written, or partly printed or partly written, addressed and delivered to one of the churchwardens at [*insert here the place*], their votes for or against the adoption of the aforesaid act for the better regulation of vestries by the rate-payers of this parish.

(Signed) "Churchwardens."

4. And be it further enacted, that the said declaration shall be to the following effect:

"I, A. B., of street, [*or* place or house,] in this parish of , vote for [*or* against, *as the case may be*,] the adoption of the act of the second year of the reign of William the Fourth, chapter 60., for the better regulation of vestries by this parish."

5. And be it further enacted, that the said churchwardens shall carefully examine the votes to them delivered as aforesaid, and shall compare them with the last rate made for the relief of the poor of the said parish, and shall be empowered to call before them and examine any parish officer touching the said votes, or any rate-payer so giving his vote, and after a full and fair summing-up of the said votes shall, by public notice according to the form and manner herein-after prescribed, declare whether or not two thirds of the votes given have been given in favour of the adoption of the said act: provided always that the whole number of persons voting shall be a clear majority of the rate-payers of the parish: provided also, that the adoption or non-adoption of this act shall be decided by such number of votes as aforesaid.

6. Provided always, and be it further enacted, that any of the rate-payers of the aforesaid parish, not exceeding five together, may inspect, at or in the vestry room, or in some convenient place within the same parish, and they are hereby empowered to inspect the votes so given for and against the adoption of this act, at all seasonable times within one month after such notice shall have been given; and the churchwardens of the said parish are hereby required

carefully to preserve the said votes, and freely to permit and allow the examination thereof by the aforesaid rate-payers of the said parish at such seasonable times within the period aforesaid.

7. Provided always, and be it enacted, that no person shall be deemed a rate-payer, or be entitled to vote, or do any other act, matter, or thing, as such, under the provisions of this act, unless he or she shall have been rated to the relief of the poor for the whole year immediately preceding his so voting or otherwise acting as such rate-payer, and shall have paid all the parochial rates, taxes, and assessments due from him or her at the time of so voting or acting, except such as have been made or become due within the six months immediately preceding such voting.

8. And be it further enacted, that notice of the adoption of this act by any parish shall be forthwith given by the churchwardens for the time being of the said parish in the *London Gazette* and in one or more of the public newspapers circulating in the county in which the said parish may be situated, and by affixing a notice of the same to the principal doors of every church and chapel within the said parish; which notice shall be to the following effect: —

"Parish of [*here insert name of parish*].

"Notice is hereby given, that the above-named parish has adopted the act of the second year of the reign of King William the Fourth, chapter 60., intituled an act [*here insert the title of the act*]; and that the numbers of the majority and minority of votes given for and against the adoption of the said act are as follows; that is to say, votes for the adoption thereof, and votes against the adoption thereof.

"Dated this day of in the year of our Lord

(Signed) " Churchwardens."

9. Provided always, and be it further enacted, that if the rate-payers shall determine, in the manner as aforesaid, against the adoption of this act, then and in that case it shall not be lawful to make another requisition for the same purposes within three years after such determination.

10. And be it further enacted, that in any parish in which public notice of the adoption of this act in the manner as aforesaid shall be so made and given, this act shall immediately become the law for electing vestrymen and auditors of accounts of the said parish in manner herein-after mentioned.

11. And be it further enacted, that if any churchwarden, rate-collector, overseer, or other parish officer shall refuse to call meetings according to the provisions of this act, or shall refuse or neglect to make and give the declarations and notices directed to be made and given by this act, or to receive the vote of any rate-payer as aforesaid, or shall in any manner whatsoever alter, falsify, conceal, or suppress any vote or votes as aforesaid, such churchwarden, rate-collector, overseer, or other parish officer shall be deemed and taken to be guilty of a misdemeanor.

12. And be it further enacted, that on some Sunday at least twenty-one days previously to the day of annual election of vestrymen, notice of election, pursuant to this act, signed by the churchwardens, shall be affixed to the principal doors of every church and chapel of the said parish, and at other usual places, in the following terms:

"Parish of [*here insert name of parish*].

"The parishioners duly qualified according to the provisions of the act of the second year of the reign of King William the Fourth, intituled an act [*here insert the title of the act*] are hereby required to meet at on the day of conformably to the provisions of the said act, and then and there to consider of and elect fit and proper persons to be vestrymen and auditors of accounts of the parish of for the ensuing year; that is to say,

Members of the Vestry.
Auditors of Accounts."

13. And be it further enacted, that the churchwardens may summon the rate-collectors to attend them on the said day of annual election, in order to assist them in ascertaining that the persons presenting themselves to vote are parishioners rated to the relief of the poor of the said parish, and duly qualified to vote at the said election.

14. And be it further enacted, that on the day of annual election for vestrymen and auditors in any parish adopting this act, each parishioner then rated,

and having been rated to the relief of the poor one year, desirous of voting, do meet at the place appointed for such election, then and there to nominate eight rate-payers of the said parish as fit and proper persons to be inspectors of votes, four of such eight to be nominated by the churchwardens, and the other four to be nominated by the meeting; and after such nomination the said parishioners shall elect such parishioners duly qualified as may be there proposed for the offices of vestrymen and auditors; and the chairman shall at such meeting declare the names of the parishioners who have been elected by a majority of votes at such meeting.

15. Provided always, and be it further enacted, that any five rate-payers may then and there, in writing or otherwise, demand a poll, which shall be taken by ballot, each rate-payer delivering to the aforesaid inspectors two folded papers, one of which papers shall contain the names of the persons for whom such parishioner may vote as fit and proper to be members of the vestry, and the other shall contain the names of the persons for whom such parishioner may vote as fit and proper to be auditors of accounts: provided always, that each rate-payer shall have one vote and no more for the members of the vestry, and one vote and no more for the auditors of accounts to be chosen in the said parish.

16. And be it further enacted, that the inspectors of votes shall deposit the said folded lists, without previously opening the same, in two separate sets of balloting glasses or boxes, one set for the vestry lists, and another for the auditors' lists; and that the said balloting glasses or boxes shall be closed at the time fixed for the termination of the voting, that is, at four of the clock of the afternoon of the last day of election.

17. And be it further enacted, That after the close of the said ballot the aforesaid inspectors shall proceed to examine the said votes, and if necessary shall continue the examination by adjournments from day to day, not exceeding four days, Sunday excepted, until they shall have decided upon the persons duly qualified according to the provisions of this act who may have been chosen to fill the aforesaid offices.

18. And be it further enacted, that if an equality of votes should appear to the aforesaid inspectors to be given for any two or more persons to fill any or either of the said offices, in that case the inspectors shall decide by lot upon the person or persons so to be chosen.

19. And be it further enacted, that if any person do forge or in any way falsify any name or writing in any paper or list purporting to contain the vote or votes of any parishioner as aforesaid so voting for vestrymen or auditors, or do by any contrivance attempt to obstruct or prevent the purposes of such mode of election, the persons so offending shall, upon information laid, and conviction before any two or more justices of the peace having jurisdiction in the parish so adopting this act, be liable to a penalty of not less than ten and not more than fifty pounds, and in default of payment thereof shall be imprisoned for a term not exceeding six nor less than three months: and any fine so levied shall be given, half to the informer who shall have informed against the person so offending, and the other half to the poor of the parish in which the said offence shall have been committed.

20. And be it further enacted, that the aforesaid inspectors shall, immediately after they shall have decided upon whom the aforesaid elections have fallen, deliver to the churchwardens, or to one of them, serving for the parish so adopting this act, a list of the persons chosen by the parishioners to act as vestrymen and auditors of accounts; and the said list, or a copy thereof, shall be affixed to the doors of the churches and chapels or other places chosen for the purposes of public notice in the said parish.

21. And be it further enacted, that if any inspector as aforesaid shall wilfully make or cause to be made an incorrect return of the said votes, every such offender shall, upon information laid by any person before two or more justices of the peace having jurisdiction in the said parish, and upon conviction for such offence, be liable to a penalty of not less than twenty-five pounds and not exceeding fifty pounds.

22. And be it further enacted, That in all parishes adopting this act the meeting of parishioners for the election of the vestrymen and auditors of accounts by the parishioners shall take place in the month of May in every year; provided always, that when a ballot is demanded at such election the same shall commence on the following day, and continue for three successive days, com-

mencing at eight of the clock in the forenoon and closing at four of the clock in the afternoon on each day: provided also, that the day on which such elections shall commence shall in the first instance be appointed by the churchwardens of the parishes adopting this act, but in every subsequent year shall be appointed by the vestry: provided always, that when by reason of the populousness of any parish the said parish shall have been or shall be divided into districts for ecclesiastical or other purposes, then and in that case the said votes shall be taken, according to the aforesaid mode of election, in some convenient place, at the discretion of the churchwardens, in each of the several districts of the said parish.

23. And be it further enacted, that in all parishes adopting this act, the vestry appointed and elected as herein-before mentioned shall, when the said act shall come into full effect, consist of a certain number of resident householders; that is to say, twelve vestrymen for every parish in which the number of rated householders shall not exceed one thousand; and twelve other additional vestrymen, that is, twenty-four vestrymen, for every parish in which the rated householders shall exceed one thousand; and twelve other additional vestrymen, that is, thirty-six vestrymen, for every parish in which the number of rated householders shall exceed two thousand; and so on at the proportion of twelve additional vestrymen for every thousand rated householders: provided always, that in no case the number of vestrymen shall exceed one hundred and twenty: provided always, that in any parish wherein a greater number of vestrymen are given by special act of parliament than the proportions aforesaid will amount to, that then the number of vestrymen shall remain the same as given by such act of parliament; and provided always, that the rector, district rectors, vicar, perpetual curate, and churchwardens of the said parish shall constitute a part of the said vestry, and shall vote therein, in addition to the vestrymen as aforesaid elected under this act: provided always, that no more than one such rector or other such minister as aforesaid, from any one parish or ecclesiastical district as aforesaid, shall *ex officio* be a part of or vote at any vestry meeting.

24. And be it further enacted, That at the first election for vestrymen after the adoption of this act, in any parish, one third of the then existing vestry, or the nearest number thereto, but not exceeding the same, shall retire from office, (such portion to be determined by lot,) and the parishioners duly qualified shall elect a number of vestrymen equal to one third of the vestry, to be chosen according to the provisions of this act; and that on the next ensuing annual election for vestrymen one half, or as nearly as may be one half, of the remaining part of the first aforesaid vestry shall retire from office (such portion to be determined by lot), and the parishioners duly qualified shall again elect a number of vestrymen equal to one third of the vestry, to be chosen according to the provisions of this act; and that on the next, that is to say, the third annual election for vestrymen, the last remaining portion of the vestry as aforesaid shall retire from office, and the parishioners duly qualified shall elect vestrymen in like manner and number as at the two preceding elections, so as to fill up the vestry to the exact number of vestrymen prescribed by this act.

25. And be it further enacted, that at every subsequent annual election those vestrymen who have been three years in office shall go out of office, and the parishioners shall elect, according to the provisions of this act, other vestrymen, to the number of one third of the total number of which such vestry shall consist, as also fill up any vacancies which may have occurred from death or other causes: provided always, that any or all of the vestrymen so going out by rotation may be immediately eligible for re-election.

26. And be it further enacted, that the vestry elected under this act in any parish not within the metropolitan police district or the city of London shall consist of resident householders rated or assessed to the relief of the poor upon a rental of not less than ten pounds; and no person shall be capable of acting as one of the said vestry unless he shall be the occupier of a house, lands, tenements, or hereditaments rated or assessed upon the afore-mentioned amount of rental within the parish for which he is to serve: provided always, that if the parish adopting this act should be within the metropolitan police district or the city of London, or if the resident householders therein should amount to more than three thousand, then and in that case the vestry elected under this act shall consist of resident householders rated or assessed to the relief of the poor of such parish upon a rental of not less than 40*l.* *per annum.*

27. And be it further enacted, that from and after the adoption of this act in any parish, the vestry shall exercise the powers and privileges held by any vestry now existing in such parish, and the authority of such vestry may be pleaded before any justice or justices of the peace, or in any court of law, in regard to all parochial property, or monies due, or holdings or contracts, or other documents of the like nature, formerly under the control or in the keeping of the said vestry of the said parish; and all parish officers or boards shall account to them in like manner as they have accounted to the said vestry; provided always, that nothing in this act shall be deemed, construed, or taken to repeal, alter, or invalidate any local act for the government of any parish by vestries, or for the management of the poor by any board of directors and guardians, or for the due provision for divine worship within the parish, and the maintenance of the clergy officiating therein, otherwise than is by this act expressly enacted regarding the election of vestrymen and auditors of accounts.

28. And be it further enacted, that all powers or duties to be performed by the vestry of any parish adopting this act may be exercised and performed respectively by the major part of such vestry assembled at any meeting, there not being less than five vestrymen present at a meeting of a vestry which consists of twelve or more elected vestrymen and not exceeding twenty-three, and not being less than seven vestrymen present at a meeting of a vestry which consists of twenty-four or more elected vestrymen and not exceeding thirty-five, and not being less than nine vestrymen present at a meeting of a vestry which consists of thirty-six elected vestrymen or upwards; and all orders and directions given and all contracts and engagements entered into by the vestrymen present at any such meeting, or the major part of them then assembled, shall be as valid and effectual as if the same were done by all the said vestrymen for the time being, and shall be binding and conclusive on all such vestrymen, provided that the same is confirmed at the next subsequent meeting of the vestry.

29. And be it further enacted, that in any case in which the vestry room of any parish in any city or town shall not be sufficiently large and commodious for any vestry meeting, such meeting shall be held elsewhere within the said parish or place, but not in the church or chapel thereof.

30. And be it further enacted, that at every meeting of any vestry, in the absence of the persons authorized by law or custom to take the chair, the members present shall elect a chairman for the occasion before proceeding to other business.

31. And be it further enacted, that the vestry of every parish adopting this act shall cause to be provided and kept a proper book or books, and proper entries to be made therein of the names of the several vestrymen who shall attend the respective meetings of the vestry, and of all orders and proceedings made or taken at such meetings; and all such books shall at all reasonable times be open to the inspection of the said vestrymen, and of any person rated or assessed to the relief of the poor of the said parish, and of any creditor on the rates of the said parish, without fee or reward; and the said vestrymen, persons, and creditors, or any of them, shall and may take copies of or extracts from such books respectively, without paying any thing for the same; and in case the clerk to the said vestry, or other person having the care of such books, shall refuse to permit or shall not permit the said vestrymen or such persons or creditors to inspect the same, or to take such copies or extracts as aforesaid, such clerk or other person shall forfeit and pay any sum of money not exceeding ten pounds for every such offence.

32. And be it further enacted, that the said vestry shall and they are hereby required to cause a book or books to be provided and kept, and true and regular accounts to be entered therein of all sums of money received and disbursed for or on account of parochial purposes, and of the several articles, matters, and things for which such sums of money shall have been so received and disbursed; which book or books shall at all seasonable times be open to the inspection of the said vestrymen, and of any person or persons rated to the relief of the poor of the said parish, and of any creditor or creditors on the same, without fee or reward; and the said vestrymen and persons and creditors as aforesaid, or any of them, shall and may take copies of or extracts from the said book or books, or any part or parts thereof, without paying any thing for the same; and in case the clerk to the said vestrymen, or other person with whom such

books shall remain, shall on any reasonable demand refuse to permit or shall not permit the said vestrymen, persons, or creditors, or any of them, to inspect the said book or books, or to take such copies or extracts as aforesaid, such clerk or other person as aforesaid shall forfeit and pay any sum not exceeding ten pounds for every such offence.

33. And be it further enacted, that in any and every parish adopting this act the parishioners duly qualified to vote for vestrymen as aforesaid shall elect five rate-payers of the said parish who shall have signified in writing their assent to serve to be auditors of accounts, which auditors shall be so elected on the first day on which the vestrymen shall be chosen after such parish shall have adopted this act, and according to the same forms of voting as are herein-before prescribed for the election of the said vestry: provided always, that no person shall be eligible to fill the said office of auditor of accounts who shall not be qualified according to the provisions of this act, as herein-before stated, to fill the office of vestryman for the said parish; and provided always, that no person be eligible to fill the said office of auditors of accounts who shall be one of the vestry for the said parish; and if any person on the day of annual election shall be chosen to be both a member of the vestry and an auditor of accounts, the said vestry at their first meeting after such election shall declare the said person incapable of acting as vestryman: provided also, that no person shall be eligible to fill the said office of auditor of accounts who shall be interested, either directly or indirectly, in any contract, office, business, or employ, or in providing or supplying any materials or articles for the parish for which he is to serve; and any person who shall be discovered, after his election, to be so interested, shall cease to be an auditor.

34. And be it further enacted, that the aforesaid auditors of accounts shall meet twice at least in each year, at the board room of the vestry, and (a majority of the said auditors being present at such meetings) shall proceed to audit the accounts of the said vestry for the preceding half year, in presence of the vestry-clerk; and the said vestry are hereby required, by their said clerk, to produce and lay before the said auditors at every such meeting a true and just statement or account in writing, accompanied with proper vouchers, of all sums of money which may have come to the hands of the said vestry or of their treasurer, and also of all monies paid, laid out, or expended by them, or by any churchwardens, overseers, surveyors, or other persons by them employed, and responsible to the said vestry, since the last period up to which the accounts of the said vestry were audited; and in all parishes in which other boards shall have controul over any part of the parochial expenditure, the said auditors shall have the same power of examining the accounts and officers thereof as of examining the accounts and officers of the vestry, and shall audit the accounts of the said boards in the same manner as they audit the accounts of the said vestries.

35. And be it further enacted, that the said auditors shall have power to summon and call before them, by a writing for that purpose, signed by any one of them, or by the clerk of the vestry of any parish adopting this act, any parish officer or other person or persons whatsoever concerned in the said accounts, and to require of him or her or them to attend the said auditors at any meeting or adjourned meeting, and to bring with them all books of accounts, writings, papers, and documents required, which may concern the said accounts, and to give such information as to the particulars of such accounts as he, she, or they shall be enabled to give: and any parish officer or other person refusing so to attend, or otherwise wilfully obstructing the purposes of such inquiry, shall be deemed guilty of a misdemeanor.

36. And be it further enacted, that the said accounts, when audited and approved by the said auditors, or by the major part of them, shall be by them signed in the presence of the clerk of the aforesaid vestry of any parish adopting this act, and the said clerk of the vestry shall also affix his signature to the same; and it shall be lawful for the aforesaid auditors to subjoin such remarks thereto as to them shall seem meet.

37. And be it further enacted, that the said accounts, when so audited and signed, shall remain at the office of the clerk of the said vestry; and that the said accounts shall after such audit be open and accessible for the examination, at all seasonable times, of any person rated to the relief of the poor of the said parish, and of any creditor on the rates thereof: provided always, that nothing in this act contained relative to the appointment and duty of auditors shall

debar the parishioners from any remedy by them before possessed by the law of the land.

38. And be it further enacted, that an abstract of the accounts of all monies received and disbursed by the vestry in any parish adopting this act shall twice in every year, within fourteen days after the same shall have been audited in manner in this act mentioned, be made out by the said vestry, either in writing or in print, and a copy of such abstract shall be delivered to all persons applying for the same, and rated or assessed to the relief of the poor of the said parish, such person paying one shilling for the same; and which copies the said clerk is hereby required to cause to be published either in writing or print, and distributed accordingly.

39. And be it further enacted, that in any parish adopting this act the vestry shall cause to be made out, once at least in every year, a list of the several freehold, copyhold, and leasehold estates, and of all charitable foundations and bequests, if any, belonging to the said parish, and under the controul of the said vestry, the said list to contain a true and detailed account of the place where such estate or charitable foundation may be situate, or in what mode and security such bequest may be invested, specifying also the yearly rental of each, and the particular appropriation thereof, together with the names of the persons partaking of their benefit (except where such benefit shall be allotted to the poor of the parish generally), and to what amount in each case, and also stating the name and description of the persons in whom such estates are vested, and the names and description of the trustees for each charity: provided always, that the aforesaid list shall be open for the inspection of the rate-payers, at the office of the vestry clerk, at the same time with the accounts, when audited according to the provisions of this act.

40. Provided always, and be it further enacted, that this act or any thing therein contained shall not extend or be construed to extend to invalidate or avoid any ecclesiastical law or constitution of the church of England, save and except so far as concerns the appointment of vestries; or to destroy any of the rights or powers belonging to the archbishops, bishops, deans, or other of the clergy of the said established church, either as individuals or as corporate bodies; or in anywise to abridge or controul their ordinary jurisdiction over or relating to any matter or thing respecting the ministers thereof.

41. And in order to remove doubts as to the meaning of certain words in this act, be it enacted, that the word "justice" shall be deemed to mean justice of the peace; and that the words "person" and "party" shall be deemed to include any number of persons or parties; and that the words "justices of the peace of the county or city" shall be deemed to include justices of the peace of any division of a county, liberty, division of a liberty, precinct, county of a city, county of a town, cinque port, or town corporate; and that the word "parish" shall be deemed to include any liberty, precinct, township, hamlet, tithing, vill, extra-parochial place, or any place maintaining its own poor; and that the word "rate-payers" shall include "ley-payers;" and that the meaning of the several words in this act shall not be restricted, although the same may be subsequently referred to in the singular number or masculine gender only.

42. And be it further enacted, that the words "church or chapel," insomuch as regards the affixing of notices as by this act directed, shall be deemed to include all places of religious worship according to the forms of the established church; and that in any parish or place not having a parish church or chapel as aforesaid, the said notices shall be affixed to some public building within the limits of the said parish or place.

43. Provided always, and be it further enacted, that nothing in this act contained shall extend to any parish not being within or being part of any city or town, in which parish there shall not be a greater number than eight hundred persons rated as householders, and having paid the rates for the relief of the poor within the year preceding that in which the provisions of this act may be desired to be put in execution within such parish.

44. And be it further enacted, that this act shall be deemed and taken to be a public act, and shall be judicially taken notice of as such by all judges, justices, and others, without the same being specially pleaded.

VICAR strictly means the person who supplies the place of another.

The priest of every parish is called the rector, unless the prædial tithes are appropriated, or in lay hands, then he is called the vicar.

VULGAR ERRORS. Erroneous notions. The following are a few of the most prominent, in reference to legal matters:—

1. That a funeral procession passing over private grounds creates a public right of way.

2. That it is lawful to arrest and detain a dead body.*

3. That first cousins may intermarry, and that second cousins may not: whereas they may both marry with each other.†

4. That a butcher cannot be sworn as a juryman on a coroner's inquisition.

5. That all persons born at sea, claim a right of settlement in Stepney parish.‡

6. That a lease for more than 99 years constitutes a freehold.

7. That a husband is punishable for his wife's criminal acts.

8. That to disinherit a child, the sum of one shilling should be bequeathed.§

WARD. The relation of guardian and ward is very similar to that of parent and child. When the care of infants is vested in the chancellor, he will compel, or rather assist, a guardian in compelling a ward to obey the reasonable desires of a guardian, in relation to education and advancement in life. A guardian can have a writ of *habeas corpus* to recover possession of his ward, if detained without the ward's consent, or he may proceed, by petition to the chancellor, to regain the custody of the infant. To abduct a ward from the custody of his guardian is a misdemeanor.

With regard to female wards, if they be placed under the control of the court of chancery, and almost any property will give the court jurisdiction, a very jealous power is exercised, it being deemed a contempt of that court to marry one of its wards without consent, wittingly or unwittingly. In cases of clandestine marriage, the court invariably commits the husband to the Fleet, and keeps him there until a settlement has been made, placing the ward's property entirely out of his reach. The court always demands the attendance of the husband in court, and not

---

* The origin of this error is noticed under ARREST.

† By our mode of computing the degrees of consanguinity, which is in conformity with the civil or imperial law, cousins-german, or first cousins, who are in the fourth degree may intermarry. But the ecclesiastical or canon law, by using a different mode of computation, reckoned those in the fourth degree by the civil law to be in the second degree by the canon law. Therefore this error has arisen by confounding the application of these two laws; for first cousins may marry by the civil law, and second cousins could not by the canon law, which has long ceased to be of force in respect of this subject. See KINDRED.

‡ The "addition" or description of a seafaring man, in indictments for offences committed upon the high seas, and in other legal proceedings, used ordinarily to be "late of Stepney, mariner," which most likely is the origin of this error, independently of the fact that the parish of Stepney has always been thickly inhabited by a seafaring population.

§ This error owes its origin to a rule of the civil law, which invalidates any will which is "inofficiose," *i. e.* wanting in display of natural affection, by the omission of a bequest to, or provision for, a child. This doctrine is still acknowledged, to its full extent, in those countries where justice is administered according to the civil law, as in Scotland, &c.

unfrequently commits him, though the marriage was had with consent of parents and friends, this being the only way to enforce a settlement. When a marriage takes place between equals in station or fortune, the court takes that circumstance into consideration, and the settlement is framed accordingly. Where a marriage is contemplated between a gentleman and a ward of court, proposals are laid (by leave previously obtained of the court) before a master in chancery, who reports upon the fitness of the marriage, and a settlement is prepared accordingly; or, in consideration of the intended husband making a settlement, the ward's property may be paid over to them both on marriage, or otherwise. Guardians misconducting themselves may be removed. — See INFANT.

WARRANTS OF ATTORNEY and COGNOVITS. These are writings, the effect of which is to enable another party to obtain a judgment in a civil action against the person subscribing them.

A warrant of attorney is an authority under seal to certain attorneys, or, indeed, any attorney, to appear for the party subscribing the same, (who by such subscription is *ipso facto*, made a defendant) in a named court, and compellable to receive a *declaration* supposed to be filed in such court, in an action of *debt* for a specific sum, which is of sufficient amount to cover a principal sum, interest, and all expenses, as due upon an account stated, or for money borrowed; and, thereupon, to *confess* judgment, or otherwise to suffer a judgment in any manner to pass against the party, in order that execution for the said sum and all other expenses may issue against him. This is often used as a security where no action is pending, and a most conclusive one it is; for it gives the holder of it (who must be the person named therein, at whose suit the proceedings are to take place, or his executors or assigns), absolute authority to levy an execution upon the defendant, or to take his person.

To this is added what is termed a "defeazance," that is, a memorandum in the nature of the "condition" of a bond, stating the terms upon which the warrant of attorney shall be *defeated* (whence the term *defeazance*). This defeazance must be written on the same paper with the warrant of attorney, and, in fact, is the only part material to be observed, it controlling the preceding formular part of the warrant of attorney in the same manner that the *condition* controls the words of the bond.

Warrants of attorney are subject to a stamp duty of equal amount with a bond for payment of money, these instruments being apt securities for this purpose.* A bond, it must be remembered, only gives an undisputed right of action; the warrant of attorney gives judgment and execution.

Judgments may be entered up upon this instrument at any time within twenty years, if the subscribing party be alive; but, after ten years old, the courts require that notice may be given the party, so that he may be able to show cause against its being put in force.

Where a female marries after having given a warrant of attorney, judgment may be entered up against her and her husband.

Persons in custody (not taken in execution), who execute this security as a consideration for their being liberated, must have the presence of an attorney, who is bound to explain the nature of this security: if this requisite is not complied with, the instrument can be set aside.

* Warrants of attorney given by a prisoner in order to effect his discharge, are only liable to stamp-duty of 1*l*.

A *cognovit actionem* is, in effect, the same as a warrant of attorney, and subject to the same regulations, as far as regards *prisoners* executing the same, and is nothing more than an unsealed writing, confessing (*i. e.* admitting) the cause of action, and authorising the plaintiff to enter up his judgment immediately, or upon certain conditions or stipulations; and this is a very usual mode of giving a plaintiff security, and of saving the farther expenses of proceeding to judgment, especially after the defendant has pleaded.

Where no proceedings have been taken, or where the defendant is taken in execution, there a warrant of attorney is the security given, though, in fact, in the former case a writ may be issued, and an *un*conditional cognovit given, which, as it requires no stamp, is a very cheap proceeding: after judgment there can be no confession, so this means will not apply in the latter case.

If cognovits express particular terms or conditions, and the sum is above 20*l.*, a stamp-duty of 1*l.* must be impressed; but this may be avoided by the cognovit being given unconditionally, and the plaintiff giving to the defendant a memorandum on a separate paper, expressing the days on which he will accept payment, as a satisfaction of the judgment, which otherwise would be entered up.

If the plaintiff and defendant are alive, the judgment may be entered up at any time within twenty years, without any notice to the defendant, or any application to the court being necessary, as is the case with respect to old warrants of attorney.

It will easily be understood that, by acknowledging judgments in this manner, by which execution can be levied the same day, the fraudulent debtor has it in his power to give one creditor a preference over another, who has obtained judgment after long litigation; or what is worse, enable a man who is no creditor at all, to hold the fruits of this collusive proceeding in trust for himself, and render detection difficult. But an act passed in June, 1822, has done much to prevent these practices. The preamble states, "Whereas injustice is frequently done to creditors by secret warrants of attorney, to confess judgment for securing the payment of money, whereby persons in a state of insolvency are enabled to keep up the appearance of being in good circumstances, and the persons holding such warrants of attorney have the power of taking the property of such insolvents in execution at any time, to the exclusion of the rest of their creditors:" The act then provides, that persons holding *warrants of attorney* or *cognovits* may file the same if they be in the king's bench, or attested copies thereof if they be in any other court at Westminster, with the clerk of the judgments and docquets, *within* twenty-one days after their execution; otherwise the same shall be void, if the defendant afterwards become bankrupt, or (as by the insolvent debtors' act) insolvent, (the cognovit or warrant of attorney being valid against the defendant himself,) unless such judgment shall have been entered up *within* the twenty-one days; all judgments being entered in a book, called the "Docquet-Book," to which every one has access, on payment of a fee of 4*d.*, for thereby the necessary publicity has been obtained.

The practical effect of this enactment is, that the assignees of a bankrupt or insolvent may recover back any goods or property seized, or the value, from the party levying it, by virtue of such invalid judgment, or from the sheriff himself, if notice of the fact is duly given to him or his officer: and creditors should also remember that no judgment, whether upon cognovit or warrant of attorney, filed or *otherwise*, is valid, or can be enforced after the insolvent's imprisonment, *i. e.* the imprisonment upon which the insolvent petitions the court.

In bankruptcy, an execution founded upon a warrant of attorney may be defeated by a *fiat* issuing within two calendar months, unless a sale has taken place, and no notice to the sheriff has been given; but this does not extend to an execution levied in pursuance of a cognovit given in order to stay proceedings upon an *adverse* suit, which (unless an act of bankruptcy intervene before sale, of which the plaintiff or sheriff has notice), cannot be impeached by the creditors, so that a cognovit *bonâ fide* given is considered as good as an adverse judgment after verdict, which cannot be impeached, unless an open act of bankruptcy take place before sale or a private act is committed, upon which a fiat is issued within two months from the levying thereof.

Warrants of attorney and cognovits are legal instruments, of which the courts will take notice, upon a summary application by motion in term time, if they are wrongfully or wickedly used, or if the consideration was illegal or grossly usurious; but this summary jurisdiction applies chiefly to warrants of attorney, which are given usually independent of any action, whereas cognovits are a proceeding in an action; yet, if an action is commenced for the sole purpose of a cognovit being given in order to enforce an illegal consideration or usurious demand, the same reason will apply, and the court interfere accordingly. In vacation time, a judge at chambers will, upon affidavit, stay proceedings till the following term, or discharge a party wrongfully imprisoned, if the wrong or illegality is apparent.

WARRANTY. The seller of goods is not liable to the purchaser, if the purchaser be disturbed by adverse claimants, or the quality is deficient, except there is an express warranty or promise of indemnity, or there has been fraud or wilful misrepresentation, or, what is the same thing, concealment.

The buyer paying a liberal price for the articles, does not *imply* a warranty. This contract should be expressed; and where the magnitude of the transaction would ordinarily induce the caution, it should be reduced into writing; but it seems that, in some cases, the law will imply or raise a contract of warranty; for instance, that provisions are wholesome; that goods sold tally and agree with the sample shown at the time of sale; that the goods answer the description of an advertisement, or particular of sale put forth concerning them; that where the custom of a particular trade or dealing establishes a warranty, the goods must answer the price given.

A warranty must ordinarily be special, and not *generally*, as to the goodness of the thing sold; it should be made at or before the actual sale, and not after it.

It is not necessary to return the goods previously to an action being commenced for damages; for the buyer may recover the difference between the sum he gave and that produced by a re-sale, or the difference between the real value (if he keep them) and the sum he paid.

It is safer, however, to offer to return the goods; and in cases where the terms of the warranty are to "take back the goods, and return the money," such offer to return must be made before action brought, and within a reasonable time after a discovery of the misrepresentation. If the seller refuse to take back the goods, they remain at his own risk, and the buyer, notwithstanding, may proceed to recover the whole sum.

As to warranty of horses, see Horses.

WASTE, and herein of DILAPIDATIONS. Waste is the committing any spoil or damage to houses or land by tenants, or those who have limited estates; for tenants in tail are privileged to do a variety of acts which in a tenant, or one whose interest is transitory or subordinate, would be deemed waste.

Waste is either actual or permissive.

Actual, or as it is often termed, voluntary waste, is committed by committing acts of positive destruction, as by cutting down timber, ploughing up ancient meadow, and pulling down houses, together with infinite other acts of deterioration.

The remedy applied for this waste, where the tenant for life is the person committing the spoil, is by injunction, to prevent the further ruin of the property, and for an account of the property wasted; or the person ultimately entitled may proceed at law by writ of waste, and recover the land wasted, with damages.

Permissive or negligent waste is the suffering damage to accrue, for want of doing the necessary acts to keep house and land in order.

Waste of this nature, when committed by a tenant for life, is remediable by application to the court of chancery, who will appoint a manager or receiver to take care of the property, or the party next entitled may bring his action of waste as in the former instance.

Tenants for years, who hold upon lease, are, by their covenants, bound to do certain repairs to the houses they occupy, and these wants of repairs are known by the name of *dilapidations*, which are recoverable against the tenants.

The estates of incumbents are liable for wants of repair to the parsonage, rectory, or vicarage, recoverable by the successor.

All tenants for years are by law bound to repair, and keep repaired, their premises, and thereby prevent dilapidations; and for that purpose may, in the country, take wood and timber sufficient for that purpose, but in modern usage, particularly with respect to houses in towns, the tenant covenants to repair.

A tenant at will, whose occupation is now enlarged to a tenancy from year to year, was never at law liable to repair; and is only bound to prevent dilapidation.

This brings us to consider what are *substantial* repairs, and what *tenantable* repairs. The first being obligatory on the lessee to perform, the latter on the tenant at will, or from year to year.

Substantial repairs, are the amendment and restoration of the main walls and vaults, the replacing of beams, girders, roofs, and other main timbers, and other essentials of an edifice; and also comprise the reinstatement of any thing that has been lost or taken away, such as broken glass, locks, keys, shelves, mantel-pieces, &c., together with reasonable papering, whitewashing, cleansing, and amendments.

Tenantable repairs are only putting in windows or doors, broken by the tenant, or during his occupation, so as to prevent waste and decay of the premises, it being incumbent on the landlord to do substantial repairs. Of course, tenants at will, or from year to year, must restore fixtures in good preservation, reasonable wear and tear excepted.

Dilapidations (as Mr. Elmes observes), are to be considered rather as a composition to be paid as *dilapidation-costs* for damage done to a house in lieu of reparation, when the expenses of complete reparation would be excessive.

WATERMEN are governed by the watermen's company, as constituted by the 7 & 8 *G.* 4. *c.* 75. (printed among the local and personal acts), and watermen offending against the provisions of that act, which amongst other things enacts, that boats carrying passengers are to be licensed, expressing the number they are allowed to carry; that the name and number are to be painted thereon; and those carrying a greater number of passengers than allowed by the licence, are guilty of a misdemeanor if one be drowned; and offending in those and other particulars, are punishable before the lord mayor and aldermen with fines, varying from 40*s.* to 5*l.*

Two justices of the peace may award satisfaction of damages done to any boat or craft, not exceeding 5*l.*

Disputes between watermen and watermen are determinable by members of the court of assistants of the watermen's company.

WATERCOURSE, the interest or right to take water in another's land, or a convenience in the free running of water from one person's land to another. This is an easement, and that species of property which is termed *incorporeal.* It is the subject of prescription, and enjoyment of this right or property for twenty years is presumptive evidence of its legality; but it is liable to be rebutted if the owner of the land was under age, a married woman, lunatic, or abroad; but the absolute right is acquired after forty years undisturbed possession.

Rights to the use of wells, and right of way thereto, drawing water from a pond, are similar rights, and may be acquired in a similar manner by undisturbed enjoyment.

The right of watercourse is not confined to individuals. This right must be acquired by deed or by length of time, which supposes a deed.

WAYS. There are four kinds of way: — 1. a footway; 2. a horseway, which includes a footway; 3. a carriageway, which includes both horseway and footway; 4. a driftway. Although a carriageway comprehends a horseway, yet it does not necessarily include a driftway: it is said, however, that evidence of a carriageway is strong presumptive evidence of the grant of a driftway.

A right of way may be either public or private: ways common to all the king's subjects are called highways. A way leading to a market town, and common for all travellers, and communicating with any great road, is a highway; but if it lead only to a church, or to a house, or village, or to the fields, it is a private way; whether it be a public or private way, is a matter of fact, and depends much on common reputation. The public may have a right to a high road as a common street, although there be no thoroughfare. The law affecting the use of a private way is as follows, wherein it is to be noticed, 1. how private ways are claimed; 2. how private ways are lost.

A private way is a right which particular persons have of going over the land of another; and this right arises either by a deed or grant, usage, which presupposes a grant, and is styled prescription, custom, or some express agreement or declaration, as under an inclosure act. A deed or grant must state expressly the way or path intended to be given, and the party who is to enjoy the same. A legal right will be presumed from long uninterrupted use by the public or parties claiming. A custom is shown as by every inhabitant of such a town or place having a way over such and such land, either to church or market. The claiming a way by agreement or reservation is, by an owner conveying land, or part thereof, to a purchaser, and keeping to himself a right of way; and by necessity an individual may have a right of way, as if there be no convenient way, when the law will sometimes suggest or imply a grant. By the general inclosure act, ways and paths may be stopped up, the commissioners first setting out private roads: and, with respect to paths deemed inconvenient, justices of the peace have power, upon previous public notice posted upon the land, to stop them up, which any person interested can apply to prevent at the quarter-sessions.

A private way may be lost by the owner opening his land, so that people pass over it continually. And although not less than thirty years will enable particular individuals to claim a way, yet a very few years will suffice to give the public a right of way; therefore, a party not meaning to give up his right of closing his land against the public (dedicate the way to the public, is the legal expression), should only give a limited permission, or do, at stated periods, certain acts of ownership, in order to demonstrate that the public are not to possess an absolute right in the way, (shutting up the way once a year on Holy Thursday, or some other particular day, is the most usual course)* ; but tenants under long leases cannot, by any act or collusion with others, bind the superior landlords by their acquiescence or permission.

It may be taken, therefore, as a general rule, that where the public have for twenty years, or private parties for thirty years or more, used the way without interruption, in the case of the public, a dedication, and to the private party or class of individuals, a licence or permission, will be presumed, and after sixty years' uninterrupted enjoyment or use by both, nothing can avail in favour of the owner of the land. It appears the law intends that a dedication to the public may be presumed from a much shorter time than is necessary to establish a right of way by individuals or particular inhabitants, owners of adjoining lands or their tenants, who may claim the right of passing and repassing across their neighbourhood, or landlord's close or field.

Public ways are highways, along which all persons may pass and repass at pleasure. The reparation of highways primarily was, and to a certain extent as to turnpike-roads, still is, incumbent on the parish; but some persons are bound by the tenure on which they hold their land, to repair part of the highways; and where there is a dispute as to the liability, the question is tried by indictment.

Highway acts have been passed from a very early period, for the purpose of keeping the roads in repair, and turnpike-roads have latterly been created, which are, in fact, nothing more than the converting parish roads into turnpike-roads, by placing bars or barriers for the purpose of gathering a toll, applicable for the purposes of the trust, viz., the keeping such roads, and adjacent roads, in repair. The turnpike-roads being placed under the management and guidance of certain trustees appointed by act of parliament, and regulated by an act universal in its operation, and controlling local acts passed at different times for the repair of particular roads.†

* An inscription upon a stone wall, or other boundary or land-mark, is a very certain mode of perpetuating the circumstances under which the way is opened, and of evidencing a limited permission of use by the public, when coupled with other acts of ownership.

† A bill is about to be introduced (in fact was introduced last session, but,

The remedy for non-repair of a highway, is to summon the surveyor before the justices of the peace, who will make an order upon him to repair such roads, unless the right be disputed, when the persons or parish said to be liable are to be indicted: upon this proceeding the right is settled.

The turnpike-road acts inflict various penalties upon persons damaging the roads, riding on footpaths, playing games, leaving waggons, laying timber, and an infinity of other acts, tending to impede the progress of travellers or endanger their persons, more especially as to cases of prevention, viz., punishing by fines, punishments and penalties, the makers of bonfires, those who erect windmills within a certain distance of the road, blacksmiths not closing their shutters at night, drivers of waggons riding on the shaft, or not using reins, or not being within a sufficient distance to have the government of his vehicle, not using skid-pans or slippers when descending hills, or descending hills with locked wheels, or driving a waggon, &c., without having a name painted upon it, and not conforming to a variety of proper regulations tending to preserve public safety and convenience, in all which cases the owner is liable, if the driver cannot be found; and these punishments, fines, and penalties, are inflicted by justices of the peace, and power given to secure *transient* offenders, damaging gates, posts, lamps, &c., in a summary manner.

Persons obstructing highways, not being turnpike-roads, are punishable by indictment as for a common nuisance; and the putting up of gates is an inconsiderate act in many ancient lanes, which, as it subjects the public to great inconvenience, has frequently been visited with this proceeding. New gates in public ways may be pulled down, and if an action of trespass be brought, the party may well justify the act.

WEIGHTS AND MEASURES. The use of heaped measure is now abolished, and all weights made of pewter or lead are not to be used.

The *stone* weight is now settled to consist of fourteen standard pounds avoirdupois, and the hundred weight is to consist of eight such stones, and a *ton* is to consist of twenty such hundred weight; and all contracts made by heaped measure, or by any other weight or measure, are made void. — See stat. 4 *&* 5 *W.* 4. *c.* 49. which abolishes all local customs with respect to weights and measures, and enforces uniformity of weights and measures throughout the country.

All articles are to be sold by *avoirdupois* weight, except gold, silver, platina, diamonds, or other precious stones, and drugs, when sold by retail, which only are to be sold by *troy* weight.

Inspectors of weights and measures are appointed.

The sale of false or deceitful balances, weights, or measures, is a cheat, or is indictable as a misdemeanor, and punishable by fine and imprisonment.

The selling of counterfeit weights and measures, and the making of them, is punishable before two magistrates, who may convict the offender in sums not less than 10*l.* or not exceeding 50*l.* for making, or not less than 10*s.* and not exceeding 10*l.* for selling them.

Ward inquests in London and Southwark have the power of inspect-

---

from particular causes, did not pass), for the purpose of amending the laws regarding turnpike-trusts. It is intended to consolidate the trusts of turnpike roads, as great expense is incurred by the present system of management.

ing weights and measures; and the city of London appoints it own inspectors or officers to view, seal, and stamp weights and measures.

False weights and measures are presentable at the court leet; but the most fit proceeding is by indictment at the sessions or assizes, for there the offender may be adequately punished.

WILD FOWL. The taking the *eggs* of snipes and wild fowl is punishable as a malicious injury before a single justice, and also punishable under the game act; but the taking of wild fowl itself is not punishable under the game act, and is not subject to any summary proceedings, the disturbing a decoy of wild fowl being only a trespass at law.

WILLS are written or verbal; but verbal wills, which must be reduced into writing, and termed nuncupative wills, are seldom, if ever, used, and are only available when a person is surprised with sudden sickness: they are, with one exception, prospectively abolished by the act 1 *Vict. c.* 26.

Written wills are either made of real or personal property.

Wills disposing of real, *i. e.* freehold property, must be attested by two witnesses, who must each sign their names in the presence of the testator: it is not necessary that they sign in the presence of each other or at the same time; though, if opportunity serve, it certainly is most advisable to adopt that mode of execution.

A will, whether of real or personal property, *must* be signed, it *may* have a seal, and indeed usually possesses this formality, and where persons (especially married women) execute a will in pursuance of a power in a settlement or deed, a seal should be affixed, independent of the two witnesses generally required by the terms of deeds creating powers of this description.

Wills of persons who were of sound mind at the time of the making are not revoked or affected by subsequent infirmity or lunacy.

Persons drunk at the time of the execution of a will, must re-execute, republish, or confirm it when sober, for a will signed under such circumstances is void.

Those who are born deaf and dumb may make a will, if it is apparent they have understanding, but not else.

A blind man may make a written will, provided the will be read to him before witnesses, and in their presence acknowledged by him for his last will; but if a writing should be delivered to a blind man, and he not hearing the same read, acknowledge the same for his will, this will not be sufficient, for it might happen that if he had heard the same read he would not have acknowledged it for his will. The best way, therefore, in such a case is, that the will be read over to the testator, and approved by him in the presence of all the attesting witnesses.

The above precautions seem in like degree requisite in the case of a person who, from defect of education or illness, cannot read.

Married women cannot devise their real estate (unless by the special custom of some manors), and they cannot, without express permission of their husbands, make a will of personal estate. But marriage-settlements often give a married woman power, by any deed or writing testamentary, signed and sealed (or *signed* only), and attested by two or more credible witnesses, to appoint, direct, or bequeath particular sums of money; if she survive her husband, she must confirm the will, else it will not operate, as the death of her husband is an implied revocation.

A few other circumstances should be noted with respect to wills.

The statutes creating government stocks, require that they should be bequeathed by wills attested by two witnesses; but wills previous to the 1st of January, 1838, bequeathing stock, are not objected to for want of this requisite.

Wills may be revoked expressly, as by making a new will, or cancelling the past one; or impliedly, as by doing various acts inconsistent with the terms of the will in relation to the property devised or bequeathed, as by marriage, contracting to sell the property itself, and by mortgaging it, though a mortgage only operates as a revocation to the extent of the incumbrance.

Wills under the influence of importunity and restraint are void, although the restraint was merely ideal; the will being contrary to the wishes of a testator being the main point.

Any fraud or imposition will vacate a will, and the courts of equity, as well as the ecclesiastical courts, have concurrent power to investigate the facts.

A felon convicted cannot make a will; but a pardon restores him to full competence.

The wife of a transported convict is, for many purposes, regarded by the law as a single woman, and she is able to make a will and bequeath property acquired by her; but if the husband return at the expiration of his sentence, all she has obtained will be his; therefore, this doctrine applies to the wives of those who are transported for life.

The will of a *felo de se* is void, as far as personal property extends; but a devise of freehold by him is good, for he forfeits his personalty only by the act of suicide: the king, upon petition, grants to the widow or next of kin, the produce of this forfeiture.

Outlaws, whether for crime or debt, are disabled from making a will: a will made previous to outlawry cannot even take effect, for all the lands and goods are forfeited.

Wills may be confirmed or republished; but, though very little will amount to a republication after an implied revocation in cases of personalty, yet a republication of a will intended to pass a real estate, must be accompanied with the same formalities as the original publication or execution.

As a man may bequeath all the personal property he may have at his death, evidently referring to future events, many persons imagine that a man may likewise devise real property thereafter to be acquired; but that is not the case; a republication of the will is necessary to contain the newly acquired property, or a codicil excuted with the same formalities must be made.

A codicil is a supplement or annexation to a will, and is taken as part of the will itself, and is generally used to add something to, or take something from, or to vary the bequests and form of the will.

The law relating to wills of *personal*, and devises of *real* estate, since the 31st December, 1837 (*i. e.* from 1st January, 1838), is regulated by the stat. 1 *Vict. c.* 26. intituled "*An Act for the Amendment of the Laws with respect to Wills*," the general object of which is to collect the provisions of several statutes relating to wills, and various legal decisions thereupon into one act of parliament, and, at the same time, to correct various anomalies and peculiar rules of construction, whereby the intents of testators had been often defeated, and which, though they had long been deemed a reproach on the law, yet were too firmly settled to be otherwise removed.

The present act particularly relates to the property which may be disposed of by will; the persons by whom wills may be made; the forms which are to be observed in making them; and the modes of altering, revoking, and reviving them, with some incidental matters.

Freehold lands were hitherto disposable by will, according to the statute of wills, 32 *H.* 8. *c.* 1., but were to be executed according to the forms directed by the statute of frauds, which passed in the year 1676, and which provided, that wills of land should be in writing, signed by the testator, or by some other person under his direction, and attested by three or four credible witnesses in his presence. There were also some, indeed very many, tenant-rights, and most copyhold property, which were, by the words or operation of the statute of wills, excepted, and therefore a devise of them was deemed void in many cases; and in those cases where the devise was allowed, it was either by special custom, the presumed surrender to the use of a will, or where the copyhold or tenant-right was vested in a trustee, who might voluntarily, or under the direction of a court of equity, dispose of the estate, as the real owner might by his will direct.

As the law previously stood, and still stands with respect to wills executed before 1st January, 1838, a will did not pass any *real* estate, which the testator was not entitled to, both at the date of his will and at the time of his death; it, therefore, had no effect upon any real estate intermediately acquired. This construction was the effect given to the word "having" in the statute of wills (repealed by the present act with others), and partly from the desire which had been entertained in the courts of favouring the heir, and consequently disregarding the wishes of testators; and this construction was afterwards carried to an extreme extent.

Personal estate, on the other hand, might be disposed of by any writing, however informal.

The ecclesiastical courts had exclusive jurisdiction over this matter, and might consider as a will that which appeared in the shape of a letter to a friend or an agent, or of a loose memorandum, or of a series of detached memoranda, if it could be deemed that such writings afforded sufficient means of collecting an intention.

Thus, an interest in land, however small, could not be disposed of by will without all the forms required by the statute of frauds; whilst an interest in *personal* estate, however large, passed by a will for which no form was required but writing.

As to the persons by whom *real* estate might be devised, no alteration is made;* but *personal* property or estate, which formerly might be bequeathed by boys of fourteen and girls of twelve years of age, if they were of sufficient discretion, is now to be disposed of only by the will of a person of full age.

With regard to the revocation of wills, and the reviving them after revocation, a great variety of rules existed. The rule of constructive revocation adopted by the ecclesiastical courts, with regard to personalty, was, that a man's will was held to be revoked by his marriage and birth of a child; and this rule was, in 1771, adopted by the courts of law and

* By the act of 34 & 35 *H.* 8. *c.* 5. *s.* 14., no person under the age of 21 years shall make a will of any manors, lands, tenements, or other hereditaments; for by the common law they are accounted "infants," and incapable of governing themselves and their affairs.

equity. Subsequent experience has shown that the rule operated against the intention of the testator, and many complicated points have occurred upon cases where the presumption of a change in the testator's circumstances were rebutted by particular facts. Litigation and uncertainty could be the only offspring of such a doctrine. There appeared, certainly, some reason in the long doubtful, and now repudiated doctrine, that the will of a single woman was revoked by her marriage, and revived upon her widowhood. As alterations in circumstances are mostly provided for by the individuals concerned, it seems to have been quite a work of supererogation for the courts to interfere.

Actual revocation of a will was (and still is) by the execution of a subsequent will, or destruction of a will with intent to revoke it, where no subsequent will was made; but circumstances often occurred where the former will, which had been superseded by the execution of a subsequent one, revived and came into operation on the revocation or suppression of that subsequent will, the re-execution of the revoked will or a codicil showing an intention to revive it, being then dispensed with. This doctrine of *constructive* revival is now abolished. An *actual* revival (*i. e.* the re-execution of the revoked will, or the execution of a codicil to that effect), is now absolutely necessary.

The other incidental matters which called for legislative interference may be more appositely noticed in the observations the editor has ventured to annex to most of the clauses, which are as follow. The act, after repealing all the statutes or sections of statutes relating to wills, proceeds to enact,

That it shall be lawful for every person to devise, bequeath, or dispose of, by his will executed in manner herein-after required, all real estate and all personal estate which he shall be entitled to, either at law or in equity, at the time of his death, and which if not so devised, bequeathed, or disposed of would devolve upon the heir at law, or customary heir of him, or, if he became entitled by descent, of his ancestor, or upon his executor or administrator; and that the power hereby given shall extend to all real estate of the nature of customary freehold or tenant right, or customary or copyhold, notwithstanding that the testator may not have surrendered the same to the use of his will, or notwithstanding that, being entitled as heir, devisee, or otherwise to be admitted thereto, he shall not have been admitted thereto, or notwithstanding that the same, in consequence of the want of a custom to devise or surrender to the use of a will or otherwise, could not at law have been disposed of by will if this act had not been made, or notwithstanding that the same, in consequence of there being a custom that a will or a surrender to the use of a will should continue in force for a limited time only, or any other special custom, could not have been disposed of by will according to the power contained in this act, if this act had not been made; and also to estates *pur autre vie*, whether there shall or shall not be any special occupant thereof, and whether the same shall be freehold, customary freehold, tenant right, customary or copyhold, or of any other tenure, and whether the same shall be a corporeal or an incorporeal hereditament; and also to all contingent, executory, or other future interests in any real or personal estate, whether the testator may or may not be ascertained as the person or one of the persons in whom the same respectively may become vested, and whether he may be entitled thereto under the instrument by which the same respectively were created, or under any disposition thereof by deed or will; and also to all rights of entry for conditions broken, and other rights of entry; and also to such of the same estates, interests, and rights respectively, and other real and personal estate, as the testator may be entitled to at the time of his death, notwithstanding that he may become entitled to the same subsequently to the execution of his will. — *s.* 3.

The only form required by the statute of wills, 32 *H.* 8., now repealed, was writing. The statute of frauds, 29 *C.* 2. *c.* 3., superadded the solemnities of signature and attestation by, at least, three *credible* witnesses. Wills of personal estate might be nuncupative, *i. e.* by *parol,* or word of mouth, and pass property to the amount of 30*l.*, and subject to various formalities, to an indefinite amount. Nuncupative wills, with the exception of mariners and soldiers, are now abolished. Mariners and soldiers were excepted from the statute of frauds, which imposed formalities and requisites on making nuncupative wills above 30*l.*, and the wills of such persons are still (see *post, sec.* 11.) excepted from the present act.

Estates *pur autre vie,* and contingent interests, were not in all cases devisable, and certainly rights of entry and conditions were not disposable by testament under the old law. But this act renders them devisable, together with all property, real and personal, of which the testator may be possessed at the time of his death.

The 4th and 5th sections provide for the fees of stewards of manors, and the payment of the various stamp-duties upon admissions and surrenders of devisees, purchasers, or tenants of customary-hold or copyhold estates, as well as of all fines payable on admittances; and also provide for the inrolment of wills affecting copyhold estates, although the proceedings upon which such fees become due are in respect of matters now unnecessary. The 6th section provides for the distribution of an estate *pur autre vie* of a freehold nature, as assets in the hands of an executor.

No will made by any person under the age of twenty-one years shall be valid. — *s.* 7.

No will made by any married woman shall be valid, except such a will as might have been made by a married woman before the passing of this act. — *s.* 8.

A married woman has always been deemed incapable of devising lands, or of making a will of personal estate. The necessary exception was, where a husband had no beneficial interest in any personal estate which the wife held as executrix, in which case she was allowed to make a will to pass such estate without the consent of the husband, which, in all other cases was, and still is, absolutely necessary. The husband, in consenting to his wife disposing of personal estate by will, must assent to one and a specific will: a general assent that his wife may make a will, will not be available. Married women, by means of "powers," may nevertheless derive a power of disposition by will in particular instances. — See *sect.* 10.

That no will shall be valid unless it shall be in writing and executed in manner herein-after mentioned; (that is to say) it shall be signed at the foot or end thereof by the testator, or by some other person in his presence and by his direction; and such signature shall be made *or* acknowledged by the testator in the presence of two or more witnesses present at the same time, and such witnesses shall attest and shall subscribe the will in the presence of the testator; but no form of attestation shall be necessary. — *s.* 9.

There were ten different modes of making wills sanctioned by the law of England, and depending on the various sorts of property intended to be disposed of. The statute of frauds, 29 *C.* 2. *c.* 3., prescribed a form for real estate, but personal property, as we have seen, might have been disposed of by any writing, however informal. Many inconveniences arose from the ignorance of testators, who not unreasonably concluded that, because two witnesses were usually called in to subscribe an attestation, the same number sufficed in this instance; and this conformity to habit frustrated many wills not prepared and executed by lawyers. An attestation by *two* witnesses at *one* time, and in the presence of the testator, to prevent the imposition of a spurious will, is by this section made sufficient: no form of attestation is rendered necessary, the bare subscription of the witnesses will be sufficient.

That no appointment made by will, in exercise of any power, shall be valid, unless the same be executed in manner herein-before required; and every will executed in manner herein-before required, shall, so far as respects the execution and attestation thereof, be a valid execution of a power of appointment by will, notwithstanding it shall have been expressly required that a will made in exercise of such power should be executed with some additional or other form of execution or solemnity.—*s.* 10.

A man may, if he pleases, give an estate to such persons as another shall appoint, and may say that such appointment shall be made, or such power be exercised by a will executed in a particular manner without any witness, or with one witness, or any number of witnesses of any particular quality; and if the mode in which the power is directed to be exercised is not strictly followed, the appointment fails; and questions, followed by great litigation, very often arise between those who claim under the appointment or defective execution of the power, and those who claim in default of appointment or non-execution of the power. Considerable benefit will arise from the effect of this clause, which enacts in substance, that powers to be executed by *will* shall be held to be duly executed, whenever a will, purporting to be made in execution of the power, shall be executed according to the forms required for a valid will by the now general law of the land, whether the forms prescribed by the power have been complied with or not.— See Power.

Provided, that any soldier being in actual military service, or any mariner or seaman being at sea, may dispose of his personal estate as he might have done before the making of this act.—*s.* 11.

Soldiers and mariners have always had the privilege of making nuncupative wills, unrestricted in amount, and discharged of the formalities formerly requisite in parol wills of personalty above 30*l*. (Nuncupative wills of *other* persons are now abolished.) But, in consequence of the frauds to which petty officers and seamen in the navy, and non-commissioned officers of marines and marines were subjected, so far as relates to their wages, pay, prize, county-money, and allowances, the* stat. 11 *G*. 4.

* The clauses which provide a mode for executing such wills are as follows:— And whereas it is expedient to establish regulations for the prevention of forgery and fraud, which have been heretofore much practised in relation to the pay of the royal navy; be it further enacted, that no will made by any petty officer or seaman, non-commissioned officer of marines or marine, before his entry into his majesty's service, shall be valid to pass any wages, prize money, or other monies payable in respect of services in his majesty's navy, and that no letter of attorney made by any such person who shall be or shall have been in the said service, or by the widow, next of kin, executors, or administrators of any such person, shall be valid or sufficient to entitle any person to receive any wages, prize money, or other allowance of money of any kind for the service of any such person in his majesty's navy, unless such letter of attorney shall be therein expressed to be revocable; and that no such letter of attorney shall be valid or sufficient to entitle any person to receive any such wages or other monies, nor shall any will made or to be made by any petty officer or seaman, non-commissioned officer of marines or marine, who shall be or shall have been in the naval service of his majesty, be valid or sufficient to pass any such wages, prize money, or other monies, unless such letter of attorney or will respectively shall contain the name of the ship to which the person execut-

c. 20., requires such wills to be attested in the presence of official persons, and superadds other solemnities. The next section (12), there-

---

ing the same belonged at the time or to which he last belonged, nor unless such letter of attorney, if made by an executor or administrator, shall contain the name of the ship to which his or her testator or intestate last belonged, and also in every case a full description of the degree of relationship or residence of the person or persons to whom or in whose favour, either as attorney or attornies, executor or executors, the same shall be made, and also the day of the month and year, and the name of the place when and where the same shall have been executed; nor shall any such letter of attorney or will be valid for the purposes aforesaid unless the same respectively shall, in the several cases herein-after specified, be executed and attested in the manner herein-after mentioned; (that is to say) in case any such letter of attorney or will shall be made by any such petty officer or seaman, non-commissioned officer of marines or marine, while belonging to and on board of any ship of his majesty as part of her complement, or borne on the books thereof as a supernumerary or as an invalid, or for victuals only, the same shall be executed in the presence of and be attested by the captain, or (in his absence) by the commanding officer for the time being, and who in that case shall state at the foot of the attestation the absence of the captain at the time, and the occasion thereof; and in case of the inability of the captain, by reason of wounds or sickness, to attest any such will or letter of attorney, then the same shall be executed in the presence of and be attested by the officer next in command, who shall state at the foot of such attestation the inability of the captain to attest the same, and the cause thereof; and if made in any of his majesty's hospital ships, or in any naval or other hospital, or at any sick quarters either at home or abroad, the same shall be executed in the presence of and be attested by the governor, physician, surgeon, assistant surgeon, agent, or chaplain of any such hospital or sick quarters, or by the commanding officer, agent, physician, surgeon, assistant surgeon, or chaplain for the time being of any such hospital ship, or by the physician, surgeon, assistant surgeon, agent, chaplain, or chief officer of any military or merchant hospital or other sick quarters, or one of them; and if made on board of any ship or vessel in the transport service, or in any other merchant ship or vessel, the same shall be executed in the presence of and be attested by some commission or warrant officer or chaplain in his majesty's navy, or some commission officer or chaplain belonging to his majesty's land forces or royal marines, or the governor, physician, surgeon, or agent of any hospital in his majesty's naval or military service, if any such shall be then on board, or by the master or first mate thereof; and if made after he shall have been discharged from his majesty's service, or if such letter of attorney be made by the executor or administrator of any such petty officer or seaman, non-commissioned officer of marines or marine, if the party making the same shall then reside in London or within the bills of mortality, the same shall be executed in the presence of and be attested by the inspector for the time being of seamen's wills and powers of attorney, or his assistant or clerk; or if the party making the same shall then reside at or within the distance of seven miles from any port or place where the wages of seamen in his majesty's service are paid, the same shall be executed in the presence of and be attested by one of the clerks of the treasurer of the navy resident at such port or place; or if the party making such letter of attorney or will shall then reside at any other place in Great Britain or Ireland, or in the islands of Guernsey, Jersey, Alderney, Sark, or Man, the same shall be executed in the presence of and be attested by one of his majesty's justices of the peace, or by the minister or officiating minister or curate of the parish or place in which the same shall be executed; or if the party making the same shall then reside in any other part of his majesty's dominions, or in any colony, plantation, settlement, fort, factory, or any other foreign possession of his majesty, or any settlement within the charter of the East India company, the same shall be executed in the presence of and be attested by some commission or warrant officer or chaplain of his majesty's navy, or commission officer of royal marines, or the commissioner of the navy, or naval storekeeper at one of his majesty's naval yards, or a fore, specially excepts the provisions of the 11 *G.* 4. from the operation of the present act.

Every will executed in manner herein-before required shall be valid without any other publication thereof. — *s.* 13.

The statute of frauds did not expressly require "publication," *i. e.* the deliberate statement by a testator, that he published and declared that (the writing) to be his will; but doubts had arisen as to the necessity of a "publication" in many cases, which this section dispels. Signature and attestation pursuant to the 9th section, are all that now is requisite.

If any person who shall attest the execution of a will shall at the time of the execution thereof or at any time afterwards be incompetent to be admitted a witness to prove the execution thereof, such will shall not on that account be invalid. — *s.* 14.

If any person shall attest the execution of any will to whom or to whose wife or husband any beneficial devise, legacy, estate, interest, gift, or appointment, of or affecting any real or personal estate (other than and except charges and directions for the payment of any debt or debts), shall be thereby given or made, such devise, legacy, estate, interest, gift, or appointment shall, so far only as concerns such person attesting the execution of such will, or the wife or husband of such person, or any person claiming under such person or wife or husband, be utterly null and void, and such person so attesting shall be admitted as a witness to prove the execution of such will, or to prove the validity or invalidity thereof, notwithstanding such devise, legacy, estate, interest, gift, or appointment mentioned in such will. — *s.* 15.

That in case by any will any real or personal estate shall be charged with any debt or debts, and any creditor, or the wife or husband of any creditor,

---

minister of the church of England or Scotland, or a magistrate or principal officer residing in any of such places respectively; or if the party making the same shall then reside at any place not within his majesty's dominions or any of the places last mentioned, the same shall be executed in the presence of and be attested by the British consul or vice consul, or some officer having a public appointment or commission, civil, naval, or military, under his majesty's government, or by a magistrate or notary public of or near the place where such letter of attorney or will shall be executed; nor shall any will of any petty officer, seaman, non-commissioned officer of marines or marine, be deemed good or valid in law, to any intent or purpose, which shall be contained, printed, or written in the same instrument, paper, or parchment with a power of attorney: provided always nevertheless, that if it shall appear to the satisfaction of the treasurer of his majesty's navy, in the case of any will or letter of attorney executed on board any of his majesty's ships, that in the attestation thereof the captain's signature hath by accident or inadvertence been omitted, and that in all other respects the execution had been conformable to the provisions and to the intent and meaning of this act, it shall be lawful for the inspector of seamen's wills and powers to pass the same as valid and sufficient.

Provided always, and be it further enacted, that every letter of attorney or will which hath been or which hereafter shall be made by any petty officer or seaman, non-commissioned officer of marines or marine, while any such person hath been or shall be a prisoner of war, shall be valid to all intents and purposes, provided it shall have been executed in the presence of and be attested by some commission officer of the army, navy, or royal marines, or by some warrant officer of his majesty's navy, or by a physician, surgeon, or assistant surgeon in the army or navy, agent to some naval hospital, or chaplain of the army or navy, or by any notary public; but so as not to invalidate or disturb any payment which hath been already made under any letter of administration, certificates, or otherwise, in consequence of the rejection of any such wills by the inspector of seamen's wills for want of the due attestation thereof according to the directions of any former act of parliament. — *ss.* 48. & 49. of the stat. 11 *G.* 4. *c.* 20., intituled 'An Act to amend and consolidate the Laws relating to the pay of the Royal Navy.'

whose debt is so charged, shall attest the execution of such will, such creditor notwithstanding such charge shall be admitted a witness to prove the execution of such will, or to prove the validity or invalidity thereof. — *s.* 16.

That no person shall, on account of his being an executor of a will, be incompetent to be admitted a witness to prove the execution of such will, or a witness to prove the validity or invalidity thereof. — *s.* 17.

The word "credible," as relating to attesting witnesses in the statute, has been the origin of litigation and dispute. The term "credible" imports that the witness is not incompetent to be examined, which incompetency may arise not only by his being convicted of perjury, or of any crime for which he has not undergone punishment, but that he has an interest under the will. The stat. 25 *G.* 3. *c.* 6. declares in effect, that the testimony of legatees should be excluded, *i. e.* a devise or legacy to a witness attesting the will was made void, so that the interest of the witness being destroyed, he was admitted to prove the execution of the will. Many other cases have occurred where persons, attesting the will, have taken a direct or indirect interest under it, and some other inconveniences have arisen from the decisions as to what were to be deemed "credible" witnesses. The omission of the word "credible" and the express declaration of the present section, have set all doubts on this head at rest.

Every will made by a man or woman shall be revoked by his or her marriage (except a will made in exercise of a power of appointment, when the real or personal estate thereby appointed would not in default of such appointment pass to his or her heir, customary heir, executor, or administrator, or the person entitled as his or her next of kin, under the statute of distributions). — *s.* 18.

No will shall be revoked by any presumption of an intention on the ground of an alteration in circumstances. — *s.* 19.

No will or codicil, or any part thereof, shall be revoked otherwise than as aforesaid, or by another will or codicil executed in manner herein-before required, or by some writing declaring an intention to revoke the same, and executed in the manner in which a will is herein-before required to be executed, or by the burning, tearing, or otherwise destroying the same by the testator, or by some person in his presence and by his direction, with the intention of revoking the same. — *s.* 20.

No obliteration, interlineation, or other alteration made in any will after the execution thereof shall be valid or have any effect, except so far as the words or effect of the will before such alteration shall not be apparent, unless such alteration shall be executed in like manner as herein-before is required for the execution of the will; but the will, with such alteration as part thereof, shall be deemed to be duly executed if the signature of the testator and the subscription of the witnesses be made in the margin or on some other part of the will opposite or near to such alteration, or at the foot or end of or opposite to a memorandum referring to such alteration, and written at the end or some other part of the will. — *s.* 21.

No will or codicil, or any part thereof, which shall be in any manner revoked, shall be revived otherwise than by the re-execution thereof, or by a codicil executed in manner herein-before required, and showing an intention to revive the same; and when any will or codicil which shall be partly revoked, and afterwards wholly revoked, shall be revived, such revival shall not extend to so much thereof as shall have been revoked before the revocation of the whole thereof, unless an intention to the contrary shall be shown. — *s.* 22.

No conveyance or other act made or done subsequently to the execution of a will of or relating to any real or personal estate therein comprised, except an act by which such will shall be revoked as aforesaid, shall prevent the operation of the will with respect to such estate or interest in such real or personal estate as the testator shall have power to dispose of by will at the time of his death. — *s.* 23.

The doubts alluded to in the prefatory remarks on this act, as to expressed and implied revocations of wills, are now entirely removed by the six last sections. With respect to the 23d section, it may be remarked, that, before the passing of this act, a man might have been possessed of the same real property, both at the date of his will, and at the time of his death, so that, by the ordinary rule, the estate would pass; yet if, in the interval he should, with the desire, and for the avowed purpose of strengthening his own title, and by that means making his gift more secure, have done certain acts, as he thought, for further assurance, the effect, as the law stood, might certainly have been to strengthen his own title, but, at the same time, to defeat the devise, for the sake of which alone he desired to strengthen his title.

Every will shall be construed, with reference to the real estate and personal estate comprised in it, to speak and take effect as if it had been executed immediately before the death of the testator, unless a contrary intention shall appear by the will. — *s.* 24.

The future law is here declared as to the *real* estate of a testator, which is now, as well as the *personal* estate, capable of being passed to the devisee, although the testator be not possessed thereof at the date of his will. As the law formerly stood, a will did not pass any real estate of which the testator was not, in legal language, *seised*, at the time of making such his will. When a testator had made or completed a purchase of real property, it was necessary for him to re-execute or "re-publish" his will, in order to devise effectually his newly acquired property: this is no longer necessary. Under this section, also, lapsed and void devises would necessarily fall into the residue of real property devised; but the next section removes all doubt, by making such declaration:

That, unless a contrary intention shall appear by the will, such real estate or interest therein as shall be comprised or intended to be comprised in any devise in such will contained, which shall fail or be void by reason of the death of the devisee in the lifetime of the testator, or by reason of such devise being contrary to law or otherwise incapable of taking effect, shall be included in the residuary devise (if any) contained in such will. — *s.* 25.

A residuary bequest of personalty carries not only every thing not disposed of, but every thing that eventually turns out not to be disposed of. The principle being, that a bequest of the residue operates upon all the personalty of the deceased, of which he was possessed at the *time of his death*, and, consequently, lapsed, void, and similar legacies are included in such residue. In real estates a different doctrine prevailed; for a will or devise of realty only affected that property of which the testator was in possession at the *date of his will*, so that the heir-at-law took such property if the devisee died in the testator's lifetime; and even a republication or re-execution of the will after the legatee's death, would not pass the devised estate to the legatee's heir. A devise of land is always deemed a specific legacy; so that, by the terms and intent of this section, a residuary devise will in future lapse as personalty, and fall into the *residuum*, and not descend to the heir as it formerly did; the lapsing of a devise of real estate, and the lapse of a bequest of personal estate being in future governed by the same rules, and having precisely the same effect. It is noticed in another place what is a "lapsed legacy," and it may here be observed, that it is a general rule that, if a legatee or devisee die in the lifetime of the testator, the legacy or devise will *lapse*, and will be lost, even if "executors or administrators" or "heirs" are named, those words being deemed surplusage. However, in sect. 32., *vide post*, it is declared, that estates tail, or *quasi* entail, *i. e.* limited to the issue, or particular issue of another, shall not lapse, if the devisee leave issue inheritable under such entail; and, by sect. 33. gifts to children or issue of the testator, dying in his lifetime leaving issue, shall not lapse if such issue be living at the testator's decease, unless in both these cases a contrary intention is declared by the will. It formerly not unfrequently happening that such devises were defeated by the death of the tenant in tail in the testator's lifetime, which defeated the gift to the issue, the remainder-man taking to their exclusion; and it was not always possible for the most careful testator to remedy this evil or chance, for the death of the person who was first to inherit might be unknown to the testator, or circumstances might intervene which rendered a republication of the will utterly impracticable. The hardship is apparent in the case of a devise to the eldest and every son successively in tail-male, and every son successively, according to seniority, in tail. If an elder son die in the testator's lifetime, leaving issue, such issue are excluded, and the estate goes to the younger branch of the family, contrary to the manifest intentions of the testator. In well-drawn wills, provisions are made as to the lapse of legacies or devises; and it is either specially declared who shall take in case the legacy or devise lapse, or that such legacy or devise shall fall into the *residuum*.

A devise of the land of the testator, or of the land of the testator in any place or in the occupation of any person mentioned in his will, or otherwise described in a general manner, and any other general devise which would describe a customary, copyhold, or leasehold estate if the testator had no freehold estate which could be described by it, shall be construed to include the customary, copyhold, and leasehold estates of the testator, or his customary, copyhold, and leasehold estates, or any of them, to which such description shall extend, as the case may be, as well as freehold estates, unless a contrary intention shall appear by the will. — *s.* 26.

A general devise of the real estate of the testator, or of the real estate of the testator in any place or in the occupation of any person mentioned in his will, or otherwise described in a general manner, shall be construed to include any real estate, or any real estate to which such description shall extend (as the case may be), which he may have power to appoint in any manner he may think proper, and shall operate as an execution of such power, unless a contrary intention shall appear by the will; and in like manner a bequest of the personal estate of the testator, or any bequest of personal property described in a general manner, shall be construed to include any personal estate, or any personal estate to which such description shall extend (as the case may be), which he may have power to appoint in any manner he may think proper, and shall operate as an execution of such power, unless a contrary intention shall appear by the will. —*s.* 27.

A general devise did not always operate so as to pass leaseholds and copyholds; in this section it is expressly stated, that a general devise of the testator's land shall not only include freehold, but copyholds and leaseholds.

With respect to sect. 27., some doubts which arose in particular instances, as to the operation of a devise when the testator had a *general* power of appointment, are removed. As to the execution of powers of appointment by will, see the observations upon sect. 10.

Where any real estate shall be devised to any person without any words of limitation, such devise shall be construed to pass the fee simple, or other the whole estate or interest which the testator had power to dispose of by will in such real estate, unless a contrary intention shall appear by the will. —*s.* 28.

The words "lands" and "tenements" did not of themselves ever legally designate the quantity of estate or interest for which they were held, notwithstanding that, in the construction of wills, a great latitude of interpretation was allowed; and although, in common parlance, when a man spoke of or mentioned his house or his lands as property he had a right to, or meant to dispose of, thereby meaning his whole and entire legal right thereto or therein; yet, if he gave by will his house or his lands to another, without adding words which imported a devise of the fee-simple or inheritance, or words, as they are termed, *of limitation*, "his heirs," the devisee, in most cases, took only an estate for life. The words "his heirs," or any language importing a devise of the inheritance, is therefore no longer required in order to pass the entire interest of the testator in the premises, which can in future be devised by any words clearly and obviously giving all the interest of the testator to the person named, unless a contrary intention shall appear by the will.

In any devise or bequest of real or personal estate the words "die without issue," or "die without leaving issue," or "have no issue," or any other words which may import either a want or failure of issue of any person in his lifetime or at the time of his death, or an indefinite failure of his issue, shall be construed to mean a want or failure of issue in the lifetime or at the time of the death of such person, and not an indefinite failure of his issue, unless a contrary intention shall appear by the will, by reason of such person having a prior estate tail, or of a preceding gift, being, without any implication arising from such words, a limitation of an estate tail to such person or issue, or otherwise: provided, that this act shall not extend to cases where such words as aforesaid import if no issue described in a preceding gift shall be born, or if there shall be no issue who shall live to attain the age or otherwise answer the description required for obtaining a vested estate by a preceding gift to such issue. —*s. 29.*

The words "die without issue," or "die without leaving issue," or "have no issue," have hitherto had different operations when applied in the same will to different descriptions of property; for these words, when applied to a bequest of personalty, meant "without leaving issue at the time of the decease of the legatee;" whereas, in devises of realty, they were always held to import a failure of issue at any indefinite period however remote. The effect of this rule was, that, in a will devising freehold and leasehold to a son, for instance, in the freehold the devisee took an estate tail, which could be disposed of at his pleasure; in the leasehold he took an interest defeasible on his own death, without issue then living. The present section of the act enables judges to construe the words according to their obvious meaning, and in the way they have been held to apply to personal estates, overturning a rule long established, but from which much litigation had arisen.

Where any real estate (other than or not being a presentation to a church) shall be devised to any trustee or executor, such devise shall be construed to pass the fee simple or other the whole estate or interest which the testator had power to dispose of by will in such real estate, unless a definite term of years, absolute or determinable, or an estate of freehold, shall thereby be given to him expressly or by implication. —*s. 30.*

Where any real estate shall be devised to a trustee, without any express limitation of the estate to be taken by such trustee, and the beneficial interest in such real estate, or in the surplus rents and profits thereof, shall not be given to any person for life, or such beneficial interest shall be given to any person for life, but the purposes of the trust may continue beyond the life of such person, such devise shall be construed to vest in such trustee the fee simple, or other the whole legal estate which the testator had power to dispose of by will in such real estate, and not an estate determinable when the purposes of the trust shall be satisfied. — *s.* 31.

These sections declare the extent of the *legal* interest which shall pass under a devise to a trustee. If words of inheritance were used, the fee-simple was, at law, vested in them for the purposes of sale, or they held it as trustees for those who had the beneficial interest or *equitable estate*. In cases where there were no words from which a devise of the fee could be collected, the doctrine was, that the trustee took an interest commensurate with the exigencies of the trust.

Where any person to whom any real estate shall be devised for an estate tail or an estate in quasi entail shall die in the lifetime of the testator leaving issue who would be inheritable under such entail, and any such issue shall be living at the time of the death of the testator, such devise shall not lapse, but shall take effect as if the death of such person had happened immediately after the death of the testator, unless a contrary intention shall appear by the will. — *s.* 32.

Where any person being a child or other issue of the testator, to whom any real or personal estate shall be devised or bequeathed for any estate or interest not determinable at or before the death of such person, shall die in the lifetime of the testator leaving issue, and any such issue of such person shall be living at the time of the death of the testator, such devise or bequest shall not lapse, but shall take effect as if the death of such person had happened immediately after the death of the testator, unless a contrary intention shall appear by the will. — *s.* 33.

In addition to the observations respecting *lapses* upon the 25th section, the reader's attention is directed to two particular instances of hardship under the old law, arising from the doctrine of *lapse*, but now remedied as far as regards future devises or bequests.

When there was a gift in tail, the testator intended the issue to take, if no act was done to bar the entail; and if the persons to whom the devise in tail was made should die in the lifetime of the testator leaving issue inheritable under the intended entail, it was probably intended by the testator that such issue should be substituted as the devisee in tail, in lieu of the person first named. The 32d section carries this probable intention into effect.

With respect to the 33d section, it often happened that a testator gave legacies to his different children as their portions, and that some of such children married and died in his lifetime, leaving issue of their own: it may fairly be inferred that the testator did not intend the portions of such deceased children to lapse, which would have the effect of depriving his grandchildren of their parent's portion; this section, therefore, provides that the legacies or portions of such of the testator's children as die in his lifetime leaving children, shall take effect.

That this act shall not extend to any will made before the first day of January one thousand eight hundred and thirty-eight, and that every will re-executed or republished, or revived by any codicil, shall for the purposes of this act be deemed to have been made at the time at which the same shall be so re-executed, republished, or revived; and that this act shall not extend to any estate *pur autre vie* of any person who shall die before the first day of January one thousand eight hundred and thirty-eight. — *s.* 34.

That this act shall not extend to Scotland. — *s.* 35.

That this act may be amended, altered, or repealed by any act or acts to be passed in this present session of parliament. — *s.* 36.

These three last sections need no explanation.

The act has not been altered or amended.

The main intentions which the act appears to have had in view, are —

1. That devises of real property should be governed by the principles established with respect to bequests of personalty.

2. That wills should not be rendered inoperative by the intervention of circumstances over which testators could have no control, or could not readily provide against.

3. That the obvious or presumed intentions of testators should not be avoided by technical defects or omissions.

WITNESS. One who gives evidence in a cause; and, being an indifferent party, is sworn to "speak the truth, the whole truth, and nothing but the truth."

The process for compelling the attendance of witnesses before courts of law, examiners in chancery, or the exchequer, or the criminal courts, is a writ of *subpœna*, commanding the witness that, *under a penalty*, he appear and testify in a certain cause, naming it, on the part of the plaintiff or defendant. Refusal or neglect, after a sufficient sum tendered for expenses, subjects the party to an attachment for contempt, or 100*l.* penalty, and damages to the party grieved. Witnesses are entitled to their expenses going, staying, and returning; and if these are not tendered with the subpœna, they may refuse to give evidence; but in and near London, it is not usual to give witnesses more than 1*s.* with the subpœna. Medical men and attornies, and those whose time is part or means of their subsistence, are also entitled to daily remuneration and refreshments while attending the court. In criminal cases, attachment is the only means of punishing a witness who refuses to attend; indeed, attachment in civil cases is the more efficacious process, as an action for damages is attended with considerable difficulties.

When the witness is in custody, he can be subpœnaed, and brought up on a *habeas corpus ad testificandum.*

Witnesses who are to appear before commissioners of bankrupt, or commissioners to examine witnesses in equity, are summoned by notice under the hands of the commissioners: they are allowed their expenses as witnesses are in other cases.

Witnesses can be summoned by arbitrators, where that power is conferred by the submission, and where courts of law have granted permission to examine witnesses upon interrogatories, when about to quit the kingdom.

Deeds or writings are producible on a writ of subpœna *duces tecum* (that you bring with you), the writings required being distinctly set forth.

The witness being in court, is sworn according to the forms prescribed by his religious persuasion; the Christian on the New Testament, the Jew on the Pentateuch, the Mahometan on the Koran, the Hindoo by a cup of water, and other heathens in such a manner as will, in their minds, create a moral obligation to tell the truth; but those who have no idea of a God or a future state, are excluded from giving testimony.

Persons convicted of infamous crimes, perjury, barratry, bribing a witness, subornation of perjury, and persons convicted of treason or felony, are incompetent to give evidence.

In considering what are infamous crimes, it is settled that it is the *offence*, not the mode of punishment, that renders an individual infamous.

But persons who have endured their punishment (except for perjury), or have the king's pardon, are competent; the crime, indeed, may be urged against his credit, but not against his competency as a witness. The judges decide who is competent; the jury decide who is worthy of credit.

Persons outlawed for criminal offences are not competent.

Unconvicted parties (supposed to be guilty of the same crime) are evidence against their companions. Where no other witnesses can be had, an informer may be a witness, although he receives part of the penalty.

Idiots, madmen, and children who are too young, or otherwise unable to comprehend a future state, or without any religious or moral impressions, are inadmissible: the court will, at discretion, postpone a trial in order that such a witness may be instructed as to the nature of an oath. A child is examined by the court before he is examined by the jury.

It is a misdeameanor to tamper with witnesses, or prevent their giving evidence.

Persons interested deeply in the event of the verdict are also inadmissible; but those for whom the verdict would be evidence are admissible on the condition that the verdict shall never be received in evidence for them.

Parties to the suit, and who may be individually liable for costs, cannot give evidence; though, when a co-defendant is acquitted, he may be immediately sworn to give evidence for the other defendants. Corporators, not liable to costs of the suit, may give evidence.

Attorneys or their clerks cannot be received to give evidence concerning confidential or any communications made to them by a client, not even after the termination of the proceedings in which those communications were made, or after the dismissal of the attorney. This privilege is the privilege of the client, not the attorney; therefore, the client may waive it, in which case the attorney or his clerk may be examined. This doctrine of privileged communication does not extend to clergymen or medical men, who, notwithstanding they are often repositories of the most confidential communications, are bound to disclose all they know, or have heard from the party, in a court of law or equity.

In criminal prosecutions, the injured parties or prosecutors, are witnesses, because the prosecution is at the suit of the king, who is injured in respect of the wrong done to one of his subjects.

In giving his testimony, a witness is not to be examined on points where his evidence tends to accuse or clear himself of a crime; nor is he bound to give any answer which would expose him to punishment, or to a criminal charge, as to convict him of usury; neither is he compellable to answer questions which are degrading to his character, although such questions may be legally asked; but a witness cannot, by law, refuse to answer on the ground only that his answer may establish a debt due from him to the king, or any other.

A witness shall not be permitted to read his evidence, but he may refer to an entry or a memorandum made by himself, *at the time the fact occurred*, to refresh his memory. A witness cannot recite his testimony again to the jury, after they are gone from the bar: if he does, the verdict will not stand, but a new trial will be granted.

Witnesses cannot be examined concerning any thing that does not relate to the issue; and where the issue itself is not perfect, the judge cannot proceed to trial.

WOUNDING. The shooting at, stabbing, or wounding any person maliciously, or with intent to commit some grievous bodily harm, is a capital felony; and if the person shot, stabbed, cut or wounded, die within a year and a day, it is murder, and punishable accordingly, unless the circumstances would only have rendered it manslaughter, had death ensued.

Maiming, which is the deprivation of a member, if it is effected by any of the above means, is punishable capitally, though, where the maim is not grievous or feloniously committed, an action will lie. Attempts to maim, with intent to murder, are also capital felonies. But see OFFENCES, and therein, of offences against the person.

A "wounding" must be committed with a sharp or edged instrument.

WRECK. Goods thrown on land after a shipwreck, which, by the custom of some manors, belong to the lord, if not claimed within a year and a day; and this franchise has its origin from a grant, or presumed grant from the crown, which last is by prescription.

The plundering and stealing from wrecks is a felony, punishable by transportation for not exceeding 15 years nor less than 10 years, or imprisonment for not exceeding 3 years. 1 *Vict. c.* 87. *s.* 8.

Goods in the possession of suspected parties may be seized under a search-warrant, and the parties stopped.

The endeavouring to procure the shipwreck of a vessel by false lights or other means, is a capital felony, 1 *Vict. c.* 89. *s.* 5.

The impeding any person endeavouring to save his life from any shipwrecked, and the maliciously destroying wrecks or any articles belonging thereto, is a felony punishable by transportation for, not exceeding, 15 years, nor less than 10 years, or imprisonment for, not exceeding 3 years, *s.* 6, 7.

The assaulting any magistrate, or other person, in the exercise of his duty, while preserving a ship or cargo wrecked or in distress, is a misdemeanor, and punishable with transportation for seven years, or imprisonment for a shorter period.

WRIT of INQUIRY. See PRACTICE.—(Div. 1.)

YARD, an enclosed space of ground attached to a dwelling-house.

By the highway acts, yards and courts cannot be taken in for the purpose of widening a highway.

It is illegal to keep a ferocious dog in a yard, with the gate open, without giving notice of the danger; for if no notice is given, the owner is liable to make compensation for any damage that may be sustained.

THE END

LONDON:
Printed by A. SPOTTISWOODE,
New-Street-Square.